THE ULTIMATE BOOK OF THE
HORSE
AND RIDER

THE ULTIMATE BOOK OF THE
HORSE AND RIDER

JUDITH DRAPER, DEBBY SLY AND SARAH MUIR

LORENZ BOOKS

First published in 1999 by Lorenz Books

© Anness Publishing Limited 1999

Lorenz Books is an imprint of
Anness Publishing Limited
Hermes House
88–89 Blackfriars Road
London SE1 8HA

ISBN 0 7548 0085 7

A CIP catalogue record for this book
is available from the British Library

Publisher Joanna Lorenz
Project Editor Felicity Forster
Designer Michael Morey
Jacket Design Mabel Chan
Illustrator Rodney Paull
Indexer Dawn Butcher
Editorial Reader Kate Henderson
Production Controllers Jessica Arendt and Ben Worley

Previously published as separate volumes, *The Book of Horses and Horse Care*,
The Practical Rider's Handbook and *Saddlery and Horse Equipment*

Printed and bound in Germany

1 3 5 7 9 10 8 6 4 2

Contents

INTRODUCTION

The World of the Horse and Rider 8

BREEDS OF THE WORLD
Introduction 24
Horses 34
Ponies 144
Types 170

HORSE AND PONY CARE
Buying a Horse 186
Keeping a Horse 194
Daily Care 222

LEARNING TO RIDE
Before Climbing Aboard 244
Sitting Comfortably 252
Mastering the Paces 268
Influencing the Horse 282
Working within each Pace 296
Preparing for Take-off 308
Cross-country Riding 328

WORLD OF THE HORSE
The Competition World 338
Non-jumping Sports 344
Jumping Sports 376

SADDLERY AND EQUIPMENT
The Saddle 396
Bridles and Bits 422
Training Aids and Gadgets 446
Grooming Equipment 458
Horse Clothing and Equipment 470
The Rider's Clothes 492

Suppliers and Acknowledgements 500

Index 502

Introduction

The World of the Horse and Rider

The horse is one of the most beautiful and complex animals, and has fascinated mankind for many thousands of years. The purpose of this book is to capture some of the magic associated with horses – why so many have devoted their lives to them. It also aims, on a more practical level, to provide invaluable information for anyone with an equestrian interest, whether you ride for pleasure or competition, are planning on buying your first horse or pony, or just love horses.

Your Horse and You

This book starts by tracing the history of the horse, from its prehistoric ancestor – the Eohippus – to the modern *Equus caballus*, that we know as today's horse.

Breeds of the World is a comprehensive pictorial guide to the diverse variety of breeds and types of horse and pony around the world, from Appaloosas to Welsh Cobs, and from hacks to polo ponies. Each breed and type is described in detail, including its main characteristics, how the breed has developed and its uses.

Buying your own horse is a major step which most people who ride will want to do at some point. The section **Buying a Horse** provides a detailed guide to the subject, from how to choose the right horse or pony to suit you and your needs, to where to look for a horse, trying it and getting it vetted.

▌ BELOW
The Shagya, a Syrian-bred Arab horse with a dished face, large wide-set eyes, a short back and high-set tail.

▌ BOTTOM
Choosing the right horse is never easy – there are so many different breeds with different temperaments and characteristics. You need to find an animal that suits you.

■ RIGHT
Owning a horse brings with it a huge responsibility; you should not consider it without making sure you are fully aware of the commitment involved in feeding, grooming, general stable management and first aid.

■ BELOW
There are a number of different types of bedding to consider for your stable. This horse is lying down on shredded paper, which provides a dust-free bed, especially good for horses with allergies to straw or respiratory problems.

■ BELOW RIGHT
The amount of feed your horse needs depends on many variables, such as how much exercise he has and how much time he spends outside grazing. When providing a haynet like this one, make sure it is tied high enough to prevent the horse from catching a foot in it.

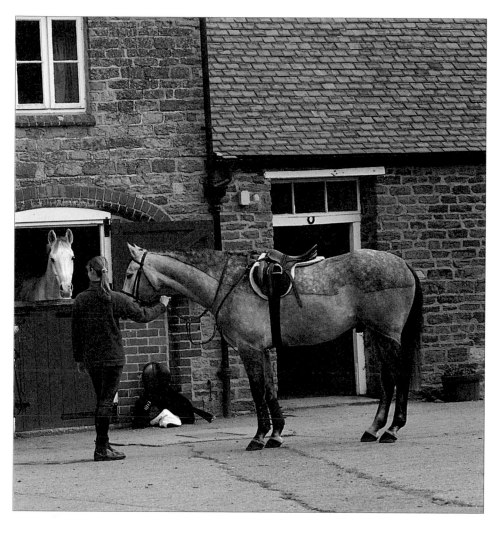

Once you have bought your new horse or pony, this is where the fun – and hard work – begins. As the owner, you are responsible for your horse's health and welfare. With this in mind, **Keeping a Horse** provides useful information on the day-to-day management of horses and ponies, whether they live in a field or are stabled, including practical information about feeding, bedding and field management.

The **Daily Care** of the horse looks at how to keep your horse healthy and ensure that he has enough exercise to keep him fit, as well as how to recognize when he may be unwell. There is a useful guide to common ailments and how they should be treated. The horse's feet are also thoroughly discussed, including the anatomy of the hooves and the typical ailments which affect them.

▌ LEFT
Once your horse is tacked up and ready, it's time to climb aboard. It's much easier to mount a horse with a helper to give you a leg-up to support you. This method is a good way to learn how to mount, and it is also far less stressful on the horse's back.

▌ BELOW LEFT
Position the stirrup iron so that your foot can go into it easily. For the near-side foot (left foot), turn the stirrup leather in an anticlockwise direction before placing your foot into the iron.

▌ BELOW RIGHT
Learning to ride requires patience and practice. Each pace – walk, trot, canter and gallop – gives you a different sense of speed and motion.

Riding horses is a demanding yet ultimately fulfilling pastime which has brought a great deal of pleasure and fun to many (although it is not without its many disappointments, as any rider will tell you!). It is important to remember that whatever your ambition, whether it be to compete at the highest level or to go on a gentle hack through beautiful countryside, riding should be enjoyable for you and your horse. The relationship between the rider and his or her mount should always be a partnership.

Learning the art of horsemanship requires dedication and patience on the part of the pupil – the rider never stops learning. Horses, like humans,

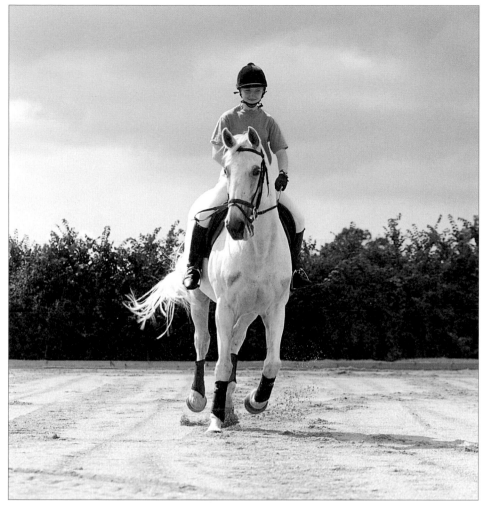

▌ RIGHT
Cantering brings with it an exhilarating feeling of speed and power, combined with a wonderful sense of freedom. The horse and rider should appear to be moving as one.

▌ BELOW
The bridle is one of the first pieces of riding equipment you will learn to use. When putting on the bridle, you should hold the horse's nose with your left hand, hold the bridle in your right hand, bring it in front of the horse's face and then gently lift it into his mouth.

are individuals, and we can learn as much from them as they can from us.

The section **Learning to Ride** will prove invaluable to anyone with an interest in riding, including first-time riders, those returning to riding after a period of time, or anyone who feels they need to do a little "revision". We look at where to learn, the basic clothing and equipment the rider needs, how to prepare the horse for riding, and how the rider communicates with his or her horse.

Although there is no substitute for actually being on a horse, when you are learning to ride the time spent in the saddle is often relatively little (it may be only an hour a week), so it is useful for the budding equestrian to be able to read and learn more about horsemanship. Such knowledge will hopefully be able to be put into practice the next time you ride.

In **Mastering the Paces** we look at how the horse moves, showing the four paces – walk, trot, canter and gallop – in detail, as well as the transitions between these paces. As the rider gains confidence and balance and learns how to coordinate himself, he

RIGHT
Show jumping is an Olympic sport, combining technical ability, athleticism and balance. Competition riding can bring out the best in horse and rider.

BELOW
Most horses can be trained to jump. This horse has jumped too high for these fences, but with practice will be able to negotiate different distances and heights.

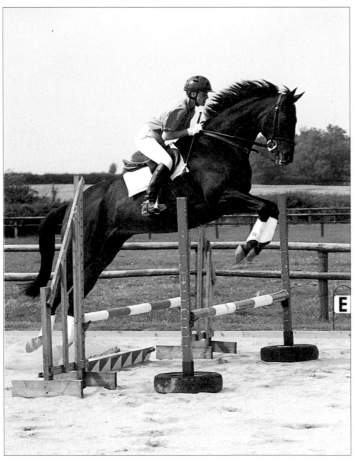

can then develop his skills and learn more about influencing his horse – for example, the half-halt, lateral work, variations within paces and the counter canter – creating and building upon the all-important rider-horse partnership.

Preparing for Take-off is a useful section on learning how to jump. Starting with simple exercises over trot poles and low fences in the arena, we progress to the exhilaration of riding around a cross-country course, how to cope with difficult terrain and preparing for the unexpected.

As your riding skills develop further you may want to take part in competitions, so in **The Competition World** we describe the wide variety of equestrian sports which exist, and how to choose one that suits you and your horse's temperament. From the pleasure and excitement of jumping or mounted games, the grace of dressage or vaulting, to the special demands of endurance riding or the thrill of taking part in a race, there's something for every rider in this section – along with the idea that the main aim of competing should be to have fun.

■ **ABOVE**
Learning to jump requires practice. This horse is jumping smoothly over a fence; the horse is collected and the rider well-positioned.

■ **LEFT**
Riders with good overall horsemanship skills can put themselves to the test by competing in horse trials or eventing.

■ **BELOW**
Taking part in a dressage competition is the perfect opportunity to show off your horse. Dressage is a very popular sport and is as enjoyable to watch as it is to partake in.

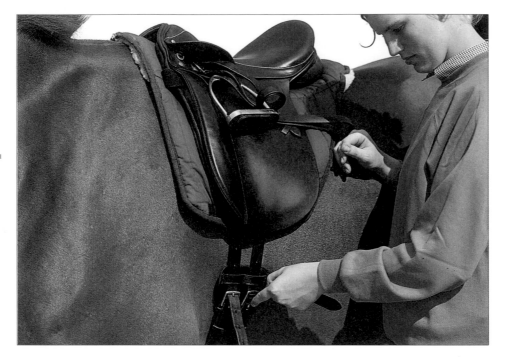

▌ **LEFT**
The saddle is one of the most important pieces of equipment you will need to buy, and because of the skill and craftsmanship involved in producing a saddle, it is usually the most expensive. Take good care of your saddle and you will enjoy it for many years.

▌ **BELOW**
It is advisable to seek professional help when choosing a new saddle, to ensure that it fits the horse correctly and is suitable for your riding needs.

Riding, like skiing, sailing and many other activities, requires specialist clothing and equipment. A visit to your local saddlery or tack shop will confirm the bewildering array of tack and equipment on sale – not all of it necessarily essential. With this in mind we have provided a detailed guide to **Saddlery and Equipment**, focusing on the everyday saddle and bridle, as well as explaining how and why many of the more unusual items of equipment are used.

The Saddle is an essential piece of riding equipment and one of the most expensive items the owner has to buy for his or her horse. There are saddles designed to suit every style of riding, so we explain which is the best for you and your chosen type

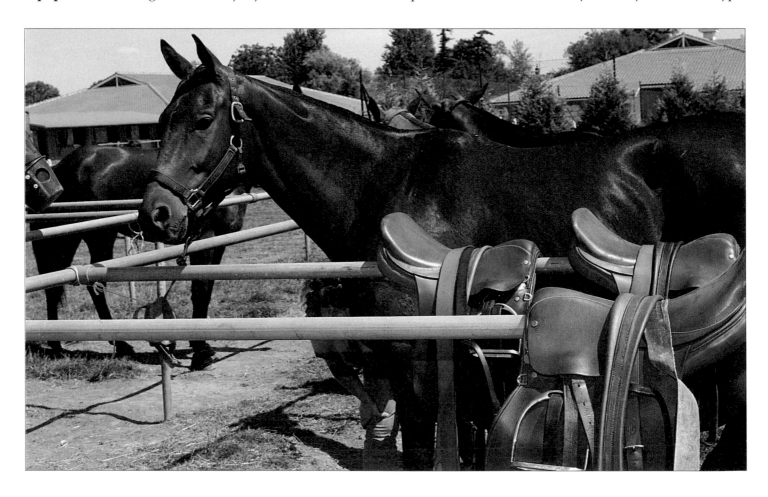

■ BELOW
Choosing the right bridle and bit can be a daunting task – they come in a huge variety of shapes and sizes. The traditional bridle is made of leather.

■ BOTTOM
Combined with the rider's legs, voice and body position, the bridle and bit provide the communication which allows the rider to control the horse.

of riding. There is also a section on essential saddle accessories including girths, stirrups, breastplates and saddle cloths, as well as a guide to saddle care.

The bridle is an equally important piece of equipment, and like the saddle should be chosen carefully, with the comfort of the horse and the safety of the rider firmly in mind. The subject of **Bridles and Bits** is a complex one and it is important to choose the right combination of tack to suit the horse and the rider – too mild a bit and you could be left with an unstoppable horse, too strong and you could unwittingly inflict pain on the horse. We explain the different types of bridle and noseband, and look in detail at bits and bitting, describing the various bit groups and the different actions they have on the horse.

▌ RIGHT
A dressage whip may be used when schooling a horse – this long whip can be used to give a gentle flick without the rider having to let go of the reins.

▌ BELOW
Not only is grooming essential for the health of your horse – removing dust, dead skin and hair, and providing massage for improving muscle tone – it also makes your horse look absolutely spectacular for competitions.

The novice rider will not need **Training Aids and Gadgets** (aids are used to develop a well-schooled, obedient horse and gadgets are used to prevent an aspect of the horse's behaviour), but nonetheless it is wise to be aware of what is available and how each item works. We explain how and when such aids are used, as well as the effect each one has on the horse.

Grooming is an essential part of the daily care of your horse, important for his health as well as his appearance. In **Grooming Equipment** we show the basic kit you will need and explain in detail how to groom your horse, from picking his feet out and daily brushing, to clipping the horse and the finishing touches required for a competition.

■ BELOW
This horse is dressed for travelling, with a poll
guard for the head, rugs to keep him warm, hock
and knee boots to protect his legs, and a bandage to
protect his tail.

■ BOTTOM RIGHT
Stable bandages provide warmth and protection.
They should always be used with padding
underneath, otherwise pressure sores may form.

The horse in the wild has evolved to withstand the
rigours of outdoor life, but many riding horses lead
an "unnatural" life. As we place greater demands on
the horse, expecting improvements in athletic
performance and transporting horses to and from
competitions, the need for special **Horse Clothing
and Equipment** has increased. From boots and
bandages to protect your horse's legs, to rugs and
blankets which keep the horse warm and dry, the
range of horse clothing is enormous. We guide you
through the maze of clothing and equipment
available, as well as providing an invaluable, step-by-
step guide to putting on boots, bandages and rugs,
so your horse will be protected from head to tail.

Finally, we come to **The Rider's Clothes**. Like the horse the rider needs special clothing and equipment for his or her chosen discipline. Much of today's riding clothing – especially competition attire – is influenced by tradition. For instance, the jacket worn by the show rider is based on the traditional coat worn by a huntsman.

This is not to say that fashion does not have an influence. As sports such as endurance riding become more popular, so new fabrics and colours are introduced to update the rider's wardrobe.

The most important considerations for any rider are comfort in the saddle and safety. Clothing for riding has developed to meet both these requirements. This section looks at the basic items that every rider needs: a protective hat, sensible footwear, and jodhpurs or breeches, and explains the correct dress for competitive riding. We also look at artificial aids (whips and spurs) explaining how and when they should be used by the rider.

We hope that you enjoy *The Ultimate Book of the Horse and Rider* and that it will prove to be an invaluable source of information for horse riders and horse lovers alike. Whatever your equestrian ambitions might be, never forget the great pleasure and satisfaction that being involved with horses can give, and that ultimately the most successful relationships between horses and people are based on mutual respect – a true partnership.

■ LEFT
For most competitions you need to wear a riding coat, breeches and boots, a shirt with a collar and tie, or a collarless shirt with a hunting tie or stock. A rider dressed for top-level dressage wears a top hat, tail coat and waistcoat.

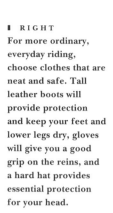

▮ RIGHT
For more ordinary, everyday riding, choose clothes that are neat and safe. Tall leather boots will provide protection and keep your feet and lower legs dry, gloves will give you a good grip on the reins, and a hard hat provides essential protection for your head.

Breeds of the World

Introduction

The lives of humans and horses have been bound together for many thousands of years. Appreciated first as just another source of food, the predecessors of the modern horse were hunted like any other wild animal. In time there came a steady process of domestication as nomadic peoples began to herd horses in the same way as they did goats and other animals. Ultimately, however, it was as a means of swift transport that the horse really came into his own. Men learnt to ride. Their whole lives were transformed. Horses became their chief means of transportation, remaining so until well into the twentieth century. Domestication, coupled with a gradual increase in human population, signalled the end of the truly wild horse. Today, even those horses which live in herds on the few remaining extensive areas of suitable grassland are not truly wild, for they are all "managed" by humans to one degree or another. Nevertheless horses retain much of the instinctive behaviour which enabled them to exist without man's intervention and it is necessary to understand what makes them "tick" if we are to enjoy our continuing association with them.

The History of the Horse

The modern horse, *Equus caballus*, belongs to the family *Equidae,* which also includes asses and zebras. *Equidae* are placed in the order Perissodactyla, to which tapirs and rhinoceroses belong and which descended from the Condylarthra, a group of primitive, long extinct mammals which were the ancestors of all hoofed mammals.

Fossil remains have made it possible to trace at least some aspects of the evolution of the modern horse over a period of some sixty million years, indicating how it gradually adapted to changes in its environment. The known history of the modern horse starts with Eohippus, also called the Dawn Horse, which is known to have lived in North America during the Eocene epoch (fifty-four to thirty-eight million years ago). An animal no larger than a small dog, Eohippus was designed for life as a forest browser moving around on soft soil. It had four toes on its forefeet, three on its back feet and pads similar to a dog's. Its small, low-crowned teeth were

suited to eating leaves and other low, soft vegetation. It would probably have had a camouflage colouring to help it to escape predators. During the Oligocene epoch (thirty-seven to twenty-six million years

ago) first Mesohippus then Merychippus, showed distinct changes: the legs became longer, the back straighter (Eohippus had an arched back) and the whole animal larger. One toe disappeared on the forefoot, leaving three toes on both fore and hindfeet. The teeth also showed signs of change, the pre-molars becoming more like true molars.

In this slow process of evolution, the most significant change of all occurred during the Miocene epoch (twenty-five to seven million years ago) when forests gave

■ PREVIOUS PAGE OPPOSITE
A Cleveland Bay.

■ PREVIOUS PAGE
A Furioso.

■ LEFT
The zebra is one of the small group of animals belonging to the family *Equidae.*

■ BELOW LEFT
The Highland Pony probably resembles Pony Type 2 of pre-domestication times.

■ BELOW RIGHT
The wiry Akhal-Teke is thought to approximate to Horse Type 3.

■ RIGHT
Horse Type 4 resembled this refined little Caspian
Pony. The Caspian was "re-discovered" in 1965.

■ BELOW RIGHT
Pony Type 1 lived in north-west Europe and looked
like the present-day Exmoor Pony.

■ RIGHT
Horse Type 4 resembled this refined little Caspian
Pony. The Caspian was "re-discovered" in 1965.

■ BELOW RIGHT
Pony Type 1 lived in north-west Europe and looked
like the present-day Exmoor Pony.

way to grassland and the horse's ancestors
became plains dwellers. This significant
change in environment called for teeth
designed for grazing, as opposed to
browsing, a longer neck to make grazing
easier, longer legs to facilitate flight from
predators and feet suitable for harder
terrain. During this time the single toe, or
hoof, began to evolve: the outer toes no
longer touched the ground and the
central toe became larger and stronger.

Then the history of the horse family
becomes somewhat more complex, with
various sub-families developing.
Eventually, however, these became extinct
and it was Pliohippus which provided the
link in the chain from Eohippus to the
modern Equus. Pliohippus evolved some
ten to five million years ago and had long
legs with a single hoof on each. Its direct
successor, Equus, the genus of modern
horse, finally emerged a million years ago.

During the Ice Ages of the Pleistocene
epoch, Equus migrated via the land
bridges which then existed to Europe, Asia
and Africa. However, the disappearance of
these land bridges (e.g. across what are
now the Strait of Gibraltar and the Bering
Strait) when the ice receded about 10,000
years ago meant that if an animal had
become extinct in one continent, that

continent could not be repopulated – at
least not without the help of man. This is
exactly what happened in America: for
some unexplained reason the horse
disappeared. It was not seen again until
European colonists reintroduced it
thousands of years later.

All members of the modern *Equidae*
family are swift runners with only one
functional toe on each foot (the modern
horse's ergot – the horny growth at the
back of the fetlock – is believed to be the

vestiges of the pad of its ancestor,
Eohippus). All live in herds and all have
cheek teeth designed to grind plant-food.

Present-day horses and ponies are said
to trace back to three distinct types,
produced by variations in their natural
environment. Northern Europe provided
a slow-moving, heavy horse *(Equus
silvaticus)* from which the world's heavy
horse breeds are derived. Then there was
the primitive Asiatic Wild Horse, survivors
of which were found still living wild as late
as 1881 (and called the Przewalski Horse);
and finally the rather more refined
Tarpan, from eastern Europe.

Later on, by the time that man began
domesticating the horse, four sub-species
had evolved: two pony types and two horse
types. Pony Type 1 inhabited the north-
west of Europe and resembled the
modern Exmoor Pony. Pony Type 2,
which was bigger and more heavily built,
lived in northern Eurasia. The Highland
Pony is probably the nearest modern-day
equivalent. Horse Type 3 was a little bigger
still, but much more lightweight in build
and suited to hot climates. Its nearest
equivalent is thought to be the Akhal-Teke.
Horse Type 4, found in western Asia, was
the smallest but the most refined and was
the forerunner of the Caspian Pony.

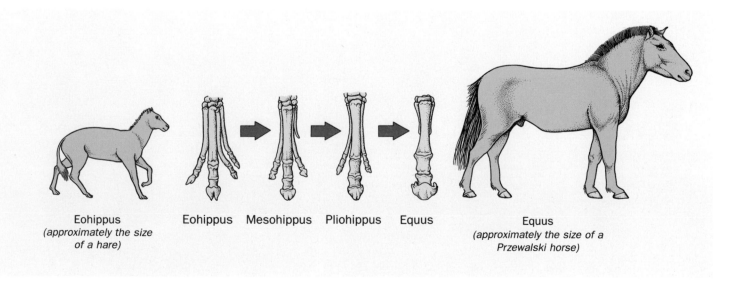

Eohippus
*(approximately the size
of a hare)*

Eohippus   Mesohippus   Pliohippus   Equus

Equus
*(approximately the size of a
Przewalski horse)*

Horses in the Wild

The horse is a herbivore, that is, an eater of plants. Like all herbivores horses are basically grass eaters. In the wild the horse is a nomadic grazer and spends up to twenty hours out of every twenty-four grazing. When food is plentiful a wild horse thrives and puts on weight; when it is scarce, and weather conditions harsh, he loses condition. Nature, as usual, has arranged for foals to be born in the spring when the weather is mild and the grass lush – thus ensuring that the mares have a plentiful supply of food, which in turn ensures ample milk for the foals. Mares come into season every twenty-one days during the spring and summer, until around September or October, and the gestation period is approximately eleven months.

Horses are by nature herd animals. In the wild they live in social groups within a larger group (the herd), each small group comprising a stallion, some mares, their foals and yearlings and perhaps one or two two-year-olds. Depending on the power of the stallion, the total size of the group is usually in the region of a dozen. Young, timid stallions and old ones who no longer have any mares often live in bachelor groups – horses do not like to be alone. Just as family life is important to them, so is friendship. Horses indulge in mutual grooming with their teeth, they play together and relax and doze together. A stallion will groom a favourite mare even when she is not in season (grooming is also used to stimulate a mare sexually) and will play with the foals – though eventually he will drive out the more mature colts who must then either join a bachelor group or begin to collect their own band of mares.

Horses communicate with each other by a number of means, both vocal and physical. Their "vocabulary" includes neighing, nickering, squealing and, more rarely, roaring. A loud neigh enables a horse to make contact with another from whom it has been separated; a quieter, lower nicker may be used by a stallion to a mare, a mare to her foal or between friends as a greeting; squeals are signs of excitement and are used when horses are in close contact, particularly sexual contact; horses may emit loud roars and screams during a fight that has serious intentions, as opposed to the sort of play-fighting indulged in by young colts, and a mare may well scream her disapproval at a stallion who pesters her when she is not ready to be mated.

Body posture is another means of communication. A relaxed horse looks relaxed: a hind foot resting, head lowered, eyes partly closed, lower lip drooping. An excited stallion prances around, head tucked in, tail raised, his whole outline saying "look at me". A startled horse looks tense and alert, signs which indicate to its companions that there is cause for alarm.

Smell is also important to horses. Mares and foals recognize each other by smell. When meeting, horses will put their noses close together, often blowing down their nostrils, before deciding whether or not to be friends. Smell also plays a part in sexual communication – a stallion smells the vulva and urine of an in-season mare and can tell the difference between the dung of another stallion and that of a mare (he will urinate over a mare's dung but add his own dung to that left by a stallion).

A horse's ears, too, being tremendously mobile, say a good deal about what he is thinking – where his attention is focused,

what mood he is in. Drooping ears indicate that the horse is in a dozy state, alert ones that something has caught his attention; ears that are turned back may show that the horse's attention is focused behind him or they may indicate submission or fear; ears laid flat denote anger or fear.

Having eyes set on the sides of his head, the horse can see almost all round him, the only blind spots being immediately behind and a little way in front of his head – he can keep an approaching object in focus merely by turning his head slightly. The horse's sense of touch is enhanced by the whiskers on his muzzle which enable him to judge how far an object is from the end of his nose and may also be useful for assessing texture, for example when he is grazing.

The horse's long legs enable him to travel at speed, essential for an animal whose natural form of defence is to run away. Since he is not equipped to fight predators such as wolves, lions and snakes, his chief means of survival is flight. This helps to explain why domesticated horses often prefer to shelter from bad weather by standing by a hedge or wall rather than making use of a specially provided man-made building: horses feel safer in the open air where they can easily gallop off if anything frightens them.

Conformation

Conformation, or the horse's overall make and shape, varies a good deal from breed to breed. What constitutes "ideal" conformation varies according to the work which the horse is required to perform. In spite of these necessary variations, however, certain guidelines can be followed when looking for desirable conformation. They relate to proportion: if a horse is correctly proportioned he will be better balanced, less prone to unsoundness and more able to perform his allotted tasks than a horse with less harmonious proportions. Indeed, many a horse with conformational defects has been condemned as "difficult" when it is simply his shape which prevents him from carrying out what his master requires.

A horse is deemed to have "correct" proportions when certain measurements are equal. For example: the length of the head, the depth of the body at the girth,

the distance from the point of the hock to the ground, the distance from the chestnut on the foreleg to the ground, the distance from the croup to the fold of the stifle and from the fold of the stifle to the point of the hock should all be the same.

The domesticated horse is required to work, which means that certain features of his conformation are of particular importance. If a horse is deep through the girth, that is from the top of the wither to below the elbow, then his lungs will have plenty of room to expand – essential for any working horse. The length of his back is also important, particularly for the ridden horse. Too long, and it will be inclined to weakness; too short, and it may restrict the action.

Starting at the front, it is important that the horse's head is in proportion to his overall size. An over-large, heavy head will upset the overall balance, putting

extra weight on the forehand, which already carries 60 per cent of the horse's total weight. Too small a head will also affect the balance. The upper and lower jaws should meet evenly at the front – if they do not this will inhibit the horse's ability to bite food such as grass. The nostrils should be large and wide, and large eyes are preferable to small ones, which experience has shown often denote a less than generous temperament. The set of the head is also important. If there is not sufficient clearance between the mandible (the lower jaw) and the atlas (the top bone in the neck), the horse will have difficulty in flexing at the poll, a requirement in the more collected gaits. There should be room for two fingers' width when the horse's head is raised.

In the riding horse the neck should be fairly long and curved. There should be no tendency to fleshiness around the

▌ LEFT
The long neck and sloping shoulder of the
Thoroughbred are associated with speed. Depth
through the girth ensures plenty of room for the
lungs to expand.

rounded and look like a matching pair.
"Boxy" upright feet are prone to jarring.
Large, flat feet may be more prone to
bruising of the sole and to corns. The
hindfeet, which bear less of the horse's
overall weight when he is stationary,
should be more oval in shape than the
forefeet. Viewed from the side the slope of
both fore and hindfeet should be a
continuation of the slope of the pastern.
The feet should point directly forwards.

throat, which again would restrict the
flexion of the head. This is particularly
important in the riding horse. A long neck
is associated with speed, a shorter one with
strength. Hence the heavy draught breeds
lack the length of neck seen, for instance,
in the Thoroughbred. The shoulder
should be well sloped (the angle of the
scapula gives the slope). Such
conformation enables the horse to take
longer strides than a straight shoulder,
which results in short, restricted action. A
straight shoulder may produce jarring,
which can be detrimental to the forelimb.
Horses with straight shoulders tend to give
an uncomfortable ride, too. The shoulder
should be muscular but not "loaded", i.e.
too heavy. The withers should be of a
good height and well defined. If they are
too high, it may be difficult to fit a saddle.
If they are poorly defined, it may be
difficult to keep a saddle in place. With
the draught horse, which must wear a
collar and for whom pulling power is
more important than extended paces, a
slightly straighter shoulder is acceptable.

The chest and body should be
reasonably broad, but not excessively so,
otherwise the horse's movement will be
affected. Narrowness in the chest, giving
the forelegs the appearance of "coming
out of one hole" is a serious fault, causing
the foreleg joints to brush against each
other. The back should rise slightly to the
croup, and be well muscled. Short, well-
muscled loins are essential: the lumbar

vertebrae have no support from the ribs,
yet it is the loins which transfer the thrust
from the engine (the hindquarters) to the
body. The croup of the fully grown horse
should be the same height as the withers
and should not be too sloping, a feature
which, combined with a low-set tail, is
usually a sign of weakness. Croup-high
horses throw extra weight on to the
forehand, thus putting more strain on
the forelimbs.

The horse's engine is in the back, that
is in the hindquarters. They should
therefore be strong and muscular. When
standing still the hindlegs should not be
stretched out behind him or tucked under
him – a line dropped vertically from the
point of the buttock to the ground should
touch the hock and run down the rear of
the cannon bone.

The forelegs should be straight and
strong, with long, muscular forearms and
large, flat knees. Short cannons indicate
strength and there should be a good
measurement of bone (the measurement
being taken around the cannon below the
knee). The amount of bone determines
the weight-carrying ability of the horse.
The amount of bone varies with the type
of horse but as a rough guide a
lightweight riding horse standing 16.2hh
should have a minimum of 8 inches
(20cm) of bone, a heavyweight horse of
the same height at least 9 inches (23cm).

The pasterns should be of medium
length and slope. The forefeet should be

COMMON CONFORMATIONAL DEFECTS

Back at the knee – where the knees,
when viewed from the side, tend to
extend backwards.

Calf knees – knees which are shallow
from front to back.

Cow hocks – hocks which, when viewed
from behind, turn inwards, as in a cow.

Ewe neck – where the top line of the neck
is concave and the lower line convex.

Herring-gutted – where the horse has an
upward slope from front to back on the
underside of the belly.

Over at the knee – where the knees
protrude forwards.

Pigeon toes – toes which turn inwards.

Roach back – where the spine has an
exaggerated upward curve.

Sickle hocks – hocks which when viewed
from the side have a concave line in front of
the hocks and a slanting cannon bone.

Slab-sided – where the ribs are flat as
opposed to "well-sprung".

Splay-footed – where the toes
turn outwards.

Sway back – where the back has an
exaggerated hollow.

Tied in below the knee – where the
measurement of bone just below the knee is
less than that farther down the cannon bone.

Colours and Markings

Equine coat colouring is controlled by numerous genes acting in combination to produce a multitude of variations in pigmentation. These genes, which are inherited, are located on paired structures known as chromosomes: the modern horse has 64 chromosomes, half of which are inherited from the sire and the other half from the dam. Some genes are dominant, others are recessive. For example, in horses chestnut is recessive to all other colours, bay is dominant to black, and grey is dominant to bay and black. The dominant greying gene can result in horses which are born with a dark coat turning progressively more grey as they

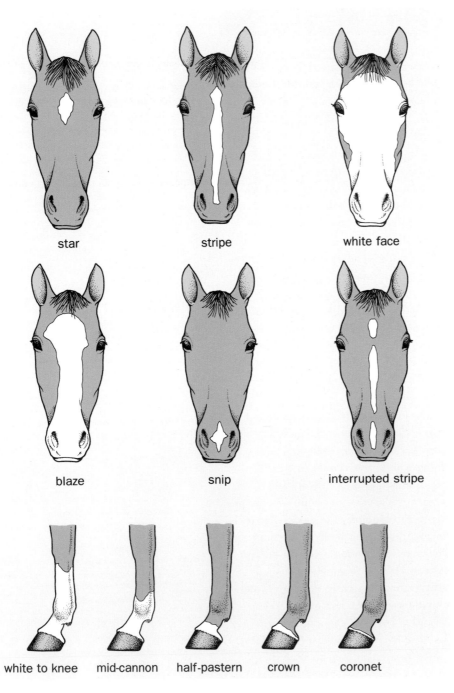

star

stripe

white face

blaze

snip

interrupted stripe

white to knee   mid-cannon   half-pastern   crown   coronet

FACIAL MARKINGS

These include: Star, stripe and interrupted stripe, snip, blaze, white face, white muzzle

LEG MARKINGS

For registration purposes leg markings are described in detail, using points of the anatomy: e.g. white to fetlock, white to knee, white to hock, etc.

Two less specific terms are also in popular use: sock (white colouring from the coronet up to the knee), stocking (white colouring from the coronet up to and over the knee or hock).

HOOF COLOURS

The horn of the hoofs can vary from blue or black to white and may be marked with dark stripes.

grow older. This is especially noticeable in the Lipizzaner, whose foals are born dark and, with rare exceptions, turn grey as they mature. Albinos occur where there is a congenital deficiency of colouring pigment. The hair is white, the skin pink and eyes often blue.

A horse is always described by its coat colouring, followed by other distinguishing features, where applicable, such as white markings and the colour of the mane and tail.

Some horses have more than one clearly defined coat colour. Broken or part-coloured horses such as piebalds and skewbalds (known as Pintos or Paint Horses in America) have irregular patches of two different colours while Spotted Horses show a variety of spotted markings. Black legs go with bay body colouring.

Horses' eyes are normally dark, although blue eyes also occur.

EQUINE COLOURS

Grey A mixture of black and white hairs throughout. The coat varies from light to iron (very dark). The skin is black.

Fleabitten Grey Grey coat flecked with brown specks.

Dappled Grey Light grey base coat with dark grey rings.

Bay Reddish coat with black mane, tail and "points" (i.e. limbs). The coat colour may vary from red to brown or yellowish.

Black All black except for occasional white marks on the legs and/or head.

Chestnut Varies from a pale golden colour to a rich, red gold. The mane and tail may be lighter or darker than the coat colour.

Liver Chestnut The darkest of the chestnut shades.

Sorrel A light-red chesnut.

Brown A mixture of black and brown hairs, with black limbs, mane and tail. A very dark brown horse may appear almost black.

Roan A body colour with white hairs interspersed, which lightens the overall effect.

Strawberry Roan Chestnut body colour with white hair giving a pinkish-red tinge.

Blue Roan Black or brown body colour with white hair giving a blue tinge.

Dun Light sandy-coloured coat with black mane and tail, often accompanied by a dark, dorsal eel-stripe extending from the line of the neck to the tail, and sometimes by "zebra markings" (stripes) on the withers and legs – the vestiges of a primitive form of camouflage. Dun can vary from yellow to "mouse", depending on the diffusion of pigment. The skin is black.

Palomino Gold coat with white mane and tail.

Spotted Small, more or less circular patches of hair of a different colour from the main body colour and distributed over various areas of the body.

Piebald Large, irregular patches of black and white.

Skewbald Large, irregular patches of white and any other colour except black.

Cream Cream-coloured coat with unpigmented skin (also known as cremello).

White Markings White markings on the face and legs and, occasionally, on the body, are a valuable means of distinguishing one horse from another and are therefore noted in detail on veterinary certificates and registration papers.

Brindle Brown or grey streaked or patched with a darker colour.

▮ OPPOSITE
ABOVE
The predominant coat colour of the Lipizzaner is grey, but foals are born dark and it takes several years for the coat to change to the typical "white" colouring associated with the breed.

▮ RIGHT
Spotted coat patterns have existed – and often been highly prized – throughout man's long relationship with the horse. Spotted horses are particularly associated with the Nez Percé Indians of North America.

Horses

There are more than 150 different breeds and types of horses in the world. The development of each of them has been influenced by man. Domestication resulted in selective breeding and, in many instances, more nutritious feeding, both of which led to an increase in the size or the quality (or both) of the horse. However, the biggest influencing factor was the work which humans required their particular horses to perform. Those who needed to move heavy loads bred for strength, while others in need of fast transportation bred for speed. The terms coldblood and warmblood (which have nothing to do with temperature) are used to describe horses. Coldblood refers to the heavy draught breeds which are believed to be descended from the prehistoric horse of northern Europe. Warmblood refers to the lighter, riding type of horse. Nowadays the term "warmblood" is used in connection with the horses being bred for competition riding. The breeds in this book are organized by continent, then sub-divided into countries within each continent.

"Wild" Horses

PRZEWALSKI HORSE

The horse no longer exists as a truly wild animal, although the Asiatic Wild Horse, believed to be one of the precursors of the domesticated horse, can still be seen in zoos in various parts of the world. The Asiatic Wild Horse (*Equus przewalskii przewalskii Poliakoff*) was "discovered" – or rather a small herd was – as recently as 1881 in the Tachin Schara Nuru Mountains on the edge of the Gobi desert by the Russian explorer Colonel N.M. Przewalski. Before that it was believed to have been extinct, over-hunted for its meat by Mongolian tribesmen. The Przewalski Horse, as it is widely known, differs genetically from the domesticated

horse, having 66 chromosomes instead of 64. In appearance it has several "primitive" features: a large head, with the eyes set high up rather than to the side of the head as in the case of the modern horse;

long ears; thick neck; heavy body with a dark dorsal strip and zebra markings on the legs. The Przewalski stands about 12–13hh and is always yellowish dun with a light-coloured nose and dark mane and

■ ABOVE
These Kaimanawa horses live in feral herds in New Zealand's North Island. Like the Brumbies of Australia they are unpopular with stockmen because they compete for food with domestic animals

■ PREVIOUS PAGE OPPOSITE
A Mustang.

■ PREVIOUS PAGE
A Trakehner.

■ LEFT
The Asiatic Wild Horse or Przewalski Horse is the only surviving race of the species from which domestic horses are descended. Its chromosome count differs from that of the domesticated horse.

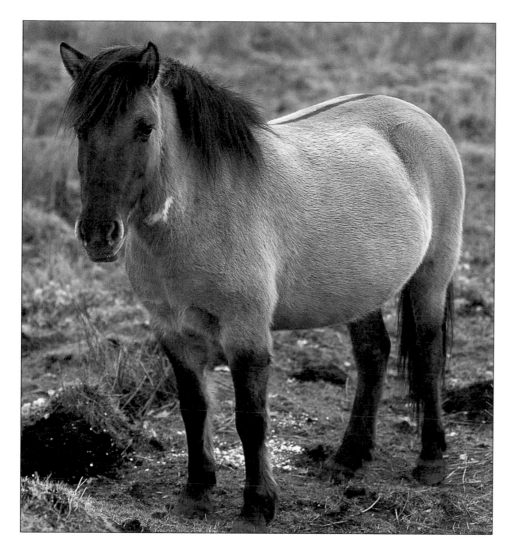

tail. The mane, which grows upright, is shed each spring and there is no forelock. Intractable by nature – it cannot be trained for riding – the Przewalski can survive on a minimum of food and endure extremes of heat and cold.

TARPAN

Eastern Europe and European Russia were the home of the Tarpan, another horse widely believed to have been an ancestor of the modern horse. It survived in the wild until the nineteenth century. One authority claims that the last true Tarpan in captivity died in 1919, in which case the Tarpan which exists today, running semi-wild in reserves in Poland, must be a "reconstruction", almost certainly bred from the Konik, which it strongly resembled. Experiments with crossing Przewalski stallions and Konik mares have also produced an animal which looks very like the original Tarpan. The Tarpan was (and is) more lightly built than the Przewalski, standing about 13hh and with

a brown or mouse dun coat, dark mane and tail and, frequently, primitive dorsal stripe and zebra markings.

BRUMBY

Australia's "wild" horse, the Brumby, is not a true wild horse, equine animals having been unknown in Australasia until the arrival of European settlers a few hundred years ago (the assumption being that because there were no land bridges linking the Americas with Australia, Eohippus and its descendants had no means of migrating there). The Brumbies which live in feral herds in the Northern Territory and, to a lesser extent, in central Australia, are descended from settlers' horses who wandered off into the bush, producing offspring that grew up under wild conditions. When rounded up and broken in some Brumbies have, over the years, been useful to man but today they are generally regarded as a pest and are culled because they compete for food with domestic animals.

See also Camargue, Mustang, Sorraia.

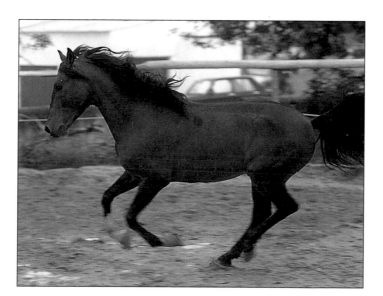

■ ABOVE LEFT
The primitive looking Konik pony is found in Poland and is a descendant of the Tarpan. Crossed with Przewalski stallions, Konik mares produce Tarpan "look-alikes".

■ LEFT
The Sorraia pony, which can be found living in semi-feral conditions in Portugal, is believed to be of ancient origin.

Arab

The oldest and purest of all horse breeds, the Arab is considered by many people to be the most beautiful equine animal in the world. With its refined head and dished profile, expressive eyes, high spirits and unique, floating action, it is undoubtedly one of the most exquisite of creatures. Although it has certainly been bred with great care for many centuries, its exact origins are unclear. Depictions of horses

in ancient art suggest that horses of Arab type lived in the Arabian peninsula as long ago as 2,000 – 3,000BC. Like the desert tribes with whom they have lived for so long, Arab horses became superbly well adapted to life in a harsh environment, having extreme powers of endurance, tremendous soundness and the ability to thrive on the most meagre of rations.

More than any other horse, it is the Arab which has influenced the development of equine

INTERESTING FACTS

The unique outline of the Arab is determined by the formation of its skeleton, which differs from other equine breeds in several respects. The Arab has 17 ribs (other horses have 18); five lumbar vertebrae (other horses have six), and 16 tail vertebrae (other horses have 18).

BREED DESCRIPTION

Height 14.2 – 15hh.

Colour Predominantly chestnut, grey, bay and black.

Conformation Small head with broad forehead, fine muzzle, concave profile, wide nostrils and small ears; deep, clearly defined jowl with the throat set into it in a distinctly arched curve; graceful, curving neck; long, sloping shoulders with well-defined withers; deep, roomy body with broad, deep chest and short, level back; high-set tail; hard, clean limbs with well-defined tendons and dense, fine bone; hard, well-shaped feet; fine, silky mane and tail.

▌ TOP
Large eyes and nostrils are typical of the Arab. The short, refined head, with its dished profile, is one of the breed's most distinctive features.

▌ LEFT
The Arab's comparatively small size belies its weight-carrying ability. Standing no more than 15hh it will nevertheless carry a fully grown man with ease.

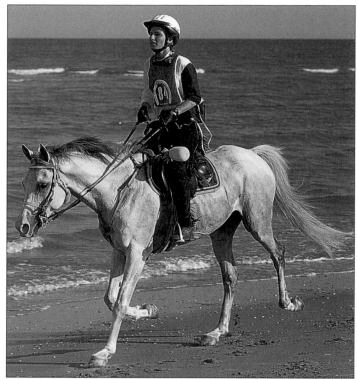

breeds throughout the world. This Arabian influence was initiated in the seventh and early eighth centuries AD when the followers of Islam spread across North Africa and into Spain. The horses they took with them were greatly superior to the native stock of other lands and so began a process of upgrading, through the introduction of

Arab blood, that was to go on for many centuries and, indeed, still goes on today.

Pure-bred Arabian horses are now bred throughout the world. As well as appearing in the show ring, they are particularly suited to the sport of endurance riding. In recent times, too, there has been a resurgence of interest in Arab racing.

▮ ABOVE LEFT
The Arab horse often appears to float over the ground. This remarkable action, coupled with a gentle temperament, makes it a popular riding horse throughout the world.

▮ ABOVE RIGHT
The breed's legendary stamina makes it the perfect choice for endurance riding which at the top level involves covering a distance of 100 miles (161km) in a day.

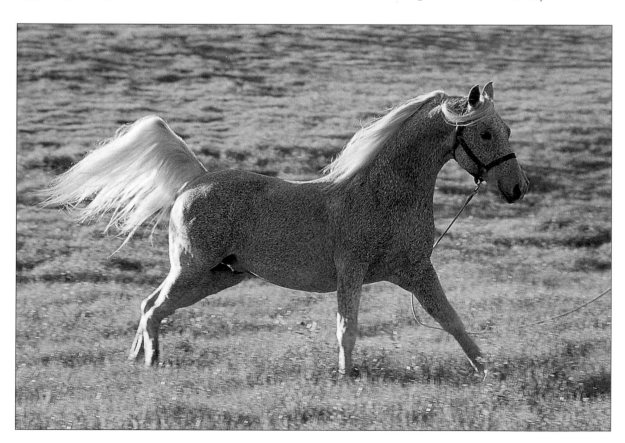

▮ LEFT
With its elegance, spirit and exceptional looks, it is easy to see why the Arab is often considered to be the world's most beautiful horse.

Barb

The Barb comes from Morocco, Algeria and Tunisia – the coastal regions of these North African countries were formerly known as the Barbary Coast, "Barbary" meaning foreign or, more specifically, non-Christian lands. Opinions differ as to the Barb's origins, lack of documentary evidence making it impossible to do more than hazard an educated guess. According to one school of thought, the Barb may trace back to an isolated group of wild horses which survived the Ice Age. If that were true, it would make the Barb an even older breed than the Arab. Another theory links the Barb to the Akhal-Teke, the horse of the Turkmens.

Although it is unlikely that the breed's true origins will ever be revealed, what is certain is that the Barb has had more influence on the development of equine breeds throughout the world than any other horse except the Arab. As with the Arab, it was the spread of Islam which led to the forerunners of today's Barbs reaching Europe from the early eighth century onwards (the first Muslim army, seven thousand strong, landed in Spain in the spring of 711). Once established on the Iberian peninsula the Barb horse played a major role in the development of the Andalusian, which subsequently became one of the major influences in horse breeding all over the world. Among the many historical references to

BREED DESCRIPTION

Height Around 14.2 – 15.2hh.

Colour Predominantly grey, bay, brown and black.

Conformation Narrow head with convex profile; arched neck; flat shoulders with well-defined withers; short, strong body; sloping hindquarters with fairly low-set tail; rather slender, but strong, limbs; narrow, but hard, feet.

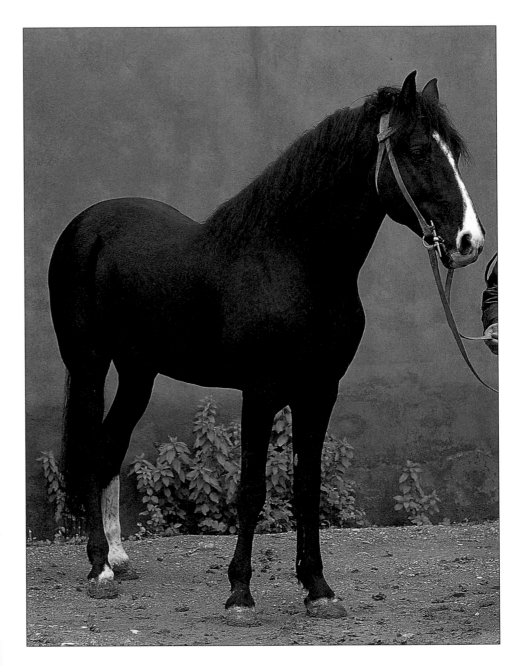

I BELOW
The Barb lacks the refinement and elegance of the Arab but is equally tough and enduring.

"Barbary" horses perhaps the most famous is Roan Barbary, belonging to the English king, Richard II (1367–1400). During the sixteenth century Henry VIII imported a number of Barbary horses into England and a century later the Barb played an important part in the evolution of the Thoroughbred. Elsewhere the influence of the Barb is still evident in the Argentinian Criollo and the American Mustang.

Despite its importance as a progenitor of other breeds, the Barb has achieved less widespread renown than the Arab, no doubt because it lacks the Arab's unique visual appeal, being much less refined and generally less impressive in appearance. Nevertheless it has the same boundless stamina and endurance, the same ability to thrive on meagre rations, the same sure-footedness – and an impressive turn of speed over short distances.

BELOW
Dressed in ceremonial attire, Barb horses and their Moroccan riders are a colourful sight at a modern "Fantasia".

INTERESTING FACTS

The most well-known Barb horses of modern times were those ridden by the Spahis, men of the Algerian and Tunisian cavalry regiments in the French army. The Spahis originally came from Turkey but were incorporated into their army by the French when the latter occupied Algiers and Tunis. Barb horses still feature in the exciting present-day North African festivals recalling these countries' military pasts.

BELOW
In the dramatic rifle-firing charge seen at North African festivals, Barb horses demonstrate their impressive speed over a short distance.

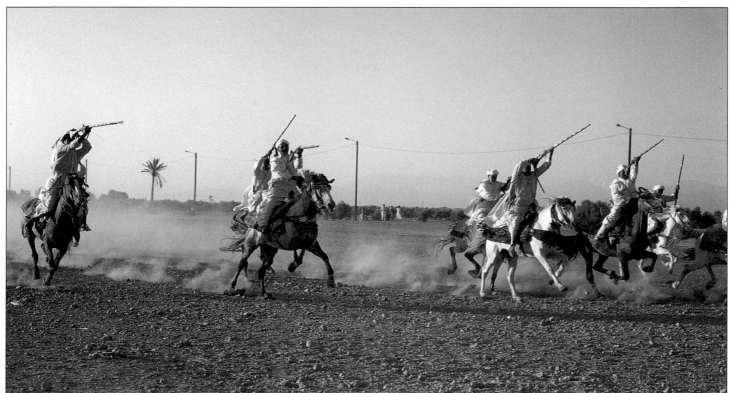

Andalusian

As its name suggests, the Andalusian comes from the sun-baked region of southern Spain which is close to North Africa. While it is without doubt an ancient breed, its origins are uncertain. Whatever native horses existed in Spain when the Muslim invaders arrived in 711 – they may well have resembled the primitive Sorraian Pony still found today in Portugal – must surely have been crossed subsequently with

■ LEFT
The Andalusian's handsome head, a more refined version of the Barb, is as eye-catching and as distinctive in its own way as that of the Arab.

the invaders' Barb horses, which were imported in such great numbers.

After the last Muslim state, Granada, had fallen to the Christians in 1492, Spain began to assume a new importance in the western world and so, too, did her horses. Taken to the Americas by the sixteenth-century

Conquistadores, Spanish horses provided the foundation stock for the majority of new breeds developed by the settlers. In Europe, meanwhile, the Spanish horse became the preferred mount of monarchs and of the great riding masters, including the Englishman, William Cavendish, Duke of Newcastle, who in the seventeenth century wrote that: "If well chosen it is the noblest horse in the world; the most beautiful that can be. He is of great spirit and of great courage and docile; has the proudest walk, the proudest trot...the loftiest gallop and is the lovingest and gentlest horse and fittest of all for a king in Day of Triumph." The Lipizzaner is a direct descendant of the Andalusian, while other famous European breeds influenced by Spanish blood include the Frederiksborg, the Friesian (which in turn

■ RIGHT
The Andalusian is not particularly tall but its compact, muscular frame is indicative of great strength.

BREED DESCRIPTION

Height 15 – 15.2hh.

Colour Predominantly grey (including "mulberry" – a dappled, purplish grey) and bay.

Conformation Handsome head with broad forehead and large, kind eyes; fairly long, thick but elegant neck; long, well-sloped shoulders with well-defined withers; short, strong body with broad chest and well-sprung ribs; very broad, strong, rounded hindquarters with rather low-set tail; medium length limbs, clean cut and elegant but strong; long and very luxuriant mane and tail.

LEFT
On point duty in present-day Barcelona. Thanks to its excellent temperament and willing nature, the Andalusian is an ideal all-purpose riding horse.

BELOW
Grey is one of the predominant Andalusian colours, along with bay. Spotted strains were once popular and were responsible for the founding of the Appaloosa breed in America.

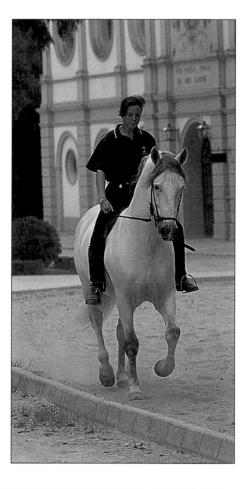

INTERESTING FACTS

The Andalusian horse's survival down the centuries, which included some pretty turbulent times, was aided by the monastic orders, particularly the Carthusians, who became especially skilful at horse breeding. In times of danger, horses were moved from the great studs to remote monasteries for safe keeping. The Carthusians were instrumental in maintaining purity of line and produced animals of consistently high quality.

influenced the Oldenburg), the Holstein and the Connemara.

The Andalusian is one of the most elegant of horses. Possessing tremendous presence, lofty paces, agility and a gentle, willing nature, it makes an excellent all-round riding horse and is particularly well suited to the movements of the *haute école* (high school). It can also be seen to great effect taking part in the colourful annual *ferias*, or fairs, of its native Andalusia.

RIGHT
The breed's proud bearing and lofty action lend themselves perfectly to the movements of the *haute école*, or high school.

Thoroughbred

The life of man has been inextricably interwoven with that of the horse for more than 4,000 years but in all that time no achievement has excelled the "invention" of the Thoroughbred. Quite apart from being the world's supreme racehorse, the Thoroughbred has played a vital part in the upgrading of numerous old horse and pony breeds and in establishing as many new ones.

Henry VIII set the process in motion during the sixteenth century when he founded the famous Royal Paddocks at Hampton Court. His daughter, Elizabeth I, founded another stud at Tutbury, in Staffordshire. Both monarchs imported horses from Spain and Italy to cross with native stock. Under subsequent monarchs – James I, Charles I and Charles II – horse breeding and racing gained impetus. By the beginning of the seventeenth century regular race meetings were being staged at Newmarket, Chester, Doncaster and Lincoln. Many noblemen took up the

BREED DESCRIPTION

Height Variable. May be as small as 14.2hh or over 17hh. Average 16 – 16.2hh.

Colour All solid colours, the most common being bay, chestnut and brown. Also grey, black and roan. White markings are permissible.

Conformation Variable, but the best specimens have excellent conformation characterized by a refined, intelligent head; elegant neck; well-sloped shoulders; short, strong body with great depth through the girth; strong, muscular hindquarters with well-set tail; clean, hard legs with well let-down hocks and a minimum of 8 inches (20cm) of bone below the knee.

■ ABOVE RIGHT
The head of the Thoroughbred is typically refined, with large eyes and nostrils. The dished profile so characteristic of its Arabian forebears is not found in the Thoroughbred.

■ RIGHT
With its well-sloped shoulders, powerful hindquarters and long limbs, the Thoroughbred is the ultimate "racing machine". The deep girth ensures plenty of room for the heart and lungs.

■ RIGHT
The bigger, slower developing stamp of Thoroughbred often makes a first-rate steeplechaser. Chasing calls for courage, stamina and speed, qualities for which the Thoroughbred is renowned.

■ BELOW RIGHT
Thanks to carefully kept records (in the *General Stud Book*) dating back some two centuries, it is possible to trace the pedigree of this foal to one of the breed's handful of foundation sires.

■ BOTTOM
Thoroughbreds hurdling at speed at Cheltenham, spiritual home of the sport of jump racing. The Thoroughbred's athletic prowess makes it equally suitable for sports such as hunting and three-day eventing.

breeding of horses for racing, sending agents overseas to seek out good stallions. Records of the time repeatedly refer to Barb, Barbary, Arabian, Hobby and Galloway horses (the Irish Hobby and Scottish Galloway were famous "running" horses of the day) – and it is on this blood that the modern Thoroughbred was founded.

The exact breeding of the Thoroughbred's forebears will never be known since horses often changed names when they

changed hands and the terms "Arabian", "Barb" and "Turk", were frequently used inaccurately. However, what is certain is that during the last quarter of the seventeenth century and the first quarter of the eighteenth, Englishmen or their agents bought a number of eastern stallions, crossed them with English mares of mixed pedigree and started a dynasty of great racehorses. The most famous of these stallions were the Byerley Turk, the Darley Arabian and the Godolphin Arabian, who are recognized as the founding fathers of the Thoroughbred. In 1791 *An Introduction to a General Stud Book* appeared and following the publication of several more preliminary editions, there came, in 1808, Volume I of the *General Stud Book*. A horse is classed as Thoroughbred if both its parents are entered in the *General Stud Book* (or in the equivalent official Thoroughbred stud books in other countries).

The Thoroughbred is a handsome horse, alert, spirited and full of presence. It has an easy, ground-covering stride at the gallop and possesses boundless courage and immense stamina, qualities which stand it in good stead on the racecourse, in the hunting field and in three-day eventing.

INTERESTING FACTS

The Byerley Turk was captured by Captain Byerley at Buda in the 1680s, ridden by him at the Battle of the Boyne and sent to England to stand at stud. His great-grandson Tartar sired Herod, one of the most important sires in Thoroughbred history. The Darley Arabian, foaled in 1700, was acquired by Thomas Darley and sent to England from the Syrian port of Aleppo. He was responsible for founding the Eclipse line – Eclipse was one of the greatest racehorses of all time. The Godolphin Arabian was foaled in the Yemen in 1724, exported to Tunis via Syria and later given by the Bey of Tunis to the King of France, who subsequently sold him to Edward Coke, from Derbyshire. He was eventually acquired by Lord Godolphin and was responsible for founding the Matchem line. The Herod, Eclipse and Matchem lines, plus the Highflyer (Highflyer was a son of Herod) are the four principal tail-male lines of the modern Thoroughbred.

Anglo-Arab

A more substantial horse than the pure-bred Arab, the Anglo-Arab is produced by mixing Arab and Thoroughbred blood. The Anglo-Arab can result from a first cross between a Thoroughbred stallion and an Arab mare or vice versa. It can also be produced by breeding Thoroughbred to Anglo-Arab or Arab to Anglo-Arab, or Anglo-Arab to Anglo-Arab. As a result of these different permutations, the amount of Arab blood varies a good deal. So, too, does the size and appearance of the horse. The biggest horses are often produced by using an Arab stallion on a Thoroughbred mare and the best examples of the Anglo-Arab will inherit the endurance and stamina of the Arab and the speed and scope of the Thoroughbred, but not the latter's rather high-strung temperament.

France has been a notable producer of Anglo-Arabs since the first half of the nineteenth century. The French Anglo-Arab traces back to two eastern stallions, Massoud (an Arab) and Aslam (which is said to be of Turkish origin). They were imported from Syria and crossed with three imported English Thoroughbred

BREED DESCRIPTION

Height Around 15.3 – 16.3hh.

Colour Usually chestnut, bay or brown.

Conformation Variable, but the best specimens tend towards good Thoroughbred conformation: intelligent head with straight profile, expressive eyes and alert ears; long neck with more prominent withers than the Arab; sloping shoulders; short, strong body – rather more sturdy than the Thoroughbred – with deep chest; somewhat long hindquarters; good, sound limbs; strong, well-shaped feet.

▌ TOP LEFT
The head of the Anglo-Arab is closer in appearance to that of the Thoroughbred than the Arab. The Anglo lacks the dished profile of the pure-bred.

▌ LEFT
The overall conformation is noticeably more Thoroughbred than Arab, although many Anglo-Arabs are more sturdily built than the average Thoroughbred.

█ LEFT
The crossing of
Thoroughbred with
Arab blood has
produced some
outstanding
competition horses in
the Olympic
disciplines, including
dressage.

mares, Daer, Comus Mare and Selim
Mare. Their three daughters, Delphine,
Clovis and Danaë became the foundation
stock of France's first breed of sports
horse. At one time the Anglo-Arab was
much used in France by the military and
as a general riding and competition horse.
More recently it has been an influential
factor in the development of the modern
sports horse, the Selle Français.

█ BELOW
In recent years French Anglo-Arabs such as this one
have achieved great success in top-level three-day
eventing, holding their own against the best of the
Thoroughbreds and Warmbloods.

INTERESTING FACTS

Before the development of the Selle
Français, the French Anglo-Arab was highly
successful in the competitive disciplines,
particularly show jumping. Many of the
horses ridden by the dual Olympic champion
Pierre Jonquères d'Oriola were Anglo-Arabs,
the most famous being the little gelding
Marquis III (a very successful Grand Prix and
Nations' Cup horse) and Ali-Baba, on whom
d'Oriola won his first Olympic title at Helsinki
in 1952. More recently French Anglo-Arabs
have been successful performers with the
French three-day event team. They include
Twist la Beige (winner of the European
Championship in 1993) and Newport and
Newlot (both European team silver
medallists).

Noriker

Bred and developed over several thousand years in the mountain regions of Austria, the Noriker is an attractive looking light draught horse. Strong and hardy, this horse is noted particularly for its calm temperament, sound limbs and sure-footedness.These characteristics make it an ideal all-round work horse over difficult mountainous terrain.

As with most horses, despite its ancient origins there was no formal breeding programme until fairly recent times. The Prince-Archbishop of Salzburg is credited with forming a stud book some 400 years ago. It was then that standards were drawn up, for both mares and stallions, and stud farms established.

Because of its toughness and capacity for hard work the Noriker became popular throughout Europe. Different strains evolved, including the Bavarian, now known as the South German Coldblood and found in Upper and Lower Bavaria. Various colour lines, tracing back to Andalusian and Neapolitan horses, also had an influence on today's breed and were responsible for the dappled and brindle colourings.

BREED DESCRIPTION

Height Stallions 16 – 17hh.
Mares 15.3 – 17hh.

Colour Brown, chestnut, black, grey and brindle. White body markings are not acceptable. Too many or too large white markings on the head and limbs are not desirable.

Conformation Straight profile, wide nostrils, medium-sized eyes; medium-length neck with thick, curly mane; good sloping shoulders; broad, deep chest; medium-length, well-muscled back; long limbs with powerful forearms, large clean joints, well-muscled second thigh and good, sound feet.

INTERESTING FACTS

The breed takes its name from the ancient state of Noricum (during the Roman Empire Noricum was roughly approximate to present-day Austria). However, the Noriker can be traced back to pre-Roman times, when a heavy war horse was developed in Thessalonica. Horses of this type were taken to Noricum by the Romans. In due course they were crossed with other coldblooded horses of the region and became admirably adapted to the harsh conditions of their new environment.

▌ ABOVE
Most Norikers are brown but the breed embraces a wide range of coat colours, including this attractive dark chestnut with flaxen mane.

▌ LEFT
The Noriker's sturdy build and good limbs and feet make it an ideal work horse in mountainous regions. Like most mountain breeds, it is a good mover, with a particularly active trot.

Belgian Draught

One of the world's finest and historically most important heavy horses, the Belgian Draught is an ancient breed, closely connected to the Ardennais. The Flanders Horse, as the breed was known during the Middle Ages, had an influence on the development of several other renowned "heavies", including the Shire, the Suffolk Punch and particularly the Clydesdale. Nowadays the Belgian Draught is also known as the Brabant, after its main breeding area in central Belgium.

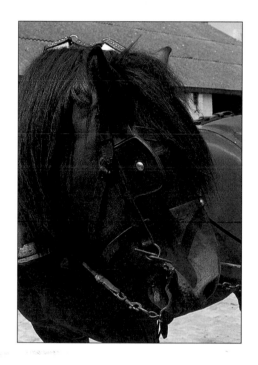

Despite widespread mechanization, this gentle giant of a horse, known for its kind nature and willingness to work, can still be found in modest numbers in many areas of Belgium and is also much appreciated in North America.

Over the years breeders have managed to maintain the excellence of these horses by a policy of strict selection and some inbreeding. The result is a handsome individual – its short neck, strong shoulders, short limbs, deep-girthed body and huge hindquarters, coupled with the most amenable of temperaments, make it the ideal draught horse for work on the land and there is no finer sight in the equestrian world than a team of these magnificent animals hitched to a smart brewers' dray.

❚ ABOVE
The Belgian Draught is an impressive horse, combining great strength with a gentle temperament and willingness to work. Despite its size, it is economical to keep.

BREED DESCRIPTION

Height 16.2 – 17hh.

Colour Predominantly red-roan with black points, chestnut and sorrel. Bay, dun and grey also occur.

Conformation Small, rather plain head but with intelligent expression; short, muscular neck; massive shoulders; short, deep, compact body; rounded, powerful hindquarters; short, strong limbs with plenty of feather and well-shaped, medium-sized feet.

INTERESTING FACTS

Towards the end of the last century there were three recognized types of Brabant horse, each based on a different bloodline. Those from the celebrated stallion Orange I, known as the Gros de la Dendre line, were mainly bay in colour. A stallion called Bayard founded the Gris du Hainaut line, with its greys, red-roans and sorrels. A third line, the Colosses de la Méhaigne, descended from the bay stallion Jean I. Today the descendants of these bloodlines all come under the general title of Belgian Draught or Brabant.

❚ ABOVE LEFT
The head is rather plain but the eyes have the kindly expression associated with so many of the heavy breeds.

❚ LEFT
Massive hindquarters are typical of the breed. These horses have docked tails.

Frederiksborg

The stud after which the Frederiksborg is named was founded by King Frederick II during the 1560s and was famous as a provider of quality horses to the courts of Europe. The stud's foundation stock came from Spain and was subsequently crossed with the Spanish horse's close relative, the Neapolitan. The horses thus produced were both elegant and spirited and well suited to the dual requirements of the day: as a mount for work in the manège and as a charger for the cavalry.

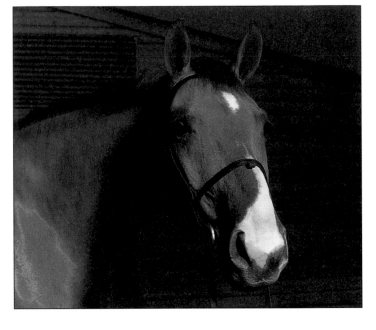

▌ RIGHT
The Frederiksborg's somewhat plain head has a kind, intelligent look about it. Most examples of the breed, like this horse, are chestnut.

BREED DESCRIPTION

Height 15.3 – 16hh.

Colour Chestnut.

Conformation Intelligent, if somewhat plain, head; short, upright neck; strong but rather upright shoulders; strong back that tends to be long; high-set tail; good, strong feet.

The breed continued to develop through the introduction of eastern and British half-bred stallions and for several centuries the Frederiksborg was one of the most sought-after horses in Europe. Eventually, so numerous were the exports of the Frederiksborg from Denmark that stock became seriously depleted, with the result that during the first half of the nineteenth century the stud turned instead to Thoroughbred breeding. This venture was not a success and in 1871 the stud was dispersed. Fortunately, however, Frederiksborgs did not disappear altogether: private breeders went on producing them, mainly for use as light harness horses.

Frederiksborgs are still bred in Denmark, although recent demands for an outstanding sports horse have led to the development of a new horse, the Danish Warmblood, based mainly on Swedish, German and Polish stallions. Frederiksborg blood does occasionally appear in today's Danish Warmblood pedigrees, chiefly through the female line.

INTERESTING FACTS

The Frederiksborg played a significant part in the development of a much more well-known breed, the Lipizzaner, famous for its association with the Spanish Riding School in Vienna. The white stallion Pluto, from the Royal Danish Court Stud, was one of the six stallions on which the Lipizzaner breed is based. Pluto was foaled in 1765, the earliest of the six. More than two centuries later his descendants are still performing at the Spanish Riding School where they can be identified by the "Pluto" prefix to their names.

▌ LEFT
The rather long back, short neck and upright shoulders are more typical of the light harness horse than the riding horse.

Jutland

Except for the feathering of its lower legs, Denmark's heavy horse bears an uncanny resemblance to the British breed, the Suffolk Punch. This resemblance is perhaps not so surprising, because the present-day Jutland was greatly influenced by the Suffolk blood introduced via the English stallion Oppenheim LXII, who stood at stud in Denmark during the 1860s.

The breed goes back much further than that, however. Heavy horses have been bred on the Jutland Peninsula for many centuries, certainly as far back as the twelfth century, when they were in great demand as war horses. Combining enormous strength with the most willing

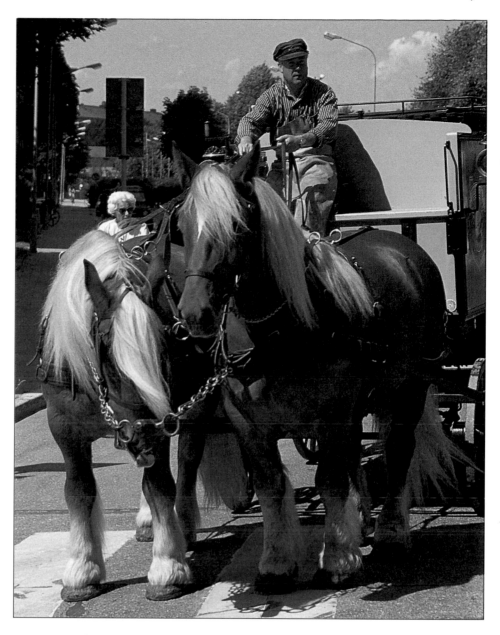

BREED DESCRIPTION

Height 15 – 16hh.

Colour Predominantly dark chestnut with light mane and tail.

Conformation Heavy, rather plain head, but with kind expression; short, thick neck; strong, muscular shoulders; exceptionally deep body with broad chest; round, muscular hindquarters; short limbs with plenty of bone.

INTERESTING FACTS

The Jutland was an influential factor in the development of the Schleswig, a draught horse which takes its name from the northernmost region of Germany and which towards the end of the nineteenth century was in demand for pulling trams and buses. Infusions of Jutland blood from neighbouring Denmark were being used by German breeders well into this century. The Schleswig closely resembles the Jutland and the Suffolk, both in build and colour. However, the use of carefully selected Boulonnais and Breton stallions from France has led to the appearance of some greys and bays.

of natures, the Jutland horse made the ideal mount for the heavily armoured knights of the Middle Ages. Cleveland Bay and Yorkshire Coach Horse blood is said to have been used in the development of the Jutland, but it is unquestionably the Suffolk which has been the dominant factor, even to its chestnut colouring.

Mechanization has reduced the numbers of these attractive horses but some can still be seen, either at shows or pulling drays in the cities or, occasionally, working the land.

▍ ABOVE
In common with all heavy breeds, the handsome Jutland has been the victim of mechanization but a few are still working.

▍ LEFT
The Jutland is usually chestnut, a colour inherited through the Suffolk Punch element in its ancestry.

Danish Warmblood

The Danish Warmblood is one of a number of horses specifically developed for use in modern equestrian pursuits, particularly the competitive disciplines of dressage, show jumping and three-day eventing.

The Danes have a long tradition as horse breeders: their first organized studs date from the fourteenth century. However, the market for horses has changed enormously this century, and especially during the last few decades. In many countries the relentless march of mechanization has transformed the horse from an essential means of transport to a "leisure" animal. In the wake of this transformation the Danes found that their native breeds – the Frederiksborg and its cousin, the spotted Knabstrup (a popular circus horse) – were not going to measure up as competitive sports horses.

To remedy this deficiency, a breeding programme was set up in 1962 to produce a new type of Danish riding horse.

BREED DESCRIPTION

Height 15.3 – 16.3hh.

Colour All colours occur.

Conformation Quality head; long, well set-on neck; good shoulders with prominent withers; muscular back and loins; long croup; strong limbs with long forearms, well-defined joints and good bone.

▌ **RIGHT**
The Danish Warmblood shows the typical conformation of the modern sports horse: well-sloped shoulders, strong back and quarters, and good, sound limbs and feet.

▌ **ABOVE RIGHT**
Like many other warmblood horses, the Danish Warmblood bears a distinctive brand mark on its hindquarters for identification purposes.

▌ ABOVE
Warmblood horses have been specifically developed for use in competitive sports such as show jumping.

▌ ABOVE RIGHT
A good deal of German blood has been used in the development of the Danish Warmblood. This is reflected in its quality head.

▌ RIGHT
Perhaps the most famous of all Danish Warmbloods is the dressage stallion Matador, winner of the silver medal at the 1990 World Equestrian Games.

Carefully selected stallions, chiefly Swedish, Trakehner, Hanoverian, Holstein and Polish, were crossed with the various local-bred mares to improve the basic stamp of horse. Stringent grading was introduced for both stallions and mares to ensure that only the best were granted entry to the stud books. The breeding programme has been a tremendous success. The resultant Danish Warmblood is a handsome individual, well proportioned and possessed of excellent paces. It combines courage with a good temperament and makes an outstanding dressage horse.

Ariègeois

The Ariègeois, which lives in the Pyrenean mountains in the south-west of France, is a breed of great antiquity. It closely resembles the horses of southern Gaul described in Caesar's commentaries on

BREED DESCRIPTION

Height 13.1 – 14.3hh (the latter is rarely attained in its native habitat, although it may be on richer, lowland grazing).

Colour Solid black. Normally no white stockings or markings on the head, although the flank may be lightly flecked with white.

Conformation Light-boned, expressive head with flat forehead, straight profile, fairly short, hairy ears and bright, alert eyes with a gentle expression; fairly short, straight neck; rather straight shoulders; long but strong back and broad chest; round hindquarters with sloping croup; short, fairly slender limbs with a tendency to cow hocks; good, strong feet..

the Gallic Wars. Its home is the high valley of the Ariège river, from which it takes its name. Well adapted to the worst excesses of its mountain environment, it is impervious to cold and outstandingly sure-footed – ice-covered mountain trails hold no terrors for the little Ariègeois.

A versatile, hardy creature, the Ariègeois has for centuries been used as a packhorse, though it can just as easily function as a small riding horse or work the land on the steepest of hill farms, where modern machinery cannot venture.

INTERESTING FACTS

The coat of the Ariègeois acquires a distinctive reddish tinge in winter. It is fine in texture, unlike the mane and tail, which are harsh to the touch and extremely thick – nature's way of offering much-needed protection from the worst of the winter weather. The Ariègeois is less well suited to heat. In summer it will seek shelter from the sun during the hottest part of the day and come out to graze at night.

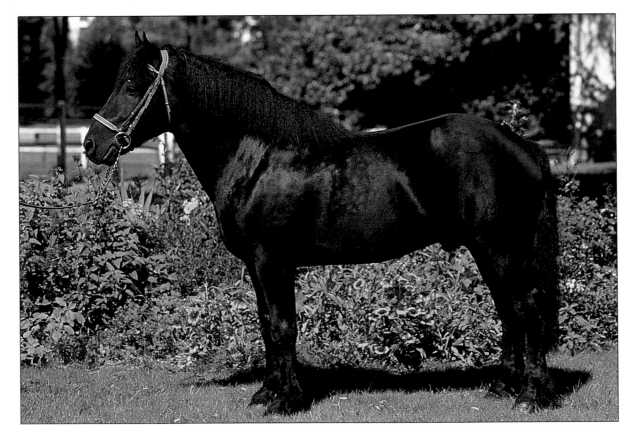

▪ **TOP**
Like all mountain breeds, the Ariègeois has very active paces. It has exceptionally strong hooves and is noted for its sure-footedness.

▪ **LEFT**
The Ariègeois has a fairly long, but nevertheless strong, back, a powerfully built neck and deep girth. The sloping croup and low-set tail are characteristic.

Norman Cob

The Norman Cob is a light draught horse, still in use on small farms in the La Manche region of Normandy. Normandy has long been famed for its horse breeding, notably at the historic studs of Le Pin (founded as a royal stud in the mid-seventeenth century) and Saint-Lô, where the ancestors of the modern Cob were bred.

Stocky and compact, like the English Cob after which it was named, the Norman Cob was developed as a distinct breed at the beginning of this century. It was at that time that the breeders of half-bred horses first began to distinguish between those animals suitable for use as riding horses, particularly for the army, and those of less quality and sturdier build, more suited to light draught work.

The Norman Cob, as the heavier type was subsequently named, became a popular workhorse, especially in the La Manche region – even the powerful Percheron failed to supplant it there.

Over the years there has been a tendency for the Norman Cob to become heavier, to cope with the work required of it, but although it is undoubtedly sturdy and muscular, it lacks the massive stature of the true heavy horse and has never lost the energetic action, particularly at trot, characteristic of the half-bred horse.

RIGHT
The Norman Cob has always been noted for its energetic action. The lively, free-moving trot is characteristic of the breed.

BELOW
The Norman Cob has the same kindly expression as the English Cob after which it is named.

INTERESTING FACTS

The tail of the Norman Cob is still traditionally docked. Down the centuries this mutilation of horses' tails has been carried out for a variety of reasons: fashion, to prevent the tail becoming entangled with harness and equipment and, in ancient times, probably to serve some ritual purpose. It used to be the fashion to dock the tail of the English Cob, but the practice became illegal in Great Britain under the Docking and Nicking Act, 1948. Quite apart from the trauma of the operation, docking deprives the horse of a vital means of protection against flies.

BREED DESCRIPTION

Height 15.3 – 16.3hh.

Colour Chestnut, bay or bay-brown; occasionally red-roan or grey.

Conformation Overall strong, stocky build with short, well-proportioned limbs.

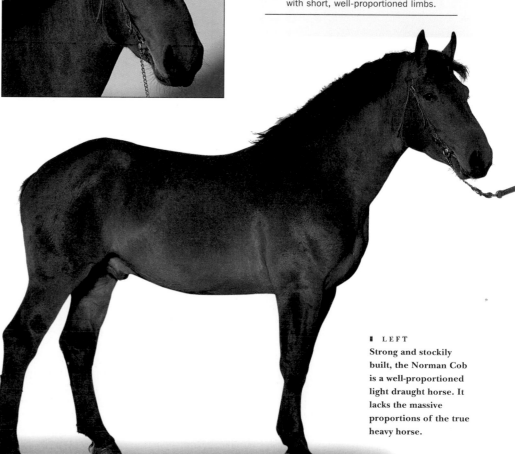

LEFT
Strong and stockily built, the Norman Cob is a well-proportioned light draught horse. It lacks the massive proportions of the true heavy horse.

Camargue

▌ BELOW LEFT
Small, strong and always grey, the Camargue has been an inspiration for artists and poets down the centuries.

▌ BELOW
The breed's ancient origins can be detected in the somewhat heavy, square head, which is reminiscent of that of the primitive horse.

The tough little Camargue, the native horse of the inhospitable wastes of the Rhône delta in southern France, was not recognized as a breed until January 1968 yet it is almost certainly of ancient origin. It bears a strong resemblance to the horses depicted in the cave paintings of Lascaux, dating from 15,000 BC. Moreover, the even older horse skeletons unearthed at Solutré in south-east France in the nineteenth century could well be those of the breed's forebears.

During its long occupation of the marshlands, the indigenous horse must

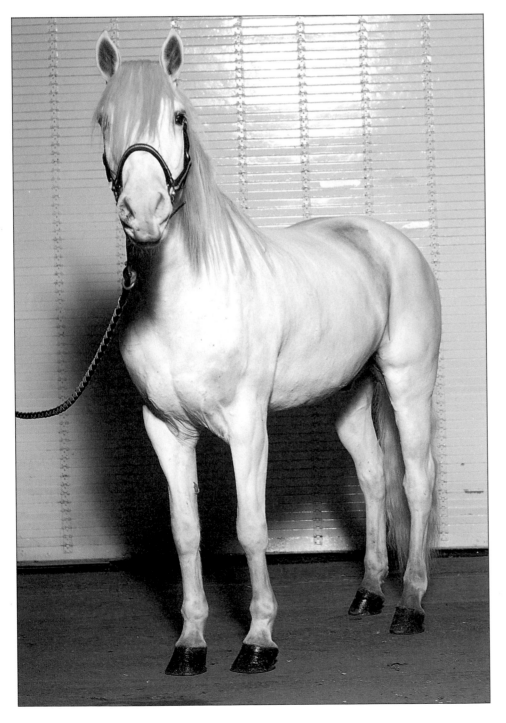

have been influenced by influxes of North African blood, but it has retained certain characteristics of the primitive horse, particularly in its rather heavy, square head.

The horses have always played an integral part in the everyday life of the Camargue, providing the guardians, or herdsmen, with strong, sure-footed mounts for their work with the herds of fighting bulls traditionally raised in the area. Despite its relatively small size, the Camargue horse has the strength and courage to carry a grown man safely over the most treacherous wetland terrain.

The herds, or *manades*, of Camargue horses, each with its own stallion, enjoy a semi-wild existence, being rounded up annually for inspection, branding of young stock, selection of suitable breeding stock and gelding of non-breeding males. Although the practice of fencing off pastureland and draining large areas for the cultivation of crops has, over the years, reduced the need for herdsmen, the horses are still very much a feature of the area. They have taken on a new role as mounts for the increasing number of tourists to the Camargue, which is famed for its wealth of wildlife.

BREED DESCRIPTION

Height 13.1 – 14.1hh.

Colour Grey.

Conformation Rather large, square head with short, wide-set ears; short neck; short, upright shoulders; fairly short back and deep chest; muscular hindquarters with short, sloping croup and long, bushy tail; strong, well-formed limbs with big knees and very hard, sound feet.

INTERESTING FACTS

The half-wild Camargue horses have long held a romantic fascination for artists and writers. In his poem "Horses on the Camargue", Roy Campbell penned these typically evocative lines:

...in a shroud of silence like the dead,
I heard a sudden harmony of hooves,
And, turning, saw afar
A hundred snowy horses unconfined,
The silver runaways of Neptune's car
Racing, spray-curled, like waves before
the wind.
Sons of the Mistral, fleet
As him with whose strong gusts they love
to flee,
Who shod the flying thunders of their feet
And plumed them with the snortings of
the sea.

▌ BELOW LEFT
Despite their semi-wild existence Camargue horses are perfectly amenable to training, as this French trick-riding expert demonstrates.

▌ BELOW
The inhospitable wastes of the Rhône delta have produced a breed renowned for its toughness, strength and sure-footedness.

▌ BOTTOM
Herding the fighting bulls reared in the region is the breed's traditional role. Despite its small size, the Camargue horse will carry a herdsman with great ease.

Ardennais

One of the world's premier heavy horses, the powerful but exceptionally docile Ardennais is of ancient origin and is named after its mountainous homeland region on the French–Belgian border.

The Ardennais used to be less massive – as late as the nineteenth century it was used not only for draught work but also for riding. Arab blood was introduced around 1810 and infusions of

BREED DESCRIPTION

Height 15 – 16hh.

Colour Roan, red-roan, iron grey, dark or liver chestnut and bay are the preferred colours. Bay-brown, light chestnut and palomino are admissible. Black, dappled grey and all other colours are inadmissible.

Conformation Straight profile with slightly prominent eye sockets, low, flat forehead, large expressive eyes, pricked ears and wide, open nostrils; medium-length neck, well set-on and generally arched; very strong shoulders; medium-heavy body with deep chest, rather short back and muscular loins; wide, rounded hindquarters; fairly short, strong and muscular limbs.

■ **BELOW**
Massively built, but extremely docile, the bigger type of Ardennais makes the perfect partner for heavy agricultural work.

Thoroughbred, Percheron and Boulonnais were added later. These attempts to improve the breed were not a great success and were abandoned, but the Ardennais nevertheless continued to be a most useful animal. Its energy and stamina made it invaluable to the military during the Revolution, at the time of Empire and particularly during the ill-fated Russian campaign. During World

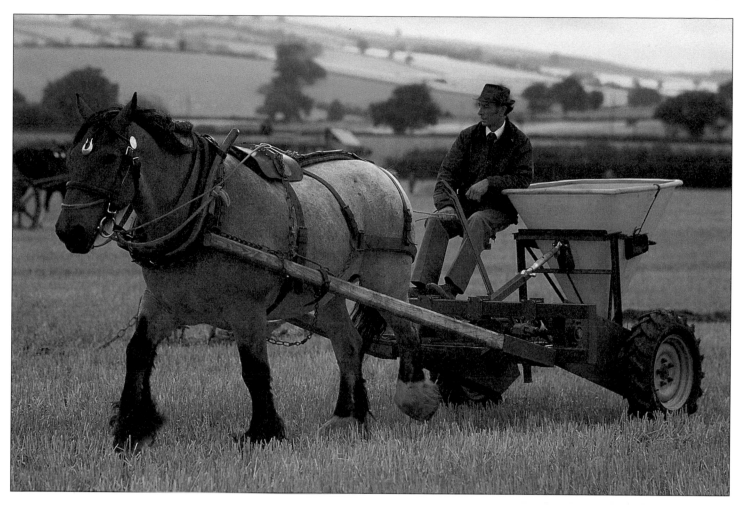

War I the Ardennais was in great demand as an artillery horse.

It was the requirements of agriculture and other heavy draught work which led to the development of a heavier stamp of horse and today, in addition to the original small Ardennais, two other types are recognized: a larger version of the Ardennais, known as the Auxois and the heavier, larger framed Ardennais du Nord (formerly known as the Trait du Nord), the result of using outcrosses to the Belgian Draught.

INTERESTING FACTS

In their writings some 2,000 years ago both the Greek historian Herodotus and the Roman emperor Julius Caesar made particular mention of the horses of north-eastern France, then known as northern Gaul, extolling their stamina and toughness. Skeletons unearthed in the region suggest that these horses stood 15hh – the height of the smaller type of Ardennais still seen today. These were the ancestors of the modern Ardennais.

▌ ABOVE
The Ardennais can still be found working on the land. Its ability to thrive on a minimum of feed makes it an economical proposition for the farmers of small holdings.

▌ BELOW
Roan is a very typical coat colouring of the breed. The eyes are invariably large, with an intelligent, gentle expression.

Selle Français

France has been well to the fore in the development of a modern sports horse, the Cheval de Selle Français (French Saddle Horse) being one of the great warmblood breeding success stories of the twentieth century. The term Selle Français came into use in December 1958 and the first stud book was published in 1965.

The French, with their great tradition of horse breeding, laid the foundations for their modern, quality riding horse as far back as the early nineteenth century, when many regions of the country began to import English Thoroughbred and half-

BREED DESCRIPTION

Height: Medium weight small, 15.3hh and under; medium, 15.3 – 16.1hh; large, over 16.1hh.

Height: Heavyweight small, under 16hh; large, 16hh and over. (The classification "medium" or "heavy" is based on the horse's weight-carrying ability, judged on conformation.)

Colour Predominantly chestnut, though all colours are permissible.

Conformation Refined head; long, elegant neck; sloping shoulders; strong body with well-sprung ribs; broad, powerful hindquarters; strong limbs with particularly powerful forearms, pronounced joints and good bone.

▍ A B O V E
A quality head, set on a long, elegant neck, is typical of the Selle Français. The breed is one of the world's most successful competition horses.

▍ RIGHT
English Thoroughbred and French Trotter blood provided the base for the Selle Français. Its harmonious proportions and overall appearance are very reminiscent of the Thoroughbred.

■ **BELOW**
Some Selle Français horses such as The Fellow (in the red colours) have the speed to take on, and beat, full Thoroughbreds on the racecourse.

■ **BOTTOM LEFT**
The breed excels at show jumping. This attractive bay mare, Miss, won team and individual silver medals at the 1994 World Equestrian Games.

INTERESTING FACTS

Although the most important influence on the Selle Français has undoubtedly been the Thoroughbred, the French Trotter has also been a factor, not least in the pedigrees of the famous show jumpers Galoubet and Jappeloup. Galoubet has trotter blood on his dam's side, albeit a couple of generations back. But the spring-heeled little Jappeloup, whose brilliant show-jumping career culminated with success in the individual championship at the 1988 Olympic Games in Seoul and a team gold medal in the 1990 World Equestrian Games, was actually by a trotter, Tyrol II, out of a Thoroughbred mare, Vénérable.

Interestingly, Jappeloup lacked the harmonious paces usually associated with the Selle Français. He was notoriously clumsy (many a human had their feet trodden on in his company) and a far from comfortable ride. This was almost certainly the result of his powerful hindquarters – he stood higher behind the saddle than in front, typical trotter conformation.

bred stallions to cross with their local, less refined, mares (the chief exceptions were the Limousin and south-west regions which specialized in breeding Anglo-Arabs). In Normandy, always a stronghold of horse breeding, two important horses evolved: a fast trotter, later to become the French Trotter (many of the half-breds imported from England came from Norfolk Roadster stock) and the Anglo-Norman. The vast majority of today's Selle Français horses trace back to the Anglo-Norman.

French Warmblood breeding differs from that in neighbouring countries, where the grading system is all-important. Success in competition by stallions, mares and their progeny or relatives forms the basis for selection in France. It is a system which, in a comparatively short space of time, has produced a highly successful competition horse, in appearance reminiscent of the Thoroughbred (which provided its most famous foundation sires) and possessing the necessary spirit to survive the cut and thrust of modern competitive sports. The Selle Français shines, above all, at show jumping where its claims to fame include Jappeloup (1987 European and 1988 Olympic Champion), Quito de Baussy (1990 World Champion), I Love You (1983 World Cup winner) and Galoubet (1982 world team gold medallist).

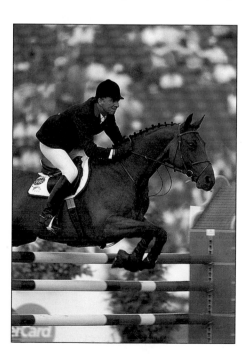

■ **BELOW**
Thanks to the Thoroughbred blood in their veins, Selle Français horses have the speed and stamina to succeed in three-day eventing.

French Trotter

France – the country with the greatest tradition of trotting racing outside the United States – developed its own strain of trotter by crossing English Thoroughbreds, half-breds and Norfolk Roadsters with robust Norman mares. The process began in the early nineteenth century. The first French trotting races, which were ridden, not driven, took place in 1806 on the Champ de Mars in Paris. As the sport began to increase in popularity, purpose-built race tracks were opened, the first being at Cherbourg in the 1830s, and the breed developed and improved. In 1861 an Imperial decree gave official encouragement to the sport, leading to the formation of its first governing body.

The Anglo-Norman developed into a fine trotter and five important bloodlines became established: Conquérant, Normand, Lavater, Phaeton and Fuchsia.

BREED DESCRIPTION

Height Average about 16.2hh. The larger horses tend to make the best ridden trotters.

Colour All colours admissible. Chestnut, bay and brown are predominant with some roan. Grey is rare.

Conformation Well-sloped shoulders, giving good ground-covering action; short, strong body; immensely powerful, often sloping, hindquarters.

▌ **TOP RIGHT**
The French Trotter has much of the Thoroughbred about its general appearance, although it is more sturdily built and rather less refined.

▌ **RIGHT**
Racing under saddle, as well as in harness, has ensured the continued quality of this old-established breed, which has played an important part in the development of the Selle Français.

The premier driven trotting race in France is the Prix d'Amérique. Its ridden equivalent is the Prix de Cornulier. Both are run over 1 mile 5 furlongs (2,650m) at the leading French track, the Hippodrome de Vincennes which, with its downhill start and testing uphill finish, is unique among raceways, which are usually flat. The Prix d'Amérique is the driven equivalent of flat racing's all-age international championship of Europe, the Prix de l'Arc de Triomphe. The Prix de Cornulier is the world's richest ridden trotting race. Very occasionally outstanding horses appear which are equally brilliant in harness and under saddle. Venutar, Masina, Tidalium Pelo and Bellino II all share the distinction of having won both the Prix d'Amérique and the Prix de Cornulier.

■ LEFT
French Trotters are sometimes used in the sport of skijoring, in which the horse pulls its human partner on skis.

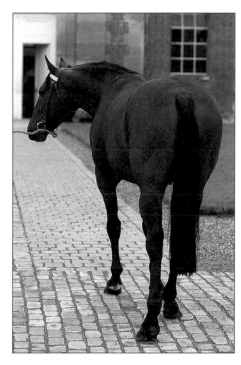

Conquérant and Normand were both by the English half-bred Young Rattler. This son of the Thoroughbred Rattler is sometimes called "the French Messenger" (Messenger being the foundation sire of the Standardbred) because of the enormous influence he has had on trotter breeding in France. Lavater was another example of the English connection, being by a Norfolk Roadster. The most prepotent of all the early stallions was Fuchsia. Foaled in 1883 he sired nearly 400 trotters and more than 100 of his sons produced winners. Some Standardbred blood was introduced over the years to give the breed more speed but the Trotteur Français Stud Book was closed to non-French-bred horses in 1937 and has only been opened a fraction in recent years to allow a very limited number of carefully selected French/Standardbred crosses to be admitted.

The French have never totally given up ridden racing. Some ten per cent of today's trotting races staged in France are under saddle and they have an important effect on breeding. Because ridden trotters race under comparatively heavy weights they must accordingly be well built horses with good balance and level action. These quality horses have played a large part in maintaining the overall standard of the French Trotter.

■ ABOVE RIGHT
Powerful hindquarters are typical of the breed, the best examples of which can trot at speeds not much less than those of the galloping Thoroughbred.

■ RIGHT
Specially designed vehicles are used to replace the bike-wheel sulky for racing on snow. Unlike pacers, trotters always race without hobbles on their legs.

Percheron

The elegant, free-moving Percheron originated in La Perche, in the south of Normandy. Its ancestors were Arabian horses brought to Europe by the Moors. The oriental influence is believed to have begun following the defeat of the Moors by Charles Martel near Poitiers in AD 732, and was continued after the First Crusade in 1099, when Robert, Comte de Rotrou, imported more Arab horses into France. Much later, during the eighteenth century, Arab stallions at the Royal Stud at Le Pin were made available to breeders of Percherons to upgrade their stock. The

■ LEFT
The Percheron has a fine head with prominent, alert eyes and wide, open nostrils.

eastern influence continued until relatively recent times, one of the most important early Percheron stallions, Jean le Blanc (foaled in about 1830), being the son of the Arab stallion Gallipoly. The Percheron's great strength and courage, coupled with its sound limbs and

■ ABOVE RIGHT
The breed is noted for its broad, deep chest, powerful forearms and excellent feet.

■ RIGHT
Well-proportioned and clean-limbed (that is, without feather on the lower legs), the Percheron is an elegant horse possessed of surprisingly free-moving paces considering its great size.

▌ **FAR LEFT**
The quality and excellent movement of the modern Percheron reflect the Arab influence on the breed.

▌ **LEFT**
Pause for a snack for a working horse. Percherons are so docile that they can be trained to work in a very short time.

▌ **BELOW**
Thanks to its good action and amenable temperament, the Percheron goes equally well under saddle and in harness.

longevity, made it tremendously popular in various fields: as a war horse, as a carriage horse and on the land. For some four decades during the late nineteenth and early twentieth centuries it was in great demand world wide, both for work purposes and as an improver of other heavy breeds. French breeders exported a great number of Percherons, which proved to be the most adaptable of horses whatever the climate. Many went to England, some to Australia (the Percheron is said to be the first heavy horse to be taken there) and South America, and the breed became particularly popular in North America, where the black coat colouring was preferred to the grey. American buyers also favoured a heavyweight horse which, together with the need elsewhere for big horses to work on the railways, encouraged the breeding of more massive animals. Despite its great size, however, the modern Percheron is very much a quality animal, retaining the long, low action of its ancestors.

BREED DESCRIPTION

Height 15.2 – 17hh. Average 16.1hh.

Colour Grey or black.

Conformation Fine head, with broad, square forehead, fine, long ears, prominent, alert eyes, straight profile and flat nose with wide, open nostrils; long, arched neck with fairly thick mane; sloping shoulders with prominent withers; broad, deep chest with fairly prominent sternum, short, straight back and loins with great depth through the girth and well-sprung ribs; long, sloping hindquarters; clean, sound limbs with prominent, powerful forearms and long, muscular thighs, large knees and hocks, small, strong fetlock joints and good, strong feet.

Breton

Short-legged and heavily built, the Breton is a surprisingly active heavy horse, with an especially lively trot: characteristics that testify to its Norfolk Roadster and, even further back, Arab ancestry. Like so many southern European horse breeders, those in Brittany used horses brought back from the Middle East by the Crusaders to cross with their more plebeian native stock adding, in more recent times, infusions of blood from England and a number of continental countries – the latter not always with successful results.

Down the centuries there has always been more than one type of Breton horse. Two were identified in the Middle Ages, the Sommier and the Roussin. The Sommier was descended from stock bred mainly in the north of Brittany and was used for pack and agricultural work. The Roussin, a much lighter stamp of animal, was found in the south and some central parts of the region and was a popular

■ LEFT
Although the Breton is prized in the French meat trade, some examples of these attractive horses can still be seen at work as draught animals.

saddle horse, noted for its comfortable, ambling gait.

Although the Breton is no longer thought of as a saddle horse, it does still come in different types – a large and small draught, and a coach-horse type known as the Postier, which is built on less massive lines than the draught horse. The Postier owes its lighter conformation and brilliant paces to infusions of Norfolk Roadster blood from England during the nineteenth century.

An early-maturing animal, the Breton is highly regarded in the French meat trade for the high yield and quality of meat it produces. However, it is still also valued as a draught animal and some Bretons can still be seen working on the land, particularly in the vineyards.

■ BELOW
Chestnut is the most usual colour for the Breton. The beautiful, kind eyes are set in a wide, somewhat square head.

INTERESTING FACTS

The Breton is a hardy, adaptable animal and a most willing worker. Because of its ability to work in hot climates, it has been used for upgrading purposes by breeders in Italy, Spain and even as far afield as Japan.

■ RIGHT
Stocky and short-legged, the Breton is nevertheless a very active mover and has been used over the years as a warhorse, draught horse, pack-horse, coach horse – and even a riding horse.

BREED DESCRIPTION

Height 15 – 16.1hh.

Colour Mainly chestnut; some red roan, bay and grey; black rarely occurs.

Conformation Squarish head with straight profile, open nostrils, bright eyes and small, fairly low-set ears; short, strong and slightly arched neck; rather short but sloping shoulders; short, broad and strong body with well-sprung ribs; very powerful hindquarters; short, strong limbs with very muscular thighs and forearms.

Boulonnais

The gentle Boulonnais, the most elegant of all the heavy horse breeds, traces back to Roman times. It is a native of north-west France and, like the Percheron, was greatly influenced by oriental blood. The Arab influence occurred more than once. First there was the arrival of the Roman armies, with their horses of eastern origin, who massed on the French coast before invading Britain. Then there were the Crusaders, who brought more eastern horses back with them. Two great noblemen in particular, Robert, Comte d'Artois and Eustache, Comte de Boulogne, are credited with importing Arab horses for use in their stables at this time. There was a slight change of direction during the fourteenth century, when Mecklenburg blood from Germany was introduced in order to breed a sturdier animal capable of carrying knights with their new, plated armour.

The term Boulonnais dates from the seventeenth century and reflects the main breeding region of that name on the north French coast. Sadly, the number of Boulonnais horses was seriously depleted during World War I because their chief breeding grounds were right at the heart of the battle zone. World War II had a second serious impact on the breed just as it was recovering. These two setbacks, plus the rapid spread of mechanization following World War II all but signalled the death blow of this fine horse. Fortunately it did survive, thanks to the efforts of a few dedicated enthusiasts, and although the meat trade features as one of the prime outlets for breeders, some Boulonnais horses may still be seen working small farms, where they can prove more effective and economical than tractors. Despite its size and substantial build, it is still possible to detect traces of the breed's Arab ancestry both in the small, refined head, with its large, expressive eyes, and in its outgoing nature.

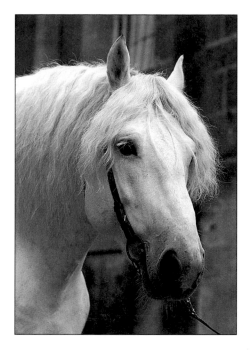

LEFT
Famous for its gentle nature, the Boulonnais is the most elegant of the heavy horse breeds.

BREED DESCRIPTION

Height 15.3 – 16.3hh.

Colour All shades of grey.

Conformation Elegant head, short and broad overall, with straight profile, wide forehead, slightly prominent eye sockets, strong, rounded, widely spaced jowls, large, bright eyes, small, erect ears, open nostrils and small mouth (in mares the head is slightly longer and less heavy); thick, often arched, neck with thick mane; muscular shoulders with fairly prominent withers; broad, straight back, broad chest and well-sprung ribs; round, muscular hindquarters with fairly high-set, thick tail; strong limbs with very prominent muscular projections in the forearms and thighs, short, thick cannons, large, flat joints and no feather.

INTERESTING FACTS

Two types of Boulonnais evolved: a large, heavy version for use in agriculture and industry, and a smaller, lighter horse suitable for less strenuous work on small-holdings and in light draught work. At one time the small type was known as the *maréeur* or *mareyeur* (fish merchant) because it was used for the transportation of fish from Boulogne to Paris. Nowadays the small type is used in agriculture, the meat trade favouring the larger animal.

BELOW
Boulonnais horses are branded with an anchor on the neck, reflecting their maritime homeland.

Trakehner

Of all the warmbloods, the Trakehner is the closest in appearance to the Thoroughbred. Organized breeding of this attractive riding horse began in 1732, when Friedrich Wilhelm I of Prussia established the Royal Trakehner Stud Administration in East Prussia (now part of Poland). A great deal of Thoroughbred and Arab blood was used to upgrade the local horses. These were descendants of the tough little Schweiken breed known to the Teutonic knights who colonized the region during the early thirteenth century. The Schweiken was a descendant of the Konik pony, which traces back to the primitive Tarpan.

Towards the end of the eighteenth century a determined effort was made to improve the Trakehner, or East Prussian, as it was also known. Inferior breeding stock at the Royal Stud was drastically weeded out, a process which led to the swift development of the Trakehner. It was soon much in demand, first as a carriage horse and subsequently as an army remount.

Renowned for its twin qualities of elegance and toughness, the Trakehner flourished for nearly two centuries – until the disastrous upheaval of World War II. During the autumn and winter of 1944 the breed suffered catastrophic losses as desperate efforts were made to evacuate the horses before the arrival of the advancing Russian troops. Of the thousands of Trakehners, many of them mares with foals at foot, who set off on the 900 mile (1,450km) journey west across Europe, few survived. Before their flight there were more than 25,000 horses registered in the East Prussian stud book. A mere 1,200 or so made it to the West

▍ **ABOVE RIGHT**
The Trakehner is noted for its refined head. Large eyes and a small, tapered muzzle enhance the overall impression of quality.

▍ **RIGHT**
The Trakehner's elegant outline owes much to the Thoroughbred influence. The Trakehner, in its turn, has been used in the development of the Dutch, Danish and Swedish Warmbloods.

BREED DESCRIPTION

Height Average 16 – 16.2hh.

Colour Any solid colour.

Conformation Refined head with large eyes and small muzzle; elegant, tapering neck; well-sloped shoulders; strong, medium-length body, well ribbed-up; well-rounded hindquarters; hard limbs with short cannons and excellent, sound feet.

INTERESTING FACTS

One of the most famous examples of the Trakehner is the show jumper Abdullah, a handsome grey stallion who competed for the United States. Ridden by Conrad Homfeld, he won a team gold medal and the individual silver at the 1984 Olympic Games and was victorious in the World Cup the following year. Abdullah was originally exported *in utero* to Canada and was foaled in 1970. After his retirement from competition he was used for breeding in many countries, thanks to the use of frozen semen.

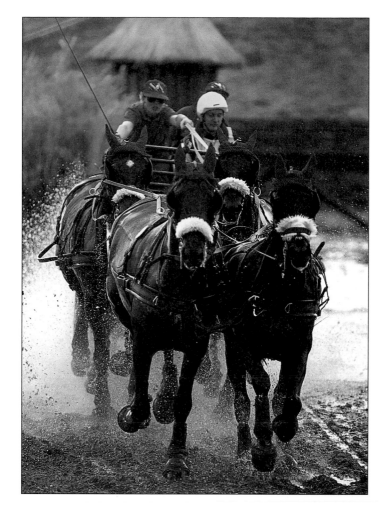

▌ LEFT
Like the Thoroughbred, the Trakehner is possessed of courage and stamina, qualities which make it suitable for tough sports such as carriage driving.

▌ BELOW LEFT
The powers of endurance which helped the breed survive the harsh times of World War II stand the breed in good stead in the modern sport of eventing.

▌ BELOW
The show-jumping stallion Abdullah demonstrated the breed's fine qualities to great advantage when winning a team gold medal at the 1984 Olympic Games.

and many of these failed to survive in the very harsh economic conditions of post-war Germany.

Incredibly, thanks to the dedicated efforts of the keepers of the original stud book, the Trakehner did not die out. The surviving equine evacuees were tracked down and re-registered in West Germany and, as breeding resumed and numbers increased, the Trakehner began to take its place in the modern equestrian world. Valued for its good conformation and action, its spirited temperament and its endurance, it has found favour both as a competition horse and as an improver of other warmbloods.

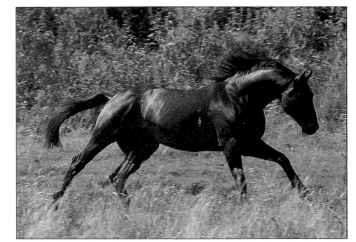

■ LEFT
Previously bred as an
all-purpose work
horse, the modern
Hanoverian has been
refined for use in
equestrian sports.

Hanoverian

George II, Elector of Hanover and King of
England, was instrumental in the
establishment of this famous German
warmblood, thanks to the foundation of
the state stud at Celle in 1735. The aim
was to provide local people with the
services of good quality stallions at
nominal fees, the original horses being
Holsteins of predominantly Andalusian
and Neapolitan blood. Thanks to the later

BREED DESCRIPTION

Height 15.3 – 16.2hh.

Colour All solid colours.

Conformation Medium-sized head, clean
cut and expressive, with large, lively eyes
and good free cheek bones; long, fine neck;
large, sloping shoulders with pronounced
withers; strong, deep body; muscular
hindquarters with well set-on tail; well-
muscled limbs with large, pronounced joints
and well-formed, hard hooves.

■ ABOVE RIGHT
Thoroughbreds and Trakehners were used
in the development of the present-day
Hanoverian. Their influence can be seen
in the breed's clean-cut head.

■ RIGHT
The Hanoverian is noted more for its
strength than its speed, hence the many
successes of its representatives in dressage
and show jumping.

A great many Hanoverians have become household names as show jumpers, among them Dollar Girl (1995 World Cup winner with Nick Skelton), Top Gun (1992 Olympic team gold medallist with Jan Tops), Walzerkönig (1988 Olympic team gold medallist with Franke Sloothaak), Deister (three times European Champion with Paul Schockemöhle), Tigre (1978 world team gold medallist with Caroline Bradley), Simona (1974 World Champion with Hartwig Steenken) and Ferdl (1960 Olympic team gold medallist ridden by Paul Schockemöhle's brother, Alwin).

▌ LEFT
Hanoverians have found favour throughout the world as show jumpers. Amadeus Z, bred in Belgium, is seen competing for Holland at the 1994 World Equestrian Games.

importation of English horses, including Thoroughbreds, the Hanoverian gradually began to show more quality, the aim being to produce a good all-purpose animal that was capable of working on the land but also suitable for ridden work and for use as a light carriage horse.

In common with so many other horse-breeding enterprises, the development of the Hanoverian at Celle was adversely affected by war. By the end of the eighteenth century the stud had over 100 stallions, but by 1816, after the Napoleonic wars, a mere thirty remained. To help make up for these losses, more outside blood was brought in, especially Thoroughbred. But the time came when the breed was tending to become too light for the work required of it and this influence was accordingly reduced.

After World War II, however, the Hanoverian had to be adapted to a new way of life if the breed was to survive and Thoroughbred blood was again introduced, along with Trakehner, to produce a warmblood suited to the demands of the leisure-horse market.

The modern Hanoverian is lighter and less coarse than of old and is noted for its good, honest temperament. In common with other German warmbloods, stallions are only licensed if they pass the required veterinary inspection and, after licensing, must pass ridden performance tests. Hanoverians are among the world's most sought-after sports horses, their strength and athleticism making them especially suitable for dressage and show jumping.

▌ LEFT
Dressage is the other sport at which the Hanoverian excels. With its great strength and true, energetic action, it is well suited to this demanding discipline.

Holstein

The Holstein is probably the oldest of the German warmbloods, dating back several centuries. As early as the seventeenth century horses bred in the region were much in demand in France, Denmark and Italy. The old Holstein horses contained mixed blood, including German, Neapolitan, Spanish and oriental. During the nineteenth century they were crossed with Yorkshire Coach Horses, a policy which helped give the breed a distinctive high knee action, great presence and an exceptionally tractable nature. Holsteins became renowned for being tough but handsome carriage horses and subsequently as army remounts.

The Traventhall Stud, founded by the Prussians in 1867 in Schleswig-Holstein, is considered the modern Holstein's birthplace. However, this stud is no longer in operation and the breeds main base is now at Elmshorn.

To produce a stamp of horse suitable for today's requirements, some Thoroughbred blood was used in the period after World War II, which resulted in a lighter type of horse with less high, "carriage-horse" action and a better shoulder. Although the infusions of Thoroughbred blood may have made the Holstein rather more excitable than it was

■ ABOVE
This handsome head, with its alert, intelligent expression, is typical of the Holstein.

■ LEFT
Formerly bred for use as a carriage horse and army remount, the Holstein was upgraded into a better-quality animal through the introduction of a certain amount of Thoroughbred blood.

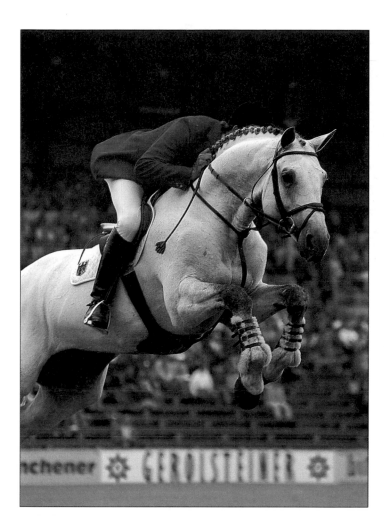

One of the most celebrated Holstein horses of all time was the big bay gelding Meteor, the only show jumper to have won a medal at three Olympic Games. Foaled in 1943, he won the individual bronze medal at the 1952 Games and four years later helped Germany win the team gold in Stockholm, where he finished fourth individually. In Rome in 1960, at the age of 17, he won a second team gold medal and finished sixth in the individual contest. Ridden by Fritz Thiedemann, an exceptionally talented all-round horseman, Meteor was an outstanding ambassador for the Holstein breed. He died in 1966 and is buried at Elmshorn, the breed's headquarters.

▌ FAR LEFT
Show jumping is a sport at which the Holstein, with its intelligent and bold character, has excelled for many years.

▌ BELOW
The breed is noted for its powerful action, which is used to good effect in Grand Prix dressage.

of old, it has, generally speaking, retained its good temperament. Its intelligence and boldness make it a first-rate mount for top-level dressage and show jumping.

Holstein horses are not bred in such quantity as some other warmbloods nor is their breeding area particularly large. Possibly as a result, there is less variation in overall type.

▌ BELOW
Originally prized as tough, active carriage horses, Holsteins can still be seen in harness in the competitive discipline of four-in-hand driving.

BREED DESCRIPTION

Height Approximately 16 – 17hh.

Colour All colours permissible. Bay with black points and brown predominate. Grey is quite common, chestnut less so.

Conformation Expressive head, well set-on and in proportion to the size of the horse, with big, bright eyes; long, muscular and slightly arched neck; long, sloping shoulders; strong back, deep, wide chest and muscular loins; strong, muscular hindquarters with well-muscled thighs, stifles and gaskins; short, strong cannon bones, flat knees, big, clean hocks, medium-length pasterns and good, hard feet.

Oldenburg

The Oldenburg, Germany's heaviest type of warmblood, was originally developed as a coach horse and was based on the old Friesian horses bred in the region between the River Weser and the Netherlands. The breed takes its name from Count Anton Gunther von Oldenburg (1603–67), who played a leading part in its development, crossing stallions from Italy and Spain with the native stock. Later breeders introduced Thoroughbred, Cleveland Bay, Hanoverian and Norman blood. The result was a big upstanding horse, measuring a good 17hh, and fairly heavily built. Unlike most large animals, however, it matured early which undoubtedly popularized it as a work horse.

■ LEFT
The Oldenburg was originally bred as a coach horse. It is the heaviest of the German Warmbloods.

BREED DESCRIPTION

Height Approximately 16 – 17hh.

Colour Predominantly brown, black and bay.

Conformation Rather plain head, occasionally with a Roman nose; fairly long, very strong neck; sloping, muscular shoulders; powerfully built body with deep chest; strong hindquarters with high-set tail; fairly short limbs with large joints and plenty of bone.

■ LEFT
Careful breeding has helped eradicate coach-horse characteristics such as upright shoulders and a long back, though some modern Oldenburgs retain the rather high knee action of their forebears.

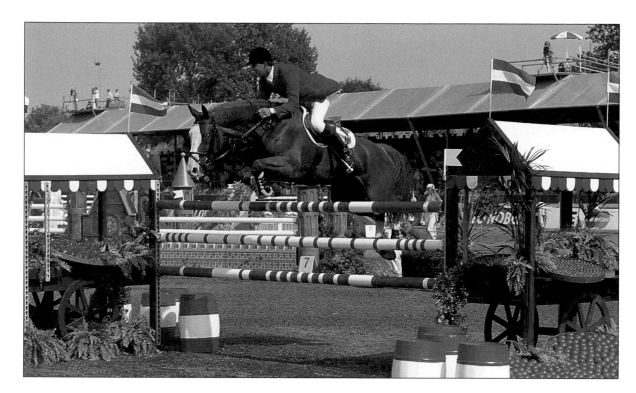

▌ LEFT
The German rider
Franke Sloothaak on
his way to becoming
World Show Jumping
Champion in 1994.
His mount is the
Oldenburg mare,
Weihaiwej.

As coach horses gave way to motorized transport in the early twentieth century, breeders had of necessity to change the type of the Oldenburg and look more to the production of a general-purpose farm horse. More recently, further infusions of Thoroughbred blood, and some Selle Français, have produced a horse which is considerably finer than its coaching ancestors and well able to hold its own in the competitive sports, working equally well under saddle or in harness. The Oldenburg still tends to be a big individual compared with other warmbloods but many of the coach-horse characteristics, such as an upright shoulder and long back, have been eliminated. The knee action still tends to be a little on the high side.

Oldenburg horses are exported to many countries and have proved particularly popular in the United States.

▌ BELOW
From coach horse to dressage horse: refinement of
the breed has been brought about through the
introduction of Thoroughbred and Selle Français
blood, making the present-day Oldenburg an
outstanding sports horse.

INTERESTING FACTS

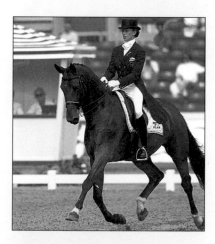

Olympic Bonfire, an Oldenburg gelding
foaled in 1983, won the World Dressage
Freestyle to Music Championship in 1994
when ridden by the leading Dutch rider,
Anky van Grunsven.

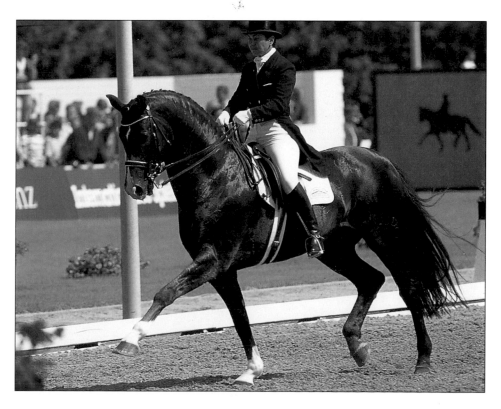

Westphalian

Closely related to the Hanoverian, the Westphalian is bred in the region of Nordrhein-Westfalen, in the north-west of Germany. Its main breeding centre, Warendorf, is famous for being the home of German equestrianism (the National Federation is based there). The area has a long tradition of horse breeding. It is known that in the early nineteenth century East Prussian stallions were made available to local mare owners to enable them to upgrade their stock. Over the years various outcrosses were made, involving Oldenburg, Hanoverian, Friesian, Anglo-Norman and trotter blood and it was not until this century that breeders finally settled for just one influence: the Hanoverian. Today's Westphalian shares the bloodlines of the present-day Hanoverian, although there are also several important ones which have developed specifically in the Westphalia region.

BREED DESCRIPTION

Height 15.3 – 16.2hh.

Colour All solid colours.

Conformation Intelligent head with good width between the eyes; well-shaped neck; deep, broad body; powerful hindquarters, although they can be a little flat.

▌ ABOVE
The Westphalian has the same clean-cut good looks as the Hanoverian, with whom it shares a common ancestry.

▌ RIGHT
The conformation is typical of that of the modern sports horse: a good length of neck, deep body and powerful hindquarters. It tends to be a little longer in the leg than the Hanoverian.

INTERESTING FACTS

Famous Westphalian horses include Rembrandt (Olympic dressage champion in 1988 and 1992, ridden by Nicole Uphoff-Becker); Ahlerich (Olympic dressage champion in 1984, ridden by Reiner Klimke); Fire (winner of the World Show Jumping Championship in 1982, ridden by Norbert Koof) and Roman (winner of the World Show Jumping Championship in 1978, ridden by Gerd Wiltfang). Rembrandt, one of the most handsome representatives of the breed, was the first horse in the history of the Olympic Games to win two individual gold medals for dressage. He was European champion in 1989 and also took the individual title at the first World Equestrian Games, held in Stockholm in 1990.

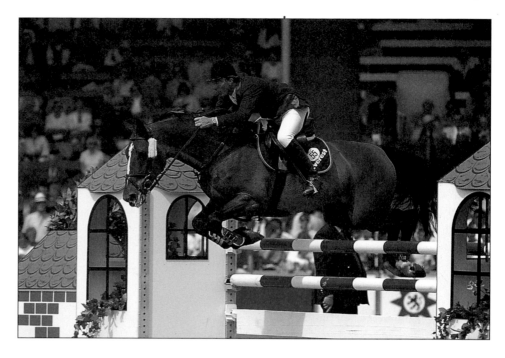

❚ ABOVE RIGHT
Two Step is a Westphalian who has found fame as a show jumper. Originally named Polydektes, he is by Polydor, one of the breed's most successful sires of competition horses.

❚ RIGHT
Ahlerich was one of the breed's most outstanding performers in the world of dressage. He crowned a gloriously successful Grand Prix career with victory at the 1984 Olympic Games in Los Angeles.

Schleswig

A sturdy, compact heavy horse, the Schleswig comes from the northernmost region of Germany, Schleswig-Holstein, which borders on to Denmark and which was, indeed, at various times actually part of that country. It is not surprising, therefore, that the Schleswig bears a marked resemblance to the Jutland, the Danish heavy breed to which it is closely related. The Schleswig was developed during the second half of the nineteenth century as a medium-sized draught horse. Infusions of lighter blood, including Yorkshire Coach Horse and Thoroughbred, were made towards the end of the century but these had no lasting effect on the breed. Popular as a tram and bus horse, and for use on the land and in forestry, the breed survived World War I (during which its homeland was under Danish rule) although it was seriously depleted in both numbers and quality. The subsequent introduction of Breton and Boulonnais blood from

France proved highly successful. The Schleswig recovered and flourished in large numbers until the years immediately following World War II. In time, however, mechanization took its usual toll, and numbers dwindled drastically. In recent years some of the surviving Schleswigs have been bred back to Jutlands, in order to increase the breed's size.

BREED DESCRIPTION

Height 15.2 – 16hh.

Colour Predominantly chestnut, occasionally bay or grey.

Conformation Large, rather plain head, but with a kind eye; short, crested neck; very powerful shoulders; rather long body, though with good depth through the girth; well-muscled hindquarters; short, strong limbs with some feather.

INTERESTING FACTS

The attractive Schleswig horse, which often has a flaxen mane and tail, is extremely powerfully built and weighs in the region of 1,766lb (800kg).

South German

This strong and agile heavy horse is descended from the Austrian Noriker, which was introduced into Bavaria, in southern Germany, towards the end of the nineteenth century. With a view to improving and developing their own stamp of horse, breeders in Upper Bavaria added some Holstein and Oldenburg blood, while those in Lower Bavaria experimented with an extraordinary variety of outcrosses, from Oldenburg and Cleveland Bay to Clydesdale and Belgian Draught. In time, however, German breeders reverted to using the original Noriker blood for upgrading purposes. Originally called the Pinzgauer Noriker, after the region in Salzburg province from which that particular strain of the Austrian heavy horse came, the German version of the breed became known as the South German Heavy Horse. Today it is bred mainly in Bavaria and Baden Wurtemburg. It still resembles the Noriker, although it is inclined to stand a little less tall. It is a

I BELOW
The South German Coldblood has a large head and, typically, a docile expression.

I BOTTOM
The South German resembles the Noriker but is a little smaller.

well-proportioned horse, with a calm, docile temperament, and can be seen in parades and at shows as well as, occasionally, at work in agriculture.

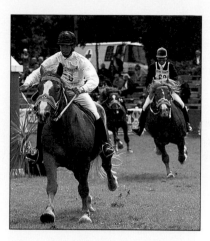

The South German heavy horse is a popular attraction at shows. As well as being used by trick riders, it takes part in races – which it clearly enjoys!

BREED DESCRIPTION

Height Around 15.3hh.

Colour Brown, bay and chestnut.

Conformation Rather large head, with kind eye; short, strong neck; powerful shoulders; strong back with deep girth; good limbs with a little feather.

Cleveland Bay

A race of bay-coloured horses was being bred, primarily for pack work, in the north east of England as far back as mediaeval times. It was the preferred means of transport of the chapmen, or travelling salesmen of the day, and was accordingly known as the Chapman Horse. Taking the Chapman Horse as their base, seventeenth-century breeders used some of the Andalusian and Barb stallions that were being brought into the country at that time to produce a fine coach horse, renowned for its active paces and great stamina. This became known as the Cleveland Bay after the area where it

was chiefly bred. As roads improved, and a faster type of coach horse became necessary, some Thoroughbred blood was introduced, usually by means of putting half-bred stallions to Cleveland mares. This lighter, faster version of the

Cleveland Bay was called the Yorkshire Coach Horse. It had its own breed society, founded in 1886, and stud book. But the coming of motorized transport signalled the demise of coach horses everywhere and the Yorkshire breed was no exception.

■ ABOVE
The Cleveland Bay is the descendant of a race of bay-coloured horses bred in north-eastern England since medieval times.

■ LEFT
A handsome, upstanding stamp of horse, the Cleveland Bay produces excellent hunters when crossed with the Thoroughbred.

Its stud book was finally closed in 1936, by which time the breed had virtually died out. Fortunately the Cleveland Bay survived, albeit in small numbers. Crossed with the Thoroughbred, the breed produces fine upstanding heavyweight hunters and excellent carriage horses. The Cleveland Bay has a true, straight and free action (high action is not characteristic of the breed), moves freely from the shoulder and covers the ground well. As well as making an excellent hunter and carriage horse, the Cleveland Bay, when crossed with the Thoroughbred, has also produced some first-rate show jumpers.

BREED DESCRIPTION

Height 16 – 16.2hh, though height does not disqualify an otherwise good animal.

Colour Bay with black points.

Conformation Bold head, not too small, with large, well-set, kind eyes and large, fine ears; long, lean neck; deep, sloping, muscular shoulders; deep, wide body, with muscular loins, powerful hindquarters and well set-on tail; clean limbs (without feather), with muscular forearms, thighs and second thighs, large knees and hocks, and strong, sloping pasterns; good, sound feet.

INTERESTING FACTS

The survival of the Cleveland Bay was aided in no small measure by Queen Elizabeth II. A colt named Mulgrave Supreme, due to be sent to the United States, was bought by the Queen, subsequently broken to saddle and to harness and then made available to breeders of Cleveland Bays, both pure- and part-bred, throughout Britain. This tremendously successful promotional exercise sparked off renewed enthusiasm among breeders. Prince Philip further enhanced the breed's profile by driving, for many years, teams of pure- and part-bred Cleveland Bays at international level.

▮ RIGHT
For many years HRH
The Duke of
Edinburgh drove a
team of Cleveland
Bays in international
four-in-hand events.
They have excellent
ground-covering
action, well suited to
work both in harness
and under saddle.

BREEDS: GREAT BRITAIN

Hackney

The Hackney, with its high-stepping action, is a native of England though it is prized the world over as a carriage horse, especially in the show ring. The Hackney horse originated in the late seventeenth and early eighteenth centuries and is a descendant of the famous English trotting horses of the time, the Yorkshire Trotter and the Norfolk Roadster. These horses had a common ancestor, a horse known as the Original Shales, who was foaled in 1755 and was by the Thoroughbred Blaze out of a mare described as a "hackney". Blaze was by Flying Childers, generally recognized as being the first great racehorse. Blaze and his progeny, notably his two sons, Driver and Scot Shales, had a considerable influence on the development of the trotters of eastern England. Despite their shared ancestry,

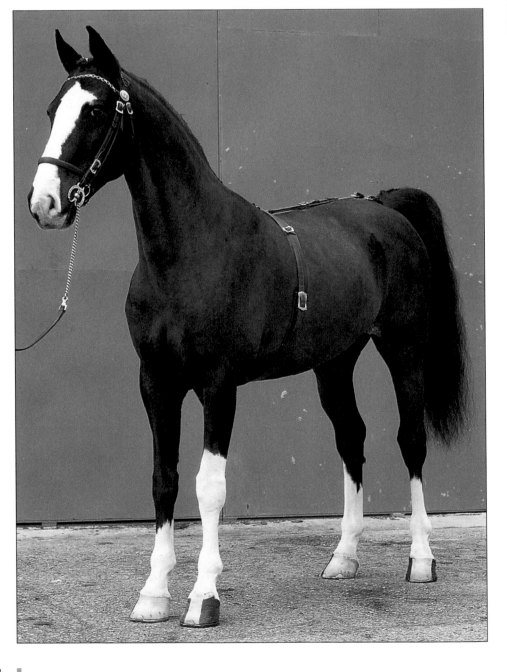

BREED DESCRIPTION

Height Hackney pony not exceeding 14hh. Hackney horse 15 – 15.3hh.

Colour Usually dark brown, black, bay or chestnut.

Conformation Small, convex head with small muzzle, large eyes and small ears; fairly long, well-formed neck; powerful shoulders and low withers; compact body, with great depth of chest; short legs with strong, well let-down hocks and well-shaped feet.

the horses bred in Yorkshire and Norfolk developed somewhat different characteristics – those of Yorkshire origin tended to have more quality than those from Norfolk, which were more cob-like in appearance – but these regional

INTERESTING FACTS

The derivation of the word hackney is doubtful but it is thought to come from the Old French *haquenée*, "an ambling horse or mare, especially for ladies to ride on", and may be related to the Old Spanish and Portuguese *facanea* and Spanish *hacanea*. In the fourteenth century the word was latinized in England as *hakeneius*.

▌ LEFT
Hackneys are popular in show rings throughout the world. Here they are being driven in an unusual three-horse combination known as a unicorn, comprising two wheelers and a leader.

distinctions later disappeared.

The Hackney pony was developed during the second half of the eighteenth century – earlier use of the term "Hackney ponies" almost certainly referred to small part-bred Hackney horses. It was the very enterprising Westmorland breeder, Christopher Wyndham Wilson, a remarkable man whose achievements included inventing the silo to store winter feed for farm animals, who was largely responsible for the development of the true Hackney pony. Wilson used a variety of pony breeds, especially the Fell, as his foundation mares, crossing them with a good-looking Hackney horse named Sir George, who was sired in 1866 and stood less than 14hh. His policy of inbreeding to the prepotent Sir George enabled Wilson to achieve his aim of developing a Hackney with real pony characteristics and in due course other breeders followed his lead. The original height limit for ponies, as recommended by the Hackney Horse Society, was 14.2hh but this was subsequently reduced to 14hh. The high-stepping action for which the Hackney is renowned was not developed until the second half of the nineteenth century, when it became the fashion to drive elegant, showy carriage horses. It is partly inherited, partly taught and can be enhanced by training.

▌ RIGHT
In classes for single turnouts the Hackney is harnessed to a lightweight vehicle with pneumatic tyres.

▌ OPPOSITE
The Hackney has a compact body, powerful shoulders and a deep chest. The limbs are strong and the feet invariably well formed.

Shire

England's most magnificent looking heavy horse is descended from the mediaeval warhorse known as the Great Horse, which was later given the name of the English Black. It was developed by crossing imported Flanders and Friesian horses with native stock to produce first a military mount and subsequently a farm and general draught horse. The introduction of the term "blacks" for these heavy horses is attributed to Oliver Cromwell, and was probably used originally to describe the imported Friesians, which are always black in colour. The main breeding areas of the

BREED DESCRIPTION

Height Stallions 16.2 – 17.2hh. Mares 16 – 17hh.

Colour Black, brown, bay or grey.

Conformation Lean head (neither too large nor too small), wide between the eyes, slightly Roman nose, large, prominent eyes with docile expression, and long, lean, sharp, sensitive ears; fairly long, slightly arched neck; deep, oblique shoulders, wide enough to support a collar; short, strong, muscular back, broad chest and wide, sweeping, muscular hindquarters with well let-down thighs; clean, hard limbs with 11–12 inches (28–30cm) of bone and broad, deep, flat hocks, set at the correct angle for leverage; fine, straight, silky feather; deep, solid feet with thick walls and open coronets.

▌ **ABOVE RIGHT**
The Roman nose, long, sharp ears, large eyes and docile expression are typical of the Shire, the archetypal "gentle giant".

▌ **RIGHT**
The magnificent Shire is descended from the medieval warhorse known as the Great Horse. It weighs in excess of 20cwt (1,016kg).

■ RIGHT
A team of twenty Shires makes a magnificent sight at an English horse show, admirably displaying the breed's tractable nature.

■ BELOW
A foal dozes in the summer sun. While Shires will never be seen in the same numbers as in olden times, the breed has enough enthusiasts to ensure its future.

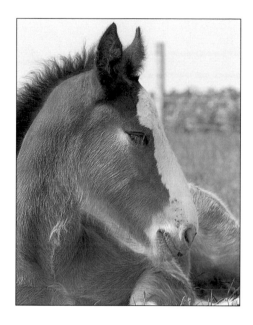

INTERESTING FACTS

One of the earliest records of a Shire stallion standing at stud is of the horse known as the Packington Blind Horse. He was named after the village of Packington, near Ashby-de-la-Zouche, where he lived between 1755 and 1770. This horse, and horses said to be his progeny, had a significant influence on the breed during its formative years.

English Black were the Fen country and the Midland shires of Leicestershire, Lincolnshire, Derbyshire and Staffordshire, from which the breed eventually took its name. In the early days the breed displayed regional variations, horses bred in the Fens tending to be bigger, heavier and somewhat coarser than those from the "Shires". Those from Derbyshire and Leicestershire were predominantly black, while Staffordshire horses were more often brown.

It was not until the late nineteenth century that the breeding of these horses became formalized, as a result of the publication of the first stud book. In 1878 a breed society was set up under the title of the Old English Cart Horse Society. The name was changed in 1884 to the Shire Horse Society and the breed has been known as the Shire ever since.

Following the formation of the breed society, the Shire went from strength to strength, competing with great success in the leading agricultural shows of the time and attracting the interest of foreign buyers. Shire horses were soon being exported as far afield as North and South America, Russia and Australia. They also became an indispensable part of daily life in Britain. With their qualities of strength, stamina, soundness and good temperament, these gentle giants could be seen ploughing the land, hauling timber and pulling farm wagons, railway vans, brewers' drays and coal carts. Although mechanization took its customary toll, a Shire "revival" began in the 1960s and today these wonderful horses can again be seen at shows, ploughing the land and, not least, pulling brewers' drays on short-haul routes in cities.

■ LEFT AND ABOVE
Shires hitched to brewers' drays are a popular sight at many British horse and agricultural shows. Some are still used for short-haul work in inner cities, where they are more economical than motorized transport.

Suffolk

Britain's oldest heavy breed, the Suffolk or Suffolk Punch, is named after the East Anglian county where it has been bred since the sixteenth century. Little is known of its origins, but as far back as 1506 there is an historical reference to a distinctive type of Suffolk horse. The Suffolk was developed as a farm horse and with its tremendously strong shoulders and clean legs (i.e. free of feather) it is ideally suited to working on the very heavy clay soils of East Anglia.

The breed is unique in that all Suffolks trace back to a single stallion, known as Crisp's Horse of Ufford, foaled in 1760.

■ LEFT
This mare shows the typical broad forehead and full, bright eyes of the Suffolk. All Suffolks are chesnut in colour – traditionally spelt without the middle "t".

■ BELOW
Although there is plenty of width between the forelegs, the hindfeet are set close together. Such conformation prevents the horse damaging crops when working in the fields.

This purity is manifested in the fact that it always breeds true to colour: all Suffolks are "chesnut" (traditionally spelt without the first "t"). Quite apart from its coat colour, the Suffolk is quite unmistakable in appearance, having a heavy body set on comparatively short legs.

■ RIGHT
With its heavy body and short legs the Suffolk admirably fits its popular name, "Punch". Its legs are always free of feather – an essential prerequisite for a horse bred to work on heavy clay soils.

BREED DESCRIPTION

Height 16 – 16.3hh.

Colour Always "chesnut", of which seven shades are recognized, ranging from a pale mealy tone to a very dark, almost brown, shade. The most common is a bright reddish shade. A little white may occur on the face and the mane and tail are sometimes pale in colour.

Conformation Quite large head, with broad forehead; deep, tapering neck; long, muscular shoulders; deep, well-rounded body with strong quarters and well-set tail; fairly short, straight limbs with plenty of bone, sloping pasterns and no coarse hair; hard, sound, medium-sized feet.

INTERESTING FACTS

The ability of the Suffolk to thrive on less rations than other working heavy horses is well illustrated by the experiences of one farmer who, during the early part of this century, compared the feed requirements of two dozen cross-bred farm horses which he used for several years on one farm, and those of twenty-five Suffolks which he used for a similar period on another. While all the horses ate the same quantities of bulk food – hay, mangolds and chaff – the cross-breds each required 75lb (34kg) of corn per week, increasing by some 14–21lbs (6.4-9.5kg) per week as they grew older, while the Suffolks, even the older ones, kept their condition on a regular 50lb (22.7kg) per week.

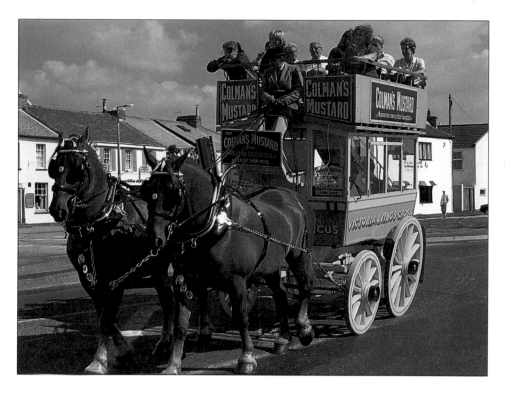

Despite its size the Suffolk is a remarkably economical horse to keep, thriving and working on comparatively small rations. It matures early – Suffolks can be put to light work at two years of age and go into full work at three. It has an exceptionally amenable temperament and it is noted for its great soundness and longevity – it is common for horses to be in use and mares to be producing foals into their late teens and Suffolks often live until they are nearly thirty. The Suffolk's remarkable qualities combined to make it one of the most popular agricultural and draught horses of all time and, not surprisingly, its popularity spread abroad. There have been Suffolks in the United States for many years and representatives of the breed have also been exported to Australia, Africa, Russia and Pakistan (where they were used to produce army horses). Like the Shire, the Suffolk survived the coming of mechanization and can still be seen occasionally working the land, pulling drays and at shows, principally in eastern England.

▌ **ABOVE RIGHT**
A pair of present-day Suffolks drawing a vehicle of yesteryear.

▌ **RIGHT**
Suffolks can still be seen at their traditional work, ploughing. Early maturing, sound, long-lived and economical to feed, the breed possesses all the attributes so vital in a draught horse in the days before mechanization.

Clydesdale

Scotland's breed of heavy horse, as its name suggests, originated in that area of Lanarkshire through which the Clyde river runs. Today's Clydesdale, which developed more recently than the other British heavy breeds, began to evolve during the second half of the eighteenth century when imported Flemish stallions were used to improve the stock, descended from pack animals, of local farmers. Before that, during the early part of the century, a breeder named Paterson of Lochlyoch had begun to produce horses which, by all accounts, bore a distinct resemblance to the modern Clydesdale, certainly as far as colour was concerned. The stallion Glancer, to whom many Clydesdales can be traced back, was out of a mare known as Lampit's Mare, who was believed to be a

BREED DESCRIPTION

Height Stallions 17.1 – 18hh. Mares 16.3 – 17.2hh

Colour Bay, brown or black. Chestnut is rare. Often with a good deal of white on the face and legs, which may run up on to the body, particularly as flashes on the stomach.

Conformation Strong, intelligent head, with broad forehead, wide muzzle, large nostrils, bright, clear eyes and big ears; long, well-arched neck; sloping shoulders with high withers; short back with well-sprung ribs and muscular hindquarters; straight limbs with forelegs set well under the shoulders, long pasterns and a fair amount of fine feather; round, open feet.

▌ OPPOSITE PAGE
The brisk, ground-covering paces of the Clydesdale make it eminently suitable for both agricultural and heavy haulage work.

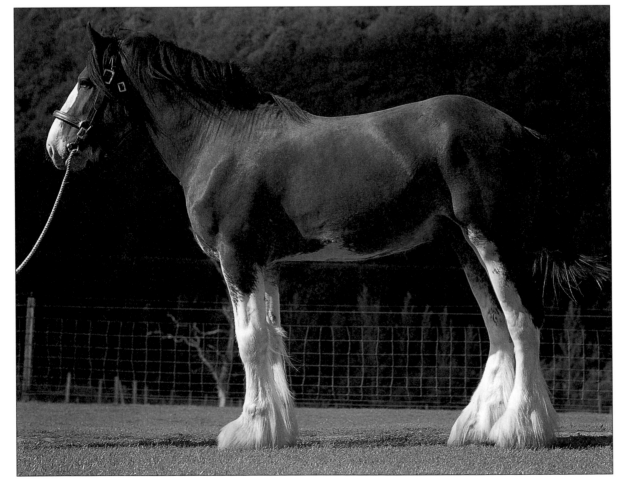

▌ ABOVE
Large, kind eyes and big ears give these Clydesdales the gentle, sensible expression typical of the breed. Unlike the Shire, the Clydesdale never has a Roman nose.

▌ LEFT
Although the Clydesdale is closely related to the Shire, it has a number of distinguishing features, the most readily discernible of which is the large amount of white often seen on the limbs and extending up to the lower parts of the body.

BELOW
Wearing traditional Scottish harness decorations, the Clydesdale makes a fine sight in the show ring.

INTERESTING FACTS

One of the most famous and influential stallions in the development of the Clydesdale was a dark brown horse named Prince of Wales, foaled in Ayrshire in 1866. He was a mixture of English and Scottish blood and had outstanding action. His stud fee of £40, by no means a small sum for those days, was well worth paying – young horses sired by him fetched anywhere from £2,000 to £3,000.

descendant of the Lochlyoch horses.

Shire blood was used in the breed's development – indeed the two leading Clydesdale breeders during the second half of the nineteenth century, Lawrence Drew and David Riddell, believed the Clydesdale and the Shire to be of the same origin, and regularly interbred the two.

The Clydesdale Horse Society was formed in 1877 and the first stud book was published the following year. By this time interest in the breed had spread to other countries and Clydesdales were soon

being exported, often in large numbers, to work the vast wheatlands of North America; others went to Australia, South America and Russia. It was, without doubt, the Clydesdale's docile nature combined with elegance and great activity that endeared it to heavy horse enthusiasts all over the world. Describing his action, the breed society says that the inside of every shoe should be made visible to anyone walking behind. The Clydesdale is an exceptionally sound horse, great emphasis having always been placed on good limbs and feet.

RIGHT
Many Clydesdales were exported to North America to work in agriculture. Their descendants can still be seen, though in rather different roles. This team is being used to haul the starting stalls at Santa Anita Racetrack.

Furioso

Hungary has long enjoyed a world-wide reputation as a horse-breeding country and as a producer of fine horsemen. The famous stud farm at Mezöhegyes, founded in 1784 by the Emperor Josef II, quickly became established as one of the great breeding centres of Europe. One of the most important breeds developed there was the Furioso, which was produced by crossing Thoroughbreds with mainly Hungarian mares. The chief influences were the English Thoroughbred stallion, Furioso, after whom the breed was named and who was acquired by Mezöhegyes in 1841, and another English horse, North Star, who was imported during the 1850s. Using these two bloodlines Mezöhegyes began producing quality carriage horses and good, heavyweight riding horses. For a time these two bloodlines were kept separate, with North Star proving a particularly successful sire of harness racehorses. He was descended from the

BREED DESCRIPTION

Height About 16hh.

Colour Any solid colour.

Conformation Fine head (denoting its Thoroughbred ancestry); well-sloped shoulders; strong back; good strong limbs and feet.

1793 Derby winner, Waxy (a grandson of the great Eclipse), and is said to trace back to Norfolk Roadster blood, which could account for his progeny's success in harness. Towards the end of the nineteenth century the North Star and Furioso strains were merged, after which the Furioso became the dominant force.

INTERESTING FACTS

The Csikos horse herders of Hungary are renowned for their trick-riding skills. Their breathtaking displays, often performed with Furioso horses, are famous all over the world.

▌ TOP
The present-day Furioso is a quality all-purpose riding horse, built on somewhat heavier lines than its Thoroughbred ancestors.

▌ LEFT
Large herds of horses, including the Furioso, have traditionally been raised on the grasslands of Hungary.

Nonius

Like the Furioso, the more heavily built Nonius evolved at the Mezöhegyes stud farm founded by the Emperor Josef II. The breed's foundation sire was an Anglo-Norman horse by the name of Nonius Senior. He was foaled in 1810, captured in

BREED DESCRIPTION

Height Large type 15.3 – 16.2hh. Small type 14.3 – 15.3hh.

Colour Predominantly bay, with some black, brown and chestnut.

Conformation Attractive, honest head; sloping shoulders; broad, strong back; strong hindquarters; sound limbs.

France by the Austrians in 1814 and installed at Mezöhegyes in 1816. Nonius was said to be by a half-bred English stallion out of a Norman mare and almost certainly had Norfolk Roadster blood in him. He was by all accounts not the most prepossessing individual and would have won no prizes for conformation, but during his sixteen years at stud he became a tremendously successful sire. Mated with mares of various breeds, including Arab, Lipizzaner, Spanish and Turkish, as well as Hungarian, he produced good quality horses, the best of which were mated back to him. In this way a distinctive type emerged – to be known as the Nonius.

During the 1860s, infusions of Thoroughbred blood were made, a policy which led to the development of two different types of Nonius: one, a large horse suited to light agricultural work and as a carriage horse, the other, a smaller, finer animal suitable for riding. In more recent times, as the need for farm horses diminished, the larger type of Nonius was used mainly for driving, a skill at which Hungarian horsemen have long excelled. Both types of Nonius combine active paces with a calm, willing temperament.

I BELOW
The head, though lacking refinement, reflects the breed's kind, tractable nature.

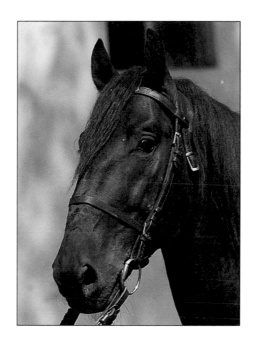

I BELOW
Thoroughbred, Norman and Norfolk Roadster blood all played a part in the development of the Nonius. Today's sturdily built individuals make good all-round riding and driving horses.

INTERESTING FACTS

There are two distinct types of harness used for driving purposes. These Nonius horses are wearing breast harness. For pulling heavy loads horses wear collars to enable them to use the full strength of their shoulders.

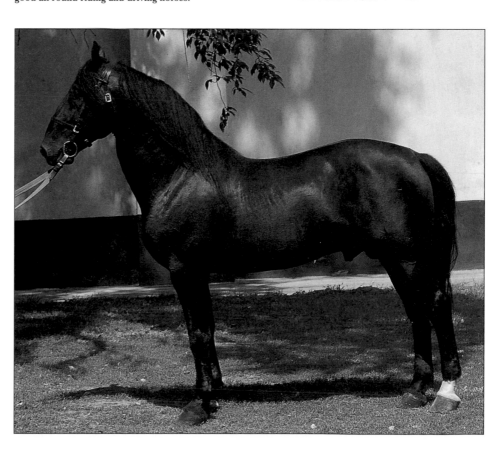

Hungarian Half-bred

The Hungarians began producing leisure and sports horses during the 1960s, continuing their tradition of breeding fine horses. They imported Hanoverians and Holsteins to cross with the Furioso and the Gidran in order to develop an animal suited to modern requirements. The Gidran, which to all intents and purposes is the Hungarian Anglo-Arab, can be traced back to an Arabian stallion known as Gidran Senior, imported into Hungary in 1816. Gidran's son, Gidran II, bred from a Spanish mare, became the foundation sire of the type which bears his name.

Initially a variety of mares were used, but later Thoroughbred blood was introduced and, subsequently, more Arab blood. This breeding policy

BREED DESCRIPTION

Height 15.3 – 16hh.

Colour Any solid colour.

Conformation Variable, but usually well proportioned with good, sloping shoulders and strong hindquarters.

▌ ABOVE LEFT
Intelligent and spirited, the Hungarian Half-bred has Arab, Thoroughbred, Hanoverian, Holstein and native Hungarian blood in its veins.

▌ LEFT
The breed was developed to meet the need for a modern competition horse. Good overall conformation and strong, sound limbs and feet are therefore essential.

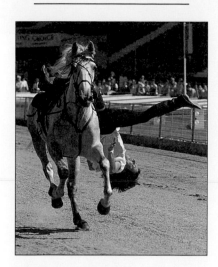

The Hungarian Half-bred has a good temperament which lends itself to training for a wide variety of activities – as this daring trick riding display proves.

▌ LEFT
Speed, stamina and a ground-covering stride make the half-bred a suitable partner for the tough sport of three-day eventing.

▌ BELOW
Hungarian Half-breds have achieved their greatest competition successes in the gruelling sport of four-in-hand driving. They have been exported to many countries for this purpose.

resulted in a quality horse with a good, ground-covering gallop. The breed was developed at Hungary's chief studs – the old-established one at Mezöhegyes; the Kisber, named after the Hungarian-bred horse who won the British Derby in 1876, and the Kecskemet, which is famous for its cross-bred driving horses, based on Lipizzaner and trotter blood.

Hungarian Half-breds have achieved outstanding success in the sport of international four-in-hand driving, where they have competed not just in the hands of the traditionally dashing and skilful Hungarian drivers but also for a number of other European nations, notably Switzerland and Britain.

Shagya

The Shagya is a strain of Arabian horse bred in Hungary and descended from a stallion of the same name. Shagya was a Syrian-bred horse, foaled in 1830 and imported to the Hungarian stud at Babolna some six years later. Shagya was used to cover quality mares which, although they were of mixed blood (including Hungarian, Thoroughbred and Spanish, as well as Arabian) were distinctly "eastern" in overall appearance. By employing the practice of inbreeding, the Babolna Stud produced the distinctive type of Arab horse seen today. The Shagya is rather taller and has a noticeably bigger frame than other Arabs (Shagya himself

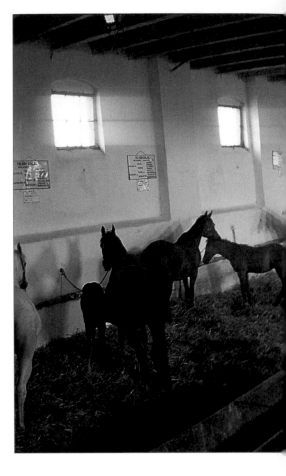

■ ABOVE LEFT
The wide-set eyes and tapered muzzle, with its large nostrils, are typical of the Shagya.

■ LEFT
The Shagya tends to have a rather more substantial frame than the pure-bred Arab, though its overall outline is very similar.

The Babolna Stud, home of the Shagya Arab, was founded in 1789 by the Emperor Joseph II. Hungary has one of the oldest traditions of organized horse breeding in the world, its first recorded stud (founded by Prince Arpad, who died in 907) dating back more than 1,000 years. During the mid-eighteenth century horse breeding began to slip into a gradual decline and it was Joseph II who was largely responsible for revitalizing it. He founded the Veterinary College in Budapest, decreed the building of the famous Mezőhegyes stud farm in 1785 and subsequently Babolna, thus paving the way for the golden age that Hungarian horses enjoyed during the nineteenth century.

BREED DESCRIPTION

Height 14 – 15hh.

Colour Predominantly grey but all other Arab colours occur.

Conformation Refined head, with dished profile, small, tapered muzzle and large eyes; elegant, curved neck; sloping shoulders; short, slightly concave back with strong loins, level croup and high-set tail; good, strong limbs with especially good, well-formed feet.

was a little taller than normal for an Arab, standing over 15.2hh). But the overall appearance, with its beautiful, dished face, large eyes, short back and high-set tail, are all characteristic of the pure-bred Arab. Combining toughness with elegance, the Shagya was bred as a riding horse and found favour as a cavalry mount in the days before mechanization. Nowadays it is bred for leisure riding and is exported to a number of countries.

ABOVE
Mares and foals at the Babolna Stud in Hungary, home of the Shagya Arab. Babolna was founded by Royal decree more than 200 years ago.

BELOW
Grey is the breed's predominant colour, although all other Arab colours also occur. Shagya Arabs often stand a little taller than their pure-bred relatives.

Icelandic

▌ BELOW
The tremendously thick mane and forelock give much needed protection against the severe weather conditions of the northern winters.

▌ BOTTOM
Stocky and compact, with short, strong limbs and notably hard, sound feet, the Icelandic horse is perfectly adapted to its harsh environment.

The little Icelandic horse is probably the purest horse breed in the world. Its ancestors were taken to Iceland by ninth-century settlers, travelling from western Norway and the north of Britain. They were small, sturdy horses who adapted well to the rigorous Icelandic climate. Later some imports were made of eastern horses, but these had such a detrimental effect upon the original stock that in AD 930 the Althing (parliament) passed a law forbidding the import of further horses. Although this law seems to have been flouted occasionally, for the last 800 years there have been no infusions of outside blood. As a result the Icelandic horse has changed little since the age of the Vikings.

It is an outstandingly tough, weather-resistant little horse (although it stands no more than 13.2hh it is always referred to by the Icelanders as a horse, not a pony). A strong swimmer – there were no bridges over Iceland's numerous turbulent rivers until the beginning of this century – it is also remarkably sure-footed. It can be seen carrying a full-grown man at speed, with ease and safety, over mountainous terrain during the traditional autumn sheep round-ups.

Some Icelandic horses are noted for their keen sense of direction and

BREED DESCRIPTION

Height 12.3 – 13.2hh.

Colour Any.

Conformation Fairly heavy head; short, well-carried neck; compact body with short back and deep girth; sloping, wedge-shaped, very strong, muscular hindquarters; strong limbs with short cannons and strong hocks; strong, well-shaped feet.

extraordinary homing instinct. After the annual round-up, while sheep are penned and sorted into each farmer's flock, horses are often turned loose and will set off alone down the valleys to their homes. There are also many recorded instances of horses that have been sold to another part of the country travelling for weeks to return to their original homes.

While some local selection of breeding stock probably took place from time to time, it was not until 1879 that Iceland undertook a practical selective breeding programme. It was begun in Skagafjördur, the country's most famous horse-breeding area. Conformation is naturally taken into account, but it is the quality of the horse's gaits which is of prime importance. These are: the fetgangur (walk), the brökk (trot – used when crossing rough country), the stökk (gallop), the skeid (lateral pace – used to cover short distances at high

speed) and the tölt (a running walk used to cover broken ground). The tölt is a gait of four equal beats – the sequence being near hind, near fore, off hind, off fore – with which the horse achieves great speed.

I **BELOW**
Notwithstanding its diminutive size, the breed is immensely strong and fast. It is a popular all-round riding horse in many countries outside its native Iceland.

INTERESTING FACTS

In days gone by horse fights were a popular form of entertainment in Iceland. Playing on the natural instinct of stallions to fight each other for possession of a mare, Icelanders would set two specially trained stallions against one another, using goads to urge them on. This pastime was so dangerous that it was a common occurrence for handlers to be injured or even killed.

Irish Draught

Irish horses are renowned for being the best hunters in the world and none more so than those produced by crossing the Thoroughbred with the versatile Irish Draught. Although there are no early formal records or stud books, Ireland's light draught horse is known to trace back many centuries, to the time when Norman horses were introduced to Ireland and crossed with the native animals, which at

▌ LEFT
A typically handsome, intelligent Irish Draught head. The breed is renowned for its innate good sense, coupled with boldness and athleticism.

that time were small of stature. Later infusions of Andalusian – and, probably, eastern – blood helped improve the overall quality (and height) of the Irish horses. The result was

very much an all-round horse, totally suited to the Irish country way of life: capable of working on the small Irish farms but active enough to be harnessed to a trap or to carry a rider safely across country. The modern Irish Draught is generally accepted to have evolved from the crossing of imported Thoroughbred stallions with the best of these country-bred mares. The numbers of these splendid horses declined in Ireland following the famine of 1847 and some heavy horses were introduced from Britain, but this tended to lead to a coarsening of the Irish Draught. To save the best of the remaining stock, in the early years of this century a scheme of subsidies was introduced by the government, for approved stallions of Irish Draught and hunter type. As a result the active, clean-legged general-purpose

▌ RIGHT
Substance and plenty of bone are the hallmarks of the modern Irish Draught. The conformation should incorporate all the features of the correctly built riding horse.

BREED DESCRIPTION

Height Stallions 16hh and over. Mares 15.2hh and over.

Colour All solid colours.

Conformation Small, intelligent head; sloping shoulders; strong body with deep chest and oval rib cage; powerful hindquarters; strong limbs with plenty of flat bone and no feather.

▌ LEFT
As a safe conveyance across the most testing of hunting countries, there is nothing to beat the Irish Draught and the Irish Draught/Thoroughbred cross.

▌ BELOW LEFT
The international show jumper Mill Pearl: a good example of the Irish Draught cross with the ability to perform at the highest level.

▌ BELOW
The breed possesses good, natural balance and the action is straight and true.

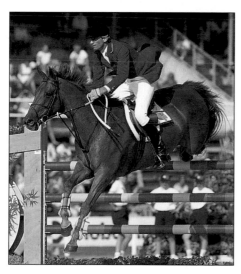

Irish Draught horse survived and in 1917 the Department of Agriculture introduced "a scheme to establish a Book for Horses of the Irish Draught type", in which 375 mares and 44 stallions were entered as being suitable and sound. The Irish Draught Horse Society was formed in 1976.

The excellence of Irish-bred horses owes much to the limestone pastures on which they are raised. The mineral-rich land contributes to the growth of strong bone and the production of good, up-standing animals. Today's Irish Draught has plenty of substance but is also an attractive looking, well-balanced, quality horse, with straight, athletic action. It is noted for its intelligence and kind temperament. It has an inherent ability to cross the most testing of hunting country with total assurance and because of its jumping prowess is a successful producer of top-level show jumpers.

INTERESTING FACTS

Since World War II many of the world's leading show-jumping horses have been Irish bred, with a fair percentage being by registered Irish Draught stallions. One of the most famous names in show-jumping breeding is King of Diamonds, an Irish Draught who sired many famous horses, including Special Envoy – who has jumped with great success for Brazil, ridden first by Nelson Pessoa then by his son Rodrigo – and Mill Pearl, ridden by the United States Olympic champion Joe Fargis.

Maremmano

Maremmano horses are bred in Tuscany and are the traditional mounts of the *butteri,* or cattlemen. Maremma, a coastal tract on the Tyrrhenian Sea extending from Piombino to Orbetello, is a former marshland which was drained in ancient times but later reverted to being an unhealthy wasteland. Drainage was reintroduced earlier this century and the area is now used as pastureland.

The origins of the Maremmano horses are obscure but it is likely that they are descended from the Neapolitan horses (founded on Arab, Barb and Spanish

▌ RIGHT
The Maremmano is a strong horse possessed of a quiet temperament, and although not particularly speedy it makes a useful all-round riding horse.

blood) made famous in the sixteenth century by Federico Grisone. Grisone was the founder of the Neapolitan riding academy and regarded as the first of the great classical riding masters after the

Greek, Xenophon (c. 430–350 BC). A good deal of outcrossing took place later – some involving imported English horses, including the Norfolk Roadster – so that the horses which became known as the

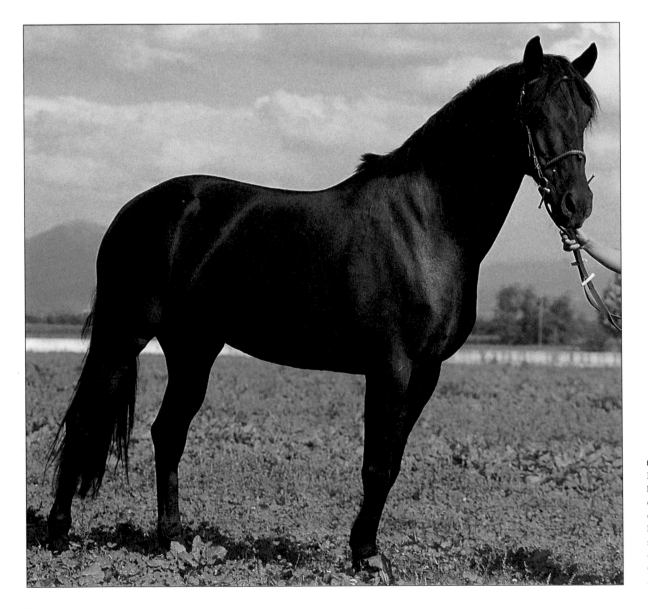

▌ LEFT
Maremmano horses vary a good deal in type and conformation. This horse is much more refined than many examples of the breed, with an especially elegant head.

∎ BELOW
A Maremmano wearing the traditional tack of the *buttero*, or Italian cowboy. Its toughness and reliability make the breed an ideal mount for working with cattle.

BREED DESCRIPTION

Height Variable, usually around 15.3hh.

Colour Any solid colour.

Conformation Variable. Overall appearance somewhat coarse, with rather upright shoulders, flat withers and low-set tail, though conformational improvements are being made through the introduction of Thoroughbred blood.

Maremmano were something of a mixture and of no fixed type. By no means the most beautiful looking of horses, nor the speediest, they are nevertheless good, honest workers, combining strength and toughness with a calm temperament. Amenable by nature and economical to feed, they have proved useful as army and police horses, as well as in agriculture – they are strong enough to perform light draught work – and cattle herding.

INTERESTING FACTS

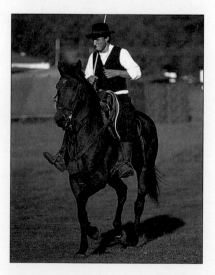

During the seventeenth century Italy became one of the world leaders for horse breeding. Most famous of all was the Neapolitan, of which the Maremmano is possibly a descendant.

Murgese

Originating from the Orfano plain and the hill districts near Gravina, the original Murgese horse can be traced back at least 500 years. During the late fifteenth and early sixteenth centuries the governor of the port of Monopoli, which for some years belonged to the Venetian Republic, kept a stock of Murgese stallions and several hundred brood mares in order to provide remounts for the cavalry. However, somewhere down the years the breed died out and the modern version dates only from the 1920s.

The Murgese is basically a light draught horse, though inferior in quality to the Irish Draught and showing no great uniformity of type. It can be ridden, but a better stamp of riding horse is produced by putting a Murgese mare to a Thoroughbred or warmblood stallion, the latter giving the progeny more quality, and paces better suited to a saddle horse.

BREED DESCRIPTION

Height 15 – 16hh.

Colour Usually chestnut, though other solid colours occur.

Conformation Variable. Overall appearance suggests a light draught horse. The head tends to be plain, though with an honest expression, and the hindquarters rather poor, with a low-set tail.

▮ ABOVE
Although basically best suited to light draught work, the Murgese can make a useful riding horse. This example of the breed has been fully trained as a police horse.

▮ TOP LEFT
Although the predominant coat colouring is chestnut, some dark colours do occur.

▮ LEFT
The Murgese is Italy's breed of light draught horse. However, it lacks definitive type and the overall quality of the light draught horse of Ireland.

Italian Heavy Draught

■ BOTTOM LEFT
The head is small with a straight profile. The eyes are large and bright, the ears small and mobile.

■ BELOW
Chestnut coat colouring with a flaxen mane and tail is typical of this attractive breed. It has inherited the active paces of the Breton, which had an important influence on its development.

Italy's premier heavy horse, the Italian Heavy Draught – also known as the Agricultural Heavy Horse – bears a distinct resemblance to the handsome Breton, which has had an important influence upon its development. The Italian Heavy Draught originated at Ferrara in the north of the country during the second half of the nineteenth century, when Neapolitan blood was crossed with Arab and Hackney

BREED DESCRIPTION

Height Stallions 15 – 16hh.
Mares 14 – 15hh.

Colour Predominantly chestnut with flaxen mane and tail. Occasionally dark bay.

Conformation Square head with broad forehead, large eyes and nostrils and small, mobile ears; muscular, slightly arched neck; well-sloped shoulders; deep chest, short, strong back with broad, slightly sloping croup; short strong limbs with muscular forearms and large joints, short pasterns and large, well-shaped feet.

to produce an active, lightweight workhorse. In due course the need arose both for a heavier agricultural animal and a heavy artillery horse, and breeders accordingly began introducing new blood, notably Boulonnais. Then, in the 1920s, pure-bred Breton stallions were used to establish the stamp of horse now known as the Italian Heavy Draught.

An attractive looking horse, stocky and muscular in build, the Italian Heavy Draught is noted for its conformation and active paces. It is capable of maintaining a good speed even when pulling heavy loads. The limbs are short and very strong with well-developed muscles and large joints. Although the need for draught horses has decreased in Italy, as elsewhere, the Italian Heavy Draught can still be seen at work on some of the smaller farms, and is also used for meat production.

INTERESTING FACTS

A stud book for Italian Draught Horses was opened in 1961. Horses accepted for registration are branded on the nearside of the hindquarters with the breed mark, a five-runged ladder within a shield.

Friesian

The Friesian is one of Europe's oldest horses and down the centuries it has had an influence on a number of other breeds, notably the Oldenburg in Germany and Britain's Fell and Dales ponies. The breed's homeland is Friesland, in the

The Friesian's friendly disposition is evident in its kind but alert expression. The rather long head is set on a well-arched neck.

north of the Netherlands. The remains of an ancient coldblood type of heavy horse have been unearthed there, from which the modern Friesian is believed to be descended. Eastern blood, introduced into the Netherlands during the time of

BREED DESCRIPTION

Height 15 – 16hh.

Colour Always black.

Conformation Rather long head, with short ears and alert expression; elegant, arched neck with long, flowing mane; powerful shoulders; strong, compact body with strong, sloping hindquarters and rather low-set, very full, tail; short, strong limbs with good bone and a fair amount of feather.

■ RIGHT
Excellent overall conformation is the hallmark of the breed. The body is compact, the limbs strong and the feet hard and sound.

104

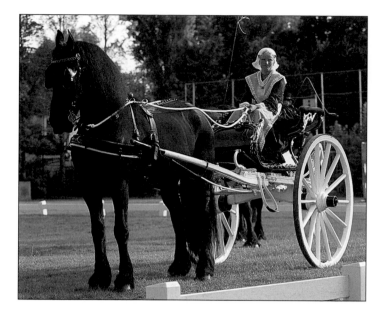

■ LEFT
An attractive turnout much appreciated throughout its native land: a Friesian driven to a traditional high-wheeled gig.

■ BELOW
Appreciation of Friesians is not restricted to Holland. This handsome team was pictured in a busy London street.

INTERESTING FACTS

The Friesians' noble bearing makes them ideal for ceremonial occasions. These horses were part of a six-strong team pulling the Dutch Royal Carriage at the opening ceremony of the 1994 World Equestrian Games in The Hague.

the Crusades, had an influence on the development of the Friesian, as did the Andalusian during the Eighty Years' War, when the Netherlands were occupied by the Spanish. The Friesian horse which thus developed was an active all-rounder, suitable for work on the land but, because of its ability to trot at speed, also useful as a harness horse and for riding.

During the nineteenth century, when trotting became extremely popular, breeders sought to improve the Friesian's already active, high-stepping trot, by outcrossing to trotters. This led to the Friesian becoming lighter in build and less useful as a farm horse. By the beginning of World War I its numbers were seriously depleted and the decline continued between the wars. However, lack of fuel during World War II led to a revival in the breed's fortunes as farmers once again turned to it for draught work.

During the second half of this century there has been a resurgence of interest in the breed and it is now very popular as a carriage horse. A well-balanced horse with proud bearing, the Friesian looks exceptionally attractive when pulling a traditional high-wheeled Friesian gig. The breed is noted for its kind temperament.

Gelderland

A number of different breeds went into the making of the Gelderland, which comes from the region of the same name in the central Netherlands and was developed during the nineteenth century. Native mares were crossed with, among others, English, French, German, Hungarian and Polish stallions to produce a good stamp of dual-purpose horse, one that was big and strong enough to do farm work or pull a carriage but not so heavy that it could not be used for riding. Hackney blood was also used in a

■ LEFT
Strong and active, the Gelderland makes an excellent carriage horse and has also played a part in the development of Holland's remarkably successful competition horse, the Dutch Warmblood.

breeding programme that was noted for its well-founded principles of selection, only horses that had proved themselves to be good, sound workers being used at stud. As mechanization spread, and horses were needed less for use on the land, breeders introduced Thoroughbred blood to lighten the Gelderland.

A typical carriage type of horse, the modern Gelderland, with its excellent

shoulders and good, free action, has been used successfully in the sport of four-in-hand driving and has also provided one of the main bases for the production of the Netherlands' sports horse, the Dutch Warmblood.

INTERESTING FACTS

The Gelderland is one of two types of all-purpose horse developed in the Netherlands, the other being its northern neighbour, the Gröningen. The Gröningen is somewhat heavier than the Gelderland. It has Friesian and Oldenburg blood in its ancestry, as well as some Suffolk Punch. Like the Gelderland, it has played an important part in the development of the Dutch Warmblood.

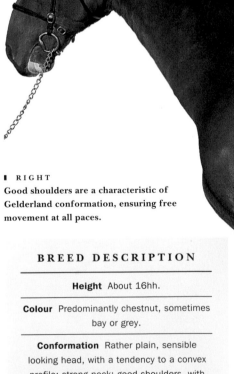

■ RIGHT
Good shoulders are a characteristic of Gelderland conformation, ensuring free movement at all paces.

BREED DESCRIPTION

Height About 16hh.

Colour Predominantly chestnut, sometimes bay or grey.

Conformation Rather plain, sensible looking head, with a tendency to a convex profile; strong neck; good shoulders, with fairly low withers; fairly long but strong body with good depth through the girth; powerful hindquarters with high-set tail; short, strong limbs with good, sound feet.

Dutch Warmblood

The production of the Netherlands' highly successful leisure and competition horse began with the selection of the best Gelderland and Gröningen mares, who were then mated with Thoroughbred stallions. The latter, also carefully selected, were imported from all over the world, including Britain, Ireland, France and the United States. Many of these came from the best racing lines, a fact which was to prove highly beneficial: as time went on Dutch breeders found that the stallions

BREED DESCRIPTION

Height 16 – 17hh.

Colour Any solid colour, with bay and brown the most usual.

Conformation Quality head, with alert, intelligent expression; good, sloping shoulders with pronounced withers; strong back and hindquarters; good, sound limbs, with plenty of bone and short cannons; good, sound feet.

who produced the best warmbloods had themselves enjoyed successful racing careers. In addition to Thoroughbreds, some Trakehner stallions were used in the early years, and a number of Holstein mares were imported and put to Gelderland or Gröningen stallions. Later on warmbloods of the type which the Dutch breeders were seeking to develop, such as the Holstein and Selle Français, were introduced into the breeding programme, and a dash of Hanoverian and Westphalian blood was added. At the same time there was a gradual decrease in the amount of Gelderland and Gröningen blood used. The result is a riding horse of harmonious proportions, with straight, true action, an easy, ground-covering stride at all paces and a good temperament.

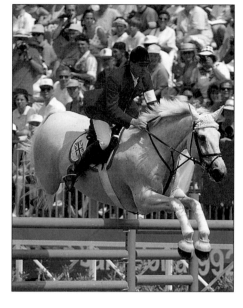

▌ LEFT
Milton is a grandson of the Trakehner Marco Polo, one of the most influential Dutch Warmblood stallions.

INTERESTING FACTS

One of the most important stallions in the breeding of Dutch Warmbloods was the Trakehner Marco Polo (1965–1976). By the Thoroughbred Poet, he was only small but he produced some top-class show jumpers. They included Marius, who was ridden with great international success by Britain's Caroline Bradley. In Britain Marius combined his competitive career with stud duties and had the distinction of siring Milton, the world's most successful show jumper.

Dutch breeders use a highly efficient, performance-based selection system to produce their horses and, despite its relative newness, the Dutch Warmblood has already demonstrated the correctness of their approach by achieving success at top international level in dressage, show jumping and carriage driving. Dutch Warmbloods have been used in the establishment of other warmblood strains, too, notably in Britain, the United States, Australia and New Zealand.

▌ LEFT
The Dutch Warmblood is a quality horse possessed of a good temperament. The correct proportions of its conformation result in excellent action, thus ensuring its suitability for modern competitive sports.

Lusitano

As its appearance suggests, the Portuguese Lusitano is a close relative of the Andalusian in neighbouring Spain. Indeed, until quite recent times the horses bred on the Iberian peninsula were regarded as being one and the same. It was not until the early years of the twentieth century that the two countries decided to establish independent stud books.

Since opening their own stud book the Portuguese have made great strides in monitoring and improving their breeding programme. They have been diligent in preserving the Lusitano's greatly admired qualities of strength and courage. These attributes led to the breed being very highly esteemed as a warhorse (the best Iberian horses have always been bred along the long frontier between

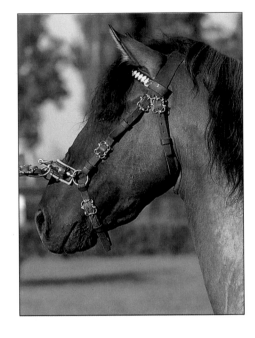

Portugal and Spain where endless battles were fought).

These same qualities also make the Lusitano an ideal mount for the demanding sport of mounted bullfighting. In Portugal, where it is considered a disgrace for a horse to be injured during a bullfight, the horses are extremely well

trained, using their inherent powers of acceleration and manoeuvrability to evade the bull.

As they have proved down the centuries, Lusitano horses are most amenable to training. Intelligent, gentle and affectionate, they work hard and enthusiastically. Possessed of good natural

BREED DESCRIPTION

Height Generally 15.1 – 15.3hh. Some horses reach over 16hh.

Colour Often grey or bay, but any true colour is found, including dun and chestnut.

Conformation Long, noble head, typically with a convex profile, finely curved nose and large, generous eyes; powerful, arched neck, deep at the base and set at a slightly wide angle to the shoulders, giving the impression of being fairly upright; powerful shoulders; short-coupled body with deep rib cage, broad, powerful loins, gently sloping croup and rather low-set tail; fine, clean legs with excellent dense bone; abundant silky mane and tail.

▌ ABOVE LEFT
This noble head and powerful, arched neck are characteristic of the Lusitano. The breed is also noted for its silky mane and tail.

▌ LEFT
The overall outline of the Lusitano is virtually the same as that of its close relative, the Andalusian.

■ BELOW
The bay colouring of this mare at the Alter Stud is typical of the Alter Real Lusitanos.

■ BOTTOM
Portugal's horses are renowned for their muscular strength, great impulsion and elevated paces.

INTERESTING FACTS

The Lusitano horse gives an exceptionally smooth, comfortable ride. Agile and intelligent, it makes the ideal mount for the mounted bullfighter.

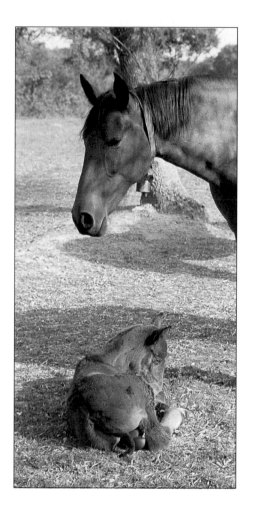

balance and with agile, elevated paces, they give a smooth comfortable ride. With their proud bearing and tremendous joie de vivre they have, not surprisingly, always excelled at high school work. However, it is not only in the manège that the breed excels. More and more Lusitanos are proving themselves well suited to modern sports such as show jumping and carriage driving. People who work with them testify to the great understanding which quickly develops between horse and human.

ALTER REAL

The Alter Real is not a distinct breed but an offshoot of the Lusitano. It takes its name from the town of Alter do Chão, in the Portuguese province of Alentejo, the world "real" meaning royal in Portuguese. The royal stud founded at Alter supplied the royal manège in Lisbon with high-school and carriage horses. The stud flourished for many years, producing a fine line of horses which were valued not

only in Portugal but all over the Peninsula. However, the stud's progress suffered serious interruption on a number of occasions, notably during the Peninsular War, and the Alter Real horses went into decline. Attempts to resurrect the strain towards the end of the nineteenth century by importing English, Norman and German blood were not successful, nor was a subsequent attempt, using Arab horses. Through the introduction of Andalusian blood at the end of the century, the Alter Real Lusitanos were finally re-established but after the fall of the monarchy in the early twentieth century, many horses were sold or destroyed. The Alter Real line would have died out but for the efforts of the d'Andrade family, who during the early 1940s saved two stallions and a handful of mares and instigated a breeding programme. Today the Alter Stud is state run and again produces horses for high school work. The Alter Real is essentially a Lusitano, although it is always bay, brown or black in colour.

Bashkir

The small Bashkir horse comes from the southern foothills of the Ural mountains, taking its name from the region of Bashkirsky where it is kept in herds. It goes equally well in harness and under saddle and for centuries has been used as a pack and general work horse as well as a supplier of meat and milk. Stockily built,

BREED DESCRIPTION

Height 13.3 – 14hh.

Colour Predominantly bay, chestnut and brown.

Conformation Massive head; short, fleshy neck; low withers; wide, deep body with broad, straight back; comparatively short legs with substantial bone; good, hard feet.

with a thick coat, mane and tail, it can survive in the open in temperatures as low as -22° to -40° Fahrenheit (-30° to -40° C). It is able to withstand ferocious blizzard conditions and will dig through snow a metre deep to find food. Furthermore, its tremendously hard feet enable it to work without being shod. The Bashkir is undoubtedly one of the hardiest breeds of

horse or pony in the world.

A type of Bashkir also exists in the north-west of the United States, prompting the theory that these horses' ancestors travelled over the former land-bridge between Asia and North America (now the Bering Strait). The horse, however, is generally believed to have become extinct on the North American continent as long ago as the Ice Age and was not reintroduced until Spanish explorers of the modern era "discovered" the land. It is therefore much more likely that the Bashkir was introduced from Russia in fairly recent times.

❚ ABOVE LEFT
The Bashkir's head is heavily built and set on a short, fleshy neck. The chest is broad.

❚ LEFT
With its stocky build, short strong limbs and exceptionally hard feet, the Bashkir is well equipped for life in a harsh environment – though, as this picture shows, it also thrives in less rigorous surroundings.

Don

Don horses were made famous by the Don Cossacks, who between 1812 and 1814 helped drive Napoleon's invading troops from Russia. The Cossacks' horses were descended from those of the nomadic steppe people and were of mixed blood. Early influences would have included the Nagai from Mongolia, the Karabakh (a type of light riding horse), the Turkmen and the Persian Arab. During the nineteenth century infusions of Orlov and Thoroughbred blood were made and outcrosses were also made to the part-bred Arab horses produced at the Strelets Stud in the Ukraine. All these crosses, used to upgrade the old Cossack strain, ceased at the beginning of this century, since when no more outside blood has been used in the breeding of Don horses.

Like most Russian breeds, the Don was traditionally reared in herds on the vast expanses of the steppes, and accordingly developed into a tough individual, capable of thriving with minimal help from humans. It was ideally suited to its original role as an army remount while nowadays it is used for general riding purposes.

Various inherent conformational defects tend to limit the quality of its paces but its strong constitution makes it a suitable mount for endurance riding.

▌ TOP
Don horses are predominantly chestnut. Calm and willing workers, they go equally well in harness and under saddle and have great endurance.

▌ ABOVE
The Don tends to lack good riding horse conformation: straight shoulders and rather upright pasterns are common faults.

BREED DESCRIPTION

Height 15.3 – 16.2hh.

Colour Predominantly chestnut and brown, often with a golden sheen.

Conformation Medium-sized head with wide forehead; average length neck; strong body with broad, straight back and loins and rounded croup; rather sloping hindquarters; straight limbs with well-muscled forearms and second thighs, but a tendency to calf knees (an inward curve below the knee), sickle hocks and upright pasterns; short, thin mane and tail.

Budenny

A breed of relatively recent origin, the Budenny was created by crossing Don and Chernomor mares with Thoroughbred stallions (the Chernomor was the horse used by Cossacks who settled in the Kuban during the eighteenth century and was similar to the Don, though somewhat smaller and lighter in build). The chief purpose was to produce a good army remount, possessed of great endurance. Breeding was centred in the Rostov region, using a process of careful selection. The best mares were bred to the

INTERESTING FACTS

Russian horses are often hot branded as an aid to identification. The chestnut horse on the facing page has also been freeze-branded on the saddle patch. This is a valuable form of individual identity marking which helps to deter horse thieves because the owner can easily be traced.

▌ ABOVE RIGHT
The Thoroughbred influence on the present-day Budenny is particularly noticeable in the refinement of head, with its lean good looks, bright, intelligent eyes and alert ears.

▌ RIGHT
The overall conformation, while showing good depth through the girth and a reasonably well-sloped shoulder, lacks the harmonious proportions of the Thoroughbred, notably in the hind limbs, which are inclined to be a bit weak.

best Anglo-Don stallions. The brood mares were both well fed and, unusually in Russian horse breeding at the time, stabled during the worst of the winter weather, thus ensuring that they produced better, healthier foals than they might otherwise have done if forced to burn up their resources merely on keeping themselves warm. The young stock were tested on the racecourse between two and four years of age.

The robust constitution of the Don horse and the excellent action of the Thoroughbred proved to be a good combination and as a result the Rostov military stud farm was soon turning out an

BREED DESCRIPTION

Height 16hh.

Colour Predominantly chestnut, some bay and brown. The coats of some Budenny horses have a golden sheen (a throwback to the Chernomor and Don horses).

Conformation Well-proportioned head with straight or slightly concave profile; long, straight neck; reasonably well-sloped shoulders with high withers; comparatively heavy body with short, straight back and long croup; fine, straight limbs, though with a tendency to small joints and rather weak hindlegs; usually well-shaped feet.

upstanding horse, with a tractable nature, which proved suitable for both riding and light draught work. Named the Budenny, it was officially recognized as a breed in 1949.

As the need for army remounts ceased and interest turned to pleasure riding and sport, more Thoroughbred was added to improve the Budenny. Although the Thoroughbred influence is quite evident in the overall light build, the Budenny has a noticeably heavier body while the legs tend to be a bit light on bone. Today the breed is used as a general purpose riding horse, especially in the sports of show jumping, dressage and steeplechasing.

▌ RIGHT
The predominant Budenny coat colouring is chestnut. Some horses have a striking golden sheen.

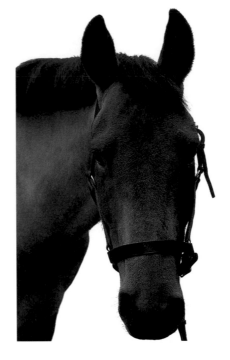

Kabardin

Sure-footedness and a well-developed sense of self-preservation are the hallmarks of the Kabardin and little wonder, for its home is the northern Caucasus, where it has for centuries been accustomed to carrying men over the toughest mountain terrain. It traces back

BREED DESCRIPTION

Height 15 – 15.2hh.

Colour Predominantly bay, dark bay and black, usually without distinguishing markings.

Conformation Long head, often with Roman-nosed profile, with sharp, mobile ears; well-muscled, medium-long neck; fairly straight shoulders and low withers; strong body, with short, straight back and short, often concave loins; strong limbs, with generally good joints, good bone and short, strong cannons, although the hindlegs tend to be sickle-shaped; good, strong feet; usually long, full mane and tail.

ABOVE
The Kabardin's head is long and Roman noses are not uncommon. The ears are very mobile and the horse has a kind, calm expression.

RIGHT
Having evolved in the mountains, Kabardin horses are very athletic and well balanced. They make good jumpers.

INTERESTING FACTS

The Kabardin's prowess at carrying a rider safely over mountainous terrain is legendary. It will pick its way unerringly over narrow, rocky mountain tracks with all the assurance of a mountain goat and has an uncanny ability to find its way in the mist or dark. Its typical mountain-horse conformation may not be conducive to speed, but its paces are nevertheless cadenced, light and smooth.

to the sixteenth century and is derived from the horses of the steppe tribes who were crossed with Turkmen, Persian and Karabakh horses. Originally the Kabardin was itself fairly small. Raised in herds, which were (and still are) grazed on the high pastures during the summer and in the foothills during the winter, it developed into a typical mountain breed: tough, sturdy and possessing great endurance.

The numbers of Kabardin horses were seriously depleted as a result of the Revolution and it was during the 1920s, when efforts were made to re-establish the breed, that a bigger stamp of horse began to be produced, one suitable as an army remount and for agricultural work. The Malokarachaev and Malkin Studs became the producers of the best modern Kabardin horses, which are used to improve stock in neighbouring areas as well as for general riding and driving purposes.

RIGHT
Despite rather straight shoulders, Kabardins make good all-round riding horses. They are agile and sure-footed.

Tersk

Like the Kabardin, the Tersk comes from the northern Caucasus, though it is a breed of more recent origin, having been developed from 1921 onwards at the Tersk and Stavropol Studs.

The Tersk is based on Strelets horses, the part-bred Arabs which were formerly bred at the Strelets Stud in the Ukraine. The Strelets was produced by crossing

BREED DESCRIPTION

Height Stallions 15hh. Mares 14.3hh.

Colour Predominantly light grey or "white" with a silvery sheen.

Conformation Fine head with large, expressive eyes and medium-length, mobile ears; medium-length neck set high on well-sloped shoulders; strong body with deep chest, wide back and muscular loins; fine legs with well-defined tendons; fine mane and tail.

INTERESTING FACTS

Nowadays most of the world's Tersk horses are produced at the Stavropol Stud. Stavropol is in the northern Caucasus between the Black Sea and the Caspian Sea.

■ BELOW
Tersk horses are invariably refined and elegant. Their predominantly light grey colouring adds to their attraction.

■ BOTTOM
The breed shows unmistakable signs of its Arab ancestry though it is usually a little taller than the pure-bred Arab.

pure-bred Arabs with, among others, high quality Orlovs and Anglo-Arabs (some Thoroughbred blood was also used, though this was not a dominant factor).

The result was a horse with a distinctly Arabian look about it but one which was bigger built than the pure-breds.

By the 1920s there were very few Strelets in existence. The few that did remain, including two stallions, were taken to the Tersk Stud in an attempt to increase their numbers. The mares were put to pure-bred Arab stallions; and various cross-bred mares, including Strelets x Kabardin and Arab x Don, were covered by the Strelets stallions. After some thirty years the new type, known as the Tersk, became fixed. It has inherited the general appearance of the Arab, though it stands a little taller, and also its elegant paces. A handsome horse, usually grey in colour, it combines a kind temperament with tremendous energy, attributes which have made it a favourite in circuses and also as a sports horse.

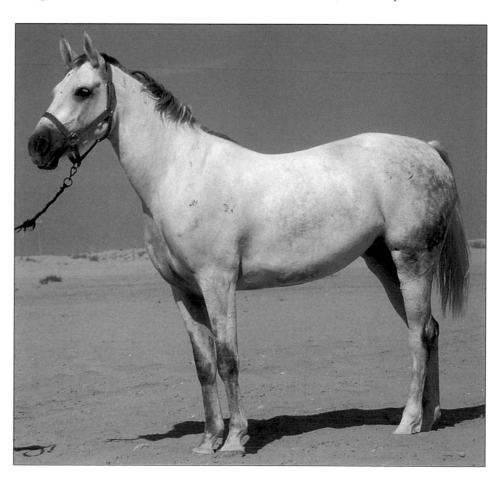

Orlov Trotter

The Orlov shares with the Standardbred and the French Trotter the distinction of being one of the world's foremost breeds of trotting horse. Indeed, before the development of the Standardbred it was probably the most famous of all trotters. Although the Orlov is less well known now outside its native land than the other two members of the triumvirate, it nevertheless plays an important role both in Russian harness racing and in the upgrading of other Russian breeds.

The Orlov takes its name from Count Alexis Orlov (1737–1809), founder of the Orlov Stud near Moscow. The Count imported from Greece a grey Arab stallion called Smetanka. Despite Smetanka's short stud career, he was to prove highly influential in the development of this popular breed. Smetanka's grey son

Polkan, bred out of a Danish mare and foaled in 1784, produced Bars I, who became the foundation sire of the Orlov Trotter.

The breed was developed by Count Orlov and his stud manager V.I. Shishkin at the then newly founded Khrenov Stud in the province of Voronezh

LEFT
The head of the Orlov Trotter is inclined to be coarse and rather small.

BREED DESCRIPTION

Height Stallions 16hh. Mares 15.3hh.

Colour Predominantly grey. Bay and black are commonly found. Chestnut is rare.

Conformation Small, often somewhat coarse head; long, often swan-shaped, neck set high on the withers; long, straight back with muscular loins and broad, powerful croup; fine, squarely set legs with a minimum of 8 inches (20cm) of bone below the knee.

LEFT
Most fast-trotting horses are fairly long in the back and the Orlov is no exception. The good measurement of bone below the knee denotes its strength.

INTERESTING FACTS

Count Alexis Orlov, the breed's founder, was a soldier famous for his courage and audacity. In 1762 he played a part in the assassination of Peter III. The Count's older brother, Grigorei, who distinguished himself during the Seven Years' War, had attracted the attention of Peter's wife, soon to become Catherine II. However, having helped place her on the throne, Grigorei found himself ousted from the Empress's favour by his fellow conspirator, the handsome Prince Potemkin. Alexis is reputed to have knocked out Potemkin's eye – and turned to horse breeding as a diversion from affairs at court!

■ RIGHT
The Russian Trotter is part Orlov, part Standardbred. It is faster on the racetrack than the Orlov.

to which the stock from the Moscow stud was transferred in 1788. Bars I was used to breed from Arab, Dutch and Danish mares as well as half-breds imported from England. Inbreeding back to Bars I was practised extensively. During the early part of the nineteenth century the breed continued to improve thanks to the systematic training and racing of trotters in Russia.

Later, as the Standardbred began to demonstrate its supremacy on the racetrack, the Russians started importing horses from America to cross with the Orlov. The resultant half-breed, subsequently known as the Russian Trotter, proved faster than the Orlov. Imports of Standardbreds ceased at the outbreak of World War I but in recent times the traffic has resumed to maintain the speed of the Russian Trotter.

■ BELOW
As well as being raced in their native country, Orlovs are well suited to the modern sport of four-in-hand driving. They are exported for this purpose.

■ BELOW
This horse, hitched to a training vehicle, demonstrates the Orlov's tremendously powerful action.

Vladimir Heavy Draught

The Clydesdale played a significant part in the development of the Vladimir, a heavy draught horse created in the provinces of Vladimir and Ivanovo, to the north-east of Moscow. During the early years of this century stallions of various heavy breeds were imported from Britain and France to cross with the local mares of the region in order to produce a good-quality heavy work horse. Among the most influential of the foundation stallions were the Clydesdales Lord James, Border Brand, both imported in 1910, and Glen Albin (1923). Shire stallions were also used, though to a lesser extent, and some Cleveland Bay, Suffolk, Ardennais and

Percheron blood is also said to have been introduced. The experiment met with success, the result being a powerfully built heavy horse, well suited to all types of heavy agricultural and draught work. Named the Vladimir Heavy Draught, it was recognized as a breed in 1946.

Its docile nature makes it easy to handle, while its active paces – no doubt inherited from its Clydesdale forebears – mean that despite its massive build it can be used to pull the famous Russian troikas. Another bonus is its early maturity: the Vladimir is so well developed by the age of three that it can start work and also be used at stud, where the stallions are noted

■ OPPOSITE ABOVE
The Vladimir Heavy Draught combines great strength with the most docile of natures – note this horse's kindly expression.

■ OPPOSITE BELOW
Clydesdale blood was used with great success in the development of this breed, which is renowned for its powerful build and active paces.

BREED DESCRIPTION

Height Stallions 16.1hh. Mares 15.3hh.

Colour Predominantly bay, also black and chestnut with white markings on head and legs.

Conformation Large, long head with convex profile; long, muscular neck; pronounced withers; wide chest, rather long, broad back and long, broad, sloping croup; long limbs; some horses carry feather.

LATVIAN

The Latvian is a powerfully built harness horse renowned for its weight-pulling ability. It is of recent origin, dating only from the early 1920s when local mares were crossed with German, English and French horses to produce an all-round worker possessed of strength, stamina and good, active paces. There are two distinct types of Latvian horse: a heavy harness type which is based largely on Oldenburg, Norfolk Roadster and Anglo-Norman outcrosses and a lighter version which has a preponderance of Hanoverian blood.

Latvian horses have good overall conformation and great freedom of movement. Stallions stand up to 16.2hh, mares up to 16hh. Black is the predominant colour of the heavier type, while most of the lighter weight horses are chestnut.

The Latvian harness horse was recognized as a breed in 1952 and although some outcrosses to Oldenburg and Hanoverian horses have been made since, these have been on a fairly limited scale. The breed is especially noted for its placid temperament which, together with its strength and energy, make it a popular working animal.

for their good fertility rate. Minus points include, in some horses, a rather long back, which is not conducive to strength, and a flat-sided rib cage (the reverse of "well sprung" or rounded ribs, which enable the lungs to work to maximum efficiency). The Vladimir is the largest of the Russian heavy breeds. Stallions have a girth of some 6 feet 9 inches (207cm) and weigh in the region of 1,688lb (758kg). Mares are only a little smaller, with a girth of 6 feet 5 inches (196cm) and a weight of 1,507lb (685kg).

INTERESTING FACTS

Other heavy horses in the former USSR include the Russian Heavy Draught, founded a century or so ago, and based largely on the Ardennais, and the Soviet Heavy Draught, which was founded by crossing Belgian Heavy Draught stallions with local harness-type mares. Both were registered as breeds in 1952. The Russian Heavy Draught is quick to mature and remarkably long lived. It was formerly known as the "Russian Ardennes".

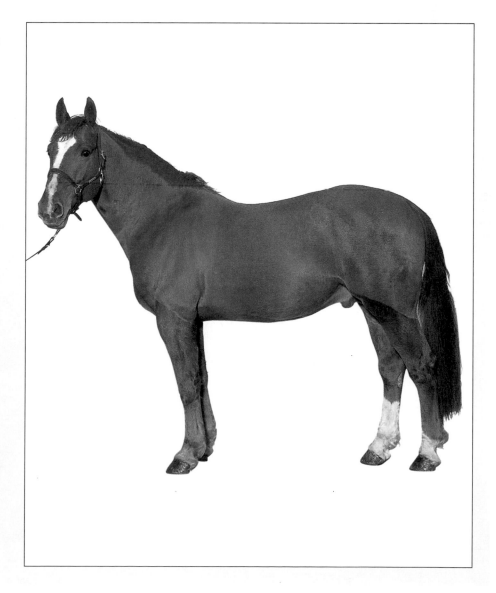

North Swedish

Forestry is the chief area of employment for the North Swedish horse, a small, compact, agile draught horse ideally suited to moving timber in confined spaces, over difficult terrain and often in inclement weather conditions.

The breed is descended from the ancient native work horse of Sweden which was influenced by the Døle horses from neighbouring Norway. At some time during the nineteenth century, outcrosses were made to horses of lighter build from outside Scandinavia but towards the end of the century there was a move to produce a heavier stamp of horse, more suited to pulling the heavier types of machinery which were then becoming available. Consequently stallions from larger breeds, such as the Clydesdale, were imported.

BREED DESCRIPTION

Height Stallions around 15.2hh. Mares around 15hh.

Colour Any solid colour.

Conformation Fairly large head with longish ears; short, crested neck; strong, sloping shoulders; rather long, but deep, strong back; rounded hindquarters with sloping croup; short, strong limbs with good bone; the mane and tail are usually very abundant.

The possibility of the old Swedish horse dying out altogether as a result of these crosses prompted interested parties to form an association to save it, the aim being to breed from the old-type stock still found in the remoter parts of the north of the country, using Døle stallions. Government support during the early years of the twentieth century aided this aim and during the 1920s performance testing was introduced as a means of selection, something which is still used today. Horses are tested for their draught aptitude as well as draught efficiency. The former test involves pulling a sled laden with logs, the judges awarding points according to the horse's performance and its condition after the work. For the efficiency test the horse is hitched to a wagon and its actual pulling power is measured by a dynamometer.

Lumbering is an area where heavy horses can prove more efficient and more cost effective than mechanized transport, and the North Swedish Horse continues to thrive in its traditional environment.

LEFT
Small and compact, the North Swedish horse is particularly strong through the neck and shoulders. Its short limbs have plenty of bone.

INTERESTING FACTS

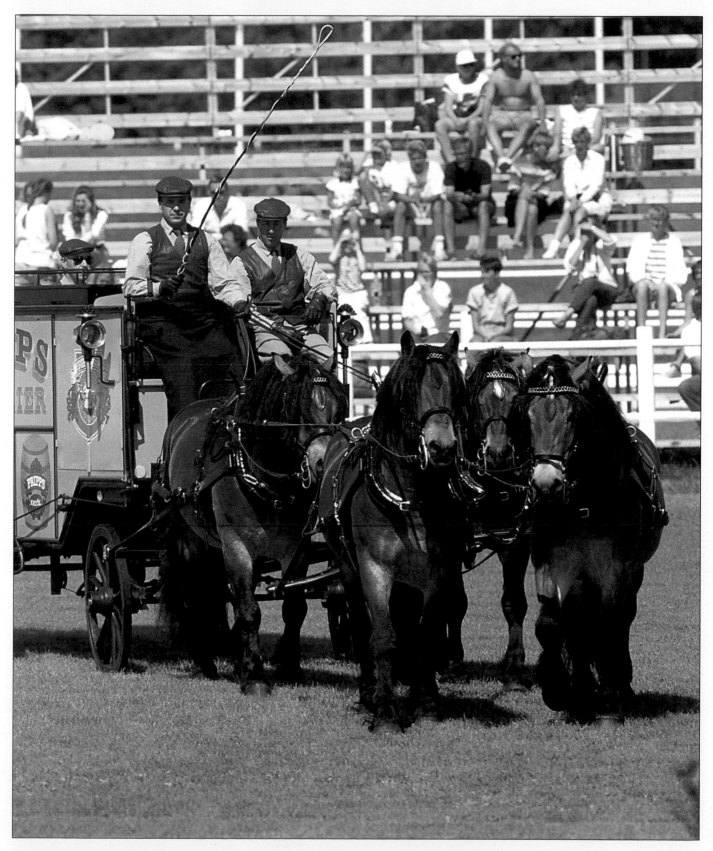

North Swedish horses make good all-round draught animals. They are, however, most often associated with agricultural work and, more especially, forestry. They begin work as three-year-olds and within a couple of years are sufficiently mature to be capable of working an eight-hour day. Stallions weigh anything from 1,440 to 1,655lb (650–750kg) and mares 1,200 to 1,545lb (550–700kg).

Swedish Warmblood

Sweden has been renowned for its fine riding and carriage horses for many centuries, so it is not surprising that the Swedish Warmblood should have had such an impact on present-day competitive sports, particularly top-level dressage.

The Skåne province of what is now southern Sweden (the area had previously been under Danish rule) was noted for its horse breeding as long ago as the twelfth century, when Archbishop Absalon raised remounts there for his cavalry. Then in the mid-seventeenth century, Charles X of Sweden founded the Royal Stud at Flyinge, to the north-east of Malmo, to supply horses for the royal stables and the

army. Down the years horses from a wide variety of breeds were used at the stud to produce a quality cavalry horse. They included Holsteins, Hanoverians, East Prussians, Frederiksborgs, Arabs,

Thoroughbreds and Oldenburgs, with the East Prussian and Hanoverian blood being particularly influential.

Officers of the Swedish cavalry mounted on Swedish horses enjoyed tremendous success in all three equestrian disciplines (dressage, show jumping and three-day eventing) at Olympic level both before and after World War I. The Swiss army bought many Swedish horses after World War II, a number of whom found fame in the dressage world. When mechanization signalled the demise of the cavalry horse it was a natural progression for the Swedes to channel their horse-breeding efforts towards leisure and

■ RIGHT
Warmblood mares with
their foals put on a
fine show to an
appreciative crowd
during the 1990 World
Equestrian Games in
Stockholm.

■ BOTTOM LEFT
Thanks to infusions
of outside blood,
including
Thoroughbred, the
breed has become a
good all-round sports
horse.

■ BOTTOM RIGHT
Swedish Warmbloods
have traditionally
excelled at the
demanding
discipline of Grand
Prix dressage.

BREED DESCRIPTION

Height 15 – 17hh.

Colour Any solid colour.

Conformation Variable, but usually a
handsome head, with wide forehead and
kind, intelligent eyes; long neck; shoulders
sometimes tend to be rather straight,
depending on the bloodline; well-
proportioned body, hindquarters and limbs.

INTERESTING FACTS

Swedish-bred dressage horses which have
found fame at the Olympic Games include
Piaff, winner of the individual gold medal in
Munich in 1972, when ridden by the West
German, Liselott Linsenhoff. Piaff's sire was
Gaspari, who competed for Sweden in the
1960 Games in Rome, where another
Swedish horse, Wald, won the individual
silver medal in the hands of the Swiss rider,
Gustav Fischer. In Tokyo in 1964 Fischer's
compatriot, Henri Chammartin, was the
individual gold medallist on yet another
Swedish horse, Woermann. Also Swedish
bred was Gauguin de Lully, winner of the
individual bronze medal at the Seoul Games
in 1988, again competing for Switzerland.

competition. There was no doubting the
Swedish Warmblood's prowess as a
dressage horse and in recent times top
jumping blood has been introduced from
France, Germany and Holland. Carefully
selected Thoroughbred stallions have also
been used on warmblood mares.

To maintain the excellence of the
breed, in terms of both conformation and
temperament, Swedish Warmblood
stallions are graded and must pass a
performance test, veterinary examination
and assessment of type, conformation and
action. There is also a system of progeny
testing, the results of which are available
to mare owners seeking a suitable stallion.

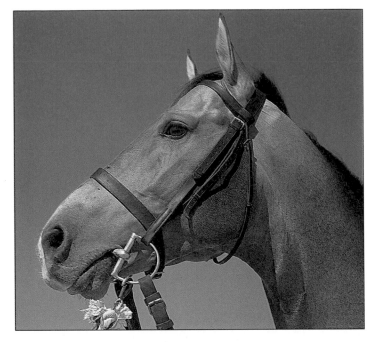

■ LEFT
The Akhal-Teke's head
is always very fine,
with large expressive
eyes and beautifully
shaped ears.

Akhal-Teke

One of the most striking looking horses
anywhere in the world, the Akhal-Teke, or
Turkmen, has been bred for some 3,000
years in the desert oases of Turkmenistan,
a region to the north of Iran and to the
east of the Caspian Sea. Although the
Turkmen people probably introduced a
certain amount of Arabian and Persian
blood at some stage, its isolated homeland
has kept the Akhal-Teke freer from
outside influences than many riding

■ BELOW
The luminous sheen
on the coat of this
horse is typical of the
breed, as is the lean
overall appearance.

▌ RIGHT
Akhal-Tekes make good all-round riding horses, their legendary stamina making them excellent mounts for competitive endurance riding.

▌ BOTTOM RIGHT
Despite being raised for centuries in desert conditions, the breed adapts perfectly well to life in the much less rigorous climate of western Europe.

BREED DESCRIPTION

Height 15.1 – 15.2hh.

Colour Bay and chestnut, often with a remarkable golden sheen; also grey and black.

Conformation Very fine head with wide nostrils, large, expressive eyes and long, beautifully shaped ears; long, straight and often thin neck set high on the shoulders; sloping shoulder with high withers; long, often weak back, shallow rib cage and a tendency to poor loins, lacking in muscle; narrow hindquarters but with muscular croup and long, muscular thighs; strong, straight forelegs with long forearm, and long hindlegs which tend to be sickle shaped with cow hocks; small but hard feet; sparse mane and tail; thin skin.

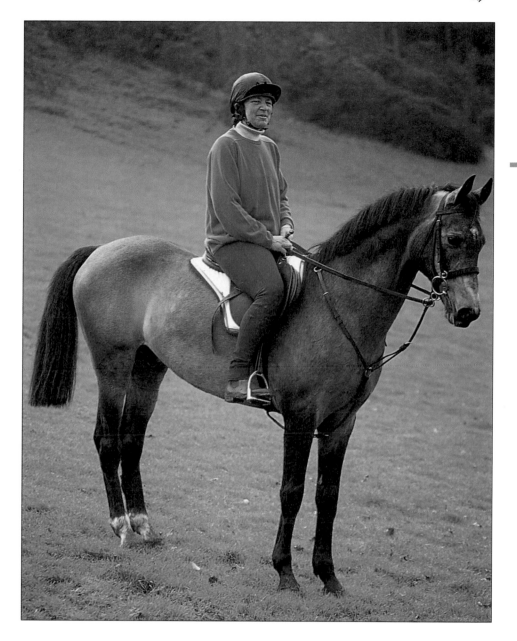

horses. Raised to withstand the extreme conditions of the desert – fiercely hot days alternating with cold nights – the Akhal-Teke developed into a tough, lean horse, whose undoubted conformational defects are offset by its fast paces, stamina and tremendous hardiness. This hardiness owes much to the rigorous lifestyle imposed upon it over many centuries. The traditional Turkmen method of horse management did not included stabling. The animals were wrapped in felt, with only their heads uncovered, and kept on tethers. Their diet included meagre amounts of dry lucerne, barley and some mutton fat. Foals were weaned very young and the horses raced as yearlings. Nowadays Akhal-Tekes are kept along more modern lines, out at grass by day and stabled by night. They are still raced, though not until they are two- or three-year-olds, as is the custom in the Thoroughbred racing world.

Spirited and athletic, they are used for general riding purposes, including show jumping and dressage, and at stud in the development of other riding horse breeds. Their phenomenal stamina also makes them the ideal mount for endurance rides, since they are capable of covering great distances, in extremes of temperature, on the most modest of rations. One of the most celebrated of all endurance rides took place in 1935, when Akhal-Teke horses travelled from Ashkabad to Moscow (their journey included crossing the Karakum desert), completing a distance of 2,580 miles (4,152km) in 84 days.

INTERESTING FACTS

The Akhal-Teke used to be renowned for its devotion to its rider – which is not surprising if one tale told about the Turkmen training techniques is true. According to this story, a young horse would be kept alone in a pit or enclosure. Stones would be thrown at it by everyone but the owner. Only he would treat it kindly and offer it food. Thus the horse learnt to trust only one man and to fear all others. This could account for the breed's sometimes difficult temperament.

Morgan

The American Morgan horse is highly unusual in that it can be traced back to just one stallion, the extraordinary little Justin Morgan, who stood a mere 14hh but who excelled in weight-pulling contests and races, both under saddle and in harness.

Justin Morgan was probably foaled in 1789 and was originally named Figure, later taking the name of his first recorded owner, Thomas Justin Morgan, who came from farming stock in Vermont but who was also a music teacher and church composer. How Justin Morgan was bred has never been satisfactorily resolved because of the lack of recorded evidence. Plausible claims have been made for Thoroughbred, Arab, Welsh Cob and Dutch ancestry. What is beyond dispute is that despite his small stature – he weighed no more than 850lb (386kg) – Justin Morgan proved himself a remarkably strong work horse, and he undoubtedly

The head of the Morgan is expressive, with large, prominent eyes and shapely ears set rather wide apart. Mares may have slightly longer ears than stallions.

worked extremely hard for a succession of owners. He was used for ploughing, as a harness horse and in woodland clearance and was never beaten in log-hauling matches against rivals weighing nearly half as much again.

He was, moreover, a wonderfully prepotent sire, passing on to his progeny all his own remarkable attributes of strength, endurance, speed and, not least, his gentle temperament. Three of his sons were to have a particular influence on

the development of the breed of which he was the founder: Sherman Morgan, foaled around 1808, Woodbury Morgan (1816) and Bulrush Morgan (1812). The Sherman Morgan line was noted for its excellent harness horses and had an important influence on the foundation of other breeds in the US: the Quarter Horse, Saddlebred, Standardbred and Tennessee Walker. The Woodbury Morgans were much in demand as saddle and parade

■ LEFT
The top line of the Morgan is distinctive. The gentle curve from the poll to the back gives the impression of the neck sitting on top of the withers rather than in front of them.

126

BREED DESCRIPTION

Height 14.1 – 15.2hh with some individuals over or under.

Colour Bay, chestnut, brown or black. No white markings permitted above the knee or hock, except on the face.

Conformation Expressive head, with straight or slightly dished profile, broad forehead, large eyes and short, alert ears; slightly arched neck; sloping shoulders and well-defined withers; compact, deep body, with short back, well-sprung ribs, broad loins and deep flank; well-muscled hindquarters with high-set tail; straight, sound legs, with short cannons, flat bone and sufficiently long, sloping pasterns to provide light, springy step; good, sound feet with dense horn; full, soft mane and tail.

horses, while the Bulrush Morgans were noted for their trotting speed.

Like so many other breeds, the Morgan horse went into decline with the coming of motorized transport, but thanks to the efforts of enthusiastic members of the Morgan Horse Club, founded in 1909, the breed survived. Today there is a thriving population of Morgan horses in the United States plus recognized breed clubs in Canada, Britain, Australia, Spain, New Zealand, Germany, Italy and Sweden. The Morgan is kept as a show horse and is also to be seen competing in a variety of spheres, such as cutting horse, stock horse and reining horse classes, hunter-jumper division, dressage and roadster and carriage driving competitions.

INTERESTING FACTS

A Morgan horse named Comanche, the mount of Captain Myles Keogh, was the only non-Indian survivor of the Battle of the Little Big Horn in 1876. He recovered from his many wounds and lived to the ripe old age of 29.

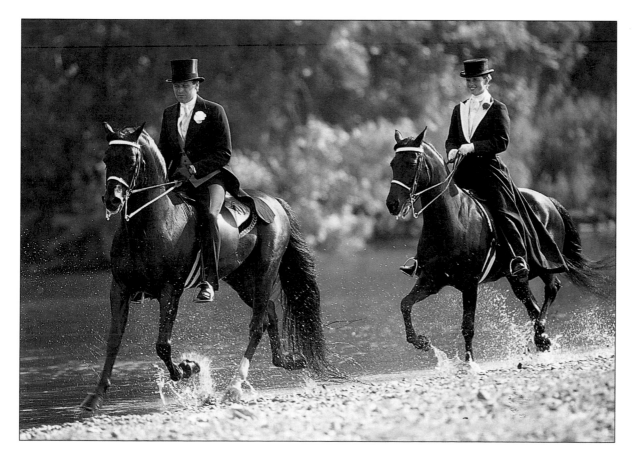

❚ ABOVE
The versatile Morgan horse is equally at home in harness and under saddle.

❚ LEFT
Morgan horses are well up to carrying the weight of adult riders. The action is straight and springy.

Quarter Horse

The Quarter Horse, as its name implies, excels at racing over a short distance – a quarter of a mile to be precise. It traces back to the horses taken to America by the Spanish Conquistadores. During the seventeenth and eighteenth centuries the waves of English settlers in the eastern states used the local Spanish-based stock to cross with their own, imported horses to produce a good, all-round work horse, suitable for every type of ridden work, for tilling the land and for work in harness. Tough and stocky, these horses became the settlers' "right-hand men". Spreading westward, they became indispensable during the great days of cattle herding when the chief requirement was for a totally dependable mount, one which was athletic and fearless working among cattle. In time these horses developed an innate "cow sense" and could anticipate the movements of a steer, stopping and turning at breakneck speed.

It was the Englishman's growing enthusiasm for racing which led to these all-purpose horses being raced in impromptu contests: on the road, in a clearing, anywhere where a couple of

▌ ABOVE LEFT
The head of the Quarter Horse is short and wide with large, intelligent eyes, alert ears and a small muzzle.

▌ ABOVE RIGHT
The chest is broad and deep, and the forelegs wide set. The muscling on the insides of the forearms gives the appearance of a well-defined inverted V.

▌ RIGHT
The breed is noted for its strong, close-coupled back and deep girth. Well-muscled hindquarters and strong, low-set hocks give the horse its tremendous acceleration.

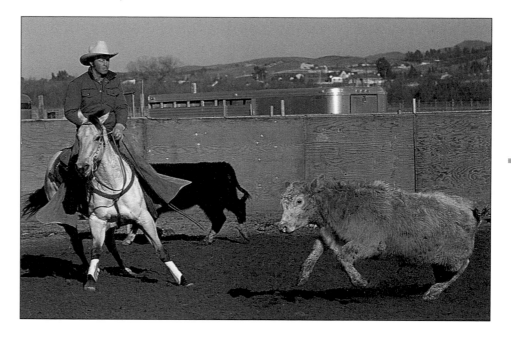

BREED DESCRIPTION

Height 14.3 – 16hh for mature stallions and mares.

Colour Any solid colour.

Conformation Short, wide head, with small muzzle, large, wide-set, intelligent eyes and medium-length, alert ears; fairly long, flexible neck; sloping shoulders and well-defined withers; compact body with broad chest, deep girth, short back, well-sprung ribs and powerful loins; broad, deep, heavy and well-muscled hindquarters with long, gently sloped croup; good limbs, with short cannons, broad, flat, low-set hocks, muscular thighs and gaskins and medium-length pasterns; oblong feet with deep, open heels.

horses could be galloped upsides for a few hundred yards. The Quarter Horse, as it was dubbed, developed immensely powerful hindquarters, which could propel it into a flat-out gallop virtually from a standing start, and the speed to sprint over short distances. Eventually, however, as Thoroughbred racing became established, interest in Quarter Horse racing dwindled. Still later, when mechanization brought about a lessening of the horse's importance in ranching, the Quarter Horse, in common with riding horses all over the world, became a leisure riding horse.

Today the Quarter Horse enjoys great popularity in Western-style competitions such as barrel racing, in rodeos and, once again, in racing over short distances. Thanks to a revival of interest in the latter sport, Quarter Horses now compete on proper tracks for big purses.

INTERESTING FACTS

The American Quarter Horse Association was formed in 1940. Its registry is now the largest of any breed in the world, with more than two million horses listed.

▌ ABOVE
Quarter Horses have an innate "cow sense" and are able to anticipate the movements of a steer.

▌ BELOW LEFT
The Quarter Horse makes an ideal mount for traditional Western sports.

▌ BELOW RIGHT
The breed is well known for its pleasant disposition and gentleness and as a result is used in a wide variety of activities.

Saddlebred

Formerly known as the Kentucky Saddler, the elegant Saddlebred was developed by the early nineteenth-century settlers in the southern states of North America. To meet their requirements for a quality utility horse, the plantation owners interbred horses of various kinds, including the Narragansett Pacer (a speedy strain of pacing horse from Rhode Island) and the Thoroughbred. The end result was a good-looking animal who gave an exceptionally comfortable ride – essential for long hours spent in the saddle on crop-inspection tours – but was equally well suited to pulling a carriage. In 1891 a group of leading breeders established the American Saddle Horse Breeders' Association and a Saddle Horse Registry was set up.

Blessed with the most amiable disposition, intelligence, speed and natural balance, the Saddlebred could (and still can) be used for all manner of different purposes, including working with cattle. Not surprisingly it has made the transition from work horse to pleasure

BREED DESCRIPTION

Height 15 – 17hh; average about 15.3hh.

Colour Usually chestnut, bay, brown, black or grey; also palomino, spotted and occasionally roan.

Conformation Well-shaped head with large eyes set well apart, small, alert ears and wide nostrils; long, arched neck; sloping shoulders with sharp withers; short, strong back; well-muscled hindquarters with level croup and high-set tail; straight, strong limbs with long, sloping pasterns; good, sound hooves, open at the heels.

▌ TOP
Everything about the Saddlebred's head suggests quality, refinement and intelligence. The neck is always long and elegantly arched.

▌ LEFT
The Saddlebred's top line is distinctive: the croup is long and level, the back short and the well-defined withers higher than in most other light breeds.

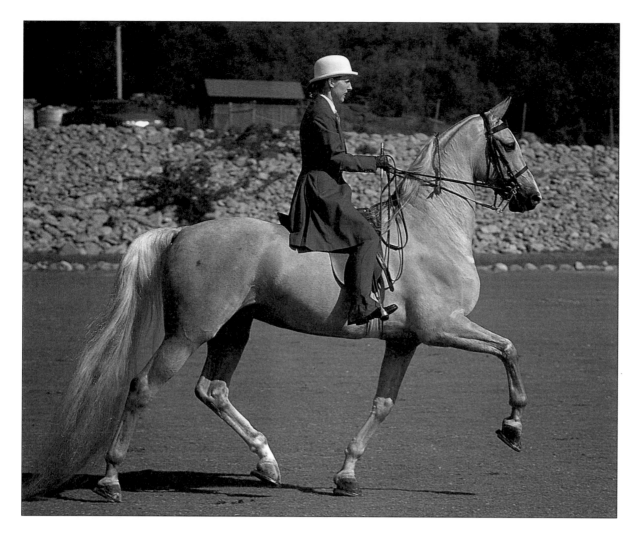

■ LEFT
Long, well-sloped pasterns contribute to the comfortable paces for which the breed is famous.

■ BELOW
As well as being popular riding horses, Saddlebreds go equally well in harness. The peculiar tail carriage is not natural, being achieved through an operation and maintained by keeping the tail in a device known as a tail set when the horse is stabled.

horse with no difficulty whatsoever and can be seen today competing in show classes under saddle and in harness.

In the show ring, ridden Saddlebreds are classified either as three-gaited or five-gaited. The three-gaited horses are shown at walk, trot and canter. The walk is springy, the trot has high action and the canter is slow, smooth and rhythmic. The five-gaited horses show these three paces plus two others: the slow gait and the rack. The slow gait is a high-stepping, four-beat gait executed in a slow, restrained manner. The rack is a fast, flashy, four-beat gait in which each foot strikes the ground at equal intervals and which is free from any lateral movement or pacing. The practice of growing the feet unnaturally long (to enhance the action), and operating on the tail to make it unnaturally high set, developed for the show ring.

Outside the artificial confines of the show ring, in its handsome natural state, the Saddlebred makes an excellent all-round riding horse – easy to train, fast, possessing great stamina and having a good jump, too.

INTERESTING FACTS

In their natural state the Saddlebred's strong hooves are well formed. For showing purposes they are grown to an unnatural length and shod with heavy shoes.

Standardbred

The American Standardbred is to harness racing what the English Thoroughbred is to flat racing and steeplechasing. During the past century or more, every country where harness racing flourishes has imported Standardbred horses to upgrade its own trotters and pacers.

BREED DESCRIPTION

Height 14 – 16hh.

Colour All solid colours, predominantly bay, brown, black and chestnut.

Conformation The Standardbred is a powerfully built horse, of rather less quality and refinement than the Thoroughbred and somewhat longer in the body and shorter in the leg. The shoulders are long and sloping and the croup invariably high.

■ OPPOSITE PAGE
The gaits are so inherent that Standardbreds often show a marked preference for the trot (shown here) or the pace over the gallop, even when they are at liberty.

Strangely enough the foundation sire of the Standardbred was a horse who only ever raced at the gallop: the English Thoroughbred, Messenger. A grey tracing back to the Darley Arabian, Messenger was foaled in 1780 and raced on the flat for three seasons, winning eight of his fourteen starts. Exported to Philadelphia in May 1788, he stood at stud in America for twenty years, covering mainly Thoroughbred mares to start with then, after racing was suppressed in New York, all types of non-Thoroughbreds. Some of his descendants became fine flat

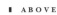

■ ABOVE
The head of the Standardbred is not exactly refined but the overall aspect is workmanlike and the expression sensible.

■ LEFT
In comparison with that other great racehorse, the Thoroughbred, the breed is rather long in the back and short in the leg. The shoulders are invariably long and well sloped, giving the horse the necessary freedom of movement.

INTERESTING FACTS

One of the greatest Standardbred trotters of all time, and the horse who did much to revive waning interest in harness racing in the 1930s, was the flying grey, Greyhound, who in 1938 trotted the mile in 1:55.25, a record that stood for 31 years. The mobile starting gate, introduced in 1946, eliminated time-wasting starts and together with greatly improved racing surfaces has contributed to the recording of increasingly faster times by both trotters and pacers.

racehorses but it was his ability to throw good trotting stock (not so much his immediate progeny as their descendants) that earned him lasting fame. His great grandson, Hambletonian, became a prolific sire of trotters and Hambletonian's four sons, George Wilkes, Dictator, Happy Medium and Electioneer, founded the sire lines responsible for virtually all harness racehorses in the USA today. Hambletonian was out of the Charles Kent Mare, who was inbred to Messenger, and descended, through her sire, Bellfounder, from the famous Norfolk Trotter, Old Shales.

In addition to the dominant Messenger line, two other important influences on the early development of the Standardbred were the Clays (descendants of a Barb stallion imported from Tripoli in 1820) and the Morgan horse. Neither produced important families within the breed but both are believed to have helped establish its characteristic gait.

The first register of trotters was published in 1871 and the term "Standardbred" was introduced eight years later when a set of qualifications was drawn up for the admission of horses into the register. The original "standard", from which the breed takes its name, was judged to be the ability of a horse to cover a mile (1.6km) in 2 minutes 30 seconds (as trotters and pacers improved, this time had to be reduced). Standardbreds race either at the pace (a lateral gait) or the trot (a diagonal pace). Up until the last couple of decades of the nineteenth century, trotters were more popular than the marginally faster pacers, but this is not so today.

ABOVE
Although the pace is one of the breed's natural gaits it is usual for pacing racehorses to wear hobbles to encourage them to maintain the lateral movement.

LEFT
Racing harness includes many items not generally seen in other horse sports. The shadow rolls on this horse's bridle are designed to prevent him from seeing and taking fright at shadows or "foreign objects" on the ground.

Missouri Fox Trotter

Although a stud book for the Missouri Fox Trotting Horse was not opened until 1948, the breed began to evolve in the early part of the nineteenth century. Settlers travelling westwards across the Mississippi river from Kentucky, Tennessee and Virginia took with them a variety of horses, including Thoroughbreds, eastern-bred stock and Morgans, and then interbred them to produce a horse suited to the conditions of their new home in the Ozark Hills region of Missouri.

The chief requirement, especially of doctors, sheriffs, stock raisers and the like, was for a horse that could be ridden for long periods, often over rough terrain, with a minimum of fatigue either to horse or rider. The answer was found in the gait known as the fox trot, in which the horse walks with its forelegs but trots behind. The Fox Trotter does not put its hindfeet down with the jarring action characteristic of the

BREED DESCRIPTION

Height 14 – 16hh.

Colour Any. Most commonly sorrel and chestnut sorrel with white markings.

Conformation Neat, clean, intelligent head with pointed, well-shaped ears, large, bright eyes and a tapered muzzle; graceful neck, in proportion to length of body; well-sloped, muscular shoulders; deep, strong body with deep, full chest and short, strong back; strong, muscular limbs; strong, well-made feet.

▌ ABOVE
This neat, intelligent looking head, with its bright eyes and well-shaped ears, is typical of the Missouri Fox Trotter.

▌ RIGHT
The body is deep, the back short and the overall impression one of compactness. Well-sloped shoulders ensure good riding action.

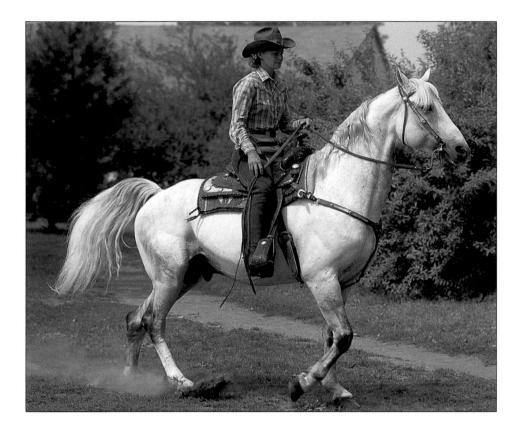

▌ LEFT
The legendary comfort experienced when riding a
Fox Trotter comes from the unusual action of the
hindfeet, which slide forward under the horse as he
puts them down, rather than hitting the ground with
a jarring action.

INTERESTING FACTS

In the fox trot the horse's hindfeet disfigure
the tracks of the forefeet, that is the hindfeet
touch the front tracks and slide forward. The
horse should travel in a collected manner,
with animation, rhythm and style. The horse's
tail is slightly elevated and moves in a
bobbing rhythm with the gait. The flat-foot
walk should also be performed with style and
animation. It is an animated four-beat gait in
which the horse overstrides its front track
with the hindfeet. The typical canter of the
Fox Trotter is collected, with the head and
tail slightly elevated.

normal trot, but slides them along under
him. The result is a smooth, comfortable
gait at which the horse can travel for
extended periods without tiring. The
ability to walk in front and trot behind is
inherited but it can also be enhanced with
training. The overall quality of the Fox

show classes in which it is judged 40 per
cent for the fox trot, 20 per cent for the
flat foot walk, 20 per cent for the canter
and 20 per cent for conformation, the only
exceptions being two-year-olds, who are
judged 50 per cent for fox trot, 25 per cent
for walk and 25 per cent for conformation.

▌ BELOW LEFT
Originally bred as a means of transport, the present-
day Fox Trotter is well suited to modern leisure
riding. It is renowned for its sure-footedness.

▌ BELOW
Unlike the Saddlebred and the Tennessee Walking
Horse, the Missouri Fox Trotter is shown with
normal-length feet. Artificial appliances such as
weights and tail sets are forbidden.

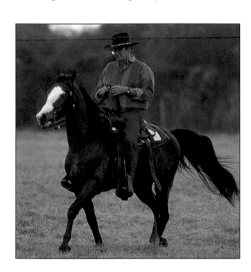

Trotter was improved over the years
through infusions of Saddlebred and
Tennessee Walker blood and today the
breed is noted for its compact, muscular
build and its sure-footedness.

Having become obsolete as a means of
transport, the Fox Trotter is now used as a
pleasure horse, being ideally suited to trail
(long-distance) riding. It is also ridden in

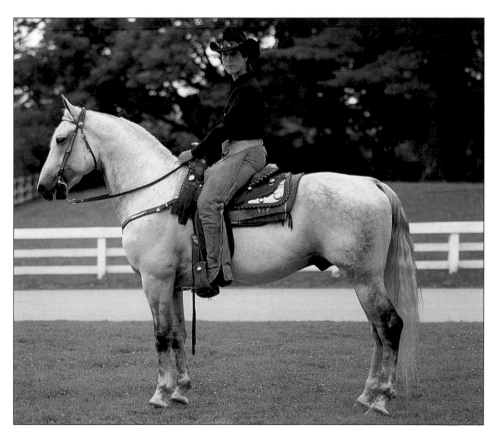

Tennessee Walking Horse

The Tennessee Walking Horse traces back to the Narragansett Pacer and, like the Saddlebred and the Missouri Fox Trotter, it was developed as an exceptionally comfortable riding horse with gaits not found in other breeds. Originally known as the Southern Plantation Walking Horse or Tennessee Pacer, it was an invaluable mode of transport for planters carrying out crop inspections, being fast, robust, comfortable under saddle and having a most tractable temperament.

The foundation sire was a horse named Black Allan, who arrived in Tennessee in

▌ LEFT
The Tennessee Walking Horse is customarily ridden in a plain bit with long shanks and on a single rein which is held with a light hand and flexed wrist.

▌ BELOW
The Walking Horse has the substance of the Standardbred and the style of the Saddlebred which are two of the breeds on which it is based.

1903. Black Allan's sire came from a line of Standardbred trotters, while his dam was a Morgan. Black Allan was crossed with the Tennessee Pacers of the time to produce the forerunners of the modern Walking Horse. Saddlebred blood was also introduced, the most important influence being that of Giovanni, who in 1914 was brought from Kentucky to stand at stud in Tennessee. By adding Saddlebred blood, breeders succeeded in producing a better quality, more refined, animal. Today's Walking Horse, which might be decribed as a somewhat more powerful version of

BREED DESCRIPTION

Height Average 15 .2hh.

Colour Any. Black and solid colours are most popular.

Conformation Intelligent but rather plain head; strong, arched neck; well-sloped shoulders; powerful body with broad chest; strong hindquarters; clean, hard limbs.

the Saddlebred, is therefore an amalgam of Thoroughbred, Standardbred, Morgan and Saddlebred blood. The Tennessee Walking Horse Breeders' Association was formed in Lewisburg, Tennessee, in 1935 and the Walking Horse was finally recognized as a breed in 1947.

Walking horses are fine all-round riding horses, their inherently kind nature making them especially suitable for novice riders. They are also popular horses in the show ring.

INTERESTING FACTS

The Tennessee Walking Horse's distinctive gaits – the flat-foot walk, the running walk and the canter – are inherited. Small foals can be seen performing the running walk beside their dams. Both walks are a loose, four-beat gait, with high action in front. As it moves, the horse nods its head in rhythm with the rise and fall of the hoofs, and the hindfeet overstride the tracks left by the front feet. The flat-foot walk should be loose, bold and square with plenty of shoulder motion. There should be a noticeable difference in the tempo between the two walks. The canter has a distinctive "rocking chair" motion.

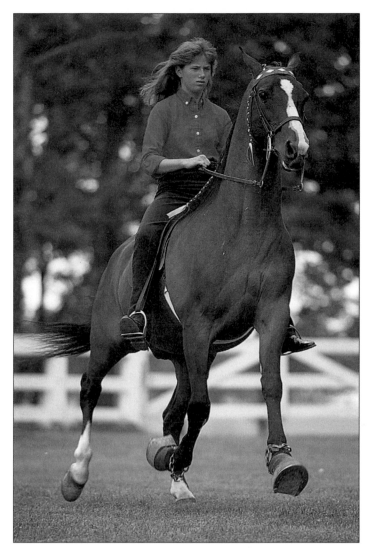

LEFT
The breed's unique gaits are inherited – young foals are seen to "walk" alongside their mothers with the ease of older horses – but are encouraged with artificial aids applied to the forefeet.

FAR LEFT
An impressive collection of Walking Horse trophies won in America, where the breed is a popular show-ring attraction.

BELOW
The exaggerated outline of the show horse is produced in part by the extra-long forefeet. The rider sits way behind the normal saddle position (on what is generally held to be the weakest part of the horse's back).

Mustang

Mustangs, the "wild" horses of North America, are descended from the horses taken to the New World by the sixteenth-century Conquistadores. As Spanish colonizers began moving north from Mexico into what is now Texas, so the Indian tribes with whom they came into contact began to have their first experience of horses. Initially, the Indians were inclined to kill and eat any horses they captured from the settlers. In time, however, as they began to realize the value of the horse as a means of transport, they learnt how to handle and ride them.

By the second half of the seventeenth century, some tribes were taking horses from the Spaniards and using them in mounted raids against the newcomers – during which they would acquire more horses. So began the gradual spread of the horse to other tribes (either by trading or by theft) and the movement of the horse

northwards. Many of the horses who subsequently ran "wild" would have done so after getting loose during skirmishes between Indians and Spaniards. Others, perhaps those who were lame or needed resting, were probably turned loose, their owners intending to round them up later. Some domestic horses put out to graze on the range simply wandered off. Gradually these horses joined together to form feral

herds, which flourished in the wide open spaces of the Great Plains. By the late eighteenth and early nineteenth centuries there were huge numbers of "wild" horses grazing the plains – one authority estimates the number to have been as high as two million.

The turning point for the Mustang, as these feral horses became known, was the westward spread of civilization. Many were

This Mustang shows unmistakable signs of its Spanish ancestry in its attractive head and luxurious growth of silky mane.

BREED DESCRIPTION

Height 13.2 – 15hh.

Colour Any.

Conformation Because of its mixed ancestry (the original Spanish stock was progressively diluted as a wide variety of settlers' horses, who either became lost or were abandoned, joined and interbred with the wild herds) there is a good deal of variation. The best are sturdily built with strong, clean limbs and feet.

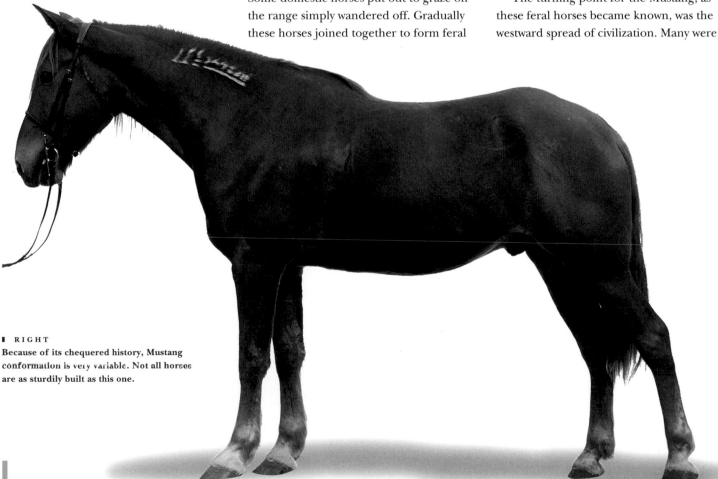

Because of its chequered history, Mustang conformation is very variable. Not all horses are as sturdily built as this one.

Centuries of living in a feral state led to the development of a tough, enduring type of animal.

INTERESTING FACTS

The term mustang probably comes from the Spanish word *mesteno*, from *mesta*, meaning an association of graziers or stock raisers. In thirteenth-century Spain *mestas* were organizations of sheep owners. Stray sheep were called *mestenos*, meaning "belonging to the *mesta*". Some etymologists think that mustang comes from the word *mestengo*, a later form of *mostrenco*, from the verb *mostrar*, to show or exhibit. Stray sheep, sometimes referred to as *mostrencos*, were shown in public to give the owner the chance to claim them. But according to the wild-horse authority J. Frank Dobie, English-speaking people in the American south-west did not know the word *mostrenco*. Dobie dates the introduction of the term Mustang to the early nineteenth century.

killed, others were rounded up for use as draught animals, some were used for cross-breeding. Large numbers were used as army remounts in the Boer War. During the twentieth century still more have been killed for the meat and pet food trades.

Public pressure led to the introduction, in 1971, of an act giving protection to wild horses in the United States and there are several ranges where they still live, albeit in much reduced numbers. Domesticated Mustangs often make good riding horses. Because of their inherent toughness, they are well suited to endurance rides.

A fine stamp of Mustang which looks well under saddle. The majority of domesticated Mustangs make good all-round riding horses.

Decorated in traditional style, these horses reflect their links with the Indian tribes who came to rely on the horses first introduced into America by the Conquistadores.

Australian Stock Horse

Horses were not indigenous to Australia and the modern Stock Horse is descended from the first imported animals, shipped over in small numbers from South Africa during the latter part of the eighteenth century. The precise breeding of these early imports is not known but they were probably of mainly Arab and Barb blood. It was not long before regular voyages began between Europe and Australia, each ship with its quota of horses aboard, and so Australia's equine population steadily grew.

BREED DESCRIPTION

Height 15 – 16.3hh.

Colour Any solid colour.

Conformation There is considerable variation, but the best types are similar to the Thoroughbred, with particularly good sound limbs and feet.

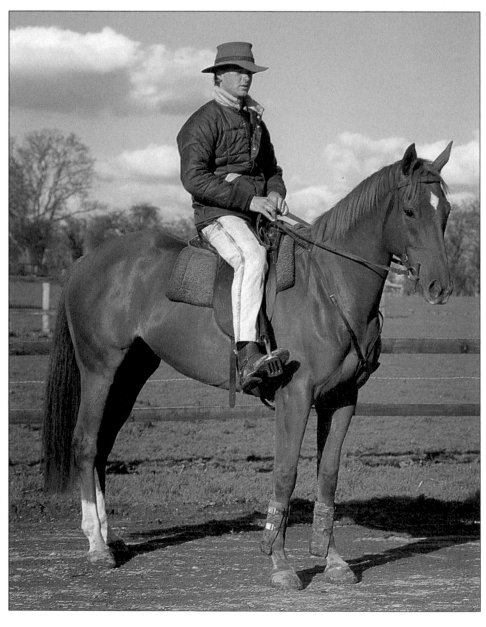

Tough horses were needed to help settlers explore their rugged new home and, not surprisingly, Thoroughbreds and Arabs were the most popular imports. Thoroughbreds were required, too, to satisfy the growing interest of the settlers in racing, a sport which rapidly gained popularity from the early years of the nineteenth century onwards.

The horse which evolved for everyday use was a tough all-rounder: hardy, reliable, of good temperament, able to work in harness or under saddle, to plough the land, clear timber, and herd cattle and sheep. Until 1971, when the term Stock Horse was introduced, it was known as the "Waler" (after New South Wales). Walers were renowned for their stamina, courage and soundness and were accordingly highly prized by the cavalry.

The present-day Stock Horse is the descendant of the Waler. It has almost certainly been influenced by a number of breeds other than the Thoroughbred and Arab – Quarter Horses, various ponies and heavy breeds such as the Clydesdale and Suffolk Punch were all imported into Australia over the years and some outcrosses would have been made – but the Stock Horse is essentially a quality riding horse. Still in demand for cattle herding, at which it excels, it can also be seen taking part in rodeos and is suitable for general riding purposes, including competitive sports.

INTERESTING FACTS

Regal Realm is one of a long line of Australian Stock Horses to compete successfully at the highest level. Ridden by Lucinda Green he won the individual gold medal at the World Three-Day Event Championships in 1982, helping Britain to take the team title. The following year he was runner-up in the European Championships, winning a team silver medal. At the Los Angeles Olympic Games in 1984 he won another team silver and finished in sixth place individually. A year later he was a member of the victorious British team in the European Championships. When he retired from international competition he returned to his native land.

▌ OPPOSITE ABOVE LEFT
The head resembles that of the Thoroughbred, which is one of the major influences in the development of the Australian Stock Horse.

▌ OPPOSITE ABOVE RIGHT
It is usual to brand Stock Horses for identification purposes. This brand is on the horse's shoulder.

▌ OPPOSITE BELOW
Many Stock Horses show the refinement and good overall conformation of the Thoroughbred. They have as a result produced some good sports horses.

▌ LEFT
There is as yet no set type within the breed. This striking-looking horse shows unmistakable signs of his eastern ancestry.

▌ BELOW
The breed was and still is a cattle-herding horse par excellence: tough, enduring, sound and good-natured.

141

Criollo

BELOW
Originally the mount of the gauchos, or cowboys, of
South America, the Criollo has achieved world-wide
fame in the world of polo.

BOTTOM
The sturdy, compact Criollo is one of the world's
toughest horses, with strong short limbs, plenty of
bone below the knee and exceptionally sound feet.

A descendant of the horses taken to South America by the sixteenth-century Spanish Conquistadores, the Criollo comes from Argentina and is one of the toughest breeds of horse in the world. Its hardiness is the result of many years of natural selection. Some of the Spanish horses and their descendants formed feral herds on the pampas, where the extremes of climate – intensely dry, hot summers and severe winters – would have proved intolerable to all but the sturdiest individuals. Those that survived adapted to their harsh environment remarkably well, no doubt helped by the fact that they were descended from Andalusian and Barb horses, both breeds noted for their endurance. The Criollo, as it became known, even developed a coat colour – Criollos are predominantly dun – which helped render it inconspicuous against

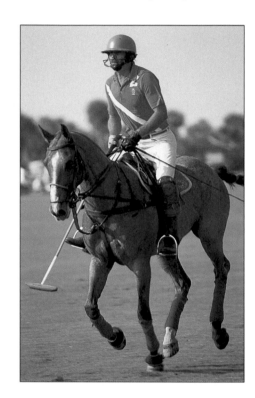

the dry pastureland of its habitat.

The Criollo became the favoured mount of the gauchos, the cowboys of the pampas, and an indispensable riding and packhorse for settlers in the huge and frequently inhospitable countries of South America. It can be found throughout the continent and although there are some variations, the result of adaptation to differences in habitat and climate, wherever it is bred it retains its basic qualities of stamina and soundness. Crossed with the Thoroughbred, the Criollo produces a fine polo pony, the Thoroughbred blood providing the extra speed required in the modern game.

BREED DESCRIPTION

Height Around 14 – 15hh.

Colour Usually dun with dark points and often with a dorsal stripe.

Conformation Medium-sized head, with wide-set eyes and alert ears; muscular neck; short, deep body with well-sprung ribs; short, strong limbs with plenty of bone and good, sound feet.

INTERESTING FACTS

The most famous example of the Criollo's extraordinary powers of endurance was "Tschiffely's Ride", a journey undertaken by the Swiss-born traveller and writer Aimé Felix Tschiffely (1895–1954). In 1925, together with two Criollos – the 16-year-old Mancha, and the 15-year-old Gata – Tschiffely set off from Buenos Aires to ride to Washington D.C. in the United States. Alternately riding one horse and leading the other as a packhorse, he completed the journey, over some of the most arduous terrain in the world, in two and a half years. The horses were then shipped back to South America, where they spent their retirement, Gata living to the age of 36 and Mancha to 40.

Peruvian Paso

The Paso (meaning "step") is another breed which owes its origins to the Barb and Andalusian horses introduced to South America by the Spaniards. The first horses to arrive in Peru were taken there in 1532 by Francisco Pizarro (c.1478–1541).

The Paso's characteristic lateral gait is thought to have been inherited from the Spanish "jennet", which was a riding horse akin to the old English ambler. The lateral movement has been preserved down the centuries; the Paso usually demonstrates a preference for it over the canter. The paso is unlike any other lateral gait in that the horse's forelegs arc out to the side as he moves. With his hindlegs he takes long, straight strides, carrying his hindquarters

■ ABOVE
Compact and well-muscled, with powerful hindquarters and short, strong limbs, the Peruvian Paso is a tremendously strong individual.

BREED DESCRIPTION

Height 14 – 15.2hh.

Colour Any, but predominantly bay and chestnut.

Conformation Intelligent looking head; fairly short, muscular neck; strong shoulders; strong body with broad, deep chest; strong, rounded hindquarters; short, strong limbs and excellent feet.

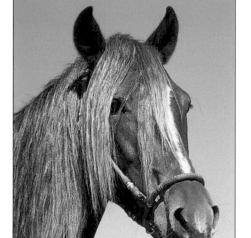

low, with his hocks well under him. This combination of flowing foreleg movement and powerfully driving hindlegs gives a particularly smooth ride. The Paso is said to be able to reach speeds of up to 15mph (24kph) and to maintain the lateral gait over rough terrain for extended periods without tiring.

Fairly small and stockily built, the Paso is noted for its sure-footedness, its ability to thrive on meagre rations and its kind nature. It makes an ideal ranch and long-distance riding horse.

■ RIGHT
Horse and rider make an attractive, workmanlike picture in their traditional Peruvian tack and costume. The Paso is up to carrying a good deal of weight.

■ LEFT
The Paso's long silky mane (and tail) is reminiscent of that of its Spanish ancestors, introduced into South America during the sixteenth century.

INTERESTING FACTS

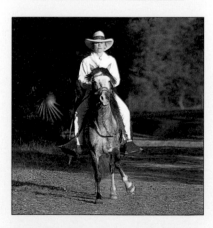

The Peruvian Paso is not the only horse to show a natural preference for a lateral gait but the curious outward arcing of the forelegs, which move rather like the arms of a swimmer, is unique to the breed.

Ponies

Broadly speaking a pony is a small horse, "small" usually meaning no higher at the withers than about 14.2hh (a hand is 4 inches). However, not all small horses can be classified as ponies. Arab horses, for example, often stand below 15hh but they are very much horses, with the proportions and characteristics of the horse. An unusually small Thoroughbred is certainly not a pony and the remarkable little Caspian, although it is classified as a pony, actually resembles a miniature horse.

True ponies have very distinct pony characteristics, which include a proportionately short length of leg in relationship to the depth of the body. True ponies are perhaps best exemplified by the Mountain and Moorland breeds of Britain and Ireland, remarkable animals which have existed in the comparative isolation of their island home for thousands of years. These ponies, which are now divided into nine distinct breeds, are possessed of extraordinary strength in relation to their size. Fashioned by a harsh environment, they are tough, sure-footed, able to exist on minimum rations and have an inherent sagacity often lacking in their larger cousins.

Haflinger

Austria's attractive Haflinger pony is named after the village of Hafling in the southern Tirol, the region where it was first bred hundreds of years ago. Its ancestors were indigenous mountain

BREED DESCRIPTION

Height Around 14hh.

Colour Chestnut with flaxen mane and tail.

Conformation Intelligent looking head, with large eyes, small ears and slightly dished profile; sloping shoulders; strong, deep body with fairly long back and muscular loins; powerful hindquarters; strong limbs and excellent feet.

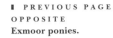

▪ PREVIOUS PAGE
OPPOSITE
Exmoor ponies.

▪ PREVIOUS PAGE
A Norwegian Fjord pony.

▪ LEFT
The "Hungarian Post" – Haflinger style! The breed combines strength with very active paces and can be trained to perform in a wide range of equestrian activities.

▪ BELOW LEFT
Haflingers are true all-rounders, equally adept at work in harness and under saddle. This handsome team was photographed in Switzerland.

▪ BELOW
The Haflinger's good temperament is easily discerned in this attractive head, with its large, kind eyes and alert expression.

horses and ponies which were upgraded with Arabian blood. All modern Haflingers trace back to a half-bred horse named El Bedavi XXII – who was bred in Austria and was a great grandson of the Arabian stallion, El Bedavi – and to El Bedavi XXII's son, Folie.

Over the years inbreeding has resulted in a pony of very definite type: small, but powerfully built, always chestnut in colour, hardy and sure-footed as befits a mountain

pony, and with the active paces of its Arab forebears.

With its amenable nature, the Haflinger makes an excellent all-round riding and driving pony. Before mechanization it was in great demand for agricultural work and as a pack-pony. Nowadays many Haflingers are used for leisure riding. The breed has been exported to a number of countries, and is especially popular in Germany and Switzerland. It is noted for its longevity.

INTERESTING FACTS

Haflingers which are entered in the breed's stud book are traditionally branded. The brand mark is the alpine flower, the edelweiss, at the centre of which is placed the letter "H".

Sorraia

Formerly used for farm work and general riding purposes, the primitive looking Sorraia survives today mainly in small feral groups. Its homeland is in Portugal in the region between the rivers Sor and Raia, tributaries of the Sorraia, which flows into the Tagus estuary from the south.

The Sorraia pony is believed to be descended from the Asian Wild Horse and the Tarpan. It bears a remarkable likeness to the latter, with its small stature and large head. The Sorraia's colouring, predominantly dun, often with an eel-stripe and zebra markings on the legs, is also typical of the primitive equine type.

The Sorraia does not have the best conformation in the world. It is, however, an extremely tough individual, able to exist on poor forage and to withstand extremes of climate. The shoulders tend to be upright, the hindquarters weak and the limbs rather long and lacking in bone, though the feet are hard and sound.

■ **LEFT**
Dun is the predominant colour of the Sorraia, Portugal's small, semi-feral pony. The breed is of ancient origin and is exceptionally hardy.

■ **BELOW**
In build and overall outline the Sorraia is not unlike the primitive Tarpan. Some selective breeding is carried out in order to preserve the original form.

BREED DESCRIPTION

Height 12 – 13hh.

Colour Predominantly dun, with black eel-stripe down the centre of the back and frequently with zebra markings on the legs and occasionally on the body; also grey.

Conformation Large, primitive looking head with convex profile; straight shoulders; poor hindquarters with low-set tail; long limbs, lacking in bone.

INTERESTING FACTS

The Sorraia is believed to be related to the Garrano, the pony of northern Portugal. The Garrano shows more quality than the Sorraia, the result of infusions of Arab blood. Although small, the Garrano is inherently hardy, and has been used for all types of farm work, as a pack-pony and for hauling timber.

Exmoor

The Exmoor is the oldest of Britain's Mountain and Moorland breeds and one of the oldest equine breeds in the world. This attractive pony has inhabited the wild moorland area of west Somerset and north Devon in the south-west of England for many centuries. Ponies of Exmoor type were certainly known during Roman times and may well have existed as far back as the Bronze Age, when they would have been used for pulling chariots. Mention is made of Exmoor ponies and their owners in the Domesday Book of 1085.

The remoteness of its habitat has meant that the Exmoor pony has been subjected to very little in the way of

"improvement" through the introduction of outside blood. The rigours of life on the moor have produced a tremendously hardy pony, strong enough to carry an adult rider in spite of the fact that the ponies stand no higher than 12.3hh.

The Exmoor Pony Society was founded in 1921 to improve and encourage the breeding of Exmoor ponies of the

traditional moorland type. By carrying out rigorous inspections, it ensures that no pony lacking true Exmoor type is registered as a pure-bred. When ponies are passed for registration, they are branded on the shoulder with the

BREED DESCRIPTION

Height Stallions and geldings not exceeding 12.3hh. Mares not exceeding 12.2hh.

Colour Bay, brown or dun with black points. No white markings anywhere.

Conformation Clean-cut face with wide forehead, large, prominent eyes, wide nostrils and clean throat; good length of rein; well laid-back shoulders; strong body with deep, wide chest, well-sprung ribs and broad, level back; clean, short limbs and neat, hard feet.

▌ TOP
The Exmoor's attractive head, notable for its large eyes, small, mobile ears and intelligent expression, is full of true pony character.

▌ RIGHT
The Exmoor is a fine stamp of pony: hard and strong, vigorous, alert and symmetrical in appearance. Its general poise indicates its good natural balance.

■ LEFT
An Exmoor foal in his native habitat. Ponies have inhabited the moor for many centuries and are totally adapted to life in a tough environment.

Society's star brand. Beneath this the pony's herd number appears, while on the nearside hindquarter there is the pony's own number within that herd.

Herds of ponies still run "wild" on the moor, although they are rounded up annually for inspection. The Exmoor's robust build and constitution make it an excellent riding pony and they are also used in the sport of driving.

INTERESTING FACTS

The most instantly recognizable features of the Exmoor are its mealy coloured muzzle and its large, prominent eyes. The latter are termed "toad" eyes because of their heavy top lids. The eyebrows are surrounded by light, buff-coloured hair.

■ ABOVE
Correctly handled and schooled, the Exmoor, for all its great strength, makes a good riding pony for a small child.

■ LEFT
The breed's inherent athleticism makes it a good all-round performance pony for an older child.

149

Dartmoor

Unlike its neighbour, the Exmoor, the Dartmoor Pony has been influenced by a number of breeds over the many centuries during which ponies have run free on the high moorland of Devon, in south-west England. Ponies are thought to have lived on the moor during Saxon times. Later the important trade route which existed between Exeter and Plymouth would have been travelled by horses of many different types, some of which would almost certainly have had an influence on the native stock. Arabs and Barbs, brought back by Crusaders, are also believed to have found their way onto the moor.

Climate and the hardships of existing in such a wild region would have ensured

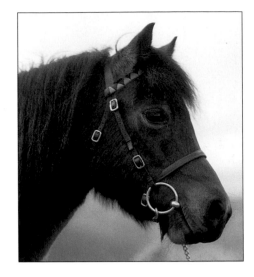

that the animals roaming the moors achieved a certain degree of uniformity, particularly with regard to size. During the Industrial Revolution the requirements of the mining industry prompted a new development: the crossing of Dartmoor Ponies with the much smaller Shetland, in order to produce animals suited to working underground. This proved to be a

highly retrograde step as far as the Dartmoor Pony was concerned. The type of riding-quality pony that had evolved began to deteriorate. In order to set matters right, new blood had to be introduced, including Welsh Mountain Pony, Polo Pony and Hackney.

The first stud book for Dartmoors was opened in 1899 and the height limits for

BREED DESCRIPTION

Height Not exceeding 12.2hh.

Colour Bay, black or brown preferred, but no colours are barred except skewbald and piebald. Excessive white markings discouraged.

Conformation Small, well set-on head with small, alert ears; strong, medium length neck, not too heavy, stallions to have a moderate crest; strong back and loins; strong, muscular hindquarters with full, high-set tail; hard, well-shaped feet.

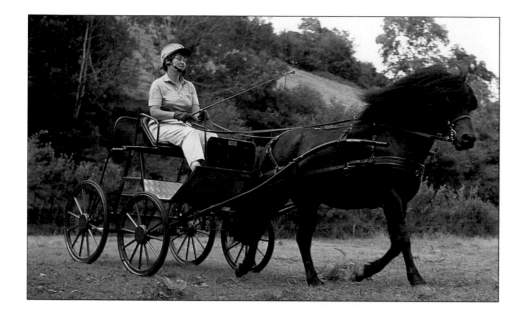

LEFT
Strength and active paces make the Dartmoor a
good harness pony.

INTERESTING FACTS

There was a steady decline in the numbers of
ponies of true Dartmoor type after World War II
and many of those found on the moor were
only poor quality cross-breds. However, in
1988 the Dartmoor Pony Society Moor
Scheme was set up in order to encourage
farmers with unregistered pure-bred type
ponies to offer them for registration and to
provide them with the services of pedigree
stallions. The aim is to establish a pool of
pure-bred ponies – hardy enough to thrive on
the moor – to which breeders can then go for
true native pony characteristics. Suitable
mares from the moor are put in large enclosed
areas known as newtakes together with a
pedigree stallion. Their female progeny are
inspected and those which pass muster are
entered in a supplementary register of the
stud book. In due course these ponies will also
be mated to a fully registered stallion, and so
on until their descendants, on inspection, can
be admitted to the full stud book.

RIGHT
Dartmoors have a
calm temperament
and make good mounts
for children.

OPPOSITE TOP
The Dartmoor's neat,
well set-on head with
its small, alert ears,
shows true native pony
character.

**OPPOSITE
BOTTOM**
The best examples of
the breed combine
quality with great
hardiness.

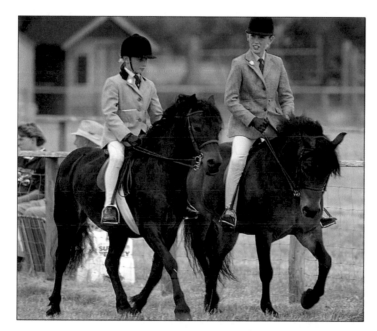

BELOW
Although Dartmoor ponies declined in number and
quality after World War II, in recent times measures
have been introduced to ensure the preservation of
a pool of hardy pure-breds.

stallions was given as 14hh and for mares
13.2hh. It was more than twenty years
before this was reduced to the present
12.2hh. Hackney blood was prominent in
a number of the foundation stallions.
However, the most influential sire of those
early years was undoubtedly The Leat, who
was by a pure-bred Arab (Dwarka, who
stood 14.1hh) out of a Dartmoor mare.
Standing 12.2hh, The Leat was a beautiful
looking pony with excellent conformation.
During his short stud career only a
handful of his progeny were registered,
but many of the best present-day ponies
trace back to him.

At its best the Dartmoor is a hardy,
quality riding pony with smooth, low, free
action. Its sound constitution, intelligence
and excellent, calm temperament, make it
an ideal pony for a child.

Welsh Mountain

The rugged landscape of Wales is home to four distinct equine breeds: two ponies, designated Section A and Section B in the Welsh Pony and Cob Society Stud Book, and two cobs, designated Section C and Section D.

At the base of all Welsh breeding is the beautiful Welsh Mountain Pony, Section A, which has thrived for many centuries in the tough environment of its native land

▮ ABOVE
The eastern influence is clearly visible in the beautiful head, with its big eyes, wide nostrils and dished profile.

▮ LEFT
The Section B is larger than the Welsh Mountain Pony but the best examples have the same true pony character. The action is straight, quick and free.

▮ BELOW
Section A ponies like this one were used in the development of the Australian Pony, which is based on Welsh and Arab blood.

BREED DESCRIPTION

Height Not exceeding 12hh.

Colour Predominantly grey, though bay, chestnut and palomino occur and any solid colour is permitted.

Conformation Small, clean-cut head, tapering to the muzzle, with bold eyes, small, pointed ears and prominent, open nostrils; lengthy, well-carried neck; long, sloping shoulders; strong, muscular back with deep girth, well-sprung ribs and strong loins; lengthy, fine hindquarters with tail well set on and carried gaily; good, strong limbs, with long, strong forearm, well-developed knee, large, flat hocks and well-shaped feet, of dense, hard horn.

and is considered by many people to be the most beautiful of all ponies. The development of the breed is obscure, but it goes back at least to the times of the Romans, who crossed horses of eastern origin with the native Welsh stock. In more recent times, particularly during the eighteenth century, some Thoroughbred, Arab and Barb blood was introduced.

The modern Welsh Mountain Pony is courageous and spirited, yet kindly, and makes a superb child's riding pony. It is also an outstanding performer in the increasingly popular sport of carriage driving. It has evolved as a supremely hardy individual, able to endure harsh weather conditions and to thrive on sparse rations. It has been used to improve other breeds, including the New Forest, and also in the development of the British Riding Pony. The Welsh Mountain Pony is popular in many countries outside its native Wales. It has been exported to Europe, the United States, New Zealand and Australia.

INTERESTING FACTS

The Welsh Pony (Section B) is larger than the Mountain Pony, though it retains the true pony characteristics. Arab, small Thoroughbred and small Welsh Cob stallions were crossed with Mountain Pony mares to develop this quality riding pony, which stands up to 13.2hh. Formerly used for shepherding and hunting, Welsh Ponies are now much in demand as children's riding ponies.

New Forest

Wild horses are known to have existed in the New Forest, in southern England, as far back as the time of Canute (c. 995–1035). The exact origins of today's New Forest Pony are, however, unknown although it has certainly been influenced down the years by a variety of other breeds. During the eighteenth century the Thoroughbred stallion Marske, the sire of the great racehorse Eclipse, was used for a time to

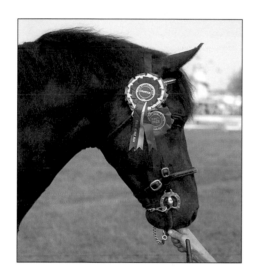

BREED DESCRIPTION

Height 13.3 – 14.2hh.

Colour Any colour except skewbald, piebald, or blue-eyed cream.

Conformation Rather large head; fairly short neck; well-sloped shoulders; deep body; strong hindquarters; straight limbs with plenty of bone and good hard, round feet.

serve New Forest mares and in the mid-nineteenth century an Arab stallion belonging to Queen Victoria was allowed to run with the herds. Hackney blood was also introduced. While these infusions of outside blood added to the pony's size, they were detrimental when it came to the preservation of true pony substance and to rectify the situation, outcrosses were made to stallions of other native breeds, including Dales, Dartmoor, Exmoor, Fell, Highland and, later, Welsh Mountain.

Today's New Forest Ponies, like many Exmoor and Welsh Mountain Ponies, still roam freely in their native habitat. Life in the Forest can be hard, the food supply often meagre and low in quality. This tough environment has produced a hardy, sure-footed animal. The pony's action is free, active and straight and its good temperament makes it easy to train. As a result they make excellent all-round riding and driving ponies. They are popular not only in their native country but also in mainland Europe, North America, Australia and New Zealand.

▌ TOP
The best type of New Forest Pony is strongly built and possesses good, well-sloped riding shoulders, powerful hindquarters and strong, sound limbs

▌ ABOVE LEFT
The New Forest's head indicates the breed's typically calm, tractable temperament.

INTERESTING FACTS

The ponies are owned by the New Forest Commoners, who carry out an annual "drift" or round-up in order to select those which are to be sold. The remaining breeding stock is then returned to the Forest.

Welsh Cob

The Welsh Cob (designated Section D in the Welsh Pony and Cob Society Stud Book) is derived from the Welsh Mountain Pony, of which it is, in essence, a larger version. It traces back at least to the twelfth century when eastern-type horses were brought back by the Crusaders and crossed with the local ponies. Subsequently infusions of Yorkshire Coach Horse, Norfolk Roadster and Arab blood were made.

Tough, sound, spirited and courageous, yet with an amenable temperament, the

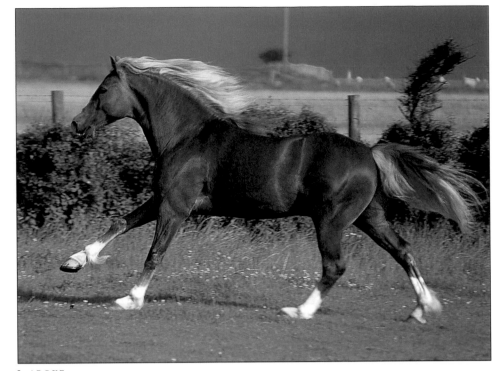

▌ ABOVE
The action is straight, free and forceful. The whole foreleg is extended from the shoulders and as far forward as possible in all paces, with the hocks well flexed, producing powerful leverage.

▌ RIGHT
The Welsh Cob Section D is described by the breed society as the embodiment of strength and hardiness.

BREED DESCRIPTION

Height Above 13.2hh – usually 14.2 – 15.2hh.

Colour Any, except piebald and skewbald.

Conformation Quality, pony head with bold, widely set eyes and neat, well-set ears; long, well-carried neck; strong, well laid-back shoulders; strong, deep, muscular body; muscular hindquarters; short, powerful limbs with long, strong forearms, strong, muscular second thighs, large, flat joints and well-shaped feet.

INTERESTING FACTS

By crossing Welsh Mountain Pony mares with small Welsh Cobs breeders produced the Welsh Pony of Cob Type (Section C in the Stud Book), a smaller version of the Cob and a marvellous all-round riding and driving pony. It shares all the characteristics of its larger cousin, but does not stand over 13.2hh. Like the Cob, it was formerly much used by hill farmers and also to transport slate from the mines of North Wales. After World War II it was in danger of becoming extinct, but its numbers have since recovered and nowadays it enjoys popularity as a trekking pony, a small hunter and as a driving pony.

❚ RIGHT
A popular attraction in the show ring, the Welsh Cob is also a good hunter and a marvellous all-round performer in competitive sports.

❚ RIGHT
A quality head, depth through the girth and strong limbs, with an abundance of flat bone, are prerequisites of this sturdy breed.

Welsh Cob was traditionally used for all manner of heavy work on the hill farms, being equally at home in harness and under saddle. It was also formerly much in demand by the army, particularly for pulling guns and other heavy equipment. Possessed of active paces and great stamina, the Welsh Cob is renowned above all for its spectacular trotting action, inherited no doubt from the Norfolk Roadster. Indeed, up until 1918, when stallion licensing was introduced, breeding stock was selected by means of trotting matches. Nowadays, not surprisingly, the breed enjoys notable success in the sport of carriage driving.

Unique among the British Mountain and Moorland breeds, the Cob has no upper height limit, but whatever its size it should retain true pony characteristics – its quality head testifying to its Welsh Mountain Pony ancestry. When crossed with the Thoroughbred (particularly the second cross) the Welsh Cob produces excellent competition horses.

Highland

One of the strongest and heaviest of Britain's Mountain and Moorland breeds, the Highland Pony comes from the Highlands of Scotland and the islands off the west coast. Ponies are believed to have inhabited the region many thousands of years ago. The modern Highland Pony, sure-footed, hardy and long-lived, evolved as a result of various outcrosses, particularly Arab and Clydesdale. The Dukes of Atholl, influential breeders of Highland Ponies for several centuries, almost certainly introduced eastern blood as early as the sixteenth century.

Until fairly recently the breed was divided into two types: a more substantial mainland type, which stood up to 14.2hh,

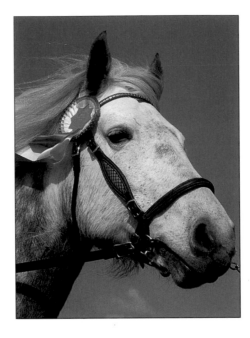

and the lighter, somewhat smaller Western Isles type. Although the Highland Pony Society, founded in 1923, no longer recognizes these distinctions, differences in type can still be discerned to some extent.

BREED DESCRIPTION

Height 13 – 14.2hh.

Colour Various shades of dun, also grey, brown, black and occasionally bay and liver chestnut with silver mane and tail.

Conformation Well-carried head with broad forehead, alert, kindly eyes and wide nostrils; strong, arched neck with clean throat; well laid-back shoulders; compact body with deep chest and well-sprung ribs; powerful hindquarters with strong, well-developed thigh and second thigh; strong limbs with short cannons, flat, hard bone and well-shaped, hard, dark hooves; silky feather, not over-heavy and ending in a prominent tuft at the fetlock; long, silky, flowing mane and tail.

The Highland is a strong, sturdily built pony, a real all-round worker which in its time has carried men to war, been the mount of shepherds, worked in harness, hauled timber, taken deer-stalkers into the hills and carried the shot stags – weighing

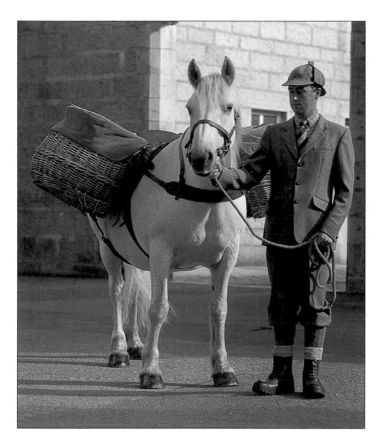

▎ LEFT
The Highland Pony is a willing worker. It is still
used on Scottish estates to carry game panniers and
to cart shot stags.

upwards of 16 stone (224lb/101kg) – back
down. It is much used for pony trekking
and makes a fine general-purpose riding
pony, well able to carry an adult. Pure-
breds can be seen taking part successfully
in a number of competitive sports,
including driving and dressage. Crossed
with the Thoroughbred the Highland
makes an excellent hunter and more than
one successful three-day event horse has
had Highland blood in its veins.

INTERESTING FACTS

One of the most striking features of the
Highland is its colouring, particularly the
various shades of dun: yellow, golden, mouse,
cream and fox (yellow dun is believed to have
been the breed's original colour). Most ponies
show at least one of the characteristics of the
primitive horse, i.e. a dorsal eel-stripe and
zebra markings on the legs. These markings
testify to the antiquity of the breed.

▎ ABOVE
Highland Ponies are noted for the beauty of their
coat colouring – including the whole range of duns
– and for the silky texture of their abundant manes
and tails.

▎ BELOW
Versatility is one of the most valuable
characteristics of the breed, which will haul
timber as easily as it will carry a rider to hounds
or go in harness.

▎ OPPOSITE TOP
The Highland Pony's
head is broad between
the eyes, short from
eyes to muzzle and
well-carried on a
strong, arched neck.
The eyes have a kind
expression.

▎ OPPOSITE
Moulded by its harsh
natural environment,
the breed is strong,
hardy, long lived and
economical to feed. It
is eminently sure-
footed over the most
treacherous terrain.

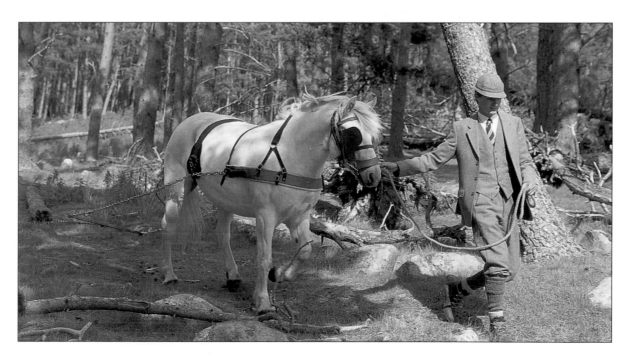

Shetland

Named after the remote group of islands situated to the far north-east of mainland Scotland and in the same northern latitude as south Greenland, the Shetland Pony is the smallest of the British native breeds. Its origins are uncertain but there have certainly been ponies in the Shetlands for many centuries and it may

■ LEFT
The Shetland's profuse growth of mane and tail afford valuable protection from the severe weather of its northern homeland.

BREED DESCRIPTION

Height Not exceeding 40 inches (102cm) at three years or under. Not exceeding 42 inches (107cm) at four years or over.

Colour Any colour except spotted.

Conformation Small, well-carried head with broad forehead, bold, dark, intelligent eyes, small, erect ears and broad muzzle with wide open nostrils; strong, deep body with short back and muscular loins; broad, strong hindquarters; strong limbs, with good, flat bone and short cannons; tough, round, well-shaped feet.

well trace back to far more distant times.

Small of stature, it is nevertheless immensely strong – one of the strongest equine animals, in relation to size, in the world. Wonderfully well adapted to the vagaries of the islands' northern climate and the poor quality grazing, the Shetland is inherently hardy. Its action is free and straight, with a characteristic lift to its joints – the result of centuries of traversing rough, rocky or heather-covered terrain. An integral part of the lives of the

islanders, the ponies have traditionally been used both under saddle and as pack animals, carrying everything from grain to peat for fuel. They were formerly much in demand for coal mining, their small size and great strength making them perfect for work underground. Breeding flourished, though there was little attempt at selective breeding before the middle of the nineteenth century.

The Shetland has also found favour far from its native islands as a children's riding pony. It can be strong-willed but it is intelligent and responds to correct handling. With its active paces and manoeuvrability, it makes a particularly good driving pony and can be seen competing right up to international level.

■ LEFT
Short-legged and stocky, the breed is noted for its great strength in relation to its diminutive size.

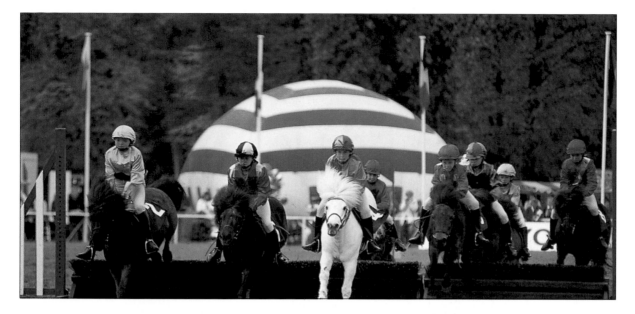

LEFT
Shetlands are very
active little ponies and
take part with great
enthusiasm in Shetland
"Grand Nationals",
which raise money for
charity.

BELOW
In spring the Shetland
begins to shed its thick
winter coat, designed
to keep out extremes
of wet and cold.

ABOVE
Shetland Ponies can be wilful, but in the hands of a
competent child they make good riding ponies.

RIGHT
Centuries of living on rough, rock-strewn terrain
have made the ponies both active and sure-footed.
Their feet are well-shaped and extremely hard.

INTERESTING FACTS

In winter the Shetland Pony grows a double
coat as protection against the inclement
climate of its native home. The coat has
"guard hairs", which shed rain and keep the
pony's skin completely dry, however severe
the weather. The mane and tail are profuse.

Dales

The Dales Pony comes from the Upper Dales (river valleys) of the eastern side of the Pennine Hills in northern England. It shares the same ancestors as its slightly larger neighbour, the Fell Pony, whose traditional home is on the western side of the Pennines. These ponies are believed to be descended from horses of the Roman period, when Friesians were introduced into northern England – this could have been the source of the Dales' predominantly black colouring. In more recent times various outcrosses are said to have been made, Norfolk Roadster among them. Some Welsh Cob blood was used during the nineteenth century and also Clydesdale. Despite the introduction of the latter, the Dales has retained its pony character, as can be seen in its neat head with its small, mobile ears.

The Dales is noted for its tremendously active paces and its great strength in relation to its size. At one time it played a vital part in lead mining, working both under- and overground, carrying loads of lead ore to the sea ports. It was also much

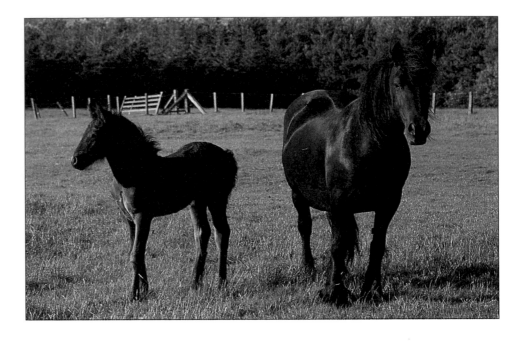

BREED DESCRIPTION

Height Not exceeding 14.2hh.

Colour Predominantly black, also bay, brown and, occasionally, grey.

Conformation Small, neat head, with wide forehead, bright eyes and small, erect ears; well-sloped shoulders; strong, deep body with short back, well-sprung ribs and strong loins; well-developed hindquarters; strong limbs with short straight cannons, good, clean joints and broad, very hard, well-shaped feet; fine, silky feather at the heel.

INTERESTING FACTS

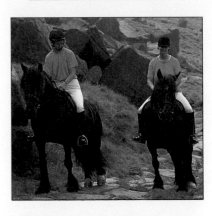

Dales Ponies are inherently sure-footed. Their forebears are said to have been used by the Romans when constructing Hadrian's Wall in the inhospitable tract of country between the mouth of the River Tyne and the marshes of the Solway Firth in northern England.

used by the army. Stamina, courage and a docile temperament, coupled with its great strength and energy make the Dales a first-rate all-round riding and driving pony. It jumps, is intelligent, has a sensible, calm temperament and can carry an adult with ease.

▌ TOP
There have been native ponies on either side of the Pennines and in the Scottish borders for many centuries. They trace back in part to the Scottish Galloway although the Dales' black colouring probably comes from the influence of Friesian blood.

▌ LEFT
The breed is particularly renowned for its strong limbs, good bone and excellent feet.

Fell

Like its relative, the Dales, the Fell Pony is believed to be descended from the Friesian which was brought to northern England during Roman times. Down the centuries it, too, was almost certainly influenced by the now extinct Galloway, the mount of border reivers (raiders, particularly cattle thieves) who needed a strong, fast, sure-footed horse for their nefarious purposes.

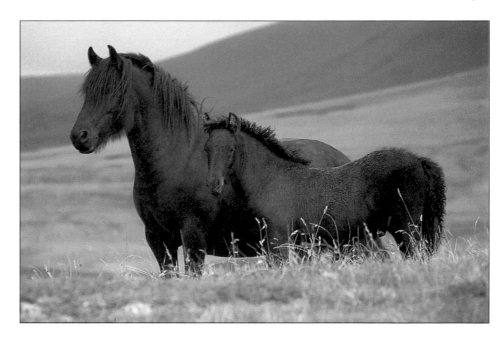

BREED DESCRIPTION

Height Not exceeding 14hh.

Colour Black, brown, bay and grey, preferably with no white markings, though a star or a little white on the foot is allowed.

Conformation Small, well set-on head with broad forehead, bright, prominent eye, small, neat ears, large nostrils and fine throat and jaws; strong neck but not too heavy, giving a good length of rein; good, sloping shoulders; strong, deep body with muscular loins; strong hindquarters with well set-on tail; strong limbs with plenty of good flat bone below the knee and well-formed feet with characteristic blue horn.

INTERESTING FACTS

HRH The Duke of Edinburgh competes in trials with a team of HM The Queen's Fell Ponies. With their lively trot and great stamina they are well suited to the marathon phase, run over a distance of 16 miles .

The Fell has evolved as a somewhat smaller, lighter pony than the Dales (official recognition of a distinction between the two did not come until 1916, when the Dales Pony Improvement Society and the Fell Pony Society were formed). The Fell is, nevertheless, enormously strong and, like the Dales, was used as a pack-pony. During the eighteenth century it transported lead, coal and iron ore to the coast, carrying up to 16 stone (224lb/101kg) at a time in panniers. Some were used in pack-trains to carry produce such as wool as far as London.

The Fell is noted for its good paces, having a fast, active walk and a swift trot. Now that it is no longer in demand for pack work, shepherding and general farm work, it has become a popular all-round pleasure pony. It makes an excellent mount for trekking, goes superbly across country, both under saddle and in harness, and has the paces to do well in pure dressage.

▌ A B O V E
Fell ponies are native to the western side of the Pennines. They are slightly smaller than their near neighbours, the Dales, but have the same inherent toughness and active paces.

▌ B E L O W
The Fell makes a first-class riding pony. These ponies, pictured at a breed performance show, were competing in show jumping and mounted games as well as in show classes.

Connemara

Elegant, hardy, intelligent, possessed of tremendous agility and jumping prowess, the Connemara is arguably the best performance pony in the world. It is Ireland's only indigenous breed; it takes its name from the wild, rocky region on the western seaboard of Ireland where ponies have existed, in one form or another, since ancient times.

How this paragon among ponies developed is unclear. One theory is that it is descended from Barb and Spanish horses introduced into the west of Ireland as early as the sixth century BC, when the Celts overran the whole of Europe. These

■ LEFT
The Connemara's beautiful head possesses great refinement. Grey is the breed's predominant colour.

horses would then have been crossed with the indigenous stock. Also, during subsequent centuries of trade between the west coast of Ireland and the Iberian peninsula it is highly likely that quantities of horses would have been imported. The breed undoubtedly does show signs of Spanish and eastern blood to this day. The suggestion that the Connemara is descended from horses of the Spanish Armada that swam ashore after being shipwrecked in 1588 is nowadays dismissed by most experts as mere fancy!

Arab stallions are known to have been imported by landowners during the middle of the nineteenth century, but it is impossible to say what influence, if any, they had on the Connemara. During the latter part of the century, however, Welsh

BREED DESCRIPTION

Height Not exceeding 14.2hh.

Colour Predominantly grey but also brown, dun, black and occasionally chestnut and roan.

Conformation Short head, often with slightly dished profile, with broad forehead, dark, full eyes, small ears; long, arched neck giving good length of rein; well-sloped shoulders; deep, compact body; strong hindquarters with high-set tail; good strong limbs with short cannons and plenty of bone below the knee; strong, sound feet.

■ RIGHT
Excellent conformation - notably the well-sloped shoulders - make the Connemara a superb riding pony, possessed of strength, free-going movement and superb balance.

Little Model was one of many part-bred Connemaras who have achieved great success in the competitive disciplines. By a Thoroughbred stallion out of a Connemara mare, Little Model, a grey, was originally trained for circus work. The British dressage rider Mrs V.D.S. Williams spent a good deal of time persuading him to "unlearn" various tricks before he could concentrate on Grand Prix work. Together they competed in the 1960 Olympics, finishing in a very creditable eleventh place. The following year they were third in the European Championships – Britain's first placing in a dressage championship. Sadly, because he was such a bad traveller, Little Model never competed abroad again although he enjoyed many successes at home.

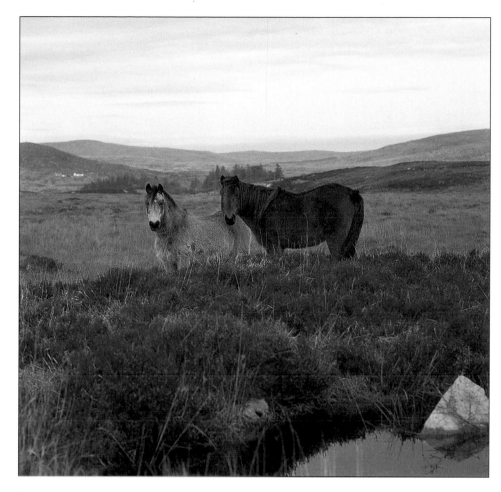

■ ABOVE
Connemaras in their natural habitat of western Ireland.

blood was certainly introduced and did play a part: one of the Welsh stallions, Prince Llewellyn, sired Dynamite out of a native mare. Dynamite in turn sired Cannon Ball (foaled in 1904), who is the first stallion listed in the Connemara Stud Book. Other attempts to "improve" the breed included the use of Thoroughbred, Hackney and Clydesdale blood.

Finally, in 1923, the Connemara Pony Breeders' Society was founded in Galway. It had the backing of the Department of Agriculture and the intention was to improve the breed from within, by seeking out the best type of mare and an appropriate number of similar quality

■ BELOW
Traditional pony power: carting seaweed in Galway.

stallions to use as foundation stock. The result of these efforts is an outstanding, quality pony of fixed type, courageous but sensible, able to excel in virtually all sports, from show jumping and three-day eventing to dressage and driving. When crossed with the Thoroughbred it produces a top-class performance horse.

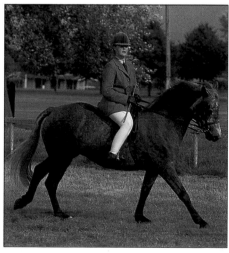

■ ABOVE
As a ridden pony the Connemara cannot be bettered. Spirited but sensible, courageous but kind, it is an ideal mount for children and adults alike.

Fjord

Norway's unusual looking Fjord Pony is believed to have inhabited Norway and probably other parts of Scandinavia since prehistoric times. At a quick glance it is not unlike the Przewalski's Horse (the Asiatic Wild Horse) in appearance, though the head is much less heavy and "primitive", being more pony-like in size and shape. Ponies resembling the Fjord are depicted in Viking art. They can be seen fighting, a pastime which was also popular in Iceland and which may have been engaged in for sport, as a form of performance testing or, probably, a combination of both.

Hundreds if not thousands of years spent in a mountainous habitat have

produced a pony that is perfectly adapted to its environment. Sturdy and muscular, the Fjord has short, strong legs with good joints and hard, sound feet. Down the centuries its inherent sure-footedness, strength, soundness and tremendous stamina have made it an invaluable

helpmate to farmers. Used to coping with severe weather conditions and undaunted by the most rugged terrain, it also proved the perfect pack-pony for use on mountain trails.

Nowadays the Fjord Pony can be found in a number of countries outside Scandinavia, including Germany, Denmark and England. It makes a good general-purpose riding pony and also goes well in harness.

BREED DESCRIPTION

Height 13 – 14hh.

Colour Most shades of dun with a black dorsal eel-stripe and, often, zebra markings on the legs.

Conformation Pony-type head with broad forehead and small ears; muscular neck; strong, deep body; fairly low-set tail; short, strong limbs with good joints, short cannons and plenty of bone; hard, sound feet.

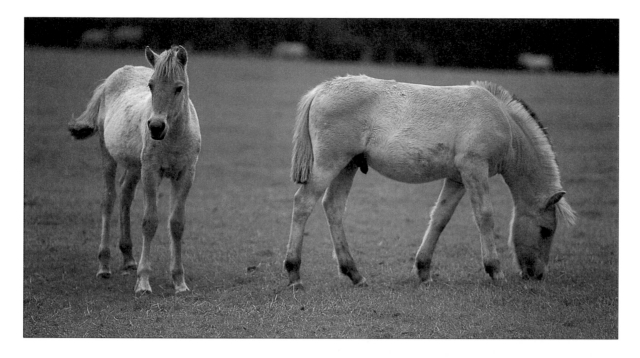

OPPOSITE TOP
The Fjord has a true pony head, with small ears,
large, wide-set eyes and a small muzzle which is
lighter in colour than the rest of the coat.

OPPOSITE
The pony's stocky build testifies to its great
strength. Deep through the girth and with a
particularly muscular neck and strong legs,
it is a great little worker in areas not accessible
to machines.

LEFT
The striking colouring
of the mane and tail,
with their black and
silver hair, is unique to
the Fjord Pony.

RIGHT
Fjords make excellent driving ponies. They have a
kind, willing temperament but are active movers
and, like all mountain breeds, exceptionally sure-
footed.

INTERESTING FACTS

One of the most distinctive features of the
Fjord Pony is its unusual mane and tail
colouring. Both mane and tail have black
hairs in the centre, with silver on the
outside. The stiff mane is traditionally cut in
a curve with the dark inner hair standing
higher than the outer silver hair.

Caspian

In 1965 an exciting discovery was made in northern Iran, in a remote, mountainous region not far from the Caspian Sea. Some three dozen miniature horses, no taller than a small pony but with the outward characteristics of a diminutive horse, were found. Detailed scientific examination revealed that these little horses had certain physical characteristics that did not match those of other horses: an extra full-sized molar on each side of the upper jaw; a scapula that was a different shape from that usually found in equine animals, and a slightly different formation of the three parietal bones in the head.

The Caspian Pony, as it has become known, is believed to be the direct descendant of the earliest equine animals that roamed the region around 3,000 BC. Bones have been excavated in Iran that point to the existence in the area of a very similar small horse at that period, a seal in the British Museum shows King Darius riding in a chariot drawn by horses of

Caspian type, and other artefacts of the period exist depicting similar small horses. It is thought possible that the Caspian is a far-off ancestor of the Arabian.

For many centuries the Caspian was mysteriously "lost". After its re-discovery a careful breeding programme was set up at studs in order to safeguard its future. Caspian Ponies can now be found in a number of European countries as well as Australia, New Zealand and the United States.

BREED DESCRIPTION

Height 10 – 12hh.

Colour Bay, grey and chestnut, with occasional white markings on head and legs.

Conformation Short, fine head with large eyes, vaulted forehead, fine tapering muzzle with large, low-set nostrils and very short ears; graceful neck; sloping shoulders; slim body with straight back and high-set tail; slim limbs but with dense, strong bone and little or no feathering at the fetlock; neat, oval, unusually strong hoofs.

The Caspian is extremely hardy, and possesses great speed and endurance as well as a kind temperament. It has dense bone and exceptionally hard, tough feet, which do not require shoeing. It makes a good riding pony and despite its small size has remarkable jumping ability.

▌ **TOP**
The skin on the Caspian's short, refined head is particularly fine. The ears should be no more than 4½ inches (11.5cm) long.

▌ **ABOVE**
On account of its small size the breed is described as a pony, although it has all the attributes of a miniature horse.

INTERESTING FACTS

Despite its lack of height, the Caspian has wonderful natural action; it can keep up with a horse at walk, trot and canter. Even at this early age the foal shows tremendous length of stride.

Riding Pony

Any pony which can be ridden is, technically, a "riding pony" but the Riding Pony which has been developed in Britain for showing purposes has evolved into a very definite type. It is essentially a child's hack, the equivalent of the adult rider's Thoroughbred show hack. It is not, therefore, surprising that small Thoroughbreds have been used in its development. Together with the Arab, the Thoroughbred was crossed with native ponies, particularly the Welsh and the Dartmoor, to produce ponies of great quality and excellent conformation. The best examples, while resembling the Thoroughbred in miniature, will not have lost the bone and substance of the native ponies and should certainly look like ponies, not small horses.

Since it is by definition a child's mount, the Riding Pony must have a sensible nature and be safe for children to ride; but since it is also a show pony, it must have presence and the long, low, graceful action of the Thoroughbred. The perfect combination of these elements, together with the retention of true pony character, is the challenge faced by all breeders of Riding Ponies. Riding Ponies may be entered in the National Pony Society Stud Book.

BREED DESCRIPTION

Height Show class divisions – up to 12.2hh, 12.2 – 13.2hh and 13.2 – 14.2hh.

Colour Any whole colour; white markings are permissible.

Conformation Fine, quality head, with large, well-spaced eyes and small ears; fairly long neck; good sloping shoulders with clearly defined withers; medium length back, deep through the girth; well-muscled hindquarters with well set-on tail; clean, hard limbs with flat joints, short cannons and well let-down hocks; good, sound feet of equal size; no feather.

INTERESTING FACTS

In the show ring, as well as the height divisions there are classes for ponies ridden side-saddle, for pairs of ponies and for novice ponies. Ponies are judged on their paces, conformation and manners but are not required to jump.

Pony of the Americas

This breed of spotted pony originated in the 1950s, the foundation sire, Black Hand, being the result of a mating between a Shetland pony stallion and an Appaloosa mare. Black Hand was the equivalent of a miniature Appaloosa. Interest in this concept of a spotted pony soon spread and the Pony of the Americas, as it became known, is now a popular all-round riding pony throughout the United States and also in Canada. It has its own breed society and stud book.

The Pony of the Americas stands no more than 13.2hh and must have one of the recognized Appaloosa colourings. It should be well proportioned, with substance, style and refinement – something like a miniature cross between a Quarter Horse and an Arabian. The pony's paces should be smooth and the action straight and free. The Pony of the Americas is a versatile performer. It is shown in Western pleasure and performance classes, as well as under English saddles and in harness. It has a kind nature and makes an ideal all-round riding pony for children.

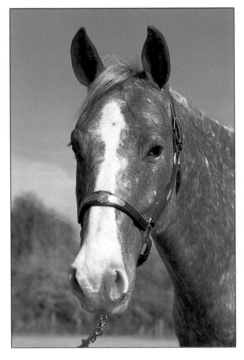

I ABOVE
The head is clean cut and the pony has a kind eye, which reflects its docile, friendly nature.

I BELOW
In overall appearance the Pony of the Americas is not unlike the Quarter Horse, but with more refinement.

INTERESTING FACTS

Leslie Boomhower, of Mason City, Iowa, was responsible for the mating of Shetland to Appaloosa which produced the breed's foundation sire.

BREED DESCRIPTION

Height 11.2–13.2hh.

Colour Normal Appaloosa markings – leopard, snowflake, blanket, frost, marble.

Conformation Clean-cut head, sometimes with slightly dished profile, with large, kind, prominent eyes and medium-sized, alert ears; slightly arched neck; deep, sloping shoulders with prominent withers; round, full-ribbed, heavily muscled body with well-sprung ribs and short back and loins; muscular hindquarters with long, level croup; strong limbs, with good clean joints; wide, well-shaped feet.

American Shetland

Shetland Ponies were first imported into America during the 1880s and quickly became popular. In 1890, when the American Shetland Pony Club was formed, there were over two hundred listed American breeders – Buffalo Bill Cody featuring prominently among them. Today there are large numbers of American Shetlands but, although they retain the name "Shetland", they do not bear a great deal of resemblance to the native "Sheltie" of Britain's Shetland Isles.

The American Shetland is the result of crossing pure-bred Shetlands with Hackney Ponies, with the addition of a little Arab and Thoroughbred blood. In appearance it is more like a Hackney than a British native pony. It is more refined than the true Shetland, being somewhat narrower and longer in the body and with longer, more slender limbs. The head, too, has lost the true pony character. Its high, extravagant action, which testifies to the infusion of Hackney blood, makes the American Shetland a popular harness pony.

BREED DESCRIPTION

Height Up to around 42 inches (103cm).

Colour Any.

Conformation Fairly long head with straight or slightly dished profile; long, graceful neck with pronounced withers; sloping shoulders; short, strong body and hindquarters; fairly long limbs.

▌ LEFT
The American Shetland usually stands a couple of inches (5cm) taller than the true Shetland. The same range of colours occurs as in the original Scottish breed.

▌ ABOVE
Due to the addition of Hackney, Arab and Thoroughbred blood, the American Shetland has lost, in varying degrees, the true native pony character of its British ancestors.

INTERESTING FACTS

The high-stepping action produced through the infusions of Hackney blood, has resulted in a pony well suited to harness classes. As with the American gaited horses, the action is enhanced by means of growing the feet longer than normal. Shetlands compete in classes for singles, pairs and tandems as well as in draught harness and under saddle.

Types

Horses and ponies with unusual or exotic coat colours and patterns have occurred throughout history and have usually been highly prized by man, regardless of their breeding. In recent times registers or stud books have been opened in some countries for the most popular of these colour types – in fact some now qualify for the title "breeds". The term "breed" is used to describe horses who have been bred selectively over a period of time and who have, as a result, developed fixed characteristics. Horses belonging to a particular breed have their pedigrees recorded in a stud book. The term "type" describes a horse bred for a particular purpose, such as hunting. Any number of permutations can be (and are) used to produce a horse suitable for riding to hounds and hunters cannot therefore be described as a breed. Horse and pony types, although few in number compared with the established breeds, nevertheless have an important role to play in the world of leisure riding.

Palomino

Throughout history man has prized horses with golden-coloured coats. Horse's with this striking colouring are depicted in works of art, often dating back many centuries, from Asia, Japan and a number of European countries. Golden horses are referred to in Homer's *The Iliad* and in Norse legend. In Spain Queen Isabella,

BREED DESCRIPTION

Height The registry of the Palomino Horse Breeders of America (PHBA) admits horses standing between 14 and 17hh.

Colour Body colour of a newly minted gold coin, with variations from light to dark. The skin is usually grey, black, brown or motley, without underlying pink skin or spots except on the face or legs. Black, hazel or brown eyes. White mane and tail with not more than 15 per cent dark, sorrel or chestnut hairs. Dorsal stripe and zebra stripes not permitted.

Conformation To be eligible for registration with the PHBA a Palomino must show refinement of head, bone, and general structure appropriate to the breeds recognized by the PHBA and be suitable for carrying Western or English equipment. It must show no pony or draught horse characteristics.

sponsor of Columbus, encouraged their breeding, as a result of which they are often referred to in that country as "Isabellas".

There are various suggestions as to the derivation of the word Palomino, now used to describe golden horses. The most likely is that it comes from Juan de Palomino, who received a horse of this colouring from Cortès. Other theories are that it comes from the name of a Spanish grape or from the word *paloma*, meaning dove. Palomino colouring features in a number of breeds, therefore the term Palomino refers to a colour type, not a specific breed.

▮ **PREVIOUS PAGE OPPOSITE**
A Paint horse with totiano markings.

▮ **PREVIOUS PAGE**
Typical Palomino colouring.

▮ **ABOVE**
Palominos always have a white mane and tail. For registration purposes the head must be of true riding horse proportions, with no pony or draught characteristics.

▮ **LEFT**
This Quarter Horse is an admirable example of the requirements of the PHBA, which call for a body colour "of a newly minted gold coin".

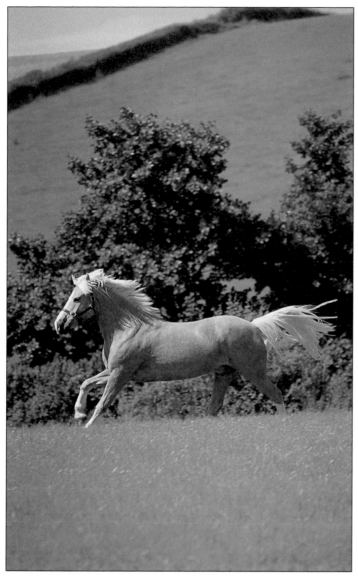

❚ RIGHT
Palominos, like this
English pony, are
found all over the
world and do not have
to be of any particular
breed to qualify for
registration as such.

❚ BELOW RIGHT
Golden-coloured
horses have been
prized throughout
history and in all parts
of the world. These
two were
photographed in
France.

INTERESTING FACTS

Palomino colouring occurs in a number of
breeds. In the United States they include the
Morgan Horse, the Quarter Horse, the
Saddlebred and the Tennessee Walking Horse,
while in Britain there are some striking looking
Palominos among the Welsh Ponies and Cobs.

cremello. Cross a Palomino with a sorrel
and the chances are still only 50 per cent –
and any Palomino colouring that is
achieved may be too poor to be eligible for
most Palomino societies. Cross a Palomino
with any other colour and the chances of
producing a Palomino foal diminish.

Despite the uncertainties involved in
breeding for colour, Palomino horses
retain their age-old appeal. Being good all-
round riding horses – conformation
should never be sacrificed for the sake of
colour – they can be seen taking part in all
kinds of activities, from cutting horse
events to trail riding.

They may occur in many parts of the
world, but Palomino horses are particularly
associated with North America, where they
were introduced by the Spanish
Conquistadores. The origin of this type of
colouring is uncertain but it is thought to
have come from the Arab – though it is not
found nowadays in the pure-bred Arabian
horse. One of the intriguing, if frustrating,
aspects of Palomino horses is that they do
not "breed true", in other words there is no
sure-fire way of ensuring Palomino
colouring in a foal. It is all a question of
genetics and the genetics of equine coat
colouring is a complicated subject,
involving dominant and recessive genes.
Put simply, mate a Palomino to a Palomino
and there is only a 50 per cent chance of a
Palomino foal. There is a 25 per cent
chance that the foal will be sorrel (a bright
chestnut) and the same chance of the
result being a pseudo-albino, known as a

Appaloosa

The spotted coat colouring of the American Appaloosa traces back to stock imported by the Spanish Conquistadores. Spotted horses became particularly prized by the Nez Percé Indian tribe who lived in the region that is now northern Idaho, north-east Oregon and south-east Washington. The word Appaloosa is derived from Palouse country, an area named after the Palouse river.

The Nez Percé are said to be the first Indian tribe to have practised systematic breeding of horses. Following the defeat of the Indians by the US army during the latter half of the nineteenth century, the horses which escaped slaughter became

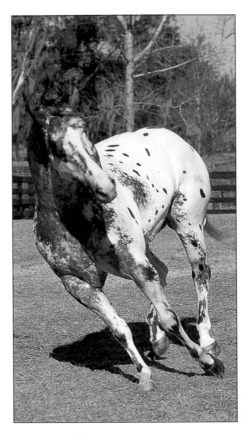

LEFT
The eye-catching markings of the American Appaloosa are derived from Spanish stock imported by the Conquistadores.

BELOW LEFT
The Appaloosa is a compact, muscular stamp of horse. The sparse mane and tail hair are characteristic of the breed.

scattered. It was not until the 1920s that efforts were made to re-establish the Appaloosa horse, using the descendants of those which survived as a basis. In 1938 the Appaloosa Horse Club was founded in Oregon. Its objectives were to collect records and historical data relating to the origin of the Appaloosa, to preserve, improve and standardize the breed and to set up a register for approved animals.

The re-establishment of the Appaloosa has been a great success and today the breed is widely used in all types of Western riding, for endurance riding and in the show ring in both hunter and jumper classes. Appaloosas are mainly associated

BREED DESCRIPTION

Height Around 14.2 – 15.2hh.

Colour Spotted. The skin is mottled (especially noticeable around the nostrils and genitalia).

Conformation The Appaloosa is a compact stamp of horse with a well-shaped neck, short, strong back, powerful hindquarters and strong limbs with extremely good, hard feet.

INTERESTING FACTS

In America gaited spotted horses, that is those who show the ability to perform an intermediate gait other than the trot (such as the rack, foxtrot, running walk or pace) are termed Walkaloosas. To qualify for registration with the Walkaloosa Horse Association, which was founded in 1983, a horse must meet one of three criteria: either be the progeny of a registered Walkaloosa stallion and mare, or show Appaloosa colouring and demonstrate an intermediate gait other than trot, or be the product of verifiable Appaloosa (colour) and Paso, Foxtrotter or Tennessee Walker blood. The Walkaloosa's colouring is typical of that found in the Appaloosa, including white sclera round the eyes. Coat patterns include, but are not limited to, leopard, blanket and snowflake. The Walkaloosa, like the Appaloosa, is noted for its kind, sensible nature and makes an outstanding pleasure and trail horse.

■ LEFT
This horse and rider, decked out in traditional style, recall the time when spotted horses were the preferred mounts of the Nez Percé Indians.

■ FAR LEFT
Spotted horses are popular in many countries outside the United States. There is a thriving Appaloosa society in Britain – this horse was photographed at the Royal Windsor Horse Show.

with the United States but they are also found in many other countries.

There are five main Appaloosa coat patterns: leopard – white colouring over the loins and hips with dark, round or egg-shaped spots; snowflake – dark spots all over a white body but usually dominant over the hips; blanket – white area over the hips without dark spots in the white; marble – mottled all over the body; frost – white specks with a dark background. Other distinguishing features include white sclera round the eyes and, often, vertical black and white stripes on the hooves. The mane and tail tend to be quite sparse.

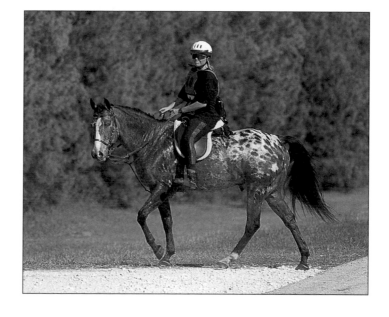

■ LEFT
Noted for its strong limbs and the excellence of its feet, the Appaloosa makes a good endurance riding horse.

Paint Horse

Horses with broken coloured coats (also known as piebalds and skewbalds) are found all over the world, though they are particularly associated with the North American Indian.

In America a horse with this type of colouring may be registered either as a Paint Horse or as a Pinto, depending on the horse meeting certain criteria. The American Paint Horse Association was founded in 1962 to provide a register for horses with individual, colourful patterns of contrasting light and dark hair and skin, and distinctive stock-type conformation. To qualify for registration with the APHA

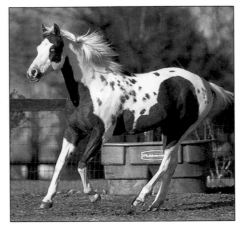

horses must be bred from registered American Paint Horses, registered American Quarter Horses or registered Thoroughbreds and must meet a minimum colour requirement. A horse with a predominantly solid-coloured coat must have a definite "natural" Paint marking, which is defined as an area of solid white hair with some underlying,

unpigmented skin. A horse with a mainly white hair coat must have a contrasting area of colour with some underlying, pigmented skin. The contrasting areas should be visible at the time the foal is born and at the time of registration.

The APHA maintains two registries, the Regular and the Breeding Stock. To be eligible for inclusion in the Regular

BREED DESCRIPTION

Because horses of various breeds are eligible for registration as Paint Horses, there is accordingly a degree of variation in the height and overall size. However, all American Paint Horses have distinct stock-type conformation. This may be generally defined as an animal whose bone and muscle construction make it highly adaptable to ranch work. It will be both versatile and athletic.

▮ TOP LEFT
This Paint horse has tobiano markings: dark colouring on the flanks, a "shield" down the neck and chest and white legs.

▮ OPPOSITE
Paint horses have always been associated with the American West. The horse on the left is an overo with a bald face.

▮ LEFT
The characteristic shape and build of the Paint horse is that of the stock horse: good overall riding horse conformation and a sturdy, compact appearance.

▌BELOW
Like the Paint horse, the Pinto has overo or tobiano
colouring (this horse is a tobiano). For registration
purposes, Pintos are divided by conformation type.

Registry the foal must have at least one "natural" Paint marking which is a minimum of 2 inches (5cm) in diameter. If a horse does not meet the required colour requirement but meets the other registration requirements (for example a solid-coloured foal resulting from a mating between two registered American Paint Horses), it may be entered in the Breeding Stock Registry.

The spectrum of coat colours in the Paint Horse encompasses all of the tones known in the horse world. The patterns range from almost total colour with a minimal amount of white to almost total white with minimal colour. The patterns are distinguished by the location of colour on the horse, the two major ones being overo and tobiano.

Overo horses have the following characteristics: the white usually will not cross the back of the horse between the withers and the tail; generally at least one and often all four legs will be dark; generally the white is irregular, rather scattered or splashy, and is often referred to as calico; head markings are often bald-

faced, apron-faced or bonnet-faced; the tail is usually one colour.

Tobiano horses have the following characteristics: the dark colour will usually cover one or both flanks; generally all four legs will be white, at least below the hocks and knees; generally the spots are regular and distinct as ovals or round patterns which extend down over the neck and chest, giving the appearance of a shield; head markings are like those of a solid-coloured horse – solid colour or with a blaze, stripe, star or snip; the tail usually displays two colours.

Horses with overo and tobiano characteristics are called toveros.

Knabstrup

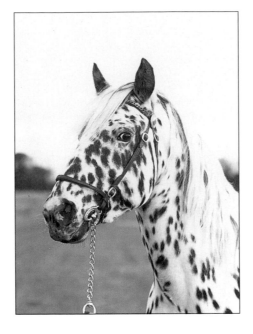

Spotted horses have been known – and have often been highly prized – since ancient times. They can be seen in early Chinese art and there were spotted strains of the Noriker (Austria's old-established light draught breed) and the Spanish horses which were so influential in the development of many of the world's modern breeds. Denmark's once-famous Knabstrup is of Spanish ancestry and dates back to the time of the Napoleonic Wars. At that time a spotted mare named Flaebehoppen was acquired by a butcher called Flaebe (hence her name). Flaebehoppen, an exceptionally fast mare possessed of great endurance, was bred by her next owner, Judge Lunn, to Frederiksborg horses and founded a line of spotted horses. Named the Knabstrup, after Lunn's estate, this strain was rather less substantial than the Frederiksborg but

BREED DESCRIPTION

Height Around 15.2 – 16hh.

Colour Mainly white, with brown or black spots of varying size over the body, head and legs.

Conformation Variable, but the best examples have reasonably good overall conformation, with a kind, intelligent head. The mane and tail are usually sparse, as in the majority of spotted horses.

INTERESTING FACTS

The breed's remarkable talents as a circus horse were demonstrated in America not so long ago when a centre-ring attraction consisted of a large Bengal tiger riding a Knabstrup horse. The horse wore protective harness – in case the big cat slipped and decided to hang on with his claws!

was tough and sound and, because of its attractive markings, became popular as a circus horse. Subsequent crossings back to the Frederiksborg reduced the number of pure-bred Knabstrup horses but examples of the breed are still to be found, though not in anywhere near the numbers of the American Appaloosa.

■ TOP LEFT
The mottled skin colouring of the lips and muzzle, so typical of all spotted horses, can be clearly seen on this Knabstrup.

■ LEFT
The characteristic white body hair with all-over dark spots, together with its intelligent, kind nature, made the Knabstrup a popular circus horse.

Spotted Pony

Spotted Ponies are known to have existed in Britain, and especially in Wales and the West Country, for many centuries. The Romans are said to have brought spotted horses into the country and some of the ancestors of today's Spotted Ponies would have been imported Spanish horses. The creation of a breed society for these striking looking animals is, however, of very recent origin. A British register for spotted horses and ponies was created in 1947 and then in 1976 the organizing society was split, with ponies up to 14.2hh coming under the aegis of the British Spotted Pony Society and larger animals being entered in the British Appaloosa registers.

To qualify for registration ponies must display some of the following features: white sclera round the eye; mottled skin – this part-dark, part-pink skin is usually most evident around the genitals, lips, muzzle, eyes and inside the ears; and striped hooves. If ponies are of solid colour but have proven spotted breeding,

INTERESTING FACTS

As with all colour types, breeding for spots is a question of genetics. Some ponies which have spotted coats when young may lose their spots as they grow older. They are known as "faders". Fading is caused by the dominant grey gene. Raised spots, that is ones that stand out above the rest of the pony's coat, rarely fade. The colour of the foal's coat cannot be used as a guide to the adult pony's colouring, since the colour often changes with the first change of coat.

BREED DESCRIPTION

Height Not exceeding 14.2hh.

Colour Leopard (spots of any colour on white or light background); few spot leopard (white base coat with few spots); snowflake (white spots on dark base coat); blanket (area of white over hips and hindquarters, with or without spots, any base colour).

Conformation Quality pony head with big, bold eyes set well apart, small, neat, well-placed ears, prominent, open nostrils and clean, well-defined throat; good length of neck, moderately lean in mares, inclined to be more cresty in stallions (slightly heavier neck allowed in cob type); good, strong, sloping shoulders, well laid back, with well-defined withers; strong, muscular body with deep girth and well-sprung ribs; lengthy, strong, well-muscled hindquarters with well set-on tail (slightly finer hindquarters in riding type); good limbs, with long, strong forearms, well-developed knee, well let-down hocks, short cannons; well-shaped, dense hooves.

they are eligible for entry in a separate register but they should preferably show some breed characteristics. Piebald and skewbald ponies are not eligible, nor are their progeny.

Spotted Ponies may be of small, riding or cob type, but all should show true pony character and must have bone, substance and active paces. They make good all-round performance ponies, both under saddle and in harness, and there is growing interest in ridden and in-hand show classes. British Spotted Ponies have been exported to Australia, North America and several European countries, including France, Germany and Holland. Indeed, the demand from overseas has led to so many good mares and stallions being exported that the breed society has now introduced performance and sire-rating awards in order to encourage breeders to keep more of the best stock at home.

▌ TOP LEFT
The British Spotted Pony has the large, expressive eyes, neat, mobile ears and open nostrils that are characteristic of all good types of pony.

▌ LEFT
Versatile and strong, the British Spotted Pony makes a good all-round riding pony and has also been used with great success in four-in-hand driving.

Hunter

As its name implies, a hunter is a horse used for riding to hounds. It is a type, not a breed, and there is no fixed "recipe" for producing a hunter. It is, however, generally accepted that the finest hunters are bred in Ireland, Britain and, to some extent, the United States.

The type of horse required for hunting varies according to the nature of the country hunted – a big, quality Thoroughbred type may be perfect for galloping and jumping over the grassland of the English "shires", but will be less than ideal for areas of heavy plough or trappy hill country, where boldness and speed are less important than steadiness and sure-footedness. Whatever the exact type of horse required, however, a hunter must have correct conformation, without which he is unlikely to stand up to the

hard work required of him. He must be well balanced and give a comfortable ride. He needs to be agile and fearless but also well mannered and controllable. He must have the necessary speed to keep up with hounds and the stamina to see him through a long day of physical exertion, often twice a week during the hunting season. He must also have jumping ability,

the exact degree depending on the type of country hunted.

The Irish hunter is often produced by crossing the Thoroughbred with the Irish Draught, while many of the best British hunters have an element of native pony blood, again laced with Thoroughbred. There is no fixed height and in hunter showing classes in Britain and Ireland the horses are divided according to their weight-carrying ability.

BREED DESCRIPTION

Height From 14.2hh upwards.

Colour Any.

Conformation Well set-on head and neck, giving good length of rein; well-sloped shoulders; strong, shortish back with well-sprung ribs and great depth through the girth; strong loins; powerful hindquarters; strong limbs with large joints and plenty of bone; strong, well-shaped feet.

▌ **ABOVE LEFT**
In the show hunter, the judge is looking for as near perfect conformation as possible. The horse must also give a good ride and be well mannered.

▌ **LEFT**
Depth through the girth is essential to allow for expansion of the lungs. Well-sloped shoulders ensure free-going action. The horse's weight-carrying ability is determined by its overall build and the amount of bone (measured round the cannon, below the knee).

Cob

The cob is a short-legged "stuffy" type of small horse, stocky in appearance and capable of carrying a heavyweight rider. Its kind, unflappable, willing nature and impeccable manners, coupled with its weight-carrying ability, make it an ideal mount for a heavyweight elderly rider – or indeed for anyone who is not particularly athletic.

As with the hunter, there is no set formula for breeding a cob. Many of the best are produced by chance, although Irish Draught blood is often used with great success, particularly when mixed with Thoroughbred. The cob's sturdy, muscular proportions are not designed for great speed, but it should none the less have active paces and be able to gallop and to jump well.

At one time the cob was used as an all-purpose horse, performing equally well in harness and under saddle. Nowadays it is most often seen as a riding horse – the best make excellent hunters.

Under British Show Hack and Cob Association

In the show ring cobs are judged like hunters and are expected to show that they can gallop. The judge rides each exhibit in turn to assess the quality of ride they give.

rules, cobs are exhibited in two weight classes: as lightweights, capable of carrying up to 14 stone (196lb/89kg) and as heavyweights, capable of carrying over 14 stone. There are also working cob classes, in which the horses must jump a working hunter-type course of fences.

The cob's mane is traditionally hogged (cut short). It used to be the custom to dock the tail of cobs but this cruel practice was made illegal in Britain under the Docking and Nicking Act, 1948.

▌ **ABOVE RIGHT**
Good conformation ensures that the cob possesses tremendous freedom of movement despite its chunky proportions.

▌ **RIGHT**
The overall impression of this most workmanlike of horses should be one of intelligence, calmness and reliability.

TYPE DESCRIPTION

Height Up to about 15.3hh (in show classes not over 15.1hh).

Colour Any.

Conformation Intelligent-looking head, with no suggestion of coarseness; fairly short, arched neck; strong, sloping shoulders; broad, deep body with short back and powerful loins; strong, well-muscled hindquarters; short, strong limbs with plenty of bone; broad, open feet.

Hack

In Britain the hack is a supremely elegant, refined type of show horse – although the word "hack" is also used to describe any horse suitable for general riding purposes (as opposed to competitive sports, such as eventing or hunting).

The term hack goes back to the days before the motorization of transport, when "park hacks" were used by the most fashionable people of the day for leisure riding, notably in London's Rotten Row, in Hyde Park. In appearance and manners the park hack was impeccable, thus complementing its elegant, well turned-out rider. In the hunting world riders formerly made use of the "covert hack", a quality horse with less substance than a hunter, to take them to the meet – their grooms having ridden the hunters on beforehand at a leisurely pace to conserve their energy for the day ahead.

❚ A B O V E
Gaiety and lightness of movement are essential attributes of the show hack.

Today's show hack is nearer to the park hack and is usually Thoroughbred, or near Thoroughbred. It is judged on conformation, presence, action, training, ride and manners – it should give a comfortable ride and its manners should be faultless. During judging, horses are usually required to give a solo show, designed to demonstrate the horse's correct training and obedience. It should include walk, trot and canter on both reins and a good halt, with the horse standing still on a loose rein.

TYPE DESCRIPTION

Height 14.2 – 15.3hh.

Colour Any solid colour.

Conformation Small, quality head; elegant neck; well-sloped shoulders with prominent withers; strong body with deep girth and well-sprung ribs; well-rounded hindquarters; good, sound limbs with at least 8 inches (20cm) of bone; good, sound feet.

INTERESTING FACTS

Hacks are shown in two height classes: small hack, for horses exceeding 14.2hh but not exceeding 15hh, and large hack, for horses exceeding 15hh but not exceeding 15.3hh. There are also classes for ladies' hacks (14.2 – 15.3hh) in which horses are shown under side-saddle.

❚ L E F T
The hack has the overall refinement of the Thoroughbred. It must give a smooth, comfortable ride and have perfect manners.

Polo Pony

The ancient game of polo is believed to have originated in Persia some 2,500 years ago. It was subsequently played in India, the Far East and Tibet, reaching the western world – England and then North and South America – during the nineteenth century. Any pony used in the game is technically a polo pony but the modern polo pony has evolved as a definite type. Many of the best animals are bred in Argentina or at least are descended from Argentinian stock.

By the beginning of the twentieth century the sport was well established in Argentina, where breeders produced suitable mounts by crossing their Criollo horses with imported Welsh ponies. After the 14.2hh height limit for polo ponies was abolished in 1919 the Argentinians began introducing English Thoroughbred blood, which produced animals of greater quality and with more speed.

The polo pony must be capable of short bursts of speed but does not require the long stride of a racehorse. Far more important is a smooth action, which makes the rider's job of hitting the ball easier, the ability to accelerate and decelerate quickly, and to make fast turns. The essential qualities of the polo pony are courage, stamina and natural balance.

▌ RIGHT
Whatever their height, polo ponies are always referred to as "ponies", not horses.

INTERESTING FACTS

Between the two World Wars some of the best polo players were to be found in India, where the game was popular both with members of the native aristocracy and in the Indian army. The game there was immortalized by Rudyard Kipling (1865–1936) in *The Maltese Cat*, the story of an inter-regimental match seen through the eyes of the equine participants. A flea-bitten grey, brilliantly quick on his feet, "The Cat" knows more about "playing the game" than most humans!

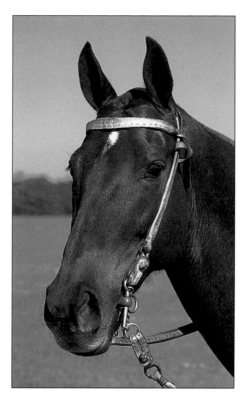

▌ FOLLOWING PAGE
Mares and foals at grass in Kentucky.

▌ LEFT
A typically intelligent looking Argentinian polo pony. It is customary to hog the mane to prevent the hair obstructing the player's stick.

TYPE DESCRIPTION

Height Around 15.1hh.

Colour Any.

Conformation Variable, the chief requirements being: fairly long, well-muscled neck; sloping shoulders with well-defined withers; strong, deep body with fairly short back and well-sprung ribs; well-rounded, muscular hindquarters; strong limbs with short cannons, good joints and plenty of bone; well-shaped, round feet.

Horse and
Pony Care

Buying a Horse

Everyone who takes part in sport on a regular basis reaches the stage when they want their own equipment. Whether it is a tennis racquet, a fencing foil, a pair of skis or a yacht, owning rather than hiring makes life easier on two counts: the equipment will be available whenever it is required and, most importantly, the owner's performance will almost certainly improve because that equipment will have been selected with their skills and limitations in mind. Riders, however, are faced with a problem not encountered by other sportsmen: their most important piece of equipment is not a man-made object which, to varying degrees, can be tailored to fit individual needs. The horse is a living creature, with a mind, will and personality of his own. He is an expensive animal both to buy and to keep. Choosing the right one is not always easy; choosing the wrong one can be disastrous, both for an owner's bank balance and for his or her confidence. The prospective horse owner should proceed with caution and the rewards will be great.

Choosing the Right Horse

Before you buy a horse make an honest assessment of your riding ability, bearing in mind that most people tend to over-estimate their skill. Talented, experienced riders get the best from all sorts of horses, even those with difficult temperaments. They can school and bring on the young horse, improve the poorly educated older one and ensure that the well-trained performer is used to the best effect. A novice rider, who has only just mastered the basics of horsemanship, can do none of these things and should choose a mount accordingly. The novice needs a correctly schooled, well-mannered mount with a kind disposition, one who will look after his rider. The term "schoolmaster" is aptly used to describe these equine paragons.

For the majority of people cost is one of the most important factors and the purchase price will be determined by a number of things: the type, size and conformation of the horse or pony; its age; its temperament and manners; its performance capabilities (either proven or potential) and its level of schooling.

■ PREVIOUS PAGE OPPOSITE
A Dartmoor pony: a suitable ride for a child.
■ PREVIOUS PAGE
A Karbardin horse: ideal for endurance riding.
■ LEFT
With the right horse, the experience of ownership will be enjoyable and rewarding for both horse and rider.

Generally speaking, an unbroken two- or three-year-old will be cheaper than a four- or five-year-old which has already received some schooling; after that the horse gradually increases in value until it reaches the age of about ten. Once into its teens, it will tend to decrease in value.

Apart from price, your choice of horse or pony will be determined by your size and weight; your riding ability; your stabling/grazing facilities; the amount of

■ RIGHT
The majority of warmbloods, specifically developed as sports horses, make fine show jumpers. This horse is a Holstein.

■ BELOW
The larger British native ponies, like this Highland, are suitable for adult riders as well as children. They are economical to keep.

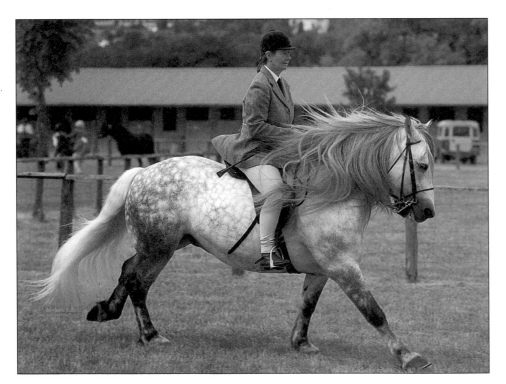

time you have to look after it, and the use to which you intend to put it. For example, there is no point in spending a lot of money on a flighty Thoroughbred if you are a nervous rider who wants to do no more than go for quiet hacks; similarly, a pure-bred Arab is not going to take you to the top in the show-jumping world. As to size, much depends on your own build – someone with long legs will certainly be more comfortable on a big horse than someone with short legs and vice versa, and it is usually easier to ride well if you are neither under- nor over-horsed. Temperament and manners are a vital consideration, too. Nervous riders need placid (though not lazy) mounts if they are not to be frightened and put off riding altogether, while a bolder rider will be able to cope with, and enjoy, a more spirited ride.

If quiet hacks out are your aim, make sure you
don't choose the horse who is too spirited.

█ RIGHT
For endurance riding,
choose a horse with
proven stamina. Arabs
and part-bred Arabs
are particularly suited
to the higher levels of
this sport.

█ BOTTOM
Experienced riders
will be able to school
young horses, but
novice riders should
learn on a more
experienced horse.

Unless you are planning to become
involved in an activity which requires a
specific breed – such as a particular
category of showing – you will have a wide
variety of breeds and types to choose from.
Always bear in mind, however, your
intended use for the horse: for endurance
riding he will need great stamina; for
eventing, stamina plus speed; for dressage,
excellent movement. While stallions often
excel in the last named discipline and are
increasingly seen in other types of equine
competition as well, they do require more
expert handling than geldings and mares,
and are not suitable for the novice horse
owner. Mares can be more moody and
take rather more understanding than
geldings (very often, though, a good
competition mare is very good indeed).
They do, of course, come into season
regularly during the summer months and
this can be a problem.

If you have good stabling and grazing
facilities, you can keep any type or breed
without a problem. Lack of stabling will
tend to determine what you can or cannot
buy, particularly if you live in a region
where the winters are cold and wet and/or
the summers excessively hot. A British

native pony will do perfectly well living out
all year round, provided supplementary
feed is given in winter, as necessary. A
thin-skinned Thoroughbred, on the other
hand, may not thrive unless he has the
shelter of a stable, at least at night. If you
wish to keep your horse at peak fitness for
competition work or hunting, you will
certainly need the use of a stable.

Then there is the question of how
much time you can devote to looking after
your horse. If you have a full-time job, and
limited time for weekday exercising, life
will be easier for you and your horse if he
can live out or at least be turned out
during the day.

If you are not planning to do a lot of
strenuous competition work, then age
need not be too much of a factor, though
of course the older the animal the more
work he is likely to have done and the
more wear and tear there will have been
on his legs and body by the time you buy
him. However, for general riding purposes
horses and ponies often go on well into
their late teens and even early twenties. A
young horse will, of course, have many
more useful years ahead of him and will
be easier to sell on for a good price.
However, young horses are not suitable
for the novice rider, who will be unable to
give them the necessary schooling.

Where to Buy

There are various ways to buy a horse. These include at a public sale, through a dealer, from a private vendor advertising in the equestrian or local press, or perhaps from the riding school where you have been taking lessons.

The novice rider is generally advised not to buy at a public sale. The problem is not that all sales are conducted by less than reputable people – that is certainly not the case – but that everything takes place so quickly and there may not be sufficient opportunity for the purchaser to ride the horse. Buying in this way calls for an expert, practised eye and it is incumbent upon the purchaser to be observant. For instance, if a horse offered for sale has an obvious physical defect, the onus is on the purchaser to see it – a subsequent plea of ignorance will not be accepted. On the other hand the horse must correspond to its description – a horse described as a show jumper must be able to jump – and the buyer is entitled to return it if this proves not to be the case (or, if necessary, to sue for damages).

Dealers are businessmen with a reputation to maintain and are unlikely to try to sell you a bad lot. Your local riding school may be able to put you in touch with one or, failing that, you may see them

LEFT
There are plenty of horses available from private vendors. Be sure to find out as much as possible about the horse.

advertising in the equestrian press. The advantages of buying through a dealer are that you will almost certainly have the choice of several horses and there should be plenty of opportunity to see them being handled and to ride them yourself. Some dealers may also allow you to try the horse at home and, if you have a horse to sell, may offer part-exchange terms.

Buying from a private vendor – and there are always a great many advertising in the equestrian and farming press as well as in local newspapers – may seem the simplest way of acquiring a horse but it is not necessarily the safest. Here the rule is *caveat emptor* (let the buyer beware), a common law maxim warning you that you cannot claim that your purchase is defective if you have not obtained express guarantees from the vendor. Many of the horses and ponies described in the "For Sale" columns are up for sale for perfectly genuine reasons but others may not be. It

is easy to compose an advertisement praising their good points but omitting their shortcomings. Just because a horse is good to box and shoe does not mean that he is quiet to clip or sensible in traffic. The brilliant jumper may refuse to go into a horsebox or trailer. The otherwise perfect equine specimen may, when you get him home, persist in jumping out of his paddock, refuse to be caught, or chew his stable, his rugs, his bandages – or all three. Often it is not so much what the advertisement does say but what it omits to say, so you must be prepared to ask the right questions.

If you have been attending a good riding school, the proprietor should be able to advise on the purchase of a horse or pony and may well have one on the premises which would suit you. The advantage here is that the instructor will have a good knowledge of your skills and limitations as a rider.

LEFT
Buying horses from sales is best left to the experts because everything happens so quickly.

Trying a Horse

■ **BELOW**
When trying a horse, ride him at different paces
and have a jump if you wish.

When you learn of a horse which you think may suit your purpose, the first step is to make an appointment to see it and try it. Always take a more knowledgeable person along with you both to offer expert advice and to act as a witness to any sale. If you have no one who will do this as a friend, it is worth paying for an expert opinion.

Explain to the vendor exactly what you want to use the horse for and ask specific questions: is the horse good to box, clip, shoe, catch, in traffic, etc. Ask to see the horse led up outside and pay close attention to how he behaves while he is having his rugs removed and his bridle put on. Note the bit which is being used. Cast an eye around the inside of the stable and the door for signs of kick marks or chewing. It may be that this is not the horse's usual box but if it is, such signs could indicate a behavioural problem. Ask to see the horse stood up outside and view him from both sides to assess his conformation before having him walked and trotted up. Make sure that he is trotted up on a loose rein both away from you and towards you (leading a horse on a short rein can help to cover up defective action).

Before you ride him, watch the vendor put him through his paces to see how he goes with a familiar rider. Then ask your expert adviser to try him. If the vendor failed to ask the horse to do certain things, such as strike off on a particular leg at canter, it may be that there is a problem, and your adviser (who should have noticed even if you have not) can look into the matter. Finally, ride the horse yourself. Does he feel right for you: not too big, not too wide, not too narrow? Is there a good length of rein? Put him through his paces, have a jump if you wish, take him out on the road to make sure he is safe in traffic and generally try to get the feel of him.

It is not easy in a relatively short time to assess whether this is the horse you really

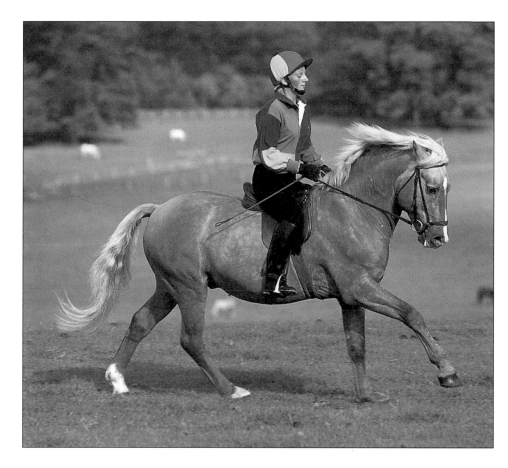

want to have on a long-term basis, so if possible arrange to have him at home on trial, say for a week. This will enable you to get to know his character, to ride him in more relaxed circumstances and also to get to know more about his general behaviour: is he well mannered in the stable, is he good in the company of other horses, will he willingly go away from other horses, is he safe in the company of dogs and in all traffic (not just cars) and so on. However well he suits you from the riding point of view, it is important that you should actually like him, too.

If you do decide to have a horse on trial, make sure that the arrangements are agreed and set down in writing – you will be responsible for feed, vet's bills and so on and will be liable for negligence.

Horses sold at public sales usually come with a warranty or warranties. A warranty is a statement of fact made before or during

a transaction – for example a horse may be "warranted sound". Privately sold horses do not always come with a warranty and if you ask the vendor for one and he or she declines, then you may have grounds for suspicion (on the other hand, in these days of increasing litigation, the vendor may simply be being extra cautious). When in doubt, consult your expert equestrian adviser and, if necessary, a solicitor. The law does give some protection to buyers of horses, as in the case of other merchandise, the big difference being that the horse is a living creature and therefore far less predictable than, say, a television or a refrigerator or a motor car.

When you do find the horse of your dreams and decide to purchase, buy him "subject to a veterinary certificate" and ask your own veterinary surgeon (not the vendor's) to carry out the inspection.

Vetting

If possible, you should be present when your veterinary surgeon carries out his examination of your proposed purchase so that he can discuss the horse with you.

The examination will begin with a preliminary visual inspection. The vet can deduce a good deal from the general attitude of the horse when approached: his stance might show signs of lameness; the condition of his stable could indicate behavioural problems such as box-walking (constant pacing round and round the stable), assuming that the vendor has not switched the horse to another box to hide the evidence; his head carriage can indicate problems of balance or vision; how he reacts to being handled will be indicative of his temperament.

The vet will take in the horse's general state of health, noting any discharges from the nose or eyes, the condition of the skin; and the presence of lesions, or heat in a

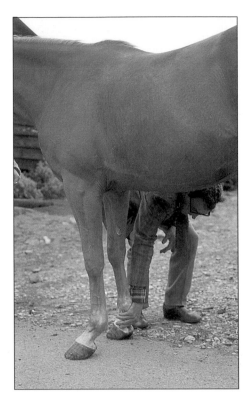

tendon or joint. He will also examine the eyes and heart.

Once outside his stable, the horse will be stood up squarely on flat ground while the vet makes a detailed appraisal of his conformation. This is followed by a manual examination of the entire horse:

the head, including the mouth and teeth, the neck, ribs, sternum, back, abdomen and the limbs. Once the horse has been examined at rest he will be walked and then trotted in hand both away from the vet and towards him to enable him to detect any signs of lameness. Turning the horse to either side on a tight circle, backing him for a few strides and lungeing him at trot on a hard, flat surface are other tests which may reveal problems of unsoundness.

Flexion tests may be carried out on the limbs, particularly if there is a suspicion of lameness. However, opinion differs on these flexion tests, as they can actually induce lameness if they are used with sufficient force.

▮ **ABOVE LEFT**
Vetting includes a manual examination of the entire horse.

▮ **LEFT**
The vet will check the horse's heart and respiratory rates both at rest and after exercise.

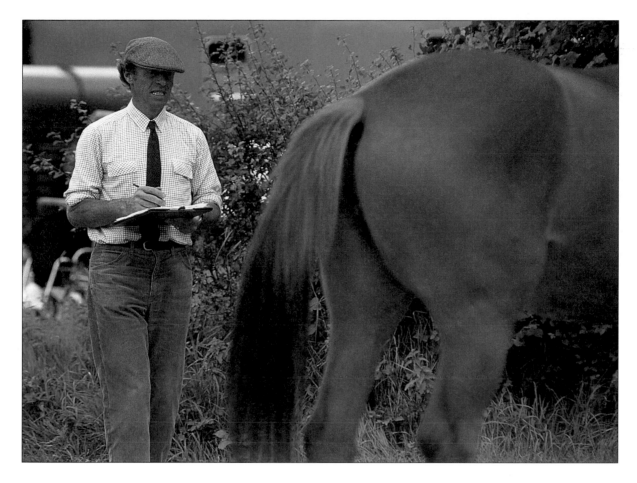

To test the horse's wind and heart he is tacked up, warmed up gently at walk, trot and canter and then given a gallop. The vet will note whether the horse dips its back when the saddle is put on and the rider mounts. Some horses habitually do this, in others it may be a sign of back problems. After exercise the vet will listen to the lungs for any signs of abnormal respiration and to the heart for any irregularity. After the horse has been cooled off he will be rested for half an hour, after which he will be trotted out again in hand. If the horse is suffering from muscular or arthritic problems, which might disappear while the horse is warm, they may well reappear after this period of rest. Signs of old lameness might also appear after fast exercise. A further examination of the heart and respiration may also be made. The vet will then complete the certificate.

The certificate includes a detailed identification of the horse, the vet's report and his opinion as to its suitability for purchase, bearing in mind the use for which it is required. It is important to remember that the certificate is not a guarantee, but an opinion expressed by a qualified person. The certificate means that the horse has been found to be free of certain disorders at the time of examination. It does not and cannot mean that the horse is and will remain completely free from disease – vets are certainly not clairvoyant. Nor does the certificate guarantee that the horse is free from so-called stable "vices" such as crib-biting or weaving. If you would like a written warranty to this effect, you must obtain it from the vendor.

Keeping a Horse

Horse ownership is a big responsibility and should not be entered into lightly. Certainly no one should consider it unless they have the necessary facilities and have first mastered the rudiments of horse care. These include a knowledge of feeding, grooming, general stable management and basic first aid. All horses and ponies need safe accommodation and daily attention – they cannot be set aside on a Sunday afternoon and forgotten about until the following weekend. Unlike small domesticated animals, who share their owners' home, they need large facilities of their own, maintenance of which takes time and money. Depending on the work required of them and their breed or type, horses can either be kept at grass or stabled, or a combination of the two (known as the combined system). The owner will therefore need access to grazing, a stable, a weatherproof storage area for feed, bedding and tools and somewhere secure to keep tack and other equipment.

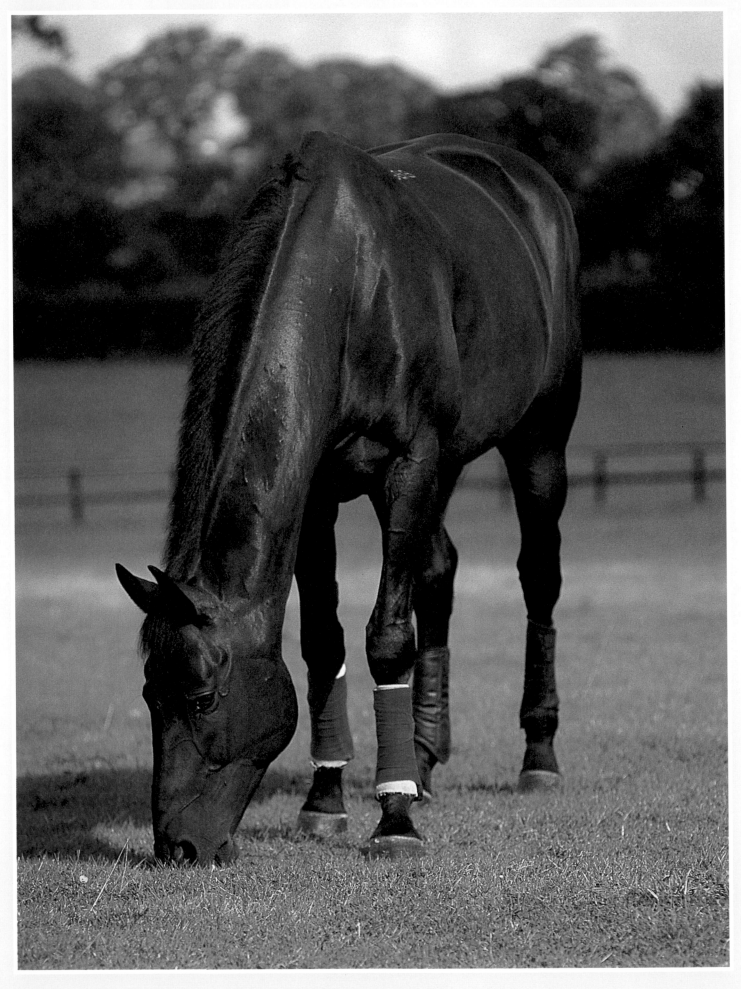

THE HORSE AT GRASS

The horse is by nature a nomadic, grazing animal, so it is far more natural – and less stressful – to keep him in a paddock than in a stable. However, a fenced paddock, no matter how large, is still an unnatural environment for a horse and certain precautions must be taken if the horse is to be safe and secure.

▮ PREVIOUS PAGE OPPOSITE Stabled horses need constant care and attention.
▮ PREVIOUS PAGE Most small ponies are quite hardy and can live outside all year round.
▮ OPPOSITE Fit horses who spend part of the day at grass should wear bandages and boots to guard against injury.
▮ ABOVE Brood mares grazing in a well-fenced paddock.

Fencing

All fields used for grazing horses must be securely and safely fenced. Since it is the horse's nature to roam, if he sees a gap he will certainly go for it. Similarly, if there is anything on which the horse can injure himself, he will find it – the domesticated horse is notoriously accident prone.

Undoubtedly the most effective (but unfortunately also the most expensive) fencing is good **wooden post and rail**. It is sturdy, long lasting and looks attractive. The wooden support posts, which should be 4 inches (10cm) square, must be driven well into the ground since horses like to rub against fencing, particularly when they are changing their coats. For a 4 foot (1.2m) fence the posts should be no less than 6 feet 6 inches (2m) in length. The fence should be constructed of good-quality wood and treated with non-toxic preservative to give protection against the weather and to discourage horses from chewing it. The top rail should be level with the top of the posts, which should be cut on a slope to allow rain to run off. Where possible the rails should be attached to the inner side of the posts. This prevents the horse banging into the

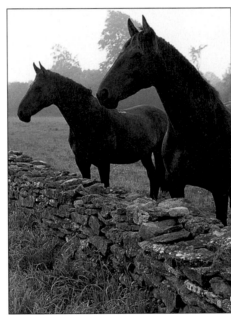

■ **LEFT**
Provided they are sufficiently high to deter the horse from jumping out, well-maintained stone walls are effective barriers.

■ **BELOW LEFT**
Fixing the rails to the insides of the support posts prevents horses pushing them off when rubbing against them.

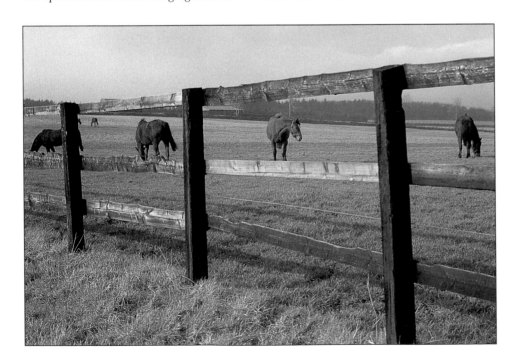

SAFETY CHECKLIST

☛ Make regular checks of all field boundaries.

☛ Repair any broken sections of boundary immediately.

☛ Keep wire fencing taut at all times.

☛ Set the lowest strand of a wire fence 18 inches (46cm) above the ground.

☛ Block off gaps in hedges with stout fencing – never use loose strands of wire.

☛ Never use pig or sheep netting – horses tend to put their feet through the squares of wire and can become caught up.

☛ Never use sheep posts, with sharp, upward pointing ends.

☛ Fence off potential danger areas, such as treacherous ground or ditches.

☛ When using electric fencing, ensure that it is visible – to humans as well as horses – by tying strips of strong plastic (for example, from feed or fertilizer bags) at intervals along the wire.

☛ Avoid metal or concrete fence posts – they will do far more damage than wooden ones should a horse collide with them.

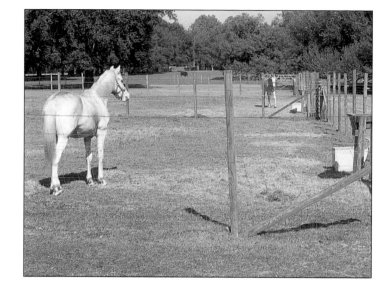

█ OPPOSITE TOP
Good-quality wooden post and rail fencing makes the perfect horse-proof boundary and looks attractive.

█ BELOW RIGHT
Rusty metal, barbed wire and concrete posts are potentially lethal to horses. Sections of poor fencing like this should be replaced.

posts when galloping about and also prevents him from pushing a rail off if he leans or rubs against it.

A tall, thick **hedge,** provided it is without poisonous trees or shrubs, can also make a good boundary. Beech and hazel are particularly suitable since horses will not eat them. Unlike a fence, a hedge provides horses with shelter in bad weather. It will, however, require regular trimming to keep it in good order – if gaps begin to appear they must be fenced off.

Probably the best boundary of all is a combination of the two: a good dense hedge with a post and rail fence running immediately in front of it.

Cheaper, less attractive but equally effective fencing can be constructed with **wire mesh**. The mesh must have small, V-shaped openings so that there is no possibility of a horse catching his foot in the holes. Mesh fencing needs to be erected professionally to prevent sagging. It is also likely to stretch when leant on.

Plain wire fencing will provide a good horseproof barrier so long as it is well constructed. It should consist of four or five strands of wire attached to stout wooden posts, with strainers at the corners to keep them taut. An alternative, and one which makes the fence more easily visible to the horse, is to use a wooden rail in place of the top strand of wire. The strands of wire should be some 12 inches (30cm) apart and the placing of the lowest strand is particularly important. It should be about 18 inches (46cm) above the ground. Any lower and the horse may put

a leg through the strands and become caught up; any higher and he may be tempted to put his head underneath. Plain wire is more suitable than barbed wire. If the latter cannot be avoided, it must be kept absolutely taut – loose barbed wire can cause dreadful injuries if any part of the horse becomes caught up in it. Horses can also cut themselves if they rub against the barbs.

█ LEFT
Electric fencing can be very useful, especially for dividing paddocks into smaller sections. Horses quickly learn to respect it.

█ BOTTOM
Curved fencing with no right-angled corners is safest for horses.

Electric fencing has its uses, especially for temporarily dividing one area of a field from another, for example when resting one section of grazing.

Stone walls will also contain horses very well, provided they are sturdy and high enough – all boundaries should be a minimum of 4 feet (1.2m) high, otherwise horses might try to jump out. Like a hedge, a wall will afford some protection against the weather.

Modern **plastic fencing**, which comes in a variety of colours, may not look as "natural" as wood but it does have certain advantages: horses do not chew it, it does not rot and it will absorb impact without causing injury. Like wire, it should be correctly strained on strong, wooden posts.

Whatever the fencing used, right-angled or sharp corners should be avoided in paddocks where horses are kept. Rounding the corners of the field makes it less likely for a horse to injure himself when galloping about, either by coming to an abrupt halt (with the possibility of jarring the legs) or actually crashing into the boundary. Acute corners can also be traps for a timid horse who might find himself literally "cornered" by a more aggressive companion.

Gates

Good access to fields is most important. Gateways must be wide enough to allow not only horses to pass through safely but also large machinery (such as a tractor and harrow) which will be required from time to time to keep the pasture in good condition. For safety's sake it is better for gates to be situated away from busy roads. Wooden and metal gates are both suitable for horse paddocks. All gates should have cross bars for added strength.

It is best to have a gate hung by an expert to ensure that it does not sag, drag on the ground or swing. Gates must open easily otherwise a horse could try to push his way out while you are still struggling to open it. The safest way to hang a gate is so that it opens inwards into the field. This

SAFETY CHECKLIST

- ☞ Make regular checks of all gates.

- ☞ Replace/repair worn or damaged catches/hinges immediately.

- ☞ Keep gates securely fastened, using chains and padlocks at BOTH ends.

- ☞ Never fasten gates with bits of rope or string – horses can bite through them and they are easily removed by thieves.

- ☞ Avoid gates less than 6 feet (1.8m) wide – horses can easily bang themselves, especially their hips, as they go through.

- ☞ Avoid gates that open directly on to a main road – it is dangerous leading a horse straight out into traffic and will also make theft easier.

- ☞ Never use flimsy metal gates – they are too easily bent and broken.

- ☞ Avoid rusty metal gates – horses can easily injure themselves.

- ☞ Avoid straining gates by climbing over them.

- ☞ Avoid feeding horses close to the gateway – the ground will quickly become poached in winter.

▌ BELOW
Gate posts must be strong. Gates should be securely fastened at both ends with sturdy chains and padlocks.

will prevent a horse pushing it open as soon as you unfasten the catch. A wooden gate should be heavy and solidly built and, like fencing, should be treated with preservative. Galvanized metal gates will

▌ BOTTOM
This broken gate is totally unsuitable for a paddock. Rusty metal may cause serious injuries and flimsy barriers encourage horses to escape.

require regular painting. Gateposts need to be very strong and should be set about 3 feet (90cm) into the ground with concrete to keep them firm. They will require strong hinges and a horse-proof catch, that is one that the horse cannot unfasten with his teeth. All catches should be easy for a person to open with one hand. There should be no protruding hooks or other fastenings on which the horse could injure himself.

Horse stealing is not uncommon and so it is vital to secure all gates. Use heavy-duty chain with a strong padlock and fit one to BOTH ends of the gate so that would-be thieves cannot simply lift the gate off its hinges. Avoid climbing over gates as it tends to weaken them. If you must, always climb over the hinge end and do it quickly.

During wet weather the ground in gateways quickly becomes poached by horses being taken in and out on a daily basis or simply pacing up and down waiting to be fed. If possible, gates should be situated on well-drained ground, and not in a muddy hollow.

Shelters

In the wild, horses make use of natural shelter such as trees, banks or rocks for protection from extremes of wind, wet or heat or to escape from flies. For horses kept in the confines of a paddock it is essential to provide an equivalent form of protection. Most domesticated horses retain their natural instinct to shelter beside a good, thick hedge or under a tree rather than going inside a confining man-made structure. But not all paddocks have hedges and trees and so a wooden shelter may be the only alternative.

Since horses are happiest when kept in company with others of their kind, a field shelter needs to be large enough to accommodate the number of horses that graze together, without risk of squabbling and overcrowding. It should be positioned on well-drained ground. If this is not possible, the floor and the area around the shelter may need a hard surface, such as concrete. The shelter should be built with its back to the prevailing wind. It must be strongly constructed and treated with preservative. The roof must be sufficiently high to give horses plenty of

head room (thus avoiding possible injury) and should slope towards the back so that rainwater runs away from the entrance. Open-fronted shelters are the safest, because it is easy for a horse to escape should he be bullied by a companion. Any fixtures and fittings, such as mangers, hay racks, etc., must be strongly made and fitted at a good height from the ground, again to prevent injury. They should be checked regularly and repaired as necessary, as should the whole shelter.

Some types of smaller field shelter are designed with a bottom door which, when closed, converts the shelter into a stable.

This can be very useful if you have no other stabling but sometimes need to keep your horse or pony inside. It can also be used as an isolation box in the event of the horse contracting a contagious illness.

A less costly type of shelter may be provided by means of a wooden screen, erected in conjunction with the fencing. Windbreak screens need to be about 6 feet 6 inches (2m) high and can either be straight or double-sided, using a corner of the field. Multi-angled screens, affording protection from different directions, can be built free-standing in the open away from the fencing.

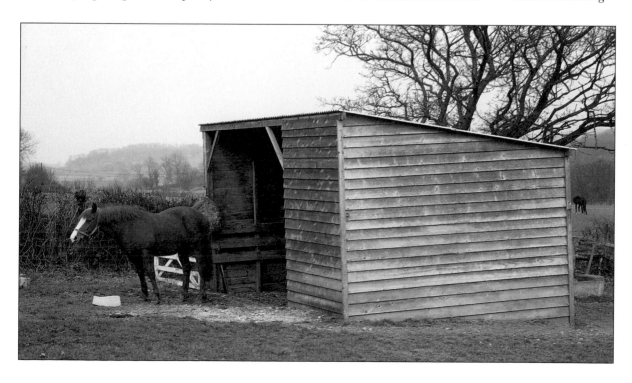

■ TOP
A well-designed wooden field shelter with high, sloping roof, wide front opening and strong kicking boards.

■ LEFT
This small shelter, with its narrow opening, is suitable for a single horse. With the addition of a door it could convert into a stable for emergency use if necessary.

Poisonous Plants, Shrubs and Trees

■ BELOW LEFT
Horses appreciate the shelter afforded by mature
trees such as this oak. But acorns, if eaten in large
quantities, can be poisonous so they should be
removed.

There are a good many plants, shrubs and trees which are poisonous to horses and ponies. Some, such as the **buttercup**, which are poisonous if eaten in large quantities when fresh, are not particularly palatable. On the other hand horses will readily eat yew, all parts of which are lethal. A quantity as small as 1lb (0.5kg) can kill a horse. All paddocks should be rigorously checked for dangerous plants before horses are put out to graze and regularly checked thereafter – remember that however well you tend your own grazing it can still be contaminated by seeds blowing from neighbouring land.

One of the most dangerous plants of all is **ragwort**, which is tall and easily recognized by its bright yellow flowers. Ragwort

SAFETY CHECKLIST

☛ Learn to recognize poisonous plants and trees.

☛ Before putting a horse in a new paddock, make a thorough check of grassland and hedges for signs of poisonous vegetation.

☛ Dig up and burn poisonous plants.

☛ Fence off any poisonous trees which cannot be removed – make sure they are well out of reach of horses or ponies.

☛ Make regular checks of all paddocks and hedges – remember that poisonous plants can spread from neighbouring land.

☛ Never leave poisonous plants which have been dug up lying about in the paddock – many plants, notably ragwort, are far more palatable to horses when wilted or dead.

☛ Practise good pasture management: a good, dense sward of grass helps prevent poisonous plants from seeding.

☛ If there are poisonous trees in the vicinity, keep an eye open for fallen twigs or branches – particularly during windy weather.

☛ If paddocks adjoin gardens, make regular checks for cuttings dumped over the fence by their owners – they may contain poisonous plants.

☛ After using chemical weedkillers keep horses off the grass for several weeks and at least until there has been a good downpour of rain.

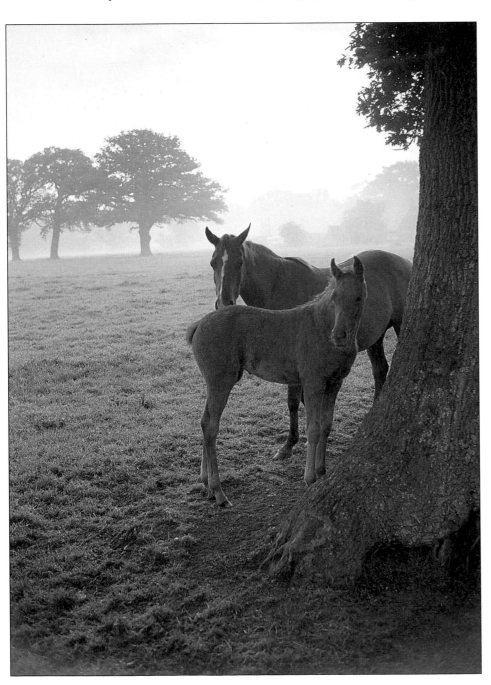

contains alkaloids which poison the liver and the effects are cumulative: small doses eaten over a long period of time are just as lethal as a large amount eaten in a short time. There is no specific treatment for ragwort poisoning and the effects are usually fatal.

Ragwort can be eliminated by spraying – the best time is between late April and late May, before the flower shoots develop and while young plants are just becoming established. Or it can be dug up, though this can be hard work. All the roots must

■ CLOCKWISE FROM RIGHT
Ragwort, yew, laurel, rhododendron and privet: all
are highly dangerous to horses. Ragwort must be
eradicated from horse pasture; the trees and shrubs
must either be removed or fenced off out of reach.

be removed from the ground and the
flower heads should be burnt. Attempting
to control ragwort by cutting it when it is
in flower to prevent the production of
seeds is unlikely to solve the problem since
the plants will often grow more vigorously
the following year. If a paddock is really
badly infested with the plant, the best
solution is to plough the land and reseed
it. The better the grassland management
the less opportunity there will be for
ragwort to become established. The
denser the sward of grass the less likely
ragwort is to seed.

Foxgloves, which like ragwort become
more palatable when they are dried in hay
than when fresh, are also lethal to horses.
As little as ¼lb (100g) may prove fatal.
Symptoms of foxglove poisoning include
convulsions and difficulty in breathing. A
horse will die in a matter of hours.

Hemlock has a similarly disastrous
effect though it takes larger quantities
(around 5–10lb or 2.5–5kg) to cause
death. All members of the **nightshade**
family are poisonous, as is **monkshood**.
Horsetails, commonly found growing in
boggy conditions, are very dangerous if
eaten in large quantities in hay. Horses do
not usually eat the growing stems.

Shrubs and trees to be avoided at all
cost include **rhododendron** (small
quantities cause death through failure of
the respiratory system), **oleander**,
laburnum (especially the seeds), **box,
privet** and **laurel**. All parts of **yew**, living or
dead, are lethal in small quantities – again
there is no known antidote. **Meadow
saffron** contains a poison which may take
time to build up in the system, by which
time the horse is beyond help, and the
poisons present in **bracken** also have a

cumulative effect which causes poor
growth, lack of co-ordination and general
loss of condition. Care should be taken if
there are oak trees in or around a horse's
paddock. The crop of **acorns** varies from
year to year. If they are eaten in large
quantities, they can be harmful. They
should be raked up and removed.

Plants, shrubs and trees which are poisonous to horses include:
Brackén, buttercup, flax, foxglove, hemlock, horsetail, lupin, meadow saffron, nightshade, purple milk vetch, ragwort, St John's wort, yellow star thistle
Box, laurel, oleander, privet, rhododendron
Buckthorn, laburnum, magnolia, yew
Acorns

Water

Horses and ponies kept at grass must have constant access to a clean supply of water. A natural supply of running water, such as a stream or river, is ideal but nowadays it is all too likely that it may be polluted. If it is not, then horses and ponies may be allowed free access provided the bottom is gravel (if it is sandy the horse may ingest sand with the water).

The approach to the drinking area must be clean, fairly flat and safe. Steep banks are not suitable since the horses will slip and slide down and the bank will eventually collapse. If the stream is narrow, this could arrest the flow of water. Any fencing that crosses the stream or river must be checked regularly to ensure that horses cannot escape from their paddock by wandering off along the waterway. Streams which are not free flowing in summer are not suitable, since the water will tend to become stagnant. Horses should never be allowed access to polluted rivers, stagnant ponds or boggy areas: these should be securely fenced off.

The alternative to running water is a man-made container. A galvanized water trough, purpose-built, fed by mains water and controlled by a ballcock provides an efficient water supply, although there is

always the problem of pipes freezing in winter. The feed pipe needs to be buried to a suitable depth and the length of pipe which is above ground will need to be well lagged. It is essential that the ballcock is enclosed so that horses cannot damage it.

If mains water is not available, troughs can be filled by hosepipe or, if convenient, by bucket. Troughs such as this with static water will require baling out every week and refilling. Smaller containers, such as old stone sinks, plastic tubs and buckets can also be used but they will need more frequent filling. The advantage of small, lightweight containers is that they are easy to clean and they can be moved about to different areas of the field to prevent wear and tear on the ground. The disadvantage is that they are easily knocked over.

| LEFT
A natural supply of running water is ideal provided it is pollution free.
| BELOW
A galvanized trough makes a suitable alternative.
| BOTTOM LEFT
All water containers must be well filled and cleaned regularly.

Standing a bucket or tub in an old car tyre is one solution to this problem.

Water troughs are best positioned parallel to a fence. Horses drink a lot so the approach to a trough will be in constant use. It should be hard – it may be necessary to lay concrete or hard core.

SAFETY CHECKLIST

☞ Check your horse's water supply every day.

☞ Bale out and clean all water containers regularly.

☞ During severe weather be prepared to break ice on water two or three times a day.

☞ Fence off all sources of stagnant water.

☞ Never place a water trough in the corner of a field where a horse may be trapped by one of its companions.

☞ Never place a water trough under deciduous trees or near a hedge where leaves, twigs and seeds can foul it.

☞ Avoid placing troughs in the middle of fields where they can become a source of injury.

☞ Recess water troughs into the line of the fence to minimize projections and the risk of injury.

☞ Never place a water trough slightly in front of a fence so that a horse could trap his leg between it and the fence.

☞ Avoid using containers such as old baths that have rough edges or dangerous projections.

Grass Management

■ BELOW
Grazing cattle with horses, or in rotation, helps control worms and weeds.

■ BELOW LEFT
Droppings must not be allowed to accumulate in the paddock. If they cannot be picked up regularly, they should be harrowed.

Careful management is required if a paddock is to withstand the horse's close-biting method of grazing and the constant wear and tear inflicted by his feet. Poor quality grazing quickly becomes "horse sick" – barren areas alternate with patches of intrusive, unpalatable weeds such as nettles, docks and thistles – and without a good grass sward it will also become badly poached in wet weather. Even good quality grazing will deteriorate if it is not given the right attention.

The ideal pasture is one that has been sown with seed selected and mixed specifically with horses in mind. A good basic mixture would contain 50 per cent of perennial rye grass, 25 per cent of creeping red fescue and 25 per cent of a mixture including crested dog's tail, meadow grass and a little wild white clover. Timothy should also be included if you intend to take hay from the paddock.

Rye grass grows well in most conditions although on poor, light soils it will decline after a few years if it is not fertilized. Two different types should be included in the mix. Creeping red fescue is particularly useful in difficult conditions (it is often used on sports grounds) and again two different types should be included. Smooth-stalked meadow grass will grow in dry, sandy soils while the rough-stalked variety, which horses find very palatable, thrives in moist, rich soils. Its dense, low growth helps prevent the intrusion of weeds and poisonous plants. Clover is useful because its root nodules contain nitrogen-producing bacteria. Its inclusion in the mix will help reduce the need for fertilizing. It is important to choose wild clover rather than one of the farm varieties, which grow very aggressively and can take over an entire paddock.

Even with the right basic mixture of grasses, the amount and quality of grazing produced will vary according to a number of natural factors. These include soil type, rainfall, wind and altitude. Soil should be

tested for its suitability to sustain grass. For example, if it is acidic it will need to be treated with lime (horses must be kept off the grazing until the lime has been washed in by rain).

The best grazing is produced on well-drained land. The installation of underground drainage is expensive but it may be essential where ground is so badly drained that it is both unproductive and easily poached by a horse's feet. Where drainage exists it is important to maintain it. Check ditches regularly, and remove any blockages which prevent water from running away freely (remember that blocked ditches on neighbouring land can prevent the free run of water from your paddock). Check all pipes leading into and out of ditches and repair as necessary.

Ideally the horses' droppings should be removed frequently as this will help to control worm infestation. Where removal is not practical, for example on large acreages, the droppings should be harrowed regularly. This should be done during warm, dry weather (which will spread out the droppings and kill the larvae). Another aid to worm control is the grazing of cattle either with the horses or in rotation. The larvae will be destroyed in the cattle's digestive system. Cattle and sheep will also help keep paddocks tidy by eating the rougher herbage. Sheep do less damage to wet ground than cattle.

Harrowing in the spring helps to pull out dead growth and make room for new, and a field should always be harrowed before the application of fertilizer. Rolling will help to firm the soil and repair poached areas. Weed control is also best carried out in spring as soon as new shoots appear. Persistent weeds should be dug out and burnt before they seed.

Pasture needs to be rested periodically. If you have nowhere else to put your horse, divide off the paddock into two or more sections. Rest one portion, graze horses in another and, if possible, graze cattle or sheep in a third.

THE STABLED HORSE

Well-designed stabling is vitally important to the
horse's health and safety, whether the horse lives in
most of the time, whether he is kept on the combined
system (that is part stabled, part out at grass) or
whether he is stabled only occasionally.

▮ OPPOSITE **All stables should have horse-proof fastenings on
the outside of the doors.**

▮ ABOVE **Roughened concrete provides a suitable surface for a
busy stableyard.**

Stables

Care must be taken with the positioning and construction of stables. This applies equally to a single stable and to a large yard. Stables should be sited so that cold north and east winds cannot blow in and should be positioned on well-drained ground. When planning new stabling, various factors should be taken into consideration. These include the supply of water and electricity as well as vehicular access. It is preferable, too, to build stables near a house, in order to deter thieves.

The most popular type of stable is the loosebox, or box stall. These are usually made of wood, concrete blocks or brick and may be roofed with wood (protected by waterproof felt), tiles, slates or heavy-duty corrugated plastic. Metal should never be used for stabling because it is hot in summer and cold in winter; it is also likely to cause injuries to the horse. A loosebox must be large enough for the occupant to be able to move about, roll, lie down flat and get up again in comfort and absolute safety. A horse standing 16hh and over needs a loosebox measuring at

■ BELOW
Good airy barn stabling provides a suitable alternative to looseboxes, especially in a hot or very cold climate. The disadvantages are the ease with which disease can spread and the fire risk.

least 12 feet x 14 feet (3.7m x 4.3m); a horse up to 16hh, 12 feet x 12 feet (3.7m x 3.7m), and a 14hh pony, 10 feet x 12 feet (3m x 3.7m). A stable of 8 feet x 8 feet (2.4m x 2.4m) is adequate for small ponies.

The roof should be sloped and fitted with effective guttering and downpipes. A high ceiling or roof is essential to prevent the horse hitting its head. If the stable has a ridge roof, the eaves should be no less than 7 feet 6 inches (2.25m) above the ground and the top of the roof should be from 12–15 feet (3.7–4.5m) high. The lowest point of a single-planed roof should be no less than 10 feet (3m) high.

Wooden kicking boards, to a height of at least 4 feet (1.2m), provide added strength and security. The stable floor should slope slightly towards the rear of the box (to aid drainage) and the surface must be hard-wearing and non-slippery. Roughened concrete is most often used. It may be covered with a special rubber material to give better purchase. Drains inside the stable are best avoided as they tend to become blocked with bedding and can also trap a horse's hoof.

For safety, the stable door must give plenty of clearance – it should be at least 4 feet (1.2m) wide and 7 feet (2.1m) high for a horse. It should be made in two halves, opening outwards, and the top half should fasten back securely for the free circulation of air and to enable the horse to see out. Only rarely is the weather so severe that it is necessary to close both halves of a stable door. The top edge of

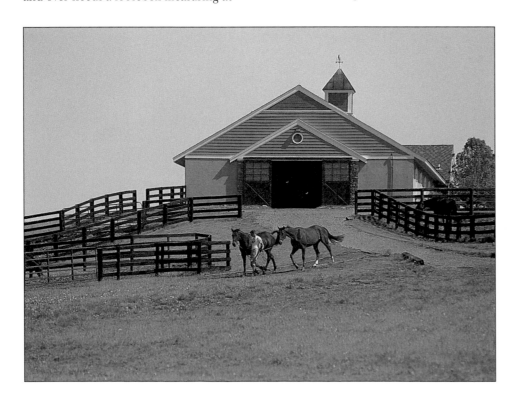

▮ OPPOSITE TOP
A well-built block of brick stables. The overhang gives extra protection to horses and humans from extremes of weather.

▮ OPPOSITE MIDDLE
Note the protective strip on the top of the doors and the kick-over bolts at the bottom.

▮ BELOW
The inside of a barn complex. With kit and equipment conveniently to hand, this type of stabling is popular with humans though it can be a boring environment for horses.

▮ BELOW
A converted container makes a poor and potentially dangerous home for a horse. Metal is cold in winter and hot in summer and the horse could easily injure himself on the makeshift door.

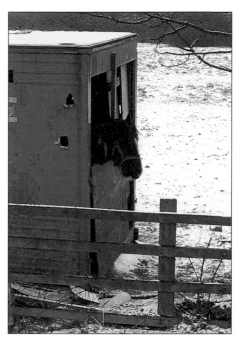

SAFETY CHECKLIST

☛ Provide adequate fire extinguishers (water and foam)/fire hose/sand buckets in the stable area – your local fire prevention officer will advise on suitable precautions. Have fire extinguishers serviced regularly.

☛ Ensure that all electrical wiring is protected with suitable conduits to prevent interference by horses and rodents.

☛ Ensure that all light fittings are out of reach of the horse.

☛ Fit waterproof switches, well out of reach of the horse.

☛ Keep stable fixtures and fittings to a minimum: two rings, one to tie up the horse, one (if required) for a haynet; water bucket or automatic waterbowl; manger.

☛ Make regular checks for protruding nails, screws, splinters etc.

☛ Make regular checks of all door bolts and hinges and keep them oiled.

☛ Fit protective grilles to all windows.

☛ Keep all drains clean.

☛ Cover open drains in the stable yard area with strong grids.

the bottom door should be securely fitted with a protective strip of metal to prevent the horse chewing the wood, and the door should have a horse-proof bolt at the top and a kick-over bolt at the bottom.

The stabled horse needs a constant supply of fresh air, so good ventilation is essential. The open top door and high roof help provide this. What the horse does not need is a draughty environment. Windows, which help ventilate and light the stable, are usually positioned on the same side of the box as the door to prevent draughts. If they are to provide maximum air and light, they should not be obscured by the top door, which tends to be the case with some stabling. Windows must be fitted with protective grilles. Additional ventilation can be provided by means of ventilation cowls in the roof, or louvre boards in the eaves. Additional light may be provided by a window in the wall opposite the door. If this is also used for ventilation, it must be above the height of the horse's head to prevent cross-draughts.

Internal stabling, where lines of looseboxes are contained within a larger building (which can be an existing barn or purpose built), is popular in some countries and is particularly useful in areas which experience extremes of heat or cold. Correctly constructed, such stabling will be warm in winter and cool in summer, but care must be taken to provide good ventilation – infectious diseases are more likely to spread in this type of stabling arrangement. Doorways and centre aisles must be wide enough to enable horses to move about without banging themselves – sliding stable doors are often the best in this situation as they do not protrude into the gangways when open. The running channels must always be kept clean.

Another way of keeping horses under cover is the yard system, where a number of horses are given the run of a large barn or a partially covered area. The yard system is labour saving, since the horses can be kept on deep litter; and horses enjoy being together with the freedom to wander about. Care must be taken, however, to choose horses who get on with each other, otherwise biting and kicking will occur.

Bedding

An ample supply of bedding encourages the horse to lie down to rest, thus taking unnecessary strain off the legs and feet; it reduces the likelihood of injuries such as capped hocks when the horse does lie down; it allows the horse to roll in comfort and protects him from injury when he does so; it reduces the jarring effect on the legs and feet that may result from standing for long periods on hard flooring; it prevents the horse from slipping up; it encourages him to stale (male horses, particularly, are usually very reluctant to stale on a bare floor); it provides warmth and insulation from draughts and it helps to keep the horse and his rugs clean.

■ BELOW
Wheat straw is less palatable than oat or barley straw and is therefore the most suitable for horses.

■ BELOW LEFT
Deep straw, well banked up the sides of the stable, provides the horse with a safe, comfortable bed.

There are a number of types of suitable bedding, all of which have pros and cons. **Straw** has traditionally been the most popular – and economical – and many people still prefer it since it makes arguably the warmest, most comfortable bed and allows free drainage. It is normally easily available though it may become scarce in wet years. Wheat straw is the best for horses, being less palatable than barley or oat straw, both of which are also likely to contain awns which can get into a horse's eyes or irritate the skin.

Straw has the advantage of being much easier to dispose of than some other forms of bedding: it can be burnt (in a safe place, well away from stabling, hay stores, etc) or contractors may collect it for use as mushroom compost. The main drawback of straw is that it may be dusty or contain fungal spores, which can cause an allergic reaction in some horses, leading to respiratory problems. This in turn can affect the horse's work performance because he will not be able to take in enough oxygen. Coughing is often the first sign of problems in this respect.

It can sometimes be difficult finding a supply of small straw bales, too,

■ BELOW
Good-quality wood shavings are a useful alternative
to straw though they provide a rather less warm
bed. They are also more difficult to dispose of.

particularly if you live in an area where there are few horse owners and therefore not much demand for the old type of bale. Straw is best bought in small bales because they are easier to handle. The large ones, weighing half a tonne or more, are difficult to manoeuvre and often present storage difficulties, especially for someone keeping horses on a small scale. It will take about four small bales to put down a good, thick straw bed in an average sized loosebox and upwards of half a bale a day to maintain the bed, the exact quantity depending on the amount of time that the box is occupied.

Aside from straw, **wood shavings** are probably the most popular form of bedding nowadays. Correctly managed, they provide a clean, hygienic bed which will not be eaten by the horse. Shavings do not have spores and, provided they are dust free (having been passed through a dust extractor by the suppliers), they can be a good alternative to straw for horses with any sort of respiratory problem.

They are packed in strong plastic bags and it is therefore possible to store shavings outside, provided there has been no damage to the wrappings in transit. Shavings do have their share of disadvantages, however. They are difficult to dispose of – being slow rotting they cannot be spread on the land – and bales are fairly heavy to handle. Shavings are also much heavier to handle when wet than straw. There is also the possibility of foreign bodies, such as sharp fragments of wood or nails, being present – though this should not be a problem with good-quality shavings. Some horses' skin may be irritated if the shavings are from wood which has been treated with chemicals and foot problems sometimes occur.

Unlike straw, which traps pockets of air, shavings pack down closely. A bed of shavings is therefore less warm than a straw bed and rather less comfortable to lie on, particularly as it is less stable than straw and more prone to exposing bare patches of floor. A shavings bed will use approximately three bales per week.

Aubiose is a fairly new and entirely natural product made from the hemp plant. It is proving particularly beneficial for horses with dust allergies and has the advantage of being exceptionally absorbent: four times more absorbent than wood shavings and twelve times more than straw. The bed is more expensive than other forms of bedding to put down initially, an average stable requiring some eight bales, but thereafter it is economical to maintain as it requires only half to one bale a week. When the bed is first laid it needs dampening with a hose or watering can to help it settle and activate its sponge-like properties.

Aubiose works by soaking up liquids in a small area at the base of the bed, in much the same way as cat litter. The top layers of the bed remain dry. It is a labour-saving form of bedding since mucking out consists simply of frequent removal of droppings and a light raking over to keep it level. It is recommended that the saturated bedding should be removed every five to ten days, depending on the horse. It is also suitable for use with the deep litter system.

Another big plus for Aubiose is the fact that it rots down to a valuable compost within five to six weeks and is therefore easy to dispose of. Its only disadvantage, apart from the initial cost, is that it is very free flowing (the particles are smaller and softer than shavings) and so it is not so easy to bank up the sides of the bed.

Shredded paper provides the most dust-free bed of all and is, as a result, often used for horses with allergies to straw or respiratory problems. It is also increasingly used for high-performance horses, such as eventers or racehorses, whose lungs need to be kept as free as possible of dust. Paper is cheaper to buy than shavings but on the other hand a deeper bed is required because it becomes saturated more quickly than either shavings or straw. On the plus side, it is light and easy to handle and

provides a really warm bed. On the minus side it is often made from printed paper and this may cause staining of the horse's coat, particularly with greys, which causes extra work for the owner or groom. It is also difficult to control a paper-bed muck heap when it is windy. Again the bed will need around three bales per week.

Peat moss may be used for bedding in areas where it is easily available . Like shavings, it is usually sold in plastic-covered bales. It, too, has its good points and its bad points. It provides a comfortable bed, is not palatable and should be reasonably easy to dispose of.

However, its main advantage over other forms of bedding is one of safety: it will not burst into flames in the event of a fire. On the other hand it is expensive, heavy to handle, needs frequent mucking out and forking over to prevent it becoming soggy and compacted and is so dark in colour that it is difficult to identify the wet areas.

Rubber matting can be used for bedding purposes but, apart from the fact that it is totally dust free when used on its own, it has more minus points than plus ones. It certainly does not look very attractive and, more important, provides

■ OPPOSITE
Hemp is a relatively new type of bedding for
horses. It is exceptionally absorbent. Rather
expensive initially, it is economical (and easy) to
manage thereafter.

■ BELOW
Rubber matting is dust free, long lasting and labour
saving but affords little comfort unless other
bedding is used on top.

■ BOTTOM
Paper, being dust free and warm, is ideal for
bedding down horses with respiratory problems.
Printed paper can cause coat stains, especially on
grey horses.

little warmth or protection from
draughts. It does not absorb wet and
if it is used without a covering of other
bedding material, the droppings will be
scattered about by the horse, who will
then lie in them and, as a result, tend
always to be dirty. There is little to
prevent a horse becoming cast (the
banked-up sides of conventional beds
help in this respect). When used on its
own its chief advantage, apart from
being dust free, is its low-cost
maintenance: after the initial outlay there
is no more bedding to purchase and the
matting should last for a number of years.
Mucking out can be done by hosepipe,
and is both quick and easy.

Management of Beds

Good management of beds is essential to keep the horse's environment healthy and to keep both the horse and his rugs as clean as possible. Stables can either be mucked out every day or you can adopt the deep litter or semi-deep litter system. The horse should be tied up during mucking out or, preferably, removed from the stable altogether. This protects him from any dust which may be disturbed while the bedding is being moved about and also makes the job easier.

Daily mucking out entails the removal of all droppings and soiled bedding. The best system is to take up the bed completely to allow the floor to dry while the horse is out. This is less of a chore with lightweight bedding materials such as straw and paper than with something heavier such as shavings.

You will need a wheelbarrow or a muck sheet, a fork and a strong yard broom with hard bristles. For mucking out a straw bed many people use a four-pronged fork for lifting droppings, but the same job can be accomplished with a three- or even a two-pronged fork. Much depends upon the skill of the wielder – the fewer prongs, the lighter the fork, the less tiring the job and the faster you can work. For mucking out shavings you will need a shavings fork, which has more prongs set closer together. The advantage of using a muck sheet is that you do not normally need a shovel. Most of the soiled litter can be forked or swept on to it and any remnants can be hand lifted, provided you wear protective gloves. When a shovel is required, it should be large and lightweight.

The muck sheet or wheelbarrow is positioned across the doorway and visible droppings collected and placed on/in it. The bedding is cleared away from one corner of the box (usually the one on the same side as the door and furthest from where the horse is tied up, though if the box is large enough the other corners may be used in rotation to ensure that all corners of the floor are dried out regularly). The floor in that corner is then swept clean. The corner is used to stack all the clean bedding – the squarer and neater the better since it will take up less room. All the droppings and wet straw are placed in the wheelbarrow or on the muck sheet and the entire floor is swept clean. Finally, a thin layer of the clean bedding is scattered across the box as standing litter. This will prevent the horse from slipping but will facilitate the drying of the floor. Assuming that the horse will stay tied up to be groomed and then exercised, the box can be left with the bed up for some time, which will help ensure that the floor – the sides as well as the centre – dries out before the bed is put down again.

An alternative, though not quite so satisfactory, method is to clear the bed completely from one wall of the box each day, thus ensuring that each bank of bedding is turned on a regular basis.

When putting down the bed again the existing bedding should be used to provide a good, deep covering to the entire floor area (right up to the door, to prevent draughts) and new bedding used to bank up the sides (with a straw bed if a

LEFT
A selection of mucking out tools: wheelbarrow, five-tined fork, shovel, shavings scoop, broom and skip. A wheelbarrow is more cumbersome to use than a muck sheet.

ABOVE
The horse should be tied up during mucking out and setting fair. (Note that, for safety, coats should be fastened while you are working with horses.)

■ RIGHT
A muck heap sited in a three-sided bunker is easier
to manage and to keep tidy than a free-standing one.

■ BELOW
Position the muck heap where there is good
drainage and easy access – for large vehicles as well
as wheelbarrows.

horse has a tendency to eat it, new straw should be covered with a layer of the used bedding which will be less palatable). Banked sides keep out draughts, help protect the horse from injury when he is rolling or lying down and may help prevent a horse becoming cast (that is stuck with his legs in such a position that he cannot get up again).

To keep the bed as clean as possible, droppings should be picked up regularly throughout the day in a container known as a skip or skep, which may be made of metal, plastic or rubber. At evening stables the bed should be set fair, that is straightened out and put tidy for the night, care being taken to bank the sides well and ensure that the entire floor area is evenly covered.

To keep a horse on deep litter the

stable needs to be large (in a small one the bed will quickly become sodden) and well ventilated. This system saves time as it involves the daily removal of the droppings only, not the wet bedding underneath. The old bed is left undisturbed and covered with fresh bedding each day. This type of bed needs careful management and is better suited to horses who are out by day as this enables the bedding to dry out more. A deep litter bed is warm in winter and may stay down for as long as six months. However, if it begins to build up too high or to smell it must be completely removed. The box should be thoroughly dried out before a new bed is started. Woodwork will tend to deteriorate more quickly with this type of bed because of the dampness in the lower layers.

A good compromise is the semi-deep litter system, whereby the droppings and the worst of the wet bedding are removed daily and the whole box given a complete muck out once a week or once every few weeks. This works well with shavings beds. With any deep-litter system, frequent removal of droppings is essential.

Management of the muck heap is also important. For convenience it should be sited reasonably close to the stables, with a dry, level approach and easy access for large vehicles. It should be downwind of the stables. A muck heap can be free-standing or contained in a three-sided bunker – breeze blocks are particularly suitable for this purpose – which makes it easier to keep the heap tidy. Make sure that there is adequate drainage away from any paths or driveways.

During mucking out the entire stable floor should be swept clean and, if possible, allowed to dry before the bed is put down again.

The sides of the bed should be banked well up the stable walls to help keep out draughts and to prevent injury when the horse lies down.

A skip is used for the periodic removal of droppings during the day. Skips may be made of plastic, metal or rubber.

Feeds

The horse is a herbivore, that is an eater of plants and especially grass and herbs. Left to live a totally natural life, the horse will spend some twenty hours out of every twenty-four grazing, slowly moving from place to place in his search for satisfying food. Horses are what are known as trickle feeders: they have comparatively small stomachs in relation to the size of their large intestines and need to top up with food at regular intervals. In the wild they put on condition when food is plentiful and lose it when it is not. The unnatural conditions imposed upon horses by man – the lack of constant access to grass and the need to burn up energy by working – mean that they must be fed suitable alternatives to grass if they are to thrive. Feeding horses is a complex subject. Like humans, horses are individuals and vary a good deal in the type and quantity of food they need to maintain health and fitness. Basically, however, the domesticated horse's diet consists of roughage, or bulk food, and concentrates.

ROUGHAGE

The usual way to feed roughage is in the form of hay, which is simply dried grass. There are two types of hay: seed hay and meadow hay. **Seed hay** is suitable for horses in hard work, because it is usually more nutritious than meadow hay. It is taken from grasses specifically sown as an annual crop, which will include top-quality plants such as rye grass and timothy. **Meadow hay** is cut from permanent pasture and is softer to the touch and often greener in colour than seed hay. It contains a greater variety of plants than seed hay (some of which may be of inferior quality) and is usually less nutritious and therefore more suitable for animals in light work.

A newer way of feeding bulk is in the form of **haylage**, which is grass sealed in plastic bags. It comes in different nutritional levels and is particularly

Seed hay (left) and meadow hay (right)

Crushed oats

Bruised barley

Flaked maize

suitable for horses with respiratory problems. Haylage may be mixed with hay or replace it altogether as the horse's bulk feed.

Chaff or **chop** is hay, either alone or mixed with one-third proportion of oat straw, which has been chopped into small pieces by passing it through a chaff cutter. It may be added to concentrates to encourage mastication and aid digestion.

CONCENTRATES

Food such as oats and barley are known as concentrates. These are the energy-giving foods which, when fed in the correct balance with the roughage, enable the horse to perform the work required of him without losing condition.

Oats have always been considered the ideal cereal for feeding to horses. The fibrous husk covering the rich seed encourages chewing and helps prevent the horse from eating too quickly, which can seriously disrupt his digestive system. The one drawback is that oats have a low calcium-to-phosphorus ratio and the horse's diet should therefore contain a calcium supplement to balance the minerals in the roughage. Oats may not be suitable for feeding to all equine animals, however, as they can have a heating effect, making them difficult to control. Oats should be lightly rolled and used within two or three weeks thereafter, otherwise they lose nutritional value.

Barley has a higher energy value than oats but is lower in fibre. It may be fed cracked, rolled, flaked (heat treated) or micronized. It may also be fed as a mash, which is prepared by pouring boiling water over flaked barley and allowing it to cool before feeding. Whole barley should never be fed unless it has first been cooked to soften it, otherwise it is too indigestible. It should be covered with boiling water and allowed to simmer for several hours until the grain has split, swollen and become soft.

Bran

Linseed (which must be boiled before feeding)

Soaked sugar beet

Molassed chop

Horse and pony nuts

Coarse mix

Maize is high in starch but low in protein and fibre. It is usually fed flaked or micronized. It can be very heating and should be fed only in small amounts.

Bran, a by-product of wheat, is high in fibre and often fed to horses who are off work or on a low-protein diet. It may be fed dry in small quantities, mixed with the horse's other feed, or as a mash. This is made by putting the bran, together with a handful of salt, in a bucket, pouring boiling water over it (not so much that the mash is sloppy), covering and allowing it to steam and cool.

Linseed, the seed of the flax plant, is rich in oil and often fed to improve the condition of the horse's coat. It is poisonous (it contains prussic acid) if not first boiled. The linseed is covered with cold water and

soaked overnight. The following day more water is added (about 4 pints/2 litres to 2–3oz/110g of linseed) and the mixture is brought to the boil and simmered for several hours. When the resultant jelly has cooled it may be added to a bran mash or to the horse's ordinary feed.

Sugar beet is a highly digestible source of energy and fibre. It has a good calcium-to-phosphorus ratio and may be used to correct the imbalance of those elements in cereals. Sugar beet pulp (the remains of the root vegetable after the sugar has been extracted) comes in cube form or shredded. Before feeding it is essential to soak it for at least twelve hours using at least double the amount of water to pulp. Cubes may require soaking for longer in more water. If it is not adequately soaked,

it will swell up in the horse's stomach, with potentially fatal results.

Molasses is a by-product of sugar. Dark and sticky in appearance and very palatable, it may be added in small quantities to the feed to supply energy, improve the condition of the coat and to tempt fussy feeders.

Concentrates which come in cube form or as coarse mixes are known as **compound feeds**. They are made from a variety of ingredients and are scientifically prepared to provide a balanced diet. Specially formulated compound feeds are available for foals, brood mares, competition horses, and so on. They are particularly useful for the novice horseman as a good-quality compound feed takes much of the guesswork out of feeding.

Feeding

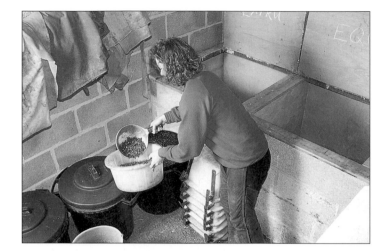

▌ LEFT
Feedstuffs should be kept in a clean feed room, in dry, rodent-proof containers. All feeds should be carefully measured.

To work out a suitable feed ration for your horse you must take into consideration his size, his age, his type and the amount and nature of the work he is doing. Feeding is both a science and an art. Science tells us much about the principles of feeding and the nutritive value of the various feedstuffs but horses are all individuals and ultimately the proof of the pudding is in their appearance and performance. You can learn to judge the correct, healthy condition for a horse of a particular breed, age, size and build doing a particular job of work by studying similar animals to your own which are being used for similar purposes (perhaps at your riding school or in local competitions).

The ratio of bulk feed to concentrates will vary according to the nature and amount of work the horse is required to do. A horse in light work does not require a great deal of energy-giving feed (it will merely serve to make him a "hot" ride). On the other hand a horse such as a hunter or an eventer needs more energy-giving feed and less bulk. For a horse in light work (doing up to about six hours a week hacking and light schooling) and for

The following is an approximate guide to total food requirements based on height (but bear in mind that it is only approximate, since horses vary a good deal in build and a finely made animal may require less food than a heavyweight doing the same amount of work):

Height	Daily feed requirement
Under 12hh	14 – 16lb (6.3 – 7.2kg)
12 – 13hh	16 – 18lb (7.2 – 8kg)
13 – 14hh	20 – 22lb (9 – 10kg)
14 – 15hh	22 – 24lb (10 – 11kg)
15 – 16hh	24 – 26lb (11 – 12kg)
over 16hh	26 – 28lb (12 – 12.5kg)

To find a more accurate yardstick it is customary to measure feed requirements against the horse's body weight (the horse requires a total daily intake of about 2-2.5 per cent of its body weight). The best way to check his weight is to use a weighbridge. Failing that you can estimate his weight by using the following formula:

$$\frac{\text{Girth}^2 \times \text{length (in inches)}}{300}$$
$$= \text{weight in lbs}$$

NB Measure the girth round the largest part of the barrel at the moment when the horse has breathed out; measure the length from the point of the shoulder to the point of the buttock.

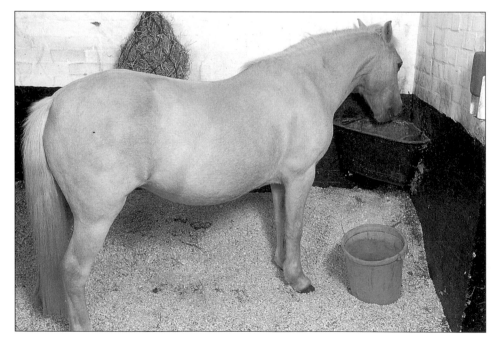

▌ TOP LEFT
Some barn-type stabling incorporates swinging feed bowls. They are labour saving in large yards with a lot of horses to feed.

▌ ABOVE LEFT
Hook on plastic mangers are useful for feeding horses kept at grass.

▌ LEFT
A large corner manger is a suitable way to feed the stabled horse. Mangers must be cleaned out regularly.

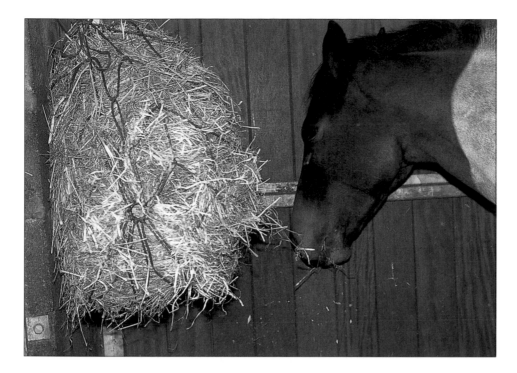

most ponies the ratio should be 30 per cent concentrates to 70 per cent bulk. For a horse in medium work (doing up to ten hours work a week, including up to two hours schooling a day, some dressage, show jumping and hacking) the ratio should be 50 per cent concentrates to 50 per cent bulk. For a horse in hard work (more than ten hours a week, or including fast work such as hunting, eventing or endurance riding) the ratio should be 70 per cent concentrates to 30 per cent bulk. These are general guidelines and all horses are different, but however hard he is working the horse should never receive less than 25 per cent bulk by weight.

Horses and ponies living out at grass during the winter require the same amount of food as stabled horses in order to maintain their health and condition during bad weather. During the spring and summer (assuming that the weather is fine) good-quality grazing should provide enough nutrition for ponies and coldblooded horses doing no more than an hour or two of light work, though it is best to check their weight regularly to make sure. During the winter, grazing will do no more than provide maintenance. In severe weather it will not even do that and the horse will lose condition if he does not receive supplementary feeding.

▮ TOP LEFT
**Haynets must be tied securely and high enough
to prevent the horse from catching a foot in
them. Feeding hay on the ground is safer and
more natural.**

▮ LEFT
**Horses should have access to salt, to counteract any
deficiency in their diet. A salt lick is a convenient
way of providing it.**

▮ FAR LEFT
**Soaking hay in clean water for a few hours
before feeding helps prevent horses inhaling
mould spores.**

Water

Water makes up approximately 60 per cent of an adult horse's body weight, the exact percentage depending on his age and condition. It is present in all his body fluids and is vital for the correct functioning of the blood, the digestion and the excretion process. A horse can survive for several weeks without food but only for a few days without water.

The quantity of water required by a horse on a daily basis varies according to his diet, the prevailing weather conditions, his work load and his general health. A stabled horse may drink in the region of eight gallons (37 litres) of water a day, although the amount may be as little as five gallons (20 litres) or as much as ten (40 litres). A horse at grass may drink less than a stabled horse because of the moisture content in the grazing. A horse will drink more when the weather is hot and humid or when he sweats as a result of hard work. A sick horse may be reluctant to drink.

It is vital for the stabled horse to have access to a constant supply of fresh, clean water, the only exception being before hard, fast work. Horses are extremely fussy about the water they drink and will go thirsty rather than drink dirty or tainted water.

Water for the stabled horse may be provided either in buckets or by means of an automatic water bowl. The advantage of using buckets is that you can easily check the amount of water the horse is drinking. Water buckets should be large and strong – heavy-duty rubber is the most resilient. Plastic buckets, though convenient because they are light to carry, are not the safest as they tend to split and can cause injury. Metal buckets are stronger but they, too, might cause injury to a restless horse.

Buckets should be positioned in a corner of the stable, not right by the door but not too far from it, either, so that they are easy to reach for refilling. The handle

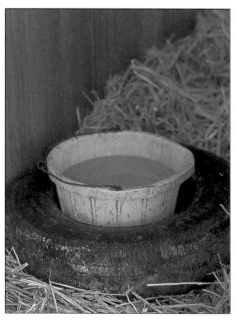

should be positioned away from the horse. Many horses can be trusted never to knock a bucket over, even when it is empty. Others get into the habit of playing with theirs. Some are just naturally clumsy and will knock a bucket over when moving about the box. Water buckets can be fixed to the wall with clips or, if the stable is roomy enough, stood in a rubber tyre.

During the day water buckets should be checked and refilled regularly. Water should be replaced rather than topped up to ensure a fresh supply. At night a big horse will need two buckets so that there is no possibility of his going short. Buckets should be scrubbed out regularly with clean water.

Automatic drinking bowls, connected to the water supply and controlled by a small ballcock, are popular in large yards because they are labour saving. However, they do have several disadvantages. Compared with buckets they are quite small and may not permit a horse to enjoy a deep drink. Unless they are fitted with a plug (which should be recessed into the bottom out of the way of the horse's teeth) they are difficult to clean. Also, it is not possible to judge at a glance how much a horse is drinking. Since water consumption, like food consumption, is an indication of the horse's state of health, this is not ideal. It is, however,

▌ BELOW
An automatic drinking bowl provides an alternative
to buckets. The bowl must be checked frequently to
ensure that the water supply is operating correctly.

▌ BELOW
The stabled horse must have constant access to
clean water. A large horse will need two buckets.

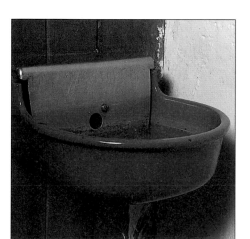

GOLDEN RULES OF WATERING

☞ Always provide the stabled horse with a
constant supply of clean water.

☞ Always water before feeding.

☞ Never work a horse hard immediately
after a long drink.

☞ After hard work (such as hunting or cross-
country) give a horse a small quantity of
water – about half a gallon (2.5 litres) every
quarter of an hour until he is satisfied.

☞ When giving electrolytes (minerals to
replace those lost during strenuous exercise)
always offer plain water as well.

☞ Keep all water utensils clean.

☞ Check automatic water bowls every day.

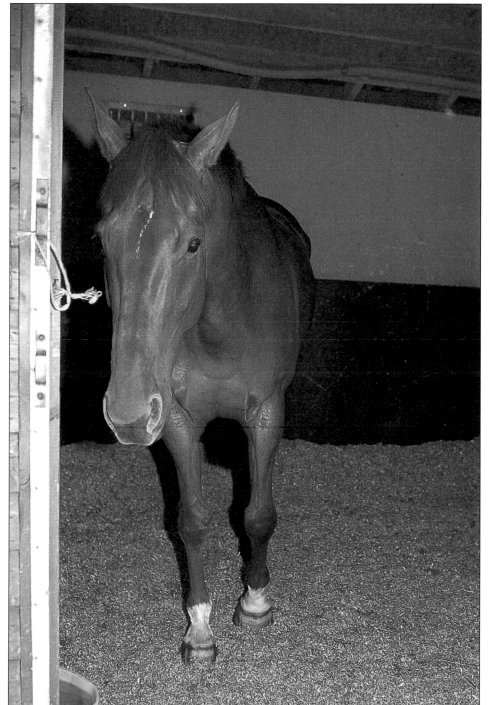

possible to install drinkers fitted with a
meter which overcomes this problem. All
projecting fixtures in a stable are a
potential source of injury to the horse and
a water bowl is no exception. Conversely,
there is every possibility of a bowl being
damaged by the horse. Drinking bowls
must be rigorously checked every day – a
blocked supply will cause the horse great
distress while an overflowing bowl with
swamp his bedding. Precautions must be
taken when fitting pipes so that they
cannot freeze in winter.

Daily Care

Horses must be kept fit and healthy if they are to perform the work required of them. Keeping them that way requires daily care and attention. It is the responsibility of the owner to ensure that the horse has sufficient regular exercise of the right type and to learn how to recognize the signs of ill-health. Every horse, whether he is kept stabled or at grass, should be checked over carefully every day to ensure that he is well, sound and has no injuries or fresh lumps or bumps. Horses are creatures of habit. They thrive on a regular routine and therefore should be visited, fed, exercised and so on, at the same times each day. Some common equine ailments and minor injuries can be dealt with by the competent horseman, others will need veterinary attention. The owner must judge when to seek expert advice, bearing in mind that the sooner treatment begins, the better the chance of a cure. Regular visits from the farrier are also an essential part of horse care. There was never a truer maxim than "no foot, no horse".

Exercise

The horse needs daily exercise for the maintenance of health and, like all athletes, when he is in work he needs additional exercise to build up and maintain condition.

Where fitness of the horse is concerned exercise is always linked to feed. A horse who is kept at grass, provided the paddock is not very small, has the opportunity to

STABLE "VICES"

Being cooped up in a stable for some twenty-two hours out of every twenty-four is unnatural and boring and may lead to a horse developing bad habits, or stable "vices". These include wood chewing, box-walking (aimless walking round and round the stable), crib-biting (in which the horse takes hold of the manger or the top of the door or some other convenient object with his teeth and swallows air) or weaving (in which he stands, usually with his head over the door, and sways from side to side). Virtually all stable vices can do harm to the horse in one way or another. All can be avoided if the horse is not allowed to become bored and frustrated.

■ **LEFT**
The stabled horse requires regular daily exercise to keep him healthy. Hacking out helps to get him fit and enables him to relax after work.

■ **OPPOSITE**
For racehorses, and other horses in hard work, a carefully planned exercise programme is essential.

■ **PREVIOUS PAGE OPPOSITE**
Most ponies, like this Haflinger, thrive when kept at grass.

■ **PREVIOUS PAGE**
Despite its size, the Suffolk Punch is an economical breed to keep.

■ **BELOW LEFT**
In their natural state, horses and ponies such as this Exmoor mare and foal have all the exercise they need.

take all the gentle exercise he needs to stay healthy. Space and the freedom to move around at will are an intrinsic part of the horse's everyday life in the natural state so the bigger his paddock the nearer it is to his natural environment and the more contented he will be.

However, the totally grass-fed horse will not be fit to do anything other than light work in summer. By keeping the horse in a stable it is possible to monitor his food intake and gradually build up his physical fitness to enable him to carry out the work required of him. But because the stabled horse is deprived of his freedom for part, if not all, of the day a good exercise regime is essential if he is to be happy and healthy and not become unmanageable.

If possible, all stabled horses should spend part of the day turned out at grass in addition to their normal work routine. There is a danger of fit horses doing themselves harm when turned out, so it is essential to have safely fenced paddocks and to fit protective boots to guard against accidents. If for some reason it is not possible to give the stabled horse his usual exercise (for example in bad weather when it may be impossible to ride on the roads), he should be turned out for a time each day or at the very least led out and allowed to eat some grass. Another alternative to ridden exercise is to work the horse on the lunge.

❚ RIGHT
For exercise purposes a simple snaffle bridle and general purpose saddle are usually adequate.

❚ BOTTOM
Horse and rider prepared to go. If the horse is to be ridden on the roads, he should be fitted with kneeboots.

Before being exercised or worked the horse should be given a quick grooming to make him neat and tidy. Stable stains should be sponged off and all remnants of bedding removed from his mane and tail. His feet should be picked out and his shoes checked.

An all-purpose saddle is suitable for general hacking out and roadwork. A numnah will protect the saddle from grease and dirt from the horse's coat and will also be more comfortable for his back.

Keeping a bridle for everyday use will minimize the wear and tear on the bridle you use for "best", e.g. for showing or competing. The bitting and bridling arrangement will depend on the horse. Most can be hacked out safely in a snaffle with a cavesson noseband. If you do need a little more control, you may prefer to fit a Grakle or flash noseband. Whether or not you use a martingale will again depend on the horse and how difficult or otherwise he is to control.

When exercising on the roads it is advisable to fit the horse with kneeboots – fitted correctly they will not impede his action. It is all too easy for a horse to slip up on tarmac and injure his knees, yet it is surprising how few people take this simple precaution. Brushing boots are another useful means of protecting the horse's legs.

A clipped horse in winter will need an exercise sheet to keep his loins warm. This is placed under the saddle to prevent it slipping back. It should be fitted with a fillet string, which passes under the tail to prevent it blowing up in the wind.

You can exercise two horses at the same time by riding one and leading one, in which case the led horse should wear a bridle and you should lead him either by the reins or on a leather lead rein run from one bit ring, through the other and into your hand. Never lead a horse on a lunge rein which could easily become tangled, and never wind a lead rein or reins round your hand. The ridden horse must always be between the led horse and the traffic and you should always ride on the same side of the road as the direction

of the traffic. Avoid riding and leading on roads where there is anything but light traffic and never ride and lead unless the horses are traffic-proof and well behaved. For maximum control the led horse's head should be at or just behind the ridden horse's shoulder.

For more serious work – schooling, dressage, jumping and so on – the horse should wear the saddle and bridle most suited to that activity and protective boots or bandages. For jumping, fit his shoes with appropriate studs to prevent slipping.

Fitness

Broadly speaking the fitness training of the horse can be divided into three distinct stages. First, there is a period of slow work designed to strengthen him up in readiness for more serious work. Second, there is the build up designed to bring him to the necessary fitness for most everyday riding activities. And third, there is the fine tuning required to bring him to a peak for physically demanding pastimes such as regular hunting, show jumping, eventing or racing.

FIRST STAGE

The period of slow work is vital and should never be rushed. The tried and tested way to make horses fit, and to prevent strains and sprains when they begin serious work, is roadwork. When the horse is first ridden after a period of rest,

■ LEFT
Hillwork builds up muscle, particularly in the hindquarters, and improves the horse's lung and heart capacity.

■ BOTTOM
Hacking out makes a welcome break from school work for both horse and rider.

he must have walking exercise only. Three-quarters of an hour a day is sufficient to begin with if the horse has been out at grass. Gradually, over a period of **two or three weeks** (preferably longer if the horse is ultimately going to be asked to do a lot of hard, fast work), this can be increased to an hour and a half to two hours a day.

Although this is slow work, the horse must not be allowed to slop along any old how. He should be kept going forward,

straight and in a good rhythm in order to start the process of building up muscles in the right places. The exercise route should be varied as much as possible to keep the horse alert and interested and he should have a day off each week to allow him to relax.

Trotting can begin during weeks **three to four**. To begin with the horse should walk for about thirty minutes before starting to trot. This will give his muscles time to warm up. His exercise period

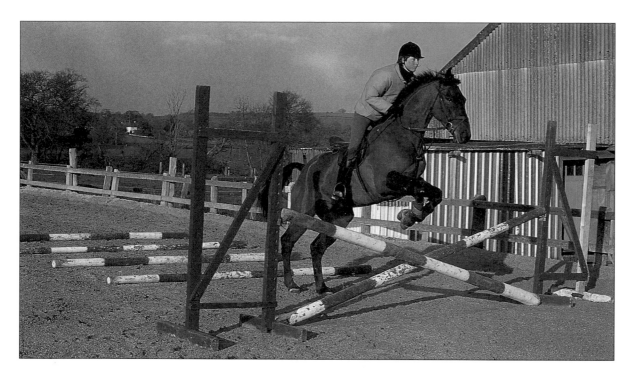

▌ LEFT
By week five the horse should be fit enough to start a little gymnastic jumping.

▌ BELOW LEFT
Serious schooling can begin when the horse has been in work for about six weeks.

should also finish at walk, in order to cool him off. The trot should be controlled and rhythmic and in the early stages the periods of trot should be short and interspersed with longer periods of walk. As the days progress and the horse begins to feel fitter, the periods of trot can be made longer. The pace must always be controlled: trotting flat out on the roads (or any other hard surface) jars the horse's legs and can lead to injury. Uphill trotting is better than trotting on the flat because it reduces the strain placed on the front legs. At all times when trotting the rider should change the diagonal regularly and, when trotting uphill, keep the weight forward.

During **week four** some periods of schooling on the flat can be introduced. They should be no longer than about twenty minutes and cantering should be kept to a minimum. To encourage the horse to relax and to continue the building-up process, he should be taken for a hack afterwards.

Week five can see the introduction of a little hillwork, one of the finest ways of building up muscle. Hacking and flatwork should continue.

By **week six** he should be ready for a canter work-out, in which he should be allowed to stride on but without going into a wild gallop. As with trotting, uphill cantering is the most beneficial.

SECOND STAGE

Once the first stage in the fitness programme is completed the horse will be in a fit state to begin more serious work. Work on the flat, incorporating suppling exercises such as serpentines and circles, should be introduced. The schooling sessions should be kept short to begin with but may be gradually increased in length as the horse becomes more toned up. Gymnastic jumping exercises over grids and on circles and elements of circles will all help to improve his athleticism.

THIRD STAGE

The type of fitness required in a particular horse is always governed by the type of work required of him. For example a show jumper needs the muscular power to clear big fences but is never required to gallop flat out for a prolonged period. On the other hand the three-day eventer needs great stamina and endurance to be able to cope with the demands placed on him.

Getting the horse fit for sports which require speed and endurance involves longer periods of canter work. Canter work must be introduced gradually and should always be carried out on good ground to reduce the risk of injury. Short periods of canter are sufficient to begin with. Later, periods of long, steady cantering may be used to bring the horse to a high degree of fitness. Only rarely is the occasional really fast galloping necessary, as for instance with the fine tuning of a racehorse or three-day event horse. The main thing to remember is that the faster the pace the more chance there is of injury occurring.

Even when the horse reaches peak fitness for the activity required of him, he should be allowed regular periods of relaxation if he is not to become sour – hacks in the countryside or spells at liberty in the paddock. During a rest day after strenuous work the horse will appreciate being led out for a bite of grass.

The Healthy and the Unhealthy Horse

Recognizing signs of ill-health in the horse is all part of good horse management. The experienced horseman can tell at a glance when something is not quite right with an animal in his or her care. Learning to recognize the warning signs means an early diagnosis which, in turn, means a better chance of successful treatment.

A change in the horse's eating habits is often the first indication of something being amiss with his health: if a normally good feeder loses his appetite, be suspicious. A change in behaviour is also a reliable early-warning signal. For instance, if a normally bright, alert horse suddenly becomes listless, it may well be the first sign of a health problem. Any form of nasal discharge, coughing or a dull "staring" coat are also indications of ill-health. A change in the consistency and frequency of the horse's droppings may also mean that all is not well.

All owners should learn to check their horse's temperature, pulse rate and respiratory rate so as to know when to call for veterinary help.

The normal temperature of the healthy horse is around 101.5° Fahrenheit (38°C). You should learn to take your horse's temperature by practising while he is healthy so that you will be capable of making a fast, accurate reading should the

All horses carry a worm burden and require regular worming. The usual method of worming is to administer an oral paste.

The horse's pulse is to be found along the edge of the lower jaw. In the healthy horse the heart rate is about 40 per minute.

need arise. The temperature is taken with a clinical thermometer which is inserted into the rectum and held there for about one minute. It is best to hold the horse's tail steady to prevent him swishing it and possibly dislodging the thermometer.

At rest the healthy horse has a heart rate of about 40 per minute. If the heart rate exceeds 60 per minute, there is definitely something wrong with the horse. To count the heart rate you need a stethoscope but failing that it is possible to count the horse's pulse rate by resting a finger over the artery situated about halfway along the bottom edge of the lower jaw. Locating the pulse will take a certain amount of practice.

In the healthy horse at rest the respiratory rate can vary from about eight to sixteen breaths a minute. To count the respiratory rate watch the horse's flanks.

Like humans, some horses have heart murmurs or faulty heart rhythms. If a heart abnormality is only present when

the horse is resting and disappears when he begins to work, there is usually no cause for alarm.

Problems with the limbs manifest themselves in various ways. Often the slightest suspicion of heat or a tiny swelling may be an indication of a serious tendon problem. Actual lameness can be detected by watching the horse as he is trotted both away from you and towards you. Watch for a sinking of the hindquarters or a nod of the head as one foot hits the ground (it will be the other limb which is causing the pain). When acquiring a new horse take note of any scars or bony enlargements so that you can distinguish new problems from old conditions or injuries.

All horses carry a worm burden which must be controlled by regular worming if it is not to cause serious damage to their health. Your veterinary surgeon will advise on a suitable worming programme.

In young horses a raised temperature and cold-like symptoms such as a nasal discharge may indicate an infestation of ascarids. These are quite large worms which can cause colic. In the adult horse the main danger comes from the large red worm, or *Strongylus vulgaris*, whose immature larvae burrow into the small arteries in the intestinal wall. The damage

The horse's temperature is taken by inserting a thermometer into the rectum. The normal temperature is about 101.5° Fahrenheit (38°C)

they cause to the walls of the blood vessels may result in a blood clot. An infestation of *Strongylus vulgaris* can cause colic and anaemia. It may also disrupt the normal movement of the bowels.

If the horse is seen rubbing his tail, he may be suffering from pin worms, which inhabit the rectum.

Cream-coloured eggs attached to the horse's hair, particularly on the legs, during summer are the eggs of the horse bot, a fly whose larvae are able to penetrate the skin and migrate to the horse's stomach. If the infestation is severe, bots can produce ulceration of the stomach wall and may affect digestion.

Every horse owner should have a well-stocked equine first-aid kit readily available at all times.

❚ LEFT AND BELOW
To detect lameness, watch the horse trotting towards you and away from you. Look for a nod of the head or sinking of the hindquarters.

❚ BELOW
Mud fever usually affects the lower legs. This horse
also has capped hocks and windgalls (painless fluid-
filled swellings just above the fetlock joints).

❚ BOTTOM LEFT
The irritation caused by sweet itch often results in
the horse rubbing the mane and tail hair at the
affected areas.

Common Ailments

Azoturia, also known as set fast or tying-up, is a stiffening up of the large muscles of the back and hindquarters. It results from the accumulation of large amounts of lactic acid. It is not always possible to determine the reason, though too much food combined with too little exercise is a common cause. The horse begins to sweat up and has difficulty in moving forwards. The muscles feel hard to the touch and the horse will clearly be in pain. Dark, red-coloured urine may be passed. The horse should be rugged up and not moved. The veterinary surgeon should be called. He or she may prescribe drugs to relieve the pain and inflammation.

In **chronic obstructive pulmonary disease** (COPD) the airways to the horse's lungs become, as the name suggests, chronically obstructed. COPD is the result of an allergic reaction to fungal spores, for instance in the horse's hay or bedding. Symptoms include a nasal discharge followed by a cough. The horse's ability to perform hard work diminishes and in time his respiratory rate at rest increases. Treatment includes rest, fresh air, antibiotics and clean stabling with dust-free bedding and spore-free feed.

Equine influenza occurs in two main strains with numerous subtypes; a serious respiratory disease, it can prove fatal. Symptoms include a horse going off his feed, a raised temperature and general cold-type symptoms. Antibiotics may help and the horse must be rested. Horses can

be vaccinated, very effectively, against many strains of flu – indeed vaccination is mandatory for most competition horses.

Grass sickness is a painful and fatal disease affecting the horse's nervous system. It is typified by loss of condition, muscle twitching, difficulty in swallowing and a green nasal discharge. In an acute case the horse may die in a few days. Others linger for weeks or months. Its cause is uncertain and it is more common in some regions than others.

Mud fever is a bacterial infection of the skin which affects the legs and/or lower body. It is most often seen on the lower legs. Raw areas develop which ooze serum and then form scabs. At the back of the pasterns and heels cracks often develop in the skin. The condition is most often seen in skin exposed to very muddy or very dry, dusty conditions. Skin with white hair is most susceptible. The best way of preventing mud fever and cracked heels is to protect the skin, when dry, with a barrier cream. Treatment involves clipping the hair from the affected area, regular washing (with antiseptic shampoo) and removal of scabs, careful drying and the use of antibiotic ointment.

COLIC

Colic is abdominal pain which may occur for a number of reasons, such as a sudden change in diet, migrating worm larvae, impaction of the intestines or, in rarer cases, a twisted gut. Signs of colic include the horse standing and looking round at, or trying to kick, its flank, sweating and/or repeated lying down and rolling.

The horse should be put in a stable on a deep bed to guard against injury if he wants to lie down and roll and the vet should be called. He or she may administer pain-relieving or relaxant drugs and/or a lubricant, depending on the type of colic. If a twisted gut is diagnosed, immediate surgery is essential to save the horse's life. Potentially life-threatening attacks of colic are accompanied by a high temperature (above 103° Fahrenheit/39°C) and raised pulse rate (above 60 per minute).

Rain scald is a skin infection caused by the same bacterium as mud fever. It occurs on the upper surfaces of the body. Like mud fever it is treated with antiseptic shampoos and the removal of the scabs which harbour the bacteria.

Ringworm is a fungal infection of the skin and hair. It occurs as small crusty, hairless patches and is infectious. An affected horse should, therefore, be isolated. Ringworm is treated with special antibiotic skin washes which should also be used on the horse's tack to kill off all traces of the infection. The stable should also be treated. Careful control is required as ringworm can affect humans, too.

Strangles is an infection of the lymph glands under the jaw caused by the bacterium *Streptococcus equi*. Affected horses have difficulty in swallowing and the glands under the jaw become swollen. The temperature may rise to as high as 106° Fahrenheit (41°C) and there is a nasal discharge. Infected horses must be kept warm and given soft food. Antibiotics may help. The abscesses in the glands should be treated with hot fomentations – once they burst the horse's condition usually improves. The pus from burst abscesses is highly contagious and horses affected by the infection should be isolated. A policy of strict hygiene must be adopted to prevent the spread of the infection on clothing and equipment. Abscesses which burst internally are very serious since they can cause pneumonia.

Sweet itch is a skin irritation caused by hypersensitivity to the bites of midges and is therefore found chiefly during the spring and summer. It usually occurs along the mane and the base of the tail, which become inflamed and sore. The irritation is such that the horse will often rub out all the mane and tail hairs at the affected places, making the skin raw. A susceptible horse or pony will suffer from sweet itch annually and must be protected from midge bites by being stabled at dusk and dawn when the insects are most active. Benzyl benzoate is used to sooth the sore areas and helps to repel the midges. Fly repellents will also help and mosquito netting should be fitted over open windows and doors while the horse is stabled. Special sheets that cover the entire neck and body give useful protection.

All horses should be vaccinated against **tetanus** and given a booster injection every other year. Tetanus is caused by a bacterium found in the soil and may enter the horse's system via a wound, especially a deep puncture wound. Typical symptoms are stiffness of the muscles, twitching, the horse standing in a stretched-out manner and, as the disease progresses, overreaction to sudden noises or movements. Eventually the horse is unable to stand and death occurs when the breathing muscles become affected. Some horses do recover from tetanus since the infection can be halted by the use of antibiotics and antitoxin. Early diagnosis is essential and the horse will need to rest in a quiet, dark stable.

Common Injuries

Back injuries, either to the bones or muscles of the back, are often the result of falls. Treatment involves rest and the use of anti-inflammatory drugs. Faradism (stimulation of the muscles by electricity), massage and laser therapy may also help.

A **capped elbow** – the term used for a bursal enlargement at the point of the elbow – is usually caused by the horse's shoe striking the elbow when he is lying down. The swelling is soft and is hot and painful when it first appears. A **capped hock** is a similar injury, caused by the horse striking his hock against something hard like the wall of his stable (perhaps through the use of too little bedding) or the partition in a horsebox (hock boots should be fitted to guard against this, particularly if the horse is a bad traveller). Unless the condition causes lameness or there is an infection, it will not require treatment. In the case of a capped elbow the horse should be fitted with a "sausage boot" (a protective ring) on the pastern. This protects the elbow while it is healing.

An **overreach** is an injury to the heel or the back of the tendon of the front legs

█ LEFT
Wounds must be thoroughly cleaned and then treated with ointment or powder. Leg wounds tend to heal less well than wounds to the body where the skin is looser.

caused by the horse striking itself with the toe of its own hindfoot. Overreaches should be carefully cleaned. An antibiotic dressing will help guard against infection. Overreaches can be serious – there is often extensive bruising – and are often slow to heal.

Splints are bony swellings found between the splint bones and the cannon bones. Although splints are most commonly found on the inner side of the forelegs, they can occur on either side of the leg and on the hindlegs. Splints often appear when a young horse first begins work. Conformation is a contributing factor. In many cases splints are associated

---

FIRST-AID KIT

The horse owner's first-aid kit should include:

- ☞ Disinfectant – for washing wounds.
- ☞ Skin swabs – small swabs impregnated with disinfectant for cleaning wounds where there is no clean water supply.
- ☞ Wound cleansing cream or liquid.
- ☞ Wound ointment or powder.
- ☞ Wound dressings.
- ☞ Crêpe bandages.
- ☞ Adhesive bandages.
- ☞ Gamgee tissue.
- ☞ Cotton wool.
- ☞ Cold packs.
- ☞ Poultices.
- ☞ Thermometer.
- ☞ Scissors (sharp, but with rounded ends for safety).
- ☞ Fly repellent.

Swollen joints can be the result of injury, infection or a dietary problem.

Fibrous tissue known as proud flesh may form a permanent blemish which will require surgical removal.

When bandaging a knee, cotton wool or Gamgee tissue should be used under the bandage.

The correct way to bandage a hock.

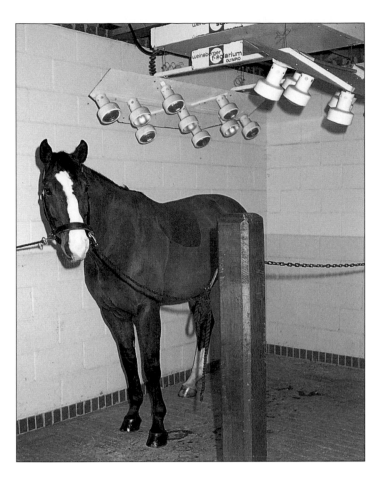

■ LEFT
Infra-red helps to relax muscles and soothe pain. This horse is enjoying a spell in a solarium.

■ BELOW LEFT AND RIGHT
Eye injuries, such as cuts and bruises, can be dangerous and require professional attention.

■ BOTTOM
Stimulation of the muscles by electricity (Faradism) is useful in the treatment of back injuries.

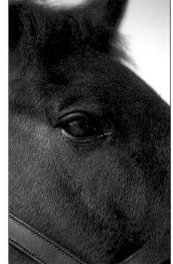

with poor foot and limb balance, in which case corrective shoeing often helps. Lameness may result, in varying degrees, while the splint is forming but often the pain associated with splints disappears in time. In the case of persistent lameness, the leg should be X-rayed to eliminate any possibility of a fracture.

Because of the strain put on the legs when galloping and jumping, **tendon injuries** are all too common in horses, particularly in the forelegs. The superficial and deep flexor tendons, which run down the back of the cannon bones, the suspensory ligament, which is immediately behind the lower part of the cannon bone, and the check ligament, situated below the knee, are all at risk. Tendon and ligament injuries are the result of sudden stress, which causes the fibres to tear. The injury causes pain, followed by heat and swelling. Cold is the most important part of the treatment: ice packs or, in an emergency, a pack of frozen peas, should be applied to the site of the injury as quickly as possible. Ice packs should be replaced frequently and the limb should be bandaged firmly, though not too tightly, for support. Laser treatment may help to reduce the swelling. The oldest – and best – treatment for all strains and

sprains is rest. A leg which has suffered a serious tendon injury is more likely to stand up to future work if the horse is given a period of twelve to eighteen months off. The veterinary surgeon can determine, by using a scanner, when a tendon injury has healed.

Horses suffer all types of **wounds** as a result of falls, accidents in the field and stable, and bites and kicks from other horses. Some, such as grazes, heal quickly provided they are kept clean and dry. Others can cause serious problems. **Puncture wounds** are often the most dangerous since bacteria may be carried deep into the wound. Although it is impossible not to notice a large, jagged laceration accompanied by a copious flow

of blood, it is easy to overlook a deep puncture wound simply because the wound to the skin is small and insignificant looking. It is important to ensure that such wounds heal from the inside out – poulticing may be necessary to draw out infection.

All wounds should be cleaned, if possible, with cold water though it should be remembered that continuous washing will not stop a wound from bleeding. The application of a pressure pad (such as a clean handkerchief) will help control the flow of blood while you are waiting for veterinary help. Large wounds may need stitching. If there is any doubt about the horse's vaccination status, he must be given a tetanus injection. If a wound needs covering to keep it clean, medicated gauze should be used as it will not stick to the wound. Wounds on the body, where the skin is loose, heal better than leg wounds which tend to develop proud flesh as they heal. Proud flesh is fibrous tissue, projecting beyond the level of the skin surrounding the wound and often forming a permanent blemish. The veterinary surgeon may advise using caustic preparations to arrest its development or it may need to be removed surgically.

Poulticing and Cold Treatments

The application of heat by means of a poultice helps to repair injury by stimulating the blood supply to the affected area. Heat also has a "drawing" effect, and will help to bring any pus to the surface.

Poultices may be made with kaolin, or specially impregnated padding can be bought. To make a hot kaolin poultice the tin of kaolin, with the lid loosened, is placed in a pan of boiling water for several minutes. When the kaolin is hot (no hotter than can be borne on the back of your hand) it is spread over a piece of lint, covered with gauze and applied to the injured area. To keep the heat in, polythene or aluminium foil is then wrapped over the gauze, followed by a piece of Gamgee tissue and the poultice is held in place with a bandage.

The poultice should be changed at least twice a day. All the kaolin must be removed from the wound before a new poultice is applied, otherwise the drawing effect of the new poultice will be lost. The main drawback of kaolin is that it is messy

to put on and remove. This problem can be overcome if you use ready-made poultices consisting of kaolin enclosed in a thin envelope of polythene.

Gamgee-type tissue impregnated with chemicals with drawing properties is also available. This must be activated by soaking in warm water. Like the envelope type of kaolin poultice it is easy to apply though it does leave a residue on the skin

which must be cleaned off before another poultice is applied.

Bran may be used to poultice the horse's foot in the case of problems such as a septic foot or corns. Boiling water is poured on to one or two scoops of bran to form a crumbly, not excessively wet, mixture. Test the bran for heat on the palm of the hand before applying it to the foot. The bran may be applied in a foot poultice boot, which is strapped on to the foot, or it may be placed in polythene and sacking and secured in place with a bandage. Horses sometimes try to eat bran poultices so it is advisable to add a little disinfectant to the boiling water to act as a deterrent. The poultice should be left on for twelve hours.

Tubbing is used for some foot wounds, which may require more regular applications of heat. Hand-hot water is placed in a non-metal bucket or tub and the horse's foot placed in it. Horses who are unwilling to cooperate by immersing their foot should be encouraged by having hot water gently splashed on their leg.

▮ TOP
Three types of equine boot designed to keep dressings in place on the horse's foot. Alternatively sacking, secured by a bandage, may be used.

▮ FAR LEFT
Gamgee-type tissue, impregnated with chemicals, makes an effective poultice. It is soaked in warm water before application.

▮ LEFT
Poultices should be removed at least twice a day. Any residue must be cleaned off the horse's skin before re-poulticing.

▍ LEFT
Inhalants are
sometimes used when
horses have respiratory
tract problems. The
bag containing the
inhalant is fitted like a
nosebag.

▍ BELOW
Hosing with cold water
helps to reduce the
swelling and heat
which accompany most
leg injuries.

▍ BELOW LEFT
Another effective
method of applying
cold treatment: a
hosepipe attached to a
"hose boot".

▍ BELOW RIGHT
Hot or cold tubbing
can be carried out by
standing the horse's
foot in a bucket –
always providing he
cooperates!

Epsom salts and antiseptic may be added
to the water. Tubbing lasts for about
twenty minutes and should be carried out
at least twice a day.

Where cold treatment is required as
opposed to heat, there are various
methods. Cold water may be applied with
a hose for regular periods of about ten
minutes. The horse should be accustomed
to the feel of the water by starting at
ground level and then gradually working it
up the foot and leg. The legs should be
bandaged between hosing sessions. Where
suitable facilities are available the hose can
be bandaged to the horse's leg. He should
be given a haynet to keep him occupied.
Walking or standing a horse in a river or
in the sea is equally beneficial.

Specially designed flexible packs, which
retain their cool temperature for quite a
long time, can be obtained. They are
cooled in a freezer and bandaged into
place. Special bandages are available, too.
These are designed to absorb water and

are flexible enough to be applied even
when the water is frozen. Another way to
apply cold to a leg is to soak bandages in
cold water (care must be taken to remove
them before they start to dry out as they

might shrink). Crushed ice in a polythene
bag or, in an emergency, a packet of
frozen peas may be bandaged round a leg.
A thin layer of Gamgee should be placed
over the leg first.

Anatomy of the Foot

Lameness in horses occurs far more often in the foot than in any other part of the limbs. This is not surprising considering the amount of strain put upon the feet of domesticated horses required to pull heavy loads or carry a rider, particularly at fast speeds or over jumps.

The term foot is used to describe the hoof – the dense horny covering – and all the structures contained inside it. The external, insensitive part of the hoof comprises the wall (the outer, protective layer of the foot); the sole (a plate of hard horn just under an inch (2cm) thick; the frog (a wedge-shaped mass of soft elastic horn), and the periople (a thin layer of epidermis between the hoof wall and the skin).

The function of the sole is to give protection to the sensitive inner structures and to help support weight. The frog performs the same functions as the sole as well as providing grip and acting as a shock absorber. The periople controls evaporation from the underlying horn.

The internal part of the hoof comprises the sensitive laminae, the sensitive sole, the sensitive frog, the perioplic corium and the coronary corium.

■ LEFT
A well-matched pair of forefeet. The toe clips steady the shoes while the nails are driven in and help to ensure an accurate fit.

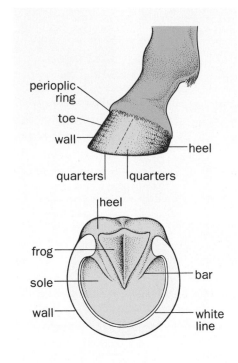

perioplic ring
toe
wall
heel
quarters | quarters

heel
frog
sole
wall
bar
white line

Laminae are interlocking leaf-like structures which attach the hoof to the pedal bone. Hundreds of sensitive (or primary) laminae dovetail with thousands of horny (secondary) laminae which grow outwards from the interior of the wall of the hoof.

The sensitive sole, which is attached securely to the lower surface of the pedal bone, is a thin layer of tissue which corresponds to the horny sole and supplies it with nutrition.

The sensitive frog supplies nutrition to the digital cushion on which it is moulded. This cushion is a wedge-shaped fibro-elastic pad situated in the hollow behind the heels. It has an important part to play in reducing concussion by expanding when the foot takes weight.

The perioplic corium or ring situated just above the coronary corium (coronary body) supplies nutrition to the periople. The coronary corium, a thick structure situated above the sensitive laminae, lies in the coronary groove and supplies nutrition to the wall of the hoof.

On the ground surface of the sole, where the sole meets the wall, is a narrow band of soft plastic horn known as the white line. This white line is of great importance to the farrier because it indicates the position of the sensitive structures of the foot and the thickness of the wall, thus helping determine where nails can be driven into the wall to hold shoes in place without encroaching on the sensitive areas.

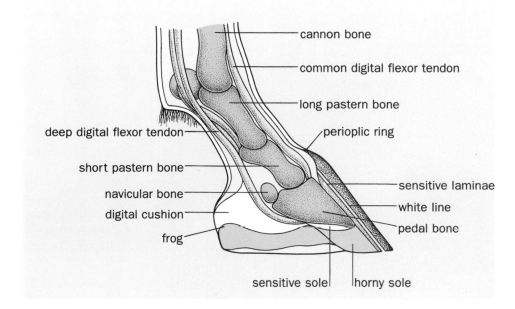

cannon bone
common digital flexor tendon
long pastern bone
deep digital flexor tendon
perioplic ring
short pastern bone
navicular bone
digital cushion
sensitive laminae
white line
frog
pedal bone
sensitive sole | horny sole

The Role of the Farrier

Horses have been shod with metal shoes for over two thousand years and although it is impossible to say for certain who first had the temerity to try nailing a shoe to the horse's hoof, it is widely assumed to have been the Celts and the Gauls.

The need to protect the feet arose when man began to use the horse as a beast of burden and for riding. The unnatural wear and tear inflicted upon the feet of the domesticated horse results in the hooves being worn down more quickly than they are renewed – this would not occur in the horse's natural state. The damage caused to the hoof is worse when travelling over hard, rough ground or in a wet environment. The latter leads to the growth of softer horn, which wears away more quickly. This explains why horses in dry, hot climates, which promote the growth of hard horn, can often do a considerable amount of work unshod without any ill effects.

The role of the farrier is of vital importance, since the horse cannot work adequately if his feet are painful. It is the farrier's job to ensure that the horse's feet are not only well and securely shod but are also correctly trimmed. The horn of the hoof is constantly growing and fitting a metal shoe to the hoof prevents excess growth being worn down naturally, as is the case with the unshod horse. The average monthly growth of horn is around ¼–⅜ inch (5–9mm) and the horse needs to have his feet trimmed about every four or five weeks, depending on the rate of growth. If his old shoes are not worn, they may be refitted – these are known as "removes".

Shoes may be fitted either hot or cold. The advantage of hot shoeing is that it ensures a better fit because the shoe can be finely adjusted to fit the foot (the shoe must always be altered to fit the foot, not vice versa). The shoe is heated in the furnace and held against the prepared hoof (which is insensitive) for a short time. The imprint it leaves indicates to the farrier any necessary adjustments required. Once these have been made the shoe is plunged in cold water before being nailed on to the foot.

It is important to remember that horses who are unshod, perhaps because they are resting, still need regular attention from the farrier. Being confined in a paddock is not the same as being free to roam in search of food, and the horse's hooves will not wear down as they would in the wild.

The farrier's work is very skilful. He must be able to trim the hoof, and drive nails into the insensitive part of the hoof wall, with great precision. One slip, and the result will be a lame horse. Nor is farriery simply about the routine trimming and re-shoeing of horses. It also involves skilled remedial shoeing, which calls for a detailed knowledge of the anatomy of the horse's limbs, including the bones, the joints, the muscles, the vascular system and the nervous system. Defective action, caused by less than perfect conformation or injury, can be greatly improved by expert trimming of the foot and the fitting of specially designed shoes. In these cases, the farrier will work in conjunction with the veterinary surgeon.

At one time it was the practice for the horse to be taken to the farrier for shoeing, which meant that the farrier had all the facilities of a permanent forge on hand. Nowadays it is usually the farrier who has to travel to the horse with a mobile forge, so the onus is on the horse owner to provide him with a suitable working area.

A dry, level surface for the horse to stand on is essential, as is good lighting. In summer, when flies are a nuisance, the horse should be in a shady area, either in a building or under a tree, and it is advisable to have some fly repellent handy.

The horse's feet should be cleaned and dried beforehand and it is the owner's responsibility to ensure that the horse is as well behaved as possible. Most horses will stand quietly. But remember that feeding or moving other horses about while a horse is being shod can make him extremely restive – and the farrier's job that much more difficult.

▌ LEFT
In order to make horseshoes, the farrier must be skilled in bending, turning and shaping metal. He uses an anvil specially designed for the purpose.

The Farrier's Tools

The farrier's tools are divided into two categories: forge tools, that is those used while making shoes, and shoeing tools, that is those used while preparing the foot and nailing on the shoe.

Forge tools include the anvil, on which the metal is shaped; various hammers and tongs; the stamp, used for making nail holes in the shoes; the fullering iron, used to make a groove round the edge of the ground surface of the shoe and the pritchel, a steel punch used to finish off the nail holes and also for carrying hot shoes to the horse's foot for fitting.

Shoeing tools include hammer, pincers, trimmer and rasp. The farrier's shoeing hammer, which has a short, curved claw, is used to drive in the nails, to twist off the points of the nails and form the clenches, and to pull out nails.

When removing shoes the farrier uses a buffer (or clench cutter) to cut off the clenches or knock them up before withdrawing the nails.

Pincers are used for raising and levering off shoes and for withdrawing nails. They are also used to turn the clenches. For trimming, a hoof trimmer, cutter or parer is used. This is a tool with a pincer-like head, one side being sharp and the other flat. To remove the overgrown wall of the hoof the flat side is placed on the outside of the wall and the sharp cutting side on the inside.

When removing ragged pieces of frog or loose flakes of sole a drawing knife is used. The searcher, a similar tool but with a thinner blade, is designed for use when cutting out corns or paring away the horn round puncture wounds.

The farrier's rasp is partly coarse, partly smooth (file cut) and has serrated edges. The farrier uses the coarse side to remove excess hoof wall and for the final levelling of the bearing surface of the foot. The coarse side is also used to finish off the clenches. The file cut surface is used to finish off the shoe and to shape the clenches. Using the serrated edges the farrier removes the sharp edge of the wall (to prevent it splitting) after the shoe has been nailed on.

STUDS

Although shoes help to give the horse added grip on grass it is often essential to fit studs in the shoes as well. Studs may be permanent or of the screw-in type (in which case the shoes are provided with screw holes by the farrier). Screw-in studs

1 Having cut off or knocked up the clenches (the turned-over points of the nails), the farrier uses pincers to lever off the old shoe.

2 Excess growth of hoof is removed with a trimmer, which has one flat and one sharp side.

3 A drawing knife is used to lower the hoof wall and remove loose flakes of sole.

4 The bearing surface of the foot is levelled with a rasp before the shoe is fitted.

5 Hot shoeing ensures a better fit than cold shoeing and causes the horse no pain.

6 Nails are driven into the insensitive wall of the foot to hold the shoes in place.

nail stamp

drawing knife

pincers

punch

clenching tongs

buffer

hoof cutters

rasp

nails

punch

shoe tongs

pincers

nail puller

drawing or nailing-on hammer

turning hammer

■ ABOVE
The farrier's tools

■ RIGHT
Screw-in studs are essential for the competition horse. After use they are removed and the holes plugged to protect the threads. A T-tap (centre) is used to clean out the screw holes before inserting the studs.

are best for competition horses because they require different types of studs according to the work they are doing and the state of the ground.

There is a wide range of studs available, varying from small ones for everyday hacking and road work (these are usually made with a tungstcn corc and are very hard wearing) to large round or square ones suitable for use in soft going and pointed ones which enhance the grip on very firm ground. There are two schools of thought about the fitting of studs: some people fit only one stud on the outside of each shoe. Others believe that this may throw the foot out of balance and so fit one on either side of the shoe.

The farrier uses the rasp to smooth the horn and shape the clenches.

Lightweight plastic shoes are a modern alternative to metal ones. They are attached to the hoof with glue.

Studs are screwed into place shortly before the horse competes. The size and shape depends on the ground conditions.

Common Foot Problems

Corns occur most often in the front feet. A corn is a bruise of the sole in the angle between the wall of the foot and the bar (known as the "seat of corn"). Corns are caused by pressure and can be the result of a stone becoming wedged, faulty shoeing or shoes having been left on too long. The shoe should be removed and the discoloured horn pared away. The condition can be complicated by the presence of infection, in which case poulticing will be necessary. Pressure can be relieved from the area by fitting a shoe on which the ground surface of the heel is lowered so that it does not make contact with the ground.

Laminitis (also known as "founder") is a painful condition resulting from inflammation of the laminae. The feet become hot and the horse adopts a typical leaning back stance in order to take the weight off the front of the forefeet.

Although the pathological cause is not yet completely understood, laminitis is associated with excessive concussion and the presence of inflammatory toxins which damage the blood vessels, particularly those in the feet. It is often the result of faulty diet (over-fat ponies, with overlong feet, kept on too rich pasture are the classic example) although it can also be caused by retention of the afterbirth in the broodmare.

An example of the farrier's skill: this defective hoof has been artificially lengthened.

Pigeon toes (those which turn inwards) cause uneven wear on the shoes.

A sandcrack may produce lameness if the sensitive part of the foot is affected.

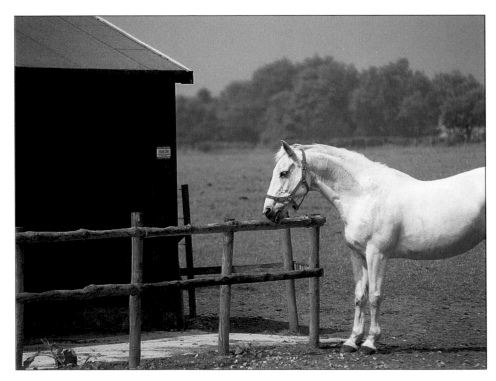

This leaning back stance is typical of a horse suffering from laminitis. He takes the weight on his heels to relieve the pain. Laminitis is one of the major causes of equine lameness, particularly in ponies.

Veterinary treatment is essential. If diet is the cause, the vet may advise a purgative. The horse should be stabled (standing the horse on sand is said to reduce the pain because it provides support to the feet). The vet may prescribe drugs (including pain killers) and if the horse or pony is overweight, he will advise on a suitable diet.

One of the dangers of laminitis is the possibility of pedal bone rotation. Except in the mildest cases, therefore, when the horse may be gently led out in hand, the horse must be given box rest.

Good foot care is vital. Corrective trimming will help restore the structures of the foot to their normal alignment and will limit the rotation of the pedal bone. Special shoes can also be fitted.

Navicular disease is believed to be the result of poor foot conformation and/or concussion, caused by hard work. Bony changes occur in the navicular bone, a small, shuttle-shaped bone which acts as a fulcrum for the deep flexor tendon before the tendon attaches to the under side of the pedal bone. In most cases both forefeet are affected.

A horse with navicular disease will put his foot on the ground toe-first as he attempts to avoid pressure on the affected area. In the early stages, lameness wears off during exercise but as the condition progresses the periods of lameness both increase and become more prolonged. As

pastern (high ringbone) or around the coronet (low ringbone). It is usually caused by injury. There is heat and swelling and the horse may have a shortened stride and tend to be more lame when turned sharply. Rest may help give relief in less serious cases. Where more serious injury is involved the horse may not become fully sound again, although some horses continue to work if given anti-inflammatory drugs.

of bruising of the toe area or pressure from the toe clip of a shoe. Sometimes it follows laminitis. Treatment involves cleaning out the cavity and filling it with tow. The farrier will be able to trim the foot and shoe it in such a way that further damage is avoided during movement.

A **sidebone** results when the lateral cartilages of the foot become ossified or converted into bone. The ossified

"Boxy" feet have an angle of more than 55° and are associated with upright pasterns.

Shoes with rolled toes reduce strain on the tendons and the navicular bone.

A plastic wedge raises the heel of a hoof which slopes too much.

time goes on, the horse may become prone to stumbling.

Although the condition is incurable, various treatments are employed to help relieve the pain. Corrective shoeing is used to raise the heels and reduce concussion to the navicular area. The horse may be given anticoagulants or anti-inflammatory drugs. Laser and ultrasound treatment may also be beneficial.

Pedal osteitis is inflammation of the pedal bone. It is often the result of jarring but can also develop after an attack of laminitis or following puncture injuries to the sole of the foot. It usually affects both forefeet and the horse will tend to shuffle when he moves. The demineralization of the bone is visible on X-ray. Careful shoeing can bring relief to what is usually an irreversible condition. Laser and ultrasound therapy may be beneficial.

Ringbone is an abnormal bony growth which occurs either at the centre of the

A **sandcrack** is a break in the wall of the hoof and may occur anywhere between the coronet and the ground surface of the foot. Sandcracks may be the result of injury, poor nutrition, an overdrying of the hoof (for instance in very dry weather), too much rasping during the shoeing process or neglect, for example lack of regular trimming by the farrier. Lameness may result if the crack is serious.

The farrier may be able to arrest the progress of a sandcrack by making grooves in the hoof wall to isolate the crack. Metal clips may also be used or, in the case of a deep crack, it may be necessary to fill it with a special bonding substance. Because the crack opens when weight is put on the foot as it is placed on the ground, a shoe with clips may be fitted.

Seedy toe is a condition in which the wall of the foot parts company with the sole at the white line. It may be the result

cartilages can be felt at the junction of the hair and the hoof in the area of the quarter of the foot. Sidebones are usually caused by concussion. Heavy or common-bred horses are the most susceptible. The horse may be lame while the cartilage is ossifying and sometimes lameness persists once the sidebones have developed because of pressure on the wall of the foot. The condition does not normally require treatment other than short-term rest but if lameness persists the farrier may be able to relieve the pressure with corrective shoeing and grooving of the hoof to allow expansion.

Thrush is caused by bad stable management (dirty bedding and failure to pick out the feet regularly). It is easily detected by the evil smell coming from the frog, which is moist and may have a black discharge. The affected area of the frog must be opened out to expose it to the air and treated with antiseptics.

Learning to Ride

Before Climbing Aboard

There are few more enviable sights in the world than a horse and rider enjoying a happy, trusting partnership. To be able to harness the spirit and beauty of an animal as majestic as the horse so that he is happy to work with you, and willing to do all that you ask of him, has to be one of life's greatest pleasures. A horse and rider in harmony appear to move by magic, but whilst the spectator may appreciate the words of Robert Surtees – "there is no closer secret than that between a rider and his horse" – anyone who has experienced some of the setbacks that can occur whilst trying to acquire the art of horsemanship may wonder whether these words were spoken with admiration, envy or in sheer frustration!

For some, horse riding is an occasional pastime, for others it is a lifelong passion – either way it should be a pleasure for both horse and rider. Learning to ride involves two living creatures – the rider is reliant on the horse's generosity and co-operation; the horse, in return, deserves fair and sensitive treatment from his rider.

If You Have Never Sat on a Horse...

If you have never so much as sat on a horse or pony, there will be a great deal to take in to start with. It will help to have an overall idea in your mind of what it is you are trying to achieve.

Once you have mounted, the means of communication with the horse are through the use of the legs, seat, hands and voice. Anything that you ask the horse to do – from simply walking forwards to performing an intricate dressage movement to jumping a huge fence – is achieved by using a combination of leg, seat, hand and, sometimes, the voice. The art of riding lies in learning to feel what the horse is doing underneath you, and understanding how to influence what he does and how well he performs by mastering this subtle combination of leg, seat and hand. These means of communicating with the horse are called aids. Leg, hand and seat aids, as well as your voice, are called natural aids and they can be backed up by the artificial aids, which are the spur and whip. The spur is a short stump of blunt metal which is worn over the rider's boot just above the heel; the whip is either a short stick or a longer schooling whip.

Ultimately, riding a horse should have the same smooth feeling of power and control as driving a high-performance sports car or a speed boat. Just as a powerful car responds instantly to a light touch on the accelerator pedal, a horse should move forwards the instant he feels a light squeeze from the rider's leg. The feeling of lightness and control which power steering in a car gives you is the same feeling that a well-schooled horse should give you through the reins. Just an inclination of your hand to guide the horse in one direction or another, or a slight squeeze and hold of the rein to help gather up all his energy and power, is all that should be needed. It takes a long period of careful training for a horse to become as responsive as this, and it takes

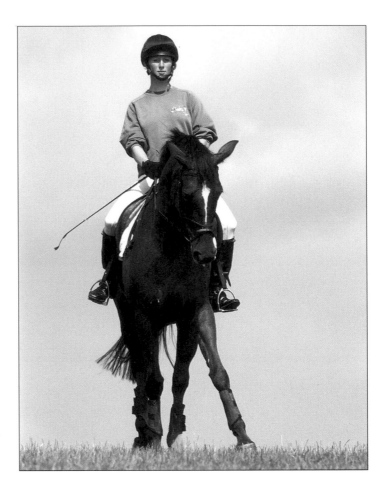

LEFT
When performing the half-pass you may have to do something different with each hand and leg, which is why attaining an independent seat should be the aim of all riders.

time and practice for a rider to get to the stage of being able to provide that training.

In the beginning, as a general rule of thumb, the novice rider should appreciate that it is the legs that are used first and foremost to instruct the horse to do something. The legs create the power, while the hands gently guide the horse in the right direction.

As a beginner, you will usually find yourself riding in a circle around an instructor. The hand and leg on the inside of the circle, i.e. the hand and leg nearest the instructor, are referred to as the inside hand and leg. The hand and leg on the outside of the circle are known as the outside hand and leg. If your inside hand is your left hand, i.e. you are going in an anti-clockwise direction, you are said to be riding on the left rein. If you are told to change the rein, this involves turning the

horse around and circling in the opposite direction, so that the inside hand is now your right hand, which means you are now riding on the right rein.

Your arms and hands are linked via the reins to the bit in the horse's mouth. This line of contact is all part of your communication with the horse, and to make life comfortable for him you must aim to relax your arms, so that as the horse's head and neck move you follow that movement. Ideally this is done whilst still maintaining a consistent but soft contact with the horse's mouth. The idea is not to let the reins keep going slack and then tight, but to relax your arms enough to follow what the horse's head and neck are doing whilst keeping a constant feel on the reins. The feel that you have down the reins to the horse's mouth is known as the contact, and the ultimate aim is to ride

AN INDEPENDENT SEAT

The key to all successful riding is to attain what is commonly known as "an independent seat". The means of communication with the horse are through your seat, legs, hands and voice – that is six different things and on some occasions you may have to do something different with each of them at the same time! To do this you must be able to sit securely and centrally in the saddle, whilst leaving your legs and hands free to communicate with the horse. This means being able to keep your balance without gripping with your legs, or hanging on by the reins, in all paces. Only then can your legs, seat and hands be used independently of each other to ask the horse to perform some of the more elaborate and enjoyable movements that he can offer you.

In an ideal world, any would-be horseman would first gain this independent seat by riding a horse or pony that is being lunged. To begin with you might hold on to the front of the saddle or to a neck strap to help you keep your balance, but as your body and muscles gradually become used to the movement of the horse underneath you, it becomes easier to remain relaxed and balanced. Various exercises without reins or stirrups will help to reinforce the balance and security of your

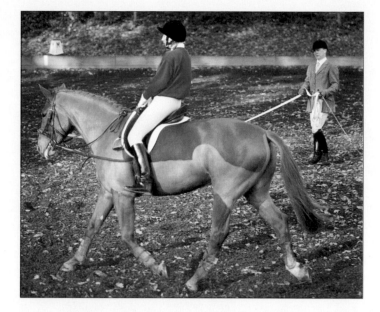

seat until you have attained true independence of hands, seat and legs at all paces. Lungeing can be a tiring and time-consuming operation, besides which, most potential riders are in a rush to enjoy more of the thrill and excitement of horse riding. But if you really want to master the

art of riding, it is time well spent, and this will be repaid when you discover how much more effective and sensitive a rider you are when you do progress to more exciting things. Remember – patience and practice are the keys to becoming a successful rider.

with a very light contact. It sometimes helps to imagine that the rein is an extension of your arm and that your hands are attached directly to the bit in the horse's mouth. As the horse's head moves your arms will have to move with him.

However ambitious or otherwise you may be, by persevering and mastering the correct techniques of horse riding, your satisfaction and enjoyment of your hobby or sport will be greatly enhanced. You may have no desire to reach the dizzy heights

of the competition world – perhaps a simple hack through the countryside is your idea of paradise – but either way, life will be more enjoyable for both you and your horse if you at least attempt to master the art of horsemanship.

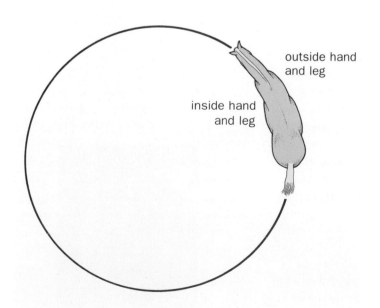

outside hand and leg

inside hand and leg

Riding on the left rein.

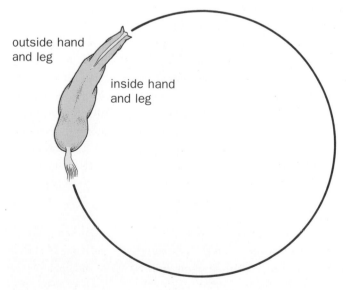

outside hand and leg

inside hand and leg

Riding on the right rein.

Understanding Horses and Ponies

The first thing that any would-be rider must appreciate is the sheer strength and bulk that a horse or pony represents. Common sense should tell even the most inexperienced person that the relationship between horse and rider cannot possibly be based on force – if it were, the horse would win every time. As a rider, you are totally dependent on the horse's co-operation, and so the partnership between horse and rider is one of mutual respect.

Much of the secret behind the successful handling of a horse or pony either from the ground or from the saddle is based on the human being in the partnership appearing both calm and confident. So before considering actually riding a horse or pony, it is well worth spending time just getting used to working with them. Most riding establishments

Spending time grooming and preparing the horse you are going to ride is all part of building up a good partnership.

would be more than happy to accept an offer of help around the yard and this is a good opportunity to learn how to feel comfortable around horses.

A horse is happiest if he is handled confidently and positively. He is far more likely to become nervous and unsure if his handler is jittery and tentative. A horse or pony should always be handled firmly, but fairly, so that he learns what is expected of him. It is the rider's job to teach the horse

Spending time helping to care for and handle horses helps beginners to feel at ease with them.

what is acceptable and what is not. The training of a horse has the same basis as the training of any other animal – when the horse does what is required he is rewarded, when he does not he is quietly reprimanded. It is vital that the handler is consistent in what he or she asks. It is not fair to drape yourself around your pony's neck, hugging and kissing him, only to turn round and wallop him when he shifts his position and accidentally steps on your toe! It is wrong to punish the horse when it was you, the handler, who put yourself in a position where you could get hurt. Although you may think it at the time, the horse would not step on you on purpose if he could avoid doing so!

Your voice is the most valuable form of communication you can have with a horse or pony. He will know from the tone of your voice whether you are pleased with him or otherwise. So it is your voice which should be used to tell the horse when he is behaving well and when he isn't. Your commands should be kept clear and

simple – if the horse does something wrong, then a stern "No" is often all it takes to let him know. A long, angry tirade will only confuse him, and wear you out. Keep it simple – "No" when he is wrong, and "Good boy" or "Good girl" when things are going well. Far too many people forget to tell the horse when they are pleased with him.

Horses, like people, have different temperaments and characters, and not every horse will get on in the same way with every person. A very sharp, nervy horse probably won't feel comfortable with an equally bolshie person – he is more likely to respond to a quieter character. An extrovert person can sometimes inspire confidence and coax a little more effort out of a horse with a more laid-back character.

NEAR SIDE, OFF SIDE

Some of the first things to learn in order to avoid confusion all round are the terms used to describe each side of the horse. If you stand facing in the same direction as the horse, his left-hand side is known as the near side, and his right-hand side is known as the off side. The horse is led from the near side; you mount and dismount from the near side. The same terms are used to describe each of the horse's limbs – if a horse is said to be lame on his off fore, this refers to the front leg on the right-hand side.

off side   near side

Where to Learn

Some children are lucky enough to be put on a pony before they can even walk – long before they are in a position to control their ponies off the leading rein, they will have developed a natural seat. This is because someone else has been in charge of the pony – all the rider has had to worry about is staying on board. It is the same principle as being lunged.

For those who haven't had that lucky start, if time and money allow, the best investment is in a course of lunge lessons at an equestrian centre with a good reputation. The advantages of this are that you will be receiving individual attention and, most importantly, you will start to acquire a deep, balanced but relaxed seat in the saddle. Lungeing will also give you the opportunity to concentrate on trying to feel how the horse is actually moving underneath you.

There is the danger of the first riding lesson being a miserable experience. Avoid any establishment where novices are put on badly schooled, bored mounts and stuck in a class with any number of other potential riders, and where inexperienced or simply incompetent instructors swagger around bawling instructions or criticism. The poor riders are expected to master

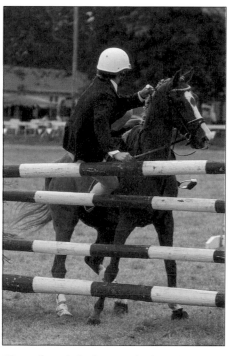

All too often a lack of communication and understanding between horse and rider leads to a lack of co-operation.

the correct riding position, keep their balance in the saddle, and manoeuvre unresponsive creatures around the arena. These new riders will either give up or become aggressive jockeys, oblivious to the reality of true horsemanship.

Lunge lessons will help the rider to develop a good seat, from which he or she will be able to communicate effectively with the horse. For any rider unable to enjoy such an opportunity, the next best thing is to opt for individual lessons, rather than group lessons. Once some of the basics have been mastered, riding in a group can be a positive and enjoyable experience, but if learning from scratch there is nothing to beat individual attention right at the beginning. This may either be at a commercial riding school or equestrian centre, or with a private individual who may give lessons using their own horses and facilities.

Always ensure that the instructor of your choice has a good reputation both for teaching ability and for being safe and responsible. In most countries there is some form of recognized teaching body and a structured system of examinations for instructors; if you have nobody to advise you, always opt for a registered and approved instructor. But if someone is highly recommended to you by more experienced riders, do not be afraid to try them even if teaching is not their profession – some people are naturally gifted teachers.

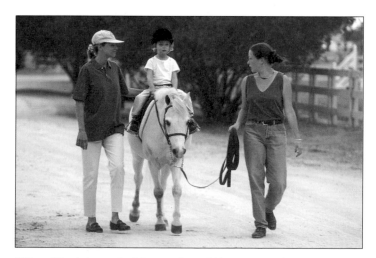

With a willing helper to lead the way, the world is yours to explore. It is a great advantage to learn to ride at such an early age. There are classes for young riders on lead reins at most local gymkhanas.

Group riding lessons are beneficial and fun once the potential rider has had a chance to master some of the basics.

Clothing and Equipment

HARD HAT

One vital item that the rider must have is a hard riding hat, also known as a crash hat or skull cap, which conforms to a recognized safety standard. Any romantic notions about feeling the wind blowing through your hair, or galloping across the prairie in your designer stetson should be dismissed – it is only fair to yourself, and to those who will have to pick up the pieces if you have an accident, that you wear the correct headgear. The design and effectiveness of riding hats has improved dramatically. A riding hat must always be worn with a safety harness to hold it in place; a traditional hard hat with an elastic chin strap is next to useless.

Hard hats come in various designs – looking like the traditional velvet hat with a built-in peak, or like a crash hat or skull cap as worn by racing jockeys and cross-country riders. The latter are more bulbous looking than the traditional type. Some of the newest styles, popularized in America, are very lightweight, vented helmets which protect the head whilst allowing the rider to stay surprisingly cool.

Whatever your standard of riding, and no matter how little or often you ride, your first priority should be to wear equipment of the highest safety standards. The highest current safety standards are the European PAS 015 and the American ASTM/SEIF 1163.

The majority of approved riding or training centres insist that their clients wear protective headgear and, similarly, whenever a rider competes he or she will generally be required to wear a proper hat. A riding hat should always be replaced once it has suffered a hard blow, either through the rider falling, or through being dropped accidentally.

RIDING BOOTS

The second most important item of clothing, from a safety point of view, is footwear. Long or short boots of some kind should be worn; it is important that they are not so wide that there is any risk of them being caught in the stirrup in the

The jockey-style crash hat or skull cap can be worn on its own, or you can fit a "silk" to it – dark blue or black for dressage and show jumping, and a colour to match your outfit for cross-country riding.

The velvet riding hat is styled on the hunting cap and looks quite formal. It is particularly suitable for show-ring riding, dressage and show jumping. A stock, which is a kind of scarf or neck tie, should always be worn for cross-country riding as it does give some support to the neck in the case of a fall.

The lightweight vented helmet is fast becoming a popular choice. If it is made to the ASTM/SEIF 1163 standard, it is just as safe as any other hat made to an accepted safety standard such as the European PAS 015. In fact, the ASTM standard hats are stronger in terms of their impact resistance.

Jodhpurs are usually made of a stretchy material and are designed to be worn with short boots.

Short leather jodhpur boots can be worn with jodhpurs or with a pair of "half-chaps" to protect the rider's lower leg.

Breeches are designed to be worn with long riding boots.

Long riding boots can be made of either rubber or leather.

It is advisable to carry a stick of some sort even if you think you are unlikely to need it. It is too late if you go out without one and your horse decides on that particular day to ignore your leg aids. From top to bottom: schooling whip, two types of riding sticks, and a hunting whip.

■ RIGHT
Whatever type of gloves you choose, make sure that they have non-slip palms; otherwise the reins will slip through your fingers.

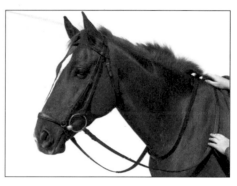

event of a fall, and they should only have a small heel – again so that there is no risk of the rider's foot becoming trapped.

There is a good range of casual and affordable boots designed for leisure riding, although they would not usually be acceptable in the competition world. For any form of competition riding, the correct turnout is long boots (ideally leather rather than rubber) or short, leather riding boots such as jodhpur boots.

GLOVES
Most riders like to wear gloves. These should have non-slip palms.

TROUSERS
For the sake of comfort, wear trousers designed specifically for riding. Any garment with a thick seam will chafe against your skin, and anything too thin or flimsy will simply wear through. Jodhpurs or breeches come in a huge variety of

If spurs have to be worn they should be as short as possible and must have a rounded or blunt end. They should never be worn by a beginner. In fact, they should not be worn until you have good control of your lower leg; otherwise you will be spurring your horse unnecessarily.

A neck strap can prove invaluable as an aid to staying in the saddle if the horse plays up or jumps awkwardly. Hold on to the strap with one hand to help keep your weight deep in the saddle, making it harder for you to be thrown off. It can also be used as an aid to help slow the horse down.

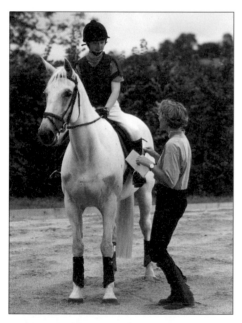

Protective clothing is important for both horse and rider. This rider is wearing a jockey-style crash helmet with safety harness, a body protector and long leather riding boots. Her horse is wearing protective leg boots to reduce the risk of injury through knocking into himself, or being scratched or cut by anything whilst being ridden.

styles and colours, and can be purchased as either competition or casual garments.

CHAPS
If short boots are to be worn, it is also advisable to wear what are known as chaps or half-chaps, which are shaped leggings made from leather, suede or waterproof material. Half-chaps are worn below the knee and protect the lower leg. They are usually fastened by either Velcro or a zip, and prevent the stirrup leather rubbing against the rider's calf. Full chaps are just like the ones cowboys wear; they cover the whole leg and are fastened with a belt around the waist. As well as offering some protection to the leg, they have the advantage of keeping the rider warm.

BODY PROTECTOR
These are padded, vest-like garments and are mandatory in most countries for sports such as horse racing and the cross-country phase of horse trials. With lightweight breatheable materials of ever-better

quality appearing on the market each year, they are nothing like as cumbersome and hot as they used to be. They can be worn either over your usual riding top, or underneath your clothes. The ones worn over the top tend to be the most convenient and are available in an array of colours and designs. In an ideal world they would be worn whenever you rode, not just when you intended to jump or compete.

NECK STRAP
A final, small piece of equipment that also adds to the rider's safety is a neck strap, which is worn by the horse. This is a leather strap (an old stirrup leather makes an ideal neck strap) worn loosely around the horse's neck. It sits just above the withers and is well positioned for you to grab hold of if you lose your balance. Neck straps can make the difference between staying aboard and hitting the deck when jumping, and have saved many a rider from being thrown off; they also prevent a horse from being "jabbed" in the mouth.

Sitting
Comfortably

Before you even get as far as sitting on a horse there is quite
a lot of groundwork to master, such as tacking up and
mounting. Riding schools vary in their approach to tacking
up for beginners. Some have the horse ready and waiting
for his rider, others feel that tacking up is all part of the
learning process and that it will give you a few minutes of
unpressurized time in which to start to get to know your
horse. If a friend is teaching you, it is all part of the fun to
help get the horse ready.

Tacking Up

The order in which the horse is tacked up varies, but any form of boots should be put on first, once the horse's legs have been checked for signs of heat or swelling. This should have been done while the horse was being groomed, but it is good practice to double check when putting on the boots – there is no point tacking up and then finding that the horse is lame!

Whether the saddle or bridle is put on next is a matter for discussion. Some riders like to put the bridle on first, so that they have better control of the horse should he pull back and break free from his headcollar. Others like to put the saddle on first so that, having removed the horse's warm rugs, the saddle goes straight on to a warm back and the horse's muscles will remain warm underneath the saddle. On a cold day, a rug should be kept over the horse's back and quarters while he is being tacked up.

Protective boots reduce the risk of injury. Hold the boot securely in place and fasten the first strap. Then fasten the second strap firmly enough to prevent the boot slipping. Tighten the first strap if it seems looser than the second strap. These boots protect the tendon area of the legs as well as the inside of the fetlocks. Many horses are prone to knocking one leg against the inside of the opposite leg – this is called brushing – and boots prevent the horse from injuring himself as a result.

PUTTING ON THE BRIDLE

1 Whilst being tacked up or groomed, the horse is usually secured by a headcollar. Before removing the headcollar put the bridle reins over the horse's head so that you have a means of holding him.

2 Remove the headcollar by lifting the headpiece forward and then gently over the horse's ears.

3 With one hand holding the horse's nose to keep his head steady, bring the bridle up in front of his face.

4 Use your right hand to hold the bridle, lay the bit over the palm of your left hand and gently lift it up into the horse's mouth. Use your thumb to press his gum in the gap where his teeth finish which will encourage him to open his mouth.

5 Once the bit is in place, keep some tension on each side of the bridle to hold it there whilst you bring the headpiece of the bridle up and over the horse's ears. Do not allow the bit to bang against his teeth as this will make him wary next time.

6 With the headpiece in place, separate the hair of the forelock from the rest of the mane (to let the bridle sit comfortably, cut a small section out of the mane where the headpiece sits). Bring the forelock forward and lift it clear of the browband.

7 Keep your hand looped through the rein so that you have a contact with the horse, and therefore control over him, and then do up the throatlash.

8 It should not be fastened too tightly – make sure you can still get four fingers of your hand between the horse's cheek and the throatlash.

9 Fasten the noseband – in this case a drop noseband which does up below the bit rings. A cavesson noseband, used for lungeing, sits higher up the horse's nose and does up above the bit rings.

10 You should be able to place one finger between the horse's chin and the noseband.

SADDLING UP

1 Place a soft, padded numnah on the horse's back. This acts as a cushion between the horse and the saddle and can relieve pressure points and reduce the risk of rubbing. It is also a warmer layer to have against the horse's skin than the leather of the saddle.

2 Keeping the saddle well clear of the horse's back, lift it so that it is poised in the right position to be lowered on to the back. Lower the saddle into place, making sure that the saddle flap on the off side is lying flat.

3 Use your left hand to lift the numnah so that it is not pulled tight over the horse's withers. It should be tucked up to lie snugly under the pommel of the saddle, clear of the withers.

4 Most numnahs have two straps that hold them in position under the saddle. The first one is usually attached to the girth straps, so pull it over the knee roll of the saddle and put it on the strap before you do up the girth.

5 Position the strap above the buckle guard, otherwise you will not be able to pull this down into the correct position. Pull the girth strap out from the buckle guard, thread through the numnah strap, then put the strap back through the buckle guard.

6 Buckle the girth to the saddle on the off side. Return to the near side, and reach under the horse's belly to catch the girth. Thread the girth buckles through the second securing strap of the numnah and fasten them, one at a time, to each girth strap.

7 Gently tighten the girth, one buckle at a time, until you can just squeeze the flat of your hand between the horse's belly and the girth. Fasten the girth equally on each side.

8 Pull the buckle guard down so that it covers the buckles – otherwise they will gradually wear a hole through the saddle flap.

9 Smooth down under the girth so that there are no wrinkles of skin caught up which might rub. Slide your hand under the girth just clear of the saddle flap and run it down under the horse's belly, taking particular care to smooth any wrinkles in the horse's elbow area.

10 A correctly fitted jumping saddle, with the girth tightened and the stirrups run up so that they don't swing and bang against the horse's sides. A jumping saddle has forward-cut flaps and knee rolls to allow the rider to keep his or her leg on the saddle even when riding with shorter stirrups.

PUTTING ON A DRESSAGE SADDLE

1 A dressage saddle has long girth straps which do up below the saddle flap. The girth must still be tightened gradually, one buckle at a time, and the skin and hair smoothed down underneath it.

2 Dressage saddles allow your legs to hang much longer and closer to the horse's sides. This gives the best possible position for you to communicate with the horse through your legs and seat.

LEADING A TACKED-UP HORSE

▌ **LEFT**
When leading a tacked-up horse, stand on his near side and bring the reins over his head. The stirrups should be run up so that they do not swing or bang against the horse's sides. Carry the excess loop of rein and your riding stick in your left hand. Have the stick pointing backwards so that you can give the horse a tap behind the girth if he refuses to walk on. You should always wear a riding hat whenever you lead a horse.

Mounting

MOUNTING FROM THE GROUND

So now it is time to step aboard. It is essential to learn how to mount correctly from the ground but, as a general rule, it is far less stressful on the horse's back to use a mounting block or be given a leg-up. Either of these methods is also a lot safer than mounting from the ground. A great many accidents occur when riders are trying to get on their horses. If you do mount from the ground, ideally an assistant should stand on the far side of the horse and, by putting his or her hand in the stirrup iron, should use some of his or her own weight to counteract your weight swinging up from the other side. This helps to reduce the amount of twisting and pulling on the horse's spine.

1 Before attempting to get on your horse you will need to put the reins back over his head, and to let down the stirrups.

2 As you pull the stirrup irons down, keep them away from the horse's sides so that they don't knock him. When they are fully down, place them gently back against his sides.

3 Stand on the near side of the horse, facing his tail, and put both reins in your left hand. It also helps to loop a finger through the neck strap and hold on to a little piece of the mane.

4 Take the stirrup iron in your right hand and turn it to face you. The stirrup should be turned clockwise, so that once you are mounted the stirrup leather lies correctly against your leg.

5 Lift your left leg and place your foot in the stirrup iron. Put your right hand on the seat of the saddle.

6 Push with your right leg to spring off the ground and, at the same time, reach to the far side of the saddle with your right hand.

Voilà! You are now mounted on your horse. Put your right foot in the stirrup and then take up a rein in each hand.

7 Once you are high enough off the ground, you will be able to grip the far side of the saddle with your right hand and this will help you to balance. Keep bringing your right leg up until it is clear of the horse's back and hindquarters.

8 At this point start to swing your right leg over the back of the horse. Bring your right hand back to the front of the saddle and rest it on either the pommel or the horse's neck to help you support and balance your upper body.

9 As your right leg starts to come down over the off side of the horse, take your weight on your hands and arms so that you don't flop down in the saddle. Lower your seat gently into the saddle.

GETTING A LEG-UP

1 If someone is going to give you a leg-up on to your horse, you should stand on the near side facing the saddle. Take both reins and your stick in your left hand – making sure you carry the stick down over the off-side shoulder of the horse otherwise you will hit your helper in the face with it as you mount up! Rest your left hand on the horse's neck or on the pommel of the saddle, and reach up with your right hand so that it is resting near the back of the saddle.

USING A MOUNTING BLOCK

It is far less stressful for both horse and rider if you are able to get aboard by using a mounting block. The horse is led alongside the mounting block so that his near side is parallel to the block. Use the stirrup to mount in the normal way. Now that you are that much higher off the ground, there is less strain on the horse's back when you step up into the stirrup.

2 Bend your left leg up from the knee so that your helper can take hold of it with both hands.

3 Sink your weight down into your right leg and when your helper gives the command be ready to spring up in the air off your right leg.

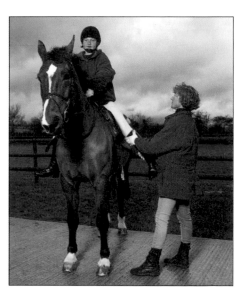

4 As you spring up off your right leg, your helper will also lift your weight by lifting your left leg up. Take your weight on your hands so that you are supporting your upper body and can control the moment when you want to swing your right leg over the horse's back.

5 As you swing your right leg over the horse's back you will need to transfer your right hand from the back of the saddle to either the pommel or the top of the saddle flap on the off side. Make sure you continue to support your upper body on both your arms.

6 With your weight on your arms you can lower your seat down gently into the saddle.

Adjusting Tack

Having learned how to tack up and mount your horse, there are one or two other small adjustments you will need to make once you are on board. The first thing you must do is tighten the girth. Although this is tightened from the ground before you mount, your weight pushing the saddle down on to the horse's back will cause the girth to need retightening. Also, many horses push their stomachs out against the pressure of the girth, and only relax again once their riders are in the saddle.

It is only once you are sitting on your horse that you can feel if your stirrups are set at a comfortable length for you; they may need adjusting. When you change from riding on the flat to jumping you will also want to shorten your stirrups whilst still sitting on the horse.

TIGHTENING THE GIRTH

1 To retighten the girth, put both reins and your stick in your right hand and bring your left leg clear of the saddle flap.

2 Reach down and lift up the saddle flap so that you have access to the girth straps.

3 Hold the saddle flap out of the way with your right hand; with your left hand, pull the buckle guard up away from the girth straps and buckles.

4 Take hold of the first girth strap and pull it up gently. Use your index finger to press the spike of the buckle through the hole.

5 Do the same to the second girth strap – make sure each is tightened by the same number of holes.

6 Pull the buckle guard back down so that it sits snugly over the girth buckles. Put the saddle flap back down and return your leg to the correct position.

HOLDING THE REINS

1 Hold the reins by allowing them to lie across the palm of your hand. The end that comes from the horse's mouth passes between your third and fourth finger.

2 It rests over the top of your first finger and is held in place by closing your thumb and fingers. You can lengthen the reins by relaxing the tension in your hand and letting them slip through your fingers.

3 This picture shows you how to hold a stick as well as your reins. When your thumb and fingers close back around the rein and stick, they are held safely in place.

ADJUSTING THE STIRRUP LEATHERS

1 Once you are in the saddle you may need to adjust your stirrup leathers in order to sit comfortably and correctly. Put the reins and stick in your right hand, and use your left hand to lift the leather flap that covers the stirrup-leather buckle.

2 Pull the free end of the stirrup leather out of its keeper if necessary, and then pull it upwards so that the buckle is released.

3 To shorten your stirrup, pull the stirrup leather upwards, as shown. To lengthen your stirrup, put your weight down into the stirrup iron and with your left hand allow the stirrup leather to slide back down through the stirrup bar.

4 When the stirrup is at the required length, push the buckle back through the appropriate hole.

5 Make sure the stirrup-leather buckle slides back into position, hard up against the stirrup bar.

6 Push the free end of the stirrup leather back through the keeper.

7 Ensure that the leather is lying flat before repeating the procedure for the right stirrup.

POSITIONING THE STIRRUP LEATHER

Each stirrup leather should be turned outwards, rather than inwards, in order to position the stirrup iron so that your foot can go into it. This allows the stirrup leather to curve smoothly across the inside of your leg. So to put your right foot (off-side foot) in the stirrup iron, give the leather a quarter turn in a clockwise direction. For the near-side foot (left foot), turn the stirrup leather in an anti-clockwise direction.

4 You should always hold both your hands at the same height, usually just above the withers and a few inches apart. The basic rule for hand position is that there should be a straight line running from your elbow, down your arm, through the wrist and hand, down the rein to the horse's mouth. It is this rule that dictates the exact position of your hands, which will therefore alter depending on what the horse is doing with his head carriage. This hand and arm position allows you to maintain a soft, elastic but consistent contact with the horse's mouth. (See The Hands which illustrates three different but correct positions.)

Dismounting

Dismounting from the horse should also be done correctly. Do not be tempted to follow the example of countless cowboys and Indians in Wild West movies by flinging your leg over the front of the saddle. If the horse throws his head up you will, at best, be knocked off backwards or, at worst, startle the horse so that he either jumps or bolts, leading to even more painful consequences. Always remove both feet from the stirrups, lean forward and swing your right leg up and over behind the saddle. As obvious as it may sound, always check that the ground where you are about to land is safe and free of obstacles before you dismount.

GETTING OFF

1 To prepare to dismount from your horse you should take both feet out of the stirrups and put both reins, and your stick, in your left hand.

2 Rest both hands on the pommel of the saddle or on the horse's neck. Lean your upper body forward.

3 Now swing your right leg up and over the horse's back.

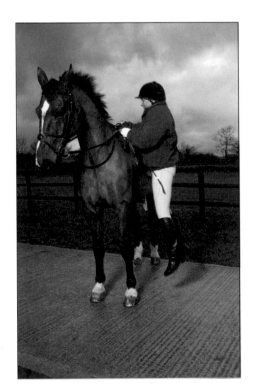

4 Swing your left leg back and out slightly so that it meets your right leg which has now swung over on to the near side of the horse. Use your hands on the saddle to help support your body.

5 Allow both your legs to drop to the ground together. Bend your knees as you land to absorb the impact.

6 Straighten up and you are ready to run up your stirrups, take the reins over your horse's head, and lead him back to his stable.

The Ideal Position

Once on the horse, you should try to adopt a proud and elegant posture. The ideal, classical position is like that of a person standing with their knees slightly bent, not sitting in an armchair. Your ear, shoulder, hip and heel should all be in line, with equal weight placed on each seat bone so that you are not tipped too far forward or sitting back on your buttocks. Always remember how heavy your head is in relation to the rest of your body – if you look down, or tilt your head to the side, or push it too far forward it will affect your, and therefore the horse's, balance. Your legs should hang long and loose down the horse's sides. When your foot is balanced in the stirrup, think of allowing your weight to sink down into your heel.

Although it is often frowned upon today by many who consider it unsafe, anyone who was fortunate enough to learn to ride bareback tends to adopt a correct position automatically. Often, it is the addition of the saddle and the stirrups which compromises what was otherwise a near-perfect position.

By practising the ideal position on the ground, you can start to get a good feel of what you are aiming for, before the added complication of the movement of the horse underneath you enters the equation. Similarly, while sitting on the stationary horse you can be shown how to follow the movement of his head and neck, so that you do not restrict the horse or harm him by pulling on the reins in an attempt to keep your balance.

Your foot should be balanced centrally in the stirrup, with the stirrup tread positioned under the ball of your foot and your weight lowered gently down into your heel.

If you sit a child on a pony bareback, his or her leg position will automatically be long and low as required for the classical position.

As soon as a saddle is introduced, note how the child adopts an armchair seat. The best way to acquire a natural, classical seat is to learn to ride either bareback or without stirrups.

1 You can practise the classical riding position on the ground. First stand straight, with your legs about 2 feet (0.5 m) apart, and your arms bent at the elbow as if you were holding the horse's reins.

2 Keeping your whole body straight and upright, simply bend your knees slightly – now you are in the classical dressage position. For jumping you simply bend your knees more. Your position on a horse should be as if you were standing with your knees bent, rather than as if you were sitting in a chair.

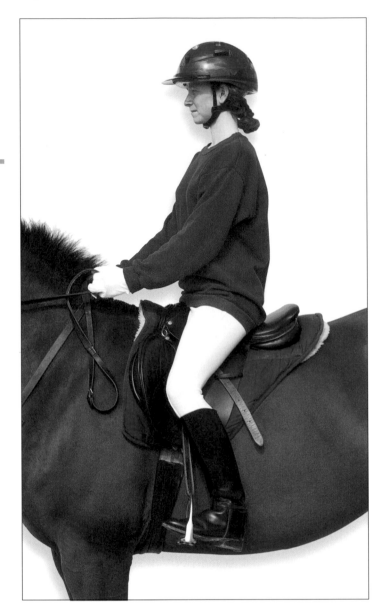

■ LEFT

Your position in the saddle should be exactly the same as the position you have practised on the ground. See how this rider appears to be standing with her knees bent rather than sitting on the saddle. Note how there is a straight line through the rider's ear, shoulder, hip and heel. Similarly there is another straight line running from the elbow, down through the wrist and hand to the rein and eventually to the bit.

COMMON FAULTS

How not to sit! You should not allow your weight to fall on to the back of your bottom as if you were sitting on a chair. Note how, when this happens, the rider's lower leg swings forward and becomes ineffective as a result.

You should not sit with your weight pitched forward. It prevents you from sitting properly and using your legs correctly – and it is painful! Note how this position causes the lower leg to slide back.

PRACTISING A SOFT CONTACT

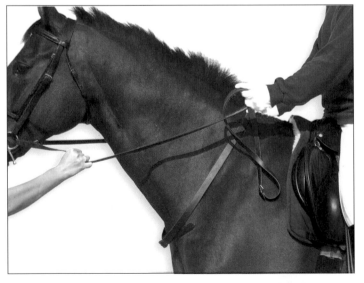

1 One of the secrets of sympathetic and effective riding is to learn how to maintain a soft but constant contact with the horse's mouth, whilst allowing him to move his head and neck freely. Take up a rein in each hand and ask a friend to hold the rein further down towards the horse's mouth.

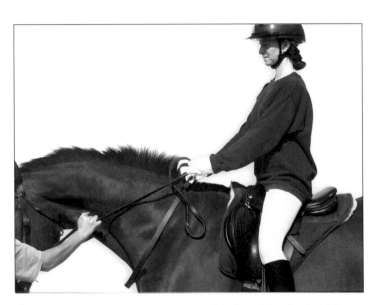

2 Ask your friend to mimic the movement of the horse's head and neck by drawing the rein forwards and then releasing it. Concentrate on maintaining the straight line from your elbow, through your wrist and hand down the rein. Keep your elbows and wrists soft and relaxed, and allow your whole arm, from the shoulder down, to be moved by the pull on the reins.

COMMON FAULTS

The Hands

Never forget that your hands are attached directly via the reins to a large piece of metal in the horse's mouth. Like your own, the horse's mouth is soft and sensitive, and you must never be harsh or abusive with your hands. One of the most important ideas to grasp is that your hands belong to the horse's mouth. Although a light, consistent contact must be maintained so that you have a line of communication with the horse, that contact should be elastic. Your hands must follow the movement of the horse's head and neck. It should feel as if you are shaking hands politely with someone; there is equal pressure and movement from each party. It is not polite to clasp someone's hand roughly and shake it violently as a terrier might shake a rat! Nor is it kind to grasp the reins and swing and tug on them. An old Spanish proverb suggests that "you should ride as if with reins of silk". This can only be achieved if the whole arm stays soft and relaxed, right from the shoulder through the elbow to the hand. The elbow opens out softly to allow the hands to go forwards as the horse's head moves.

A common fault is to have stiff, straight arms and to turn the wrists and hands outwards. You can see from this position how harsh it all looks, and how impossible it would be to keep a sympathetic contact with the horse.

A similar error is to carry your hands so that the thumbs are pointing downwards – again this prevents you maintaining a soft, consistent contact with the horse's mouth.

The exact position of the hands, how close they are held to the withers, depends upon the horse's head carriage. There should always be a straight line from the elbow, through the wrist, down the rein to the bit; so if the horse is working with his head quite low, the hands must be carried a little lower and to either side of the withers in order to keep this straight line.

When the horse is working in a rounder outline, the hands can be carried a little higher; and when you find yourself riding a highly schooled horse who carries his head and neck higher still, your hands should be carried a few inches above the withers. The rule of thumb is to be aware of keeping the straight line from the elbow, through the rein to the horse's mouth.

You must adjust your arm position, following the horse's head and neck, so that you maintain an imaginary straight line from your elbow, through your wrist and hand, down the rein to the bit. This horse is working in a good outline in trot and you can see how the straight line is maintained.

When you encourage the horse to stretch and lower his neck, you must still keep the straight line. This rider has allowed her arms and elbows to be drawn forwards and down so that the line is maintained.

Here the horse is working with more pronounced flexion and bend through his neck. In this case you should raise your lower arms and hands slightly to maintain the line.

The Legs

The most important way that you can communicate with the horse is through the legs and seat. Your legs should hang long and relaxed around the horse's sides, with no tightness in the knee joints in particular. It is the insides of the calves which squeeze against the horse to ask him to move either forwards or across to one side or the other. If you run your hand down the inside of your leg just below the knee, you should feel the slight outward bulge of your calf muscle; it is this part of the leg which is used to communicate with the horse.

Check that your stirrup length is correct by allowing each leg to hang long and loose, and free of the stirrup. You should then only need to turn your toe up slightly to find the stirrup. This is the position that you should be aiming for,

Ask a friend to adjust the stirrup leather so that you only need to turn up your toe to find the stirrup iron. It may take some time for you to be able to ride comfortably with such a long stirrup length as your muscles will need to supple up and stretch, but this is what you are aiming for.

although at first it is likely to produce too much pull down the back of the thigh and calf muscles. Until your muscles have toned, stretched and strengthened sufficiently, it is sensible to ride with the leg in as long a position as is still comfortable. With time, and particularly as you begin to find your balance on the horse and the beginnings of an independent seat, you will gradually find it easier to ride with the leg in a longer position.

Keep your knee joint relaxed and let it fall away from the saddle slightly, which will allow the leg to hang correctly around the horse's side. Contrary to popular belief, you should not grip with the knees as doing so will effectively push your seat up and out of the saddle. Equally, if you hold your knees tightly against the saddle, you cannot squeeze the horse's sides with your legs. The knee and the toe have to be turned slightly outwards to allow the inside of the calf to press against the horse's sides; which you will need to do to apply a leg aid correctly.

A common fault is for the lower leg to be drawn back and upwards in order to press against the horse's side, but this is an

To find the correct stirrup length that will allow you to adopt the classical position for flatwork, you should sit deep in the saddle and just allow your legs to hang long and loose without putting them in the stirrups.

This is the classical position viewed from the front. You can see how the rider's legs would completely encompass the body of the horse; it is this position that allows the leg to support the horse at all times, and from which you can communicate with the horse through your leg aids.

LEFT
To apply the leg aids correctly you need to be aware of exactly what your lower leg is doing. When the horse is moving at the pace you wish him to, keep your legs gently in contact with his sides, but do not actively do anything. The lower leg and the knee joint should remain soft and relaxed.

ineffective means of communication. The lower leg must lie close to the girth; it will come into contact with the part of the horse's belly which is fractionally behind the girth. For some movements, such as turning, or when the rider wants to control the horse's hindquarters, the lower leg is used a few inches further back behind the girth. But the leg is always used in the same way – with the weight down in the heel, the knee and toe turned out slightly and with a squeeze or nudge inwards, not backwards. If you conjure up in your mind a picture of an old-fashioned, bow-legged horseman, you will have a good idea of how the rider's legs are used against the horse's sides, and why some riders end up looking bow-legged!

COMMON FAULTS

When you wish to apply a leg aid, simply squeeze your lower leg inwards. Allow your knee to come slightly away from the saddle so that your lower leg may close in against the horse's side. Your weight remains gently pushed down into your heel. Again you can get a feel for this by asking a friend to push your leg inwards against the horse's sides. Having your leg held in the right position will give you a feel for what you are trying to achieve. Until your muscles are used to this movement it will seem difficult, and you will not be able to apply a very strong leg aid. Your thigh and calf muscles will need to stretch and strengthen before your leg aids can be truly effective.

Picture one shows a bad leg position – see how the lower leg is pushed forward and away from the horse's sides. This is usually a result of the rider adopting an armchair seat in the saddle. It leads to the leg aids being incorrectly applied.

In picture two, instead of squeezing inwards this rider has drawn her lower leg back and, as a result, her weight has come out of her heel and her heel is higher than her toe. At this point it is very easy for the stirrup iron to slip off your foot. This type of leg aid is ineffective – the lower leg is simply being brushed backwards across the horse's side and is not being applied to the more sensitive area just behind the girth. A horse that is ridden like this will never be able to differentiate between an aid to move forwards and an aid to move his quarters, when the rider's lower leg is applied further back behind the girth.

Lungeing Exercises

One of the best ways to encourage an independent seat is to be lunged. When the horse is lunged, the handler on the ground can control the horse's speed and direction, leaving you free to concentrate fully on your position. Lunge lessons are given at most riding establishments. It is important that the horse you ride is calm and steady on the lunge, and that the person who is lungeing you is capable and confident in what they are doing. A lungeing cavesson should be used over the horse's usual bridle. This is like a padded headcollar with a reinforced piece on the noseband which has rings attached to it. These take the lunge line. The handler should maintain a position which allows the lunge line, the lungeing whip and the horse to form a triangle.

The voice rather than the lunge whip should be used to ask the horse to move forwards. The lunge whip should only be used to back up the voice if the horse does not respond, and then should be moved quietly so that the horse does not suddenly shoot forwards. He should be allowed to settle into a steady rhythm; this

The handler keeps a contact with the horse via the lunge line. The lunge whip can be used behind the horse's hindquarters to encourage him to move forwards, or it can be flicked towards his shoulder to keep him out on the circle. Both rider and handler should wear a riding hat; the handler should also wear gloves.

will make it easier for you to relax and find your balance. Both horse and rider should be allowed periods of rest during these exercises.

Lungeing should only ever take place on a secure surface. If you only have a field and it is hard and rutted, or deep and wet, the horse is likely to injure or strain his tendons if he is made to work on it. Lunge lessons should not last for more than 20–30 minutes, and work should be carried out in both directions. Working on a circle is tiring and stressful to the horse's limbs, and once you are tired or sore you will not be able to do anything more to improve your position. If anything, it will get worse as you tense up with effort. If you are struggling, it is much better to stop than to keep on until you reach the point of exhaustion or frustration.

RIDING WITHOUT STIRRUPS

Although work without stirrups is usually carried out on the lunge, or in an arena or *manège*, if you have the opportunity to hack out regularly, it is worth making yourself ride for a few minutes each time without stirrups. Normally, the stirrups would be crossed over in front of the saddle so that they don't bang against the horse's sides, but this is not advisable out on a hack in case you need the stirrups back in a hurry. You should only ride without stirrups on a hack at walk. At this pace they should not swing so much that they knock the horse's sides or elbows. Equally, you can quickly slip them back on if necessary. After only a few minutes of riding without stirrups, when you put your feet back in them they often feel too short – that is the time to let the stirrup leathers down a hole so that gradually you can ride at a longer length.

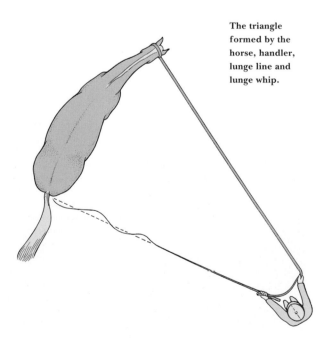

The triangle formed by the horse, handler, lunge line and lunge whip.

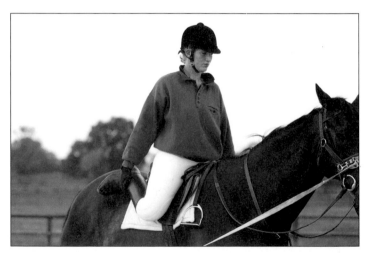

To help stretch the thigh muscles, practise this simple exercise. Bring your feet up under your bottom and hold them in position with a hand around each ankle. This has the added advantage of helping you to keep your shoulders up and straight, and it automatically puts your seat in the correct position in the saddle. When you take your stirrups back after these exercises, you may feel that you want to lengthen the stirrup leathers. This is a good sign and is the start of the path towards attaining the classical position.

STRENGTHENING EXERCISE

1 Practise riding without stirrups and, to help build up your confidence and balance, spread your arms out to either side.

2 To help strengthen and supple your upper body, twist first round to the left...

3 ... and then back to the right.

HOLDING THE LUNGE LINE

1 It is important that whoever is going to lunge you knows how to do this safely and correctly. One of the biggest risks to the handler is getting his or her hands trapped in the lunge line should the horse panic and try to run away. The safest way to hold the lunge line is not to loop it around your hand but to do the following: lay the end of the lunge line across the palm of your hand. Do not put your hand through the loop that most lunge lines have on the end.

2 Lay the lunge line, in equal loops, backwards and forwards across the palm of your hand. Continue to loop the line across your palm until it is the desired length, i.e. you are the distance you want to be away from the horse.

3 Now you can close your hand around the loops and keep a contact with the horse as he moves. If you want to let more lunge line out so that the horse can work on a larger circle, just open your hand and allow one loop to fall away. If the horse did panic and pull away you could close your hand tight around the line and try to stop him. But if he has built up too much speed and is determined to get away, the lunge line will be pulled out of your hand, and you will be free of it. If it is looped around your hand and the horse bolts, the loops will tighten like a noose around your hand. You will either be dragged or have your fingers torn off. Either way the horse will escape if he is determined, so it is better to let him go if you have to and at least remain in one piece and in a position to retrieve him.

"ROUND THE WORLD" EXERCISE

◗ LEFT
The horse or pony you learn to ride on should be a sensible and calm one. This young rider is making the most of her pony's kind nature to have some fun, whilst also increasing her confidence on horseback. Exercises such as this one – called "Round the World" – should only ever be carried out on a quiet pony and with someone on the ground to hold the pony's head.

Mastering
the Paces

Having climbed aboard, it is now time to experience some
forward motion! The first thing you will suddenly be aware of
is just how much the horse moves underneath you. The horse
has four legs to operate and, at walk, these move one at a
time. As each shoulder or hindquarter swings the appropriate
leg forward, you will feel it. Each pace that the horse can offer
you – walk, trot, canter and gallop – will give a different
sensation of speed and motion, and you must learn to absorb
it, and to remain balanced on the horse at each pace, whilst
still maintaining the correct, classical position. To the outside
eye, horse and rider should appear to be moving as one.

Absorbing the Movement

In an attempt to follow the movement of the horse, many riders end up trying too hard and do too much with their bodies. This, instead of creating a picture of harmony, actually looks completely unco-ordinated; the horse appears to be moving to one beat, and the rider to another. It is also uncomfortable.

The first thing to bear in mind is that your seat belongs to the saddle which, in turn, belongs to the horse's back. The saddle will mimic the movement of the horse's back and you should imagine that your seat is glued to the saddle. Sit deep in the saddle, with your weight taken equally on each seat bone. When striving for a deep, balanced seat, it sometimes helps to imagine that your legs have been cut off, about half way down the thigh; therefore it is the top half of the thighs and the seat itself which embrace the saddle. By sitting up straight and keeping the shoulders balanced above the hips, your weight sinks

down into the saddle. This allows the legs to hang long and loose around the horse's sides, with the foot supported softly by the stirrup. The arms follow the movement of the horse's head and neck, and this is achieved by keeping the elbows soft and relaxed with your shoulders remaining still. If your seat is glued to the saddle, and your shoulders, head and neck remain still, the only part of your body that is free to move is the area between your hips and your ribcage. So the hips and stomach are rocked gently forwards and back by the movement of the horse. It is by being soft and supple through the hips, the lower back and the stomach that you are able to move as one with the horse. Always remember that it is the horse that moves your body, and so your body must remain relaxed to allow it to be moved by the horse. You should not create any additional movement yourself – this is most likely to happen if your body is tense.

THE WALK

The walk is described as a four-time pace because the horse moves each leg individually; if you listen to his footfalls you hear four separate hoofbeats. In trot, the horse moves his legs in diagonal pairs, so this is known as a two-time pace.

The sequence of footfalls in walk is as follows: outside hind, outside fore, inside hind, inside fore. The horse should take strides of equal length and he should look energetic and purposeful. If you watch a horse walking you will see that his whole body is in action; the movement flows through the muscles of the hindquarters, up over the back, and through the shoulders and the neck. The horse should look supple, athletic and powerful. Although the walk is the horse's slowest pace, he does use his neck to quite a degree, which means you must be particularly aware of allowing your arms to follow the movement so that you do not restrict the horse.

MOVING WITH THE HORSE

At walk the rider allows his hips and stomach to be rocked gently forwards and back by the push of the horse's hindquarters beneath him. Notice how the rider is maintaining a straight line from the elbow, through the lower arm, and down

the rein to the bit. A light but constant contact is kept with the horse's mouth by allowing the arms to follow the natural movement of the horse's head and neck as he walks.

HALT TO WALK AND WALK TO HALT

Transitions

Changing pace on a horse, whether it be from halt to walk, or from trot to canter etc, is known as performing a transition. Like changing gear in a car, whether you are increasing or decreasing pace, it should appear smooth and effortless.

Transitions are achieved by a subtle balance of the use of the hand and leg. Use your lower leg to activate the horse's hindquarters, which is where his power comes from. You can then use your hands to guide that power in whichever direction you wish.

■ REFINING THE USE OF THE LEGS AND HANDS

To walk forwards, squeeze your legs against the horse's sides and allow your hands and arms to be drawn forwards. If the horse ignores you, give him a sharper nudge with your heels. If this is ignored, give him a tap with the schooling whip or stick behind your lower leg. If you have to

COMMON FAULTS

If the rider decides to do nothing with her legs and simply pulls on the reins in an effort to slow down you can see what happens – the horse resists the request to slow down and throws his head and neck in the air in order to fight the pull of the rider; this is described as the horse hollowing against the rider. The whole picture looks tense and uncomfortable. The rider must first ask with the legs and then only use as much hand as is absolutely necessary to achieve the desired result.

1 At halt the rider still keeps a light contact with the horse's mouth and lets the legs hang long and loose by the horse's sides. The lower leg is in contact with the horse but is not actively doing anything. Note how a straight line is maintained from the shoulder to the hip to the heel. The position would be better still if the rider kept her chin up – a common fault of many riders is the tendency to look down!

3 To prepare to return to halt, the rider squeezes her legs inwards against the horse's sides and at the same time reduces the degree to which she allows her arms to follow the movement of the horse's head and neck. On a well-schooled horse this very slight blocking of the free forward movement will be enough to halt the horse.

do this, you must be very quick to keep the soft forward movement of the hands. The horse may jump forwards if he is tapped with the whip, and he must not then be punished by being pulled in the mouth. Remember to reward the horse for obeying and going forwards. With practice, he will listen to you and a squeeze with your legs will be sufficient.

To halt the horse, squeeze with the legs but do not allow your hands to be drawn forwards so much. The horse will realize that his forward movement is being blocked and will either slow down or

2 To go forwards to walk, the rider squeezes both legs against the horse's sides and, at the same time, allows the hands and arms to go forward to follow the forward movement of the horse's head and neck. Once the horse is walking positively forwards the rider allows her legs to relax against the horse's sides. The arms and hands are drawn gently forwards and back by the movement of the horse's head and neck. This movement is led by the horse. The rider does not pull back on the reins.

4 On a less responsive horse the rider will have to continue to reduce the degree to which the hands follow the horse's head and neck to the point, where they are held still, which will completely block the forward movement. As soon as the horse halts, the rider should soften the hands as much as the horse will allow whilst still remaining at halt. Until the horse halts, the rider's legs remain actively against the horse's sides, gently pushing him up into the hands. Once he has halted, the legs relax and remain gently in contact with his sides.

shorten the steps he is taking. Continue to decrease the forward movement of the hands until, if necessary, they are returned to the normal halt position and do not move forwards at all. This complete blocking will halt the horse.

As with the leg aids, the long-term aim is to use as light and gentle an aid as possible. To begin with you may have to block completely with your hands but, with practice, the horse will become more attentive until only a slight reduction of the forward movement of the hands is enough to halt him.

Changing Direction

You cannot continue in a straight line forever, so once you are confident with forward movement you must be able to change direction.

When the legs are used together either on or fractionally behind the girth, and the hands are also moving together, the horse is kept in a straight line. To go around a corner, or to turn, the horse has to bend through his body. In order to achieve this, the hands and legs must be used individually. If one leg is allowed to slide further back behind the girth this will make the horse move his hindquarters away from the leg in question, i.e. if your right leg is used behind the girth, the horse will be encouraged to move his quarters across to the left, and vice versa. So, to make the horse turn, one leg is used in the normal place to encourage him to keep moving forwards, and the other leg is used further back behind the girth to control the hindquarters.

The horse should never be turned sharply – any turn should be thought of as part of a circle, so to turn right think about circling away to the right. Then the right hand and leg are referred to as being on the inside, while the left hand and leg are now on the outside.

TURNING RIGHT

1 Horse and rider are about to turn off a straight line and away to the right. The rider has moved the right hand a few inches away from the withers, towards the right. This is called opening the hand, and it invites the horse to turn his head and neck to the right in preparation for the turn.

2 The rider's inside (right) leg is used on the girth to keep the horse moving forwards; the outside (left) leg is used behind the girth to stop his quarters swinging too far to the left. The left hand and arm soften so that the horse keeps bending to the right. The right hand stays to the right of the withers, inviting the horse to move that way.

3 As soon as the horse has turned as far round to the right as the rider requires, the hands and legs return to their normal position.

4 To turn right, the rider's inside (right) hand is moved a little to the right of the withers – opening the hand; the inside (right) leg remains on the girth, encouraging the horse to move forwards.

5 The outside hand is softened so that the horse can bend his head and neck away to the right, whilst the outside leg is used behind the girth to control the degree to which the hindquarters move.

TURNING LEFT

1 To turn left, the rider opens the inside (left) hand a few inches to the left to invite the horse to turn his head and neck in that direction.

2 The outside (right) hand is softened forwards to allow the horse to turn away to the left, while the outside leg is used back behind the girth to control the swing of the hindquarters.

3 As soon as the horse is heading in the required direction, the rider's hands and legs return to the normal position.

4 To turn left the inside (left) hand is opened out to the left to ask the horse to turn his head and neck to the left, while the inside leg is used on the girth.

5 The outside (right) hand must be allowed to soften forwards to allow the horse to turn away to the left. The outside leg is used behind the girth in order to control the hindquarters.

rider's hands follow movement of the horse's head and neck

rider's legs both used on the girth to send the horse forward

outside hand controls the degree to which the horse's head and neck bend to the right

inside hand opens outwards to bend the horse's head and neck to the right

outside leg behind girth bends the horse's quarters around inside leg

inside leg on the girth – the point around which the horse's body must bend

■ **RIGHT**
Riding forwards on a straight line.

■ **FAR RIGHT**
Bending the horse so that he can turn right.

Forwards to Trot

The trot is the next pace that the horse can offer you, and many new riders find this one of the hardest to master. When the horse trots the rider feels a far more powerful force of movement from beneath than is experienced at walk. In order to feel comfortable at this pace, you must try to keep your body relaxed so that it absorbs the movement, rather than tensing up and being bounced around by the horse.

■ THE RISING TROT

When the horse trots you can either sit deep in the saddle the whole time – which is known as the sitting trot – or you can rise out of the saddle with each stride, in time with the beat of the trot. It is far less tiring – and more comfortable – for the new rider to learn the rising trot, than it is to master the sitting trot. Once you feel at ease at this pace, and are able to stay relaxed and balanced, then is the time to practise the sitting trot.

When the horse trots, he is springing from one diagonal pair of legs to the other. To rise to the trot, allow the spring from one pair of legs going forwards to lift your seat out of the saddle. The seat returns to the saddle as the other pair of legs springs forwards. So as the horse moves each pair of legs in a one-two, one-two, one-two beat, you are sitting and rising to the same beat: up-down, up-down, up-down.

THE TROT

The trot is a two-time pace – the horse springs from one diagonal pair of legs to the other. If you listen to his hoofbeats, you only hear two footfalls within each complete stride. The outside hind and the inside foreleg move forwards together; this is followed by a brief period of suspension, and then the inside hind and outside foreleg move forwards as a pair.

PRACTISING THE RISING TROT

1 Rising to the trot can be practised when the horse is stationary. The rider sits in the normal classical position, attempting to keep the knee-joints in particular as long and relaxed as possible. Keeping the lower legs as still as possible, the rider should think of just allowing her hips and stomach to swing forwards.

■ RISING ON THE CORRECT DIAGONAL

When riding in rising trot in a circle, the rider is meant to rise in time with a particular diagonal pair of the horse's legs. The easiest way to explain what this entails is for you to look down and watch the horse's outside shoulder for a few minutes once you are in trot. You should be rising out of the saddle as the outside shoulder goes forwards. As it comes back, you should sit again.

The reason for bothering to rise on the correct diagonal will become clear later when you are concerned with improving the quality of the horse's work. The horse

2 The seat only comes out of the saddle enough to allow the seat bones to be clear of the saddle. The hips are then allowed to return lightly to the normal sitting position. The shoulders and arms remain still – the rider should think of allowing the hips and stomach to swing forwards and up towards her elbows.

will find it easier to balance himself on a turn or circle if the rider is in the saddle when the inside hindleg and the outside foreleg are touching the ground. As the horse uses his legs in diagonal pairs, this is achieved by sitting as the outside shoulder comes back, and rising as it goes forwards. When you change the rein and circle in the opposite direction, it follows that you must also change the diagonal, i.e. rise as the new outside shoulder goes forwards. Changing the diagonal is achieved by sitting for an extra beat before rising again. So instead of sit-rise, sit-rise, you would sit-rise, sit-sit-rise and this will put you on the correct diagonal.

▌ RIGHT
In sitting trot the rider retains the correct classical position, allowing her stomach and lower back to absorb the movement of the horse. Note the straight line through the shoulder, hip and heel, as well as the line from the elbow, down along the rein to the bit.

COMMON FAULTS

A common mistake in rising trot is actively to try to push the body up and down. This causes the shoulders and arms to bob up and down, which is disconcerting and uncomfortable for the horse as it is his mouth which suffers if there is excessive movement of the hands and arms.

Another common mistake in rising trot is for the rider's shoulders to tip forwards. This puts the rider off balance and means the hands are often rested on the horse's neck in an effort to regain balance. If the hands are resting on the neck, they cannot keep a soft but continuous contact with the horse's mouth. The shoulders must stay upright, just as they do when the rider is stationary; only the hips should move forwards. If the shoulders remain balanced and in line with the rider's heels, the rider will not be pushed off balance by the movement of the horse.

■ THE SITTING TROT

In sitting trot you should remain sitting deep in the saddle, maintaining the same classical position as when stationary and at walk. The movement of the horse is absorbed by the stomach and lower back, so that you remain deep in the saddle without being bounced up and down. As you feel the horse's legs springing forwards underneath you, try to think of allowing your ribcage to sink down towards your hips. This means that the stomach and lower back act like a concertina: as the horse springs along in trot the stomach and lower back are either contracting or expanding to absorb the movement. You must stay relaxed so that your legs can hang long and loose by the horse's sides, and your arms can still stay soft and maintain a light contact with the horse's mouth. It helps to make a conscious effort to keep breathing – you would be surprised how many riders hold their breath as soon as they concentrate too hard on something. Steady breathing helps you relax.

In sitting trot the knees should be long and loose.

Gripping with the knee makes your seat insecure.

COMMON FAULTS IN THE SITTING TROT

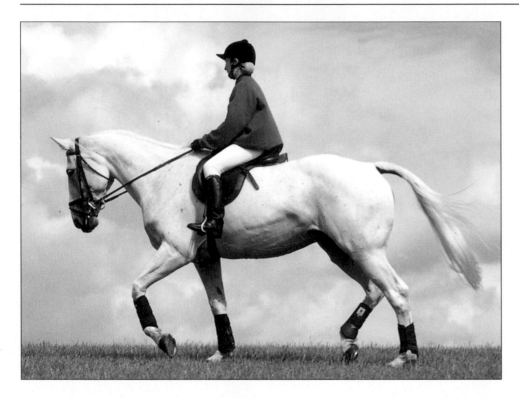

▌ LEFT
Back to the armchair position! How not
to sit – the lower leg has slipped forwards
and the rider is now sitting on the back of
her seat. The line from the shoulder
through the hip to the heel has been lost.

▌ LEFT
If you fall into the armchair position your
body is unable correctly to absorb the
movement of the horse. You will be
bumped up and down and, as a result, you
will find your hands and arms bobbing up
and down as well. It's uncomfortable for
both horse and rider.

FROM WALK TO TROT TO WALK

1 The horse should be walking forwards actively and attentively before the rider asks for trot. See how the rider is keeping a contact with the horse's mouth without actually pulling or restricting him. The rider's legs are in contact with the horse's sides but are not being used actively. By keeping both the legs and the hands in contact with the horse in this way, you will be keeping open your lines of communication.

2 To ask for trot, the rider squeezes both legs actively against the horse's sides and softens the hands forwards so that the horse feels free to increase the pace and go forwards into trot.

3 Once the horse is settled in trot, the rider's legs and hands return to just being in contact with the horse. The leg is there to squeeze the horse forwards should he slow down, and the hand is there to guide him.

4 To return to walk the rider sits deep in the saddle and squeezes the legs against the horse's sides. (If the rider had been in rising trot, she would return to sitting trot to achieve this.)

5 Then, instead of softening the hands forwards, she keeps the hands still so that the horse's forward movement is blocked, bringing him back to walk.

6 As soon as the horse settles in walk, the hands and legs relax sufficiently to keep just a light contact.

On into Canter

It is at canter that the new rider will first experience the true exhilaration of riding a horse. The feeling of speed and power as the horse eats up the ground with each stride gives a real buzz. But despite the increased speed, the rider generally finds this a very smooth pace.

■ CANTERING ON THE CORRECT LEG

If you watch a horse cantering in a circle, he should appear to be leading each stride with his inside foreleg. In practice, the inside foreleg is actually the last leg to be moved by the horse within each canter stride, but to the observer it does appear

■ LEFT
In canter, the rider sits deeply in the saddle and allows the hips to be rocked forwards and back by the movement of the horse. The arms and hands must stay soft and relaxed so that they can follow the movement of the horse's head and neck. Note once more the straight line through the ear, shoulder, hip and heel, and again from the elbow, down the rein to the bit. At all paces, the correct classical position should be maintained.

THE CANTER

The canter is a three-time pace, with the legs working in the following sequence: outside hind goes forwards, then the inside hind and outside fore go forwards together, followed by the inside foreleg. There is then a period of suspension when all four feet are off the ground, before the stride pattern is repeated – outside hind, inside hind and outside fore together, then inside fore.

to be leading the stride. When this is the case, the horse is said to be cantering on the correct leg, or the correct lead. So when cantering on the right rein, i.e. circling to the right, the inside (right) foreleg should appear to be leading; and, when cantering on the left rein, the inside (left) foreleg appears to be leading.

To ask the horse to canter forwards on the left lead you should use the inside leg

on the girth and the outside leg behind the girth, whilst opening the left hand slightly to keep the horse bent left, and just keeping a feel on the outside rein to stop the horse simply accelerating in trot. To canter on the right lead the aids are reversed; the right leg is used on the girth, the left leg is used behind the girth, and the right hand is opened slightly to bend the horse to the right.

Cantering on the correct leg. This horse and rider are circling on the left rein and you can see how the horse's inside (left) foreleg appears to be leading.

Cantering on the wrong leg. Here you can see that, although the horse is still circling to the left, it is the outside foreleg that appears to be leading the stride.

FROM TROT TO CANTER TO TROT

1 Before asking the horse to canter, the rider must go into sitting trot and be sure that the horse is working forwards actively and attentively.

3 Once the correct canter is established, with the left leg leading, the rider just keeps her outside leg in place behind the girth to encourage the outside hind to keep initiating the canter stride. The inside leg remains on the girth, so that the horse's body is bent around the rider's inside leg as they progress around the circle.

6 The rider reduces the degree to which she allows her hands and arms to move forwards with the horse's head and neck, so that the horse's forward movement is blocked. You may have to keep a slightly stronger feel in the outside hand to help bring the horse back to trot.

2 To ask the horse to go forwards into canter on the left rein, i.e. to canter on the left lead, the rider sits deep, presses the inside (left) leg on the girth, but asks more actively with a squeeze or a nudge of the outside leg back behind the girth. This is because it is the horse's outside hindleg that starts off the stride, so the rider activates this leg by using her own outside leg behind the girth. The inside hand is opened out slightly to the left to encourage the horse to keep a bend to the left, but the outside hand may have to keep more of a feel than usual on the outside rein to prevent the horse from simply trotting faster. In this picture the outside hind is just about to take the first step of the canter stride.

4 The arms and hands move forwards with the movement of the horse's head and neck, and the rider sits deep in the saddle, allowing her hips to be rocked by the horse's stride.

5 In order to return to trot the rider sits deep in the saddle and closes both legs against the horse's sides.

7 As soon as the trot is established the rider softens her hands forwards again to follow the movement and allows her legs to hang softly by the horse's sides. She must be ready to squeeze the horse forwards again into a more active trot if he tries to slow down any more.

COMMON FAULT

A common fault when asking the horse to canter is for the rider to tip forwards and look down over the inside shoulder. As soon as the rider's shoulders drop forwards she is pushed off balance, and then the hands tend to drop down on to the horse looking for support. The rider must stay sitting upright and use her hands and legs independently to ask for the transition to canter. Leaning forwards simply unbalances both horse and rider, and this makes the job harder.

CANTERING IN THE FORWARD SEAT

By taking the weight out of the saddle, the rider can encourage the horse to relax his back and put a little more life and swing into his paces. In canter this is often done out on a hack so that the horse is allowed to bowl along effortlessly under his rider. In a schooling session, the rider may take his weight out of the saddle to help the horse relax and use his back more. This is often done when the horse is being warmed up before he is asked to jump. It is called riding in the forward seat, and the rider simply lifts his seat bones out of the saddle and allows his weight to sink down into his heels and the stirrups. The rider will need to have gained a good sense of balance to do this, and will also need quite strong leg muscles, as it really stretches the backs of the calves. If you feel you keep tipping back in the saddle, you probably need to bring your shoulders slightly further forwards. If you feel you are tipping forwards on to the horse's neck, you need to raise your shoulders and check that your lower leg has not slipped backwards, which will in turn push your weight forwards.

Full Speed Ahead – The Gallop

Riding your horse at the gallop is an invigorating and exciting experience, but for it to be safe and enjoyable for both horse and rider you must develop a well-balanced, secure seat and feel confident about controlling your horse. Balance and security are important because if you lose

At gallop the horse is at full stretch – he lengthens out his body and neck, and each leg is fully extended as it powers forwards over the ground. The rider tucks his upper body in behind the horse's neck so that the outline of the two is as streamlined as possible. The seat is taken out of the saddle, which means the rider's weight is dropped down into the heel and is also pushed further back to allow the rider's upper body to tuck in behind the horse's neck. The rider's arms extend forwards as the horse stretches his neck forwards within each stride. It is usual to ride with shorter stirrups when galloping as this makes it easier for the rider's weight to be lifted out of the saddle. The lower leg remains on the girth unless the stirrups are pulled up very short, in which case the lower leg is usually pushed forwards in front of the girth with the weight well down in the heel, as demonstrated by any race rider.

THE GALLOP

The gallop is a four-time pace with the legs working in the following sequence: near hind, off hind, near fore, off fore. Because the walk is also a four-time pace it is often said that if a horse has a good walk he will also be a good galloper. Watch race horses walking around at the track and you will appreciate this!

balance at this pace you will either topple off, or end up hanging on to the reins. The horse will fight this pressure on his mouth and you may find yourself no longer in control. At this pace the horse is at full stretch and, to allow him to use

himself fully, you should bring your weight up out of the saddle, push your seat further back and tuck your upper body in behind the horse's neck, very much like a race jockey but without quite such short stirrups.

HIGH SPIRITS

Most horses enjoy a good gallop and will quite often let their riders know this by popping in a high-spirited leap or buck. If the rider is able to sit this out, it is no more than clean, harmless fun, but it becomes less amusing when it is sufficient to unseat the rider. When cantering or galloping, always keep a contact through the reins with the horse's mouth in order to help balance him. If the horse becomes playful and over-excited in his work, it is even more important to maintain this contact.

STOPPING A HARD-PULLING HORSE

It is often at the faster paces, canter and gallop, that the horse becomes over-excited to the extent that he is less responsive to his rider, particularly when it comes to slowing down again. Whilst in theory it should be possible to stop a horse at any pace by using the subtle balance of hand and leg, in practice the horse's excitement can override his desire to listen to his rider. If you find yourself struggling to slow down a galloping horse, make sure your lower leg is pushed forwards whilst still squeezing both legs against the horse's sides. The slightly forward lower leg position allows you to brace yourself against the stirrup. When a horse gets strong, it is easy to be pulled forwards out of the saddle; the lower leg slips back putting the rider in a very vulnerable position. Shorten up the reins as much as you can and put one hand, still holding the rein, tight into the horse's neck. Use the other hand

to keep a strong hold on the other rein and, by gradually giving and taking this rein, the horse will start to listen again and will slow down. If you keep a continuous pull on the rein, the horse will simply lean on the bit and become stronger still – give and take the rein to prevent him doing this. Circling the horse will also cause him to slow down.

Influencing the Horse

There is a subtle difference between learning to ride and actually influencing the horse. The new rider will spend the early period of training simply learning how to sit correctly balanced on the horse, and mastering the basic aids which will enable horse and rider to proceed at walk, trot and canter, to halt and to circle left or right. Until you achieve this balance and the resultant independent seat, you will be little more than a passenger on the horse. Once you have acquired an independent seat, you can concern yourself with how well or otherwise your horse is performing underneath you. Riding a horse should be a pleasure for both parties – the ultimate aim is to be mounted on a co-operative horse who will respond to your lightest instruction. When this is achieved, those observing you may well marvel at that closest of secrets – the one between a rider and his horse.

MOVING TO THE LEFT

Control of the Horse

Use your hands and legs to control and influence the horse's shoulders, hindquarters, head and neck. When making a turn or circling, the horse's shoulders and hindquarters are controlled by the rider's use of the legs. When combined with the hands, this can be taken further still to move the horse in a number of different ways. The rider's leg can be used behind the girth to encourage the horse to move sideways (laterally) away from the leg, or to control the swing and direction of the quarters. The use of the leg on the girth encourages the horse to bend around the leg and allows the rider to control the horse's shoulder.

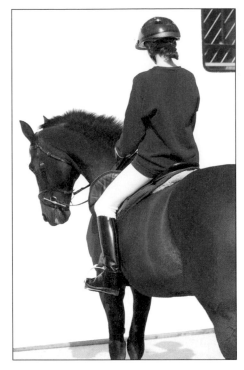

1 Whilst at halt, if the rider keeps a light feel on the outside rein (the right rein), opens out the inside rein a few inches and squeezes the horse's side with her inside leg on the girth while the outside leg remains relaxed, the horse will bend his head and neck to the left.

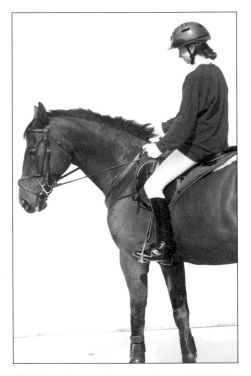

2 If the rider actively presses the outside (right) leg against the horse's side, but blocks the horse's forward movement by not softening her outside hand forwards, and just holds her inside leg against the horse's side behind the girth to keep the hindquarters still, the horse will step across to the left. His hindquarters remain still because the feel from the inside leg stops him stepping across with his hindlegs, but he will move his shoulders and forelegs across to the left. To straighten up again, the rider presses her left leg against the girth to push the horse's shoulders back over to the right. The left hand prevents the horse from stepping forwards, and the right hand is opened out to the right to invite the horse to step over to the right. The left leg stays back behind the girth to keep the horse's hindquarters still.

MOVING TO THE RIGHT

1 Similarly at halt, if the rider keeps a light feel on the outside (left) rein and opens the inside hand whilst pressing the inside leg against the girth, the horse will bend his head and neck to the right.

2 If the rider brings her outside (left) leg back behind the girth whilst blocking any attempt by the horse to move forwards with the outside rein, and keeps her inside (right) leg on the girth to keep the horse's shoulders stationary, then as she presses her outside leg against the horse he will swing his quarters over to the right. To straighten the horse up again the aids are then reversed – the right leg is used behind the girth to push the quarters back over to the left, whilst the right hand prevents the horse from stepping forwards. The left leg is used on the girth to make sure the shoulders remain still. Once the horse is straight again, the rider's legs and hands return to the normal position.

The Rider's Goal – To Lighten the Forehand

If you watch a horse showing off loose in a field you will see how proud and active he can look: his neck is high and arched, and he will use his hindquarters powerfully to produce round, elevated paces. As soon as a young or unschooled horse is asked to carry a rider, this picture can change dramatically: the horse's outline becomes flatter and longer, his steps lose their spring and he may lean on the bit by carrying his head and neck low, so that the rider always has a horrible, heavy feel in the hand; alternatively, he may carry his head high in an effort to evade the effect of the rider's hand on the rein and the bit. The rider has to teach the horse how to rebalance himself so that he can comfortably deal with the unbalancing effect of a rider on his back and regain his proud, elegant and light bearing.

An unbalanced horse usually takes advantage of the fact that the rider is holding the reins and will lean on the bit, so the rider is in effect helping to carry the weight of the horse. When this happens the horse is said to be on his forehand, i.e. more of the combined weight of the horse and the rider is carried on the horse's shoulders and forelegs than on the hindquarters and hindlegs. If you piled a lot of heavy weights on to the front of a car it would become heavy to handle, and similarly the horse becomes heavy in the rider's hand and is difficult to steer and control. If the weight is taken off the front of the car and loaded on to the back, suddenly the car is light and manoeuvrable in front.

The rider's aim is to encourage the horse to carry more of the weight on the hindquarters than on the forehand. In order to do this the horse has to lower his hindquarters and allow his hindlegs to step much further under his body. When he does this, his shoulders, head and neck are automatically raised and this is called lightening the forehand, or transferring the weight from the forehand to the hindquarters.

ENGAGING THE HINDQUARTERS

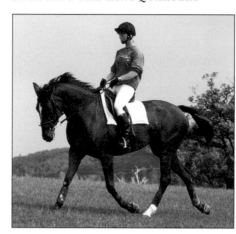

1 A young or unschooled horse will carry himself in a long, low outline; see how low the head and neck appear to be, and how long and flat the overall picture is as a result.

2 The rider has used her legs and seat to encourage the horse to bring his hindlegs further underneath him, and just keeps enough of a contact on the rein to prevent the horse speeding up. The effect of the rider's legs pushing the horse up into the contact maintained by the hand is that the horse starts to bend and flex his hocks more, so that they can step further underneath the body. This is called engaging the hocks or hindquarters.

3 Various schooling exercises, combined with the horse learning to become more responsive to the leg and seat aids, gradually allow the rider to encourage the horse to use his hindquarters more.

4 The horse's outline is now rounder, and the forehand has been raised slightly higher than the hindquarters so that the horse is carrying more of the weight on the hindquarters and has lightened the forehand. Asking the horse to transfer the weight in this way, from the forehand to the hindquarters, is always brought about by greater use of the rider's legs, not by pulling the horse's head and neck up and in with the reins. The rein contact should remain soft and elastic, only blocking sufficiently to prevent the horse from speeding up when the leg is applied, instead of engaging the hindquarters more as is required.

Control and Motion – Introducing Lateral Work

When first learning to ride, you are concerned primarily with being able to send the horse forwards into walk, trot, canter and gallop, and being able to halt. As your skills develop, you learn how to make the horse move sideways, either by moving his whole body or just his shoulders or hindquarters. This is known as lateral work, and is invaluable for a novice rider as it teaches him or her to feel and influence the horse's movement. For the horse, it is used as a suppling exercise and to encourage him to work more actively with his hindquarters.

LEG YIELDING

Lateral movements include leg yielding, quarters-in (both described here), shoulder-in and half-pass (see Developing Lateral Work). All horses should be introduced to these exercises as part of their overall training programme. Practise them at walk and, once you have mastered control of the shoulders and hindquarters, you will realize just how manoeuvrable the horse can be.

■ LEG YIELDING

In this exercise the horse is asked to move forwards and sideways at the same time;

the inside hind and foreleg cross over in front of the outside hind and foreleg.

■ QUARTERS-IN

In this exercise the horse continues walking in a straight line but he brings his quarters in to one side. If working on a sand surface, the horse's hoofprints would leave three lines of tracks: the inside line is formed by the inside hind, the middle line is made by the inside fore and the outside hind (which follow each other), and the outside line is made by the outside fore.

■ REIN BACK

The rein back is when the horse is asked, quite literally, to walk backwards. It should only ever be performed in walk although, when frightened, the horse will be quite capable of running backwards at a respectable speed!

Although the rein back is not a lateral movement, it is all part of teaching horse and rider the full extent of the control and motion they can achieve.

The horse should step backwards, in a straight line, moving his legs clearly and positively in diagonal pairs – inside fore and outside hind together, followed by outside fore and inside hind together.

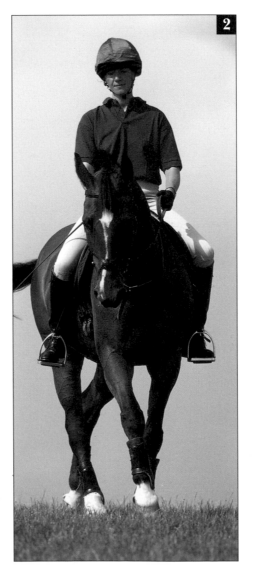

▮ LEFT
To leg yield across to the left, as this rider is doing, she brings her right leg behind the girth which tells the horse to move sideways; her left leg remains on the girth, encouraging the horse to keep moving forwards as well as sideways. The right hand is opened a few inches which encourages the horse to keep a slight right bend through the body; the left hand keeps enough of a feel on the rein to prevent the horse bending too far to the left and, combined with the push from the right leg behind the girth, invites the horse to step sideways. To leg yield away to the right the aids are reversed – the left leg is used behind the girth, the right leg on the girth, the right rein keeps enough contact to invite the horse to step to the right, and the left rein is opened a few inches to encourage the horse to keep a slight bend through his body.

QUARTERS-IN

▌ RIGHT

In these pictures the horse is being asked to bring his quarters into the left whilst continuing to walk forwards in a straight line. The rider uses her outside (right) leg behind the girth to move the quarters across slightly. Her inside leg stays on the girth to encourage the horse to keep moving forwards and to prevent the shoulders moving out of line. The left hand is opened slightly which, combined with the pressure from the left leg on the girth, encourages the horse to keep a bend through his whole body. The outside hand takes up enough of a feel to keep the horse's shoulder moving forwards in a straight line.

Quarters-in to the right is achieved by reversing the aids – the left leg is used behind the girth, her right leg, now the inside leg, stays on the girth, the right hand is opened slightly and the left (outside) hand takes up enough of a feel to keep the horse's shoulders moving forwards in a straight line.

REIN BACK

1 The rein back can only be successfully performed if the horse is calm and relaxed when at the halt.

2 The rider squeezes both legs against the horse's sides, but makes sure that she blocks the horse's forward movement by not allowing her hands to move forwards. Because the legs are applied actively, the horse knows he has to move somewhere. The rein contact is telling him he cannot go forwards and so he goes backwards. Some horses, as demonstrated here, understand what is required more easily if you apply both legs behind the girth, and then lift your seat bones off the saddle. This encourages the horse to step back underneath you as required.

3 Having taken one step back with one diagonal pair of legs, the horse proceeds to step back with the remaining diagonal pair. The horse should only be asked to step backwards for a limited number of steps. As a reward, allow him to walk forwards again whilst making a fuss of him.

Acceptance of Contact

Right from the start the horse has to learn to accept, without tension or resentment, the fact that the bit in his mouth is attached, via the reins, to the rider's hands, and that there will always be a light but sympathetic contact between the two. It is vital that you achieve a balanced, independent seat so that you are not tempted to hang on to the reins in an effort to balance yourself. Your priority is to learn to follow the movement of the horse's head and neck so that you are able to keep a constant but sympathetic contact with his mouth. In the early stages of training, you should not concern yourself with how the horse is carrying his head and neck, but only with learning to feel,

BASIC PRINCIPLES

Before you can hope to achieve a lightening of the forehand, there are a number of basic principles that you and your horse must master. These form the basis of all horses' training and progression, whether or not you are dealing with a horse who has never been properly schooled, and are as follows:

■ Acceptance of the rein contact.
■ Free forward movement.
■ Maintaining a rhythm.
■ Bend and flexion through the body.
■ The use of half-halts to engage the hindquarters and rebalance the horse. Once you have mastered these principles, you will be equipped with the means to ride your horse to the maximum of his potential.

follow and maintain the contact. Once the horse knows that the contact is constant, but kind, he will learn to accept it. Your elbows must remain soft and relaxed so that the contact can be maintained. It may be necessary to open the hands out a little wider than usual so that there is no obstruction – whatever the horse does with his head, you can follow it with your hands.

COMMON FAULTS

How often have you seen a horse slopping along like this? The rider is not keeping a contact with the horse's mouth and, although she is actively using her legs, the horse is completely ignoring the aid and continuing to plod along in a lethargic and uninterested manner.

The horse must respond the same way in all paces. Here, in trot, we can see the result of the rider failing to keep a contact with the horse's mouth, and the horse blatantly ignoring the rider's leg aids. The rider is working hard with her legs whilst the horse is being extremely lazy with his!

FOLLOWING THE HORSE'S HEAD AND NECK

▮ **RIGHT**
In the early stages of training, the rider should not concern himself with the position of the horse's head and neck – only with learning to follow their movement so that a soft but constant contact is maintained.

Free Forward Movement

The horse also has to learn to respect the rider's legs, i.e. when you use your legs against the horse's sides, he must respond by going forwards if both legs are used together or by moving away from the leg if used as a lateral (sideways) aid. The vast majority of problems experienced both on the flat and over jumps are caused by the horse ignoring, or being slow to react to, the rider's leg aids. The horse's first reaction should always be to move forwards. Once the horse respects the leg and is willing to maintain free forward movement without you continually having to reapply the leg aids, he is said to be in front of the leg and on the aids – he is attentive and ready to react to his rider's commands instantly.

In the early stages of training, you should use your voice combined with a squeeze from both legs to ask the horse to move forwards. If the horse does not respond, use your voice again, backed up with a sharp nudge with both heels against the horse's sides. If this is still ignored, squeeze your legs against the horse, use your voice to ask him to walk on and give him a tap with the schooling whip or stick behind your leg at the same time as the leg aid is applied. You must be ready to allow forward movement with the hands, particularly if the horse jumps forward when the schooling whip is used. As soon as he moves forwards, reward him by praising him verbally. You should then relax your legs against the horse's sides. As soon as he slows down again, repeat the process. Gradually the horse will learn to respond to the first light aid.

KEEPING A SOFT CONTACT

1 Here the rider has shortened her reins sufficiently to keep a contact with the horse's mouth. She has applied the leg again and backed it up with a tap from the schooling whip. Already the picture is one of greater alertness and activity.

2 The rider maintains the contact and uses the leg once more to ask the horse to walk on a little more energetically.

3 This time the horse responds instantly; the rider's leg can relax and the horse maintains the forward movement without further nagging. Note how the horse's outline is now much rounder and shorter as he begins to lighten his forehand.

4 In trot, the rider takes up contact with the horse's mouth and backs up her leg aids with a tap from the schooling whip.

5 Immediately the horse offers much more in the way of forward impulsion. Now that he is thinking forwards, see how he lengthens his steps and voluntarily raises his head and neck into a rounder, shorter outline.

6 The rider can relax her legs and enjoy the free forward movement that the horse is offering her. But as soon as he drops back from this pace, the rider starts the process over again.

Maintaining a Rhythm

Now that the horse accepts the contact and moves forward willingly from your leg, both you and he need to learn to maintain an even rhythm in all your work. This rhythm must not be too slow or the work will lack impulsion and power; neither must it be too fast or the horse will tend to become unbalanced and will be pushed on to his forehand. Aim for a rhythm in each pace which gives you the feeling of free forward movement without feeling rushed. The ultimate aim is to use a light squeeze from the legs to ride the horse up into this rhythm; then to relax and enjoy the experience whilst the horse willingly maintains the rhythm, without continual nagging from either hand or leg.

Once the horse is responding quickly to the leg you are half way there. Some horses have naturally rhythmic paces and will automatically maintain the rhythm. Others will need a reminder from leg, voice and/or schooling whip to keep up to the rhythm, or they may need to be slowed down. Having got the horse thinking forwards, be careful not to dampen his goodwill by restricting him with the reins if he goes too fast. The use of a neck strap to slow the horse is a better method to use; it prevents the horse from learning how to lean on the bit or to fight you by shortening and tensing his neck.

By pulling on the neck strap instead of blocking with the reins, you can slow the horse down. Practise in the arena, first using the strap to bring the horse from walk to halt, and then from trot to walk etc. Once the horse understands its use, this method can be used to steady him within any pace. But remember that you must still use your legs and voice, if necessary, in the same way as you would do if you were going to use the rein contact to slow down.

USING THE NECK STRAP

1 Here the rider is introducing the neck strap by using it to bring the horse back from trot to walk. She has put the reins in one hand and holds the neck strap in the other.

2 The rider then uses her legs with a light squeeze against the horse's sides, whilst using her voice and a firm pull on the neck strap to slow the horse down. Although the rider wants to slow down, the leg is still applied because it encourages the horse to bring his hindlegs further underneath him so that he can keep his forehand light. If the leg is not used, the horse will simply shift his weight on to the forehand and will become heavy and unbalanced in the rider's hand.

3 The horse comes back quite happily to walk without the need to block with the rein. He is rewarded with a pat and praise from his rider.

4 When working in trot, if the horse has a tendency to speed up out of the desired rhythm the rider can just loop a finger through the neck strap and take a pull on it until the horse slows the rhythm down again.

5 When the horse responds, the neck strap is released and he is praised by his rider.

Bend and Flexion

In all the horse's work, the rider is striving to ensure that the horse's hindlegs follow in the same tracks as his front legs, i.e. his quarters are not allowed to swing out or his shoulder to fall in. This is referred to as straightness in the horse, which is a term that causes some confusion. For the horse to be straight, i.e. for his hindlegs to follow in the same tracks as his forelegs, when working on a turn or a circle he has to bend through his body; his whole body must form a slight, continual curve around the rider's inside leg. So in order to be straight the horse has to bend!

The degree of bend that the horse shows through his body is dependent on the size of circle or turn you are riding. For example, to ride a 65½ foot (20 m) circle the horse shows only a slight bend through his body, but to manoeuvre himself around a 33 foot (10 m) circle there will be a greater degree of bend.

ACHIEVING BEND

1 The rider should concentrate on making sure that the outside hand is really following the horse's movement in a soft, allowing way, whilst still maintaining a light contact. This ensures that the horse's forward momentum is not stifled by a restricting outside hand. The rider then opens the inside hand, setting it in the open position by simply tensing the muscles of the arm, not by pulling back on the rein. The inside leg is used on the girth to keep the horse pushed out on to the circle, and a firmer contact is only taken up on the outside rein if the horse falls in on the circle, i.e. allows the circle to get smaller and smaller. If he does this, the rider must keep pushing the horse out with the inside leg and draw him back out on to the original circle by using the outside rein.

2 The rider should now feel the horse bending through the body and neck; if the horse resists and does not respond by offering some bend through his body, the rider simply opens the inside rein out further and sets it there – still without pulling back on it. The inside leg is kept on, and should be backed up with a tap from the schooling whip if the horse continues to fall in on the circle rather than bend through the body.

3 As soon as the horse offers the bend, i.e. when you can see a glimpse of his inside eye and nostril, use both legs against his sides to encourage him to bring his hocks further underneath him and to flex through his topline. When you feel the horse relax his poll and jaw so that the nose is lowered and his face is on the vertical, soften the inside rein and allow it to follow the movement in the same way as the outside rein. Praise the horse verbally – this is his reward for yielding to your leg and hand. The horse is now beginning to work in self-carriage, i.e. he is carrying more weight on his hindquarters and is lightening his forehand. Note that his head and neck are higher and more arched than in picture one; this is a result of the hocks being brought further under him.

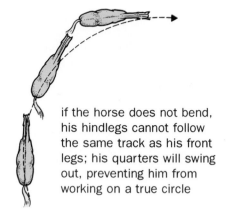

the horse bends through his body so the hindlegs follow the same track as the front legs

if the horse does not bend, his hindlegs cannot follow the same track as his front legs; his quarters will swing out, preventing him from working on a true circle

■ LEFT
How a horse goes around a corner.

The more the horse has to bend his body the more he has to use his hocks, and the inside hindleg in particular has to step much further across and under the horse's body in order to follow in the track of the inside foreleg. Having ridden simple turns and circles, you will know that the inside leg is used on the girth with an open inside hand to encourage the horse to bend around the inside leg, whilst the outside leg is used back behind the girth to prevent the quarters swinging out. The outside hand is used to prevent the horse bending his head and neck too much to the inside. On an unschooled horse the aids have to be exaggerated

until he realizes what it is you are asking him to do. Once the horse is willing to offer you the bend through his whole body, you can ask him to flex right through his topline so that his whole outline becomes soft and round and he offers you no resistance whatsoever. The horse's topline describes the area from the top of the tail, over the hindquarters, back, withers and neck, and on up to the poll. When the horse flexes through his topline, his hindquarters are lowered as his hocks come further underneath him, he stays soft through his back, arches his neck and relaxes his poll and jaw so that the head is carried in a relaxed manner; the horse will

lower his nose so that a vertical line could be drawn down the front of his face.

The horse should be introduced to this work in trot – it is very easy to stifle his forward momentum if it is first asked for in walk. Ride forwards into trot, bearing in mind the principles of having a horse who will respond happily to your leg and settle into a rhythm without being nagged by your leg or hand.

With time and practice, you will find that the horse will become more and more responsive to the request to bend and flex. After a while, you will not need to open the inside hand in such an exaggerated fashion; simply moving the hand over

OBTAINING THE CORRECT DEGREE OF BEND

  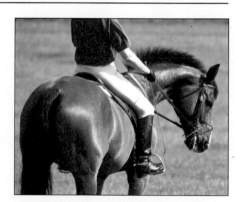

The rider should only ask for a slight bend through the horse's body and neck, so that the outside of the horse makes a continual curve around the rider's inside leg. The rider only needs to see a glimpse of the horse's inside eye and nostril to know that the bend is correct.

A common fault is for the horse to bend only through the neck from the withers, so that his body is still straight. In this position the horse can avoid having to step under himself more with his hindlegs, so his quarters will swing out as he goes around a corner. If his hocks are not underneath him, he can neither turn correctly nor flex through his topline when asked. The rider must use the outside rein to reduce the degree of bend in the neck, the outside leg to keep the hind-quarters from swinging out, and should reinforce the inside leg by tapping the horse with the schooling whip behind his or her lower leg.

Another fault is for the horse to tilt his head towards the inside. He is allowing the rider's inside hand to draw his nose to the inside but is ignoring the outside hand, so instead of bending through the neck and poll, the horse simply tilts his head to one side. More contact should be taken up with the outside rein to correct this.

BEND AND FLEXION – THE OVERALL PICTURE

1 The horse is ridden forwards into trot; the rider opens her inside hand and closes her inside leg on the girth to ask the horse to bend around her leg. The outside hand stays soft and allows the horse to move freely forwards, unless it has to be used to prevent him bending too much through the neck.

2 Here the horse has responded by curving his whole body around the rider's inside leg; see how the neck looks more relaxed and softer than in the first picture. This is because the horse is working willingly, without resistance.

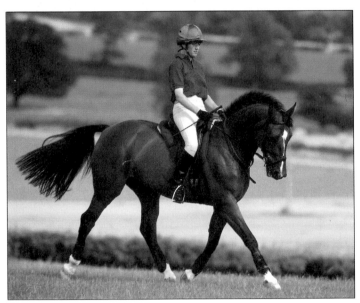

3 Now that the rider has obtained the correct amount of bend, she closes both legs against the horse's sides to encourage him to be more active and step further under himself with his hindlegs. The horse is now flexing through his topline, i.e. his quarters are lowered and his back and neck are round and soft, which in turn raises and lightens his forehand.

4 The result is a picture of power with softness, and roundness with activity. See how the horse is bent around the rider's legs; he is also using his hindquarters actively which allows his forehand to be light and elevated. The increased power shows in the way the horse is stretching his front legs forwards, and matching this up behind by stepping under himself further with the hindlegs. His neck is carried higher and is more arched than in the first picture but he remains soft and light in the rider's hand. This is the start of self-carriage.

about an inch will be sufficient. Much further down the line in the horse's training, it will also only be necessary to take up a feel on the inside rein and to close the legs against the horse's sides to achieve bend and flexion.

Once the bend and flexion are established in trot, you can strive for the same result in both walk and canter. But the vital thing to remember with this training method is always to reward the horse by softening the inside hand the instant that he offers you even the tiniest degree of flexion and relaxation. To begin with it will be a case of working quite hard to ask the horse to bend and then to flex, followed by the reward of softening the inside hand as soon as he does so. He may only offer you the bend and flexion for a few strides before you have to repeat the process and ask again, but as he begins to understand what is wanted and his topline muscles up as a result of the work, he will offer it to you for longer periods.

Gradually you will be doing less asking and more rewarding; you will find yourself riding for longer with both hands soft so that the horse is working on a light contact. But you will need to be persistent and consistent in your training.

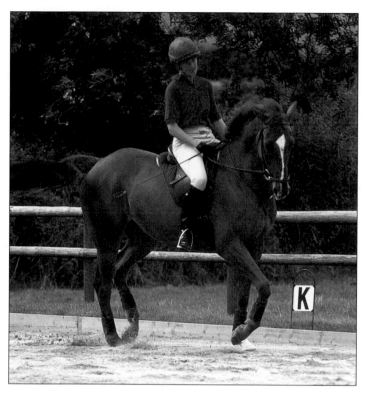

This horse has offered the rider the required degree of bend and flexion – note the arch of his neck and how his forehand appears lighter and higher than his hindquarters. You can see how he is really flexing his hock as he goes to step forwards with his hindleg and, most importantly, note how the rider has softened the inside rein so that the horse is holding this outline himself.

▌ RIGHT
As soon as the horse responds to the rider's aids by bending through his body and then flexing through his topline, the rider must soften the inside hand and praise the horse verbally as a reward. This is the only way that the horse can know that he has responded to the aids in the right way.

▌ RIGHT
While the inside hand is being softened, it can also be used to pat the horse's neck as further praise.

CORRECT USE OF THE INSIDE HAND

It is vital to ask the horse to bend his whole body around your inside leg by opening the inside hand and using the inside leg to keep the horse out on the circle. By using your hand and leg in this way, when the horse does respond he will produce a continuous bend through his body, neck and head. You may have to open your inside hand very wide, you may have to back up the inside-leg aid with a tap from the schooling whip, and your outside hand may have to take up more of a contact to stop the horse bending his neck too far to the inside, but, when the horse drops his resistance, relaxes and responds to these aids, he will be working correctly.

If the horse is slow to respond and refuses to offer the requested bend, it is very tempting to cheat! If you cross your inside hand over the horse's withers instead of opening the hand out and backing it up with the inside leg, the horse will instantly bend, but this bend will only be from the withers, it will not be right through the body. The crossing over of the rider's hand cuts off the horse's forward impulsion and cuts off the bend at the withers. So whilst you will be able to see the required glimpse of the inside eye and nostril, it will not be backed up by the correct use or position of the horse's hindquarters.

Crossing the inside hand over in this way is something that many riders, even at high levels

of competition, are tempted to do. Some do not realize that it is a false measure and are satisfied with the false bend that the horse offers them, but their future is limited and their potential will not be fully realized. The temptation to cross the hand over is simply a sign that the horse is not respecting the rider's inside leg and/or the outside hand. So instead of giving in to the temptation, use it as a reminder to yourself to use your inside leg and outside hand correctly,

even if this means not continuing with the exercise until the horse is prepared to move away from the inside leg (see Free Forward Movement). Always go back and correct the underlying fault if any training exercise is not progressing well. Never think that a short cut such as crossing the hand over or losing your temper will pay long-term dividends. Get the basics right and then you will have something permanent to build on. Be consistent, and be quick to praise your horse.

When asking the horse to bend, you must open your inside hand and use your inside leg.

If you cross your inside hand over, the horse will bend only from the wither.

Working Within Each Pace

Once both horse and rider have begun to understand the basics of a correct and acceptable way of working in each pace, the rider can take the horse's performance further. Having mastered the principles of free forward movement and obtained a degree of bend and flexion, you can further influence the horse by seeking to improve his paces. Plenty of horses have a pleasant enough way of going – they are able to maintain a round outline and a good rhythm in each pace – but this can be nurtured to produce a horse who puts real power and flair into his work. The use of half-halts and the introduction of lateral work help the horse to become more balanced and bring him nearer to working in self-carriage.

The Half-halt

The half-halt describes what happens when the rider closes his or her legs and hands momentarily against the horse. This serves to rebalance the horse in whatever pace he is working; the rider's legs push the horse's hindlegs underneath him further whilst the hand blocks any acceleration in pace which the horse might offer. The power that the legs have created is trapped by the rider's hand so that, instead of accelerating, the horse lowers his hindquarters and elevates his forehand slightly, becoming better balanced and lighter in the rider's hand. The half-halt can be used to (1) rebalance

HALF-HALT AT TROT

1 This horse is producing an active trot, and is maintaining a good outline; considering that he is only young the overall picture is soft and round. The rider is sitting quietly with the leg aid on, but only needs to maintain a light contact with the reins to the horse's mouth.

2 Now the horse is becoming unbalanced. He has probably overpowered himself with the push from his hindlegs and is poking his nose forward and starting to lean on the bit in an attempt to balance himself. The soft, round outline is disappearing.

3 To rebalance the horse, the rider uses a half-halt. She closes her legs on the horse's sides and pushes him up into her hand which, just for a second, is blocked against the horse's forward movement. In effect, the horse's body is squashed up together; his outline becomes shorter because his hindlegs are pushed further under his body so he is able to carry more weight on them, which in turn lightens and elevates his forehand.

4 The horse is rewarded by the rider relaxing the leg and softening the hand again. The softening, or giving of the rein, has been exaggerated in this picture to show that once the horse is using his hindquarters and hocks more actively he is able to carry himself and remain light in the rider's hand (self-carriage). So although the rein is completely loose, the horse is maintaining his own balance and a correct outline.

HALF-HALT AT CANTER

1 Here you can see how this horse is falling on to his forehand at canter. The impression in the picture is that the horse's weight is falling forwards and that he is leaning on the bit and, therefore, on the rider's hands for support.

2 The rider uses a half-halt to rebalance – she closes her legs against the horse's sides and blocks any forward acceleration with her hands.

3 Now the horse is balanced and light in the rider's hands. In picture one the hind-quarters appear higher than the shoulders (on the forehand). Now the shoulders are higher than the hind-quarters (the forehand is elevated and lightened).

the horse in any pace, (2) warn the horse that the rider is about to ask him to do something such as change direction and (3) build impulsion within each pace which can be stored to produce collected work, or released to produce extended work.

■ ACHIEVING THE HALF-HALT

Every horse will respond to a combination of hand and leg. You have to find out what combination is needed for your horse to obtain the desired result. Too much hand and the horse will either resist by throwing his head up, or he will simply slow down. Too much leg and the horse will try to accelerate and be pushed on to his forehand, which will unbalance him.

First, practise the half-halt at walk. At a given point, close your legs against the horse's sides and reduce the degree to which you allow your hands to follow the contact, as if you were about to halt. Just as you sense the horse is about to halt, soften

THE RIDER'S SEAT AS AN AID

The rider's body weight can be used, through the seat, to influence the horse – it can create or block the amount of impulsion that the horse is working with. If you think about using your seat as an aid too soon, there is a risk that you will simply become stiff in the body and will no longer be able to move with the horse. The use of the seat will develop naturally once you have achieved that all-important independent seat. If you think back to the use of the hands and arms, and how these stay soft and relaxed so that they follow the movement of the horse's head and neck, that is how you should think of your own body weight. Just as you can change

the degree to which your hands follow the head and neck movement, for example when asking the horse to slow down or halt, your body weight can be used either to encourage the horse to use himself more actively, or to slow him down. Letting the seat move freely with the horse encourages active movement; reducing the degree to which the seat moves with the horse slows him down. The use of the body weight or seat should always be subtle and sympathetic. The feel for its correct use will come naturally once an independent seat has been achieved, and once you understand how and why you need to influence the horse.

your hands forward again, keeping your legs on the horse's sides so that he continues in walk. Once you get the feel of how much leg and hand is needed to produce this effect of almost but not quite halting the horse, you will have achieved a half-halt. Then practise it at trot and at

canter. Each time, act as if to bring the horse back to the slower pace and, at the last second, allow him to continue in the original pace. Once you have mastered the half-halt, you can use it more subtly to forewarn the horse that he is about to be asked to do something different.

TOO MUCH HAND

If the rider makes the mistake of using too much hand and not enough leg, the horse will soon let her know by not offering the desired response. Here the rider has tried to rebalance the canter by raising and pulling back with the hands, with no back-up from the leg. The horse responds by simply falling back into trot.

Developing Lateral Work

The shoulder-in and half-pass are the most useful lateral-work exercises in terms of encouraging the horse to use his hocks more actively and effectively underneath him. The mistake that many people make is to think of them simply as requirements of a dressage test. This is not how they should be viewed – lateral work is used to improve the horse's overall way of going. These exercises teach the horse to respond to different uses of the hand and leg, to be supple through his body, and to place his hocks further underneath him in an effort to carry more of his body weight on the hindquarters rather than on the forehand.

COMMON FAULT

A common mistake is for the rider to ask for too much angle so that the horse works on four tracks instead of three, i.e. each leg is put down in a separate track. The rider has crossed her inside hand over the horse's withers so that the horse is only bending from in front of the withers, through the neck, instead of through the body and neck. The whole point of the exercise has been lost; the horse is not supple through the body, only through the neck, and the hindlegs are not being encouraged to take any extra weight at all. To correct this mistake the rider needs to take up more contact in the outside hand to reduce the bend in the neck, use the outside leg to stop the quarters swinging round any further, and the inside leg to push the shoulders back towards the track which will reduce the angle of the horse's body until he is working correctly on three tracks.

■ SHOULDER-IN

The shoulder-in is similar to quarters-in, in that the horse moves on three tracks, but here it is the shoulders that are brought in, not the quarters, as the horse continues to move forwards. The footfalls are as follows: the inside track is made by the inside foreleg, the middle track by the outside foreleg and inside hindleg together, and the outside track is made by the outside hindleg.

It is quite difficult in shoulder-in for the new rider to keep the horse moving forwards in a straight line. The horse may try to swing his quarters out one way, or may drift sideways instead of holding the position and moving forwards in a straight line. If you are working in an arena it helps to do the following: as you bring the

SHOULDER-IN

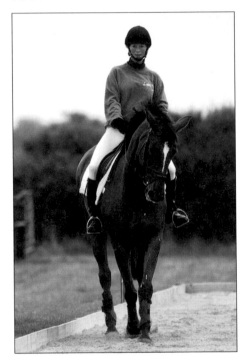

1 It is easiest to practise lateral movement in an arena so that you have a straight edge to work along; here the rider is about to ride shoulder-in in trot down the long side of the arena. She has already ridden a 33 foot (10 m) circle in trot in the corner that she is just coming from. This circle gives the rider an idea of the correct amount of bend that the horse should hold throughout the shoulder-in. To start the shoulder-in she goes to ride another 33 foot (10 m) circle, but, as soon as the horse's front legs have left the track to start the circle, she uses the outside hand to prevent him continuing on the circle, and the inside leg to keep him moving forwards along the side of the arena.

2 As the horse progresses down the long side of the arena in shoulder-in, you can clearly see how he is working on three tracks (inside fore, outside fore/inside hind, outside hind). This exercise encourages the horse to be supple as he has to maintain a bend through his body and neck; it also introduces the horse to the idea of carrying more weight on the inside hindleg. As the inside hindleg touches the ground, you can see that it is placed directly under the horse's belly and beneath the rider. So at this point the horse is carrying much of his body weight, as well as the weight of the rider, on that inside hindleg.

3 To help keep the horse moving forwards in a straight line whilst in shoulder-in, the rider should look straight ahead and think of her outside hip as pointing the way forwards.

HALF-PASS

1 To ride the half-pass, shown here in walk, the rider would turn down the long side of the arena and ask the horse to go into shoulder-in. Instead of continuing in shoulder-in, he would then use the outside leg back behind the girth to push the horse's hindquarters across until they are almost directly in line with the shoulders. The outside leg stays in place telling the horse to move sideways, whilst the inside leg also keeps him moving forwards. The outside hand controls the degree of bend through the horse's body and neck whilst the inside hand remains open, inviting the horse to step forwards and sideways.

2 In half-pass the horse must remain bent around the rider's inside leg so that he is bent in the direction in which he is moving. In this picture, the rider's outside leg can clearly be seen in use behind the girth to push the horse sideways. Half-pass can be ridden in walk, trot and canter.

3 This picture shows how, in half-pass, it is the outside hindleg which has to come across and under the horse, thereby having to take the weight of both his own body and the rider's. The exercise also encourages the horse to be supple through his body and, in particular, through his shoulders.

horse's shoulders in off the track, make sure you are looking ahead yourself and think of your outside hip as a pointer; if you imagine keeping your hip moving forwards in a straight line, the horse's outside shoulder will move forwards on the same line. The correct position for the rider in shoulder-in is for the hips to stay parallel with the horse's shoulders, but for the shoulders to be held straight as if you are riding forwards in a straight line as normal. You should look straight ahead.

■ **HALF-PASS**

In half-pass the horse moves diagonally across the arena, taking good-sized steps forwards and sideways, and keeping his body bent in the direction in which he is moving. His shoulders are allowed to be just fractionally ahead of his hindquarters as he makes this movement. His outside hind and foreleg cross over in front of his inside hind and foreleg.

COMMON FAULT

A common mistake is for the horse to try to make life easier for himself by not maintaining the correct bend. See how the horse is now bent to the outside which, in effect, means he is now simply leg yielding. The rider needs to ride the horse forwards in a straight line so that he knows straightaway that his response was not acceptable. Shoulder-in should be re-established, and the rider should use the outside leg to bring the quarters over and to keep the horse stepping sideways. As soon as the horse offers the wrong bend again, he must be ridden forwards in a straight line and the process repeated. The rider may need to tap the horse with the schooling whip just behind the inside leg to make sure he is listening to this leg and remains bent around it.

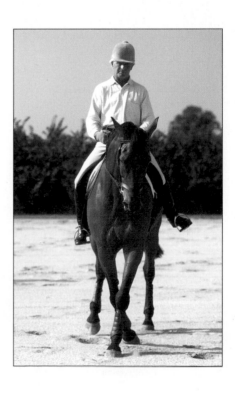

Variations Within Each Pace

The horse is capable of a number of variations of each pace, e.g. in trot or canter the horse can work in a collected, working, medium or extended pace, and he can work in collected, medium or free walk. As the horse's responsiveness to his rider increases and his training progresses, he should be able to offer all of these variations smoothly and without resistance. When asking the horse for variations within each pace, think in terms of asking for more power and impulsion rather than more speed.

MEDIUM WALK

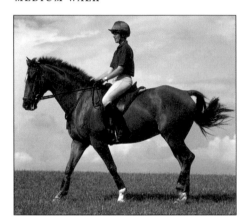

The medium walk is the pace the horse naturally offers his rider – the sort of pace that would be produced out on a hack. The horse takes long, relaxed steps and he overtracks, which means his hind feet step further forwards than the hoofprints left by the front feet.

▌ RIGHT
The medium paces require the horse to work with increased impulsion so that he takes longer, rounder steps than he would do in the working paces. He lengthens his whole frame slightly whilst still keeping a round outline.

WORKING TROT

The working trot is the pace the horse naturally offers his rider. It is an active pace with the horse maintaining a round outline whilst working in a forward-thinking rhythm. It is the sort of trot the horse would produce out hacking – relaxed but active. The same is true of the working canter.

COLLECTED TROT

In the collected paces, which can be either walk, trot or canter, the horse shortens his whole outline by lowering his hindquarters and bringing his hocks further under him, and by elevating his forehand so that his neck is raised and arched. The horse takes shorter, rounder steps, with greater elevation.

MEDIUM TROT

EXTENDED TROT

In the extended paces the horse stretches his whole frame and takes steps of maximum length with maximum impulsion. As with all the variations in pace, the horse must still remain in balance and in a rhythm. This horse could still afford to lengthen and stretch his neck a little more forwards so that the overall picture was of a longer frame.

FREE WALK

◗ LEFT
The free walk is often asked for in a dressage test – the rider offers the horse a long length of rein and the horse stretches his head and neck down and takes long, relaxed steps forwards, with his hind feet overtracking his front feet. Because the horse has been taught always to expect a contact between his mouth and the rider's hand, when the rider offers him a long length of rein, he stretches his head and neck down to seek out the contact he is used to feeling. To allow the horse to stretch his head and neck fully, the rider allows her arms and hands to go forwards and down so that there is still a straight line from her elbow, through the arm, down the rein to the bit.

EXTENDED CANTER

In the extended canter the horse lengthens his whole frame and fully extends his legs to take the longest possible steps whilst still remaining in balance. The horse in these pictures needs to lengthen his neck a little more and to take his nose forwards a fraction so that he is not behind the vertical.

Achieving Collection and Extension of the Paces

Producing these variations within each pace involves bringing together the techniques and principles with which you should, by now, be familiar. Whether the horse is working in the collected, medium or extended paces, he has to maintain the same rhythm in his work. In other words, you do not slow the horse down in order to achieve collection, nor should you go faster in order to extend the horse. To achieve collection, the rider uses the half-halt so that the horse's hocks are pushed further underneath him whilst the hand prevents him from accelerating. The trapping by the rider's hand of the power produced by the use of the leg causes the horse to shorten his frame and put that power into taking shorter, higher steps. Medium or extended work is achieved by first using half-halts to collect the horse and then releasing that power and energy in varying degrees by softening the hand forwards, which enables the horse to lengthen his frame and his stride. Whether the resulting pace is medium or extended depends on the degree to which the rider softens with the hand whilst continuing to ask for more power and drive from the hindquarters. To be able to produce these variations in pace, you have to develop a feel for creating and storing energy for collected work, and for directing that energy forwards into either medium or extended work.

COLLECTING AND EXTENDING THE HORSE

1 When practising collecting and extending the horse, it is easier to work within the confines of an arena. The short side of the arena which provides two corners in close proximity to each other is a good place to ask for collection, whilst the long side, or even across the diagonal, provides room for extending the paces. This rider is using half-halts to collect the horse as he progresses through the corner of the arena and begins to turn across the diagonal. A corner is a good place to start to ask for collection, as the horse has to bring his inside hindleg further underneath him in order to negotiate the turn anyway. Note the raised, arched neck and the way the hock is being raised and flexed.

2 As the horse starts to cross the diagonal, the rider continues to collect the energy that was built up as they came through the turn. The horse's outline remains relatively high and short.

4 The outline is now lower and longer as the horse extends his limbs forwards to cover as much ground as possible with each stride.

3 Once the horse is completely straight, the rider asks the horse to extend. He continues to ask for impulsion and drive from the hindquarters by keeping his legs actively on the horse's sides, but now he releases that stored power by softening the hands forwards so that the horse can lengthen his frame and strides. Note how the horse's hindquarters are still lowered, and how the first surge of released energy has really elevated his front end as the horse begins to extend his steps.

▮ RIGHT
Teaching the horse to counter canter.

Introducing Counter Canter

Counter canter is a movement required in many dressage tests, and it demonstrates the horse's suppleness, balance and obedience. Counter canter involves the horse cantering with the left leg leading whilst being worked on the right rein, and vice versa. The horse must keep his head and neck bent over his leading foreleg, so that he is in fact bent in the opposite direction to that in which he is moving.

Counter canter is introduced by cantering on the left rein across the diagonal to the opposite track. As the horse reaches the other side and turns on to the right

COMMON FAULTS

In this picture, the horse is still cantering with the right leg leading but, instead of maintaining the bend of his head and neck to the right, he has bent to the left, i.e. he is now bent in the direction in which he is travelling. The rider must correct this by opening the right hand and closing the right leg on the girth to ask the horse to maintain the bend to the right.

Another common mistake is for the horse to bend his neck too much to the right. This causes him to lose balance and his whole body drifts back to the track instead of following the path of the 16½ foot (5 m) loop. When this happens the horse's hindlegs are not following in the same tracks as the front legs – the horse is simply falling sideways or falling out through the shoulder. If the rider now took up more contact on the outside (left) rein to straighten out the bend of the head and neck, used the left leg behind the girth to stop the quarters swinging out to the left, and opened the right hand whilst keeping the right leg on the girth to encourage the horse to bend his neck to the right, the correct counter canter would be restored.

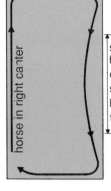

shallow loop where horse is ridden in counter canter – still on the right leg but travelling towards the left

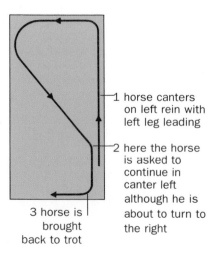

1 horse canters on left rein with left leg leading

2 here the horse is asked to continue in canter left although he is about to turn to the right

3 horse is brought back to trot

rein, he should be asked to maintain the canter with the left leg leading for a few strides, before being brought back to trot.

Once horse and rider are comfortable with this, shallow loops can be ridden in canter down the long side of the arena;

whilst the horse is on the track he is cantering as normal, whereas whilst he is negotiating the shallow loop he is in fact in counter canter, provided he maintains the original bend of his head and neck over the leading foreleg.

RIDING A 16½ FOOT (5 M) LOOP IN COUNTER CANTER

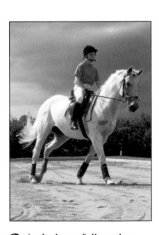

1 The horse canters around the arena on the right rein with the right leg leading as normal. Instead of continuing down the long side of the arena, the rider turns the horse off the track and rides a smooth 16½ foot (5 m) loop along the long side. As the horse negotiates the first curve of the loop he must continue to canter on the right leg.

2 With his head and neck slightly bent to the right, he starts to follow the loop around to the left. He is therefore bent away from the direction in which he is moving. The horse's body must remain straight – his hindlegs must follow in the same tracks as his forelegs, with only his head and neck showing a bend to the right.

3 As the horse follows the loop around to the left and back towards the track, he must still maintain the canter on the right lead, with his neck bent to the right.

Riding a Flying Change

The flying change is when the horse changes directly from cantering with the left leg leading to cantering with the right leg leading, and vice versa. It is called for in some dressage tests and can be built upon in more advanced dressage so that the horse can literally change from one leg to the other on every stride, almost as if he were skipping! For the everyday rider, the flying change is most useful when jumping a course which requires changes of direction at canter. For example, instead of landing over a jump with the left leg leading, then having to come back to trot before picking up canter on the right lead in order to turn right to the next fence, the rider can

simply land, take a few strides forwards in canter and then ask for a flying change as he turns towards the next jump.

Before the horse can be asked to perform a flying change, he must be responsive and obedient to the leg, and his canter must be balanced and able to show a degree of collection. He should willingly perform walk-to-canter transitions, be able to produce 33 foot (10 m) circles in canter, and work in counter canter before progressing to a flying change.

Some horses can tend to become excitable or nervous when they are introduced to this movement, so be sure to teach it carefully and patiently.

CHANGING THE LEAD

1 This movement is best taught by asking the horse to change from counter canter back to normal canter. This horse has been down the long side of the arena on the right rein, and has then cantered a half-circle so that he is now cantering across the diagonal with the right leg leading.

2 As the horse nears the track and the ensuing left-hand corner, the rider must indicate to the horse that he must change from right canter lead to left canter lead. The rider momentarily blocks the horse's forward momentum by closing and setting the left hand, whilst at the same time changing her leg aids from asking for right canter to asking for left canter, i.e. the rider's left leg is now applied on the girth, and the right leg used behind the girth to tell the horse to put his right hindleg down on the ground first. Remember that if the right hind starts the stride off, it is the left foreleg that appears to be leading. In this picture, you can see how the rider's left hand has blocked the horse's forward momentum so his forehand is elevated as a result.

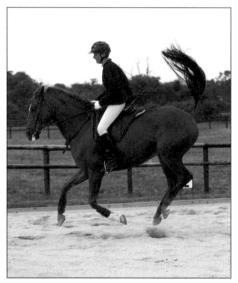

3 In this picture, the horse is in the period of suspension that follows each canter stride, and it is only at this point that he is able to perform the flying change. So the blocking of the forward movement makes the period of suspension just a fraction longer, giving the horse time to re-arrange his legs so that he lands on the opposite lead, i.e. he changes from the right lead to the left lead. This young horse has overreacted to the rider changing the position of her leg aids (bringing her left leg back on to the girth and using her right leg behind the girth). He has flicked up his back end higher than his forehand which unbalances him. As he strengthens up and becomes more relaxed about the exercise he will make a smoother flying change.

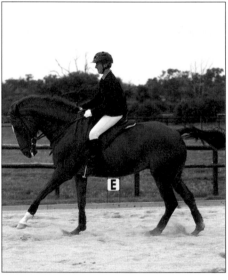

4 As a result of the rider changing her aids from asking for canter right to asking for canter left, the horse has landed on the left lead as required and can now continue to canter around the arena on the left rein.

Riding a Dressage Test

Once you have practised everything that has been discussed in this book so far, it will be good for both you and your horse to go out and put it all to the test by riding in some dressage competitions. These can be anything from small, local affairs to affiliated competitions.

Always make the effort to learn your dressage test off by heart, but do not practise it continually on your own horse because he will learn it himself and will start to anticipate the next movement instead of waiting for your instructions. At some competitions you are allowed to have your test read out to you, but if you are having to concentrate on instructions being read out, you cannot possibly concentrate 100 per cent on getting the best out of your horse.

Your horse should be well groomed and have his mane plaited for a dressage competition. You should wear a pair of white or beige jodhpurs or breeches, long or short riding boots, a riding jacket and a shirt and tie or stock.

All dressage tests begin with the horse and rider coming down the centre line of the arena, and all but preliminary tests require the rider to halt the horse and salute the judge. This first movement is the first impression that the judge will have of you – the only thing the judge can see from that angle is how straight your horse is as he comes down the centre line. So concentrate on riding the horse forwards in a good active pace, as it is easier to ride a straight line if the horse is moving forwards with impulsion. (Think of how a bicycle wobbles if you pedal too slowly – the same happens to a horse if he lacks impulsion.) A good straight halt will earn you good marks and put the judge in a good frame of mind for the rest of your test. Be ready with both hands and legs to correct any attempt the horse may make to drift one way or the other as you squeeze him forwards from your legs into a blocking hand and into halt.

▌ RIGHT
Notice how this young rider is looking across the arena to the marker where she has to make her next move. Keeping your head up and looking ahead to where you have to go next helps improve the accuracy and timing of the different movements you have to perform.

Once the horse halts, keep a feel against his sides with your legs and down the rein with your hand. This will keep him on the aids and attentive to your next instruction. Female riders bow to the judge by putting both reins in their left hands, and bowing their heads as they drop their right hands to their sides. Male riders are usually required to remove their hats unless these are fitted with a safety harness. The reins are put in the left hand and the hat is removed with the right hand and lowered to one side as the rider bows his head. Do practise this at home, otherwise your horse is likely to shy away as you lower your hat to his side. When

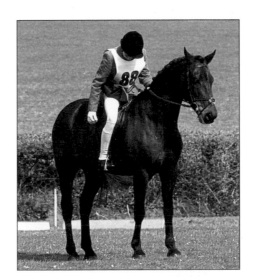

Every single dressage test includes at least one – and usually two – halts and salutes. A nice straight halt and a confident, unhurried salute create a good impression, and are aspects of the test that can be practised at home.

you are ready to ride on again, concentrate first and foremost on straightness and maintaining a constant rhythm.

The various movements in a dressage test have to be carried out at the markers which are set around the arena. The correct point at which to carry out the next movement is as your shoulder is level with the marker. Always look up and think ahead to the next marker. Insist that the horse stays out on the track and uses the whole arena; do not be tempted to cut corners. If you ride the horse correctly around each corner, you will automatically be rebalancing him and asking him to use his hindlegs more actively. Remember to balance the horse during and before each new movement, with a half-halt if necessary. All tests end with another turn down the centre line and a halt and salute for the judge. No matter how well or badly the test may have gone, always perform this movement with good grace and manners. Remember that each movement in the test is marked separately, so that if you make a mistake in one movement all is not lost. If you keep your head and improve upon the mistake in the remaining movements, you will pick up marks again. Never give up – there are always more good marks to be earned. On top of all that, do make a conscious effort to smile. It will immediately fill you, and the judge, with confidence and, more importantly, it will help you to relax and to stay that way.

Preparing for Take-off

One of the best things about riding is to experience the exhilaration of riding a horse over fences. A lot of new riders are put off jumping through lack of confidence but, if you have developed any sort of feel for riding, jumping should simply be a natural and enjoyable progression.

All too often, when faced with a fence to jump, horse and rider seem to forget the basics they have been practising up until then. Balance and rhythm are abandoned as they career towards the obstacle! The secret of safe, enjoyable and successful jumping is to carry into the jumping arena the principles learnt and mastered whilst riding on the flat.

Rhythm and Balance

The two most important things for the would-be show jumper to keep in mind are rhythm and balance. If you can concentrate on keeping the horse balanced and in an even rhythm all the way to the fence, you have very little else to worry about.

You have already discovered how to encourage the horse to work in an even rhythm and to be responsive to your leg. Just because a jump appears in your path does not mean that anything changes – the horse must still be obedient enough to stay in the rhythm that you have dictated and, provided that you learn how to stay in balance with the horse throughout, clearing the fence comfortably and confidently will come naturally to both of you.

Horse and rider can practise working in a balanced rhythm by simply trotting and cantering over poles on the ground. This kind of work can be mixed in with your usual flatwork training so that the horse learns to remain calm and to apply

WORKING OVER TROT POLES

1 The horse is ridden in an active working trot through the corner and down to a line of trot poles set approximately 4 feet (1.25 m) apart, which gives the horse room to put his feet down between each pole as he takes each stride.

2 The horse must stay balanced and in the same rhythm as he approaches the line of trot poles.

3 The rider softens his hands forwards so that the horse is able to stretch his head and neck forwards as he negotiates the poles.

4 The horse should maintain exactly the same rhythm throughout the whole exercise – do not allow him to slow down at the end of the poles. Ride him through the next corner correctly, insisting he bends around your inside leg and maintains his balance and rhythm, and repeat the exercise.

WORKING THROUGH CANTER POLES

1 Exactly the same exercise should be practised in canter, except now the poles are spaced out approximately 10 feet (3 m) apart to give the horse room to canter over them.

2 The rider must keep the horse balanced and in the same rhythm through the corner and all the way up to the poles.

3 As the horse negotiates the poles, the rider simply softens the hands forwards so that the horse's head and neck are not restricted.

4 As when working over trot poles, the horse should maintain the same rhythm throughout the whole exercise.

5 As the horse completes the poles and canters on to the next corner, exactly the same rhythm and balance must be maintained throughout.

the same rules learnt on the flat to his jumping work. Far too many horses are allowed, and often encouraged, to become overexcited and go too fast when they are asked to jump. The horse should be taught to use power to clear fences, not speed.

USING POLES AND LINES OF FENCES

Trot and canter poles are often used to help introduce horse and rider to jumping. They should be spaced out in such a way that the horse can easily negotiate them, without having to stretch himself or shorten himself up. Trot poles are usually set about 4 feet (1.25 m) apart and canter poles 10 feet (3 m) apart. But if these distances do not suit your horse then, at this stage in his training, alter them to suit him. Adding lines of fences to the poles forms what is called a jumping grid. Gridwork is used to introduce the horse to the idea of jumping. Later in his training, it is used to increase his athleticism and to improve the way in which he jumps. It trains him to jump more carefully so he is less likely to injure himself or to knock fences down.

■ INSIST ON CONSISTENCY

It is only with practice and patience that you will teach the horse to carry out this exercise. Most horses thoroughly enjoy the idea of jumping but it is important to teach the horse to contain his enthusiasm so that he still remains obedient, balanced and in a rhythm.

A young horse who is being introduced to this work for the first time should have no reason to rush or get excited, provided he has been taught the basic principles throughout his flatwork training.

An older horse who already knows about jumping may get excited if he has been allowed to do so by previous riders, but practice and perseverance will teach him to keep an even rhythm.

If the horse really is inclined to rush, you should keep circling around the outside of the poles until he settles into a steady rhythm. If he still rushes as soon as he is allowed to go to the poles, simply circle him away from them again and keep repeating this exercise until he maintains the same rhythm. Alternatively, you can bring the horse back to walk and insist

that he walks over the poles until he is prepared to keep the same rhythm in both trot and canter.

The opposite problem may occur with an inexperienced or nervous horse who may want to slow down on the approach to the poles until he is confident about what they are. The first few times the horse is introduced to the exercise, he should be allowed to slow down to give him time to take everything in. After that, insist that he maintains the same rhythm. It may be worth choosing a slow rhythm in trot so that the horse does not feel he is being hassled, but do insist that the horse sticks to this rhythm throughout. Once he is confident, the pace can be picked up a little and a slightly faster rhythm maintained throughout. The horse should never be rushed through these exercises – his pace should be active and yet balanced.

In jumping it is the power of the horse that is critical, not his speed. As a rider you are trying to create and store power and energy on the way to the fence so that all that power can be used by the horse to clear the fence.

Jumping Fences

It is your job to bring the horse to the fence in a balanced rhythm, to remain in balance with him over it, and to land in balance so that you can continue to the next fence.

Most riders attempt to do far too much on the approach and over a fence, which only unbalances and distracts the horse. When jumping in canter, keep a light seat on the approach to the fence. About 22–33 yards (20–30 m) away, whilst still retaining exactly the same rhythm, lower your seat deeper into the saddle and actively close your legs against the horse's sides. Keep your shoulders slightly forwards. Having closed the legs more against the horse's sides, you may have to take a slightly stronger contact in the hand to prevent the horse accelerating. As the horse takes off over the fence, remain in the same position but close your knees and lower legs tighter against the horse's sides to help you remain still in the saddle, and stretch your hands and arms forwards to allow the horse to stretch his head and neck forwards over the fence.

BASIC TECHNIQUE

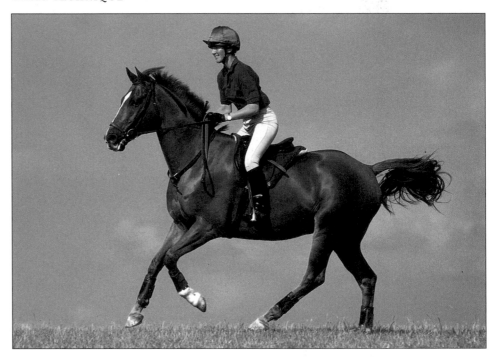

1 Here the rider is in the forward seat. Note how her seat bones are raised just off the saddle so there is less weight directly on the horse's back. This encourages the horse to remain soft through his back and to bowl along actively beneath her. The rider keeps her shoulders slightly more forward than they would be when cantering on the flat, but it is this position that allows the weight to be taken off the saddle whilst still allowing the rider to keep her balance. The lower leg is closed on the horse's sides, and the rider's weight is now taken by the stirrup iron. The horse is producing a light, active canter with his forehand nicely elevated.

2 As the rider approaches a fence, she lowers her seat into the saddle but keeps her shoulders in the forward position. The lower legs are closed more firmly against the horse's sides so that his hocks are pushed under him, but the rider's hands prevent him from accelerating. The aim is to collect the horse so that he has plenty of energy to power himself over the fence.

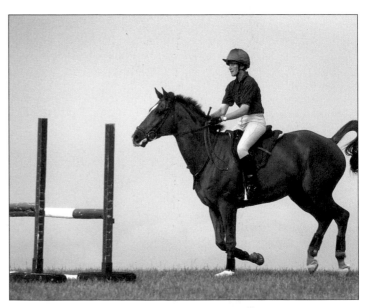

3 Just before the horse takes off, the rider softens her hands forwards so he can lower his head and neck to produce a supple, clean jump. The rider's seat is still deep in the saddle, her lower legs are closed against the horse's sides, her heels are pushed down and, at this point, she also allows her knees to close against the saddle to keep her body balanced as the horse jumps.

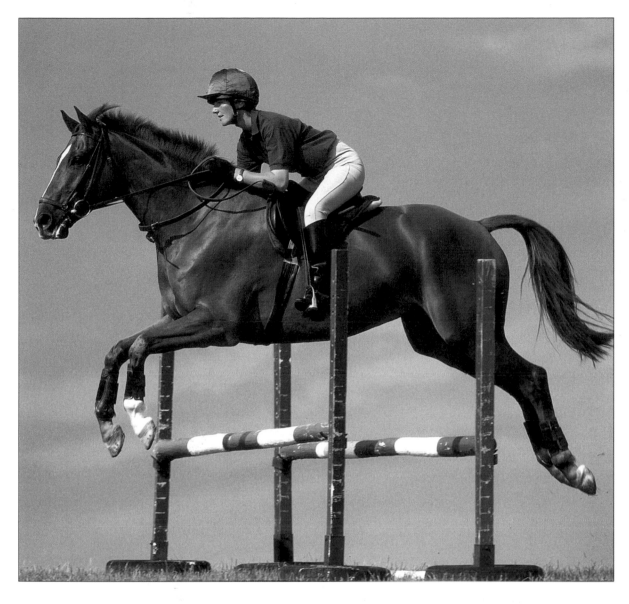

4 As the horse takes off, all the rider does is to allow her hands and arms to stretch forwards to follow the movement of the horse's head and neck. The rider remains perfectly still and balanced over the horse and, in this way, leaves the horse free to jump athletically and comfortably over the fence.

5 By adopting this technique over a fence, the rider is able to remain in balance with the horse; this means that, as they land, the two of them are still balanced and ready to face whatever comes next. If another fence were to follow immediately, they would both be in the correct position to tackle it.

6 Horse and rider look equally balanced on the approach and on landing over the fence. If horse and rider can maintain this same rhythm and balance around a whole course, they have every chance of producing a clear round, be it across country or in a show-jumping arena.

COMMON JUMPING FAULTS

GETTING IN FRONT OF THE MOVEMENT
These two pictures show one of the most common faults of which any number of riders, of all standards, are guilty. Faced with a fence, many riders seem to be overwhelmed by an irresistible desire to anticipate when the horse is going to take off and to "jump" with him! Instead of sitting quietly and maintaining their position, the rhythm and the balance, they fire their seat out of the saddle, hurl their upper body up the horse's neck and generally do about ten times more than they need to. The effect on the horse is both unbalancing and distracting. This can result in the horse hitting the fence with his front legs because the rider has loaded too much weight on to his forehand or, worse still, the horse may be tempted to put his feet back down again in front of the fence. The horse is then unable to jump at all.

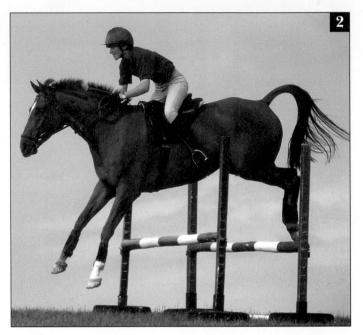

You can see how easy it would be for the horse to put his front feet back down on the ground and, because the rider has come right out of the saddle and thrown all her weight forward, she would have very little chance of staying on board. In the second picture, the rider is still in a relatively weak position; her weight is balanced on her knees instead of being pushed down into the stirrups and her heels, with the result that her lower leg has slid backwards.

The rider is going to be out of balance with the horse as he lands and will not be in a very strong position to regain the balance and rhythm that they started with. If the horse stumbled as he landed, because the rider is not supporting her weight in her lower legs and heels, she would probably be thrown forwards. Again she may well fall off or at the very least she would not be able to help the horse recover as well as if she had maintained her balance.

IN TIMES OF TROUBLE!
Whilst the horse must not be allowed to rush towards his fences, it is just as important that he is not allowed to slow down to the point that he runs out of impulsion and stops. If you sense that the horse is reluctant to keep progressing forwards to a fence, you must adopt a more aggressive style of riding to encourage the horse to keep going. In this situation it is more important than ever that you keep your seat in the saddle the whole time. If you are tempted to anticipate the take-off and get in front of the movement, the reluctant jumper is presented with the ideal opportunity to stop dead!

In these pictures, the rider has pressed both legs very firmly against the horse's sides. If necessary, both heels should be used to kick the horse forwards. The seat remains deep in the saddle and the rider arches her back slightly to allow her seat as well as the legs to drive the horse forwards. The rider must not throw her hands forward at the horse as often happens – she is trying to ride the horse up into the contact so that while contact is maintained it does not actually restrict the horse's forward movement.

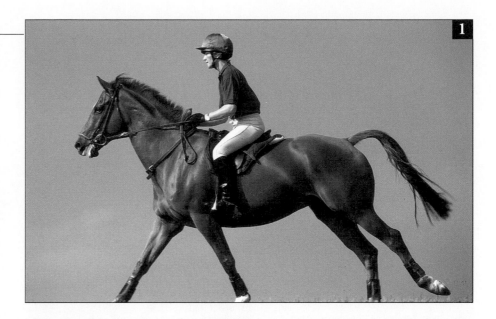

CHASING THE HORSE INTO THE FENCE

Another fault commonly adopted by any number of riders is to chase or rush the horse into the fence. The rider is meant to maintain the same rhythm and balance as he or she rides from fence to fence, but many people feel unable to wait for the fence. As soon as they are a few strides from it, they drive the horse forwards, immediately unbalancing the horse and pushing him on to his forehand.

This approach usually results in the horse taking off much too far away from the fence and really having to stretch to clear it. In these pictures, even the horse looks angry at this unwanted interference from his rider. If the horse is made to jump like this, he is likely to knock fences down. He is being made to use speed to clear the fences rather than power and the athleticism of his body. If he is ridden like this across country, particularly to a very upright fence, he will find it difficult to get his front legs up in the air quickly enough and risks hitting the fence; if it is a solid cross-country fence, this may well be enough to unseat his rider or, at worst, would cause the horse to fall as well.

▌ RIGHT, TOP TO BOTTOM
In the first picture the horse's canter stride is already plenty long enough, but in the second you can see that the rider has continued to drive the horse, stretching out his frame and stride even further. Compare the look of this canter to the approach made in the first pictures in this chapter. In those pictures the canter looked light and active, and the forehand was elevated. In these pictures you can see how flat and stretched out the canter is and how all the weight is falling on the forehand.

Maintaining Balance and Position

The easiest way to learn to maintain the correct position whilst jumping is to learn how to stay in balance with the horse – and the easiest way to learn that is to remember always to maintain the same rhythm when jumping. Having already practised maintaining the rhythm, balance and your position over trot and canter poles, this exercise can be extended to include your first jump about 14 feet (4.25 m) away from the last pole. You should simply concentrate on keeping the horse trotting in a balanced, even rhythm through the trot poles and on to the fence. The horse will fit in three trot strides after the last pole and will be perfectly placed to pop over the fence.

If you find that you cannot resist the temptation to "jump" as the horse jumps, or if you feel yourself tensing up as the fence gets nearer, try the same exercise without looking at the fence at all. It's quite simple, and the horse will cope perfectly well without your eyes looking out for him, provided you do still maintain the same even rhythm.

POSITION AT TAKE-OFF

1 Think about maintaining the correct position, keeping your seat in the saddle as you approach the trot poles but allowing the shoulders to be carried forwards a little.

2 Close the knees and lower legs against the horse's sides just in front of the fence, and soften the hands forwards.

3 As the horse takes off, allow the hands and arms to go forwards in order to follow the movement of his head and neck.

LOOKING AWAY FROM THE FENCE

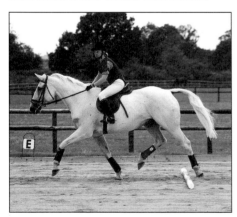

1 Once you have lined the horse up in front of the row of cross poles, look to one side so that you cannot anticipate the fence itself.

2 Keep the rhythm throughout, sit deep in the saddle, allow your shoulders to move forwards a little, and close your legs and knees against the horse as he trots over the last trot pole (you will feel him do this).

3 As you feel him take off, just allow your hands and arms to follow forwards.

Trotting and Cantering to a Fence

Having experienced your first jump it is now just a case of getting the feel of cantering to a fence whilst maintaining the same principles as described already. This is most easily done by extending your existing line of trot poles and small fence to include a second fence which the horse will jump from canter. This should be placed approximately 18–20 feet (5.5–6 m) from the first fence; this allows the horse to trot to the first fence, land and take one canter stride before taking off over the second fence.

Many riders at this stage feel tempted to interfere in an effort to help the horse, but the grid is set up to allow the horse to find his own way through. The biggest help you can be to your horse is to maintain the even rhythm and balance.

JUMPING TWO FENCES

1 The horse remains in trot over the cross poles and up to the first fence, just as he did in the previous exercise. The rider retains the same position and rhythm throughout.

2 Having allowed forward movement with the hands and arms over the fence, the rider now makes sure his legs are closed against the horse's sides to encourage him to canter forwards in the same rhythm. As the horse lands, the rider's hands return to the normal position.

3 Here the horse takes the one canter stride that brings him up to the second fence; the rider continues to concentrate solely on keeping his position and the same rhythm.

4 The horse clears the fence, but the rider has anticipated the jump and has allowed his lower leg to slide back a fraction and brought his seat out of the saddle. The next time he comes to this fence it would be good practice for the rider to look away so that he cannot anticipate what is going to happen!

MAINTAINING BALANCE

▌ RIGHT
This is another horse and rider completing the same exercise. In the second picture you can see why it is so important for the rider always to soften the hands forwards on the last stride in front of the fence – see how this horse has really stretched his head and neck forwards towards the jump before taking off. This is to be encouraged as it helps the horse to produce a powerful, athletic and round jump.

In the last two pictures you can see how this rider has kept her seat in the saddle, which has allowed her to land in balance with the horse and ready for the next challenge.

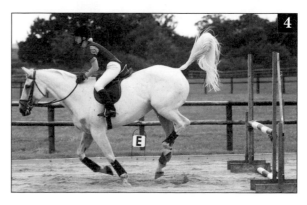

The Circle Exercise – Balance, Rhythm and Trust

Trotting poles and grids make it easier for the horse and rider to keep their rhythm and balance – the real test is whether or not they can maintain the same principles when cantering to a single fence. One of the best ways to ensure this is to practise this very simple exercise. Build a small jump somewhere that allows you room to canter in a large circle to it, say on a 33 yard (30 m) circle. Pick up a canter and just practise maintaining a good, even rhythm as you canter around the circle, bypassing the jump to begin with. When you feel settled enough to jump, make sure that you stick to the same rhythm – don't speed up or slow down just because you are thinking of jumping. As you come on to the last quarter of the circle before the jump, sit deep into the saddle, close your legs against the horse's sides and contain him in the same rhythm with your hand, and then look away from the jump. Maintain the rhythm and allow the horse to look after the jump. As you feel him take off, allow your hands and arms to go forwards to follow the contact. Have a friend standing in the middle of the circle to check you do not look at the jump.

Practise jumping at different speeds on the circle – the faster you go the further away from the fence the horse will take off, the slower you go the closer he will

FINDING THE RIGHT RHYTHM

1 On the last quarter of the circle the rider sits deep in the saddle, closes the legs and hands to collect the horse whilst still maintaining the same rhythm, and then looks away from the fence.

2 The rider continues to look away from the fence, concentrating only on keeping the same rhythm and balance. Note how the horse, left undistracted by his rider, is totally focused on the fence.

3 The horse has the fence measured up and is about to take off.

4 The rider allows his arms and hands to follow forwards whilst the horse clears the fence.

get before take-off, provided you maintain the same rhythm. This exercise will help you find the rhythm from which your horse jumps best. Once you get the idea of

trusting the horse and waiting for the fence, you can go back to looking where you are going, but return to this exercise whenever you get the urge to interfere.

LEARNING TO TRUST THE HORSE

1 Nine times out of ten, if the rider looks at the fence at this stage he or she feels obliged to interfere by either checking or chasing the horse. This simply distracts and unbalances the horse.

2 The rider is trusting her horse to do the job; note how the horse is fully concentrating on the task in hand and is about to clear the fence.

3 A horse can jump as big a fence as you wish in this way. Provided you keep the rhythm and balance, he will do the jumping.

Improving Horse and Rider's Jumping Ability

In the same way that, when learning to ride, the rider is more concerned about his or her own position and balance than about how well the horse is going, when learning to jump you must first master the art of keeping a balanced, rhythmic approach before worrying about trying to improve the horse's actual jumping ability.

Gridwork can be used to help in both instances – jumping the grids allows you to concentrate on improving your own balance and position, and can also be used to improve the horse's agility and ability over a fence.

Some horses are naturally more careful jumpers than others; some horses tend to throw long, flat jumps, whilst others may have a tendency to jump very high but with little scope to clear spreads. In either case, gridwork exercises can enhance the horse's performance.

◼ GRIDWORK AND JUMPING DISTANCES

When gridwork is first introduced, the distances should be set to suit the horse. Once the horse is confident with the exercise, the distances can be altered – either lengthened or shortened – to improve the horse's technique. So with a horse who tends to throw a long, flat jump

the distance should gradually be reduced so that he has to collect himself up and use himself more athletically, while a horse who is very short striding should be encouraged to stretch out a little by using longer distances.

You may well wonder why it is necessary to alter what the horse does naturally. The reason is that, in the competition world, show jumps and cross-country fences are built to set measurements and distances. The course designer has to build fences that can be jumped safely by different sizes and types of horse, so he has to find an average distance to use and build his fences around that. For example, an average measurement used in course designing is based on the assumption that the horse will cover 4 yards (3.65 m) with every canter stride. Extra room has to be allowed for the distance away from the fence that the horse will take off, and further distance must be allowed on the other side of the fence for the horse to land. A rule of thumb is 4 yards (3.65 m) for one canter stride, plus 2 yards (1.9 m) for take-off and 2 yards (1.9 m) for landing. If the course designer wants the horse to fit in one stride between two fences, he will place the fences 8 yards (7.35 m) apart. To fit in two

GRIDWORK DISTANCES

As a general guide, the following distances can be used in grids:
A bounce distance (where the horse doesn't take a stride between two fences but lands and takes off again immediately)
    from trot – 3–4 yards (2.75–3.65 m)
    from canter – 4–4$\frac{1}{2}$ yards (3.65–4 m)
One-stride distance approached
    from trot – 6 yards (5.5 m)
One-stride distance approached
    from canter – 6–8 yards (5.5–7.35 m)

strides the fences would be placed 12 yards (11 m) apart – two canter strides equal two by 4 yards (3.65 m), plus 2 yards (1.9 m) for landing over the first fence and 2 yards (1.9 m) for taking off at the second fence.

If your particular horse is to fit in the same number of strides as the course designer intended, he needs to cover the ground that the designer has based his figures on. Higher up the competition ladder, the course designer may include an extra-long or an extra-short distance, to test riders' ability to adjust the distance their horses cover. Some riders may choose to collect up their horses and fit in three strides; others may push for two.

**Jumping distances
(right to left)**

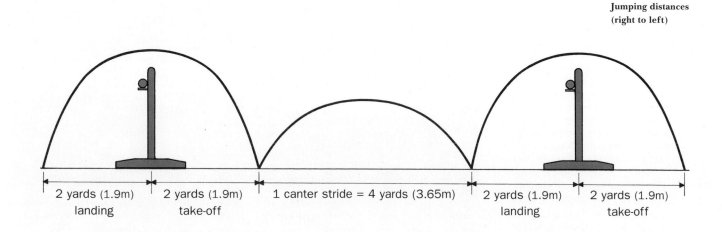

| 2 yards (1.9m) landing | 2 yards (1.9m) take-off | 1 canter stride = 4 yards (3.65m) | 2 yards (1.9m) landing | 2 yards (1.9m) take-off |

BOUNCE GRID

Gridwork Exercises

Jumping grids can be adapted and altered as much as your imagination allows, the only confines being that you use distances that are acceptable and safe for the horse. But you should always have some aim in mind when designing a grid, otherwise you may dishearten the horse or simply end up undoing with one exercise any improvement you had created with another. So don't just go blindly on – feel the difference the grid is making to the horse and change it accordingly. And if the horse throws a truly fantastic jump early on in the session, it sometimes pays to stop at that point rather than risk undoing the good work you have just created.

It is very helpful to have someone knowledgeable watching you from the ground. Sometimes they can see, better than you can feel, exactly what the horse is doing as he progresses through the grid.

▌ RIGHT, TOP TO BOTTOM
The fences in this bounce grid have been set at 10 feet (3 m) intervals. The horse is introduced to the exercise by first using one bounce, i.e. two fences. This horse has approached this exercise in canter, but if the horse has never seen a bounce before you may prefer to shorten the distance and approach in trot, so that the horse has more time to work out what to do. When he is confident about tackling this, an additional fence can be added to make it a double bounce.

As you can see, a bounce distance means that the horse lands over one fence and immediately takes off over the next without taking a stride in between. It is a good exercise for improving the horse's physical and mental agility. He has to think quickly in order to organize himself correctly. Another advantage of this exercise is that it helps to make the horse confident enough to tackle lines of fences in competition. If he is used to seeing – and picking his way through – lines of poles and fences in front of him at home, he will feel more confident when faced with a complicated combination of fences in a competition.

Practising with a bounce grid also improves the rider's balance and ability to follow the movement of the horse.

■ THE COMBINATION GRID

This grid aims to improve the way the horse jumps. It starts with the horse trotting to a small cross pole, set one canter stride away from a spread or parallel fence. This is set on a distance that suits the horse's natural stride. The distance to the parallel is increased gradually, by up to 2 feet (0.5 m), and the fence is altered to become an ascending parallel, i.e. the back pole is raised higher than the front pole. Once the horse is jumping well through this, it is altered again. This time the distance is shortened gradually, up to 2 feet (0.5 m) less than the original distance, and the fence is adjusted to make it a descending parallel, i.e. the back pole is now lower than the front pole. An ascending parallel encourages the horse to be neat and careful with his hindlegs over a fence; the descending parallel teaches him to be neat and careful in front whilst still being able to stretch forwards to clear the spread.

SQUARE PARALLEL

The horse is brought to the grid in trot. The two trot poles are set 4 feet (1.25 m) apart and are, in turn, 8 feet (2.5 m) away from the small cross pole (the first jump). These serve to bring the horse into the grid balanced and straight. He takes one canter stride before jumping the parallel.

ASCENDING PARALLEL

The approach through the trot poles and the cross pole remains exactly the same. But the one-stride distance to the parallel (now ascending) has been increased. To encourage the horse to take a longer stride to help him cover the distance to the parallel, the rider simply "clicks" to the horse and closes her legs against his sides to tell him to stretch forwards. The horse responds by taking a longer stride than he did in the first grid sequence. In the last picture you can see how the horse is really using his hindquarters, and has snapped up his hindlegs to make sure he clears the back pole.

RIDER'S WEIGHT

Here the horse tackles the same grid and, from this angle, the interesting point to note is shown in the last picture. The rider has, to some degree, thrown her body weight forwards and up the horse's neck, rather than keeping her seat in the saddle. Note how she has pitched her weight to the left-hand side and look at the effect this has had on the horse's left foreleg.

Because the rider's weight is loaded over the horse's left shoulder, it is harder for the horse to bring his left foreleg up as quickly and cleanly as the right foreleg. It would therefore be very easy for the horse to knock this fence down with the trailing foreleg. To avoid this, the rider's weight must stay balanced centrally in the saddle.

DESCENDING PARALLEL

The approach to this exercise is the same as before, but the one-stride distance is shortened to less than it was in the very first grid, and the parallel is now descending. The horse has to land over the cross pole, collect and shorten his stride and then be quick and neat with his front legs to clear the front pole of the descending parallel. The previous exercise will have reminded him to be really tidy with his hindlegs, so this exercise should produce his most impressive jump. Note in the last picture how very neat and tidy this horse has been with his front legs – exactly the aim of the exercise.

■ THE DOUBLE OF PARALLELS

This exercise is aimed at helping the horse who tends to throw a high, but not necessarily very wide, jump. Two parallel fences are built one stride apart, with the distance set to suit the horse's stride, i.e. approximately 8 yards (7.35 m). The horse is cantered through this once or twice and then the distance between the two fences is shortened by simply making the two parallel fences wider – the back rail of the first fence and the front rail of the second fence are moved 1 foot (30 cm) or so towards each other. This encourages the horse to throw a wider jump than usual over the first spread; he must land and shorten himself up to fit in one stride before having to throw another scopey jump over the second spread.

INTRODUCING TWO PARALLELS

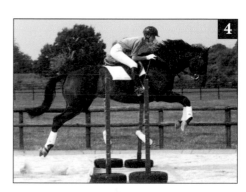

The exercise is introduced by cantering the horse to two parallels, set one stride apart at a distance to suit the horse's stride. Note how soft and sympathetic the rider's hands are – allowing the horse to use himself without restriction.

ADJUSTING TO THE JUMP

Now the spreads have been made wider so that the distance between the two fences has become shorter – the two green jump wings have been moved in towards each other. In the first picture you will see that the rider has been caught out by the huge jump that the horse has thrown – she really needed to allow her arms and hands to go forwards more so as not to restrict the horse.

Having thrown such a big jump, the horse now has to shorten and balance himself quickly in order to clear the second fence. Note the improved position of the rider's hands.

Riding Related Distances

Over a whole course of fences, two of them will often be placed on what is called a related distance. This means the designer intends the competitors to ride a set number of strides between the two. Combination fences refer to jumps which are one or two strides apart, whereas related distances refer to jumps which are anything from three to, say, six strides apart.

Gridwork exercises at home will have shown you whether or not your horse has a naturally short or long stride, and you should use this knowledge to your advantage when faced with combinations or related distances. If the horse has a naturally short stride, you will need to encourage the horse to open out his stride; you may need to ride with more pace than, say, the rider whose horse has a long, ground-covering stride. Whatever the case, when riding combinations or related distances the aim is to maintain an even stride length between the fences, not to land over the fence and then have either to check the horse or to chase him forwards towards the next element.

Watch a number of horses tackling a related distance and you will start to see how it rides best. Some riders may approach in a short, collected canter and fit in an extra stride, whilst others may let their horses jump, canter and jump out of a longer stride and fit in one stride less. If you practise the options at home you will learn which approach suits your horse, but whatever the number of strides you opt for they should be of an even length. So, to fit in the maximum number of strides, approach in a more collected canter, with a little less pace. To fit in the minimum number of strides, approach on a longer stride with more pace.

TAKING FIVE EVEN STRIDES

These two fences are set 60 feet (18.25 m) apart, and in this first exercise the rider intends to fit five strides between them. She approaches in a reasonably collected canter which encourages the horse to jump in quietly over the first fence. As she lands, the rider successfully maintains the same rhythm that she had on the approach, and this allows the horse to fit in the five even strides as required between the two fences.

TAKING FOUR EVEN STRIDES

Now the rider needs to open the horse out a little to fit in only four strides, so she approaches on a longer stride and in a stronger rhythm than previously. The horse jumps in more aggressively which helps him to make up some of the distance required. The rider again thinks about keeping the horse going forwards and up to the rhythm that she had on the approach. This allows the horse to take four strides of even length between the fences.

TOO MUCH PACE

This rider, attempting the same exercise, shows how not to do it! Her plan was to fit in five strides, but instead of coming on a quieter rhythm than normal she has ridden the horse strongly into the fence so that he throws an extravagant jump. She is now going to struggle to fit in the five strides and resorts to checking the horse back, i.e. using her hands to make the horse continually shorten his stride. In the last-but-one picture, you can see how the horse is objecting to this treatment by throwing his head up and resisting the rider's hand. The horse has kindly cleared the fence for her but could easily have knocked it down, or even refused. Once the horse throws his head up, his eye is taken off the fence and he is unable to judge what he needs to do. It also makes him tense and hollow so that he cannot be as athletic. As you can see from these pictures, instead of taking five strides of even length, this horse's strides were being gradually shortened. Having made the initial mistake of coming in with too much pace, the rider may have been wiser to allow the horse to continue in the stronger rhythm and to fit in only four strides. Practising these exercises at home will give you a feel for how to get the distance right on the day and for how best to react when things go wrong.

Riding a Course of Fences

Successfully riding a course of show jumps is simply an extension of the principles practised at home – except that you need to concentrate for longer. Instead of having to keep the rhythm and balance over just one or two fences, you have to maintain them around the twists and turns of a course. But the principle is exactly the same – choose your rhythm and stick to it. Keep the horse balanced, especially on the turns, and maintain that balance and rhythm every inch of the way around the show-jumping course.

However large or small the course you are about to jump, always take the opportunity to walk it so that you can measure the distances between fences and decide the exact line that you intend to ride.

■ RIDING YOUR ROUND

As soon as you are allowed to enter the arena, pick up the canter you will be jumping from and give the horse a good canter around and in between the fences. Always be aware of being in the right position to carry on cantering around to the start markers and the first fence once the signal is given. You will be eliminated if you blatantly show your horse the fences

before you start, but if there is a particularly spooky fence in the arena it is a good idea to happen to canter past it on your way to the first fence!

Once the bell sounds, stay relaxed and just concentrate on holding the rhythm and balance all the way around the route you have planned to ride.

Fences can come up on you very quickly once you are jumping in a competition arena, so look up and ahead the whole time. Look for the next fence before you have even landed over the previous one. If you have to land over a fence and then turn, say, right to the next fence, open your right hand slightly once you are in the air over the first fence, and just bring your left leg back behind the girth at the same time, to encourage the horse to land and canter away with the right leg leading. If you fail to get to the turn with the correct leg leading, either ask the horse for a flying change or bring

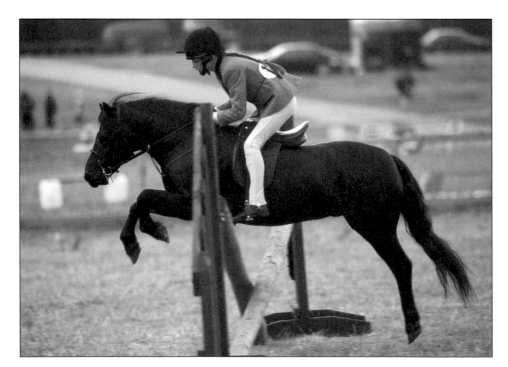

Make good use of the practice jump. Keep it very low to begin with so that you both get a confident and happy start to your warm-up. Then gradually raise it to the height of the fences in the ring. If you have an upset of any sort, put it back down and jump it a few times until you are both confident again.

WATCH THE OPPOSITION

If there is time, try to watch several other horses and riders negotiate the course. Listen out for the judges' signal to start – usually a bell, buzzer or horn – and remember that you must start within thirty seconds of hearing it.

Watch to see whether or not each of the distances between the fences is riding as you envisaged. Are the horses finding the distances long or short?

Note the turns that the other riders make to the fences and see which route appears to give the horse the best chance of clearing the jump.

❙ RIGHT
The aim is to have a happy partnership, as well illustrated here.

WALKING THE COURSE

At all show-jumping competitions the rider is given the opportunity to walk around the course before the class starts. Make the most of this time to note the following relevant points:

■   Find the start markers. You have to pass through these once the judges give you the signal to start, or you will be eliminated.

■   Walk the route you intend to ride. Do not simply take the shortest line from fence to fence in order to learn the order of the course. Walk exactly where you intend to ride and memorize it.

■   As you walk, note the conditions of the ground – are there any poached or slippery areas to try to avoid? Pace out the distances between any combination or related-distance fences. Remember that 8 yards (7.35 m) equals landing, one stride and take-off. Every stride after that takes 4 yards (3.65 m). So a one-stride distance between the fences is 8 yards (7.35 m), a two-stride distance is 12 yards (11 m) etc.

■   As you walk any turns, ensure that you really are allowing enough room to get the horse straight and lined up for the next fence. Do not be tempted to cut corners at this stage.

■   Relate the distance that you measure out to the knowledge you have of your own horse's stride length. You will know from practising at home whether your horse covers the ground easily or whether you need to open him out in order to fit in the designated number of strides.

■   Note where the finish markers are. You have to pass through these once you have jumped the last fence.

him back to trot and then pick up the correct canter lead. If you simply let the horse canter on around the corner on the wrong leg he will be less balanced. There is also a risk that he will attempt to change on to the right lead but may only change his front legs, rather than the hindlegs as well. This is called cantering disunited and is very unbalancing for horse and rider.

If you have to pass the entry/exit gate during your round, just be aware that your horse may be tempted to try to rejoin his friends in the collecting ring. Keep the leg on and back it up with a tap from your stick if the horse drops back from the rhythm you asked for.

If you do have a refusal or a runout, make sure you go far enough away to give your horse a good approach on your second attempt. It is very easy to panic and just swing the horse back round and fire him at the fence again, which will only invite a second refusal. Turn him away, pick up the canter and make a good, balanced turn back to the fence. Do not be tempted to go faster and chase the horse into the fence – that will only push him on to his forehand and make it easier for him to stop again. Think of collecting him up and riding him from a strong, determined leg up into your hand. Contain the power you are creating and channel it towards the fence. Keep the rhythm consistent and do not get in front of the movement.

Make use of the turns to collect and balance the horse. Remember that to go around a corner properly he has to bring his inside hindleg further underneath himself, which in turn helps to lighten and elevate his forehand.

After jumping the last fence and passing through the finish markers, bring the horse quietly back to walk, make a fuss of him and leave the arena at walk.

If disaster strikes and you have a really bad round, remember that losing your temper is not going to improve things. Never punish the horse after his round – the time for a smack is the instant that the horse misbehaves. And never ever punish your horse with a yank at his mouth, or a jab with the spurs. If things have gone wrong, the place to put them right is back at home. Learn from what happened – analyse the mistakes and use exercises at home to correct them. Then come out another day and do it right!

Once you start jumping a course of fences, you will find that everything comes up on you very quickly. You must keep looking ahead to the next fence so that you can plan your turns accordingly.

Cross-country Riding

Riding across country is a true test of a horse-and-rider partnership – whether it be the genuine article when you are quite literally crossing the open countryside and jumping whatever natural hazards block your path, or the more organized version of riding a course of cross-country fences. Cross-country riding requires bravery and fitness from both horse and rider, as well as obedience and trust from the horse. Cross-country fences do not fall down, very often the horse cannot even see where he is going to land, and he cannot judge the depth of any water which he might be required to jump into. Far from being a sport for the reckless and slapdash, if the partnership is to survive it needs trust, obedience and technique.

Cross-country Jumping

■ BELOW
When galloping across country your weight should be kept out of the saddle, unless riding downhill or directly on the approach to a fence. This allows the horse to stretch out underneath you unhindered by your weight in the saddle.

Jumping cross-country fences involves exactly the same principles of rhythm and balance that have already been discussed. The two main differences are:

■ You are generally required to ride across country at a faster pace than you would ride a course of show jumps. It is harder to balance a horse when he is travelling fast, so the rider has to work harder to achieve the same balance as when show jumping whilst travelling in the faster rhythm.

■ The terrain and the types of fence that you have to jump are far more varied than when show jumping. The cross-country course designer will use the natural terrain of the countryside to add to the questions he is asking of horse and rider. He might place a fence right on the brow of a hill, or on a hillside. He may set the course so that the rider has to cross some rougher, more undulating ground on the approach to a fence, making the job of balancing the horse harder still. If you are riding across country while out hunting, for example, you will have no idea of what kind of terrain or fences may come up next. Whatever the countryside throws at you, you have to find a way of crossing it.

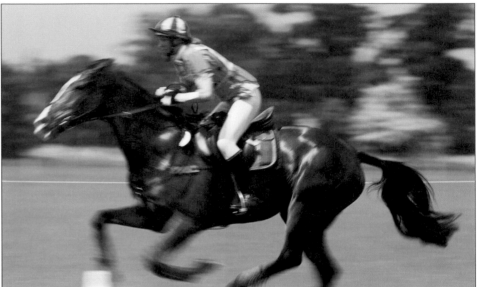

SPEED ACROSS COUNTRY

When riding in a cross-country competition there is nearly always what is called an optimum time to aim for, laid down either by the appropriate rule book or by the event organizer. Anyone exceeding the optimum time will incur time penalties. This often results in riders trying to ride the course faster than they are truly capable of doing. It may be good to be competitive but it is always better for the horse, and for the rider's long-term success, for horse and rider to cross the country safely rather than fast. You should never ride faster than you can ride safely.

Remember that you will ride a better round, and probably record a faster time, if you settle in a rhythm and jump from that rhythm, than if you set off hell for leather and then have to fight for control in front of every fence. So think long term – ride your horse safely so that he learns how to deal with things properly and, just as importantly, so that his enjoyment and confidence grow. Gradually you will find you are recording good times across country without realizing you are even trying. That is how you produce a good cross-country horse.

DOWNHILL APPROACH

As you approach an uphill fence you should elevate your shoulders so that you lighten the horse's forehand; this makes it easier for him to get his front end up in the air and clear of the fence.

On the downhill approach to this fence, the rider keeps his seat well back in the saddle, and uses his legs and hands to keep the horse pushed up together so that he does not fall on to his forehand. Just in front of the fence the rider elevates his shoulders slightly to lighten the horse's forehand further and to make it easier for the horse to get his front end up and over the fence. The rider must land in balance with the horse, ready to restore the balance and rhythm immediately.

Coping with the Terrain

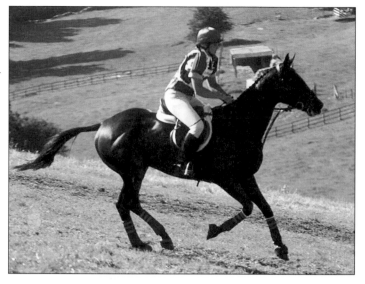

■ LEFT
Just as when working
on the flat or show
jumping, the cross-
country rider must
keep the horse
balanced between her
legs and hands, over
all kinds of terrain.

Keeping the horse balanced and in a rhythm across all kinds of terrain is the secret of good cross-country riding. When galloping on the flat in between fences you should adopt a forward seat, i.e. raise your seat off the saddle so that your weight is carried down through your lower legs into your heels and the stirrup irons.

In the same way that you use a combination of legs and hands when riding on the flat to keep the horse balanced and in a rhythm, do the same across country. You must be physically fit and strong to do this as you not only have to support your own weight by keeping your seat out of the saddle, but you must also continue to use your lower legs effectively to keep the horse pushed up into the hands so that he is balanced. In front of a jump, do the same as you would when show jumping – lower your seat into the saddle, close the legs and hands sufficiently to squeeze the horse up together and to keep him in the same rhythm, and then let your hands follow the horse's movement over the fence.

When galloping uphill, shift your weight further forwards so that the horse's hindquarters are free to propel him up the hill. Still adopt the forward seat, but bring your shoulders further forwards to keep your weight forwards. Although

uphill fences can look imposing, they generally jump very well as the horse is already actively using his hocks. On the approach to an uphill fence, slightly elevate your own shoulders, and drop your seat down into the saddle. This has the effect of driving the horse's hocks up underneath him and lightening his forehand so that he is able to raise his front end easily to clear the fence.

Downhill fences are harder to negotiate. When running downhill the horse is more likely to fall on to his forehand, which unbalances him and usually results in him leaning on the rider's hands for support. With all his weight falling on to his forehand he may not be able to raise his shoulders and forelegs quickly and cleanly enough to clear the jump. A good number of cross-country falls occur at downhill fences simply because the rider has failed to follow the golden rule of maintaining

balance and rhythm. So when riding downhill, keep your seat in the saddle, your weight well down in your heels and your lower legs pushed slightly forwards. There should be no need to lean back unless it is an exceptionally steep slope. Do not let the horse pull his head and neck down because in so doing he will pull you forward out of the saddle and then all your weight, as well as the horse's, is loaded on to the forehand. Keep your shoulders up, use your legs and seat to drive the horse's hocks under him and use a stronger contact to balance the front end. Elevate your shoulders more in front of the fence to help the horse lighten and raise his front end, and give his head and neck plenty of freedom over the fence. As you land, keep your own weight back so that you don't get pushed on to the horse's shoulders. Take up contact, close the lower legs and work on rebalancing the horse and restoring the rhythm again.

Preparing for the Unexpected

When competing at a cross-country event, the rider walks the course and is therefore familiar with the terrain and the questions that the fences ask. The horse, however, has no idea what is coming next, and it is your task to use your knowledge of the course to prepare the horse.

Having left the start box, settle the horse into a good strong canter. Any straightforward single fences are jumped out of this canter; you simply have to maintain the same rhythm and balance and allow the horse to run and jump out of his stride. But when you know a more complicated jump is coming up, you must prepare the horse for it. So if you know that after the next rail there is a ditch to be jumped just one stride from it, prepare the horse for this unexpected obstacle. On

the approach to the rail, slow the horse and collect him up so that his stride is shorter but he is still in an active rhythm. Hold this strong, more collected canter all the way to the rail. An experienced horse will take this as a signal that there is more to this fence than meets the eye. It gives him time to realize that a ditch follows the rail. On an inexperienced horse, this same action will help focus the horse's attention on the fence, and will give him time to see the ditch on the other side. However, you must be prepared for the horse to be wary of the ditch, and you may need to ride more aggressively so that he keeps going and tackles both the rail and the ditch that follows.

Similarly if the next fence is followed by a step down, or involves a combination

of various obstacles, always re-collect and balance the horse on the approach. If, having walked the course, you know that the distance between two fences is very tight, shorten the horse's stride on the approach and keep this new rhythm all the way to the fence so that the horse jumps it tidily and has room to take the designated number of strides. If there is a long distance between the fences, open the horse's stride out well before he gets to the jump and hold the new rhythm all the way to the fence. On landing you may need to send the horse forwards actively in order to encourage him to continue the opened-out stride on the approach to the second fence.

Landing over a drop or into water also requires some warning for the horse, and

JUMPING INTO WATER

On the approach to this log into water, the rider has shortened the horse's stride and really pushed him up together. This has elevated the horse's forehand and has helped to focus him on what is coming up. Just in front of the log, the rider is ready with a strong leg to insist that the horse keeps going now that he has spotted the water on the landing side of the fence. The rider keeps her upper-

body weight back as the horse drops down into the water, and she slips the reins through her fingers to allow the horse the full use of his head and neck. Once in the water there is not enough time for the rider to shorten the reins back up; she therefore draws her elbows back behind her, which in effect takes up the slack in the reins and allows her to regain the contact and control.

you should rebalance and collect him on the approach. As the horse lands, use your own body weight to help balance him. Make sure you don't get tipped forwards; keep your body weight back by keeping your own shoulders elevated. Although the reins will have slipped through your fingers so that the horse's head and neck are not restricted over the jump, you still need to keep a contact with his mouth so that you can help balance him again as

you land. If the horse trips or stumbles as he lands, or if he is taken by surprise by the size of a drop, or by landing in water, you can use the contact through the reins to support the horse and to keep his head up slightly, and you may well be able to save him from falling. In contrast, if you have tipped forwards and let the reins go loose, if anything untoward should happen on landing both you and the horse are likely to fall.

▮ ABOVE LEFT
When jumping into water, you must keep your weight well back. However, at the same time it is vital that you let the reins slip through your hands so that you do not restrict the horse's use of his head and neck. Note how this rider maintains a contact so that he can help to balance the horse as soon as they have landed in the water.

▮ ABOVE RIGHT
When cantering through water the rider must keep a contact with the horse's mouth so that the horse can remain balanced and light on his forehand.

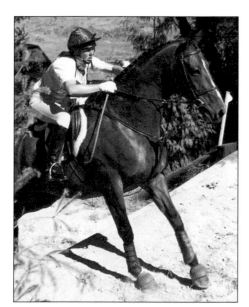

It is quite difficult to stay in balance with a horse when he jumps up on to a step or bank. The idea is to keep your seat close to the saddle, but with your weight just raised out of it so that the horse feels he can really use himself. Your upper body needs to fold forwards and your hands must also move forwards so that, once again, the horse has enough freedom of the rein to stretch and use himself as he jumps.

PATIENCE AND DETERMINATION

A lifetime can be spent mastering the art of horsemanship because, like any artist or craftsman, it is perfection that you are seeking. You may not wish to take your riding to the highest levels but you should never close your mind to the opportunity to improve. You may have no ambition to compete seriously but you should always have pride in the care and well-being of your horse. Enjoy him to whatever degree you wish but always repay him by making sure you know how to care for him. Every horse and pony, whatever his job in life, deserves to be looked after properly.

Those who do wish to strive for perfection will need patience and determination in equal measure. Patience is vital because all horses are individuals, and some will react and learn more quickly and easily than others. You must be prepared to take time to teach the horse the basics so that you have a strong foundation to build on later. A horseman should always be working for the long-term good of the horse, not for short-term gain.

Determination is needed because somehow horses always seem to create as much

heartbreak as happiness. Things do go wrong – some horses simply aren't cut out for the sport for which they were bought. In the same way that not all human beings can cope with the same pressures or stresses in life, horses vary in their degree of tolerance and aptitude. Many a failed competition horse has become someone else's adored hack or hunter. So always be realistic about what you are asking of the horse. If he really isn't up to the job, it is kinder to sell him to someone who will appreciate his other talents, rather than for both of you to endure a life of frustration and misery.

Horses do go lame or become ill, often just before your main target of the season, and riders have accidents with a similar degree of bad timing! Years of work and preparation can appear to be wasted when such things go wrong, but if you have trained and prepared your horse thoroughly and carefully your chance will come.

You will never stop learning about how to get the best from your horse. Even the top riders continue to go to people more experienced than themselves for help and advice – and remember that they never stop practising their art either.

COPING WITH AN EARLY TAKE-OFF

This rider has taken quite a risk at this widespread fence by asking her horse to take off very early. On a less scopey horse there is every chance that this sort of riding will result in a fall, as the horse may be physically unable to clear the spread of the fence and will land on it. In the first picture the rider has kept the horse balanced and in an even rhythm, but in the second picture she has suddenly opened the horse out and asked him to take off. Had she maintained the rhythm and balance all the way to the fence, the horse would have been able to fit in another stride and would have taken off a little closer to the fence. As it is, having stood the horse right off, the rider has reacted in the correct way over the fence. She has kept her body weight balanced over the middle of the horse and has slipped the reins, so that he can really stretch himself out and clear the fence.

TACKLING TWO CORNERS – 1

This horse and rider are tackling a combination of two corners set three strides apart. See how the rider lands over the first corner and, using his knowledge of his horse's stride length, he sits quietly and lets the horse take three even strides to the second corner.

TACKLING TWO CORNERS – 2

Another horse and rider tackling the same combination. Note how this rider, having landed over the first corner, knows that she has got to open her horse's stride out in order to make up the three strides to the next fence. She has sat down in the saddle and is really riding the horse forwards. Knowing her horse very well, she has even dropped the rein contact with his mouth, and thus lessened her control, to encourage him to stretch everything forwards in order to reach the fence. In this instance, it has paid off for her because she knows her horse well enough to trust him. Usually at a fence like this, which demands accuracy, you cannot afford to drop the rein contact in this way as the horse is then free to run out if he so wishes.

■ WHEN THINGS GO WRONG

Successful cross-country riding requires an ability to cope with the unexpected – even though you may have walked the course and know exactly how you intend riding everything, sometimes the horse has other ideas. Despite your best intentions he may jump or react differently from how you imagined. Then you need to know what to do to make the best of the situation. For example, if your horse is normally long striding you might expect him to make up the distance in a combination easily, but if there is something in that combination that makes the horse back down, such as a ditch under the jump, suddenly you may not be on the stride pattern you imagined. Experience will teach you whether it is best to shorten your horse's stride and let him fit in an extra one, or whether you are better off riding even more aggressively, forcing him to open up his stride again and to take on the fence. Some horses jump very big over ditches, or off drops, and this may alter the distance to the next fence.

Most importantly, if and when the unexpected happens, you are of most help if you can stay in balance with the horse and give him the necessary freedom of his head and neck. This all comes down to having an independent seat. If you can stay balanced without needing to hang on to the reins, and can at the same time keep thinking ahead and judging what you need to do to help the horse, you are the best asset he can have. A horse can jump out of some seemingly impossible situations, and can correct seemingly disastrous misjudgements, if his rider is not hindering him. The golden rule is to maintain rhythm and balance.

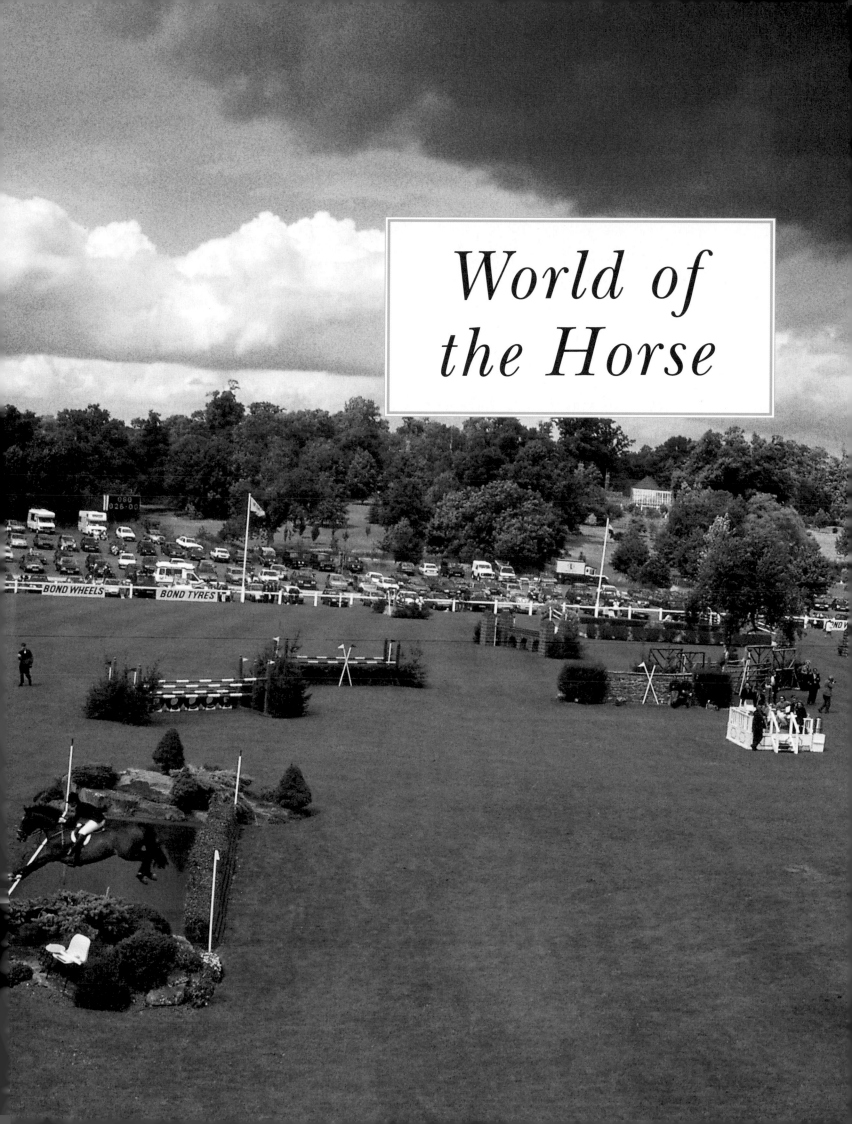

World of
the Horse

The Competition World

Competing with your horse can be as low key or as serious as you wish to make it. Some riders make a living out of riding and competing with horses, others simply enjoy giving the family horse a quick wash and brush-up once a year for a local show. Whatever you opt for within that scale, there are certain things to be aware of. Before attempting any form of horse sport you must be sure that your horse is fit and mature enough, both mentally and physically, to take part. He should be sufficiently well schooled to be obedient to your commands, and should have seen enough in his daily hacks and general training regime not to be overawed by the competition scene.

Most horses should be versatile enough to take part in any number of sports at the lower levels. But if you decide to take up a particular sport seriously, check out the requirements and skills needed to ensure that you are both suited to that sport.

Types of Competition

▌ BELOW
There are so many opportunities to compete; all abilities and tastes are catered for, from the rough and tumble of mounted games...

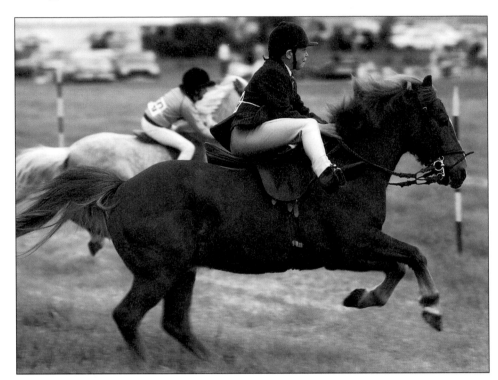

The wide range of horse sports that is now available means there is something to suit all types of horse and rider. From the more genteel, such as showing and dressage, to the rough and tumble of team sports such as polo and horseball, all manner of skills, both mental and physical, are tested. Some sports are judged very subjectively. Dressage and showing, for example, are reliant on the opinion of the particular judge on the day. Others are out-and-out contests of stamina and tactics, such as horse racing and endurance riding. In show jumping and cross-country-riding competitions, the skills of each horse and rider are not only pitted against their fellow competitors, but also against the questions set by the course designer. However great or small your competitive streak, there is something to suit all tastes.

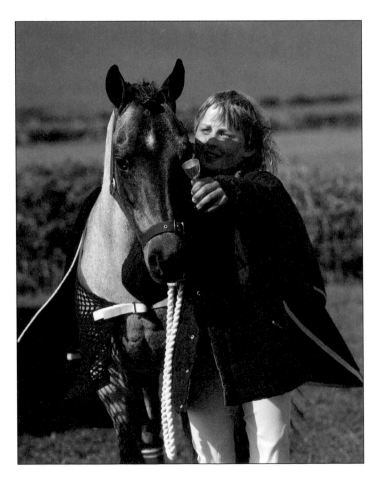

▌ LEFT
The main aim of competing at any level is that it should be fun. It is not so much the winning as the taking part – although everybody likes to win sometimes!

WELFARE REQUIREMENTS

■ All affiliated competitions will state the age at which horses or ponies are allowed to compete in that particular discipline. For example, event horses are not allowed to compete in one-day events until they are five years old. You will need to be aware of such restrictions before planning a competition season with your horse.

■ Competition horses must have an up-to-date vaccination certificate which proves that they have received their annual vaccination booster.

■ As a rider and competitor you have a responsibility to your horse and to other competitors to ensure that, if you suspect your horse is suffering from something contagious, he is kept isolated from other horses. Obviously if your horse is clinically ill you would not consider taking him to a competition but some diseases, such as ringworm or mild viruses, do not greatly affect the horse's general well-being. When this is the case you should not be tempted to hope for the best and still go – you must keep your horse at home, away from other horses, until he is fully recovered.

■ BELOW
...to the sheer
elegance of dressage...

■ RIGHT
...and the test of all-
round horsemanship,
eventing.

■ AFFILIATED AND UNAFFILIATED COMPETITIONS

Most countries have a good selection of organized horse sports, and these are usually split between what are regarded as affiliated and unaffiliated competitions. The **affiliated competitions** are generally stricter and require horse and rider to be registered as members of that particular sport's governing body.

At the top end of the scale, the International Equestrian Federation (FEI) governs all international competitions involving the sports under its jurisdiction – dressage, show jumping, carriage driving, eventing, vaulting and endurance riding.

The FEI controls their rules, and approves the programme of events at regional, championship and Olympic level.

Each country's own national federation is, in turn, answerable to the FEI. They organize competitions for all levels of experience within their own country.

Unaffiliated competitions, usually run along the same lines as the affiliated competitions, are put on by individuals who are happy about taking on the organizational responsibility. To enter these you do not need to be a registered member of any governing body, but you will need to be familiar with the affiliated

rules as these are often used. Many of the riders who compete in the affiliated competitions will take advantage of the more relaxed atmosphere at unaffiliated shows to introduce a young horse to the sport. The unaffiliated competitions also act as an introduction to the sport for novice riders.

■ RESTRICTIONS

Many sports split their competitions into classes for either different age groups of riders, or different standards or sizes of horse or pony. Pony classes are restricted either to recognized pony breeds or to any equine standing under 15hh. Showing classes are classified by size and type of horse or pony – working hunter, show hack, cob etc.

The affiliated organizations run competitions for horses of the various grades recognized by their governing body, e.g. event horses are graded from novice through to advanced, dressage horses from preliminary through to grand prix, and so on.

Local unaffiliated classes are divided up into rider age groups, size of horse or pony, or prize money or placings previously won. The novice class may be restricted to horses or ponies who have

never been placed in any competitions, the next class may be limited to horses who haven't previously won a competition. The open class, as its name suggests, is open to any grade of horse or pony and is usually the most competitive of all.

To avoid disappointment and embarrassment or, worse still, elimination, do make sure you have read the rules and regulations of any competition you intend entering and comply with them.

The happy winner of a show class salutes his appreciative audience.

Choosing a Sport

It is a good idea to find out if you enjoy and have an aptitude for a particular sport by entering unaffiliated competitions before going to the expense of registering with an affiliated body.

If, for example, you decide that dressage appeals to you, start out by competing quietly against friends and neighbours at local unaffiliated shows. Having decided that this sport really is for you, register with your national federation and start to work your way up through the grades of affiliated competition. If you have the talent, dedication and time to commit to the sport, there is nothing to stop you reaching the top. If your sights really are set on the giddy heights of world championships or the Olympics, do remember that competitors at this level not only have to qualify to take part but also have to be selected by their national federation to enter as individuals or team members.

If you are lucky enough to be able to take your sport that seriously, you should investigate the opportunities that your national federation offers. Most countries that have an affiliation to the FEI also offer training to their members, as well as competitions culminating in international championships for riders of different age groups. The sports of dressage, show

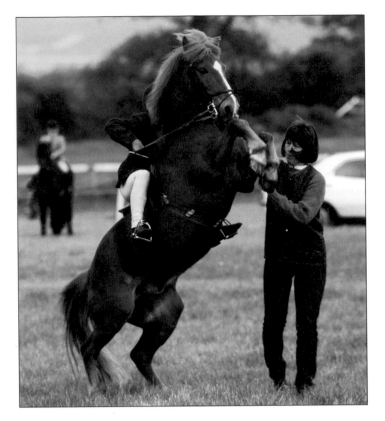

▪ LEFT
When choosing a sport to take part in, it is important to consider the suitability of both your own and your horse's temperament. For some riders the excitement becomes too much – can you cope with this? Will it add to your fun or will it worry you?

▪ ABOVE AND BELOW
If you wish to compete regularly then some form of transport is going to be necessary. This can be a vehicle and trailer or a horse lorry, either of which can be purchased, hired or shared. Not only will the trailer or lorry provide a safe haven for your horse in between classes, it will also tend to become the social centre of the event.

EQUIPMENT NEEDED FOR ALL EQUESTRIAN SPORTS

▪ You should wear a recognized safety helmet or crash hat complete with safety harness for all horse-riding activities. If you intend riding and jumping across country, you should also wear a body protector.

▪ Each sport has its own recognized and accepted style of dress. Dressage, show jumping and showing classes require the rider to be turned out in a riding jacket, jodhpurs or breeches, short or long riding boots and a hard hat. For cross-country riding, you can wear a sweat shirt or jumper instead of a riding jacket.

Polo, horseball and polocrosse require breeches and long leather boots to be worn, along with a shirt instead of a riding jacket, plus protective padding such as knee pads.

Endurance riders wear either standard jodhpurs or breeches, or more lightweight ones for hot conditions, as well as waterproofs for wet weather. They are not expected to wear riding jackets but dress according to the weather conditions.

▪ Your horse or pony will need a well-fitting saddle and bridle, and it is also advisable to protect his legs against strains or knocks by using boots or bandages.

▪ You will need water, buckets, sponges, sweat scrapers and towels so that the horse can be washed and dried off if he is hot and sweaty after competing.

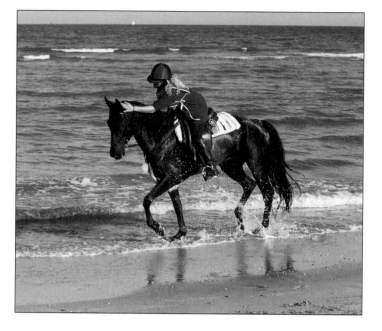

This competitor rewards her horse with a pat and a paddle at the World Equestrian Games Endurance competition. Endurance competitors are allowed to dress according to the weather conditions.

jumping and eventing have championships specifically for pony riders, juniors and young riders. When you reach the age of twenty-one, you have to join the senior ranks.

Within the other equestrian sports there is usually a very good choice of competition designed to cover all levels of ability and ambition. In the showing world this ranges from local shows to regional competitions, right through to national championships. For some of these classes, your horse or pony may have to be registered with a breed society or showing association; these, in turn, help to govern and organize the various competitions, local and national.

Team sports such as polo, polocrosse and horseball require greater organization and facilities, as does learning the skills of vaulting. To take part usually entails joining a local club.

▌ BELOW
Whether you have a good or a bad day, you must always put your horse's or pony's needs first. Make sure he has time to relax and enjoy the experience as well.

▌ BELOW
Equestrian sports involving jumping offer variety and fun. Show jumping, for example, has classes available for anyone from leading-rein contenders, through junior classes as shown here, to international senior competitions.

TRAVELLING EQUIPMENT

Once you decide to compete regularly, unless you are very lucky in having regular competitions held within hacking distance, you will need to transport your horse in either a horse lorry or trailer. The horse must be kept safe and comfortable when travelling.

■ There should be bedding on the floor to cushion his legs and to help soak up any urine or droppings he produces.

■ He should be secured with a headcollar and rope which is tied through a piece of string attached to the fixed tie ring. This is so that, should the horse fall or struggle, he will be able to free his head and neck – otherwise he may injure himself very badly.

■ He will need a selection of rugs or blankets, chosen according to the weather conditions on the day, so that he becomes neither too hot nor too cold on the journey.

■ He should wear protective boots or bandages on his legs, a tailguard or bandage (or both) to protect his tail from rubbing, and a poll guard to protect the top of his head.

■ You should offer your horse water to drink during the journey, and a haynet, although this should be taken away at least an hour before he is due to be ridden. Take food and hay for him to eat during the day and on the journey home, and keep a check on how warm or cold he is whilst travelling.

Non-jumping Sports

Horse sports are so varied that they are difficult to
categorize. For the purposes of this book, they are split into a
selection of non-jumping and jumping sports. To make it to
the top of any one, you need to specialize. But most riders
enjoy taking part in a number of different activities, so first
look at the different things you can try. Unless you have your
heart set on one particular sport, it is worth experimenting to
find out what really suits you and your horse. The discipline
and perfectionist nature of dressage may suit your personality,
or perhaps you would prefer the more light-hearted approach
of mounted games. Once you have outgrown those, there are
team games such as horseball, polo and polocrosse to enjoy,
or perhaps Western riding appeals to you. Whoever you are,
whatever your ability, there is bound to be something
to which you can aspire.

Mounted Games

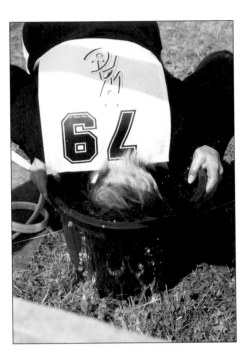

BELOW
Some games rely on your pony's skills; others are down to the rider. In "Apple Bobbing" you have to retrieve an apple from a bucket of water without using your hands!

If you can envisage a cross between party games and a race on horseback, you will have some idea of what mounted games involve. Although adults do compete, it is primarily a sport for children – the energy, enthusiasm and agility that this sport requires ideally suit youngsters and their ponies. The beauty of these games is that there is one to suit every type and ability of pony and rider.

Mounted games can be organized for fun between a group of friends or as a serious form of competition, with regional, national and international championships provoking great rivalry between the various clubs and associations taking part. But at whatever level they are played, mounted games will help to develop your riding skills, your confidence in handling yourself and your pony and, most importantly, the realization that riding is fun.

■ HOW MOUNTED GAMES BEGAN

Surprisingly for a sport that is now dominated by children, mounted games were first played by adults. It was in India that the games we are familiar with today developed. They were then known as gymkhanas, which translated as gymnastic or athletic displays on horseback. The word gymkhana is still used in many countries today to describe the sport. The British Army, which was based in India in the late nineteenth century, adopted the games, although their mounts included donkeys, mules and camels. The games, such as "Kiss the Girl", "Tent Pegging" and "Grab the Hat", were a popular and light-hearted way not only of helping to keep horse and rider fit and supple, but also of fostering strong regimental loyalty.

When the soldiers returned to Britain, they introduced the games to their home country where they proved most popular with children, their small, nippy ponies being ideal mounts for the games. The Pony Club, which was formed in 1929 and quickly grew to become a world-wide organization with over 100,000 members, developed and spread the benefits of the games. Pony Club Mounted Games are now played in over twenty-five different countries at interbranch, interstate and international level.

For those who do not wish to lose out on the enjoyment of mounted games once they are over Pony Club age, there is the International Mounted Games Association. This holds an annual World Mounted Games Championship in a different host country each year, and membership of the Association goes up to the age of twenty-one.

Other opportunities to play mounted games are offered at local shows and gymkhanas, where there are classes for leading-rein competitors as well as for older children.

■ SKILLS REQUIRED

To enjoy mounted games for the fun and entertainment they offer requires no great skill on the part of horse or rider. But if you want to be the winner of many ribbons, or to make it on to a team and compete more seriously, certain skills are necessary.

Your pony will need to be fit, obedient, agile and unflappable – he will encounter

A flying start is a big advantage, whatever race you are in. Practise at home by gradually asking your pony to go straight into canter from walk, and then from halt.

▌ LEFT
Another great asset is the ability to vault on to a moving pony. It is a bit easier than it looks – if you time it properly the pony's forward motion helps propel you through the air and up on to his back.

asset, as is the ability to dismount at speed without losing balance and falling over.

You must be able to control your pony with only one hand on the reins, as the other hand is often needed to do whatever the game entails. If the pony can be taught to neck rein, i.e. to respond to pressure on the neck from the rein rather than to a feel on the bit, controlling him with both reins in one hand will be easy.

■ TRAINING THE MOUNTED-GAMES PONY

Obedience in the form of fast reactions is what is required of the mounted-games pony. He must be able to start and stop quickly, turn tightly and, amidst all the excitement of the race, remain stock still while his rider carries out whatever task the game requires.

You cannot begin to improve your pony's responsiveness until he is working obediently to the basic leg and hand aids. Unless he is already at the stage where you can quietly ask him to go forwards in walk, trot and then canter, to halt, to turn left or right and to move to the side, i.e. leg yield, he is not ready to be asked to do

THE RANGE OF GAMES

Each year more and more ingenious games are developed to test the pony's and rider's speed, agility, co-ordination, fitness and sense of humour!

The easiest games are designed for young riders whose ponies are being led – musical mats, musical chairs and musical statues. The children are led around on their ponies until the music stops, when they must leap off and pounce on a chair or mat. One chair or mat is taken away each time so that the rider who finds him- or herself without a chair or mat is out. In musical statues the pony, rider and leader must remain absolutely still when the music stops. The first to move is out – more often than not it is the pony who doesn't have the patience or desire to remain still.

For those who want to test their speed and agility there are the races. These can be as simple as a bending race, where horse and rider thread their way between a line of poles, or as complex and extravagant as such team races as the "Dragon Race". There are even games that include the fun of jumping. In "Chase Me Charlie", the competitors follow each other over a jump. If they clear it they stay in the game, if they knock it down they are out. The jump is raised each time until only the winner remains. "Barrel Elimination" involves jumping over a line of barrels. After each round, one barrel is removed so that the jump becomes narrower and narrower until there is only one barrel remaining to be jumped over. If the pony stops or runs out to either side, he is out of the game.

all kinds of strange objects in the varied races on offer. Most riders opt for a pony who for most other sports would be considered a touch too small for them, but a smaller pony makes it easier to reach down to deposit or retrieve objects and to mount and dismount on the move.

As a mounted-games competitor, you too will need to be fit and agile. Good co-ordination and balance are called for, as well as a good turn of speed as, in many games, the rider may be dismounted and leading the pony for much of the race. Similarly, the ability to vault on to your pony while he is cantering along is a great

▌ LEFT
It takes a tolerant pony and two agile riders to manage this feat!

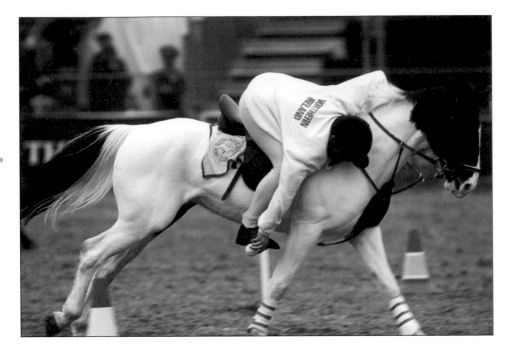

▌ LEFT
It helps to be fit and supple and to have good
co-ordination. Here the rider has to retrieve a
tennis ball from the top of the cone.

NECK REINING

In countries where horses have always been used for herding livestock, such as America, Australia, New Zealand, parts of Africa and the Far East, neck reining is commonly used. This allows the rider to carry both reins in one hand. To turn the horse to the right, the rider simply brings his left hand, which is holding the reins, over to the right-hand side of the pony's neck. The reins press against the left-hand side of the pony's neck, the pony moves away from the pressure and so turns to the right. Do the opposite to turn left.

In most European countries, ponies need to be taught to respond to neck reining. If you apply the correct leg aids before you bring the rein across the pony's neck, and at the same time incline your body weight slightly in the direction you want to go, the pony will quickly get the idea of responding to neck reining.

anything beyond this. As in all things, establish the basics first and it will be easy to teach your pony any number of new skills.

THE QUICK START

To have any chance of winning you need to get a good start – your pony should be able to leap forwards from halt to full speed ahead. He will already know how to go up through the paces to canter; now he needs to speed up the process. You should first practise going forwards into trot from halt, and then try halt to canter. The correct aids should still be applied and they should be backed up by the voice, and, if necessary, a tap behind the leg with the schooling whip, rather than resorting to giving the pony a great thump with your heels. If you teach the pony to go forwards by kicking his sides with your heels, he will gradually become less responsive and will certainly be spoilt for any other activity. Treat this training in the same way as your flatwork – you are still looking for a quick response to a light aid.

THE QUICK STOP

Similarly, the pony must be able to come back rapidly from flat out to halt whenever required. This is not achieved by simply hauling hard on the reins. As in your flatwork training, ask the pony to halt by using your legs to drive him up into your hands which, on this occasion, do not soften or yield to him, so he is brought back to a halt. Using your voice to ask

him to "Whoa" will also help him to understand and respond more quickly to the request to stop. Shift your weight slightly further back in the saddle as you ask your pony to halt. This will help push his hindquarters further under him and allow him to sit down on his hocks so that, when he halts, his forehand is still light and elevated, ready for the all-important quick getaway.

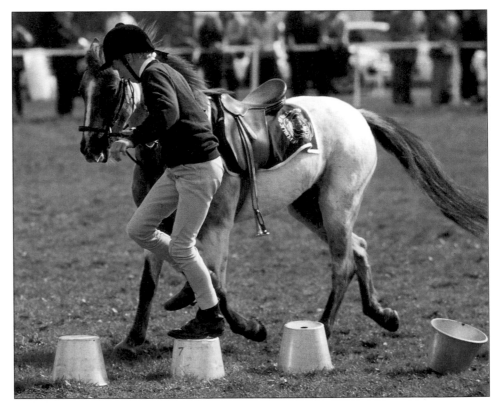

In the stepping-stones race the rider has to tackle the stepping stones before vaulting on to the pony and racing for the finishing line.

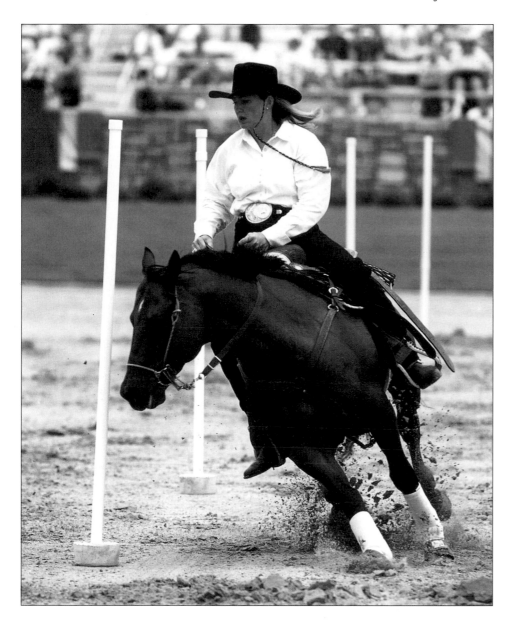

■ LEFT
LEFT
Mounted games aren't just for children and small ponies – here an American Quarter Horse shows how good he is at bending.

pressure on the right-hand side of the pony's neck. It is sometimes helpful to use the reins slightly higher up the pony's neck when you would like him to turn particularly sharply.

GETTING USED TO THE EQUIPMENT

In a serious mounted-games competition your pony will face any number of strange objects. He must be prepared to go up to whatever the target of the game is, he may have to go under a washing-line strung with clothes, or a post hung with signboards – all manner of items have to be acceptable to him. He must allow his rider to carry flags, buckets, swords and balloons without being worried by them. He must be accustomed to noise and the general hustle and bustle, including a very noisily appreciative audience, which is all part of a mounted games competition.

All these strange and startling things should be introduced to the pony at home. As long as you give him time to realize that none of these peculiar objects is going to

TURNING

Your pony will need to be able to turn quickly and sharply, and this can be practised at home by using a barrel as a turning point. Practise first in trot, riding up to and around the barrel, keeping your pony as tight to the barrel as you can. Remember that it is your outside hand and leg that will prevent the pony from drifting away from the barrel. Once you have mastered a tight turn in trot using both hands on the rein, try it in canter. When the pony is familiar with what is required, try it with the reins in one hand. To turn tightly to the left around the barrel, your right leg will be back behind the girth to keep the pony's quarters close to the barrel, your inside leg will be used on the girth to make the pony bend through his body and you will bring your rein hand across to the left, so that there is

The "Dragon Race" is one of the most spectacular – the riders have to kill the dragon by bursting the balloons attached to him. Then they can rescue the damsel in distress.

harm him, he will soon accept them.
There is no point using force – his trust
has to be won and this takes time and
patience. When you show your pony
something new, allow him time to make
up his own mind that it is harmless. Do
not force him to approach this strange
object too quickly. Reward and reassure
him all the time that he is prepared to
face it, even if he is still not very close to it.
Only become stronger in your riding if he
actually turns away from the object. Then
you must be positive and use your legs and
hands to turn him back. Once he is facing
it again, reward him. Let him know you
are displeased each time he tries to turn
away, and gradually he will realize that you
are determined that he will meet this new
thing. Usually curiosity takes over and he
will dare to get closer and closer. Take
things slowly – go one step at a time –
and this will ensure that your pony's
confidence and enjoyment increase.

THE CHANGEOVER
Many races require a fast changeover of
equipment – usually a baton – between
two riders. This has to be practised, firstly
to accustom the pony to the idea of
another pony and rider bearing down on
him at great speed – the last thing you
want is your pony shying away. Secondly,
both riders involved need to know how to
hand over the item without dropping it. It
should be held at arm's length so that the
receiving rider has a good view of the

target to be grabbed. The riders should be
positioned so that the receiver can grab
the baton with his or her best hand (the
right hand if he or she is right-handed)
and the first rider should not release the
grip on the baton until he or she is
positive that the second rider has taken
hold of it. It is quicker to turn around and
hand it over again than for the baton to be
dropped and the rider to have to dismount.

■ PRACTICE FOR THE RIDER
Once you are familiar with even a small
number of mounted games, you will
realize that a wide range of skills is called
for. All demand dexterity and agility, but
some demand more specialist skills. If you
are a good shot you will excel at games
such as the "Hi Lo Race", where a tennis
ball has to land in a high net, or the
"Sharpshooters' Race", where a soft ball is
thrown at a line of comic models until it
succeeds in knocking their heads off. In
the "Sack Race" you will need to be able to
race along, leading your pony, while your
feet and legs are trapped in a sack!

All these strange skills can be practised
on foot at home, with simple homemade
equipment. Practising the races on foot will
also help to promote your overall fitness
and agility, which will be all to the good
when you try them out on horseback again.

VAULTING ON AND OFF
To be a truly successful mounted-games
player you will need to master the art of

mounting and dismounting at speed. A
small pony coupled with a rider with long
legs have the advantage here, although
there is an art to vaulting on which makes
it easier than it looks. The trick is to use
the momentum created by the pony's
movement to help lift you into the saddle.
To begin with, practise mounting a
moving pony with someone leading the
pony so that he can be kept straight and at
a steady speed. You should run beside the
pony, who will be trotting or cantering,
keeping level with the pony's shoulder.
Stretch your right hand over the pony's
back and take hold of the front of the
saddle flap on the far side. Your left hand
is holding the reins and can be rested on
the pony's withers. As the pony's near-side
foreleg touches the ground, spring
upwards and swing your right leg over his
back. If your timing is good, the pony's
forward momentum will help to lift you up
into the air.

To dismount from a moving pony,
organize yourself so that you land facing
forwards and are immediately able to run
forwards so that you do not lose your
balance. If you have ever stepped off a
moving bus or carousel platform, you will
know that unless you start running as soon
as your feet touch the ground you will fall
flat on your face.

Take both feet out of the stirrups, put
your right hand on the pommel of the
saddle and your left hand on the pony's
neck. Lean forwards over the pony's neck
and swing your right leg up and over his
back. Use your hands to push your body
clear of the pony's side and to help
balance yourself as you land. Make sure
you land running.

For those competing seriously, team-
training sessions will be necessary, possibly
even with a coach, here it is possible to see
which riders and ponies are best suited to
which games, and also to discuss team
tactics – an important weapon on the
road to victory.

The Games

As you will have gathered, any number of mounted games can be dreamed up. The Pony Club probably has the most comprehensive list, which is used for their national and international competitions. It has a good rule book, including – to avoid any breakdown in international relations – an Official International Exchange Visits rule book. Despite the fact that mounted games are meant to be fun, they can become very competitive, so it is always safest to be sure everyone is agreed on the same rules. The following is a selection of team games. Most can be adapted to suit team or individual competitions, but do not feel you have to be limited to these. Let your imagination run riot!

SACK RACE

Gallop your pony to the end of the arena where there is an empty sack. Jump off the pony, get inside the sack, and make your way back to the start, hopping, shuffling or tripping along, whilst still leading your pony. One trick is to rest an arm across the pony's withers as this will help support your weight and keep you upright. The other hand holds the sack up around you. Jump forwards, allowing the pony to take your weight and to carry you forwards a little way before landing again.

An even more amusing adaptation of this game is the "Big Sack Race". Four team members gallop to the end of the arena where a fifth team member is holding a huge sack. She takes her team-mates' ponies whilst all four of them climb into the sack and, *en masse*, wriggle their way back to the start.

GROOM'S RACE

This calls for an additional skill – the ability to control two ponies at once. You have to ride your own pony, and lead one of your team-mates' ponies, up through a line of bending poles. At the changeover point your team-mate mounts her own pony, and leads the third rider's pony back through the line of poles. And so it goes on until all the riders and ponies have had their turn and are back at the start.

LAUNDRY STAKES

One pair of riders gallops to a washing-line, carrying a basket of laundry between them. They hang out the washing and gallop back, handing the empty basket to the second two members of the team. They have to gallop to the washing-line, remove the washing, and bring it back safely to the start in the laundry basket.

ROPE RACE

Set off at a gallop through a line of bending poles carrying a piece of rope about 3 feet (1 m) long. At the end of the arena, one of your team-mates grabs the end of the rope and you both gallop back through the bending poles together. At the other end you drop your end of the rope and a third rider picks it up; the second and third rider hold the rope and gallop through the bending poles, and so on. Be careful not to allow your pony to tread on the heels of the one in front.

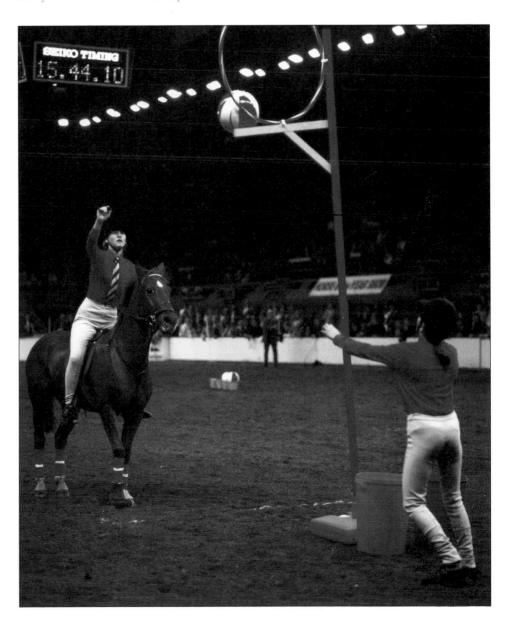

▌ BELOW
The "Basketball Race" is another favourite at the Pony Club games.

▌ BELOW AND OPPOSITE
The greatest opportunities to play mounted games are provided by the Pony Club, which is an international youth organization. These groups of riders from many different countries are taking part in the annual Euro Camp.

BALLOON RACE

A bunch of balloons is tied to a post. Gallop to the post, collect a balloon, · gallop back and pass it to your team-mate. He or she gallops with it to the post, collects a second balloon and hands both balloons to the third rider. This goes on until the last team member crosses the line with all the balloons in his or her hand.

FISHING RACE

You are given a fishing rod, which is actually a piece of wood with a hook on the end. Gallop to a bin full of wooden fish with rings in their noses, hook a fish, gallop back to the start and hang it on a peg. Your team-mate then sets off, catches a fish, brings it back, and so on until all the fish are caught.

BALL-AND-RACQUET RACE

You have to balance a tennis ball on a tennis racquet whilst riding your pony as fast as you can through a line of bending poles. You then hand the racquet and ball to your team-mate who races through the bending poles, and so on.

STEPPING STONES

Race to a line of stepping stones – usually a line of upturned buckets or similar – dismount and negotiate the stepping stones whilst leading your pony alongside. Then remount your pony before crossing the finishing line.

SHARPSHOOTERS' RACE

This race calls for another asset – a pony willing to carry two riders on his back! At the start of the race sit bareback on your pony. When the whistle goes your team-mate has to jump up behind you, and you race to the far end. Your passenger jumps off and has to throw soft balls at a row of comic figures until their heads are broken. Your passenger has to remount, and you both race for the line where the next pair of riders is ready to set off.

FIVE-FLAG RACE

Gallop with a flag in your hand to a pot at the end of the arena. Put the flag in the pot. On your way back, grab another flag from a line of pots and hand it to

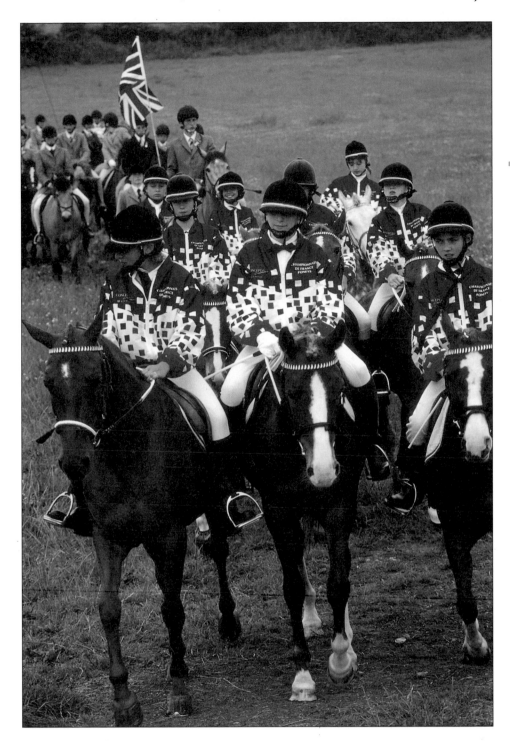

your team-mate. He or she gallops to the far end and puts it in the furthest pot along with the first flag. On the way back, he or she grabs another flag from the line of pots to hand to the next rider, and so on.

DRAGON RACE

This is one of the most spectacular races to watch. It requires some quite elaborate equipment in the form of the dragon, and so it usually tends to be reserved for major championships.

The centre piece is a model dragon with balloons attached to him. For added effect he is often made to puff great clouds of smoke. One team member plays the part of the damsel in distress, captured by the fearsome dragon. Her team-mates are the knights attempting to rescue her. As a gallant knight, you race to the damsel and collect a token from her, which you tie to your lance. You then attack the

IMPORTANT RULES

Most competitions are run under Pony Club rules. Points to note:
■ Ponies must be at least four years old, and not more than 14.2hh.
■ If you weigh more than 117 lb (53 kg) when dressed for riding, your pony must be over 12.2hh.
■ Your pony must wear a snaffle bridle and a conventional saddle; racing saddles are not allowed. Whips or spurs are not allowed; nor may you use the baton or your hand to encourage your pony to go faster.
■ Riders must wear recognized safety helmets with a proper safety harness.
■ The winner of the race is the pony who manages to get his head across the finishing line first.
■ If the race involves leading the pony, the winner is the first rider across the line provided he or she still has hold of the pony. In a race involving pairs of ponies, the placing is judged from the moment that the second pony's head crosses the line.

dragon by bursting a balloon. When the last knight succeeds in bursting the final balloon, the damsel is rescued and led to the finish on her pony.

BENDING RACE

In contrast to the "Dragon Race", this requires the minimum of equipment – just a line of flexible poles pushed into the ground at intervals. You have to ride your pony in and out of the poles, turn tightly at the end and either race for the finish or thread your way back through the poles. Barrels can be used instead of poles.

EGG-AND-SPOON RACE

Holding a spoon with a boiled egg resting in it, you have to race through a line of bending poles, out and back, without losing the egg.

These are just a sample of what is on offer if you take up mounted games. More important than the games themselves is the opportunity they provide to ignite a spark of interest in children, so that their enthusiasm for horses and riding, for fun or for sport, may continue long after they have outgrown the fun of mounted games.

Dressage

The simple aim of dressage is to produce a horse who can carry his rider easily, is supple, balanced, correctly muscled, active, eager and responsive to his rider's most subtle command – yet far too many people look down on dressage as an opt-out for those who are too scared to jump!

If you wish to succeed in any horse sport, you have a far greater chance of doing so if your horse is a well-schooled and responsive ride. Whatever sport or sports you decide to take part in with your horse, you should discipline yourself to practise the art of dressage, even if you never set foot or hoof in a competitive dressage arena.

Your horse cannot perform to the best of his ability, nor be a true pleasure for

you to ride, unless he has had some help and training to improve his balance and responsiveness. A horse is a far greater joy to hunt, to jump, to hack out or to compete with in any form, if he is able to balance himself so that he carries more of

his weight, and that of his rider, on his hindquarters, which in turn will lighten his forehand.

■ THE HISTORY OF DRESSAGE

As far back as the fourth century BC, Xenophon, a Greek, wrote a book on training the riding horse. Prior to that, most interest in training lay in driving horses for chariots, rather than in riding.

From the sixteenth century onwards, a succession of excellent European horsemen laid down the foundations of classical riding and training as we know it today. The aim of these early trainers was to improve the lightness and balance of the horse. Much of the work involved training from the ground using long reins, so that the horse learnt the movements without the hindrance of a rider. Only after that was the rider taught how not to hinder the horse!

Interest in dressage fluctuated over the following centuries. In Great Britain there was far more interest in hunting and cross-country riding which, in those days, was performed very much on a wing and a prayer. The horses jumped what they were asked to jump either because they were naturally bold or because their riders were able to use enough brute force to get what they wanted. School riding or dressage was laughed at. Typically, instead of the good influencing the bad, in this particular instance the British attitude drifted across to France after the Napoleonic Wars and

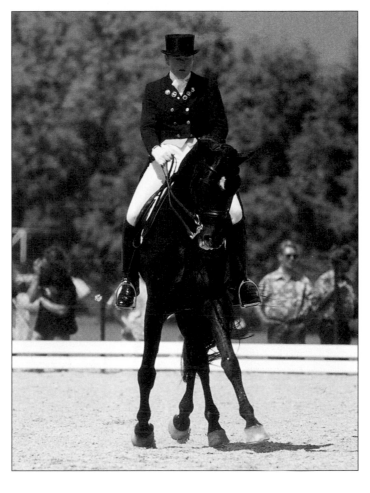

the interest in dressage faltered there for a while. The nineteenth century saw a revival of interest in Europe. The principles laid down centuries before were refined and adapted, but the basic requirements of free forward movement, suppleness, obedience and lightness of the forehand remained and are still the aim of dressage riders today. In many other parts of the world such as America, Argentina, Africa, New Zealand and Australia, the horse was still primarily used either as a beast of burden or as a stock animal for the herding and control of large herds of livestock. But the influence of the great riding masters, particularly those of the Spanish Riding School in Vienna and the Cadre Noir in France, spread throughout the world until dressage became a truly international sport and a passion for many riders.

▮ LEFT
This experienced and impressive combination is performing one of the more advanced dressage movements – the half-pass.

▮ BELOW RIGHT
Size and layout of the dressage arenas used for lower-level tests (left) and for advanced tests.

▮ DRESSAGE AS A COMPETITIVE SPORT

Dressage is an Olympic sport, and its governing body is the FEI. It is therefore affiliated, and there are various levels of competition for affiliated members. However, dressage is a popular and easy sport to organize which means that many unaffiliated competitions are run by various show organizers.

Dressage tests are split into the internationally recognized FEI tests and national tests, devised by each individual country. The national tests generally start with the lowest level, preliminary or novice, progressing through elementary to medium and advanced tests. Unaffiliated shows normally only offer classes up to elementary level, and may also make use of the simpler dressage tests taken from the sport of eventing. Most countries hold national and regional championships as well as participating in the international

20 x 40m

20 x 60m

FEI competitions. All tests are ridden in a dressage arena, which is a rectangle marked out by boards and letters. The letters signify where various movements should be carried out. The lower-level tests are performed in the minimum-sized arena of 22 x 43¾ yards (20 x 40 m), whereas more advanced tests are carried out in an international-sized arena of 22 x 65½ yards (20 x 60 m). The marker letters are always the same. At the Olympic Games and other FEI championships, the arena must have an all-weather surface of sand, but at other competitions it may be of grass, or may be indoors.

Lower-level tests are judged by just one person, who awards marks for each set

FEI TESTS

- Prix St George
- Intermediare 1
- Intermediare 2
- Grand Prix
- Grand Prix Special
- Free Style Test – this is the same standard as the Grand Prix but is performed to music.

movement in the test, plus an overall mark for the horse's way of going and the rider's performance. The judge stands behind the C marker, directly in line with the centre line of the arena. Higher-level competitions are judged by three or even five judges. Each judge sits to one side or the other of the centre-line judge and awards his or her own marks. These marks may well vary, as each judge will see the test ridden from a different angle. The final mark is taken as the average of all the judges' marks.

In all dressage competitions, you are given a precise time at which your test will start. You must work out how much loosening up and schooling work your horse needs so that he is well prepared for his test at the allotted time. Once you are sent over to the appropriate arena, you must not enter it until the judge signals you to start, usually with a bell or horn. You can ride around outside the arena, continuing to work on keeping your horse balanced, calm and attentive, until the judge's signal. Enter the arena at A, proceed down the centre line to X, the half-way point, halt and salute the judge. A female rider is required to put both reins

in the left hand, bow the head, and drop the right hand to the side. A male rider is expected to remove his hat and bow likewise. After this, you can proceed down the centre line and into the first movement of the appropriate test. The test always ends with another trip down the centre line to halt and salute once more. Then proceed at a free walk, giving the horse a long rein, and leave the arena at A. After that it is a case of waiting for your mark to be put up.

■ WHO CAN DO DRESSAGE?

Any rider can, and should, practise dressage, even if you choose not to compete. Once your horse is basically obedient, can maintain a rounded outline and can work in a reasonable rhythm in walk, trot and canter, he is equipped to perform the simpler dressage tests. The lower-level tests only require the horse to work in medium walk, working trot and canter, and may require some lengthening of the horse's stride. The horse must be able to produce a good halt, as all tests end with a halt and salute to the judge, and the vast majority of tests also start with one. A few of the very basic tests allow the

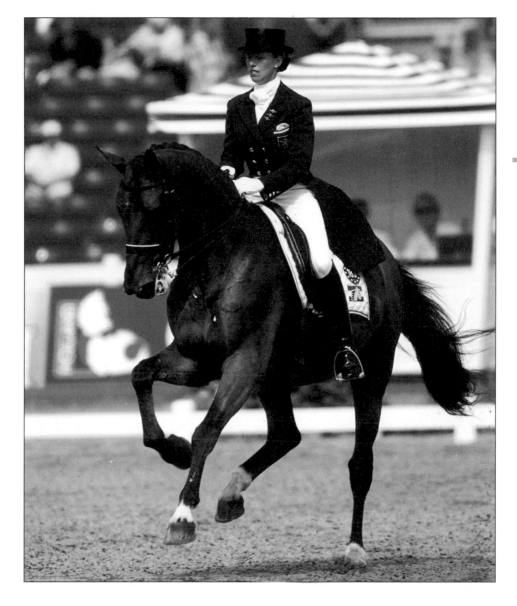

▌ RIGHT
The aim of dressage is simply to produce a fit,
supple, obedient horse who is so responsive that his
rider appears to be doing nothing.

▌ BOTTOM
16½ foot (5 m) loops.

horse to enter the arena and carry straight
on with the test. You will need to be able
to ride basic schooling movements such as
65½ or 49¼ foot (20 or 15 m) circles, and
serpentines or half-circles, but none of
these is outside the scope of a reasonably
well-schooled horse.

International tests have to be ridden
from memory, as does the dressage test in
horse trials, but lower down the scale you
are allowed to have the test read out to
you. It is well worth making the effort to
learn the test, both out of respect for the
judge who has given up a day to come and
mark you, and because to ride a really
good test you need to concentrate fully on
getting the best out of your horse, not
wondering what command is going to be
called out to you next. The movements of
the test should become second nature to
you if you are to ride your horse to the
best of your ability.

▉ SKILLS REQUIRED

To be successful in any equestrian sport
you need to develop a secure independent
seat but, in dressage, it is equally important
to develop "feel". You should be able to feel
exactly what the horse is doing underneath
you. Is he straight, is he giving you the
correct bend, are his hocks really coming
underneath him, is he relaxed enough

through his neck and jaw? This feel can be
developed with experience, but some riders
are simply never able to accomplish it. Be
patient and dedicated. The correct training
of a dressage horse is a very long, careful
process – there are no short cuts.

Any horse who has been correctly
schooled is already doing dressage, and can
therefore compete, but some horses find
this discipline easier than others. A calm
temperament helps, along with a
willingness and quickness to learn. If the
horse has good conformation and naturally
good paces, he is going to find his work
easier than a horse who has an awkward
build and therefore struggles to move as
freely. The horse should be forward
thinking, and ideally he should have
naturally active hocks – some horses have
naturally "lazy" hocks and will find it harder
to use their hindquarters. Finally the ideal
dressage horse should have presence – he
should make people want to stop and watch
him. But don't be deterred if your horse
lacks some of these qualities. Careful and
consistent training can do wonders for the
most unpromising candidate – it just takes
more time and determination.

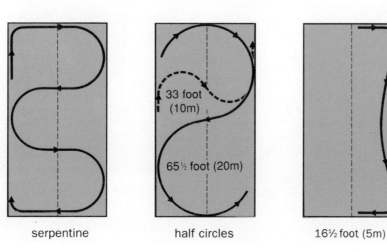

serpentine   half circles   16½ foot (5m)

The World of Showing

The showing scene probably offers a wider range of opportunities for all types and abilities than any other equestrian sport. If you are the sort of person who takes pride in appearance, manners and performance – both yours and your horse's – you will enjoy exploring the showing world.

There are no Olympics or world championships for showing, but there is ample opportunity to compete. In most countries there are regional and national championships for the different categories of show horses and ponies.

If you wish to compete at the higher-level shows, you will need to register your horse with the appropriate society. Which you register with depends on the type of horse you own and which classes you wish to compete in. It usually means registering with a breed society, a show-pony society, or a hunter or hack society or association. Small, local shows do not usually require their entrants to be registered with anyone.

■ LEFT
Mountain and moorland ponies are shown off in a more natural state than their show-pony colleagues. Their manes and tails are left full and unplaited or braided; their legs are not trimmed either. It is probably harder to produce a well-turned-out native pony than it is to produce his show-pony counterpart who may be plaited, braided, clipped and trimmed.

Different countries vary in the interest and opportunities that are afforded to showing. In terms of expense and facilities required, it is a relatively easy sport to cater for. A grass enclosure and some respected judges are all that most classes require. Generally speaking, there are classes available to suit all ages and types of horse and rider.

■ **IN-HAND SHOWING**
Mares and foals, yearlings, and two-, three- and four-year-old horses and ponies can all be shown "in-hand", i.e. they are led by their handlers and are judged on how smartly they are turned out, their conformation, their manners and paces, and their potential suitability for adult life. As the handler, you are expected to be

very smartly dressed yourself, and your horse should be sensible and obedient enough to stand in line with the rest of the class, and to walk and trot in-hand when he is required to do so by the judge.

Your horse should appear in the ring without a saddle, and with no boots or bandages of any sort. He can be led with either a headcollar or a bridle.

You can practise all the requirements at home, teaching your horse to halt squarely and to remain still, and to walk and trot calmly beside you when asked.

EQUIPMENT NEEDED

For nearly all showing classes, apart from side-saddle, you can use your normal saddle and bridle. If given the choice, a saddle which is not too forward cut is usually more appropriate. It shows off your horse's shoulders and front end rather than covering them up, and gives you more chance of impressing the judges. At higher levels of competition it may be more appropriate to wear either a top hat or a bowler hat instead of a traditional hard hat. The showing world in general strives to uphold tradition and standards, and it is worth bearing this in mind when you are buying any clothing or equipment. Keep everything clean, tidy and workmanlike and you won't go far wrong.

Pony and rider showing off their paces in the Working Hunter Pony class.

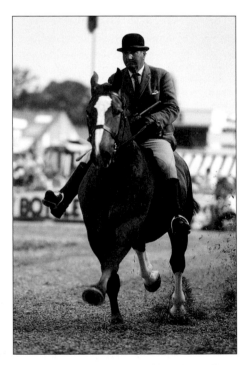

In many classes you have to be able to show off your horse at the gallop despite the confines of the arena. A safe, all-weather surface is provided for this show cob.

You may find yourself competing against "professional" showmen who will arrive with a whole string of horses or ponies to enter. This is Great Britain's Robert Oliver.

■ BELOW
In most showing classes all the competitors ride around together while the judge assesses them. They are then called into line, after which they may be asked to give an individual show.

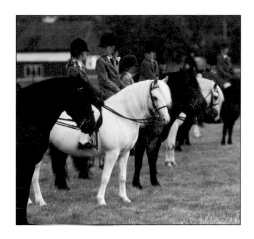

SUCCESS IN THE SHOW RING

To maximize your chances of success in the show ring it is worth making use of a little ring craft. All this involves is using your common sense to ensure the judge gets the best chance to view your horse. When you are all parading in the ring together, make sure you keep some open space around your horse. If everyone is bunching up, circle away to make some more room for yourself. Do not hold your horse back and make him tense, as this will restrict his pace. Let him stay in his natural rhythm and circle away to make room.

If you are called to give an individual show, remember that the aim is simply to demonstrate your horse's paces, obedience and general way of going. Have something planned before you go in; do not do too much in walk as this takes up so much time, and the judge will have had plenty of opportunity to view your horse in walk already. Make sure you demonstrate trot and canter on each rein. Keep your movements simple and smooth so that your horse is able to stay in a rhythm and in balance, and to show himself off to the best of his ability. Think of it as a short but sweet dressage test, using the same degree of accuracy and concentration in the show ring as you would do in the dressage arena.

■ BREED CLASSES

Some classes are restricted to particular breeds so that the entrants can be judged on their trueness to type. Each breed of horse or pony should have certain characteristics which identify him as being true to type. These characteristics are listed by the appropriate breed society. Breed classes can be judged either as in-hand or as ridden classes and, once again, turnout, manners and conformation are the key criteria.

Some breeds have very specific traits which they are judged on; for example, the Tennessee Walking Horse on his walk.

If the class is ridden, you are expected to wear jodhpurs or breeches with the appropriate short or long boots, a shirt and tie or stock, and a hunting, show or

■ ABOVE
Many of the bigger shows are held indoors, with classes going on late into the evening. Your horse will have to become accustomed to spotlights and a far more claustrophobic atmosphere than he will have experienced at an outdoor show.

■ LEFT
Many classes are judged in-hand, which means that the horse is led rather than ridden.

When showing in-hand your horse must be trained to trot quietly alongside you when required.

hacking jacket. A skull cap with a cover, or a traditional velvet hat, should be worn.

■ **TYPE CLASSES**

These classes are not restricted to breeds but to types of horse and pony. Within each type, the classes are usually split by height or weight. The type of horse or pony might be working hunter, show hunter, show hack, cob, riding horse, ladies' hunter etc. The hunter and cob classes will probably be further divided into lightweight, middleweight and heavyweight, whereas the working-hunter and hack classes are usually split according to height.

The classes designated "working", such as the working hunter pony, involve the competitors completing a course of fences. These are usually rustic show jumps as opposed to solid cross-country fences, but may include a stile, brush

fences, a water ditch or a bank. It is usual for each competitor to jump their round, before the whole class is called into another arena where the judge will watch each one perform a short show designed to show off the horse's paces, obedience and general presence. In very competitive classes, unless you jump a clear round you may not even be called back into the second arena for further judging.

In the other showing classes the usual procedure is for the whole class to walk, trot and canter together in a large arena watched by the judge. They are then all called into a line and all, or some, may be asked to perform an individual show in front of the judge. Additionally, the judge may want to ride your horse him- or herself, and to see him, untacked, walked and trotted up in-hand. A showing class may take a long time to judge and it is on these occasions that your horse's manners and patience will be put to the test.

Breed classes are popular with many competitors. These Arab horses will be judged on their breed characteristics as well as their paces, manners and general condition.

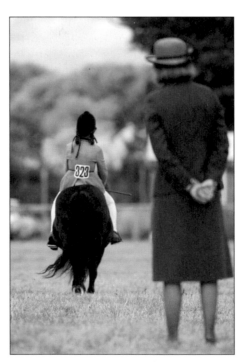

The judge may study your performance from a variety of angles.

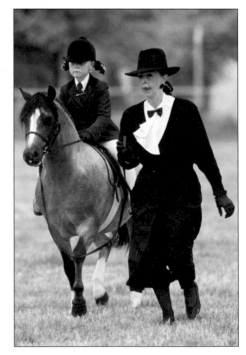

Sometimes you will find yourself eligible for several different types of class. This young rider on her Welsh mountain pony can enter the leading-rein class as well as the Welsh mountain breed class.

LEFT
Everybody loves to dress up – showing classes often offer the chance to compete in fancy dress.

■ BELOW
Side-saddle riding is growing in popularity. Here Jennie Loriston-Clarke gives a superb side-saddle dressage display.

■ BELOW
It takes a competent side-saddle rider to be able to jump well – note how this rider is giving her horse a good length of rein so that he is not restricted.

■ SIDE-SADDLE CLASSES

Riding side-saddle, as opposed to astride, used to be the only acceptable way for a lady to be seen on a horse, but, as competitive sports became more popular with both sexes, riding astride became the norm. However, the elegance and splendour of side-saddle riding have made a comeback in many countries, and shows are held specifically for side-saddle riders. Additionally, some lady riders of show hunters have enhanced their appearance and their prospects in the show ring by competing side-saddle against the majority of astride riders. Many riders take up side-saddle having ridden astride for years; others are taught to ride side-saddle in the first place – both approaches seem to be equally successful.

It is, however, an expensive sport in terms of the equipment needed – a side-saddle and riding habit will cost more than a conventional saddle and riding outfit. Second-hand equipment may prove even more expensive, as the more authentic saddles and habits are in great demand. But if you enjoy creating a real spectacle, there is nothing to beat the elegance of a well-turned-out side-saddle rider.

It takes a good horsewoman to jump successfully – too many seem unable to give their horses sufficient freedom of head and neck, but this is also true of a good many astride riders, male and

female! Many ladies still hunt side-saddle although, presumably for safety reasons, riders are not allowed to compete side-saddle in horse trials.

Although much to do with side-saddle riding is judged on turnout and overall

appearance, some classes are judged on equitation, i.e. on how well you ride your horse. This is a popular class with those who have taken the trouble to learn to ride well, and who have schooled their horses carefully and skilfully.

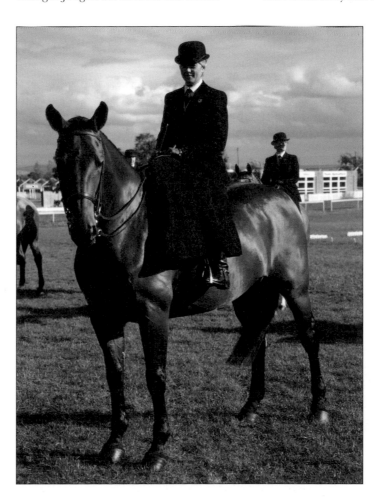

■ LEFT
Equitation classes are popular, as riders are judged on how well their horses perform for them rather than on how expensive or well bred they look.

Endurance or Long-distance Riding

▌ BELOW
The horse's weight is checked at the beginning and end of the ride so that the amount of condition he has lost can be judged.

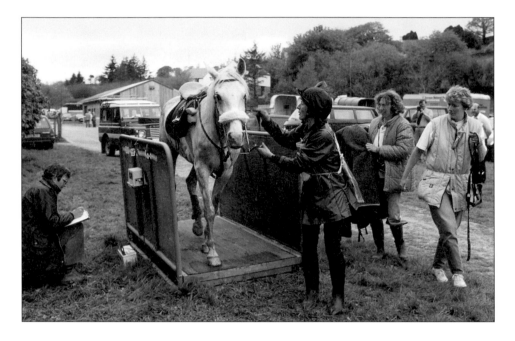

There are two types of long-distance riding – endurance riding (which has FEI status) and trail riding. Trail riding does not involve racing – the idea is to complete the ride with your horse still in good condition. Trail rides vary from about 25 miles (40.25 km) to over 100 miles (160 km). Endurance riding does involve racing – it is a competition against the clock which tests the speed and stamina of the horse. It also tests the rider's horsemanship and judgement of pace, and of his or her horse's well-being. Each competition is split into a number of phases, each one being usually just under 25 miles (40 km) long. At the end of each phase the horse is checked by a veterinary surgeon for sores on his back or in his mouth, overreaches, and general well-being; his heart rate is monitored.

Competitions vary in length, but an international event which takes more than one day is usually over a minimum distance of 50–62 miles (80–100 km). A championship one-day competition usually covers nearly 100 miles (160 km)

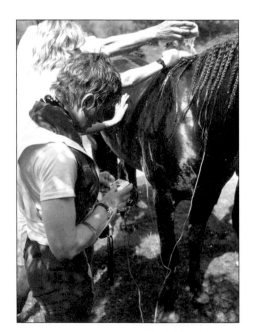

The horse's pulse rate is monitored at intervals throughout a long-distance ride; the horse has to finish in good condition.

with a winning riding time of somewhere between ten and twelve hours.

▌ DEVELOPMENT OF THE SPORT

For many centuries the horse has been used to transport man and his possessions over great distances. Most countries can boast feats of great endurance riding – there has always been someone who has wanted to go further than those before him on the back of a horse – but endurance riding as an organized competitive sport did not start in earnest until the 1950s.

Endurance riding today puts the horse's welfare first and foremost with strict veterinary checks. The organizers have the authority to eliminate any competitor whose horse shows signs of having had enough. Before this, some of the earliest long-distance races tested the horse's endurance to the limit, with equine contestants literally being ridden until they dropped. The care and attention lavished on today's endurance horses is some recompense for the suffering endured by the horses who gave their all in previous centuries.

Interest in competitive endurance riding spread most quickly in Europe and America. The first endurance rides were actually organized to demonstrate the suitability of different types of horses as cavalry mounts. It was in California in 1955 that competitive endurance riding started.

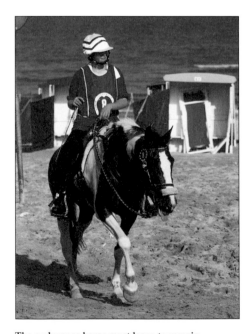

The endurance horse must learn to remain balanced, settled and in a rhythm, even on the lightest rein contact.

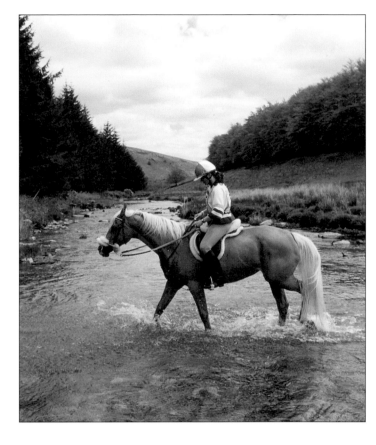

| RIGHT
All kinds of natural hazards have to be tackled.

TACTICS

To succeed as an endurance rider you will
need to be happy with your own company,
have a good rapport with your horse and
your back-up team, and an awareness of
winning tactics. Who is ahead of you, who
is behind you, are you keeping up with the
pace, how can you avoid overtiring your
horse, how can you help him if he does tire?
What is your strategy at the checkpoints and
the meeting points *en route* where your
horse is allowed to be refreshed? Whose
horse can still put in a sprint for the finish,
and how far ahead of them do you need to
be to make sure you sprint over the line first?

| BELOW
**Endurance or long-
distance riding is
suitable for many
different types
of horses.**

EQUIPMENT AND
BACK-UP TEAM

Numnahs or gel pads are essential under
saddles to reduce the risk of any rubbing or
bruising, and purpose-designed endurance
saddles can be purchased. Stock or
Western-type saddles are popular as far as
rider comfort is concerned. Many horses are
ridden in hackamores (bitless bridles) to
reduce the risk of sores or bruising, but
these take practice and skill to use.

A good back-up team of between one and
three helpers is essential during an endurance
competition. They, as well as you, must be
able to map read so that you all follow the
same route and arrive at the same meeting
points. They carry and provide everything that
horse and rider may need along the way –
food, water, clothing, spare tack (especially
numnahs and girths as these may need
changing several times during a ride), spare
horseshoes, a first-aid kit, a tack-repair kit, a
torch, and a grooming kit and towels.

Interest was sparked by the ride
undertaken by Wendall T. Robie and a
group of friends. They followed the old
mining and emigrant trails over 100 miles
(160 km) from Squaw Valley, through the
Sierra Nevada range and on to Auburn.
This trail became the world's first official
endurance ride, and was named the
Western States Trail Ride.

Today the popular sport of endurance
riding, which has been approved as an
international discipline since 1982, is
governed by the FEI.

■ THE ENDURANCE HORSE

The main requirements of any endurance
horse are that he has strong, dense bone,
strong, healthy hooves, and a willingness
and confidence to tackle whatever he is
faced with because he will encounter all
kinds of natural hazards on a long-
distance ride. He should have a light,
ground-covering action, and be balanced
and sure-footed over all manner of
terrain. He should be trained to settle into
a steady trot or canter when required, and
should accept a loose rein with minimal
contact. A calm temperament means he
will take less out of himself.

Western Riding

Western riding is predominant in countries where the horse is still used to work cattle, such as America, Argentina, Australia, New Zealand and parts of Africa. It also has a growing following in other countries where riders are keen to enjoy the experience of riding a light, balanced, responsive horse, along with the novelty of trying many of the Western riding skills.

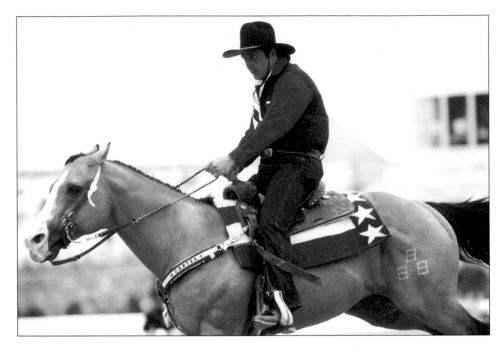

■ WHAT IS WESTERN RIDING?

America is the home of Western riding, which developed directly from the needs of the early pioneers. They depended on horses for their survival – for transport, for hunting food, and later for herding and managing vast herds of cattle. They had to be able to sit comfortably, for very long hours, in the saddle. They also needed horses who were both fast and responsive and yet also calm and easy to handle. The skills that horse and rider had to learn in order to earn a living in those times form the basis of the Western-riding competitions held today.

In Western riding you adopt a longer leg position than is usual for general riding. The reins are held in one hand, leaving the other free to rope cattle, fire a gun etc, and the horse is controlled mainly by the seat and weight, rather than by hand and leg. A Western horse is not ridden in an outline. He carries himself in a relaxed, but light and balanced manner, with his rider keeping the reins virtually slack. The weight of the reins is used as an aid, rather than the contact with the horse's mouth.

Western-riding competitions test everything from how the horse feels to

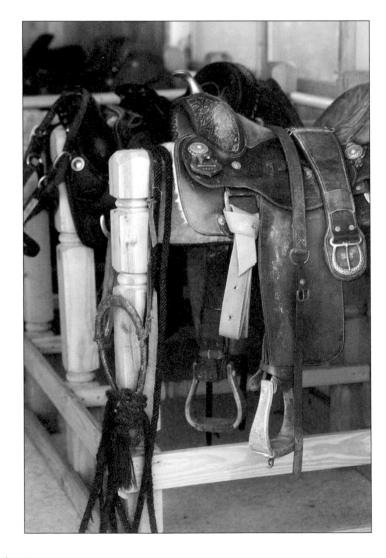

■ ABOVE
In Western riding it is the seat and weight distribution of the rider that are used to control the horse, rather than the hand and leg as is usual in English riding.

■ LEFT
Western tack is designed to offer comfort, practicality and security to riders spending many hours in the saddle.

EQUIPMENT NEEDED

Many riders simply enjoy riding in the Western style – hacking or long-distance riding – without going as far as competing.

A Western or stock-type saddle adds authenticity and comfort to the proceedings but is not essential during the training of horse and rider. Similarly, a standard bridle and bit can be used, rather than the simpler Western-style bridle which may or may not be bitless. But once Western tack is used, no doubt you will want to be properly kitted out too. Cowboy boots, which have a raised, supported instep and a higher heel than a standard riding boot, along with a pair of long, leather chaps are the two essentials.

■ **RIGHT**
In cattle-cutting competitions the horse has first to "cut" a selected calf out from the rest of the herd, and then to prevent the selected animal from rejoining the herd. This Quarter Horse is using his own "cattle sense" rather than his rider's instructions to keep the calf he is facing from joining the herd behind him.

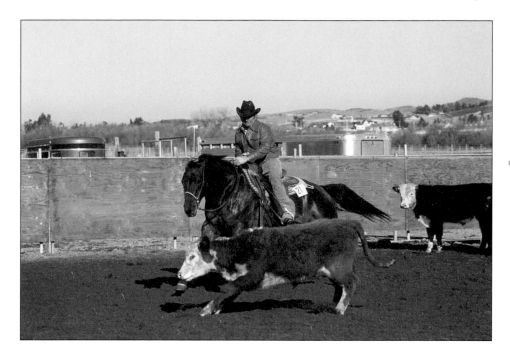

ride, his ability to perform complex reining exercises and his skill at cutting out and controlling cattle, to his ability to race through a line of barrels. There are World and European Championship titles to be won, as well as numerous regional and national events to compete in.

Many Western riders get caught up in the whole Western phenomenon. As well as learning the ridden style they may also practise other "Wild West" skills, such as trick roping, whip cracking, knife and axe throwing, as well as the fast draw and gun spinning. It is amazing what sitting in a Western saddle can do to the imagination of even the most retiring rider!

■ THE WESTERN RIDING HORSE

Any horse can be converted to Western riding, but not all horses will have the temperament or inherent traits for all the Western-style competitions. The American Quarter Horse is a popular and successful choice – he has the speed, stamina, agility, intelligence and in-bred "cattle sense" to succeed. Other American types, such as the Appaloosa, the Paint horse and the Pinto, also feature strongly. But any horse with natural balance and agility, who can be taught to respond to weight and seat aids rather than being held between hand and leg as is usual in English-style riding, can be taught Western skills.

■ SKILLS REQUIRED

As a rider you must have good balance, the patience to build a rapport with your horse which allows your commands to appear invisible to the onlooker and, if you are to become involved in cattle-handling skills, the overall fitness and

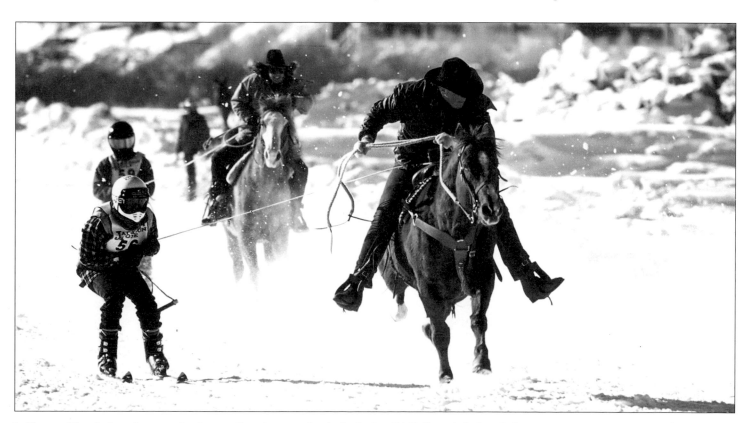

In Western riding the horse is expected to be versatile and co-operative. At the Cowboy Ski Challenge in Jackson Hole, Wyoming, the horse demonstrates his ability to carry out any number of duties, from providing the power for the skiers...

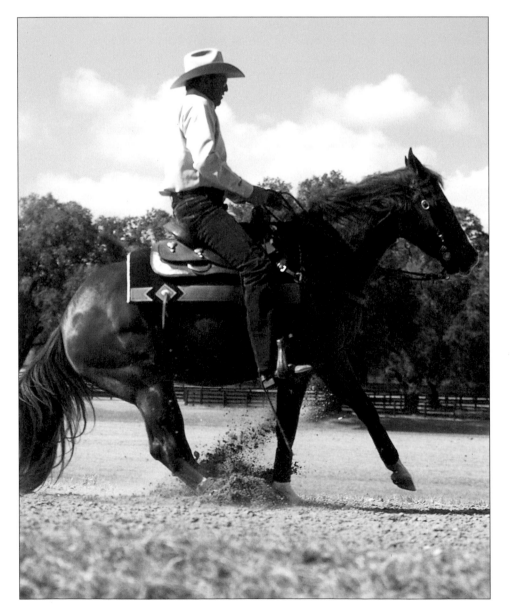

toughness which these require. For most
Western showing classes, the horse has to
be taught the jog and the lope – these are
basically a slow, smooth trot and canter.
These paces were developed for rider
comfort and to reduce wear and tear on
the horse's legs and joints. For most
equestrian disciplines, the horse is trained
to put spring and elevation into his paces,
but for Western riding the paces are
smooth and flat, with less knee and hock
action than normal. Other classes require
the horse to be taught various Western
moves – the rollback which is a fast 180°
turn, the spin or pirouette which is a 360°
turn, the side pass (lateral work), the rein

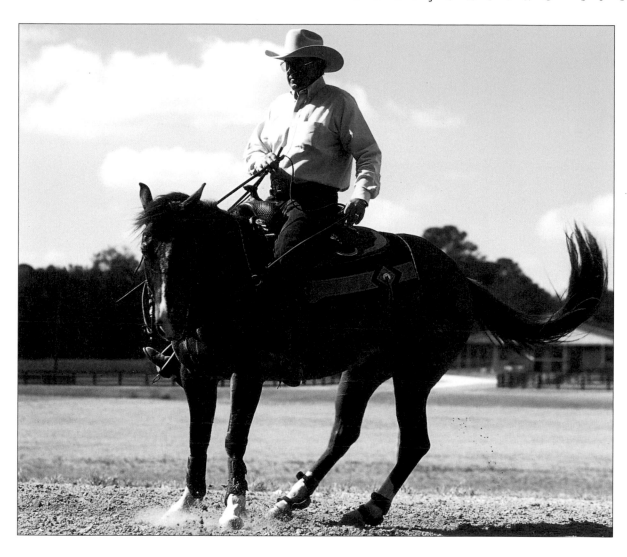

■ LEFT ·
The spin is one of the many Western skills that the horse has to learn.

back, the sliding halt, and the flying change.

■ SHOWING CLASSES
These are the easiest Western classes to train for and take part in.

■ The **Western Pleasure** class is the simplest. The horse is judged on how much of a pleasure he is to ride. He must work in all paces on both reins, with the rider keeping the reins in one hand and a minimal contact. He is judged on how smooth his paces and transitions are, and on how calm and responsive he is to his rider's commands.

■ The **Trail** class tests the horse's ability to cope calmly with the sort of hazards he might encounter when riding the trail. There are a number of tasks you and he will have to perform in the ring, such as opening and closing a gate, backing through or round an obstacle, and jumping some logs. You may have to carry an object, and your horse may have to allow himself to be hobbled (tied up) on his own.

■ The **Western Riding** class imitates some of the tasks a ranch horse might have to carry out. The horse must demonstrate a good walk, jog and lope, and may have to tackle various tasks or obstacles similar to those also found in the trail class.

■ The **Reining** class tests some of the most advanced Western-riding techniques. The horse demonstrates at speed a pattern of various Western movements – turns, circles, spins, flying changes, rollbacks and sliding halts. All of these movements are performed from the lope – the slow, smooth canter.

■ CATTLE-HANDLING CLASSES
These require more extensive practice, training and facilities than the Western showing classes.

■ In the **Cutting Horse** class, the rider indicates to a judge which calf he is going to separate from the herd. The calf has to be "cut out" from the herd and driven out into the arena. The rider must then adopt

a loose rein and leave the job of preventing the calf from rejoining the herd to the horse. The cutting horse must be fast, athletic, brave and clever. The ability to outwit and outperform the calf is called "cow sense" and is thought by many to be an inherited trait, rather than an acquired skill.

■ The **Working Cow Horse** class is judged in two sections: first the horse performs a reining pattern which demonstrates the various Western movements, and then he has to hold, manoeuvre and control a cow within the arena, turning it several times as well as driving it along a fence line.

■ **Barrel Racing** is a fast, furious, grown-up version of that most popular of mounted games, the bending race! Horse and rider race around a course of barrels – they are allowed to touch the barrels but not to knock them over.

■ Other competitions, such as **Steer Wrestling** and **Calf Roping**, demonstrate and test the skills still required by the working cow pony and rider.

Vaulting

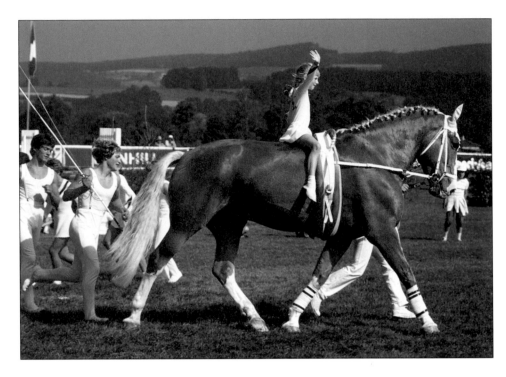

The sport of vaulting is probably most simply described as gymnastics on horseback. Although it is now recognized as an international sport, governed by the FEI since 1982, it developed from an early teaching method which was used to accustom novice riders to the movement of the horse, and to instil a sense of balance and confidence.

Cavalry schools in particular used vaulting exercises to teach new recruits to develop their balance whilst the horse was in motion. Vaulting also served as a good fitness and strengthening exercise for riders, as well as giving them confidence when on horseback.

■ SKILLS REQUIRED

If you wish to be a vaulter you will need to have good natural balance, be naturally athletic and have an air of grace and elegance. The sport also requires confidence – it takes a brave person to carry out many of the exercises with poise.

The horse needs to be quiet-natured, strong, unflappable and able to hold a steady, rhythmic, balanced canter on the lunge throughout the exercise.

The main disadvantage of the sport is that the vaulter always requires help – someone has to be on hand to lunge the horse and, unless you are to compete only as an individual, you will need a partner or even a full team of eight to work with. Riders interested in vaulting therefore really need to join a club, although much of the actual gymnastic work can be practised on a wooden horse.

■ THE COMPETITIONS

International vaulting competitions are made up of team, individual and pair

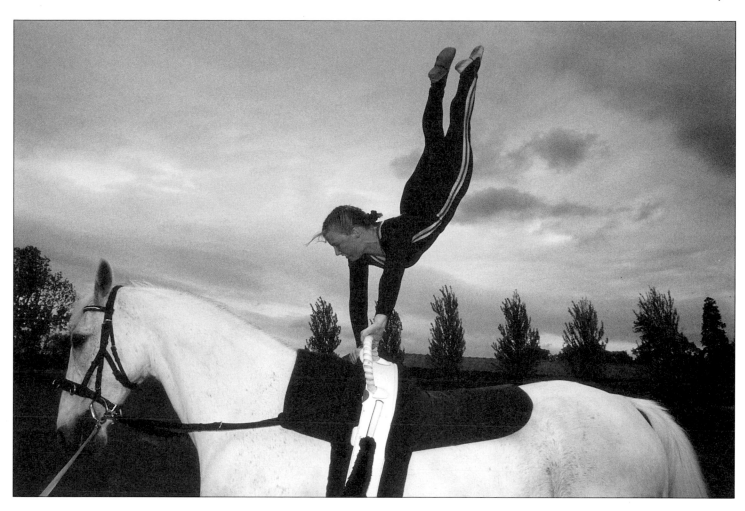

classes. The upper age limit for team vaulters is eighteen, but there is no upper age limit for individuals. A team comprises eight vaulters, one horse and one lunger, and a reserve vaulter. Both the individual and the team competitions include a compulsory and a free-style test.

The horse always works on the left rein, in canter, and must complete a circle of no less than 42½ feet (13 m) in diameter.

There are two classes of international competition – CVI one star, and CVI two star. The World Championship is held every two years, and there are also intercontinental championships, including classes for all-male, all-female and mixed teams.

DISPLAY TEAMS

As well as taking part in competitions, vaulting teams are now often called upon to provide displays at shows and exhibitions. Such demonstrations are certainly an exciting, elegant and colourful way in which to entertain a crowd of spectators.

▌ ABOVE
It takes a good athlete to maintain the grace, poise and balance of a gymnast whilst on a moving horse.

▌ LEFT
The team horse must maintain a consistent rhythm throughout all the exercises.

Polo

Of all the team ball games played on horseback, polo is the most widely played and recognized. The sport of polo carries an unashamedly glamorous image. It has always been expensive to take part in, mainly because of the string of ponies that is needed if you are to be a professional player. Despite the growing number of polo clubs, and the opportunities for children to learn to play provided by the Pony Club, polo remains an expensive sport, the greatest opportunities being open to the wealthy or the very talented.

Polo is thought to have originated in Persia about two-and-a-half thousand years ago. Its popularity spread to China, Japan, Tibet and Manipur, where British soldiers learnt the game and wrote home about it. Soldiers in England started playing their own version based on the description they had been given, and British settlers took the game to Argentina. The late 1800s and early 1900s saw the foundation of many polo clubs, including London's Hurlingham which was the first in the Western world. Hurlingham's rules later became universal. Polo is now played all over the world.

■ LEFT
Polo is only too happy to flaunt its reputation for wealth and glamour. Spectators gather at the Palm Beach Polo Club.

■ THE GAME

Polo is played on a grass – or snow – pitch which is 901 feet (274 m) long by 600 feet (183 m) wide. Most of the pitch is framed with low boards to help keep the ball in play, and there is a goal at either end, 24½ feet (7.5 m) wide. Indoor polo is also growing in popularity.

There are four players in each team, each of whom has a specific role. The Number One is the front player; his job is to keep well up the pitch to take forward passes and to shoot at goal. When he is not in a position to score, he tries to keep the opposing team's back player (their Number Four) away from the goalmouth so that one of his team-mates may have a chance to score.

The Number Two is another front player; he is usually the most influential attacking player. He works closely with his Number One to keep moving the ball up the field to maximize their chances of taking a shot at goal.

The Number Three player is the link between the two forwards and the back. He is central in turning the play back from defence to attack and must be an extremely versatile player, able to defend, attack and score. He is usually the strongest and most experienced player in the team and is often the captain.

EQUIPMENT NEEDED

To play polo you must be properly dressed – breeches, long boots, helmet with optional face guard, and knee protectors. You will also need your own polo mallets.

You must have at least two ponies – there is no longer a height restriction but polo mounts are still referred to as ponies. The rules insist that ponies wear standing martingales and that they have their tails tied up so that there is no risk of them becoming caught up in anything. The polo pony needs to be brave, responsive, quick-thinking, agile, fast and tough.

■ LEFT
Practice makes perfect. Even the most complex shots can be practised without getting on a horse – at least not a real one.

The Number Four is the back player; his main task is to defend the goal but he must also be a good hitter, able to send the ball long and hard up the field to give his forwards a chance of attacking goal.

A full polo match is divided into six seven-minute periods called chukkas. One pony should only ever be used for two chukkas per game, and should never have to play two consecutive chukkas.

Each player uses a mallet (a bamboo stick with a wooden head) to drive the ball down the pitch to the opposition's goal. The opposing team is obviously doing its utmost to prevent any progress down the pitch and to turn the ball back so it can drive for a goal of its own.

All polo players are given a handicap – this varies between -2 goals and +10 goals. The handicap indicates the player's value to the team, not the actual number of goals he has or is expected to score. Teams are given overall handicaps which dictate at which level they play – high goal, medium, intermediate or low goal.

■ SKILLS REQUIRED

To succeed as a polo player you should be quick-thinking, fit, have very good co-ordination and balance, be physically and mentally tough and have good anticipation of how play is going to proceed.

There are four main playing strokes to be mastered, as well as a further eight subsidiary strokes. The four main strokes are the off-side forehander, off-side

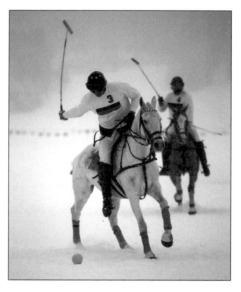

backhander, near-side forehander and near-side backhander. These strokes can be practised on a wooden horse as well as on your pony. Would-be players spend many hours simply "stick and balling", i.e. cantering up and down a pitch, hitting a shot, chasing the ball and trying another stroke – up and down, round and round, gradually getting a better result every time.

The rules of polo are quite complex and the game itself is fast moving, with the direction of play changing all the time. As a player you need to have an intimate understanding of the rules, as well as a continual awareness of where everyone is in relation to the direction of play.

Horseball

Horseball is for those who enjoy a real contact sport – it resembles a cross between rugby football and basketball played on horseback. There are two teams of four players. The ball is about the size of a football and has leather loops sewn to it to use as handholds. The ball is thrown between the players and can be pulled from your opponents' hands, but if it drops to the ground it must be picked up without dismounting: riders have to bend down and scoop the ball up off the ground by grabbing hold of the leather loops. Whenever a rider is retrieving the ball off the ground the other riders have to keep a distance as a safety precaution; otherwise they are offside. The stirrups are tied together under the horse's belly, making it easier for the rider to reach down.

A goal is scored by throwing the ball through a suspended loop which has a net attached to it. The game is started, and restarted after a goal, by a throw-in similar to that used in rugby. The ball is tossed in the air between two riders who each strive to grab it first. The game can be played

■ LEFT
Horseball has grown rapidly in popularity in recent years, as a game for both adults and children.

■ BELOW LEFT
The ball is moved rapidly down the arena towards the goal. In order to score, the ball has to be thrown through a high loop with a net attached.

EQUIPMENT NEEDED

The joy of playing horseball is that the equipment required for the sport is cheap and simple. The ball can be made by having leather loops sewn to a normal football and the goal can be made from an old netball post, using a hoop and a haynet. If you are going to play bareback, whoever sews the loops to your football can also be asked to sew handholds to a surcingle, which will hold a numnah in place on the horse's back and give you some security.

indoors or outdoors, and is a sport enjoyed by both adults and children.

Because the ball can only travel as far and as fast as you can throw it, horseball does not require the same speed from its contestants as, say, polo. For this reason any horse or pony who is well behaved in company, i.e. can be trusted not to kick out or nip an opposing pony or rider, and who is reasonably well schooled, can be introduced to the game.

The greatest advantage of horseball is that, because the equipment is relatively cheap and easy to make, it is ideal as a fun, impromptu game for a group of friends on horseback. At the other extreme it can be played fast, furious and mean by teams with their hearts set on regional and national championship glory.

PONY CLUB HORSEBALL

The Pony Club adopted the game with enthusiasm as the organizers could see its potential as a fun way of improving riding skills and confidence. To make it additionally beneficial as a training exercise, at Pony Club level horseball is played bareback. You sit on a numnah held in place with a surcingle which has two handholds. When you have to reach down to scoop the ball off the ground, you can use the handholds to help keep your balance. To ensure that the ponies don't get pulled in the mouth, you have to drop the reins when you catch the ball.

Polocrosse

Polocrosse is based on the mounted game of polo and on lacrosse, a ball game that is played on foot. Whilst polo originated in the Far East and lacrosse in North America, both were introduced to Europe by returning servicemen and travellers. Polocrosse was first played in 1932 in London. It was used as an exercise to encourage better riding skills and was originally played by teams of two indoors. It quickly developed into a four-a-side

■ LEFT AND BELOW
Ponies and riders need to be athletic and versatile, as well as unflappable!

EQUIPMENT AND SKILLS NEEDED

To play polocrosse you need one horse and a polocrosse racquet. The only other necessary equipment is protective boots and bandages for your horse's legs. All kinds of horses and ponies play the game, from Shetland ponies to thoroughbreds, making it a good family game. You need to have a safe and secure seat in the saddle; beyond that, it is just a case of practising your catching and throwing skills, which can be done on the ground as well as mounted.

outdoor game. In 1938, an Australian couple who watched the game in England took the idea back home with them to Australia, where it became the fast and exciting game that it is today. Polocrosse is played in many different countries around the world, and there are numerous inter-club championships as well as a World Championship.

■ THE GAME

Polocrosse is played between two teams of six, all of whom are equipped with a long-handled racquet which has a net on the end of it. A soft rubber ball is the object of play; it is caught in the net of the racquet and passed between players by throwing or bouncing it.

The game is split into six chukkas, each lasting for eight minutes. Each team is divided into two and they alternate for

each chukka so that only three of the six team members are on the field at one time. The game is played on a large area slightly bigger than a rugby field. The pitch is divided by penalty lines over which the ball must not be carried – the player must either bounce and retrieve it, or throw it to a team-mate.

There is a goal at each end consisting of two poles 8 feet (2.5 m) apart. The ball must be thrown between these in order to score. Only the Number One player is allowed to shoot at goal. The defending Number Three player is allowed in the goalscoring area to protect the goal and to tackle the attacking Number One. The Number Two players are only allowed in the midfield area.

■ BELOW
Many younger riders are introduced to team ball games on horseback by the Pony Club. Polocrosse is a popular alternative to polo, although the Pony Club fields many high-quality polo teams as well.

Driving

Horses and ponies are well designed for the task of pulling a vehicle of some kind or other. Remember that a horse has to be taught how to re-arrange his balance and posture in order to carry a rider, whereas pulling something comes more naturally.

Driving is great fun – although many riders find it more nerve-racking than riding – and it can be undertaken in as simple or elaborate a way as desire and finances allow.

■ DRIVING FOR PLEASURE

Many a family pony has been converted from riding to driving once the children have outgrown him. Given a patient and common-sense approach, most horses and ponies of an equable nature will convert to driving; many even show a preference for it, though there are always exceptions.

The first stage in training a driving horse is to accustom him to wearing blinkers. He should be lunged and long reined in these, and finally hacked out in them. After that, introduce him to the rest of the harness. The next stage involves

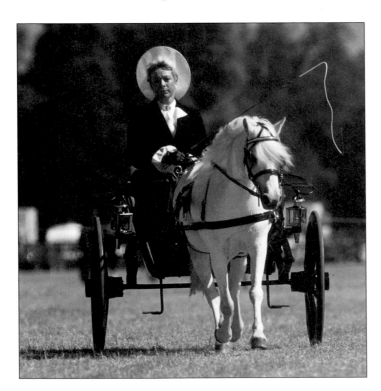

getting him to pull something safe, such as an old tyre. It is not the weight of what he is pulling that is likely to bother him, but his awareness of something following behind him and the noise it makes. Once he is comfortable with this he is well on the way to being introduced to a simple cart of some sort. Straightforward as it all sounds, experienced help should always be sought in the training process.

Driving clubs will provide a social dimension to a leisure activity which can otherwise be quite a solitary one.

■ COMPETITION DRIVING

The world of competition driving revolves around the show ring and driving trials. Show-ring driving follows a similar format to ridden showing classes; driving trials resemble ridden horse trials and consist of three disciplines – a dressage test, a marathon and an obstacle competition.

In show-ring driving, the full turnout of horse or pony, his harness, the cart, the furnishings and the appearance of the driver and groom are all judged, as well as the behaviour and way of going of the whole team. Competing in driving trials requires far more time, practice and equipment than show-ring driving.

Harness racing, which involves specially bred trotters or pacers pulling a lightweight racing cart, is another specialist sport which attracts a great spectator following. The horses can travel at a tremendous speed in trot, and race each other around a big circuit. The

▮ ABOVE
The second phase of driving trials is the marathon, in which competitors cover a set route following various roads and tracks. This phase incorporates a hazards section where cross-country-type obstacles have to be negotiated.

▮ LEFT
In show-ring driving the overall turnout and performance of the competitors is judged. This smart little Welsh mountain pony is creating a good all-round impression in the ring.

■ OPPOSITE
For competition
purposes a team
of four is about as
complicated as you
want to get, but horses
can be driven in larger
teams than this.

■ BELOW
Driving horses and ponies, and the vehicles they
pull, come in all manner of shapes and sizes, and
can be driven in different ways. This pair of ponies
is being driven abreast.

■ BELOW
This pair is being driven in tandem, i.e. one behind the
other.

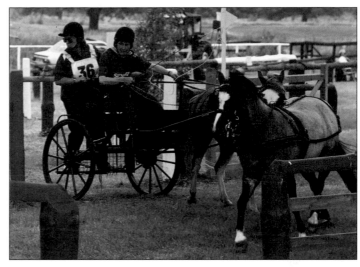

necessary equipment is relatively
inexpensive as the carts are lightweight
and basic in design, but it is a fiercely
competitive sport.

SHOW-RING DRIVING CLASSES

■ In **Private Driving** classes the
competitors may be sent off for a drive
around the surrounding roads with the
judge following in a car to see how they
react and behave.

■ **Light Trade** classes are for horse-drawn
vehicles which were, or still are, used for
trade purposes, such as deliveries of
goods. An additional requirement in these
classes is for the horses to stand still
unattended, which they would have to do
while their goods were being unloaded.

■ The **Concour d'Elegance** class is judged
more on overall poise than on close detail.

■ **Scurry Driving** is a popular class at many
British shows. Pairs of ponies, which must
be either 12hh and under, or between
12hh and 14.2hh, are harnessed to small,
four-wheeled vehicles carrying a driver
and groom. They race around an obstacle
course marked out by cones, which
involves tight turns and high speeds and a
lot of noise from the spectators. Any cones
knocked over are penalized by adding
extra seconds to the overall race time. The
groom has to play a very active role –

leaning out to either side to help maintain
the vehicle's balance as it swings around
the corners.

■ Additional show-ring classes include the
likes of **Ride-and-Drive** competitions and
Heavy Horse classes. There may also be
the opportunity to put on a display to
entertain the public.

DRIVING TRIALS

■ For the first phase, you have to perform
a simple dressage test within the confines
of a large arena; this is given a mark based

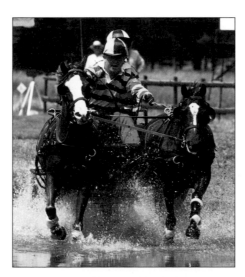

**Water is a popular hazard in driving trials. This pair
of ponies is negotiating a simple water crossing with
great enthusiasm.**

on the performance and on the overall
presentation.

■ The marathon, which comes next,
involves covering approximately 15½ miles
(25 km) in about two hours. There are five
different sections and two compulsory ten-
minute breaks.

– The first section can be completed at
any pace, but trotting is usually sufficient
to make the time.

– The second section must be
performed in walk and is followed by a
ten-minute rest.

– The third section usually involves
a stretch of more arduous terrain and
a fast trot is required to make the time;
cantering is not allowed.

– The fourth section is another walk
section, followed by a ten-minute break.

– With the fifth section the excitement
really begins. This involves negotiating
various man-made or natural hazards at
speed, as this section is timed.

■ The final phase is the obstacle or cone-
driving competition. This tests the horses'
obedience and the driver's ability to drive
accurately between sets of cones which
mark out the course. Once again, this
section is timed.

■ The overall winner is the one with the
best combined score over the three
different phases.

Jumping Sports

Jumping needs confidence, rhythm and balance. Once you have a fair degree of these three skills you can start to discover the world of jumping sports. Show jumping offers competitions for fun as well as for fortune seekers, and provides an excellent and safe way to practise your jumping skills and gain experience. Once you feel confident over show jumps – which fall down if you hit them – you may want to try your hand at jumping solid obstacles. Hunting and hunter trials provide you with the opportunity to do this – and when you are feeling confident enough you can progress to team chasing or eventing. For the brave and robust there is race riding – the ultimate way to jump at speed.

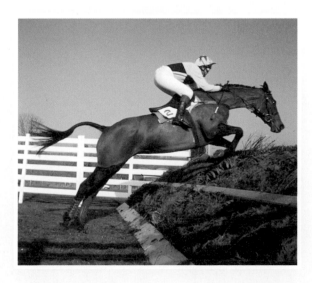

Hunting

There is little to beat the exhilaration of riding fast across country. You and your horse must tackle whatever is thrown in your way – balancing your horse over all kinds of terrain with the wind making your eyes stream, mud splattered in your face, encouraging him over every manner of obstacle, letting him jump out of his stride and land running, looking eagerly ahead for the next challenge.

The thrill of it usually lifts the spirits and the courage of all horsemen and women. The hedge that you sailed over effortlessly when running behind hounds may look completely unjumpable when viewed in cold blood! There is neither judge nor winner, except in the hearts and minds of those taking part. Hunting, for many, provides an opportunity to tackle much greater challenges than they might otherwise contemplate.

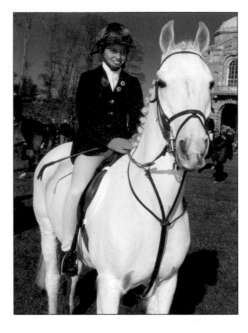

▌ **ABOVE**
Hunting etiquette requires that you and your mount are smartly and tidily turned out. Your horse's or pony's mane should be plaited (braided), your tack should be gleaming, and you should be kitted out in clean jodhpurs, boots and jacket.

▌ **BELOW**
The hounds are controlled by a huntsman; he is usually assisted by a whipper-in who helps to keep the hounds together as a pack.

■ DIFFERENT TYPES OF HUNTING
HUNTING QUARRY

Ever since man learnt to ride a horse he has used the horse's speed and agility to his advantage, including in his hunt for food. Today, hunting on horseback is a country sport rather than a means of survival. Hunting live quarry for sport is a controversial subject on which many people hold strong views. Some consider it has a valuable role to play in the conservation of the countryside and in the management of the wildlife it hunts; others think it is cruel and an outdated way to control wildlife. Hunt meets often attract protesters from various animal rights organizations and are often not publicized.

A wide variety of animals is hunted from horseback around the world. The most common ones are the fox and stag in

▌ LEFT
You are never too young or too old to go hunting. Many children are taken out, and an abundance of youthful pensioners still hunts regularly.

edges of fields, through gates and along tracks. A good knowledge of the local countryside helps in the task of keeping up with the hounds. If you are crossing country that has been planted with crops, only the hounds and huntsman are allowed to take the direct line after the prey. The field have to find a way round which minimizes any damage to the crops; an intimate knowledge of your surroundings makes this easier. Etiquette demands that you follow the lead of the field master, but after a good run behind hounds the field often gets split up and strung out, and it is up to you to find the hounds again.

The hounds will either succeed in catching their prey or they will lose track

England and Ireland, the wild boar in other parts of Europe, and the coyote in North America and parts of Africa. The hunting of any of these animals relies on the co-operation and permission of the landowners whose property is crossed.

Packs of hounds are bred and trained to pick up the scent and track down the hunted animal. The hounds are controlled by a huntsman and whipper-in, who are the only people actively involved in the work of the hounds. The hunt followers, or field as they are often known, are sometimes helpful in observing the whereabouts of the hounds or the direction the hunted quarry has taken, but their main role is to help pay for the upkeep of the hunt's hounds, horses and hunting country. In return for an annual subscription and a "cap" – an additional donation to hunt funds made on the day of the hunt – the hunt follower enjoys seeing hounds at work and the thrill of the chase.

In fox hunting, after a convivial half an hour or so at the meet, the huntsman heads off with the hounds to the first cover. This is usually a piece of woodland or scrubland where a fox is likely to be found. The field follow, led by the field master whose instructions you must obey at all times – and who you should avoid overtaking! The hounds are "cast" into the cover, i.e. sent in to hunt around until they find the scent of the fox. Some days are good scenting days and the hounds can easily follow the scent; other days are not so good.

Once the hounds are on the scent of their quarry, they will follow it across all manner of country. The mounted followers keep up as best they can, the bravest and most talented jumping everything in their path, the rest finding a way around the

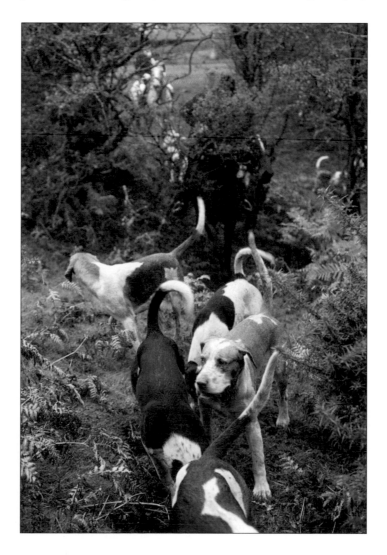

▌ LEFT
Whether you are hunting foxes, coyote, hare, or with drag or bloodhounds, nothing very exciting happens until the hounds pick up the appropriate scent and set off.

■ LEFT
Out hunting there will always be those who want
to jump obstacles and those who want to go around
them. The choice is yours, but should be based
on an appreciation of ability – yours and your
mount's – rather than on pride.

of it, or may have to be called off if the fox crosses land that the hunt doesn't have permission to cross. In any case the hounds are taken to another cover to see if they can pick up the scent of another fox, and so it goes on.

Most hunt meets are organized for mid-morning, and hunting continues until late in the afternoon. At about lunchtime "second horses" are arranged. This means that the huntsman, whipper-in and master will change on to fresh horses who have been brought by lorry to a pre-arranged point. Their first horses are taken home, washed and dried off, rugged up, fed and stabled. Hunt followers may also change

on to second horses if they have another horse and have been able to organize someone to deliver it for them.

Whilst hunting is a thrilling way of enjoying cross-country riding, it carries a lot of risks because there is no time to check out what you are about to jump. Many a horse and rider have fallen when, having taken off over what looks like an innocuous hedge, they see in mid-air that there is a wire or timber fence running alongside it on the far side. A scopey, quick-thinking, focused horse can usually get himself out of such a muddle, but only with experience which can be painful in the making.

DRAG HUNTING

This involves a pack of hounds and mounted followers but, instead of hunting a live quarry, the hounds follow a trail that has been laid earlier in the day by someone dragging a bag laced with a strong scent that the hounds have been taught to pick up and follow.

Drag hunting gives you the chance to ride fast across country, behind hounds. It is safer and more predictable than hunting live quarry because you are following a pre-set course. The jumps will be either safe, natural features or man-made fences. A knowledge of the country is not necessary as the course the hounds take is pre-determined. Many hunts offer days specifically for the novice or nervous, when they will make sure the jumps encountered are smaller than usual.

Subscriptions from the field help to pay for the upkeep of the hounds and kennels.

BLOODHOUNDS

Hunting with bloodhounds is another form of drag hunting. This time the hounds are following the scent of a man

EQUIPMENT NEEDED

Your horse should be well turned out with his mane plaited (braided). He will need a good, strong set of tack, as a good-quality saddle and bridle will add to your own safety. Hunting entails long hours in the saddle, often in bad weather conditions. The last thing you want is for a rein or stirrup leather to snap when you are in the middle of nowhere, riding at a flat-out gallop and heading for a large and solid post-and-rail fence!

Put an especially well-padded numnah under the saddle to make it more comfortable for the horse and to reduce the risk of him being rubbed.

Whether or not your horse wears boots to protect his legs is a matter of personal choice. Your horse's legs are at great risk of being knocked or scratched out hunting, but many boots, once they are wet and muddy and have been worn for several hours, start to rub anyway. You will need to decide which is the lesser of two evils.

As a rider you are expected to be smartly turned out. You should wear traditional-coloured breeches or jodphurs, teamed with either long riding boots or short jodhpur boots. You must wear either a hacking jacket (tweed jacket) or a plain blue or black jacket. A crash cap with blue or black velvet silk should be worn and this should have a well-fitting safety harness. If you wear a hacking jacket it is correct to wear a shirt and coloured stock (similar to a cravat or broad neck tie) held in place with a stock pin. A plain cream or white stock should be worn with a blue or black jacket.

Gloves should be worn and a stick carried. You should carry in your pockets some good, thick string, such as baling twine, and a foldaway penknife so that you can help make repairs to any gates or fences that get broken by the less able jumpers in the field. A day's hunting can end up being a very long day – find room in your pockets

for a couple of sandwiches or a bar of chocolate to keep you going.

If you are going to hunt a lot, a hunting whip and a pair of wire cutters are worth buying. A hunting whip is a shaped cane with a long leather lash on the end. The cane is useful for helping you to open and shut gates, and the lash, if let down so that it hangs by your horse's legs, can be used to prevent hounds from going right underneath your horse where they are more likely to get kicked or trampled. A leather carrying pouch can be fitted to your saddle in which to put a pair of wire cutters. No matter how diligent you are, when you are crossing unknown country it is possible to get caught up in one of the hazards of agriculture – wire netting or barbed wire. A pair of wire cutters is invaluable to cut your own horse free or to help anyone else unfortunate enough to be caught out.

■ BOTTOM
At the end of a long, hard day's hunting the field is
greatly diminished. It is one of the most satisfying
feelings in the world to be amongst the few left at
the end of the day.

■ BELOW
Ladies traditionally only ever rode side-saddle, and
the elegant picture it creates is one reason for a
growing number of people returning to the habit.

who sets off some time before the hunt
starts. The runner will follow a previously
agreed trail, making this form of hunting
as safe as drag hunting. You might find the
thought of a pack of bloodhounds bearing
down on a fleeing man alarming, but they
will not harm him when they catch him.
He will most likely be smothered in wet,
warm licks by his friendly canine pursuers.

■ SKILLS REQUIRED

Hunting suits all types of horse and pony –
it seems to inspire the less cautious to be
even braver, but it can also cause a great
deal of over-excitement. It is important to
have developed a reasonably strong and
secure seat and to be able to balance your
horse in order to help him tackle the
varied terrain and obstacles that you will
encounter. Whether you are riding around
a cross-country course or are genuinely
crossing the country out hunting, the
approach to jumping is the same: keep the
horse balanced and in a rhythm. Keep in
contact with the horse with your legs, seat
and hands so that you can help balance
him as he negotiates the unexpected.

Those brave and able enough to jump
everything in their path will take the most
direct line, following the lead of the field
master. But there are plenty of others who
will find their way around as best they can
so as not to have to jump too much.
Consider your own riding ability and the
experience of your horse before deciding
which party to join. When you do get the
chance to jump, always give your horse
room to see what it is you want him to do.
Don't follow blindly behind the horse in
front – your horse will not be able to judge
the fence and, if the horse and rider in
front fall or refuse, you will have a

problem. In a crowded gateway, or if there
is a queue of riders waiting to jump a
narrow fence, slow your horse down well
beforehand, so that you don't run into the
back of everyone else. Wait your turn and
give your horse room to make a good,
balanced approach, and the chance to see
what the fence involves.

Your horse needs to be fit, as he will be
required to gallop and jump, often with
little chance to rest. He should be well
mannered; he must accept other horses all
around him. If you have even the slightest
suspicion that he may panic or kick out,
keep him out of the crowd. It is your
responsibility to prevent your horse
from hurting anyone else. A young or
inexperienced horse should be introduced
quietly to the hunting field. It is often a
good idea to avoid the first hour of the
meet when all the horses are fresh and
excited, and perhaps join the hunt later
in the day. Keep the horse moving and
thinking forwards but do not allow him to
get caught up in the crush of the field
until he is used to all the sights and
sounds. It is considered an unforgiveable
sin to let your horse kick a hound, so be
constantly aware of where the hounds
are in relation to your horse. Keep his
hindquarters turned away from the
hounds if they approach or pass by you.

In the excitement of the chase do not
overlook your horse's well-being. At all
times, keep in mind how tired he might
really be – horses get very caught up in
the excitement of the chase and may not
appear to be tired, as their excitement and
adrenalin gives them additional stamina.
But this should not be abused – think of
how fit your horse really is, and how much
galloping and jumping he has done. Do
not keep him out for too long – there will
always be another day. Think responsibly
about what you ask him to jump. Never be
tempted to jump wire – find a gate
instead. Look out too for hazards such as
rabbit holes and discarded farm machinery.

Hunter Trials and Team Chasing

For those who want to be judged on their cross-country-riding skills, there is the option of competing in hunter trials and team chases. In a hunter trial you may ride the course as an individual or as one of a pair. In team chasing there are four team members to motivate each other.

In hunter trials you are expected to tackle a course of cross-country fences, the height of which varies depending on the class you enter. Some competitions cater for leading-rein riders, others offer a range of classes varying from about 2 feet 6 inches to 3 feet 9 inches (0.75–1.2 m). The organizers decide upon an optimum time, which is based on horse and rider tackling the course at what is commonly described as a fair hunting pace. Within the course there is usually an additional timed section which often includes a gate that has to be opened and shut – not jumped! The winners are the horse and rider who jump clear and complete the course nearest to the optimum time – which is not revealed to the riders until after the competition. If more than one rider finishes on the optimum time, the winner is the fastest one through the timed section.

▌ ABOVE
Water is one of the most common problems encountered at a hunter trial. There is no reason why it should be feared provided it is introduced quietly and calmly. This pony looks a bit tentative and needs to gain more confidence before he is likely to tackle water with enthusiasm.

▌ BELOW LEFT
Hunter trials offer a huge variety of challenges for all ages and abilities. Even leading-rein riders can take part, provided their helpers are as agile as their ponies!

■ SKILLS REQUIRED

The main difference between hunting and competing in a hunter trial is that at a hunter trial you have to jump alone and in cold blood. You do not have the rush and excitement of hounds running and the rest of the field following to give you confidence. You and your horse have to be prepared to jump for the fun of it, although some classes are open to pairs in

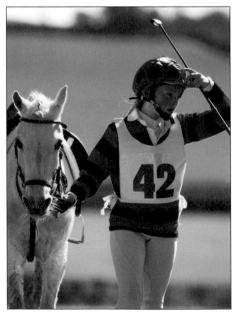

▌ LEFT
Cross-country riding is tiring for both horse and rider, but it is always a kind and correct gesture to dismount and lead your horse or pony once you have pulled up over the finish line.

❚ **BELOW**
This horse and rider have both taken a good soaking at the water hazard, but the joy of team chasing is that, provided the rest of the team got through, there is still a chance of winning. It just means there is a little consolation for the faller – his team will have galloped away into the distance!

❚ **LEFT**
Competing as a pair is a good way of introducing an inexperienced or nervous horse or rider to the thrill of cross-country riding, as they can gain confidence from their partners.

Once you are up to speed it is a case of staying in that rhythm and keeping the horse balanced.

■ TEAM CHASING

Team chases are held over a variety of different-sized cross-country courses. Teams of four riders set off around the course, and progress is timed from the moment a team sets off to the moment the third rider crosses the line. So if one member of your team is left behind you are still in with a chance of winning.

The winning team is the one whose first three riders complete the course in the fastest time. Penalties are not given for falls or refusals – it is all judged on speed. For this reason the number of falls can be quite high. If the lead horse falls and the others are coming too fast and too close behind, at least one other member of the team is likely to fall also. But there is never any need to give up hope – even if one of the team stops or falls, provided the team can make up time somewhere else they still have a chance of a place. Regional and national championships are held.

which case a less confident horse can take a lead from his bolder partner. Some horses make marvellous hunters but will not jump an inch outside the hunting field. Remember to let your horse take his own line out hunting – do not just blindly follow the horse in front. If you have balanced him and helped him so that he regards hunting and cross-country jumping as fun, there is no reason why your hunter should not happily complete a hunter trial for you.

In the timed section you will have to open and shut a gate quickly without

dismounting. It should be easy if your horse has learnt to listen and respond to your hand and leg aids. You just need to be sure that your horse will rein back, and move over to the right or left when you ask him, and you can practise all these skills at home.

To win the competition you will need to have a good sense of speed and timing. If you have hunted, try to think of the speed you travel at when hounds are running, and to go at that same speed on the hunter-trial course. You will know the terrain, having already walked the course.

EQUIPMENT NEEDED

To compete in a hunter trial you need to be kitted out in your hunting attire, although most organizers allow you to wear a sweat shirt or jumper instead of a jacket. They will, however, insist that you wear a proper safety helmet and harness, as well as a body protector.

Your horse will need his usual saddle and bridle, as long as these are clean and in good condition, and his legs should be protected with either boots or bandages.

A normal riding stick or hunting whip may be carried; for hunter trials a proper hunting whip may help in opening and shutting the gate quickly in the timed section.

❚ **RIGHT**
Team chasing involves a team of four riding fast and furiously across country. The competition is based on the time it takes for the first three team members to complete the course.

Show Jumping

The sport of show jumping involves tackling a course of artificial jumps, as opposed to natural cross-country jumps. It takes place in an arena which can be grass or have an all-weather surface, indoors or outdoors. An Olympic sport governed by the FEI, it is also a popular unaffiliated sport with any number of classes being held at local shows.

Show jumping requires accuracy and care. Almost every horse or pony can jump, but they do not all have the technique or the will to clear the fences.

Show jumping developed from the "leaping competitions" which were held at various shows in Europe and America during the late nineteenth century. There were high-jump and long-jump competitions for horse and rider but the idea of jumping a course of fences was, at the time, mainly restricted to natural cross-country fences. Jumping was first included in the Olympic Games in Paris in 1900. It incorporated the high and wide competitions plus a timed competition over a course of artificial show jumps. In 1907, the first International Horse Show was held at Olympia in London, England, and the show jumping proved to be very popular. From then on competitions were organized throughout Europe and America for major trophies such as the

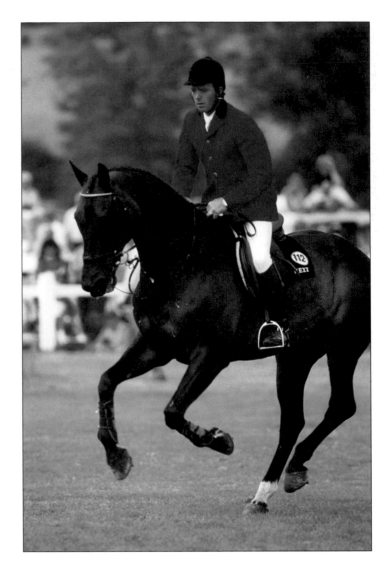

■ LEFT
Teaching your horse to go well on the flat is as important to his success as teaching him how to jump correctly; look at the beautifully round and elevated canter that this show jumper is producing – with a canter like this, jumping the fence is almost a formality.

■ BELOW LEFT AND RIGHT
If you can invest in a few jumps of your own, or team up with some friends to share them, there is much that can be practised at home. A simple thing to practise is always looking towards the next fence. This helps you to judge your turns and your approach. Once you have taken off over a fence you should be looking towards your next target; as you ride around the course you should always be looking towards where you have to go next.

Nations Cup. This began as a military competition open to three officers of the same nationality who had to compete in uniform. Today it is open to four riders of the same nationality, male or female, military or civilian.

■ SHOW-JUMPING COMPETITIONS

The simplest form of unaffiliated competition is the Clear-round Class. This is an excellent way of introducing an inexperienced horse and rider to the sport. Each rider pays a small fee to tackle a course of jumps. If you jump a clear round you win a rosette, but the real usefulness of the competition is that if you jump a fence badly you can turn around and jump it again. Most organizers of these classes are extremely tolerant and will even lower a fence for you if your horse continually refuses. In a proper competition you would be eliminated after three refusals.

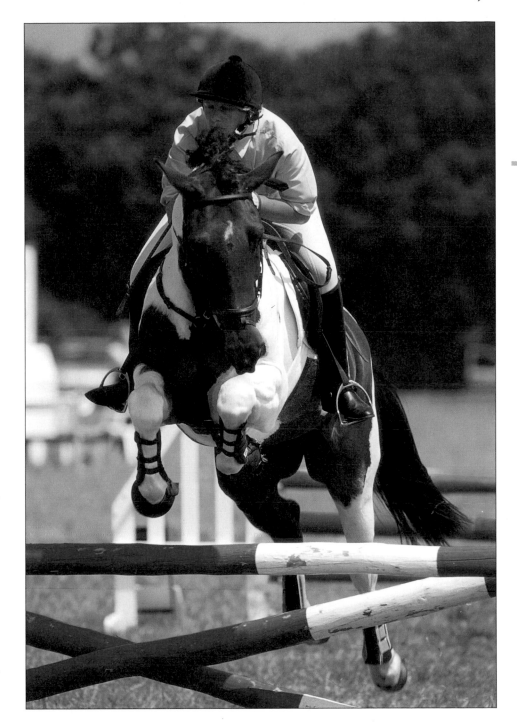

■ RIGHT
It is important that the horse learns to jump straight, unless his rider is asking him to turn in the air. In this picture you can see that the horse is looking in the opposite direction from his rider, suggesting he has a tendency to jump crookedly. Gridwork and the use of V-poles help to teach the horse to stay straight.

The next stage is the two-round competition. Each competitor tackles the same course of fences and if you jump a clear round you go through to the jump off. This is ridden against the clock and the fastest clear round wins.

Fences in unaffiliated classes start as low as the organizer wishes. There may even be leading-rein classes with jumps only 18 inches (45 cm) high. Fences usually go up to about 3 feet 11 inches (1.2 m). Affiliated competitions start with a novice class with fences at about 3 feet 3 inches (1 m) and continue through the grades to courses with jumps which are well over 6 feet (1.8 m) high.

There are also other types of jumping classes such as "Take your own line". This involves a course of fences which each have a different value in terms of points to be won. You jump as many fences as you can in the time allowed, in any order you like, with the aim of accumulating the maximum number of points. The *Puissance* involves jumping a short course of fences; these include a wall, which is always the highest jump. The fences are gradually raised until nobody is able to clear the wall.

Derby competitions have cross-country-type obstacles in the arena, such as banks and ditches. Some shows also hold relay

EQUIPMENT NEEDED

To develop your show-jumping skills you need to have access to at least three or four sets of show-jump wings and poles. Other than that, all that is needed is a reasonably flat surface to practise on, which can be a grass paddock when ground conditions permit, or an outdoor or indoor arena with an all-weather surface. Your horse needs only his usual saddle and bridle and should wear protective boots of some sort. Most show jumpers use open-fronted boots on the front legs so that the tendon area is protected but the horse will feel the knock if he hits a pole, and short fetlock boots behind. To compete you

will need to wear breeches or jodhpurs with riding boots, and a show or hacking jacket. A shirt and tie, or stock, is worn underneath the jacket.

Whilst almost any horse or pony can be persuaded to pop around a show-jumping course, once the fences get bigger you do need a horse who is athletic and balanced. There are plenty of horses who will clatter their way around a course, gaily sending poles flying without appearing to be the least bit bothered by the experience. There is a great deal you can teach a horse but, at the end of the day, he has to want to clear the top pole.

competitions between teams of show jumpers, or for added entertainment they may build two identical courses side by side over which competitors race. Time faults are added for knock-downs.

One of the advantages of show jumping is that jumping a course of fences does not take as much out of a horse as, say, a day's hunting or a hunter trial, so the show jumper can compete far more frequently than many other sports horses. You could compete in a couple of different classes on the same day and, provided your horse is fit enough and enjoying his work, you might compete nearly every weekend. In

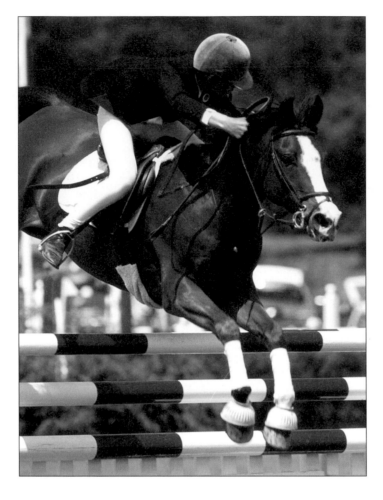

▮ RIGHT
Riders all develop their own jumping style as they gain confidence and experience, but one of the things you must always do, no matter what your technique, is to ensure that you give your horse plenty of freedom of his head and neck. Your hands must always move forwards when the horse is jumping over the fence.

theory this offers horse and rider the chance to gain experience relatively quickly.

■ SKILLS REQUIRED
Flatwork training is as important to the show jumper as jump schooling. A balanced, rhythmic and elevated canter is essential if the horse is to jump successfully. Whatever it is you are jumping, your chances of clearing it safely are mainly reliant on how good an approach you give the horse to the fence. The horse must be able to negotiate corners and turns whilst still keeping his rhythm and balance, so he needs to be supple and responsive.

How much actual jump training you do depends on what suits your horse. Naturally careful horses are best not jumped too often – just enough to keep them in practice and their muscles toned up. A horse whose technique needs tidying up may be jumped up to three or four times a week.

Jump training rarely involves jumping huge fences. It concentrates on improving the horse's technique and ability over

smaller fences – this reduces the risk of injury or loss of confidence. Gridwork is used to make the horse more supple, and to influence his technique and the shape he makes as he goes over a fence to maximize his chance of going clear.

The distances between fences in a grid can be shortened to encourage the horse

to shorten up his stride and snap his front legs up quickly and neatly as he takes off. They can also be lengthened, which encourages the horse to stretch and to lengthen his stride and jump.

Poles can be rested on the fence or on the ground in such a way as to encourage the horse to stay straight as he jumps; many horses have a tendency to veer off to the left or right. Gridwork also gives you a chance to concentrate on tidying up your own position and to improve your balance.

The ability to lengthen or shorten your horse's stride and to react quickly when he jumps into a combination or related distance in a different way from the one that was planned, is an essential skill for the successful show jumper. Some riders have a natural eye for a stride, which means that as soon as they land over one fence they are able to gauge whether they need to alter the horse's stride length in order to meet the next fence on a good stride. Those not born with this skill can develop a good eye by practising riding different distances between fences at home, and getting a feel for the pace at which they need to approach the first

▮ LEFT
This little pony is showing superb technique – see how tightly he has snapped up and folded his front legs, which gives him every chance to clear the fence.

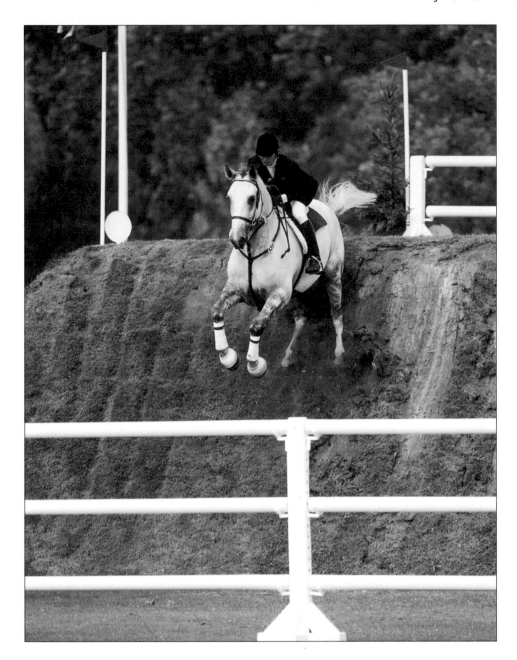

Show-jumping competitions usually just involve jumping over fences. However, in Derby classes cross-country type obstacles are introduced; this is the world-famous Hickstead Derby bank.

horse and rider to progress through the grades. They can go as far as their ability, time and/or finances allow them.

For those looking for greater rewards, show jumping also offers very good opportunities. Through the FEI there is a training and team-selection programme for pony riders, juniors, young riders and seniors. There are also Pony Club and riding club competitions and championships. To be considered for team selection usually involves informing the appropriate selection committee of your interest and then entering a number of specified competitions where your performance will be noted by the selectors. If you are a likely candidate for a team place, you may be invited to attend various training courses – but remember that the ability to operate as part of a team is as important as being a good enough competitor to warrant selection.

In show jumping the horse has to be taught to jump *over* water, whereas in cross-country riding you are always trying to encourage your horse to jump *into* water.

fence in order to fit in the required number of strides to the next fence.

Among the most important attributes the rider needs are patience, a cool head and confidence – if you have all three of these you will no doubt succeed in whatever sport you choose!

■ **OPPORTUNITIES**

In all sports there are those who compete purely for their own enjoyment and entertainment, and those who compete with a view to being selected for team competitions and, who knows, maybe ultimately the Olympics. Show jumping caters extremely well for both types of competitor. For the less ambitious there are no end of unaffiliated and affiliated classes and competitions which still allow

Eventing

The sport of eventing, or horse trials as it
is also known, is really a complete test of
all-round horsemanship on the part of the
rider, and of all-round performance on
the part of the horse. Horse and rider are
tested on their ability to compete in the
disciplines of dressage, show jumping
and cross country. The dressage test
demonstrates that the horse is supple,
obedient and calm; the show jumping
proves his agility and carefulness over
fences; the cross country proves his
boldness, speed and stamina. The sport is
split into one-day events and three-day
events. At a one-day event the order of the
phases is usually dressage, show jumping
and cross country. At a three-day event
the cross country, combined with some
additional tests of the horse's speed and
endurance, is held the day after the
dressage. The show jumping is held on the
final day, testing whether the horse still
has the necessary energy, agility,
obedience and desire to clear the show
jumps following the tough test of his
stamina the day before on the speed and
endurance phase.

■ HOW THE SPORT
DEVELOPED

Eventing was started in Europe by
cavalrymen, when they were not away
fighting wars! The sport was originally
named "The Military". It evolved as a way
of testing the skills a cavalry horse would
need – the dressage represented his
suitability for parade duties, the cross
country reflected the need to cross any
terrain to seek out, confront or escape the
enemy, and the show jumping showed that
after the rigours of battle the horse was
still fit, willing and obedient, ready to
march on to the next challenge.

The first Olympic three-day event was
held in 1912. Then and for some years
afterwards the sport remained the domain
of the military. It spread from country to
country through international military

A THREE-DAY EVENT

Day one	Dressage
Day two	Speed and endurance:
	Phase A roads and tracks
	Phase B steeplechase
	Phase C roads and tracks
	Phase D cross country
Day three	Show jumping

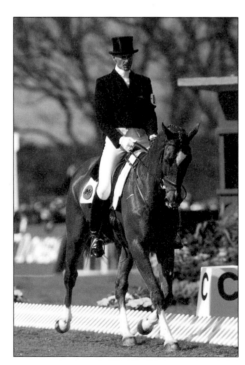

The sport of eventing involves three very different
disciplines, all of which must be completed
successfully in order to win. The dressage test
comes first. Whilst this is simpler than a pure
dressage test, it must be remembered that it is
being ridden on a horse who has been prepared
physically and mentally for the cross-country phase.
He knows what is coming next, so it is harder for
him to settle to the discipline of dressage.

competitions and, as events became more
numerous, the interest of civilian riders
was aroused. Now eventing is a popular
sport in any number of countries around
the world.

■ ONE-DAY AND THREE-DAY
EVENTS

At a one-day event you have to complete a
dressage test, a course of show jumps and
a cross-country course, all on the same
day. The penalties incurred in each
competition, or phase, are added
together, and the winner is the rider
incurring the lowest number of penalties.
One-day events are an end in themselves
for many riders, but their true purpose is
to prepare horse and rider for the more
demanding three-day event.

A three-day event can actually last for
four or five days, depending on the
number of entrants. All the horses are
stabled together at or near the event for
its duration. Before the competition
begins there is a veterinary inspection,
where any signs of lameness, injury or
illness will result in elimination before you
have started. The next one or two days are
taken up with everybody completing their
dressage tests.

The second part of the competition –
the speed and endurance section – starts
on the following day. Phase A, roads and
tracks, involves completing a set route
within a set time. This is usually achieved
comfortably at trot, although a very short-
striding horse may have to canter some of
the way in order to avoid time penalties.
This takes you to the start of the steeplechase, which is Phase B. All on your own

OPPOSITE
In one-day events the show-jumping phase comes
after the dressage, before the cross country. At a
three-day event it is the final phase, testing the
horse's agility and obedience after the rigours and
excitement of the cross country the day before.

you have to gallop around a circuit
of steeplechase fences, again within a set
time. The finish of the steeplechase takes
you on to Phase C, another set of roads
and tracks, which is meant to serve as a
recovery period after the steeplechase. A
steady trot has to be maintained for much
of the way if you are to finish inside the
time. You then find yourself in the ten-
minute box which is a roped-off area near
the start of the cross-country course. Here
the horse is allowed to rest for ten
minutes. He is usually washed off, has his
tack re-adjusted and checked for security
and comfort, and is then walked quietly
around so that he does not stiffen up
before the cross country, which is Phase D.
In the ten-minute box, vets check the
horses over and eliminate any who are
already overly tired or are stressed.

After the ten-minute rest you set off on
the cross-country course, which is judged
in the same way as at a one-day event.
There are penalties for any refusals, falls
or runouts, and also for exceeding the set
time. The following day there is another
veterinary inspection where any horse who
appears to have suffered from his
exertions of the day before is withdrawn
or eliminated from the competition.

This is followed by the final phase,
the show jumping. This is usually run
in reverse order of merit, so that the
overnight leader jumps last. Any penalties
incurred for refusals, knock-downs or
exceeding the time are added to the
dressage and to the speed and endurance
penalties to give a final score. The winners
of three-day events do indeed prove
themselves and their horses to be
successful, all-round competitors.

■ LEVELS OF COMPETITION
Eventing is governed by the FEI and there
are various levels of affiliated competition.
There are also Pony Club, Riding Club
and unaffiliated competitions although
these rarely offer classes at higher than

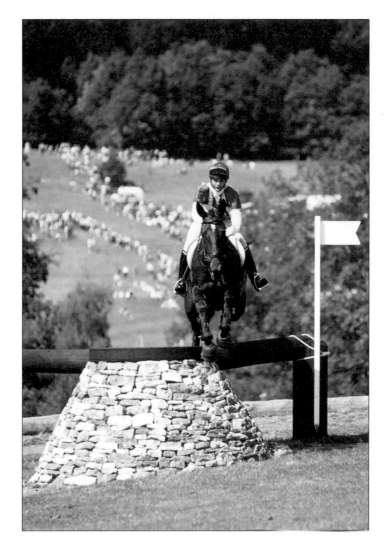

LEFT
The cross-country
phase is the most
important, and
should be the most
influential, of the
three phases. For
most event riders it is
the favourite phase.

**BELOW LEFT
AND RIGHT**
At a three-day event,
the competitors have
to tackle two roads and
tracks phases, as well
as a steeplechase
course, before they
even set out on the
cross-country course.
There is a ten-minute
rest period between
the end of the second
roads and tracks and
the start of the cross-
country test.

affiliated intermediate level. Affiliated
one-day events are graded into different
levels along such lines as novice (or below,
such as preliminary or pre-novice),
intermediate and advanced. These
classifications or grades refer to the ability
of the horse, not the rider, so in the same
novice class you may find a sixteen-year-
old riding in his or her first event
competing against the reigning Olympic
champion. For many this is all part of the
charm and attraction of the sport. It is far

more of an achievement to perform well
against such experienced riders, even if
you don't win, than it is to take first prize
in a class where you knew your rivals
weren't up to much anyway.

Affiliated three-day events are classified
as one star (novice), two star (about
intermediate level), three star
(intermediate to advanced level) and four
star (advanced and championship level).

In between the one-day events and the
three-day events are the occasional two-day

LEFT
During the ten-minute rest the horse is cooled down as much as possible by washing him off. His tack is checked over and re-adjusted if necessary.

events. These are limited in number and are usually only offered at novice level, but provide a great introduction to three-day eventing for the inexperienced rider or horse. You perform your dressage and show jumping on day one, and on day two you complete a shortened speed and endurance phase. This still consists of roads and tracks, steeplechase, roads and tracks, ten-minute halt and the cross-country course, but the speeds and distances are less than for a three-day event.

Every horse has to qualify to take part in a three-day event. For each grade there are a set number of one-, two- or less rigorous three-day events which horse and rider must have completed to a set standard. You usually need to have gone clear on the cross country, or at least have

incurred only a limited number of penalties. This adds another dimension to the sport as it allows you to compete with your horse's long-term future in mind. You may well go to a one-day event and come away without a prize, but if you were able to go clear on the cross country you will have achieved a qualification towards your target of the three-day event.

■ **SKILLS REQUIRED**
Bearing in mind what is required for dressage, show jumping and hunter trialling will give you some idea of the myriad skills the successful event horse and rider need. But before you are put off just think of it in terms of good basic training equalling good all-round performance. If you have put some effort

into schooling your horse well on the flat, and have carried through the same principles of rhythm, balance and responsiveness into your jump training, you are well on the way to producing a capable and successful event horse. Jump training, whether over show jumps or cross-country fences, requires the same technique and skills. The only difference is the speed at which you ride across country, and the fact that the natural terrain you have to cross makes it harder to maintain your rhythm and balance than when you are jumping in an arena. An

EQUIPMENT NEEDED

It is possible to compete in events with a minimal amount of tack and equipment but, because of the three disciplines involved, there is a greater chance that you will need to invest in various bits and pieces. Many horses are better ridden in different tack for each phase – a horse may perform happily in a snaffle for his dressage test but may need a double bridle or a gag for the cross country. Some horses need different tack for the show jumping as well. You should use a breastplate or girth and a safety girth with your saddle for the cross-country phase. You may also want to use different types of boots or bandages for the show-jumping and cross-country phases – show-jumping boots do not offer enough protection for cross country. If you can afford it, a dressage saddle for the dressage phase will help your seat and position enormously; some riders even opt for different show-jumping and cross-country saddles although this is a little excessive. In fact, it is now possible to buy saddles with interchangeable knee rolls which allow the same saddle to be converted from a dressage model to a jumping model.

You will need jodhpurs, breeches and boots, plus a show or hacking jacket and a recognized crash hat. You must also wear a body protector on the cross-country phase. At advanced level you are expected to perform your dressage test in a top hat and tailcoat – these are expensive when new, but can often be bought secondhand.

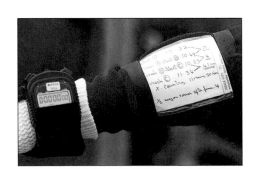

ABOVE
You have to keep note of how much time you can allow yourself on the roads and tracks phases, the steeplechase and the cross-country course. Exceeding the optimum time incurs time faults. Most riders record all their times on a card which they carry on their arm, along with a stopwatch.

LEFT
At advanced one-day events and at three-day events the horses have to carry a minimum weight of 165 lb (75 kg). This includes the rider's clothing and the horse's saddle. If you weigh in under that, you will have to carry lead weights in a weightcloth under the saddle.

■ RIGHT
This horse is about to unseat his rider, having thrown a very big but steep jump into the water at Badminton. In the circumstances, the rider has done well to keep her weight back and at the same time has slipped the reins to give the horse every chance of coping with the situation.

■ BELOW
Blyth Tait, the 1996 Olympic gold medallist, demonstrates how to slip the reins but still keep a contact so that the horse has some support to help balance him as he lands.

additional factor is the variety of fences you will meet on a cross-country course. Once your horse is familiar with show jumps he is unlikely to be fazed by anything he meets in the arena, unless you approach it badly. But the awkward obstacles that can be built into the natural terrain on a cross-country course are numerous, and each time the horse competes he may well be faced with something he has never encountered before. Cross-country training should concentrate on building up confidence and trust, and making the right decision about the approach you should take.

Water is one hazard which seems to cause more trouble than most. In the horse's early training it is important that he is never frightened in water. This means carefully choosing any water hazard you ask him to enter. Don't ask him to splash through a river unless you know it has a safe, secure bottom. If he willingly enters water for you, and then finds himself floundering in deep mud he is going to be frightened and he is not going to trust you next time you face him with water. So do not abuse his trust and willingness. Similarly do not allow the overbold or exuberant horse to frighten

himself – make him approach water quietly and calmly so that he puts in a sensible jump which allows him to land in a balanced and controlled manner. If your horse is introduced to water like this, and if you take care always to be in a good position to support and balance him as he lands in water, he should never have reason to refuse to tackle a water complex.

Fitness is another necessity for both horse and rider. As long as they are regularly hacked out and given some schooling and jump training, most horses and ponies will be fit enough to complete a novice one-day event. Once

you want to do more than this, special attention has to be paid to the horse's fitness and training routine. This requires knowledge and experience of how to achieve fitness without subjecting the horse's vulnerable joints and limbs to unnecessary wear and tear. You will also need to be fit, as a tired rider is of little help to a tired horse.

The event rider perhaps needs more determination and persistence than other equestrian competitors, simply because it is a lot harder to get three things to go well all on the same day than it is to get one specialist discipline to come right.

■ LEFT
Commonly known as "hailing a cab", this rider has thrown her arm behind her in a tactic which many riders find helps them to keep their weight back behind the horse when jumping down into water.

Race Riding

Race riding, either on the flat or over fences, offers the best opportunity to experience the full power and speed that a horse can produce. The racing industry revolves around the thoroughbred horse and, to a lesser degree, the Arab horse. Point-to-pointing, the occasional unofficial horse or pony race and the growth in Arab racing all give the amateur rider the chance to experience the thrill of race riding, and the chance to race for the fun of it. Professional jockeys are either retained or employed on a freelance basis by race-horse trainers. They often work for a big training yard in order to supplement their income, exercising and schooling the race horses, as well as racing them competitively if they are offered the ride.

■ POINT-TO-POINTING

This is an amateur sport which tends to thrive wherever hunting thrives. A horse which is to go point-to-pointing has to qualify by going out hunting for a set number of days. The amateur status of the sport, and the fact that a great many who take part own just one horse which they hunt and race, all adds to its fun and social atmosphere. It is popular with spectators, even in winter when they usually end up standing around in the wet and cold, eating the traditional picnic in

■ LEFT
The ability to sit tight when the unexpected happens is a great asset. Note how this jockey has kept his upper body back and is still looking up and ahead, which is a great aid to keeping in balance when racing.

■ BELOW LEFT
Race horses have to be supreme athletes – the greatest care and attention is lavished on them to keep them in peak condition. For a change of scene, these race horses are being exercised on the beach; another day it may be over grass or all-weather gallops, or just hacking along the roads.

the car park. There are yards where the owner makes a living out of training and racing either his own or other people's point-to-pointers, and this makes some of the races very competitive.

In most point-to-points the horses jump standard brush fences which may occasionally have a ditch in front, but some courses include banks and water as well. This reflects the sport's origins when riders simply raced each other from one point, usually a church steeple, to another point somewhere in the distance. The standard of riding varies considerably; anyone who has seen the differing standards on the hunting field will know what to expect in a point-to-point race. It

is for this reason that in point-to-pointing there are more falls than in professional steeplechasing or hurdling. The point-to-point course is usually an oval-shaped track marked out over an area of grassland. The fences are well spaced out around the course and, because they make use of natural terrain, some courses are much flatter than others. Competitors quickly discover which tracks suit their particular horse best.

■ ARAB RACING

This is a well-organized sport which involves flat races between Arab horses. The racing is fast and competitive, but the sport is still small enough to allow you to

EQUIPMENT NEEDED

To ride in any of these races you will need to wear an acceptable crash hat, lightweight breeches and boots, and a jumper reflecting your racing colours. In a point-to-point you are allowed to wear hunting kit. A body protector is compulsory for some types of racing, and advisable for all types. Goggles are a handy accessory, as a faceful of mud half-way around the course does little for your ability to steer your horse home. A weightcloth will also be needed. A horse can be raced in his ordinary saddle but most jockeys opt for a lightweight racing saddle.

■ BELOW
Despite its amateur status – which means the greatest reward is the fun to be had rather than the prize money to be won – the risks of point-to-pointing are probably greater than in either professional racing over jumps or flat racing. Falls are frequent.

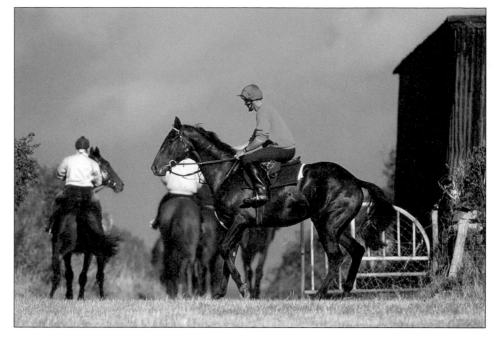

train and compete your own horse with success. Races vary in length, which means horses tend to specialize in either the short, faster races, or the longer, slightly slower ones.

■ PONY AND HORSE RACING

There are a few pony and horse races held in most countries which give ordinary riding horses and their jockeys a chance to demonstrate their speed – or lack of it! Most of these are unofficial, although a few countries do have a national body which registers competitors and organizes races for them.

■ PROFESSIONAL FLAT AND JUMP RACING

The international racing scene is divided into flat races, hurdle races, steeplechase races and timber or cross-country races. Flat racing is mainly to test pure speed – many of the races are short sprints where

speed rather than stamina counts most. Jump racing requires stamina, jumping ability and speed.

■ SKILLS REQUIRED

To race ride you need to be fit, have good balance and a feel for jumping at speed. These can all be practised at home if you intend racing just for fun. But if you want it to be more than that, the best place to learn is in a big racing yard, even if you only help out there at weekends. The more thoroughbred race horses you are able to ride, even if only on exercise, the better your fitness, position and balance will become.

Flat-race jockeys are generally quite short and also have to be lightweight. Jump jockeys, who ride with their stirrups a little longer, can be taller but need to keep their weight down so that they do not force the horse to carry more weight than he has been allocated.

■ ABOVE
If you fancy a career with horses, a job in a good racing yard can offer great variety, good experience and good friends.

■ BELOW LEFT
Dirt-track racing is common in America.

SUCCESS IS DOWN TO YOU

Competing with your horse can and should be an enjoyable experience for both of you. But if you take a look around you will see that this is not always the case – unhappy horses and riders abound at all kinds of events. Some horses are always going to be more talented than others; some will be more co-operative than others. But there will also be those who, either through lack of schooling or understanding, or simply through bad riding, do not fulfil their potential. Not everyone can afford the horse or pony of their dreams. Some think that this is exactly what they have found, only to be disappointed when things don't go to plan. A few horses, no matter how well ridden, simply lack the necessary ability or character to succeed at certain sports.

When things aren't going as well as you would like, remember too that very few talented riders are born – they have to be made. Riding has to be worked at; it doesn't just happen. You cannot be blamed for lacking a particular skill or aptitude for a specific sport – we are all made differently – but you can be blamed if you don't bother to work at your basic riding skills. So if you are going to ride, strive to ride well. GOOD LUCK!

Saddlery and Equipment

The Saddle

The saddle is one of the most important pieces of equipment
for the ridden horse, and, because of the skill and craftsmanship
involved in producing a saddle, it is usually the most expensive.
The earliest type of saddle, first developed thousands of years
ago, was nothing more than a simple blanket kept in place with
breastplate and girth. The modern saddle, however, is a
sophisticated piece of equipment. It has evolved as a result of the
demands of modern equestrianism, whether it be the Western
saddle designed to withstand the rigours of cowboy life; the
dressage saddle designed to give the rider an elegant yet
effective position; or the minuscule racing saddle.
The saddle's design and fit can have a tremendous effect
on both the horse's performance and the rider's position.
An ill-fitting saddle can cause the horse considerable discomfort
and even physical damage. When choosing a new saddle,
therefore, it is always advisable to seek professional help –
a trained saddler will be able to ensure that the saddle
fits the horse correctly.

Points of the Saddle

Virtually all saddles are built upon a solid framework called a tree. This framework was traditionally made from beech wood but is now available in laminated wood, and even fibreglass and plastic. It is the shape of the tree and the placing of the metal stirrup bars riveted to the tree which determine the size and shape of the saddle. The seat of the saddle is given shape by stretching a webbing and cotton fabric over the tree. Serge or a synthetic fabric is stretched to form the seat shape and a wool or synthetic stuffing provides the padding below.

cantle — seat — waist — pommel — skirt — D ring — saddle flap — stirrup leather keeper

▌ BELOW
Under the saddle flap. Most saddles have three girth straps. The first two are fixed to the web strap attached to the tree and the third is fixed independently.

point of tree — knee roll — saddle flap — buckle guard — sweat flap — girth straps (billets)

▌ ABOVE
The general purpose saddle is the standard model for the sport. The moderate features make it suitable for all riding disciplines at a non-professional level. Specialist saddles develop individual characteristics of the general purpose saddle according to the needs of the particular discipline.

fixed head

leaping head

The side-saddle is designed
to give an elegant riding
style and was at one time
the only type of saddle used
by ladies. The conventional
saddle is now the norm for
both sexes, but side-saddle
riding has made a comeback
and is often a feature of
shows and competitions.

front of swell

horn

seat jockey

seat

front of cantle

back of cantle

back
jockey

surcingle

girth

tie strap holder

breastcollar dees

cheyenne roll

skirt

■ RIGHT
The Western saddle is
designed to offer comfort,
practicality and security to
riders spending many hours
in the saddle. The ornate
leatherwork turns the saddle
into an elaborate piece of
riding equipment.

flank strap

hobble strap

fender

stirrup leather

stirrup

Riding and Competing Saddles

Saddles are available in a number of shapes and styles to suit the many equestrian disciplines at every level of competition from novice to professional.

The **leather general purpose (GP) saddle** is designed to be used across the board of riding activities. It is ideal for pleasure riding, hunting, novice cross-country and show jumping and basic dressage. A less expensive alternative to the leather saddle is the **synthetic general purpose saddle**, which is lighter in weight than the leather type, and easier to clean.

For most riders, the general purpose saddle is perfectly adequate for jumping. However, if you are riding at a competitive level and tackling larger fences, you may prefer the specialist design of the jumping saddle. The saddle flaps of the **Crosby close-contact jumping saddle** are more forward cut than those of the general purpose saddle. This enables you to keep your legs close to the saddle even when riding with a short stirrup length.

The **event saddle** is very similar in style to a general purpose saddle and can be used for all phases of horse trials, although some riders prefer to have an additional saddle for the dressage phase. Many famous riders have become involved in the design of saddles and the event saddle illustrated was developed by the international eventer, Mary King.

The **Albion Selecta** is a multi-purpose saddle which aims to combine the general purpose saddle with a dressage and a jumping saddle. It features easily removable knee pads which allow the saddle to be adapted for all riding disciplines from pleasure riding to jumping, dressage, cross-country and working hunter events.

The **polo saddle** has a relatively flat seat, extra-long sweat flaps and no knee and thigh rolls. It is designed specifically for the game of polo, during which the horse travels at speed and the rider needs to be able to move with ease to hit the ball.

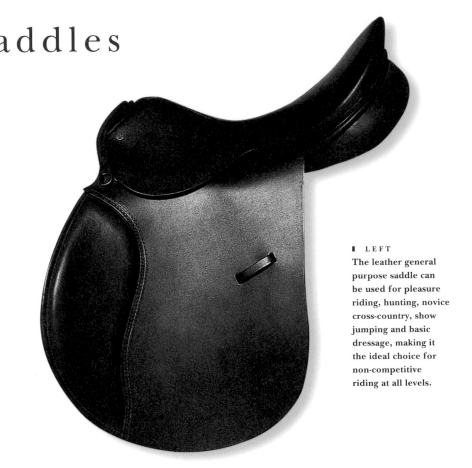

▮ LEFT
The leather general purpose saddle can be used for pleasure riding, hunting, novice cross-country, show jumping and basic dressage, making it the ideal choice for non-competitive riding at all levels.

▮ RIGHT
The synthetic general purpose saddle is a modern alternative to the leather saddle. While it can be put to all the same uses, the synthetic material means it is cheaper, lighter and easier to clean.

▌ ABOVE
The polo saddle has a flat seat, extended sweat flaps and no knee or thigh rolls, all of which allow the rider freedom of movement when striking the ball.

▌ BELOW LEFT
Event saddle. This is similar in style to the general purpose saddle and can be used for all phases of horse trials.

▌ RIGHT
The Crosby close-contact jumping saddle. The saddle flaps are more forward cut than those of the general purpose saddle. This allows the rider to carry his legs closer to the saddle, and makes his position more secure.

▌ LEFT
Albion Selecta saddle. Easily removable knee pads allow the saddle to be adapted to different riding disciplines.

Showing Saddles

There are a number of saddles designed specifically to improve the horse's performance in showing competitions.

The purpose of the **showing saddle** is primarily to enhance the appearance of the show horse rather than to increase the comfort of the rider. The saddle is straight cut to show off the horse's shoulder and is simple in design, since it is the horse rather than the tack that is being judged. The showing saddle is a specialized piece of equipment and not always very comfortable; many riders prefer to use a dressage saddle for showing classes.

The **dressage saddle**, designed for riding and schooling horses on the flat rather than over jumps, has longer and straighter flaps than the general purpose saddle. This allows you to carry your legs in a longer position and closer to the horse's body. To eliminate bulk under your legs, longer girth straps (billets) are fitted and used with a short dressage girth.

The **Saddlebred saddle** is for showing American Saddlebreds and other gaited horses. It features a cut-back pommel (called a "cow-mouth") and very wide saddle flaps, which enable the rider to sit much further back in the saddle than usual.

For showing classes in which the horse is required both to jump and to be ridden on the flat, the **working hunter saddle** is ideal. The seat is deeper than the showing saddle, and padded knee rolls give a more secure seat which is helpful when jumping.

The **side-saddle,** first developed for ladies in the fourteenth century, allows the rider to carry both legs on the near (left) side of the horse, with the left foot in a stirrup and the right leg hooked over the pommel. The flat seat has a suede or doeskin cover for extra grip. Although no longer in general use, shows often feature ladies' hunter classes for side-saddle riders.

▌ ABOVE
The flaps of the dressage saddle are longer and straighter than on the general purpose saddle, allowing the rider to keep his legs in an extended position and closer to the horse's body.

▌ ABOVE
The shape of the side-saddle allows the rider to adopt a more elegant position, with both legs on the near (left) side of the horse.

■ ABOVE
This showing saddle in
split hide, designed by
producer and rider Lynn
Rusell, is specially shaped
to suit larger show horses
such as cobs and hunters.

■ RIGHT
The design of the
Saddlebred saddle enables
the rider to sit far back in
the saddle. In a show this
riding style will help to
enhance the well-shaped
conformation of the
Saddlebred horse.

■ RIGHT
The working hunter saddle
is a compromise between a
showing saddle and a
jumping saddle.

Trail-riding and Working Saddles

Saddles which are to be ridden over long periods of time need to have an element of comfort incorporated into the design.

The **endurance saddle**, as its name suggests, is designed for long-distance rides. The seat has extra padding and the saddle panels have extra width, thereby spreading the rider's weight over a greater area and reducing the risk of localized pressure points on the horse's back. Additional D rings are fitted to the saddle so that equipment, such as lead ropes and sponges, can easily be accommodated.

The **Australian stock saddle** is a utilitarian saddle designed for the comfort of both horse and rider during the hours spent driving cattle. The weight distribution properties mean that modified versions of this saddle can also be used for endurance or trail-riding.

The **Western reining saddle** is higher in front than the standard Western saddle, preventing the rider from being thrown forward when the horse performs the characteristic sliding stop. **Western pleasure saddles** are lighter in weight than working saddles and have only one cinch attachment. Comfortable and secure, these saddles are ideal for long-distance or trail-riding.

The **parade saddle** is an ornate working saddle featuring highly intricate metal and leatherwork. These decorative saddles are specially designed for use in carnival or rodeo parades.

The **trooper** or **Cavalry saddle** is built around a steel and wood tree and is the traditional choice of the armed forces because of its strength and durability.

The **military fan saddle** is designed for working horses, such as those used by the mounted police. The saddle tree distributes the rider's weight evenly for comfort during long periods of work, often when the horse is stationary.

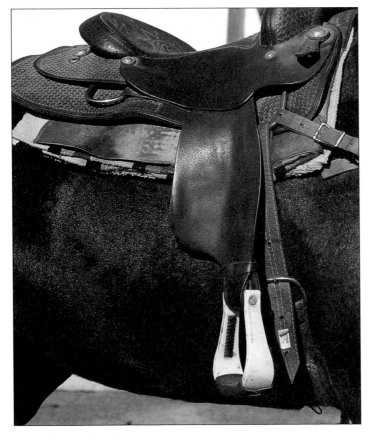

▌ ABOVE
The Australian stock saddle is built for comfort and durability. The rider may spend several hours driving cattle on the plains, and the even spread of his weight in the saddle will become a significant factor for both horse and rider.

▌ ABOVE
The high front of the Western reining saddle prevents the rider being thrown forward and out of the saddle when the horse performs the dramatic reining halt, which is a feature of this riding style.

■ ABOVE
The deep seat makes the
Western pleasure saddle
comfortable and secure
for long-distance riding.

■ ABOVE
Endurance saddle. This is designed specifically for
long-distance riding, with the comfort of both horse
and rider in mind.

■ RIGHT
The elaborate parade saddle
features intricately detailed
leatherwork, and makes a
splendid sight at carnivals
and rodeos.

■ RIGHT
The trooper (Cavalry)
saddle is constructed around
a steel and wood tree. It is
the traditional saddle of the
armed forces because of its
durability.

■ RIGHT
The military fan saddle is
designed to distribute the
rider's weight evenly in the
saddle. This becomes an
important feature when the
ridden horse is motionless
for long periods of time.

Racing Saddles

Horse racing, and flat racing in particular, requires a highly unusual riding style that makes specific demands on the saddle.

The saddle used in flat racing is crouched over rather than sat on, and for this reason it has a flat seat and is fitted with very short stirrup leathers. **Leather racing saddles** are necessarily light; they come in a variety of weights, starting from as little as 325g/11oz. Saddles for National Hunt racing (racing over jumps) are heavier and larger in size than the saddles used for flat racing. **Synthetic racing saddles** are becoming increasingly popular for dirt and all-weather track racing, where the sand used for the track's surface can cause damage to leather tack.

As the name implies, **race exercise saddles** are used when exercising racehorses rather than when actually racing them. Because the question of weight does not apply, the exercise saddle is usually heavier and larger than the racing saddle, and comes with a full or half-tree in leather or synthetic material. The full-tree saddle illustrated features "todsloan" saddle flaps, named after the American jockey James Todhunter Sloan, who pioneered the style of riding with shorter stirrup leathers.

▌ LEFT
The flat seat and short stirrup leathers are characteristic of saddles used for flat racing. The jockey rides crouched over the saddle with his head tucked well in for a more streamlined position.

▌ RIGHT
Race exercise saddles are larger and heavier than racing saddles. Exercising the horse requires a more functional saddle than the lightweight type worn for the race.

Learner Saddles

For beginners taking their first lessons in equestrianism, a specially adapted saddle can be a huge advantage, not least because of the additional safety features which these saddles incorporate.

The **pony saddle**, designed for young children and smaller ponies, has removable panels to vary the amount by which the child is "wedged in", and a hand support for extra grip. The **felt-pad saddle** also includes the safety handle feature, and this can be very helpful for nervous children. The simple design consists of a soft felt pad with a leather covering and built-in webbing girth and stirrup bars.

The **Riding for the Disabled Association (RDA) saddle** will enable physically or mentally disabled children and adults to ride in safety. The loop fitted to the front of the saddle gives the rider something to hold on to without needing to grip and pull at the reins too tightly, thereby damaging the horse's mouth.

▌ LEFT
The pony saddle makes an ideal choice for small children who are just learning to ride.

▌ LEFT
The felt-pad saddle is a beginner's saddle for children. It consists of a soft felt pad with a leather covering and built-in webbing girth and stirrup bars.

▌ RIGHT
The design of the RDA saddle enables the physically and mentally disabled to ride with safety and confidence.

Ceremonial Saddles

The Royal Mews at Buckingham Palace in London houses a large collection of saddles, bridles and harnesses belonging to the Royal Family. Much of the saddlery and equipment in this beautiful collection is of a unique historical interest.

Queen Elizabeth II's love of horses is well known and many of the gifts she receives are related to the subject of riding. The Portuguese ceremonial bridle was presented with a saddle to HM the Queen by the Portuguese government on a state visit to Portugal in 1957. The bridle has solid silver bit and fittings.

The Alamo saddle was presented as a gift to the Queen from the actor John Wayne, who directed and starred in the film *The Alamo*. The saddle had been used by the actor during the making of the film. The design of the saddle is highly ornate and features tooled fenders and decorated *tapaderos* (toe covers).

Although ladies traditionally sat to the near (left) side when riding side-saddle, it was not uncommon for young ladies learning to ride to use a saddle designed for riding on the off (right) side, as demonstrated by a pair of side-saddles belonging to Princess Mary.

Queen Victoria's side-saddle was used by the monarch in the latter half of the nineteenth century. To allow for a less restrictive riding style, the design features a pommel on either side of the saddle, so that the saddle can be ridden on either the near or the off side.

A hunting saddle used by the Prince Consort, HRH Prince Albert, during the mid-nineteenth century, is elaborately detailed in gold thread and features a holster for carrying a pair of pistols, which in those days would have been carried for the prince's personal protection.

The Kaiser's bridle, a gift from Wilhelm II of Germany, has not been used since the diamond jubilee of Queen Victoria in 1898. The lavish design features gilt trim on the bits, solid gold buckles and gold thread embellishment on the bridoon rein.

The bridle worn by Queen Elizabeth II's horse, Burmese, at the annual military ceremony, Trooping the Colour, is based on the traditional military bridle and combines a headcollar with a bridle. The detailing on the bridle is gilt and the reins are decorated with gold thread. The elaborate saddlery traditionally worn for Trooping the Colour includes gilded stirrups on the Queen's side-saddle.

▌ LEFT
The ceremonial bridle presented to Queen Elizabeth II by the Portuguese government.

▌ RIGHT
The elaborate Alamo saddle, a gift to Queen Elizabeth II from the American actor, John Wayne.

▌ RIGHT
The Kaiser's bridle was presented to Queen Victoria by Wilhelm II of Germany.

■ LEFT
A highly decorative
gilded stirrup from the
side-saddle ridden by
Queen Elizabeth II at
Trooping the Colour.

■ LEFT
A pair of side-saddles,
originally belonging
to Princess Mary, show
how the side-saddle
could be designed to
let the rider sit on the
off side.

■ BELOW

The military-style bridle worn
by Queen Elizabeth II's horse at
Trooping the Colour.

■ LEFT
A hunting saddle used
by the Prince Consort,
HRH Prince Albert, in
the nineteenth century.

■ BELOW
Queen Victoria's side-
saddle, with the double
pommel design, allowed
the Queen to ride off
either side of the saddle.

■ BELOW
Traditional detailing on a bridle
worn by Queen Elizabeth II's horse
at ceremonial parades.

Girths, Cinches and Surcingles

GIRTHS

Girths are used to keep the saddle in place on the horse's back. They are available in leather and synthetic materials: although expensive, leather girths are very durable if well cared for, while cotton and synthetic girths are cheaper and generally less hardwearing.

The **Atherstone girth** is padded and has a contoured shape to prevent it rubbing the horse's elbow. It is an ideal choice for general or competition use. The Atherstone is also available with strong elastic inserts at one or both ends, which allows the girth to stretch as the horse expands his ribcage when galloping. Take care not to overtighten an elasticated girth as it can still cause the horse discomfort, even though it stretches.

The **Balding girth** is made of a single piece of leather split into three. It was originally developed for polo ponies: the special shape helps to minimize chafing and girth galls.

The **three-fold leather girth** has become less common since the arrival of synthetic alternatives. It comprises a single piece of leather which is folded around a piece of oiled fabric. The girth is fitted with the open side away from the horse's elbow to prevent pinching. The oiled fabric helps to keep the leather supple.

The **Humane girth** has girth tabs which slide through special loops allowing the girth to move with the horse. The **Cottage Craft girth** is an inexpensive foam-padded, cotton girth which is both comfortable for the horse and easy to wash. **Cord girths**, made from thick cotton cords, have an open design which helps to reduce sweating while the cord strands themselves help to keep the girth in place.

Neoprene girths are available for general purpose and dressage saddles. The fabric (commonly used for wet suits) does not absorb sweat and helps to reduce rubbing. **Narrow-webbing girths** are often used on show horses and ponies, as they

■ **ABOVE**
leather Atherstone girth

■ **LEFT**
Atherstone girth with elastic inserts

■ **RIGHT** three-fold leather girth

■ **ABOVE** Balding girth

■ **RIGHT** Humane girth

■ **RIGHT** Cottage Craft girth

■ **RIGHT** neoprene girth

■ **RIGHT** Wintec girth

■ **RIGHT** dressage girth

■ **RIGHT** Cottage Craft dressage girth

are less obtrusive than traditional girths. They consist of two narrow strips of webbing and a small section of textured rubber to prevent the girth slipping.

The **dressage girth**, also known as the **Lonsdale girth**, is shorter than a traditional girth as it is designed for use with the dressage saddle, which has longer girth tabs (billets).

The **Fitzwilliam girth**, used with a side-saddle, features an extra balance strap to prevent the saddle from slipping. The **leather stud-guard girth** is useful when competing in show-jumping events or horse trials. It is designed to prevent horses fitted with studs from injuring themselves when they snatch up their forelegs over a fence.

Racing girths are made from elastic or from webbing with elastic inserts, allowing the horse the freedom to expand his ribcage at a full gallop.

Accessories can be fitted to the girth as aids to the horse's comfort. The **fleece girth sleeve (cover)**, a soft fleece or sheepskin sleeve which slides over the girth, helps to keep the girth clean and minimize rubbing and galling. **A girth extender** is a short leather strap used to lengthen the girth. **Girth (buckle) guards** are fitted over the **girth tabs (billets)** on the saddle to prevent the girth buckles from rubbing and damaging the saddle flap. A **stud guard** is a pad of leather which is fitted to a standard girth to protect the horse when jumping, in the same way as a

■ **RIGHT**
narrow-webbing show girth

■ **RIGHT**
leather stud-guard girth

■ **ABOVE**
A racing saddle fitted with a surcingle.

■ **RIGHT**
Western fleece cinch

■ **RIGHT**
Western strand (string) cinch

■ **RIGHT**
neoprene cinch

■ **LEFT**
A surcingle fitted
over the saddle
for cross-country
riding.

■ **RIGHT**
all-elastic racing girth

■ **RIGHT**
racing girths

■ **RIGHT**
Fitzwilliam side
saddle girth

stud-guard girth. The **sheepskin seat saver**
is fitted over the saddle to make it more
comfortable to ride for long periods of
time – ideal for endurance or trail-riding.

■ **LEFT**
girth extender

CINCHES AND SURCINGLES
Western saddles are held in place with
cinches rather than girths. Cinches are
attached to the saddle by a large buckle
at each end and are available in a range
of materials: **neoprene** and **padded fleece
cinches** help to reduce chafing, while
strand cinches, made from cord or woven
horse hair, prevent the horse sweating.

■ **LEFT**
all-elastic racing surcingle

■ **LEFT**
tubular racing surcingle

Racing surcingles, in elastic or webbing
with an elastic insert, go over the top of
the saddle. They are used in addition to
a racing girth to provide extra security
in the event of the racing girth breaking.
For the same reason, the **overgirth** or
surcingle is fitted over the saddle for the
cross-country phase of horse trials.

■ **ABOVE**
fleece girth sleeve
(cover)

■ **LEFT**
leather stud guard

■ **RIGHT**
sheepskin seat
saver

■ **RIGHT**
girth (buckle) guard

Breastplates and Cruppers

BREASTPLATES AND BREASTGIRTHS

The breastplate and breastgirth are designed to stop the saddle slipping back, and are especially useful for high impact disciplines such as galloping or jumping.

The sturdy **hunting breastplate** is made from leather or leather and elastic. Two straps are attached to the D rings on the saddle, while a strap passes through the horse's front legs and loops around the girth. A ring at the chest allows a running martingale to be fitted if necessary. The **racing breastplate** is a lightweight version of the hunting type, while the **Western breastplate**, made of tooled leather, is heavier than the English type and is used with the Western saddle only.

The breastgirth is a simple strap which is passed around the horse's chest and attached to the girth on either side of the saddle. The **leather breastgirth** is commonly used on polo ponies, while the **elasticated** or **Aintree breastgirth** allows for the movement of the horse during strenuous exercise, in particular when jumping across country. The **continental breastgirth** is similar to a normal breastgirth but is fitted to the saddle D rings rather than to the girth.

A **sheepskin sleeve (cover)** can be fitted over the chest strap of a breastgirth to prevent it from rubbing the horse.

The **neck strap** is a useful attachment for novice riders or for those training young horses. A strong leather strap, such as a stirrup leather, is fitted around the base of the horse's neck. It is useful for jumping as it gives the rider something to hold on to without pulling at the reins and risking damage to the horse's mouth.

CRUPPERS

A crupper can be fitted to prevent the saddle from slipping forward and is generally only needed on ponies. A strap is passed under the tail and attached to the back of the saddle.

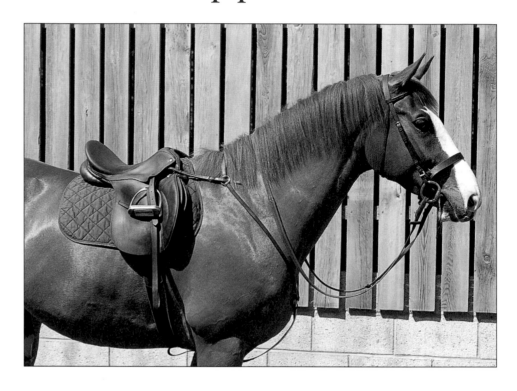

▌ ABOVE
The hunting breastplate is used to prevent the saddle slipping back when the horse is galloping and jumping.

▌ LEFT
The racing breastplate is a lightweight alternative to the hunting type, but it is designed to serve the same purpose.

▌ BELOW
Western breastplate

Polo ponies are often fitted with leather breastgirths.

The modern elasticated breastgirth allows the horse greater freedom of movement.

The continental breastgirth is attached to the D rings of the saddle, rather than to the girth.

A sheepskin sleeve (cover) can be fitted over a breastgirth to prevent the strap rubbing the horse.

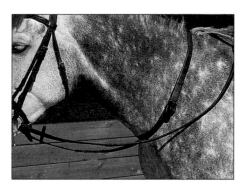

A neck strap is a useful attachment for the rider to hold on to when jumping or galloping, and can help make a nervous rider feel more secure.

HOW TO ATTACH A BREASTGIRTH

Attach the strap from the breastgirth to the girth just under the buckle, above the numnah strap to prevent it slipping down. Pass it under the first strap and round the second strap.

❚ ABOVE
A crupper is often worn by ponies and smaller horses to prevent the saddle slipping forwards.

FITTING A LEATHER BREASTPLATE

1 When the breastplate is in place, check that the fit allows room for a palm's width at the chest.

2 You should be able to fit four fingers under the strap which passes over the neck.

3 The breastplate keeper should be pushed tightly up to the girth so that there is no loop in which the horse could catch his foot.

Stirrups

Stirrups, also known as irons, are available in a variety of styles but are almost always made from stainless steel, which is extremely strong. For safety, the stirrup should be wide enough to allow about 1–1.5cm/½in on either side of the rider's foot to avoid the foot getting caught in the stirrup in the event of a fall.

The most common English stirrup is the **Prussian side open bottom**, also known as a **hunting iron**. Very useful for dressage and jumping are heavier models such as the **fillis stirrup**, which give the rider more balance. The **off-set fillis** is a popular choice for jumping. The eye of the stirrup is set to the inside, which encourages the knee and thigh to be pressed into the saddle for extra grip.

Alternatives to steel become necessary when weight is important. Contemporary choices include the **carbon-fibre stirrup** which is both light and strong, and features graphite treads for extra grip. **Polymer** and **Flexi-ride stirrups** are designed specifically for endurance and trail-riding. The rubberized material absorbs concussion, enhancing the rider's comfort when riding for long periods of time. **Cradle-bottom racing stirrups**, which are designed purely for racing, are made from lightweight aluminium.

Western stirrups consist of a wooden or Ralide frame covered in leather; a more decorative design is made from inlaid wood. For parades, a toe cover called a *tapadero* can be fitted to the stirrup. The **side-saddle stirrup** features a round eye through which the stirrup leather passes, allowing greater flexibility of movement for the rider's leg.

Rubber treads can be fitted into stirrups to provide extra grip for muddy boots or when riding in wet weather. The treads lie flat inside the stirrup, although angled or wedged treads are also available for dressage and jumping.

■ ABOVE
Prussian side open bottom stirrups are the traditional English riding stirrups.

■ ABOVE
Fillis stirrups are solid and heavy, and are used to help the rider balance in the saddle.

■ ABOVE
The eye of the off-set fillis stirrup is set to the inside, pressing the knee towards the saddle.

■ ABOVE
Cradle-bottom racing stirrups are made from lightweight aluminium.

▌ A B O V E
leather-covered Western stirrup

▌ A B O V E
inlaid wood Western stirrups

▌ A B O V E
Toe covers can be fitted to ordinary stirrups. They are commonly used in endurance and trail-riding events and will prevent the rider's foot sliding through and getting stuck in the stirrup.

▌ A B O V E
Polymer and Flexi-ride stirrups are designed to increase foot comfort when endurance or trail-riding.

▌ L E F T
Carbon-fibre stirrups are lightweight but extremely strong.

▌ A B O V E
The round eye of the side-saddle stirrup allows the lower leg greater flexibility.

 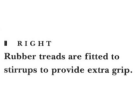

▌ R I G H T
Rubber treads are fitted to stirrups to provide extra grip.

SAFETY STIRRUPS

In the event of a fall, the rider risks serious injury if his foot becomes caught in the stirrup. Safety stirrups are designed to prevent this by allowing the foot to be quickly released from the stirrup.

The **Australian Simplex** or **bent-leg stirrup** has a bent outer leg on the iron, encouraging the early release of the foot. The **Peacock safety stirrup** has a strong band of rubber fitted to the outside of the stirrup, which is pulled off if the foot gets caught. The **precision riding stirrup** is a new design which self-aligns to the position of your foot to increase comfort and security.

STIRRUP LEATHERS

English leathers are traditionally made from top-quality English dressed hides. **Extending leathers** have a small hook attachment which allows the stirrup to be lengthened for mounting. **Racing leathers** are lightweight and made from leather and nylon web. **Jumping** or **double-sided stirrup leathers** are reinforced with nylon to strengthen the leather and prevent it from stretching. The **side-saddle leather** has a hook adjustment to alter the length at the base, near the stirrup. **Dressage leathers** are a smart single thickness of leather with a buckle at the base, allowing the legs to be carried closer to the horse.

ABOVE
Australian Simplex safety or bent-leg stirrups. The bent leg of the iron is fitted to the outside.

ABOVE
Peacock safety stirrups. In the event of a fall, the rubber is pulled off to release the foot.

ABOVE
Precision riding stirrups self-align for safety and comfort.

RIGHT
Jumping stirrup leathers, also known as double-sided stirrup leathers, are reinforced with nylon for extra strength under extreme pressure.

LEFT
Top to bottom:
synthetic stirrup leathers, racing stirrup leathers, English stirrup leathers

RIGHT
Side-saddle stirrup leathers.

Numnahs and Saddle Cloths

Numnahs and saddle cloths are fitted under the saddle to stop the saddle rubbing the horse's back and to absorb the concussion caused by movement. They help to keep the underside of the saddle clean by absorbing sweat and grease from the horse's body. Numnahs are saddle-shaped whereas a saddle pad or cloth is normally square or rectangular. A numnah or saddle cloth should never be used to make an ill-fitting saddle fit, and if not kept scrupulously clean they can rub the horse's back, leading to sores and even skin diseases.

Lightweight **quilted cotton numnahs** are ideal for protecting the saddle from sweat. They are held in place with straps which go round the girth and girth tabs. Available to fit general purpose and dressage saddles, they come in a variety of colours, although white is traditional for competitions.

The materials from which numnahs and saddle pads are made are chosen for their comfort-inducing properties. The **wither pad** is a small, oval pad in fleece or sheepskin which is placed between the wither and the saddle. The **pure new wool numnah**, fully washable with a cotton backing, is designed to relieve and prevent pressure sores. The **sheepskin numnah** absorbs impact and allows heat from the horse's body to pass through it. The **non-slip numnah**, made from neoprene, is designed to absorb concussion and to prevent the saddle from slipping.

Modern choices often include unique features which make them more attractive to the rider. The **Poly pad** is a thick, quilted pad which provides extra protection for the horse's back. Unlike many other numnahs or saddle cloths, it stays in place without the need for straps or loops. The **Coolback numnah** or saddle cloth features a special lining which draws sweat away from the horse's back. The **Proteq saddle pad** is a unique concept,

▌ LEFT
A saddle cloth or numnah for a general purpose saddle.

▌ BELOW
A Poly pad is a thick quilted pad which provides extra protection from the saddle. It is also available as a wither pad.

A quilted cotton saddle cloth and numnah for a dressage saddle.

▌ LEFT
Navajo fleece pad

▌ BELOW
pure wool numnah (*left*) and sheepskin numnah

▌ ABOVE
fleece wither pad

▌ BELOW
The Navajo saddle blanket is often used with Western or polo saddles.

incorporating thousands of tiny poly-styrene beads. When the saddle is in place the air is pumped out of the pad, so that the beads mould to the configuration between the saddle and the horse's back.

Western and polo saddles are traditionally fitted with the **Navajo saddle blanket**. The **Navajo fleece pad** is a Western blanket pad with a fleece lining.

The **racing weight cloth** is fitted between the numnah and the saddle. It features a series of pockets in which lead weights can be placed to ensure that the rider is carrying the correct weight for the race. Weight cloths are also used in the speed and endurance phases of horse trials.

New products designed to fit between the saddle and the numnah now make use of highly effective synthetic materials. These include the **Pro-lite relief pad**, which incorporates a visco-elastic gel and latex rubber to absorb impact, and the **gel pad**, which contains thermoplastic elastomer gel for shock absorbency. Flat or moulded **shock-absorbing pads** can be placed under the saddle to help distribute the rider's weight more evenly over the horse's back.

■ ABOVE
Aerborn Coolback numnah. This saddle cloth has a special lining which absorbs sweat from the horse's back.

■ ABOVE
The gel pad contains a thermoplastic elastomer gel to aid shock absorbency.

■ ABOVE
Placed under the saddle, the moulded shock-absorbing pad helps to distribute the rider's weight evenly.

■ ABOVE
The flat shock-absorbing pad is used to help distribute the rider's weight along the horse's back.

■ LEFT
The Proteq saddle pad incorporates thousands of tiny polystyrene beads, which help mould the pad to the horse's back.

■ ABOVE
The Pro-lite relief pad uses visco-elastic gel and latex rubber to absorb impact and concussion.

■ ABOVE
Lead weights can be added to the pockets of the weight cloth to ensure the jockey carries the correct weight for the race.

Saddle Bags

Saddle bags, pouches or panniers are lightweight bags which can be fitted to the saddle, positioned behind it and hung over either side of the horse. They are functional accessories used to carry the provisions needed on rides of several hours or more.

The **trail pad**, a fleece pad incorporated into a canvas cloth with pockets, is ideal for endurance and long-distance pleasure rides. The fleece numnah sits comfortably on the horse, while the canvas overlay is suitably sturdy.

As its name suggests, the **hunting canteen** was traditionally used to carry the refreshments necessary for a day's fox hunting. The smart leather pouch is just the right size to hold a flask of warming liquor.

Argentinian saddle bags are handwoven from wool in traditional patterns. They are used by *gauchos* to carry food when riding for days at a time out on the *pampas*.

I BELOW
trail pad

I LEFT
hunting canteen

I ABOVE
Argentinian saddle bag

419

Saddle Care

A good saddle is a costly piece of equipment and it is important to look after it properly, not only because it is expensive to repair but because a damaged saddle may harm your horse's back.

HOW TO CARRY A SADDLE

LEFT
The saddle should be carried in either of the two ways shown: over the forearm with the back of the saddle nearest the elbow (*far left*), or against the side of the body with the hand holding on to the pommel (*left*).

HOW TO STORE A SADDLE

Once you have removed the saddle from the horse, it can be placed over a fence or saddle rack before being returned to the tack room. (If you leave the saddle over a stable door, the horse will most probably nudge it off.)

You can also put the saddle on the ground, pommel down and with the seat facing the wall. Place the girth between the pommel and the ground to protect the leather.

Saddles are best kept on saddle racks in a clean and dry tack room – damp conditions will damage the leather. Do not leave sweaty numnahs or girths attached to the saddle; remove and clean them before putting them away separately.

HOW TO CLEAN A SADDLE

1 Place the saddle on a stand. Remove the stirrup leathers, girth and numnah. With warm water and a dampened sponge, work all over the saddle removing any mud, sweat and general dirt. Take care not to let the leather get too wet.

2 Whilst cleaning, check the saddle for wear and tear. Pay particular attention to the stitching, especially where the girth tabs (billets) are joined to the saddle.

3 Don't forget to clean the underside of the saddle as this can get sweaty even if a numnah or saddle cloth has been used.

4 Allow the leather to dry slightly before applying the saddle soap. Use a fresh sponge and work the saddle soap into the leather with a circular rubbing motion. Cover the entire surface of the saddle, including under the saddle flaps.

SADDLING UP

1 Place a numnah or saddle cloth on the horse's back, making sure it is positioned sufficiently high up the horse's withers.

2 Lift the saddle over the horse's back and carefully lower it into position on top of the numnah or saddle cloth. Ensure both saddle flaps are lying flat against the horse's sides.

3 Pull the numnah or saddle cloth up into the gullet of the saddle so that it is clear of the horse's withers.

4 Numnahs usually have straps to anchor them to the saddle and stop them from slipping. Attach the top straps to the saddle's girth tabs (billets) through which the girth is fitted above the girth guard before doing up the girth.

5 Buckle the girth to the off side (right) of the saddle first and pass it through the bottom strap on the numnah. Move back to the near side (left) of the horse, reach underneath him and take hold of the girth.

6 Pass the girth through the retaining strap on the numnah before buckling to the saddle girth tabs on the near side.

5 Remove dirt and grease from the stirrup leathers with a sponge. Apply the saddle soap and check the stitching for wear. Check that the leathers have not stretched: because we mount from the near side, one leather will become longer than the other if they are not switched regularly.

7 Tighten up the girth gradually (it should be equal on both sides) until there is just room to fit the flat of your hand between the girth and the horse's side. Picking up the horse's feet, one at a time, and pulling them forward will also help you to judge if the girth is comfortable for the horse.

8 Once the girth has been tightened, slide the buckle guard down over the girth buckles to prevent them from rubbing against and damaging the saddle flaps. Slide your hand round the horse's belly under the girth to ensure that there are no wrinkles in the horse's skin.

Bridles and Bits

Along with the saddle, the bridle and bit are the most important pieces of equipment for the ridden horse. Combined with the rider's legs, voice and body position, the bridle and bit provide that important line of communication which allows you to control the horse.

Bridles are traditionally made of leather. However, synthetic bridles, which come in a choice of vivid colours, are becoming much more popular, especially in the sports of flat racing and endurance riding.

The variety of bits available can be bewildering, and choosing the right bit for a horse is almost a science in itself. To simplify matters, bits are divided into five groups which are categorized by their action, based on the area of the horse's head to which pressure is applied. The five groups are: snaffles, doubles, pelhams, gag snaffles and bitless bridles. It is important to make an accurate judgment over your choice of bit: a bit that is too weak will result in the rider having no control over the horse, while one that is too severe will encourage the horse to fight against it.

Snaffle Bridle

The snaffle bridle is a simple, basic bridle which is suitable for most types of riding. In particular it is the appropriate bridle for horses in the early stages of training. The noseband is not essential and need not be fitted; however, many horses, especially those with longer heads, tend to look better with the noseband in place. By changing the bit or fitting a different type of noseband, the action of the bridle can be made stronger, so that the rider has greater control over the horse and the way in which he carries his head.

headpiece (crownpiece)

browband

throatlatch

cheekpieces

noseband

eggbutt snaffle

reins

▮ RIGHT
The snaffle bridle is the standard type of bridle used with all single bits.

Double Bridle

The double bridle is basically the same in design as the snaffle bridle, although the addition of an extra bridoon sliphead means that two bits can be used simultaneously with two sets of reins. Unlike the snaffle bridle, which can be used with a variety of nosebands, the double bridle should only be fitted with a basic cavesson noseband so that the action of the curb is not interfered with.

headpiece
(crownpiece)

browband

bridoon sliphead

throatlatch

cheekpieces

noseband

▌ RIGHT
The double bridle, in expert hands, allows precise control over the horse's way of going. It is always used with two bits and two sets of reins.

loose-ring bridoon bit

sliding cheek curb bit

bridoon rein

curb chain

curb rein

Western Bridle

The traditional Western bridle is fastened with narrow leather thongs, which enabled the cowboy to carry out running repairs on any items of broken tack himself when he was miles from the nearest saddler. Western bridles are referred to as either "one-ear" or "split-ear". The headpiece (crownpiece) of a split-ear bridle is made from a single piece of leather which has slits cut into it to fit over each ear. This is to prevent the bridle from being pulled off accidentally. The one-ear bridle incorporates a definite loop which fits over one of the horse's ear. The reins of the Western bridle are not joined at the end. This is to avoid the risk of the horse getting a foot caught in the reins if they trail on the ground.

throatlatch

headpiece (crownpiece)

browband

cheekpieces

Western curb bit

reins

RIGHT
split-ear Western bridle

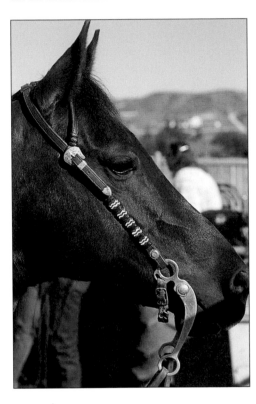

BELOW
one-ear Western bridle

Endurance 2-in-1 Bridle

The endurance bridle is a combination of a headcollar (crownpiece) and a standard bridle. The cheekpieces and reins can be quickly unclipped to leave just the headcollar in place. The headcollar can also be ridden as a Scawbrig, a type of bitless bridle, by attaching the reins to the noseband. The endurance bridle (also known as the combination bridle) has proved popular with endurance riders because of its practical design: the bit can be removed quickly to give the horse a drink during competition, while the reins very usefully double as a lead rope.

RIGHT
endurance 2-in-1 bridle

THE MAIN POINTS OF CONTROL

Bits, bitless bridles and certain types of nosebands will all act on specific parts of the horse's head.

The poll – the headpiece (crownpiece) of the bridle applies pressure here when a gag or curb bit is used.

The nose – bitless bridles and specific types of nosebands affect the nose.

The mouthcorners – snaffle bits bring pressure on the corners of the horse's mouth and lips.

Side of the face – bits with full cheeks, D rings or large racing rings affect this area.

Curb groove – the curb chain fitted with a pelham or Weymouth bit affects the curb groove.

Roof of the mouth – bits with ported mouthpieces affect this area.

Tongue – all bits apply pressure to the tongue.

Bars – all bits affect the bars, a sensitive part of the horse's mouth between the incisors and premolar teeth.

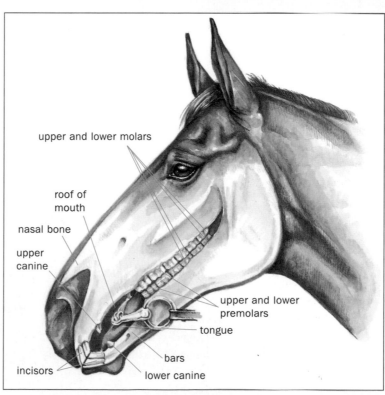

Snaffle Bits

The snaffle bit is the largest of the five bit groups. It contains a wide variety of different types of bit which vary in strength of action from very mild to severe. Snaffle bits act on the tongue, the bars and the corners of the mouth; some also act on the roof of the mouth. Snaffle bits encourage the horse to raise his head and bring it back towards your hands for greater control. In its basic form the snaffle is the most commonly used bit for horses in the early stages of schooling. Any well-schooled horse should go happily in a snaffle bit.

While all snaffles have the same basic action, different cheek- and mouthpieces will affect the action and severity of the bit. The single-jointed **eggbutt snaffle** has rounded edges where the rings join the mouthpiece to prevent the lips being pinched. The fixed cheek rings keep the bit relatively still in the horse's mouth.

The rings of the **loose-ring snaffle** allow the bit to move more freely in the horse's mouth, which some horses prefer. This type should be fitted slightly wider than the eggbutt snaffle, and can have rubber bit guards fitted over the rings to prevent it from pinching the horse's lips.

The **full-cheek snaffle** has extended cheekpieces which prevent the bit from sliding through the horse's mouth, and help to steer the horse by bringing pressure against the side of his face. This type of bit should be fitted with leather **fulmer keepers** attached to the cheekpieces of the bridle, to hold the bit still in the mouth and to prevent a cheekpiece from accidentally getting stuck up the horse's nostril. The **fulmer snaffle** is similar to the full-cheek but has loose, rather than fixed, bit rings.

The **half-spoon cheek snaffle** has spoon-shaped cheeks which extend downwards to put pressure on the outside of the lower jaw, helping with steering. The **D-ring snaffle** is often used on racehorses in preference to a fulmer

❙ ABOVE
D-ring snaffle

❙ ABOVE
full cheek snaffle

❙ ABOVE
eggbutt snaffle

❙ ABOVE
half-spoon cheek snaffle

❙ ABOVE
loose-ring snaffle

❙ ABOVE
Filet Baucher snaffle

snaffle. Like the fulmer, the shape of the cheekpieces prevents the bit being pulled through the mouth. By bringing pressure on the sides of the horse's face it can also help to steer the horse.

The **Filet Baucher** or **hanging cheek snaffle** has separate rings to which the cheekpieces of the bridle are attached so that the bit is suspended in the horse's mouth. Unlike other snaffles, the cheekpieces will exert some pressure on the horse's poll.

❙ ABOVE
fulmer keepers

TYPES OF MOUTHPIECE

Snaffle bits come with a variety of mouthpieces which vary in the severity of their action.

The **straight bar mouthpiece** usually comes with non-riding bits such as stallion-showing bits or in-hand bits, and acts primarily on the tongue and lips.

The **mullen mouth** is a mild, simple unjointed mouthpiece, more curved than the straight bar. The mullen mouth rests on the bars of the mouth, exerting less pressure on the corners of the mouth and a more uniform pressure on the tongue.

When pressure is applied to the reins, the **single-jointed bit** squeezes the corners of the mouth in a nutcracker action, as well as applying pressure to the bars, the tongue and the roof of the mouth. Single-jointed snaffles have either a narrow, solid mouthpiece or fatter hollow mouthpiece (this latter type is known as the German snaffle). As a general rule of thumb, the fatter the mouthpiece, the milder its action.

Double-jointed mouthpieces feature a central link, which comes in different shapes and sizes. The nutcracker action is less severe than with single-jointed bits. However, these bits still act on the bars and corners of the horse's mouth.

The **French link** has a kidney-shaped link in the middle of the mouthpiece. It increases the flexibility of the bit, stops the horse from leaning and encourages him to soften his mouth.

The **Dr Bristol** incorporates a flat plate link which is much more severe in action than the French link. It is used in vigorous competition events such as jumping or cross-country. The plate applies strong pressure on the horse's tongue unless the head is carried in the position needed for the rider to control him. No small amount of pain will be inflicted on the horse if the bit is misused and it should only be used by experienced riders on particularly boisterous horses.

▮ ABOVE
hollow mouth

▮ ABOVE
Dr Bristol

▮ ABOVE
KK training

▮ ABOVE
KK correction

▮ ABOVE
French link

▮ ABOVE
copper roller

▮ ABOVE
Waterford

▮ ABOVE
magenis

▮ ABOVE
cherry roller

▮ ABOVE
twisted mouthpiece

▮ ABOVE
W or double mouthpiece

The **KK training bit** has a central lozenge-shaped link which is designed to shift pressure away from the lips and corners towards the centre of the horse's mouth to give a milder bit action.

The **Waterford bit** has a multi-jointed mouthpiece made up of a series of bulbous links. Because of the number of links, this mouthpiece is extremely flexible, which discourages the horse from leaning on it.

Roller mouthpieces feature a series of rollers in either steel or steel and copper. Because of the movement, these mouthpieces are used to discourage the horse from leaning on the rider's hands. There are two main types of roller mouthpieces: the **magenis** is a strong bit which features small rollers set into a squared-off mouthpiece; the **cherry roller** has rollers across the length of the mouthpiece and will encourage the horse to play with the bit, keeping his mouth relaxed. The more rounded shape of the mouthpiece means it has a kinder action than the magenis. Another roller mouthpiece, the **copper roller**, is similar to the cherry roller except that the rollers alternate between copper and steel. The copper is included to encourage the horse to salivate and relax his jaw.

The **twisted mouthpiece** is very severe, putting sharp pressure on the horse's tongue and the corners of his mouth.

Ported mouthpieces allow more room for the horse's tongue than other types of mouthpiece, while placing more contact on the bars. Bits with a high port will also act on the roof of the horse's mouth, causing the horse to raise his head.

The **KK correction bit** is a training bit made from Aurigan (a copper alloy) and is designed for strong, pulling horses.

The **W** or **double mouthpiece** has two thin, single-jointed mouthpieces attached to a set of bit rings. Strong bits like this are best left to expert riders because of the damage they can do to the horse's mouth.

Double Bits

Double bits are a combination of two bits: the **bridoon** (a snaffle bit) and a **curb bit**, also known as a **Weymouth**, which is fitted with a curb chain. The bridoon acts in exactly the same way as the snaffle, raising the horse's head, while the curb bit acts on the horse's poll and curb groove. Combining these two bits in one bridle enables you to fine tune your horse's head and neck carriage. A double bridle is used on horses who are already well schooled, particularly for dressage. It is also considered the correct bridle for the show ring. The curb bit comes with a mullen or ported mouthpiece. The length of the cheekpieces on curb bits varies but in general, the longer the cheekpieces, the greater the poll pressure.

▍ ABOVE
An eggbutt bridoon
(top) with a fixed-
cheek Weymouth
(below).

▍ LEFT
A loose-ring bridoon
(top) with a sliding-
cheek Weymouth curb
(below).

Pelham Bits

The pelham is a compromise between a snaffle and a double bridle, combining the actions of both. As well as exerting pressure on the horse's mouth, pelhams also act on the poll and curb groove. Unlike the double bridle, it has only one mouthpiece and can be ridden with pelham roundings, the short pieces of leather linking the top and bottom rings, so that only one set of reins is needed (although it is more correct to ride with two). It is ideal for a show horse whose mouth is too small for a double bridle.

The **mullen-mouthed pelham** is the most popular pelham mouthpiece and also the mildest in action. The **jointed pelham** is very strong, the jointed mouthpiece having a direct action on the horse's tongue. The **Rugby pelham** has a loose-ring link for the bridoon rein, and as a consequence it brings greater pressure on the horse's curb and poll. The **Scamperdale pelham** is ideal for horses with fleshy lips. The mouthpiece is shaped so that it bends back at either end. This helps to keep the cheekpieces of the bit away from the horse's lips to prevent chafing. Unlike most other pelhams, the **globe pelham** is fitted with only one set of reins, which are attached to the lower rings.

The **kimblewick**, also known as the **Kimberwicke** or **Spanish jumping bit**, comes into the category of pelhams although it has less leverage action than a pelham and is ridden with only one set of reins. The **slotted-cheek kimblewick** (shown here with a hinged, copper, quarter-moon mouthpiece) enables you to choose at what height to attach the reins. The lower they are fitted, the greater the curb action of the bit. The **rounded-cheek kimblewick** has a similar action to a snaffle bit when the rider's hands are held high: lowering the hands emphasizes the curb action.

▌ ABOVE
jointed pelham

▌ ABOVE
Scamperdale pelham

▌ ABOVE
Uxeter hinged copper kimblewick

▌ ABOVE
mullen-mouthed
pelham

▌ RIGHT
globe pelham

▌ ABOVE
Cambridge mouth kimblewick

▌ ABOVE
Rugby pelham

▌ ABOVE
pelham roundings

▌ ABOVE
slotted-cheek kimblewick

Gag Snaffles

This group of bits encourages the horse to raise his head by raising the bit in his mouth, as well as acting on the corners of the mouth and the poll. Gag snaffles are popular bits for strong, fit horses ridden across country and for those who like to put their heads down and gallop off. Like the pelham, the gag snaffle should be fitted with two sets of reins (although they can be used with only one set, attached to the roundings). One set is attached to the bit ring like a snaffle, the second set to the roundings which pass from the cheekpieces through the bit rings. This enables the rider to utilize the strong gag action only when it is actually needed.

The **Balding gag** has loose-ring cheekpieces through which gag roundings pass. The **Cheltenham gag** is similar in design but features eggbutt bit rings. With both types of gag, the larger the bit ring, the more severe the bit's action.

The **half-ring**, or **Duncan gag**, is a particularly strong type of gag as it can only be used with one set of reins, which is fitted to the gag roundings.

The **Dutch gag**, also called the **continental** or **three-ring gag**, can be used with one or two sets of reins. The bridle cheekpieces are attached to the top rings to produce poll pressure. The reins can be fitted to any of the three lower rings: the lower the reins are fitted, the stronger the leverage action on the horse's mouth.

The **American gag** should also be used with two sets of reins (one set fitted to the central rings and the other fitted to the lower rings). As the gag (lower) rein is used, the mouthpiece slides up the cheekpieces, encouraging the horse to raise his head.

Gag roundings, or **running cheeks**, are leather or nylon straps which are attached to the cheekpieces of the bridle and then passed through the bit rings and attached directly to the reins. As the rider takes a contact on the reins, the bit slides up the roundings and the horse's head is raised.

▌ ABOVE
Balding gag

▌ ABOVE
Dutch gag

▌ ABOVE
Cheltenham gag

▌ ABOVE
Gag roundings: the top two are of leather, the bottom two are nylon.

▌ ABOVE
American gag

The Bitless Bridle

Although not a bit at all, bitless bridles, also known as hackamores, make up the fifth bit group. Instead of acting on the horse's mouth, bitless bridles apply pressure to the horse's nose as well as to the poll and curb groove. They can be used on horses who have injured their mouths but need to be kept in ridden work. Although bitless bridles have no influence on the horse's mouth, they can still be severe in inexperienced hands.

The **English pattern** or **Blair hackamore** has a padded noseband, metal cheeks and a leather curb strap (which is fitted slightly higher than a normal curb chain). Take care when fitting the English hackamore: if it is too high, the cheekpieces may rub the horse's cheeks; if it is too low, it can interfere with his breathing.

The **German hackamore** has a rubber-covered metal noseband, often worn padded with sheepskin, and a curb chain . The longer cheekpieces of the German hackamore have a stronger leverage action than the English pattern. Both types of hackamore can be used in conjunction with a bit by simply adding an extra sliphead to the bridle.

The **bosal** forms an integral part of Western training and riding. It is usually made from plaited (braided) rawhide and is used with a normal or one-ear bridle. The reins are attached directly to the "heel" knot at the back of the bridle.

■ ABOVE
English pattern hackamore

■ ABOVE
German hackamore

■ ABOVE
Western curb bit

■ ABOVE
high port correction bit

■ ABOVE
fixed-butt snaffle

■ LEFT
loose shank bit with silver inlay

■ ABOVE
Billy Allen bit

■ RIGHT
The bosal in use.

WESTERN BITS

With their long cheekpieces and ported mouthpieces **Western curb bits** can appear severe, but in practice the Western horse is ridden with such a light contact that this is not the case. The horse is systematically trained, first using a bosal, then a combination of bosal and bit, and finally a bit alone. Western riders traditionally ride with just the weight of the rein itself maintaining the contact. Western bits are usually made out of sweet iron. This is

"warmer" than stainless steel, and the rusting that naturally occurs encourages the horse to salivate.

The **high port correction bit** has loose shanks which allow the cheekpieces to swivel at the butt of the mouthpiece. The high port acts on the roof of the horse's mouth when a contact is taken.

The **low port bit** has silver inlay, a chain and a plaited (braided) nylon curb strap. The angle of the shank on the bit determines the severity of the leverage

action, with a more angled shank giving a milder leverage action.

The **Billy Allen bit** has a jointed mouthpiece with a central roller, which lessens the nutcracker action of the mouthpiece. It is used as a transitional bit between the shank snaffle and a curb bit.

The **fixed-butt snaffle** is similar in action to an English eggbutt snaffle – the fixed butt keeps the bit still in the horse's mouth while the single joint has a nutcracker action on the horse's tongue.

Unusual Bits

There will always be bits that do not fit neatly into specific categories or those which have evolved with a specific sport in mind. Here are a few examples.

The **citation bit** forms part of a combination bit and bridling system called a Norton bridle. It has two mouthpieces, the thinner of which is attached directly to the noseband via the links on the bit rings. This is a highly specialized bit and bridle and is strictly for experienced hands only.

The **scourier** or **Cornish bit** has two sets of bit rings, one of which passes through holes in the mouthpiece. The inside rings are attached to the bridle while the outer

rings are attached to the reins. This, combined with a grooved mouthpiece, results in a very severe bit.

The **Wilson snaffle**, like the scourier, has two pairs of bit rings. This bit is used for driving. Its action is similar to that of the scourier – pressure applied to the reins causes the bit rings to squeeze on the sides of the horse's mouth.

The **wind-sucking bridoon** or **flute bit** has a wide, hollow mouthpiece pierced with a series of small holes. It is designed to stop the horse from gulping down air when crib biting or wind-sucking.

The **tongue bit** incorporates a flat metal plate which prevents the horse from evading the bit by getting his tongue over the mouthpiece.

The **butterfly bit** is not a bit as such, but an attachment which clips on to the mouthpiece of an existing bit to increase the severity of its action.

The **loose-ring racing snaffle** has much larger bit rings than normal snaffles. The larger rings prevent the bit from being pulled through the horse's mouth. They can also help to steer the horse in a chosen direction by bringing pressure on the side of the face.

■ ABOVE
scourier

■ ABOVE
tongue bit

■ ABOVE
citation

■ ABOVE
wind-sucking bridoon

■ ABOVE
mouthing or breaking bit

■ ABOVE
loose-ring racing snaffle

■ ABOVE
Wilson snaffle

■ ABOVE
butterfly bit

Training and Showing Bits

Some bits are specifically designed for training young horses and for leading and showing horses in-hand.

The **chifney**, also known as an **anti-rearing bit**, consists of a ring which sits in the horse's mouth and is attached to a separate headstall. It is often used when leading stallions and racehorses in the parade ring.

The **Tattersall ring bit**, similar to the chifney, is useful for leading boisterous youngsters. The bit is held in place by a headstall which is attached to the two metal loops on either side. The lead rope is attached to the rear of the ring.

Mouthing or **breaking bits** are designed to encourage young horses to play with the mouthpiece. They can have a single or unjointed mouthpiece and feature small metal "keys" in the centre of the mouth-piece with which the young horse plays.

The **horseshoe stallion bridoon**, which looks similar to the **overcheck bridoon**, is designed for showing stallions in-hand.

▌ RIGHT
Top to bottom: **chifney; Tattersall ring bit; horseshoe stallion bridoon; overcheck bridoon**

▌ ABOVE
A Thoroughbred yearling with a Tattersall ring bit fitted to a leather headcollar.

BIT MATERIALS

Bits are available in a wide variety of metals, alloys and synthetic materials. The following materials are listed in order of common usage.
Stainless steel is strong and easy to clean. Steel is the most popular choice of bit material. One of the disadvantages of steel is that it is a "cold" metal which does not encourage salivation.
Rubber is used to cover metal bits to soften their action. However, rubber is not particularly hardwearing and is easily chewed.
Vulcanite or vulcanized rubber is harder wearing than rubber but heavier and not as flexible.
Polyurethane and **nylon** bits are flexible if unjointed. These materials are also used to cover jointed metal bits. A mouthpiece using polyurethane or nylon can be very mild in action and often has an

copper alloy

vulcanite

happy mouth

rubber

copper and steel

apple scent to make it more appealing to horses.
Copper mouthpieces warm up to the horse's body temperature more quickly than steel but are less hardwearing. They are designed to encourage horses with dry mouths to salivate.
Copper alloy bits are designed to combine the qualities of copper with the strength of stainless steel. Manufacturers claim that they improve the contact between the rider's hands and the horse.
Brass alloy bits are claimed to have the same qualities as copper. They are a combination of brass with silicon and aluminium.
Sweet iron mouthpieces rust very quickly when allowed to get wet, thereby encouraging the horse to salivate.

nathe

stainless steel

brass alloy

sweet iron

Curb Chains and Lip Straps

Curb bits and pelhams should always be fitted with a curb chain or strap. The curb chain brings pressure on the horse's curb groove. The chain or strap itself should be fitted so that it is brought into action when the shank of the curb bit is at an angle of 45 degrees.

The **Western leather curb strap** is used with a Western curb bit. The **single-link curb chain** is light in weight but, because of its design, can pinch the horse's skin; the **double-link curb chain** is preferable to the single-link type as it is less likely to do this. A **leather curb chain** is designed to be fitted to an English curb bit. The **elasticated curb chain**, like the leather curb chain, has a milder action than the metal type. The **rubber-covered chain** is more comfortable for the horse than an uncovered curb chain, and has a milder action on the curb groove.

All English curb straps or chains should be fitted with a fly ring through which a **lip strap** passes. The strap, attached to either side of the curb bit or pelham, helps to keep the curb chain in place.

Fulmer keepers are small leather straps which are fitted to the cheekpieces of a snaffle bridle. They are used to prevent the upper cheekpiece of a full-cheek snaffle from tipping forward. They also help to keep the bit raised in the horse's mouth, preventing the horse from getting his tongue over the bit.

Leather pelham roundings can be fitted to pelhams and certain types of gag bit when only one set of reins is used.

▌ ABOVE
Western curb strap

▌ ABOVE
double-link chain

▌ ABOVE
single-link chain

▌ ABOVE
leather curb chain

▌ ABOVE
elasticated curb chain

▌ ABOVE
rubber-covered chain

▌ RIGHT
Lip strap fitted to a Weymouth bit.

Nosebands

Nosebands are available in a variety of designs, from those chosen purely for aesthetic reasons, to corrective nosebands which offer more control, acting in conjunction with the bit to increase the strength of the bit action or to prevent the horse evading it.

The **cavesson** is the simplest noseband design available. It is the only type of noseband to use with a double bridle and can also be used with a standing martingale. When fitted correctly, it should have little or no action on the horse's head. The cavesson should be fitted loosely enough to allow room for two fingers under the noseband.

Rope cavessons are much more severe in action than leather ones and are more commonly seen on polo ponies or strong show jumpers. The **continental** or **cinchback cavesson** is designed to be fitted

▌ LEFT
cavesson noseband

▌ BELOW
continental cavesson

▌ LEFT
rope cavesson
noseband

more tightly than a traditional cavesson to discourage the horse from opening his mouth. It can be used with a double bridle and for this reason is often used for dressage or showing.

The **dropped noseband** is fitted with the back strap passing below the bit. It is designed to prevent the horse from opening his mouth and evading the bit. The dropped noseband (when fitted correctly) can increase pressure on the horse's poll as well as on the nose and lower jaw. The dropped noseband should not be used if a standing martingale is fitted. Take care not to fit it below the base of the nasal bone as this can restrict the horse's breathing.

The **flash** is based on the cavesson noseband but has an additional strap which is fitted below the bit. It was originally developed for riders who wanted a noseband which closed the mouth like a dropped noseband, but which could be used alongside a standing martingale. The flash noseband is fitted slightly higher and tighter than the cavesson. Attachments are available which can transform an ordinary cavesson into a flash noseband.

The **Grakle** or **figure-of-eight** takes its name from the eponymous winner of the British 1931 Grand National steeplechase. The Grakle should be fitted snugly so that the top strap goes around the horse's jaws above the bit (resting just below the facial

bone) while the lower strap passes below the bit, keeping the mouth closed. The Grakle puts pressure on the horse's nose (where the straps cross) and helps to stop the horse from crossing his jaws.

Take care that the central point does not lie below the nasal bone as this will cause discomfort to the horse. There should be a short strap fitted at the back of the noseband to keep the straps in place.

I **ABOVE**
Left to right:
**dropped noseband;
flash noseband;
Grakle or figure-of-
eight noseband**

I **LEFT**
Mexican Grakle

❚ BELOW
Australian cheeker

❚ RIGHT
sheepskin noseband

The **Mexican** or **high-ring Grakle** is fitted higher than a normal Grakle, above the cheek bones. It sits higher up the face and is thought to be more effective at preventing the horse crossing his jaws.

The **Kineton** or **Puckle noseband** is a severe noseband which derives its name from its designer, a Mr Puckle of Kineton. Metal loops pass under the bit so that when a contact is taken up, strong pressure is brought to bear on both the nose and the bit, encouraging the horse to lower his head. As with the dropped noseband, take care not to fit it too low.

The **sheepskin noseband**, often used on racehorses, is basically a cavesson noseband covered with a sheepskin sleeve. It encourages the horse to lower his head, which he must do if he is to see over the noseband.

The **Australian cheeker** is a rubber attachment which fastens to the headstall of the bridle and either side of a snaffle bit. It helps to keep the bit raised in the mouth, preventing the horse from getting his tongue over it. It is thought that being able to see the central strap encourages the horse to back off the bit.

The **controller** or **combination noseband** combines the action of a dropped and a Grakle noseband. The two straps help to keep the horse's mouth closed and discourage him from opening his mouth. The front strap is adjustable and is fitted like a dropped noseband. For very strong horses, the front strap can be reinforced with a strip of metal.

❚ BELOW LEFT
Kineton noseband

❚ BELOW RIGHT
controller noseband

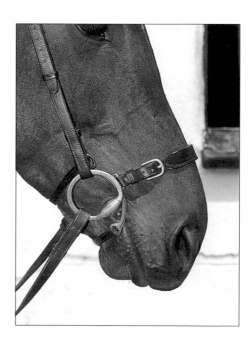

Reins

The reins provide the vital line of communication between your hands and the bit in the horse's mouth.

Plain leather reins are very smart and make an ideal choice for showing. They are often used with double bridles as they are not bulky. A thicker rein is fitted to the bridoon with a thinner rein used for the curb. A disadvantage of plain leather reins is that they can be slippery, especially if allowed to get wet. **Plain leather dressage reins** incorporate small leather "stops" which help to improve grip.

Laced leather reins have thin strips of leather laced through them to improve grip. **Plaited (braided) leather reins** are easy to grip but are more expensive than laced reins and with use they will stretch.

Rubber-covered reins are the popular choice for everyday riding because of their durability. They are very easy to grip, even when wet, and for this reason are often used for racing, eventing and general riding. **Half-rubber reins** are less slippery than plain leather ones, and are more attractive and less cumbersome than rubber-covered reins. **Continental reins** are made of webbing with leather stops to improve grip. **Rubberized webbing reins** are lightweight and incorporate rubber for improved grip.

Plaited (braided) cotton reins are light in weight and reasonably easy to grip. **Plaited (braided) nylon reins** are slightly cheaper than plaited cotton reins, but can be very slippery and will stretch easily. **Western reins** are traditionally ridden split, without being secured at the end with a buckle, to prevent the horse catching his foot if the reins trail on the ground once the rider has dismounted.

■ ABOVE
Plain leather double reins, bridoon.

■ ABOVE
Plain leather double reins, curb.

■ ABOVE
plain leather dressage reins

■ ABOVE
continental reins

■ ABOVE
laced leather reins

■ ABOVE
plaited (braided) leather reins

■ ABOVE
plain leather reins

■ ABOVE
plaited (braided) cotton reins

■ ABOVE
plaited (braided) nylon reins

■ ABOVE
half-rubber reins

■ ABOVE
rubber-covered reins

Western reins

Rein Attachments

There are a number of ways in which reins can be attached to the bridle, depending on the reason the horse is being tacked up. For instance in showing classes, where appearance is of the utmost importance, reins will often be stitched on to the bit.

Although this makes changing the bit difficult, it does look much neater than billets (stud hooks) or buckles.

Billets are small metal hooks which fasten into a small hole in the rein to attach it to the bridle. The billet and billet

hole should be checked regularly for wear and tear. **Buckles** are a secure way of attaching reins but can look bulky. Western reins are attached to the bit by **hide thongs**. **Loops** are a less secure method of fastening reins than buckles.

▌ BELOW
Looped fastening reins

▌ BELOW
Buckle fastening on synthetic reins.

▌ BELOW
Western reins

▌ BELOW
leather reins with buckle fastening

Browbands

The browband helps to keep the bridle in position on the horse's head. It is very important that the browband is fitted correctly as a browband fitted too loosely looks untidy and may not be effective in preventing the bridle from slipping back. If fitted too tightly, the browband can pinch the horse's ears, thereby forcing him to shake his head. Available in a wide range of designs, browbands are always highly decorative.

The **plain browband** is ideal for horses with heavier, coarser heads. **Padded browbands** feature a raised central section, which suits larger warmblood heads. A raised strip of coloured **plaited (braided) leather** can add contrast to an otherwise plain bridle. **Velvet-covered browbands** are available in a wide choice of colours and can be selected to match your outfit. They are popular for showing hacks and children's ponies. A delicate browband, the **plaited (braided) Arab**, is specially designed to suit the finer features of the Arab horse. **Clincher browbands** have studs (clinchers) in silver or brass. They come in all sorts of decorative designs which feature metal bobbles and small, mirrored strips. **Diamanté browbands** are popular for horses competing indoors where the light catches the stones. The **chain browband** is best suited to horses or ponies with extremely fine heads. The **bit motif browband** incorporates a gilt snaffle design. **Western browbands** can be very simple in design, with little or no ornamentation, although highly decorative browbands with silver detailing are often used for showing or parades. Not all Western bridles feature browbands: the one ear and split ear bridles do not require a browband to keep them in place.

■ LEFT
padded browband

■ LEFT
plain browband

■ LEFT
Top to bottom:
silver clincher;
brass clincher;
bobble clincher;
mirrored clincher

■ LEFT
velvet-covered browband

■ LEFT
plaited (braided) Arab browbands.

■ LEFT
diamanté browband

■ LEFT
bit motif browband

■ LEFT
chain browband

■ LEFT
Top to bottom:
ornate Western browband; plain knotted Western browband

Bridle Accessories

There is a range of items which can be fitted to the horse's bridle or halter. Many of these pieces are corrective items designed to discourage the horse from a bad habit, while some are aids to improve his comfort.

▌ RIGHT
Bit guards are rubber disks which can be fitted to loose-ring bits to prevent them from pinching the horse's lips. They also help to keep the bit positioned centrally in the horse's mouth.

▌ BELOW
The pricker pad is a leather pad with sharp bristles. It is fitted to one side of the bit against the side of the horse's face to discourage the horse from leaning to one side.

▌ ABOVE
Rein stops should always be fitted when a martingale is used. They stop the martingale rings slipping down towards the bit and getting stuck.

▌ ABOVE
A face net is a fine mesh net which is fitted over the horse's head. It can help protect the horse from flies when he is turned out in the field.

▌ ABOVE
Blinkers are mainly used on racehorses. They block the horse's view to either side, helping him to concentrate and thus improve his racing performance.

▌ RIGHT
Martingale stops are fitted to running and standing martingales to stop the central strap slipping through the chestpiece.

▌ ABOVE AND RIGHT
Fly fringes are attached to the bridle to protect the horse's face from flies when ridden or in the field. The type with earpieces is also sometimes used on show jumpers competing indoors as it can help to muffle spectator noise. A simpler fly fringe can be fitted to the horse's headcollar to protect him from flies when turned out in the field.

▌ RIGHT
The tongue guard is a rubber attachment which fastens to the bit. It is used to prevent the horse getting his tongue over the bit.

443

Putting on a Bridle

1 Stand on the near (left) side of the horse and hold the headpiece (crownpiece) of the bridle in your right hand. Place your left hand (holding the bit) under the horse's muzzle.

2 Press your thumb firmly but gently against the bars of the horse's mouth to encourage him to open his mouth.

3 Guide the bit gently into the horse's mouth, taking care not to bang it against his teeth. Draw the bridle up with the right hand and, using the left hand, guide the left and then the right ear under the headpiece of the bridle.

4 Separate the mane under the headpiece (a small section of mane, called a bridle path, can be clipped from this area) and bring the forelock out over the browband.

5 Fasten the throatlatch. It should be loose enough to allow you to fit four fingers between the throatlatch and the horse's cheeks.

6 Fasten the noseband (in this case a cavesson) so that it passes underneath the cheekpieces of the bridle. It should be loose enough to allow you to place two fingers underneath the noseband.

Bridle Care

A leather bridle should be cleaned regularly to keep it in top condition and to prolong its life. Remove sweat and grime every time the bridle is used and once a week dismantle it completely for a thorough cleaning. A synthetic bridle can be simply wiped down with a damp cloth or immersed in water. Check the stitching and billets (stud hooks) regularly, paying particular attention to where the bit is attached to the bridle at the reins and the cheekpieces.

1 Hang the bridle from a suitable hook, undoing all the straps from their keepers.

2 Wipe the bridle down with a damp sponge to remove dirt and grease.

3 Use a clean sponge to rub in lightly moistened saddle soap.

4 Wipe the bit, or rinse it under running water. Do this each time it has been used to prevent a build-up of saliva and food.

A correctly put up bridle. Cross the throatlatch over the front of the bridle, loop up the reins and fasten the noseband around it.

▌ LEFT
Jockeys will often tie a knot at the end of the reins. This is a safety measure in case the buckle joining the reins were to break during the race.

Training Aids
and Gadgets

There is a saying that gadgets and training aids are fine in the hands of experts but that experts have no need for them. This may apply in an ideal world but every horseman or woman, however expert, will encounter problems when schooling and training horses and may occasionally need additional help in the form of an aid or a gadget.

A training aid is a piece of equipment used to develop a well-schooled, obedient horse to improve his performance, while a gadget is a piece of equipment which prevents or restrains an aspect of the horse's behaviour which makes him dangerous or difficult to ride.

A degree of skill is required when using training aids or gadgets. The equipment must be fitted correctly, and you must be aware of its strength and severity. Only use it when it is specifically required, never as a matter of course. Training aids and gadgets in the wrong hands can damage the horse physically and psychologically.

Martingales

Martingales are designed to assist the bridle in controlling the horse. They prevent the horse from raising his head beyond the point at which the rider can control him.

The **running martingale** consists of a neck strap and a second strap which is attached to the girth and passes between the horse's front legs before dividing into two pieces. At the end of each of these straps is a small metal ring through which the reins pass. **Rein stops** should be fitted to the reins, below the bit, to prevent the martingale rings from getting caught on the bit. When the horse carries his head in the correct position no pressure is felt. However, when he raises his head above a certain point, the martingale restricts the movement of the reins which in turn causes the bit to bear down on the bars of the horse's mouth. The running martingale should be fitted so that the rings are in line with the withers to prevent it putting any pressure on the

reins when the horse's head is held in the correct position. It should not be used in conjunction with a curb bit.

The **bib martingale** is a variation on the running martingale. The two straps of the martingale are joined by a triangle of leather. This is to prevent an excitable horse from getting caught up in the straps; the design is often used on racehorses.

The **combined breastplate and martingale** is a traditional heavyweight hunting-style breastplate used to stop the saddle from slipping back. The breastplate has a central ring to which a running martingale attachment is fixed.

The **standing martingale** has a single strap which is attached to the girth, passes between the horse's front legs and is fixed to the back of the noseband (a cavesson or the cavesson part of a flash noseband). Like the running martingale, it has a neck strap. When correctly fitted it should be possible to push the martingale strap up into the horse's gullet.

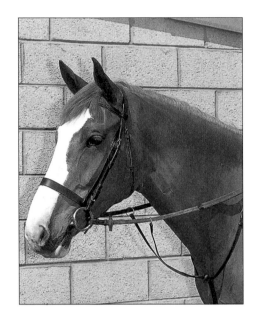

▎ ABOVE
running martingale

▎ BELOW LEFT
combined breastplate and martingale

▎ BELOW RIGHT
bib martingale

▌ LEFT
standing martingale

▌ LEFT AND BELOW
The Irish martingale is used to prevent the reins being thrown over the horse's head in the event of a fall. It is often used on racehorses, as shown here on Desert Orchid.

A **rubber martingale stop** should always be fitted to running and standing martingales to stop the martingale from slipping through the neck strap, which could result in the horse getting a foot caught in the straps.

The **Market Harborough** consists of a leather strap attached to the girth, which passes between the horse's front legs before dividing into two straps with a clip at each end. These straps pass through the bit rings and are clipped on to one of a series of rings on the side of the reins. Like the running martingale, the Market Harborough will only put pressure on the bit (and as a consequence on the bars of the horse's mouth) if the horse brings his head up beyond a certain point. The Market Harborough should only be used with an ordinary snaffle.

The **Irish martingale**, unlike other martingales, has no direct action on the horse's head carriage. It consists of a short piece of leather with a ring at either end

through which the reins pass. The Irish martingale is used to prevent the reins from being pulled over the horse's head in the event of a fall. It can also be used for horses who have a habit of suddenly tossing their heads in the air – "star gazers" – resulting in the reins being thrown over their heads.

▌ LEFT
Market Harborough martingale

Training Reins

Training reins are used when schooling the horse to help him develop the correct musculature for ridden work, or as a corrective aid to encourage the horse to carry himself well.

Running reins, also known as **draw reins**, are long pieces of leather or webbing with a loop at each end which fit around either side of the girth; the reins pass through the bit rings (from the inside to the outside) and up to the rider's hands. Running reins encourage the horse to lower his head, bringing it towards the vertical to promote the correct development of his back muscles. Running reins should only be used with an ordinary snaffle bridle to which an independent set of reins is also attached, and the rider must be quick to release the pressure on the running reins when the horse lowers his head. It is important that the horse is ridden forwards or there is a danger that he will become over-bent (with his head held behind the vertical).

A more severe method of fitting running reins is to attach them to the

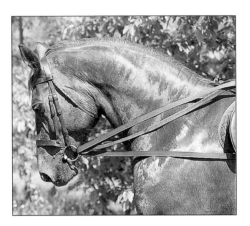
Running reins attached to either side of the girth.

Attach running reins at the chest for more control.

girth at the chest before passing them through the front legs up to the bit and back to the rider's hands. Fitted in this way the running reins (more correctly referred to as draw reins) impart a stronger leverage action on the horse's head.

An **overcheck rein** has a centre buckle and passes over the horse's poll, through the bit rings to the rider's hands. Overcheck reins will encourage the horse to raise his head by raising the bit in his mouth, rather like a gag snaffle.

The **De Gogue schooling system** is used for ridden work or lungeing. A strap from the girth passes between the horse's legs and divides into two cord straps. A piece of leather with pulleys on either side is fixed to the headpiece of the bridle. The cord straps go over the pulleys and down to the bit. For ridden work, short reins can be attached to the straps (with a second independent set of reins also fitted). For lungeing, the cords pass through the bit rings and clip on to the chest strap.

The De Gogue schooling system for lungeing or ridden work.

The Chambon system for lungeing or loose schooling only.

The Abbot Davies balancing rein.

▌ LEFT
Two ways of attaching the
elastic training rein.

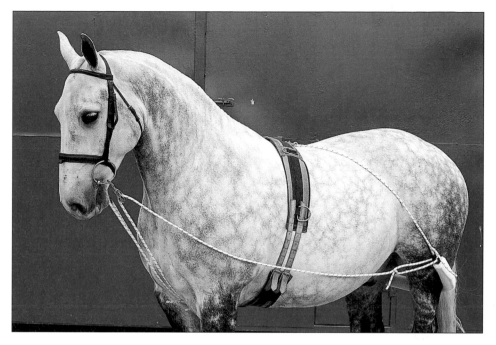

The **Chambon** is a schooling system consisting of a poll pad fitted over the top of the horse's head, to which pulleys are attached on either side. A strap is attached to the lungeing roller which passes up between the horse's front legs before dividing into two cords. The two cords fit over the pulleys and are clipped on to the bit rings. The Chambon encourages the horse to lower his head and neck and round his back, which in turn encourages engagement of the hindquarters. The Chambon can be used on horses which are being loose-schooled but is not designed to be ridden in.

The **Abbot Davies balancing rein** encourages the horse to develop the muscles of his back and hindquarters by raising his neck at its base. A combined system of pulleys and straps will prevent the horse leaning. It can be fitted from tail to mouth but more commonly, or in the latter stages of training, it is fitted from girth to mouth or mouth to ears.

The **Harbridge** aims to encourage the horse to work correctly by discouraging leaning, enhancing self-carriage and generally stimulating softness in the horse's back. It is not dissimilar in appearance to a running martingale. A strap attached to the girth passes through the horse's front legs and divides

into two pieces of elastic which are clipped on to the bit rings. It should be used for flat work only, and is not suitable for schooling over jumps.

The **Schoolmasta training aid** is designed for horses which lean on the bit or have a tendency to over-bend and carry their heads behind the vertical. The system works independently of the rider's hands: straps clipped on to either side of the bit are attached to a pulley fitted to a special numnah, and this helps to correct the horse's posture.

The **elastic training rein** fits over the horse's poll, passes through the rings and clips on to the girth at the side or at the chest. The rein is designed to promote self-carriage without putting pressure on the horse's mouth.

The **Pessoa training system** aims to give the horse a rounded outline. It consists of a roller and pulleys attached from the roller to the bit rings, and to a strap passed round the hindquarters. As with all training equipment, skill and experience are needed for it to be used successfully.

The Harbridge has two elasticated
straps which clip on to the bit.

The Schoolmasta training aid is used in conjunction with a specially
adapted numnah.

Lungeing and Long Reining

Lungeing is a method of exercising or training the horse from a single long rein. The horse is worked in a circle, at a distance of 20m/66ft from the handler, in both directions and in walk, trot and canter.

The **lunge cavesson** is an essential piece of lungeing equipment. It is fitted over a bridle if side reins are to be used. A lunge line is attached to the central ring on the noseband. The cavesson should fit snugly so that it does not slip when in use.

Lungeing and **breaking rollers** are necessary when side reins or long lines are used. In the examples shown here, the top roller has large rings through which long-reining lines are fitted. Side reins can be attached to the smaller D rings. A crupper prevents the roller slipping forward; a breastgirth keeps it from slipping back. Lungeing the horse with side reins fitted

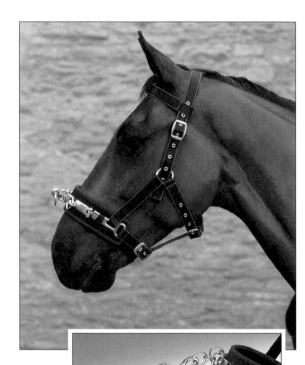

■ LEFT AND BELOW
Shown here are two examples of a lunge cavesson, in leather (*left*) and webbing (*below*).

enables the handler to influence the horse's outline and general way of going by containing impulsion. Working the horse on long lines enables the trainer to teach the young horse to respond to the feel of reins before a rider is introduced.

The **Elwyn Hartley-Edwards breaking roller** is a webbing and leather roller designed specifically for training the young horse. It features a built-in crupper to prevent the roller from being pulled forwards as the horse is worked.

Side reins are attached to the roller and clip on to the bit rings to encourage the horse to work in a correct outline. There is some debate as to whether elasticated or non-elasticated types are better. Some trainers feel that a rein that "gives" is better than a fixed type, while others suggest that elasticated reins can encourage the horse to evade the contact of the reins.

■ BELOW
Top to bottom: **Leather breaking roller, leather lunge roller and web lunge roller.**

■ BELOW
Top to bottom: **Rubber side reins,
continental pattern side reins,
leather side reins with elastic
inserts, nylon side reins.**

Continental pattern side reins in
leather have rubber inserts which allow
the reins to "give" as the horse moves.
Leather side reins are available, many
with elastic inserts. Leather side reins
can be costly but if well cared for they
will last longer than synthetic ones. **Nylon
side reins**, with or without elastic inserts,
are a cheaper alternative.

The **lunge line**, available in cord or
webbing, is attached to the central ring
on the lunge cavesson by means of a
spring clip or a buckled strap. The lunge
line enables the handler to control and
guide the horse around a circle.

■ ABOVE
**The Elwyn Hartley-Edwards breaking
roller shown fitted with side reins
and a crupper.**

■ LEFT
lunge lines

LUNGEING CAVESSON FITTED OVER A BRIDLE

The cavesson has been fitted over a bridle with the noseband removed. The reins have been twisted and looped through the throatlatch to prevent the horse accidentally getting caught in them. The side reins are attached to the bit rings: these should only be attached when the horse is being lunged. Start with the side reins fitted loosely and adjust them as the horse warms up.

HORSE TACKED UP FOR LUNGEING

Lungeing roller fitted with a breastplate.

USING A SADDLE INSTEAD OF A ROLLER

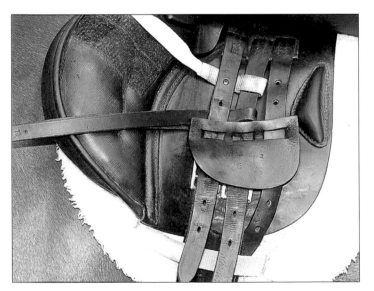

1 Side reins can be fitted to the girth straps on a saddle instead of the roller. They are useful if you plan to ride the horse after it has been lunged or if the horse is being lunged with a rider on board. The side reins pass round the second girth strap and under the first. This will prevent them from slipping down.

2 The stirrups can be removed from the saddle or, if the horse is to be ridden, they can be held securely in place by looping the stirrup leather around the stirrup and securing it with the spare end.

Lead Reins and Ropes

Lead reins and ropes are essential items of equipment when handling horses.

Lead ropes are inexpensive and sturdy, and are the practical choice for everyday use. They are clipped on to the horse's headcollar or halter so that he can be secured when travelling, or when being groomed or tacked up. Cotton and plaited (braided) nylon lead ropes come in a variety of colours: choose one to match your horse's headcollar.

When securing a horse with a lead rope, always use a quick release knot to allow the horse to be untied quickly in an emergency. Tying a horse directly to a fixed object, such as a gate or metal tie ring, can risk injuring him if he decides to pull back suddenly. Instead, attach the rope to the fixed object with a loop of bailing twine. If the horse pulls back suddenly, the twine will break and the horse will be released unhurt.

Leather and **webbing lead reins** are very smart and are commonly used for showing horses in-hand. The leather type has a double chain attachment called a **Newmarket chain**, which clips on to either bit ring and gives the handler greater control over the horse. The webbing lead rein is popular for showing and attaches directly to the headcollar or halter.

▌ BELOW
plaited (braided) nylon lead rope

▌ BELOW
cotton lead rope

▌ BELOW
webbing (*top*) and leather lead reins

Headcollars and Halters

Headcollars and halters are indispensable items of tack which are used to lead horses in-hand or to secure them when travelling or in the stable. Some are also designed to control or restrain horses.

The best-quality **leather headcollars** are made from English leather and, like all good-quality leather tack, they will last for years if well cared for. As an extra feature, you can attach a brass plate engraved with your horse's name.

Synthetic headcollars are ideal for everyday use. They are extremely strong, although this can be a problem – if the horse is turned out in one and gets caught on a branch, gate or fence, the synthetic headcollar will not break easily. The **synthetic rope halter** is made of strong nylon cord and fastens simply by tying. **Rope halters** are commonly used for showing young stock in-hand.

The **Controller headcollar** can be used for horses with a tendency to pull when led in-hand. The headcollar is designed to apply pressure on the nose when the horse pulls against the handler.

The **"Be-Nice"** halter, popularized by the American trainer, Monty Roberts, will train the horse to be led in-hand. The halter tightens around the horse's head and applies pressure to the poll when the horse resists being led. It should never be used to secure the horse.

The decorative **Western show halter** is made from leather with engraved silver detailing. The **in-hand bridle** is halfway between a bridle and a headcollar. It has short leather straps to which a bit is fitted and is used, as its name implies, for showing horses in-hand. The **rolled Arab slip** is a delicate halter which will enhance the fineness of the Arab head in in-hand showing classes. The **foal slip** is designed as a first headcollar for young foals. The short strap which hangs down is used instead of a separate lead rope.

A leather headcollar makes a very smart piece of equipment. A brass plate engraved with the horse's name can be fitted as an extra feature.

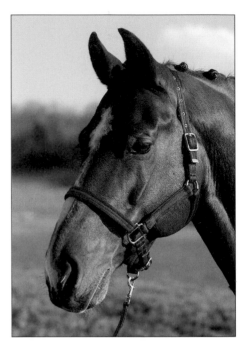

The synthetic headcollar is strong, durable and easy to care for. It is available in many colours and is a popular choice for children's ponies.

The unusual design of the synthetic rope halter means that it can be fastened without buckles.

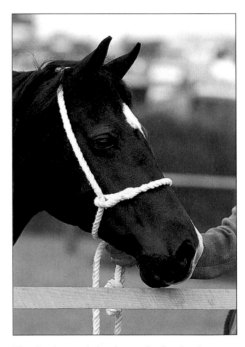

The simple rope halter is popular for showing young horses in-hand.

▌ ABOVE LEFT
controller headcollar

▌ ABOVE MIDDLE
"Be Nice" halter

▌ ABOVE RIGHT
Western show halter

▌ LEFT AND
RIGHT
foal slip

▌ ABOVE LEFT
in-hand bridle

▌ BELOW LEFT
rolled Arab slip

Grooming Equipment

Regular grooming is an essential part of good horse management. It is not simply a question of making the horse look smart. Far more important is the fact that thorough brushing helps keep the horse healthy by removing accumulated dust, dead skin and hair, and helping to keep the pores open and clean. During hard work the horse's skin excretes waste matter in the form of sweat. It is important that the skin and coat are kept clean to enable this system to work efficiently. A good, strenuous grooming also serves as a massage, improving the horse's muscle tone. In addition, grooming helps to keep the horse's tack and rugs clean, which in turn prevents sores. While the stabled horse needs daily grooming both before and after exercise, the grass-kept horse requires far less attention. Although the areas under the saddle and bridle must always be cleaned before tacking up, only the worst of the mud or grease should be removed elsewhere for appearances' sake. Horses and ponies who live out need the natural grease and dirt in their coats to help keep them warm and dry, especially in winter.

Grooming Kit

The **dandy brush** has long, stiff bristles and is used for removing dried mud and stable stains (where the horse has lain in its droppings or wet bedding) from the legs. It is too harsh to use on the horse's body or on the mane and tail.

The **body brush** has shorter, finer bristles than the dandy brush and may be used on the horse's entire body (and legs). It has a loop for the hand (leather or canvas are the most comfortable). The best body brushes have a leather back which is less likely than wood or plastic to hurt the horse if you inadvertently knock him with it while grooming. Leather, being softer and flexible, also sits more comfortably on the hand.

The body brush is cleaned after every few strokes by drawing the bristles across the teeth of the **metal curry comb**. The

metal curry comb should never be used on the horse.

For dampening down the mane and tail the **water brush** is used. This usually has a wooden back and has softer bristles than the dandy brush.

Two **sponges** are required, one for cleaning the eyes and nostrils, the other for use on the dock and the gelding's sheath. The sponges should never be interchanged (having two different colours prevents them being muddled up). They should be washed out after each use.

The **hoof pick** is a vital piece of equipment, used for cleaning out the horse's feet. The end of the pick should be blunt to prevent damage to the foot. Hoof picks are easily dropped and lost in the bedding. It is a good idea to tie a piece

▌ **RIGHT**
The grooming kit should include trimming scissors, thinning scissors and mane combs for use when trimming the heels, and when pulling the mane and tail.

▌ **PREVIOUS PAGE OPPOSITE**
Quarter marks put the finishing touch to a show pony.

▌ **PREVIOUS PAGE**
Grey horses, like this Percheron, take more keeping clean than dark-coloured horses.

▌ **CLOCKWISE FROM LEFT**
Body brush and metal curry comb; dandy brush; water brush; rubber and plastic curry combs; 'cactus' cloth.

of brightly coloured twine to the handle to make it easier to locate.

A **stable rubber**, usually made of cloth, is used, slightly dampened, to give a final polish to the horse's coat. A piece of chamois leather or jute sacking is equally effective for this purpose.

A **rubber** or **plastic curry comb**, which like the body brush is fitted with a loop for the hand, may be used for removing dried mud from the coat. Care must be taken when using it on bony areas such as the legs.

A **sweat scraper** is used to remove excess water from the horse's coat after washing him down. It consists of a blade of rubber attached to a metal frame with a handle. Again care must be taken not to knock the bony parts of his body.

Also in the grooming kit will be a **metal mane comb** which is not actually required for the grooming process but for use during trimming the mane and tail. The mane comb may have thick, widely spaced teeth or thin, closer ones.

All grooming tools should be kept tidily in a container designed for the purpose. Brushes should normally be kept bristle-side up (the bristles will last longer that way). They should be kept clean by regular washing. Since hot water may soften the glue which holds bristles in place, the whole brush should be plunged into cold water after cleaning and stood bristle-side down while it dries (this is particularly important for wooden-backed

brushes as the wood will deteriorate if it is left wet for long periods). All other items of grooming equipment should also be kept scrupulously clean.

For **wisping** – a form of massage involving a rhythmic thumping of the muscles of the neck, shoulders and quarters – a pad is required. Traditionally wisping was carried out with a hay wisp, made by twisting a rope of hay into a firm pad. Nowadays special pads are obtainable, often made of leather.

Sometimes the horse may need to have his mane and tail washed and occasionally his whole body. Buckets, sponges, an appropriate horse shampoo (if necessary), sweat scraper and towels will be required.

Electric groomers, which operate like a household vacuum cleaner, are useful for removing grease and dirt particularly from a horse who has not been clipped. Because of the noise horses must be introduced to them carefully and the tail should always be plaited up out of the way to avoid the possibility of the hair becoming caught up if the groomer has a rotating brush. An electric groomer is not suitable for use on the horse's head. While electric groomers are useful for removing dust and dirt, they do not provide the same massaging effect as a good hand grooming.

▌ RIGHT
A good hoof pick is an essential item of equipment. The one on the left is fitted with a brush which is used after the pick to remove remnants of dirt from the feet.

Grooming Technique

The stabled horse needs a thorough grooming every day. This is best carried out after exercise when the horse is warm. The pores of the skin will be open and grease and dirt will be easier to remove. The horse should be tied up during grooming.

Each **foot** should be picked up and carefully cleaned out with the hoof pick. The pick should be used from the horse's heel towards the toe to avoid damaging the frog. Dirt from the feet should be placed in a skip, not in the horse's bed.

The body brush is used to clean the horse's entire **body,** starting with the neck and working down to the shoulders and the front legs, along the body, over the hindquarters and down the hindlegs. Use the brush – in the left hand for the nearside, in the right hand for the offside

– with brisk, firm strokes and after every few strokes clean the bristles on the metal curry comb, which is held in the other hand. Periodically the dirt should be tapped from the curry comb. This should be done in the doorway or just outside the stable, not into the bedding. Care should be taken when grooming not to bang the horse's bony projections, for example those of the hips and legs, and the brush should not be used with too much pressure over the loins. Having completed

one side, move round to the other side of the horse and repeat the process.

The body brush is also used to clean the **head,** which should be done very gently. The horse should not be tied up for this, in case he pulls back. The headcollar should be fastened round his neck, leaving his nose free.

Brush out the **mane** and **tail** with the body brush, taking care not to break the hairs. The tail should be held away from the horse's body with your free hand and

▌ LEFT
A very sweaty or dirty horse may be washed down provided he can be dried quickly to prevent chilling. Excess water is removed with a sweat scraper.

1 Grooming begins with picking out the feet. The hoof pick shold always be used from the heel towards the toe.

2 Remnants of dirt may be removed from the area round the frog with a brush.

3 The hoof wall should be kept clean – a stiff brush may be used to remove mud and other forms of dirt.

1 The body brush is used to give the entire body a thorough grooming. It should be used in the direction of the lie of the coat.

2 The curry comb is held in the spare hand and used for cleaning the body brush – never use it on the horse.

3 The dock should be sponged each time the horse is groomed. Use a different sponge from the one used for the eyes and nose.

1 Tail bandages are made of elasticated cotton and are about 3 inches (8cm) wide and 10 feet (3m) long.

2 The bandage is started high up, as near as possible to the top of the dock.

3 A loose flap is left at the top and then turned down and bandaged over. This helps prevent slipping.

4 The bandage is applied down the length of the dock and up again. It should not be fitted too tightly

5 The bandage is secured with tapes and the dock should be eased into its natural shape.

brushed out a lock at a time. Any tangles should be teased out with the fingers. A very muddy tail will need washing. To finish off the mane and tail, dip the bristles of the water brush in clean water (not the horse's drinking water) and go lightly over the mane to "lay" it down smoothly. Do the same to the top hairs of the tail. A pulled tail should be bandaged for an hour or so afterwards to keep it tidy.

Use a damp sponge to clean the horse's **eyes** and **nostrils** and another for the **dock.** In the case of geldings the **sheath** will need sponging out once every couple of weeks or so to remove the greasy discharge which accumulates and can cause the horse discomfort. Special solutions can be obtained for this purpose or you can use a mild soap and warm water. Use the same sponge that is used for cleaning his dock. The easiest time to give him a thorough clean in this area is when he is staling. Do it carefully and gently – and beware of being kicked should the horse object. If you are unable to catch the moment when the horse is staling, clean out the sheath by gently inserting the sponge inside it and cleaning all round. Rinse the whole area several times and dry off with a towel.

The finishing touch to the whole grooming process is applied by running a damp stable rubber or other cloth over the entire coat to add a final polish. Wisping with a hay wisp or pad, when done, takes place after regular grooming since its purpose is not to clean but to **massage.** The pad or wisp is applied in

GROOMING TIPS

☛ Never try to groom a sweaty horse – walk him about until he is dry.

☛ Never try to brush off wet mud – either hose it off or let it dry first.

☛ To dry off a wet horse in the stable cover him with a sheet or rug made of "breathable" material or put a layer of straw along his back and quarters with a rug over the top (this is known as "thatching").

☛ To remove dried mud use a dandy brush or rubber curry comb but not too roughly – it may be necessary to remove mud from sensitive areas of skin, such as inside the hindlegs, with your hand.

☛ In cold weather keep a clipped horse warm during grooming by turning his rugs back and forward (as when quartering) rather than removing them altogether.

☛ Give all rugs and blankets a thorough shaking every week – it is pointless to put dusty rugs back on to a clean horse.

☛ Never stand directly behind a horse.

☛ Never sit or kneel on the floor to reach the lower parts – always squat or bend so that you can move quickly if he does.

☛ Keep a watchful eye open for any skin injuries or tell-tail lumps or bumps, particularly on the legs, which could warn of impending soundness problems.

☛ With the grass-kept horse clean the area under the saddle and brush off the worst of the mud for appearances' sake but do not attempt regular, thorough grooming.

much the same way as a brush, but with a firmer thump (though not too hard). It is used on the large muscular areas of the horse (the neck, shoulders and quarters). It is said to improve the circulation and muscle tone. It should never be used on the more tender areas, such as the loins, nor on the bony areas, such as the legs.

A thorough grooming will take from half to three-quarters of an hour, depending on the initial cleanliness of the horse's skin and coat – and the strength and endurance of the groom! Grooming is most effective if you stand a little away from the horse in order to put your weight behind the brush.

A less comprehensive type of grooming called **quartering** is used to prepare the horse in the morning for exercise. Its purpose is to remove any surface dirt accumulated during the night and to make the horse generally presentable. Quartering involves unfastening his rugs, turning them back over his loins and giving his front half a quick brush over, then turning his rugs forward and doing the same to his hind end. Any stains and bedding marks should be removed, if necessary by using a damp sponge or water brush. The damp areas should be dried off with a stable rubber or a towel. The mane and tail should be brushed through and all traces of bedding removed. The feet should be picked clean and the eyes, nostrils and dock sponged. Quartering takes between ten and twenty minutes, depending on the horse's size and how dirty he is.

Types of Clip

In winter horses grow a thick coat to protect them from the weather. A horse with a thick coat who is required to do anything other than light work will sweat excessively and, as a result, be very uncomfortable, lose condition and run the risk of catching a chill if he is not carefully dried off after exercise. Clipping off the thick winter coat of the stabled horse removes these problems and also makes it easier to keep the horse clean and looking smart. A clipped horse must be kept warm with blankets and rugs. A clipped horse who spends some time out at grass will need a waterproof New Zealand rug.

There are different ways of clipping a horse or pony, depending on the work he is required to do and the type of coat he grows. A **full clip** involves removing the coat from the entire body and the legs. A thick-coated horse may be given a full clip when he is first clipped and then at subsequent clippings have his legs left unclipped. Leaving the hair on the legs affords some protection from knocks. The full clip is usually only used for horses in very fast work, such as racing, or sometimes for a show horse being prepared for early spring shows.

The most usual clip for other horses doing hard work is the **hunter clip** which involves leaving the hair on the legs and the area under the saddle. Again the reason for leaving legs and saddle patch unclipped is to provide protection. Care must be taken to dry off the saddle patch thoroughly after work.

As its name suggests the **blanket clip** involves leaving an area of the horse's back, loins and quarters unclipped (and also the legs). The hair is removed from the neck, shoulders and belly and all or part of the head. A blanket clip is suitable for a horse doing a fair amount of medium to hard work.

Horses who are kept out, and stabled horses not in hard work, may be given a low **trace clip,** which consists of removing the hair from the underside of the neck, between the forelegs, the belly and the upper part of the hind legs. Medium and high trace clips, which involve removing more of the body and neck hair are suitable for stabled horses in steady work.

With the **chaser clip** the hair is removed from the head, the lower part of the neck, the chest, the belly and the upper part of the hindlegs. The clip finishes just behind the ears. It is often used on steeplechasers (hence its name). Many Thoroughbred horses have fine coats which may not require total removal even when they are in hard work.

There are various other partial clips suitable for the grass-kept horse used only for light work such as occasional hacking. These include the **bib clip** and the **apron clip.** In the bib clip the coat is removed only from the jowl, down the underside of the neck down to and including the front of the chest. In the apron clip an area above the forelegs and extending back under the girth area of the body is also removed. These areas, together with the flanks and the inside of the hindlegs, are usually the first to become sweaty. A tough animal, such as a native pony, could probably live out without rugs after having a bib or apron clip though in very adverse weather he might need to be rugged. When clipping the hair from the hindquarters an inverted V is left at the top of the tail. The unclipped leg hair is sloped at the top from front to back.

The horse's head is a particularly vulnerable spot because of its thin covering of skin and hair. Many people leave the head unclipped or simply clip the lower half which effectively removes the hair from the sweatiest part (i.e. the jowl) while leaving the top half with protection from the weather. Many horses dislike having their heads clipped at all. This can be caused by a number of reasons, from fear of the sound or feel of the clippers to painful conditions such as toothache or an ear infection.

▌ ABOVE
This horse has been blanket clipped. The clipping lines should be carefully marked on the horse beforehand, using chalk or a damp bar of saddle soap.

▌ ABOVE RIGHT
The area above the tail is finished off in a neat V shape. Care must be taken not to cut into either the mane or tail hair.

▌ LEFT
The Irish clip involves removing the hair from the belly and chest and part of the shoulders and neck. This horse has had his head clipped, too.

▌ OPPOSITE PAGE
A trace clip is suitable for stabled horses not in hard work. The body and neck may be clipped higher or lower depending on the amount of work the horse is doing.

▌ LEFT
For the horse in hard work the hunter clip is most suitable. A full or part saddle patch (as here) should be left to protect the back.

465

Clipping and Trimming

Clipping horses is hard work and can be dangerous. It should never be carried out alone. The beginner should learn the techniques by watching an expert at work. If in doubt, find someone else to clip your horse, at least to begin with so that you can find out how he behaves.

Having decided on the type of clip, all lines (for example the leg lines and saddle patch) should be marked on the horse's coat with chalk or a damp piece of saddle soap. To mark the saddle patch put the horse's usual saddle on his back, without its fittings, make sure it is in the position where it lies when he is being ridden, and draw round it. It is better to make the saddle patch a little larger than it will finally need to be to make allowance for any mistakes when clipping the edges. A badly positioned saddle patch will spoil the look of the horse.

Start clipping at the front of the horse, on the neck or shoulder, and work your way backwards section by section. The clippers should be used against the lie of the coat (broadly speaking from the back of the horse towards the front) with long, sweeping strokes. Each stroke should be parallel to the one above or below it and should slightly overlap the previous one.

Take care when clipping the top line of the neck not to cut into the mane. Clip a short bridle path out of the mane just

▌ RIGHT
Essential clipping and trimming equipment: electric clippers, electric and battery driven trimmers, spare clipper blades, oil, small brush (for cleaning clogged blades) and screwdriver (for changing fuses if necessary).

behind the ears where the headpiece of the bridle lies. This does not need to be very long: 2 inches (5cm) is adequate.

After the neck and shoulders clip the body and finally the hindquarters. Be particularly careful when clipping awkward places such as the delicate skin below the stifle and the folds between the front legs. The stifle skin should be held with your spare hand to straighten out the folds. An assistant should hold each foreleg up and forward in turn to stretch the folds of skin. Holding up a foreleg will also help prevent a horse from fidgeting or kicking. When clipping between the hindlegs be particularly watchful in case the horse does try to kick out. Keeping hold of his tail will help to prevent this.

The most difficult part of the horse to clip well is the head. If a horse is really frightened of having the clippers near his

head it is far better to leave it unclipped. If the horse's head is to be clipped, first remove the headcollar. If he will not stand still without some form of restraint a halter is easier to work round with the clippers than a headcollar. Where you start will depend very much on the horse but the cheeks are probably the best place. Rest the clippers, switched off, against the cheekbone for a few moments until the horse becomes used to their presence. Then if he does not object switch on and work carefully over both cheeks, underneath from the chin to the throat, up over the front of the head and over the forehead. Because the head is so bony the clippers should be used as lightly as possible to reduce vibration. Be particularly careful when working near the eye.

Some people clip off the horse's whiskers round his muzzle but since these

The mane is shortened and thinned by means of pulling, using a mane comb. Remove only a few hairs at a time to prevent soreness and damp the mane down afterwards.

To neaten an untidy tail, pull hair from the sides and centre of the dock, preferably when the horse is warm and the pores are open.

A mane comb and sharp, round-ended scissors are used to trim excess hair from the pasterns and fetlocks of unclipped legs. Take care not to leave "steps" of hair.

▌ RIGHT
Holding up a foreleg smooths out skin creases and also stops the horse fidgeting.

▌ MIDDLE RIGHT
Proceed carefully and gently when clipping the head.

▌ BOTTOM RIGHT
Holding the tail helps prevent a horse from kicking. The tail is bandaged to keep it clear of the clipper blades.

are used as sensors it is preferable, and kinder, to leave them alone.

To trim the ears, hold each one in turn and run the clippers along the outside edge only. Never try to clip the hair from inside the ear as the horse needs this as protection from insects and dirt. Never clip the eyelashes. Be careful when clipping the top of the head not to cut into the forelock.

If the horse's legs are left unclipped it will probably be necessary to trim his fetlocks and pasterns to make him look tidy. Use a mane comb and scissors (with rounded ends for safety) to remove excess feather, taking care not to create "steps" of hair but to leave a smooth line. Trim any thick hair from around the coronet.

If the horse's head is left unclipped, long hairs around the jaw may also be removed with scissors and comb. Scissors may be used to trim the long hairs from the edge of the ears.

Manes are kept neat by means of pulling, which involves plucking out strands of hair until the mane is the desired length and thickness. If the horse finds this too uncomfortable, it is possible to tidy up the mane with a thinning comb but never be tempted to use scissors which will give a very unsatisfactory result. Pulling can usually be achieved if you take your time and do only a small section of the mane at a time, spreading the whole job over a number of days.

An untidy tail can also be improved by pulling out some of the hairs from the top of the dock. Hair should be removed from the sides and, to a lesser extent, from the

centre. As with the mane, it is best to remove a few hairs each day to prevent soreness. After pulling, the tail should be dampened with a water brush and bandaged to make the hair lie flat (do not leave the bandage on overnight). A pulled

CLIPPING AND TRIMMING TIPS

☛ During clipping feel the underside of the blades every few minutes – if they are becoming hot, switch off and allow them to cool down before continuing.

☛ During clipping clean and oil the blades every ten to fifteen minutes.

☛ During clipping keep the horse warm by throwing a rug over the clipped areas – a cold horse will fidget more than a warm one.

☛ Always clip in good light conditions – start in the morning.

☛ Never try to clip a sweaty or dirty horse.

☛ For the best results do not clip until the horse's winter coat has "set" (i.e. is fully grown) – usually mid-autumn.

☛ To gauge the correct position and angle of leg lines measure one hand's width from where the foreleg joins the chest (for the V) and two hands' widths below the elbow; measure four hands' widths below the top of the stifle on the hindleg and two hands' widths above the point of the hock.

☛ Accustom a nervous horse to the feel of clippers by running hand clippers (i.e. non-motorized ones) over him.

☛ Have clippers serviced, and the blades reground, regularly.

☛ Ask your veterinary surgeon to administer a sedative to a horse who is really dangerous to clip.

☛ Pull manes and tails when the horse is warm, either on a hot day or after exercise – the hair will come out more easily while the pores are open, which is easier for you and more comfortable for the horse.

☛ Pull hair, whenever possible, from the underside of the mane – this will encourage it to lie flat.

tail will need regular pulling if it is to keep its neat shape. A horse who lives out during the winter should not have his tail pulled – the hair at the top of the dock is there to protect him from rain and snow. To trim the bottom of the tail, raise the horse's dock to the position where he carries it when he is on the move. With your other hand hold the hair at the bottom of the tail and then cut off the hair to the required length. The end of the tail should be parallel to the ground when the horse is moving.

Final Touches for Turnout

Plaiting, or **braiding, the mane** makes the horse or pony look smart, particularly if he has an untidy mane and is to appear in public. In some showing classes it is expected that the horse will be plaited. In others, such as those for Mountain and Moorland ponies and Arabs, the mane is never plaited. It is easier to plait a mane that has been pulled – a very thick, uneven mane will result in ugly, untidy plaits.

The mane hair is divided into equal bunches, each of which is dampened and then plaited, turned under and secured close to the crest of the neck, either by sewing with thread or with rubber bands. Sewn plaits are the most secure and are therefore more suitable for the horse engaged in lengthy periods of work such as hunting or eventing. Rubber bands are suitable for sports such as show jumping, where the mane does not need to remain plaited for long.

The plaits need to be fairly tight to look tidy and stay put, but beware of plaiting too tightly. If you do, it can cause the horse discomfort, particularly if he is required to stretch his neck a lot, for example when he is doing fast work or jumping.

A horse's appearance may be greatly improved by clever plaiting: making the plaits in the dip of the neck bigger than

A plaited forelock gives the head a neat appearance. Plaits should be tight enough to prevent them dropping out but not so tight that they cause the horse discomfort.

Quarter marks add the finishing touches to a well-groomed horse or pony. A chequered pattern may be made with a mane comb and stencil.

the others will help disguise a ewe neck; a small number of plaits will make a long neck seem shorter; conversely, a short neck will look longer if the mane has lots of small plaits. The appearance of a horse with a very untidy mane can be improved if the mane is hogged, or clipped off altogether. A hogged mane looks best on a horse of fairly heavy build, such as a cob – in Britain cobs are always shown with a hogged mane. Manes grow quickly and will need re-hogging every few weeks.

Plaiting, or **braiding, a tail** looks complicated but is not too difficult once you have had a little practice. For successful plaiting the tail must have long hair at the top – it is not possible to plait a pulled tail. The hair must be clean, well brushed and dampened before plaiting begins. When the plait is complete it should be carefully dampened with a sponge and then protected with a tail bandage. To avoid damaging the plait the tail bandage must be removed by unwinding, not by sliding it down.

In very muddy conditions, for instance when riding across country in wet weather, it may be more comfortable for the horse to have his tail put up so that it cannot become clogged with mud. To put up a tail, start plaiting from the top in the usual way. When you reach the end of the dock,

1 Plaiting a mane using needle and thread: the end of each plait is secured with thread.

2 The plait is folded or rolled up until it is close to the crest and stitched firmly.

3 Finished plaits should be the same size. Using larger or smaller plaits can help disguise a poorly shaped neck.

1 To plait a tail begin high up, using one bunch of hair from each side and one from the centre.

2 Plait down to the end of the dock, using thin bunches of hair from alternate sides.

3 At the end of the dock, stop adding side bunches and continue plaiting the long hair.

divide the rest of the tail into three and continue plaiting to the end of the long tail hairs. The bottom of the plait should be secured with a thick rubber band or needle and thread. The plaited tail is rolled up under the dock and carefully sewn to hold it in place.

For smart occasions, such as showing and racing, the horse's coat may be decorated with **quarter marks.** These are applied on the hindquarters and may be drawn in with a comb, a brush, or by means of brushing over a plastic stencil. All three methods involve producing a pattern by brushing patches of the coat in different directions.

There are various other "tricks of the trade" which will enhance the appearance of a show horse. Chalk may be brushed into white leg markings. It is also useful for disguising any dirty marks on a grey coat, particularly those acquired during travelling, when there is no time to wash and dry the horse before his class. A little baby oil or Vaseline may be rubbed around the eyes and nostrils – this will accentuate the quality of the head. Human hairspray may be used to help control an unruly mane. The horse's coat may be given a final polish with coat gloss, which is specially made for the purpose.

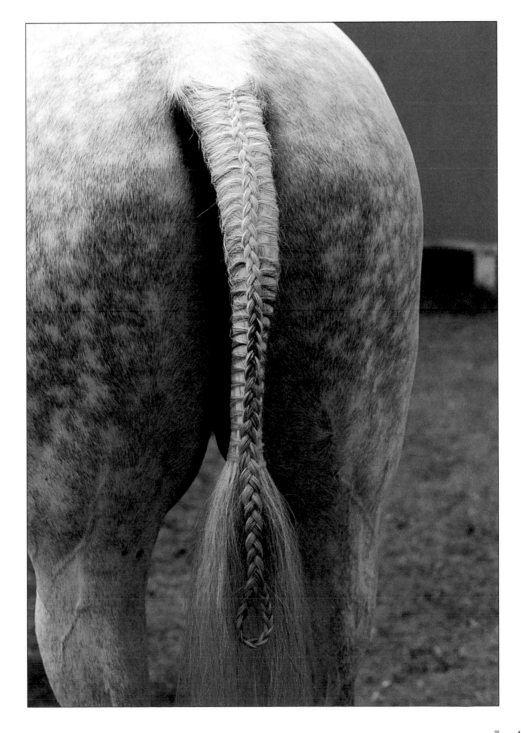

▌ RIGHT
The end of the plait is secured with needle and thread, tucked under and sewn in place to give a smart appearance.

Horse Clothing and Equipment

The ridden horse needs a variety of clothing and equipment to keep him warm, clean and dry, and to protect him from injury. Rugs are a necessity for clipped horses and for fine-skinned, hot-blooded types such as Thoroughbreds. Modern rugs are lighter in weight than their predecessors, making them more comfortable for horses to wear and easier to clean. They are also more effective at keeping the horse warm, dry, cool or clean.

There is always a risk that a horse may be injured during exercise or when he is competing or travelling to and from shows. To minimize the risk there is a range of equipment and clothing available to protect him literally from head to tail.

Turnout and Stable Rugs

TURNOUT RUGS

Turnout rugs are used to keep the horse warm and dry when turned out in the field. Turnout rugs are made from tough synthetic fabrics. Modern turnout rugs incorporate state-of-the-art breathable materials which are highly water- and windproof but still allow moisture to pass from the horse's body through the rug, preventing the horse from getting overheated.

The **New Zealand turnout rug** is a heavyweight canvas turnout rug, so-called because it was first developed in New Zealand. The self-righting type has breast and leg straps which help the rug to stay in place, whatever the horse gets up to.

The **Wug** and **Gladiator turnout rugs** are made from synthetic material. Both feature an extended neck which helps to keep the horse warm and dry.

■ LEFT
The Wug turnout rug, with its extended neck, is made from a tough yet lightweight material.

■ LEFT
The Gladiator turnout rug features a useful neck cover.

■ LEFT
The New Zealand rug is a heavyweight proofed canvas turnout rug.

▌ **BELOW**
The stable synthetic
rug can be used as a
day or night rug.

▌ **RIGHT**
quilted foal rug

STABLE RUGS

Stable rugs keep the horse clean and
warm in the stable. The models available
range from lightweight cotton rugs for
summer to thick quilted rugs for winter.

Melton day rugs are made of wool
and are available in a range of colours.
A woollen rug will keep the horse warm
but it can be heavy and less breathable
than modern fabrics, and is more
difficult to clean. Woollen rugs can be
personalized with the owner's initials or
a sponsor's logo.

The **synthetic stable rug** is a modern
alternative to the traditional woollen rug.
New fabric technology means that stable
rugs can be both lightweight and warm,
allowing any sweat from the horse's body
to pass through the fabric. Because they
are easy to wash, synthetic stable rugs also
work well as night rugs.

Under rugs (blanket liners), available
in different thicknesses, are designed to
be fitted under a horse's stable rug to
provide extra warmth during the cold
winter months. Extra warmth may also
be provided by a **horse blanket** fitted
under a stable or night rug.

Jute rugs, traditionally used as night
rugs, have a natural fibre outer layer and
a blanket lining. Their main disadvantage
is that they are very heavy.

▌ **RIGHT**
The woollen Melton
day rug is effective
at keeping the horse
warm, but is heavier
than rugs made from
synthetic fabrics.

▌ **BELOW**
The Jute rug is a
natural fibre rug
traditionally used
as a night rug.

Sheets and Coolers

SHEETS

Sheets are made from lighter materials
than turnout or stable rugs. A sheet can
be used either in the summer months
when the temperatures are higher, or
immediately before or after exercise.

Summer (stable) sheets, made from
linen or cotton, are lightweight rugs used
to help keep the stabled horse clean.

Paddock sheets are shaped rugs in
cotton or wool, so-called because they are
used to keep racehorses warm while being
paraded in the paddock before the race.
The paddock rug is held in place with a
surcingle and breastgirth. It can double as
an exercise sheet, also called a half-sheet
or quarter-sheet, to keep the racehorse's
hindquarters warm during early morning
exercise on the gallops.

Many exercise sheets are designed to
keep the horse warm and dry while active,
and are particularly useful for clipped
horses. The synthetic polypropylene fabric
used for the **wicking exercise sheet** will
only allow moisture to pass through if
the horse begins to sweat. This type of
exercise sheet is worn under the saddle.

❚ BELOW
A linen summer (stable) sheet can be used to keep
the stabled horse clean during warmer weather.

❚ BELOW
paddock sheet

COOLERS

Coolers are multi-purpose rugs, often
incorporating the latest developments in
fabric technology. They allow the horse
to dry off quickly after exercise or bathing
without the risk of catching a chill because
of a wicking effect which allows moisture
to pass from the horse's body through the
fabric. Cooler rugs are ideal for those
horses with a tendency to sweat profusely
when travelling.

The non-absorbent breathable fabric
of the **Coolmasta rug** makes it suitable
for use as an anti-sweat rug, a travelling
rug or a stable rug. The polypropylene
fabric of the **Universal wicking rug** allows
dampness from the horse's body to pass
through the rug to prevent chills, as does
the **fleece rug**. The **Combi sweat (anti-
sweat) rug and fly sheet (scrim)** is a fine-
mesh rug. The knit of the cotton fabric
creates air pockets which help the horse
to dry off quickly. These rugs can be used
on a stabled horse under a lightweight
summer sheet to speed up the drying
process after exercise.

▌ ABOVE LEFT
Universal wicking rug. A multi-purpose rug which lets body moisture through the fabric to prevent the horse catching a chill.

▌ ABOVE RIGHT
Coolmasta synthetic rug. A cooler which is versatile enough to be used as summer (stable) sheet, anti-sweat rug, travel or day rug.

▌ RIGHT
Fleece rug. While moisture evaporates away through the rug, the fleece fabric ensures that the horse's body temperature does not drop.

▌ BELOW
Combi sweat (anti-sweat) rug and fly sheet (scrim). A fine mesh rug which can be used under a summer sheet to speed up drying.

▌ BELOW RIGHT
Rain sheet. This waterproof rug (cover) will keep the horse dry at shows and competitions.

Specialist Sheets and Rugs

▌ BELOW
Continental waterproof exercise sheet

Besides the basic types of rug, an increasing number of rug products are available for more specific needs.

Exercise sheets will keep thin-skinned horses warm and dry during exercise sessions. The **continental waterproof exercise sheet** has a lightweight outer shell with a twill lining and can be fitted over the saddle in wet weather. The **fluorescent exercise sheet** ensures that both horse and rider are easily seen by other road users, and is especially useful for anyone who has to ride on roads at times of poor visibility.

The **rain sheet** is a lightweight synthetic sheet which covers the horse from ears to tail. The sheet will keep the horse dry at competitions and shows but should not be used on horses turned out in the field.

New-born foals do not normally require rugs. However, the **quilted foal rug** can be very useful in helping to keep a sickly foal warm in the stable.

The **rug bib (blanket bib)** is fitted under the rug to prevent it from rubbing the horse's shoulders, leading to sores and bare patches in his coat.

Hoods can be fitted to rugs to provide extra warmth and to help keep the horse clean. The **outdoor hood**, made from

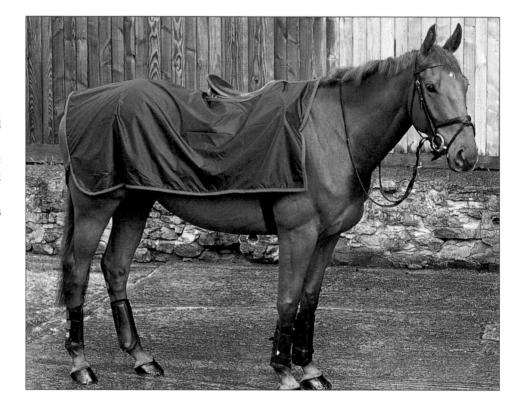

a synthetic material, can be fitted to a turnout rug. The **lycra hood** is used in the stable to keep the horse clean.

Chest extenders are panels of fabric with straps which can be buckled on to the horse's existing rug to provide a better fit.

▌ BELOW LEFT
fluorescent exercise sheet

▌ BELOW RIGHT
wicking exercise sheet

▌ ABOVE
A rug bib is fitted
under the rug to
prevent the rug
from rubbing.

▌ ABOVE
golden stripe horse blanket

▌ BELOW
lycra hood

▌ BELOW
under rug

Fitting a Rug

Whatever type of rug you use, it is important that it is fitted correctly. Rugs are often left on for long periods of time and an ill-fitting rug can cause rubbing and discomfort. Rugs are sized according to their length, with the measurement based on the length of the horse taken from the centre of the chest to the tail.

HOW TO PUT ON A RUG

1 Stand on the near (left) side of the horse. Fold the blanket in half widthways and place it over the horse's neck. Fold the rug back over the horse's hindquarters.

2 Fasten the cross surcingles, but not too tightly: there should be room for the width of a hand between the horse's belly and the straps. These straps should be fastened first so that there is no risk of the rug ending up hanging around the horse's neck, or worse still, his legs.

HOW TO REMOVE A RUG

To remove the rug, undo the leg straps first, then the chest straps and finally the cross surcingles. Fold the front of the rug over the horse's hindquarters and slide off carefully.

3 Next fasten the chest straps: there should be room for a hand's width at the chest.

4 Finally, fasten the leg straps. Fitted correctly, the straps should hang clear of the horse's legs so that they do not rub, but should not be loose enough for the horse to get his leg caught.

■ RIGHT
Modern turnout rugs allow horses to spend time out in their field whatever the weather. It is important to remember that turned out horses should have their rugs checked at least once a day, as the rug can slip and become uncomfortable for the horse.

Rug Rollers and Surcingles

Most modern stable rugs have surcingles already fitted but separate rollers and surcingles can be used to keep in place those rugs which do not incorporate their own. A separate roller or surcingle is also necessary when more than one rug at a time is worn, to keep them both in place.

Rollers and surcingles should be fitted snugly enough to secure the rug, but they should not be so tight as to be uncomfortable for the horse after long periods of time. Correctly tightened, there should be just enough room to allow four fingers between the roller or surcingle and the rug.

Surcingles used to secure rugs differ significantly from surcingles used to secure saddles, since the needs of the turned out horse and the ridden horse are not the same. The **rug surcingle** is designed for comfort. It is wrapped in protective padding and replaces the buckles and clasps of the saddle surcingle with thick rounded straps, to allow the horse the freedom to sit or roll.

The **elasticated surcingle** fits around the horse's girth. If you are using one of these, it is a good idea to fit a pad over the withers to prevent pressure sores. The **elasticated roller** has padding built in to the area in contact with the withers, as does the **jute surcingle**, which fastens with strong leather straps.

The **anti-cast roller**, made from webbing and leather, has a large metal hoop on the top which prevents the horse from getting cast or wedged when rolling in his stable (stall).

Elasticated surcingle. This type should be used with a pad over the withers to prevent pressure sores.

Elasticated roller. This type has padding built in to protect the withers.

Jute surcingle. This type has built-in padding and fastens with strong leather straps.

Webbing anti-cast roller. The large metal hoop on the top prevents the horse from getting cast.

Boots

Boots are designed to protect the horse's legs when travelling, turned out or being ridden, and a wide choice is available. Many equestrian activities place extreme demands on the horse's legs and protection is needed to prevent injury. Some horses are also predisposed conformationally to striking themselves accidentally while being exercised.

Brushing boots, also referred to as **splint boots**, have a reinforced pad along the inside of the boot to prevent injuries caused when one leg knocks against the other. The boot should start just below the knee and finish just below the fetlock (or ankle) joint. **Hind brushing boots** are longer than **fore brushing boots** to protect the hind cannon bone. **Leather brushing boots** have buckle and strap fastenings. They are tougher than synthetic boots but must be looked after to maintain their condition. **Synthetic brushing boots** are held in place with Velcro straps. They are lightweight and easily washed.

Leather brushing boots. These are used to prevent injuries inflicted as the horse is being brushed.

Synthetic brushing boots. These particular boots are fleece lined to prevent rubbing.

Sesamoid boots. These boots protect the base of the horse's fetlock.

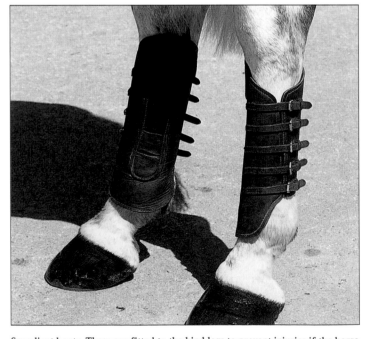

Speedicut boots. These are fitted to the hind legs to prevent injuries if the horse were to accidentally kick himself while galloping.

Speedicut boots are fitted to the hind legs and are designed to protect against injuries that occur when one leg strikes another during fast work. When the horse is travelling at high speed, the vulnerable area is the upper part of the leg, hence the boot's extra length.

Tendon boots are designed to protect the tendons which run down the back of the horse's lower foreleg, so are normally open-fronted. The boots should start high enough to protect the tendon and extend low enough to protect the fetlock joint. **Leather tendon boots** have buckle and strap fastenings and may be lined with sheepskin to prevent rubbing. **Synthetic tendon boots** usually have strap and clip fastenings.

Open-fronted boots are popular with show jumpers because they protect the vulnerable part of the horse's leg while still allowing him to feel the poles of the jump.

Sesamoid boots protect the base of the fetlock joint and are often used on

❚ BELOW
Leather tendon boots protect the tendons which run down the back of the horse's leg.

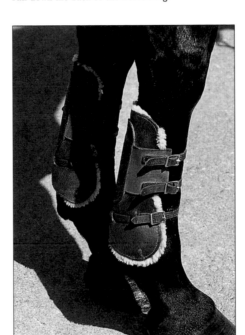

❚ BELOW
Synthetic tendon boots are cheaper and easier to clean than the leather boots.

racehorses that are trained or run on all-weather or dirt tracks. The base of the fetlock would be damaged if unprotected as it touches the ground as the result of the forces exerted when galloping.

Fetlock boots are shortened versions of brushing boots, fitted to the hindlegs. **Skid boots** are used for Western riding, and are fitted to prevent fetlock injuries which can occur when the horse makes sliding halts.

Fetlock boots. These are a shortened version of the brushing boot, and are normally fitted to the hindlegs only.

Skid boots. These are fitted to prevent injuries to the fetlock when the horse comes to a sliding halt.

Free knee boots prevent damage to the horse's knees when jumping. Because of their design – they can flip up – they are not suitable for road work or travelling. **Skeleton knee boots** have a lower strap fitted which prevents the pad from flipping up in the event of the horse falling. They are not suitable for jumping as there is a risk that the horse could get a hoof caught in the back strap.

The **coronet ring**, also called an anti-brushing ring, is fitted to one of a pair of legs to prevent brushing injuries. A **sausage boot**, also referred to as a **shoe-boil boot**, is used on stabled horses to prevent injury to the elbow when the horse lies down.

Overreach boots, or **bell boots**, prevent overreach injuries. An overreach is caused by the toe of the hind foot striking into the heel or coronet of the front foot. **Pull-on rubber overreach boots** can be difficult to get on but, once on, stay in place well. A disadvantage of this type of overreach boot is that they can flip up, in which case they will not protect the heel and coronet. **Velcro-fastened rubber overreach boots** are easier to put on and take off. **Petal boots** are less likely to flip up because of their segmented design. They are made up of a series of tough plastic segments or petals which are attached to a strap fitted around the coronet.

Covering boots are felt shoes which fit over the mare's hind feet. They are used on mares being covered, to avoid risking injury to the stallion should the mare try to kick him.

▌ LEFT
Free knee boots. Because of their design, these boots are not suitable for roadwork or travelling.

▌ ABOVE
Skeleton knee boots. These have a lower strap fitted which prevents the pad flipping up.

▌ RIGHT
Sausage boot. These are used on stabled horses to prevent injuries to the elbow.

▌ ABOVE
Coronet ring. This is fitted to one leg to prevent brushing injuries.

■ LEFT
Protection is necessary to guard against the hazards encountered during the cross-country phase of a one-day event. Because the horse is jumping fixed objects, it is vital that his legs are protected with boots or bandages.

■ ABOVE
Mare's covering boots. These felt shoes are fitted over the mare's hind feet to protect the stallion should she lash out at him.

■ ABOVE
Velcro-fastened rubber overreach boots. This type is easier to put on and take off than the pull-on variety of overreach boot.

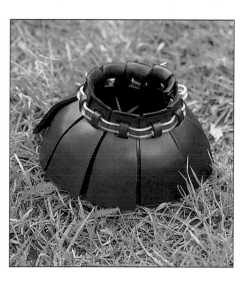

■ RIGHT
Pull-on rubber overreach boots. These moulded boots will sit securely on the hoof, but they do flip up easily and can offer no protection when this happens.

■ LEFT
Petal boots are made up of a series of tough plastic segments which are attached to a strap.

EXERCISE BOOTS

Exercise boots, such as brushing boots, are much more convenient to use than exercise bandages (polo wraps) as they are quicker and easier to put on.

▌ BELOW
Skid boots are worn by reining horses to protect the base of the fetlock joint from injury as he comes to a sliding halt.

FITTING BRUSHING BOOTS

1 Never kneel down when putting on or taking off boots – always crouch so that you can get out of the way quickly should the horse suddenly move. When fitting boots with two straps, fasten the top strap first.

2 On most boots, straps fasten from the front to the back. For boots with more than two straps, fasten the middle strap first, then the top strap and finally the bottom strap or straps.

3 Be careful not to over-tighten boots as this is uncomfortable for the horse and can damage the tendons in his lower legs.

4 When removing boots, undo the bottom strap before unfastening the top one.

THERAPY BOOTS

These boots are designed to keep in place poultices, which are used to draw out dirt from a wound, and otherwise to assist in the treatment of injuries.

Rubber over-shoes fit over the horse's foot. One of these can be used to cover a foot bandage or poultice, or to protect the unshod hoof during ridden work. The **Tenderfoot sox** is used to hold a foot poultice in place.

A **tendon-hosing boot** fitted to the horse's lower leg allows cold water to be trickled down the leg to help reduce swelling caused by stresses, strains or injuries. If something more than a trickle is needed **aqua boots**, covering the entire lower leg and foot, are attached to a compressor which forces water to move around inside, massaging the lower leg.

Magnetic therapy boots are available in various designs. They incorporate thin, flexible magnetic pads which, when placed over the injured area, are said to assist in the repair of muscle, tendon or bone damage.

◾ **LEFT**
rubber over-shoe

◾ **LEFT**
magnetic therapy boots

◾ **BELOW LEFT**
tendon-hosing boot

◾ **BELOW RIGHT**
aqua boots.

Bandages and Pads

LEFT
travelling or stable bandages

BELOW LEFT
exercise or tail bandage

BELOW RIGHT
polo wraps

BANDAGES

Like boots, bandages can be used to protect the horse's legs during exercise or travelling as well as for first-aid purposes.

Travelling or **stable bandages** are non-stretch bandages usually made of wool or acrylic and used for warmth and protection. To prevent pressure sores developing on the leg, they should always be used with padding underneath.

Exercise or **tail bandages** are lighter in weight than stable bandages. They are usually slightly elasticated and are held in place with ties. When used to protect the leg during competitions, in particular horse trials, they can be stitched in place. They will help to smooth the tail hair down as well as protecting the tail while the horse is travelling to the competition.

Polo wraps are made from strong, shock-absorbent felt. Unlike traditional bandages, polo wraps do not require padding underneath.

A **cohesive bandage** is a stretchy bandage which sticks to itself. It can be used as an alternative to an exercise bandage or for holding dressings and poultices in place.

PADS

Bandages should never be applied directly to the leg (except for polo bandages) but should be used with bandage pads to help reduce the risk of pressure sores developing on the legs.

Felt pads are hardwearing and shock absorbent, but they do not mould easily to the shape of the horse's leg. **Cotton quilted pads** are easily washable and hardwearing but, like felt, do not mould easily to the horse's leg. **Porter boots** are hard-shelled leg protectors which mould to the shape of the horse's leg and are held in place with an exercise bandage. They are used instead of pads to protect the leg from injury during competitions.

ABOVE LEFT
stable bandages

ABOVE RIGHT
Porter protector

LEFT
cohesive bandage

PUTTING ON AN EXERCISE BANDAGE

EXERCISE BANDAGES

Exercise bandages and polo wraps are used to protect the horse's legs during exercise or work. A great deal of skill is required to apply bandages which are neither too tight (which can lead to damaged tendons), nor too loose (when they can unravel and cause the horse to fall). Exercise bandages must always be applied over some sort of padding, such as a Gamgee, Fybagee or Porter boot.

1 Place the padding around the leg, making sure that the edge of the pad lies between the tendons, on the outside of the leg. The padding should start just below the knee or hock and finish just below the fetlock joint. Wrap the pad around the leg firmly, from front to back, making sure that there are no lumps or wrinkles.

2 Bandage in the same direction as the padding and start just below the padding at the top.

3 Do one complete turn with the bandage around the top of the padding before working down the leg. Exercise bandages are elasticated so be careful not to pull the bandage in too tightly.

4 Make sure that the bandage stays smooth and that the tension is even.

5 At the bottom of the leg the bandage should follow the same angle as the fetlock joint so that it forms a V at the front of the leg. This will ensure that the movement of the fetlock is not restricted.

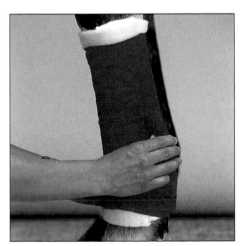

6 Continue to wrap the bandage around the leg, working back up to the top of the padding.

7 Secure the bandage by fastening the ties with a simple knot. The knot should be flat and sit on the outside of the leg. For competitions, stitch the bandage to ensure that it stays in place. Cover the stitched end with insulating tape.

8 The bandage should be firm enough not to slide down but not so tight that it could damage the tendons. You should just be able to slide your finger inside the bandage.

Travelling Equipment

Special clothing can be used to protect the horse from injuries incurred during transportation in a horse truck or trailer.

A **tail guard** prevents the horse from rubbing his tail when travelling. Linen and cotton tail guards are secured with strips tied to the surcingle. The padded tail guard is fitted with Velcro fastenings.

Shaped travel boots can be used instead of travelling bandages to protect the front and hindlegs, from the coronet up to the knee and hock. **Travel boots** are simple square wraps which give protection to the lower leg.

Hock boots, made from leather and felt, are fitted over the top of travel bandages to protect the hock from injury, in the same way that **knee pads** are used to protect the knees. **Felt travel pads** under travel bandages will do the same job.

A **poll guard**, made from leather with a felt lining, provides protection for the sensitive poll area of the horse's head. It is attached to the headcollar or halter.

Shaped travel boots. These are designed for front or hindlegs to protect them from the coronet right up to the knee or hock.

Travel boots. These simple square padded wraps are effective in protecting the lower leg.

Hock boots. These are fitted to protect the hock joint from injury during transit.

Knee pads. These can be used with travel bandages to protect the knees from damage.

HORSE DRESSED FOR TRAVELLING

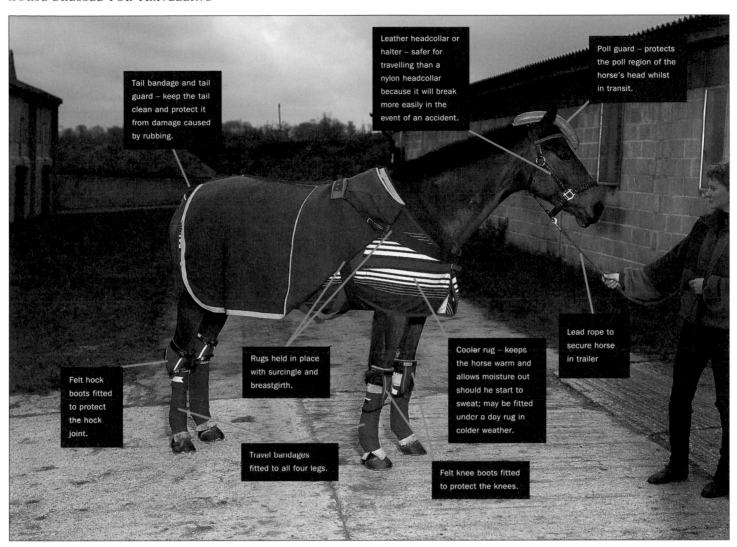

Tail bandage and tail guard – keep the tail clean and protect it from damage caused by rubbing.

Leather headcollar or halter – safer for travelling than a nylon headcollar because it will break more easily in the event of an accident.

Poll guard – protects the poll region of the horse's head whilst in transit.

Felt hock boots fitted to protect the hock joint.

Rugs held in place with surcingle and breastgirth.

Cooler rug – keeps the horse warm and allows moisture out should he start to sweat; may be fitted under a day rug in colder weather.

Lead rope to secure horse in trailer

Travel bandages fitted to all four legs.

Felt knee boots fitted to protect the knees.

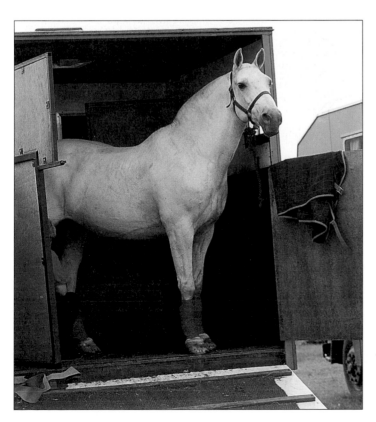

LEFT
Horses are very vulnerable to minor injuries when travelling on the roads. While a complete set of travelling equipment is not always necessary, your horse should be fitted with leg protection and a rug. Regular safety checks should also be made on the trailer itself.

Shaped travel pads can be used in conjunction with travel bandages to protect specific parts of the legs when the horse is in transit.

Corrective Equipment

The following pieces of equipment may be used on the horse to discourage or prevent bad habits when he is stabled or turned out to grass.

A **plastic muzzle** may be used on a horse who is on a strict diet but needs to be turned out. The muzzle prevents him from eating large amounts of food, while the holes in the design allow him to breathe and drink. Plastic muzzles are also useful for horses who bite, chew their rugs or eat their bedding. The design of the **leather muzzle**, made of thick strips, allows the horse to breathe and drink but, like the plastic muzzle, it prevents him from nibbling his rug and biting.

A **bib** is attached to the headcollar and sits below the horse's chin. Like the muzzle, it is fitted to prevent the horse from chewing his rugs or bandages. A much more restrictive item is the **neck cradle**, which should be used only as a last resort to stop a horse from chewing.

A **cribbing collar** is a strong leather strap which is fitted tightly around the horse's throat to prevent him from crib biting and wind-sucking. The collar will not cure the condition, but will stop him doing it while it is fitted.

The design of the leather muzzle allows the horse to breathe and drink but will not allow him to bite and chew.

A plastic muzzle may be used on a horse on a diet who nonetheless needs to be turned out.

▮ LEFT
The neck cradle offers a last ditch attempt to stop a horse chewing rugs or bandages.

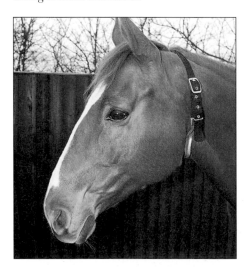

Cribbing collar. This is fitted around the horse's throat to prevent crib biting and wind-sucking.

▮ LEFT
The plastic bib is a mildly restrictive piece of equipment which will help to dissuade the horse from chewing his clothing.

What are Vices?

There are a number of pieces of equipment used on horses to prevent or discourage vices (as described on the opposite page) but what are vices and what causes a horse to exhibit them? A vice is chronic, habitual behaviour displayed by the horse, for example box walking, weaving (when the horse rocks from side to side swaying its head), windsucking (the horse sucks in air and swallows it) or crib biting (similar to windsucking except that the horse will also take hold of an object with his teeth).

Most vices are displayed by stabled horses (although not exclusively) and are thought to be a result of boredom or nervousness on the part of the horse. It is also possible that vices are copied by one horse from another.

Before resorting to equipment to stop a vice, it is always worth investigating the possible causes. For example, if a horse is bored being kept in his stable for long periods, try turning him out for part of the day, or increasing the amount of hay in his diet to keep him occupied.

If a horse persistently chews his rugs or bandages it is possible that they may be irritating him in some way. His bandages may have been applied too tightly or his rug may be irritating his skin. In any case it is always worth trying to eliminate the possible causes of a vice before trying to treat the symptoms.

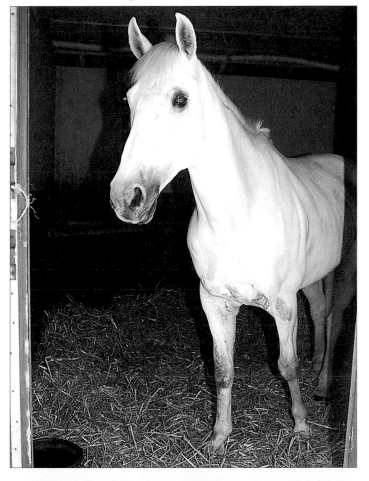

▌ LEFT
It is always better to prevent vices rather than deal with them once the bad habits have formed. Horses can easily get bored if they are kept in a stable all day, and this can lead to chronic stress-induced behaviour. Make sure your horse is turned out as much as possible, to give him exercise and to add variety to his routine.

▌ BELOW
Check your horse and his rugs. If they are chewed, it may be a sign that the horse is uncomfortable or that his skin is irritated. It may help to remove the rug for a time, loosen it, or try a different material.

▌ ABOVE
If your horse is stabled for long periods, make sure he has fresh supplies of hay. This is not only good for his diet, but will also keep him occupied.

The Rider's Clothes

Like the horse, the rider requires specialist clothing for his or her safety and comfort. There is a wide variety of riding clothing available, with new designs and developments always coming on to the market. However, there are a few basic items which are essential for anyone who rides. A protective riding hat should always be worn when riding, lungeing or long reining horses, to reduce the risk of injury to the head. The wearing of a body protector is also a sensible precaution when jumping or riding horses which you know to be unpredictable. Riding boots (short or long) should be worn, because they are designed to prevent the rider's foot getting caught in the stirrup in the event of a fall. Many riders choose to wear gloves: those which have non-slip palms are better as they prevent the reins from slipping through the hands. Gloves, however, should always be worn when lungeing, long reining or leading horses by hand, to prevent injury to the hands should the horse suddenly pull away. Jodhpurs or breeches are a sensible choice for riding as their design prevents rubbing caused by the saddle or stirrup leathers.

Clothes

When working with horses, whether you are on the ground or riding, safety is the keynote. Horses are big, strong animals and there is always an element of danger, however calm and placid they might normally be. Therefore care should be taken even when choosing clothes for mundane, everyday chores such as mucking out.

Neat clothing which is well fitting without being too tight is the easiest to move around in. A long-sleeved shirt with a sweatshirt or sweater, depending on the weather, and a pair of comfortable trousers, jeans or jodhpurs are ideal for stable work. Avoid overtight trousers as they make bending down difficult. Dark colours will stay looking smart longer. Long sleeves are preferable to short ones since they give some protection from nips from equine teeth. Sleeveless suntops and vests should definitely be avoided.

Footwear is of great importance since a misplaced hoof can do a great deal of damage to a human foot. "Trainers" give little protection, nor do most rubber boots, though sturdy Wellingtons are as good as anything for mucking out, particularly if you wear thick walking-boot socks inside. At other times a pair of leather jodhpur boots will probably afford the best protection and will certainly enable you to move more quickly than when wearing Wellingtons. Some boots are now fitted with protective toecaps.

Coats and body warmers, when worn, should be kept fastened – a flapping coat can frighten a nervous horse and there is also the danger that it might become caught up on some "foreign body". Some horses are nervous of noisy waterproof fabrics, so avoid wearing them around the stables.

Long hair should be tied up, again to avoid the possibility of scaring a horse or becoming caught up. This is particularly important in windy weather. Avoid wearing jewellery: rings, earrings,

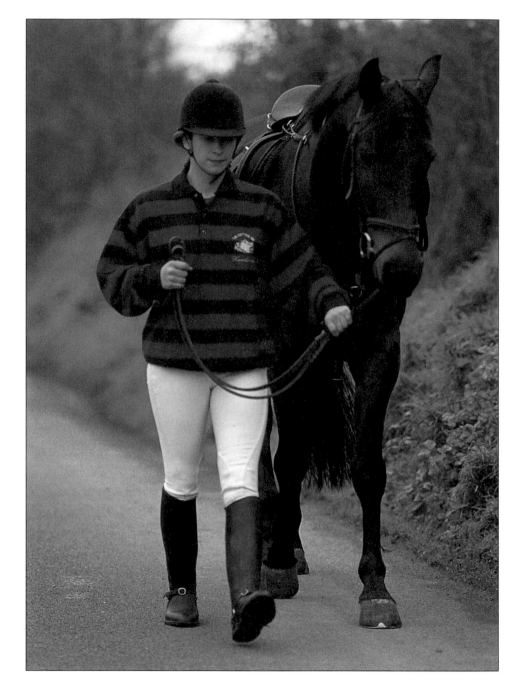

noserings and the like can all cause nasty injuries if they become caught up.

Most well-trained horses are safe to lead about, in and out of their stables, down to the paddock, etc. But if you have any doubts whatsoever about a horse's good behaviour (when handling a young horse, for example) take precautions: wear a hard hat, correctly fastened, in case he rears up and strikes out, boots to protect your feet and a pair of gloves.

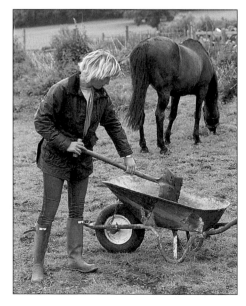

▌ ABOVE
A sweatshirt, breeches, boots and a hard hat make a suitable outfit for everyday exercise.

▌ LEFT
Neat, workmanlike clothes enable you to carry out daily chores in comfort and safety.

Safety Gear

Riding has always been and always will be a risk sport. But modern safety equipment is constantly improving and everyone who rides should ensure that they wear the best available protective gear, which includes hat, body protector and boots.

The most vulnerable part of the rider is the head and it is irresponsible to get on to a horse, or to lunge or long rein or otherwise handle an unpredictable young

❙ LEFT
Fluorescent clothing is a wise safety precaution when riding on the roads. The message on the tabard helps to alert drivers.

SAFETY CHECKLIST

☞ Wear a correctly fitting hard hat with the chin strap fastened at all times when mounted.

☞ Replace a hat that has been subjected to impact in a fall – it may not give sufficient protection next time.

☞ Always ride in your own hat – a borrowed hat is unlikely to fit you correctly.

☞ Wear safe footwear at all times when mounted.

☞ Always use the correct stirrup iron size – about 1 inch (2.5cm) wider than your boot – to prevent your foot becoming stuck.

☞ Wear fluorescent garments – hat cover, tabard/body warmer etc – fitted with retro-reflective strips when riding on the roads and fit your horse with similar high visibility leg bands.

☞ Avoid riding on the roads in poor visibility and after dark.

☞ Never ride in jewellery.

☞ Always fasten tiepins horizontally or at an angle, never vertically.

☞ Always ride with your coat fastened.

☞ Never take off a coat or sweater while mounted – while you are taking your arms out of the sleeves you will have no control over the horse should he make an unexpected move.

☞ If you have less than perfect eyesight, wear soft contact lenses if possible. If not, seek your optician's advice on the safest type of spectacles.

horse, without wearing a **hard hat** securely fastened with a **chin strap**. Your country's national federation (for example in Britain the British Horse Society, in the United States the American Horse Shows Association) will advise on the most up-to-date safety standards. The **jockey skull**, or **crash hat**, is generally considered to give maximum protection and is therefore recommended (and obligatory under the rules of most sports) for all riding which involves fast work or jumping. The **chin harness** must be correctly adjusted and fastened at all times. It may be worn on the point of the chin, with a chin cup, or under the chin, whichever is most comfortable. The alternative is the traditional **hunting cap** which must have a soft peak (a hard peak can cause facial, head or neck injuries in a fall). All riding

hats should be correctly fitted (many retailers are trained in hat fitting).

Body protectors are designed to protect the torso and the shoulders in the event of a fall. They should fit well, feel comfortable and not restrict the rider's movement.

Riding boots and **jodhpur boots** are designed to prevent the foot from sliding right through the stirrup iron or otherwise becoming caught up in the iron in the event of a fall – a potentially fatal situation. They have smooth soles and a clearly defined heel. Leather boots afford the best protection from knocks, for example when riding across country, but rubber ones fashioned in the same style are suitable for everyday riding. Wellington boots, trainers and other boots or shoes with ridged soles and little or no heel should never be worn for riding.

❙ LEFT
A jockey skull or "crash hat", with a correctly adjusted chin harness, gives the head maximum protection. It is fitted with a silk cover.

❙ LEFT
A body protector should be worn when jumping fixed fences and by people needing special protection (for example, an older person with more brittle bones).

Riding Clothes

By and large all riding clothes are designed for comfort and protection. Only with the odd item of equipment (such as the top hat for dressage) is clothing dictated by fashion.

Most riding clothes are based on hunting attire, which evolved over a long period and led to the design of an entire outfit which would give protection from wet, cold and the many knocks experienced when travelling at speed across country. Long leather boots keep the feet and lower legs dry and give maximum protection from painful encounters with gateposts or other fixed objects. Breeches keep the upper legs warm and dry and protect the insides of the knees from chafing against the saddle. A well-fitting jacket made of a good stout tweed or twill gives warmth and a certain amount of waterproofing while at the same time affording complete freedom of movement – essential for all riding, but particularly for jumping and riding at speed. Gloves keep the hands warm and dry and give a secure grip on the reins. A hunting tie or stock helps protect the neck in the event of a fall. A hard hat, correctly secured with a chin harness, protects the most vulnerable part of all, the head.

For everyday riding there is a wealth of suitable clothing to choose from which is both cheaper than more formal attire and suited to frequent immersion in the washing machine. **Jodhpurs**, which extend down the leg to the ankle, and are usually worn with short, elastic-sided leather jodhpur boots, are cooler in summer than breeches and long boots. They come in a range of materials, from lightweight cotton suitable for hot climates to thermal material for wear in extremes of cold. Instead of jodhpur boots, jodhpurs may be worn with **half-chaps**, which cover the leg from below the knee to the foot, or with full **chaps**, which extend up to the thigh.

Close-fitting **riding trousers** are also suitable for everyday wear. Like jodhpurs,

they come with "strappings" – reinforcements at the knee and thigh. Some garments are also fitted with an inset seat panel made in an extra-grip material.

Rubber **riding boots** are a cheaper alternative to leather ones, though they can be cold in winter, when an inner sole

or an extra pair of socks may be required.

Casual **riding coats** such as waxed or quilted jackets, blousons and body warmers are fine for everyday riding and may be worn with a shirt and/or sweatshirt or sweater. Modern waterproof materials are light and comfortable to wear and the more expensive ones have the advantage of being "breathable". Waterproofs come in a range of lengths and may have added features such as storm collar and cuffs, fleecy lining and pommel flap. Noisy waterproof materials should be avoided as horses tend to be frightened of them, particularly on a windy day.

There are **gloves** for every occasion, specially designed for the rider. Special features include reinforced rein fingers, pimple palm grips and lycra inserts for extra flexibility.

■ LEFT
Everyday riding clothes should be neat and safe. Dark colours are more practical than the light shades worn with traditional hunting dress.

■ BELOW LEFT
Chaps are a good alternative to boots. This rider is prepared for roadwork – note the fluorescent tabard and the horse's protective boots.

Clothes for Competition

For most forms of competitive riding it is usual to wear a riding coat with breeches and boots, a shirt with a collar and tie or collarless shirt with a hunting tie or stock. The rules of some sports also stipulate the wearing of spurs. A hat is obligatory and although the bowler hat (derby) is still seen in show classes and the top hat in dressage, the trend is more and more to the safer type of hunting cap and, even more so, the jockey skull. The latter is usually worn with a dark-coloured silk cover.

For cross-country riding the jacket is replaced by a sweater or shirt, according to the weather, which may be in the rider's own colours, as may the hat silk.

Endurance riding is one area where tradition holds less sway, partly because the sport is of fairly recent origin (at least in an organized competitive way) and also because at the higher echelons riders are not only in the saddle for very long periods but also spend some of the time on their feet, running alongside their horses to give them a breather. Breeches and boots would be too hot and uncomfortable so this is the one sport where runningshoes are permitted. However, as a safety precaution, riders are required to use enclosed-type stirrup irons to prevent their feet slipping right through.

▌ LEFT
Correct dress for top-level dressage includes a top hat, tail coat and waistcoat.

▌ BELOW
Most riding gear, for women as well as men, is based on clothes developed for the hunting field.

▌ BOTTOM LEFT
The clothes worn for endurance riding are less formal than in other competitive sports.

Whips and Spurs

Whips and spurs (referred to as artificial aids) can be used by the rider to reinforce the leg aids.

The rider uses a whip just behind his or her leg if the horse does not respond to a command from the leg. Whips should only be used in these circumstances and not as an alternative to the leg, or as a punishment.

Shorter, thicker whips are used for show jumping and cross country. Longer, finer whips are ideal for schooling horses on the flat, because they can be used to give a gentle flick without the rider having to take his or her hands off the reins.

Hunting whips are not used on the horse, but are traditionally carried out hunting. They usually have a bent top which is very useful for pulling gates shut,

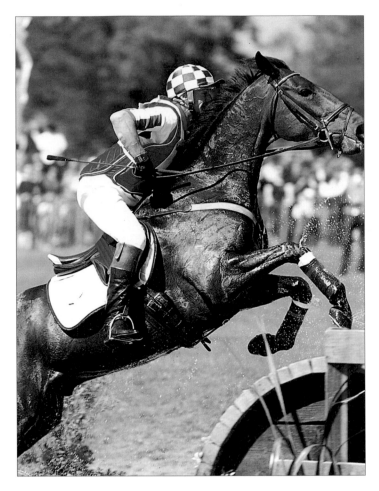

and a plaited leather thong and cord lash which is carried looped round. For showing horses, a simple malacca or leather-covered cane is often carried.

Spurs can be worn to emphasize the rider's leg aids. The most common type of spur used for English riding is called a Prince of Wales spur. It has a short blunt-ended neck which, when fitted, points downward. The spur fits snugly around the back of the rider's boot and is held in place with a strap. Spurs are also available with rowels (small metal discs fitted to the tip of the spurs) which give them a much sharper action. Spurs should only be used by experienced riders who have an independent seat and can maintain control when the spur is applied to the horse.

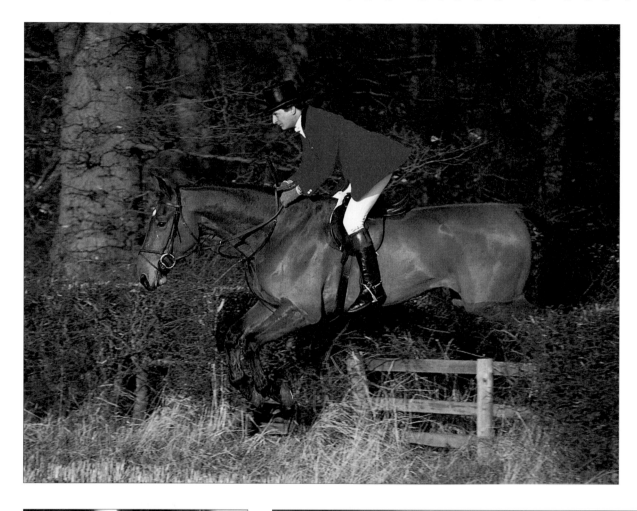

▌ LEFT
The hunting whip is not used on the horse, but is carried as a hunting tradition, and is sometimes used for pulling gates shut. It is much longer than the show-jumping or cross-country whip.

▌ ABOVE
Spurs, like whips, can be used to emphasize the rider's leg aids. They should only be used by experienced riders.

▌ RIGHT
A show-jumping whip, used for encouraging the horse to move forward if he doesn't respond to the rider's leg aids.

Suppliers and Acknowledgements

The authors would like to thank the many individuals and breed societies who kindly provided information for use in the breeds section of this book, particularly:

The American Morgan Horse Association, Inc; The American Paint Horse Association; The American Saddlebred Horse Association, Inc; The British Spotted Pony Society; Vivienne Burdon; The Cleveland Bay Horse Society; The Clydesdale Horse Society of Great Britain and Ireland; The Exmoor Pony Society; The Hackney Horse Society; The Haflinger Society of Great Britain; The Highland Pony Society; The Irish Draught Horse Society (GB); Sylvia Loch (author of *The Royal Horse of Europe,* J.A. Allen, 1986); The Lusitano Breed Society of Great Britain; The Palomino Horse Association of America, Inc; The Pinto Horse Association of America, Inc; Valerie Russell; The Suffolk Horse Society; The Walkaloosa Horse Association; The Walking Horse Owners' Association of America, Inc; The Welsh Pony and Cob Society.

We are grateful to the following for allowing their horses, ponies and stables to be photographed:

HORSES: EUROPE
Arab – Sariah Arabians, Dorking, Surrey
Barb – Haras Regional de Marrakech, Morocco
Thoroughbred – Mrs M Blackburn, c/o Catherston Stud, Whitchurch, Hampshire
Anglo-Arab – Woodlander Stud, Raglan, Gwent
Danish Warmblood – Catherston Stud, Whitchurch, Hampshire
Ariègeois – Bob Langrish, photographer
Norman Cob – Haras National Le Lion d'Angers, Loire, France

Camargue – Laurent Serre, Camargue, France
Selle Français – Haras National Le Lion d'Angers, Loire, France
French Trotter – Haras National Le Lion d'Angers, Loire, France
Percheron – Haras National Le Lion d'Angers, Loire, France
Breton – Haras National Le Lion d'Angers, Loire, France
Hanoverian – Mrs S Bray, Nuneaton, Warwickshire
Holstein – Mr Luetzow, Wokingham, Berkshire
Oldenburg – I Brendel, Trenthide, Dorset
Westphalian – Marlow Building Co Ltd, Marlow, Buckinghamshire
Hackney – Georgina Turner, Ipswich, Suffolk
Shire – Lingwood Shire, Brentwood, Essex
Suffolk – Randy Hiscock, Shaftesbury, Dorset
Shagya Arab – Sonia Lindsay, Okehampton, Devon
Icelandic – Edda Hestar, Salisbury, Wiltshire
Friesian – Harrods, London
Gelderland – Mr Luetzow, Wokingham, Berkshire
Dutch Warmblood – Mrs C Hughes, Doncaster

Don – Russian Horse Society, Epsom, Surrey (standing) Mrs June Connolly, Droitwich, West Midlands (action)
Budenny – Mrs Marcus, Beoley, Redditch, Hereford & Worcester (action)
Kabardin – Mrs June Connolly, Droitwich, West Midlands
Orlov – George Bowman Jnr, Penrith, Cumbria
Vladimir – Russian Horse Society, Epsom, Surrey
North Swedish – Jan Gyllensten, photographer, Sweden
Akhal-Teke – Viscountess Bury, Plumpton, Sussex
Knabstrup – Mrs Ann Peruzzi-Smith, Diss, Norfolk

HORSES: UNITED STATES
Morgan – Betty Gray, Orange Lake, Florida
Quarter Horse – Quiet Oaks Farm, Ocala, Florida & Derby Daze Farm, Ocala, Florida
Saddlebred – Boca Raton Equestrian Center, Del Ray Beach
Standardbred – David McDuffee & Tom Walsh Jnr, South Florida Trotting Center
Missouri Fox Trotter – Sandy Hart, Winter Haven, Florida

Tennessee Walking Horse – Mrs Carol Worsham, Dunnellon, Florida
Mustang – Cindy Bowman, Dunnellon, Florida
Peruvian Paso – Annette Ward, Alachua, Florida
Pony of the Americas – Cynthia Bunnell, Eustis, Florida
American Shetland – Caroline Proctor, Ocala, Florida
Palomino – Holmes Quarter Horses, Brandon, Florida
Appaloosa – Classic Acres Farm, Ocala, Florida
Paint – Brooke Hamlin, Ocala, Florida

PONIES
Haflinger – Millslade Farm Stud, Bridgwater, Somerset
Exmoor – Mrs J Freeman, Wareside, Hertfordshire
New Forest – Shirley Young, Salisbury, Wiltshire
Shetland – Mr & Mrs E House, Bincombe Shetlands, Bridgwater, Somerset
Dales – Mrs B Powell, Farnham, Surrey
Connemara & Welsh Cob – Miss S Clark, Dorking, Surrey
Fjord – Mrs Murray, Ottery St Mary, Devon
Caspian – Henden Caspian Stud, Chippenham, Wiltshire

STABLE MANAGEMENT
Catherston Stud, Whitchurch, Hampshire
Stretcholt Farm Stud, Bridgwater, Somerset.

We would also like to thank the following for facilities and equipment, and for riding for photographs:

FACILITIES AND EQUIPMENT
Philip Wellon for the use of land at Vine Farm; Aubiose UK Ltd for the outdoor arena; HAC TAC Ltd for supplying close-contact breeches.

RIDERS

Amanda Colbourne, Thomas Cooper, Janine Cornish, Charles Daniel, Kate Eckley, Janice Peglar, Sarah Rees-Elford, and Jeremy Russell.

The following companies supplied the tack and equipment featured in this book:

UNITED KINGDOM

Aerborn Equestrian Ltd
Pegasus House
198 Sneiton Dale
Nottingham NG2 4HJ

Albion Saddlemakers Co Ltd
Albion House
55 Caldmore Road
Walsall
West Midlands WS1 3NA

Clyst Equestrian Ltd
Teko House
Furnham Road
Chard
Somerset TA20 1AX

Keenthorne Saddlery
Nether Stowey
Bridgwater
Somerset

Miller Crosby Ltd
30 Birchbrook Industrial Estate
Shenstone
Nr Lichfield
Staffordshire WS14 0DT

Proteq™ Worldwide Ltd
Graingers
West Ashling
Chichester
West Sussex PO18 8DN

The Royal Mews
Buckingham Palace
London SW1W

Shires Equestrian Products
15 Southern Avenue
Leominster
Herefordshire HR6 0QF

Stylo Matchmakers
International Ltd
Holybrook Mill
Harrogate Road
Greengates
Bradford
West Yorkshire BD10 0QW

Wychanger Barton Saddlery
The Haywain
Burlescombe
Nr Tiverton
Devon EX16 7JY

UNITED STATES

Whitman Saddle Manufacturing
5272 West Michigan
Kalamazoo
MI 49006

Libertyville Saddle Shop Inc.
P.O. Box M
Libertyville
IL 60048-4913

Fennell's Horse Supplies
Red Mile Road
Lexington
KY 40504

Drury's Saddlery and Supplies
1638 Danville Road
Harrodsburg
KY 40330

We are also grateful to the following for allowing their equipment, horses and stables to be photographed:

Betty Howett
Bossington Stables
Bossington
Nr Minehead
Somerset

Mrs Mary King
School House
Salcombe Regis
Devon EX10 0JQ

Bob Mayhew
Dumpford Manor Farm
Trotton
Hampshire GU31 5JR

Lynn Russell
Durfold Farm
Plaistow Road
Surrey EV8 4PQ

Sarah Rowe
4 Cleal Cottages
Broadway
Ilminster
Somerset TA19 9RD

Margaret Swords
White Horse Lodge
Over Stowey
Bridgwater
Somerset

Hannah Washer
Fulbrook Cottage
Fiddington
Nr Bridgwater
Somerset

Megan Williams
The Moat House
Longdon
Nr Tewkesbury
Gloucestershire

Index

Page numbers in *italic* refer to the illustrations

A

Abbot Davies balancing reins *450, 451*
Abdullah (Trakehner show jumper) 69, *69*
Agricultural Heavy Horse 103, *103*
Ahlerich (Westphalian dressage champion) 77, *77*
aids (communication with horse) 246
   see also hands; legs (rider's)
ailments, common 230–1
Aintree breastgirths 412, *413*
Akhal-Teke *26*, 124–5, *124, 125*
Alamo saddle 408, *408*
albinos 33
Albion Selecta saddles 400, *401*
Ali-Baba (show jumper) 47
Alter Real 109, *109*
Amadeus Z (Hanoverian show jumper) *71*
American breeds of horse 126–39
American breeds of pony 168–9
American gag snaffles 432, *432*
American Shetland Pony 169, *169*
Andalusian 42–3, *42, 43*
Anglo-Arab 46–7, *46, 47*
Anglo-Norman 61, 62
anti-cast rollers 479, *479*
anti-rearing bits 435, *435*
Appaloosa 174–5, *174, 175*
aqua boots 485, *485*
Arab 38–9, *38, 39*, 46, 64, 68
Arab racing 39, 392–3
Ardennais 58–9, *58, 59*
Ardennais du Nord 59
Argentinian breeds of horse 142
Argentinian saddle bags 419, *419*
Ariègeois 54, *54*
Asiatic Wild Horse 27, 36–7, *36*
Aslam (Turkish stallion) 46
Assateague Pony 37
Atherstone girths 410, *410*
Aubiose bedding 212, *212*
Australian cheekers 439, *439*
Australian Simplex stirrups 416, *416*
Australian Stock Horse 140, *140, 141*
Australian stock saddles 404, *404*

Austrian breeds of horse 48, 146
Auxois 59
azoturia 230

B

Bablona stud, Hungary 94, 95, *95*
back injuries 232, *233*
balance, and jumping skills 310–11, *310, 311*, 316, *316*, 318
Balding gag snaffles 432, *432*
Balding girths 410, *410*
bandages and pads 486–7, *486, 487*
   tail *463*
   travel 488, *489*
   see also poultices
Barb 40–1, *40, 41*
Bars I (Orlov Trotter stallion) 116, 117
Bashkir 110, *110*
Bavarian 48
Bayard (Brabant stallion) 49
"Be Nice" halters 456, *457*
beds:
   bedding materials 210–13, *210, 211, 212, 213*
   management of 214–15, *214, 215*
behaviour:
   changes in 228
   vices 193, 224, 490–1
Belgian Draught 49, *49*
bell boots 482, *483*
bib martingales 448, *448*
bibs 490, *490*
billets (stud hooks) 441
Billy Allen bits 433, *433*

bits 246, 423
   double 430, *430*
   gag snaffles 432, *432*
   materials 435, *435*
   pelham 431, *431*
   and points of control 427, *427*
   putting on *254, 444*
   snaffle *426*, 427, 428–9, *428, 429, 433, 433*
   training and showing 435, *435*
   unusual 434, *434*
   Western 433, *433*
Black Allan (Tennessee Walking Horse stallion) 136
Black Hand (founding Pony of the Americas stallion) 168
Blair hackamore 433, *433*
blankets 473, *477*
   see also rugs
Blaze (Thoroughbred stallion) 82
blinkers *443*
bloodhounds 380–1
body brushes 460, *460*, 462, *462*
body protectors (rider's) 251, *251, 495, 495*
Boomhower, Leslie 168
boots (horse's) 480, *480*, 481–2, *481, 482, 483, 484*
   brushing 225, *254*, 480, *480, 484*
   exercise 484
   kneeboots 225, *225*, 482, *482*
   porter 486, *486*
   putting on *254, 484*
   sausage 232, 482, *482*
   therapy *234, 235*, 485, *485*
   travel 232, 488, *488, 489*

boots (rider's) 250–1, *250*, 494, 495, 496
bosals 433, *433*
Boulonnais 67, *67*
bounce grid *320*
"boxy" feet 31, *241*
Brabant 49, *49*
braiding:
   manes 468, *468*
   tails 468–9, *469*
bran 217, *217*
   as a poultice 234
branding 112, 140, 146
breaking bits *434*, 435
breaking rollers 452, *452, 453*
breast harnesses *91*
breastgirths 412, *413*
breastplates 412, *412*, 448, *448*
breeches *250*, 251
Breton 66, *66*
bridles 225, 423
   accessories 443, *443*
   bitless *426, 427*, 433, *433*
   browbands 442, *442*
   care of 445
   ceremonial 408, *408, 409*
   curb chains 436, *436*
   double 425, *425*
   endurance 2-in-1 426, *426*
   lip straps 436, *436*
   nosebands 437–9, *437, 438, 439*
   points of control 427, *427*
   putting on 254, *254, 444*
   rein attachments 441, *441*
   reins 440, *440*
   snaffle 225, *225*, 424, *424*
   Western 426, *426*
   see also bits; headcollars
bridoon bits *425*, 430, *430*, 434, *434*, 435, *435*
bridoon reins *425*
bridoon slipheads *425*
British breeds of horse 80–9
British breeds of pony 148–61
browbands *254*, 424, 425, 426, 442, *442*
Brumby 37
brushing boots 225, *254*, 480, *480*, 484, *484*
buckle guards *255*, 398, 410, *411*
buckles 441, *441*
Budenny 112–13, *112, 113*
buffers 238, *239*
Bulrush Morgan (Morgan stallion) 126, *127*

Burmese (Elizabeth II's horse) 408
butterfly bits 434, *434*
Byerley Turk (stallion) 45

C

calf knees 31
Camargue *29*, 37, 56–7, *56*, *57*
Campbell, Roy 57
Cannon Ball (Connemara
  stallion) 163
canter 278, *278*
  common faults 280, *280*
  counter 305, *305*
  extended *303*
  fitness training 227
  in the forward seat 280, *280*
  from trot to canter to trot *279*
  half-halt at *299*
  to a fence 317, *317*, 318, *318*
canter poles 311, *311*
cantles *398*, *399*
capped elbow 232
capped hock 232
carriage horse breeds:
  Cleveland Bay *24*, 80–1, *80*, *81*
  Friesian 104–5, *105*
  Gelderland 106, *106*
  Hackney 82–3, *82*, *83*
  Holstein 72–3, *73*
Caspian Pony *27*, 166, *166*
cast 215
Cavalry saddles 404, *405*
Celle Stud, Germany 70, 71
chaff 216
Chambon schooling system *450*,
  451
changing direction 272
Chapman Horse 80
chaps 251, 496
chaser clip 464
cheekpieces *424*, *425*, *426*, 428,
  430, 432
Cheltenham gag snaffles 432
Chernomor 112
cherry roller mouthpieces 429,
  429
chifneys 435, *435*
chin harnesses 495, *495*
chukkas 371
cinchback cavesson
  nosebands 437–8, *437*
cinches 411, *411*
citation bits 434, *434*
Clays 133
clench cutters 238
Cleveland Bay *24*, 80–1, *80*, *81*

clincher browbands 442, *442*
clipping and trimming 464
  techniques 466–7, *466*, *467*
  types of clip 464, *464*, *465*
clothing (horse's) 471
  coolers 474, *475*
  fitting and removing a rug 478,
    478
  rug rollers and surcingles 479,
    479
  sheets 474, *474*
  specialist sheets and rugs 476,
    476, *477*
  stable rugs 473, *473*
  travelling 488, *488*, *489*
  turnout rugs 472, *472*, *478*
  see also bandages and pads; boots
clothing (rider's) 250–1, *250*, *251*,
  493, 494
  for competition 342, 497, *497*
  riding 496, *496*
  safety gear 495, *495*
clover 205
Clovis (Anglo-Arab mare) 47
Clydesdale 88–9, *88*, *89*, 118
coats (horse's):
  Shetland Pony 159
  and signs of ill health 228
coats (rider's) 494, 495, 496
Cob 181, *181*
cohesive bandages 486, *486*
cold treatments 235, *235*
coldbloods 35
colic 231
Colosses de la Méhaigne Brabant
  line 49
Comanche (Morgan horse) 127
Combi sweat (anti-sweat) rug and
  fly sheets (scrims) 474, *475*
combination bridles 426, *426*

combination fences 324
combination grid 321, *321*, 322
combination nosebands 439, *439*
competition 340, 393
  affiliated and unaffiliated 341
  choosing a sport 342–3
  dressage 354–7, *355*, *356*, *357*
  driving 374–5, *374*, *375*
  endurance riding *343*, 362–3,
    362, *363*
  equipment needed 342, 343
  eventing 388–91, *388*, *389*, *390*,
    391
  health and welfare
    requirements 340
  horseball 372, *372*
  hunter trials 382–3, *382*
  mounted games 346–53, *346*,
    347, *348*, *349*, *351*
  polo 370–1, *370*, *371*
  polocrosse 373, *373*
  race riding 392–3, *392*, *393*
  restrictions 341
  show jumping 384–7, *384*, *385*,
    386, *387*
  showing 358–61, *358*, *359*, *360*,
    361
  team chases 383, *383*
  vaulting 368–9, *368*, *369*
  Western riding 364–7, *365*, *366*,
    367
compound feeds 217, *217*
Comus Mare (Thoroughbred
  mare) 47
concentrates, food 216–17, *216*,
  217, 218–19
Connemara Pony 162–3, *162*, *163*
Conquérant (French Trotter
  bloodline) 63
continental breastgirths 412, *413*

continental cavesson
  nosebands 437–8, *437*
continental gag snaffles 432, *432*
continental reins 440, *440*, 453
Controller headcollars 456, *457*
controller nosebands 439, *439*
Coolback numnahs 417, *418*
cooler rugs 474, *475*
Coolmasta rugs 474, *475*
copper roller mouthpieces 429,
  429
cord girths 410
Cornish bits 434, *434*
corns 240
coronet rings 482, *482*
corrective equipment 490, *490*
Cossacks 111
Cottage Craft girths 410, *410*
counter canter 305, *305*
covering boots 482, *483*
cow hocks 31
"cow-mouth" pommels 402
cradle-bottom racing stirrups 414,
  414
crash hats 250, *250*, 495, *495*
creeping red fescue 205
cremello colouring 173
crib biting 491
cribbing collars 490, *490*
Criollo 142, *142*
Crisp's Horse of Ufford (Suffolk
  stallion) 86
Crosby close-contact jumping
  saddles 400, *401*
cross-country skills and
  techniques:
  coping with early take-off *334*
  coping with terrain 331, *331*
  eventing 388, *389*, *389*, 390–1
  hunter trials 382–3
  hunting 381
  jumping 330, *330–1*
  jumping into water 332, *333*
  preparing for the
    unexpected 332–3, *333*, 335
  speed 330
  tackling two corners *334–5*
  team chases 383
croup *30*, 31
crownpieces *424*, *425*, 426, *426*,
  427, *444*
cruppers 412, *413*
Csikos horse herders, Hungary 90
curb bits *425*, *426*, 430, *430*, *433*
curb chains/straps *425*, 436, *436*
curb groove *427*, *427*, 430, 431, *433*

curb reins *425*
curry combs 460, *460*, 461, 462, *462*
cutters, hoof 238, *239*

D
D rings 398, 404, *428*
Daer (Thoroughbred mare) 47
Dales Pony 160, *160*
Danaë (Anglo-Arab mare) 47
dandy brushes 460, *460*, 463
Danish breeds of horse 50–3
Danish Warmblood 50, 52–3, *52*, *53*
Darley Arabian (stallion) 45
Dartmoor Pony *28*, 150–1, *150*, *151*, *186*
Dawn Horse 26, *27*
De Gogue schooling system 450, *450*
Deister (Hanoverian show jumper) 71
Delphine (Anglo-Arab mare) 47
dirt-track racing *393*
disabled riders, saddles 407, *407*
dismounting 260, *260*
docking of tails 55, 181
docks 463
Dollar Girl (Hanoverian show jumper) 71
Don 111, *111*
d'Oriola, Pierre Jonquères 47
double bits 430, *430*
double bridles 425, *425*, 430
double mouthpieces 429, *429*
double-jointed mouthpieces 429, *429*
double-link curb chain 436, *436*
double-sided stirrup leathers 416, *416*
Dr Bristol mouthpieces 429, *429*
Dr Le Gear (Percheron) 65
draw reins 450, *450*
drawing knives 238, *238*, *239*

dressage 47, 71, 354, 356–7
dressage girths 410, *410*
dressage reins 440, *440*
dressage saddles 402, *402*
    putting on *255*
dressage stirrup leathers 416, *416*
Driver (Hackney stallion) 82
driving 374–5
    driving trails 374, *374*, 375, *375*
    show-ring driving 374, *374*, 375
dropped nosebands 438, *438*
droppings:
    mucking out stables 214, 215
    in paddocks 205, *205*
    signs of ill-health 228
Duncan gag snaffles 432, *432*
Dutch breeds of horse 104–7
Dutch gag snaffles 432, *432*
Dutch Warmblood 107, *107*

E
ears:
    indication of mood 29
    trimming 467
East Prussian 68
eating habits, changes in 228
Eclipse Thoroughbred line 45
eggbutt snaffle bits *424*, 428, *428*, *430*
El Bedavi (Haflinger ancestor) 146
elbow, capped 232
Elwyn Hartley-Edwards breaking rollers 452, *453*
endurance 2-in-1 bridles 426, *426*
endurance riding 362
    development of the sport 362–3
    endurance horses *39*, 125, *187*, *189*, 362, 363
    equipment and back-up team 343, 363, 497
    tactics 363
endurance saddles 404, *405*
English Black 84–5

English Cob 55
English pattern hackamore 433, *433*
English stirrup leathers 416, *416*
Eohippus 26, *27*
equestrian centres 249
Equidae 26, 27
equine influenza 230
Equus 27, *27*
ergot 27
event saddles 400, *401*
eventing 388, *388*, *389*, *390*, *391*
    development of 388
    equipment 390
    levels of competition 389–90
    one-day and three-day events 388–9, *388*, *389*
    skills required 390–1
evolution of the horse 26–7, *27*
ewe neck 31
exercise 224–5, *224*, *225*
    fitness training 226–7, *226*, *227*
exercise bandages 486, *486*, 487, *487*
exercise boots 484, *484*
exercise sheets 225, 474, 476, *476*
Exmoor Pony 27, *144*, 148–9, *148*, *149*, 224
extending stirrup leathers 416
extension and collection of gait 304, *304*
eyes 29, 30
    cleaning 463
    colour 33
    injuries *233*

F
face nets *443*
Faradism *233*
farriers 237, *240*
    tools 237, 238–9, *238*, *239*
feeds and feeding 216, 218–19, *218*, *219*

amount needed by Suffolk breed 87
concentrates 216–17, *216*, *217*
daily requirements 218
feeding habits and signs of ill-health 228
roughage 216, *216*
feet:
    anatomy 236, *236*
    common problems 240–1, *240*, *241*
    conformation 31
    evolution 26, 27, *27*
    farriers and 237, 238
    grooming 462, *462*
    see also hooves
FEI (International Equestrian Federation) 341, 355
    dressage tests 356
Fell Pony 161, *161*
felt-pad saddles 407, *407*
fences for jumping 311, 324, 385
    see also jumping skills
fencing for paddocks 198–9, *198*, *199*
fenders (saddles) *399*
Ferdi (Hanoverian show jumper) 71
fetlock boots 481, *481*
fights, horse 97
figure-of-eight nosebands 438–9, *438*
Filet Baucher snaffle bits 428, *428*
fillet strings 225
fillis stirrups 414, *414*
Fire (Westphalian show jumper) 77
first-aid kits 232
fitness 224
    training 226–7, *226*, *227*
Fitzwilliam girths 410, *411*
fixed-butt snaffle bits 433, *433*
Fjord Pony *145*, 164–5, *164*, *165*
Flaebehoppen (Spotted mare) 178
Flanders Horse 49
flank straps *399*
flash nosebands 225, 438, *438*
flat racing *393*
fleece cinches 411, *411*
fleece girth sleeves (covers) 410, *411*
fleece rugs 474, *475*
Flexi-ride stirrups 414, *415*
flute bits 434, *434*
fly fringes *443*
flying change 306, *306*, 367

Flying Childers (Thoroughbred
    racehorse) 82
Flyinge Stud, Sweden 122
foal rugs *473*, 476
foal slips 456, *457*
foals 28, 29
Folie (Haflinger stallion) 146
forehand, lightening the 285, *285*
forelegs *30*, 31
founder (laminitis) 240, *240*
fox trot 134–5, *135*
foxgloves 203
fox-hunting 378–9
Frederiksborg 42, 50, *50*
free knee boots 482, *482*
French breeds of horse 46–7, 54–67
French link mouthpieces 429, *429*
French Saddle Horse *see* Selle
    Français
French Trotter 61, 62–3, *62, 63*
Friedrich Wilhelm I of Prussia 68
Friesian 42, 76, 104–5, *104, 105*
frog (hooves) 236, *236*
full-cheek snaffle bits 428, *428*
fullering irons 238
fulmer keepers 428, *428*, 436
fulmer snaffle bits 428
Fuchsia (French Trotter
    bloodline) 63
Furioso 25, 90, *90*

G
gag roundings 432, *432*
gag snaffles 432, *432*
gaits:
    collection and extension 304,
        304
    fox trot 134–5, 135
    Icelandic horses 97
    Peruvian Paso horses 143, *143*
    Saddlebred horses 131
    Tennessee Walking Horses 137,
        137
    transitions 271, *271*
    variations within each 302, *302–3*
    Walkaloosa horses 175
    see also canter; gallop; trot; walk
Gallipoly (Arab stallion) 64
gallop 281, *281*
Galloway Horse 45
Galoubet (Selle Français show
    jumper) 61
Gamgee tissue *232*, 234, *234*
Garrano 147
Gaspari (Swedish Warmblood
    dressage horse) 123

Gata (a Criollo) 142
gates, paddock 200, *200*
Gauguin de Lully (Swedish
    Warmblood dressage
    horse) 123
gel pads 418, *418*
Gelderland 106, *106*
geldings 189, 463
general purpose (GP) saddles 225,
    398, 400, *400*
General Stud Book 45
genes 32
German breeds of horse 68–79
German hackamores 433, *433*
Gidran 92
Giovanni (Saddlebred
    stallion) 136
girth extenders 410, *411*
girth guards 410, *411*
girth sleeves (covers), fleece 410,
    411
girth straps 255, *398*, 402, 410
girths *399*, 410–11, *410, 411*
    tacking up 255
    tightening when mounted 258,
        258
Gladiator turnout rugs 472, *472*
Glancer (Clydesdale stallion) 88
globe pelham bits 431, *431*
gloves 251, *251*, 496
Godolphin Arabian (stallion) 45
Grakle nosebands 225, 438–9, *438,
    439*
grass management in
    paddocks 205
grass sickness 230
Great Britain:
    breeds of horse 80–9
    breeds of pony 148–61, 167
Great Horse 84
Greyhound (Standardbred
    trotter) 133
gridwork 311, 319–20
    bounce grid *320*
    combination grid 321, *321, 322*
    distances 319
    double of parallels (oxer) 323, *323*
    square parallel (oxer) grid *321*
Gris du Hainaut Brabant line 49
Grisone, Federico 100
Gröningen 106
grooming 459
    before exercise 225
    clip types 464, *464, 465*
    clipping and trimming 466–7,
        466, 467

equipment 460–1, *460, 461*
    final touches for turnout 468–9,
        468, 469
    techniques 462–3, *462, 463*
Gros de la Dendre Brabant line 49
gymkhanas 346

H
Hack 182, *182*
hackamores 433, *433*
hacking out 224, 225, 226, 227
Hackney 82–3, *82, 83*, 169
Haflinger Pony 146, *146, 222*
half-chaps 251, 496
half-halt 298–9, 304
    at canter *299*
    at trot *298*
    too much hand *299*
half-pass 301, *301*
half-ring gag snaffles 432, *432*
half-spoon cheek snaffle bits 428,
    428
halt:
    halt to walk 271, *271*
    a hard-pulling horse 281
    quick forwards from 348
    quick stop 348
    sliding *366*
halters 456, *456, 457*
Hambletonian (Trotter
    stallion) 133
hammers, farrier's 238, *238, 239*
hands 246
    bend and flexion 292, 293, *293,
        294, 295, 295*
    common faults *263*
    cross-country riding 332, 333,
        333
    flying change *306*

half-halt 298, *298*, 299, *299*
half-pass *301*
    inside and outside 246
    jumping fences 312, *312–13,
        314, 316, 317*
    leg yielding *286*
    maintaining a rhythm 290, *290–1*
    moving to left and right 284, *284*
    quarters-in (haunches-in) *287*
    rein back *287*
    riding position 259, 262, 263,
        263
    shoulder-in *300*
    soft contact 262, 288, *288*
    stopping a hard-pulling
        horse 281
    transition 271, *271*
    from trot to canter to trot *279*
    walk to trot to walk *277*
    when changing direction 272,
        273
hanging cheek snaffle bits 428,
    428
Hanoverian 70–1, *70, 71*, 76
Harbridge training reins 451, *451*
harnesses 91
hats, hard 250, *250*, 495, *495*
haute école (high school) 43
hay 216, *216*, 219
hay wisps 461, 463
haylage 216
haynets 219
headcollars 426, *427*, 456, *456, 457*
headpieces 424, 425, 426, 444
health and ill-health:
    cold treatments 235, *235*
    common ailments 230–1, *230*
    common foot problems 240–1,
        240, 241

common injuries 232–3, *232, 233*
competition requirements 340
poulticing 234, *234*
signs of 228–9, *228, 229*
heart abnormalities 228
heart rates 228, *228*
heat treatments 234–5, *235*
hedges 199
hemlock 203
hemp bedding 212, *212*
Herod Thoroughbred line 45
herring-gutted 31
high port correction bits 433, *433*
high school (*haute école*) 43
Highflyer Thoroughbred line 45
Highland Pony *26*, 156–7, *156, 157, 188*
high-ring Grakle nosebands *438*, 439
hillwork *226, 227*
hindlegs 30, 31
hindquarters 31
  engaging 285, *285*
history of the horse 26–7
hobble straps *399*
Hobby Horse 45
hock boots 232, 488, *488, 489*
hocks:
  capped 232
  correct method of
    bandaging *232*
hogging of manes 181
hollowing against rider *271*
Holstein 72–3, *72, 73, 188*
hoods 476, *477*
hoof picks 460, *461, 462*
hoof trimmers 238
hooves 236, *236*
  colours 32, *32*
  evolution 27, *27*
  see also feet
horns (saddles) *399*
horse bots 229
horse fights 97
horseball 372, *372*
  equipment 372
  Pony Club 372
Horses on the Camargue (Campbell) 57
horseshoe stallion bridoons 435, *435*
horseshoes and shoeing 237, 238, *238*
horsetails 203
hose boots *235*, 485, *485*
hounds 379, 380–1

Humane girths 410, *410*
Hungarian breeds of horse 90–5
Hungarian Half-bred 92–3, *92, 93*
Hunter 180, *180*
hunter clip 464, *465*
hunter trials 382, *382*
  equipment needed 383
  skills required 382–3
hunting 378, *378, 379, 380, 381*
  with bloodhounds 380–1
  drag hunting 380
  equipment needed *378,* 380
  hunting quarry 378–80
  skills required 381
hunting breastplates 412, *412*
hunting canteen 419, *419*
hunting caps 495
hunting irons 414, *414*
hunting saddles 408, *409*
hunting whips *250,* 498

I
I Love You (Selle Français show jumper) 61
Icelandic 96–7, *96, 97*
ill-health:
  cold treatments 235, *235*
  common ailments 230–1, *230*
  common foot problems 240–1, *240, 241*
  common injuries 232–3, *232, 233*
  poulticing 234, *234*
  signs of 228–9, *229*
independent seat 247, *247*
influenza, equine 230
inhalants 235
in-hand bridles 456, *457*
in-hand showing 358, *359,* 360, *360*

injuries:
  common 232–3, *232, 233*
  see also health and ill-health
inside hand and leg 246, *247, 295*
  see also hands; legs (rider's)
instructors, riding 249
International Equestrian Federation *see* FEI
International Horse Show 384
Iranian breeds of pony 166
Irish breeds of horse 98–9
Irish breeds of pony 162–3
Irish clip 465
Irish Draught 98–9, *98, 99*
Irish martingales 449, *449*
irons *see* stirrups
Islam 39, 40
Italian breeds of horse 100–3
Italian Heavy Draught 103, *103*
Italian Saddle Horse 102

J
jackets, riding 494, 496, 497
Jappeloup (Selle Français show jumper) 61
jaws 30
Jean I (Brabant stallion) 49
Jean le Blanc (Percheron stallion) 64
jockey skulls *250,* 495, *495*
jodhpur boots *250,* 495
jodhpurs *250,* 251, 496
jog 366
jointed pelham bits 431, *431*
jump racing 393
jumping distances 319, *319*
jumping saddles 400, *401*
jumping skills and techniques:
  cantering to a fence 317, *317*

circle exercise 318, *318*
common faults 314–15, *314, 315*
cross-country 330, *330–1, 332, 333, 334, 335, 381, 382–3, 390–1*
fitness training 227, *227*
improving 319, *319*
jumping fences 312, *312–13*
maintaining balance and position 316, *316, 317*
race riding 393
related distances 324, *324, 325*
rhythm and balance 310–11, *310, 311*
riding a course of fences 326–7, *326, 327*
show jumping *385,* 386–7, *386, 387*
jumping stirrup leathers 416, *416*
Justin Morgan (Morgan stallion) 126
Jute rugs 473, *473*
Jutland 51, *51,* 78

K
Kabardin 114, *114, 187*
Kaimanawa horses *36*
kaolin poultices 234
Kecskemet Stud, Hungary 93
Kentucky Saddler 130
Kimberwicke bits 431, *431*
kimblewick bits 431, *431*
Kineton nosebands 439, *439*
King of Diamonds (Irish Draught show jumper) 99
Kipling, Rudyard 183
Kisber Stud, Hungary 93
KK correction bits 429, *429*
KK training bits 429, *429*
Knabstrup 178, *178*
knee pads 488, *488*
knee rolls 398, 402
kneeboots 225, *225*
Konik 37, *37*
kumis (milk drink) 110
Kyrklund, Kyra 53

L
laburnum 203
laced leather reins 440, *440*
lameness:
  common foot problems 240–1, *240, 241*
  detecting 228, *229*
  splints and 233
laminae 236, *236*

laminitis 240, *240*
Lampit's Mare (Clydesdale ancestor) 88
lateral work 286
  half-pass 301, *301*
  leg yielding 286, *286*
  quarters-in (haunches-in) 286, *287*
  rein back 286, *287*
  shoulder-in 300–1, *300*
Latvian 119, *119*
laurel 203, *203*
Lavater (French Trotter bloodline) 63
Le Pin Stud, Norway 55, 64
lead reins and ropes 455, *455*
leading horses:
  for exercise 225
  a tacked-up horse 255
learner saddles 407, *407*
Leat, The (Dartmoor Pony stallion) 151
left:
  moving to the *284*
  turning *273*
left rein, riding on the 246, *247*
leg yielding 286, *286*
legs (horse's) 29
  clipping and trimming 466, *466, 467, 467*
  conformation *30*, 31
  markings 32, *32*
legs (rider's) 246, 264–5, *265*
  bend and flexion *292, 293, 294, 295*
  common faults *265*
  cross-country riding 331
  flying change *306*
  from trot to canter to trot *279*
  half-halt 298, *298, 299, 299*
  half-pass *301*
  horse's response to 289, *289*
  inside and outside 246
  jumping fences 312, *312, 314, 316, 317*
  leg yielding *286*
  maintaining a rhythm 290, *290*
  moving to left and right 284, *284*
  quarters-in (haunches-in) *287*
  reinback *287*
  riding position 261, 264–5, *264, 265*
  shoulder-in *300*
  stopping a hard-pulling horse 281, *281*
  transition 271, *271*

walk to trot to walk *277*
  when changing direction 272, *272, 273*
lessons, riding 249
ligament injuries 233
lightening the forehand 285, *285*
linseed 217, *217*
lip straps 436, *436*
Lipizzaner *32*, 33, 42, 50
Little Big Horn, Battle of the 127
Little Model (part-bred Connemara dressage champion) 163
loins *30*, 31
long-distance riding *see* endurance riding; trail riding
Lonsdale girths 410, *410*
looseboxes 208
loose-ring racing snaffle bits 434, *434*
loose-ring snaffle bits 428, *428*
lope 366
low port bits 433, *433*
lunge cavessons 266, 452, *452, 454*
lunge lines 267, 453, *453*
lunge whips 266, *266*
lungeing:
  exercises 266, *266*, 267
  learning to ride 247, *247*, 249
  reins 452–3, *452, 453, 454*
lungeing rollers 452, *452, 454*
Lusitano 108–9, *108, 109*

M

magenis mouthpieces 429, *429*
magnetic therapy boots 485, *485*
maize *216*, 217
Mancha (a Criollo) 142
mane combs 461
manes:
  grooming 462, 463, *466, 467*
  hogging 181
  plaiting or braiding 468, *468*
mangers *218*
Marco Polo (Trakehner stallion) 107
maréeur 67
Maremmano 100–1, *100, 101*
mares 28, 29, 189
mareyeur 67
Marius (Dutch Warmblood show jumper) 107
Market Harborough martingales 449, *449*
Marquis III (show jumper) 47

Marske (Thoroughbred stallion) 153
Martchem Thoroughbred line 45
martingale stops *443*, 449
martingales 225, *443*, 448–9, *448, 449*
massage 461, 463
Massoud (Arab stallion) 46
Matador (Danish Warmblood dressage stallion) 53, *53*
meadow grass 205
meadow hay 216, *216*
meadow saffron 203
meat trade 66, 67, 103
Melton day rugs 473, *473*
Merychippus 26
Mesohippus 26
Messenger (Thoroughbred stallion) 132–3
Meteor (Holstein show jumper) 73
Mexican Grakle nosebands *438*, 439
Mezőhegyes Stud, Hungary 90, 91, 93

military fan saddles 404, *405*
milk yields 110
Mill Pearl (Irish Draught show jumper) 99, *99*
Milton (Dutch Warmblood show jumper) 107, *107*
Miss (Selle Français show jumper) *61*
Missouri Fox Trotter 134–5, *134, 135*
molasses 217, *217*
monkshood 203
Morgan 126–7, *126, 127*, 133, 173
mounted games 346
  the games *346*, 347, *348, 349, 351–3, 351*
  how they began 346
  practice for the rider *347*, 350
  rules 353
  skills required 346–7
  training the pony 347–50
mounting 256
  from the ground 256, *256*
  from a leg-up *257*
  from a mounting block *257*

mouth:
  and bits 428, 429, 431, 432
  points of control 427, *427*
  rider's hands and 263
mouthing bits *434*, 435
mouthpieces 429, *429*
  see also bits
movement:
  absorbing 270, *270*
  free forward 289, *289*
muck heaps 215, *215*
muck sheets 214
mucking out 214
mud fever 230, *230*
Mulgrave Supreme (Cleveland bay
  colt) 81
mullen mouthpieces 429, *429*,
  430
mullen-mouthed pelham bits 431,
  431
Murgese 102, *102*
Mustang 34, 37, 138–9, *138, 139*
muzzles 490, *490*

N

nails, horseshoe *238, 239*
Narragansett Pacer 130, 136
Nations Cup 384
Navajo saddle cloths *417*, 418
navicular disease 240–1
Neapolitan 50, 100, *101*
near side 248, *248*
neck 30–1, *30*
neck cradles 490, *490*
neck reining 348
neck straps 251, *251*, 412, *413*,
  448, 449
  use of 290, *290–1*
neighing 28
neoprene 410, *410, 411*
Netherlands breeds of horse 104–7
New Forest Pony 153, *153*
New Zealand turnout rugs 472,
  472
Newlot (three-day eventer) 47
Newmarket chains 455, *455*
Newport (three-day eventer) 47
nickering 28
night rugs 473
nightshade plant family 203
Nonius 91, *91*
Nonius Senior (Anglo-Norman
  stallion) 91
Norfolk Roadster 82
Noriker 48, *48*
Norman Cob 55, *55*

Normand (French Trotter
  bloodline) 62, 63
North Star (Thoroughbred
  stallion) 90
North Swedish 120, *120, 121*
Norton bridles 434
Norwegian Fjord Pony *145*, 164–5,
  164, 165
nosebands 225, *424, 424, 425, 425*,
  437–9, *437, 438, 439, 444*
  fastening *254*
  points of control 427, *427*
noses 30, *427, 427*, 433
  cleaning 463
  discharges 228
novice riders 188, 190
  saddles 407, *407*
numnahs 225, *255*, 417–18, *417,
  418*

O

oats 216, *216*
off side 248, *248*
off-set fillis stirrups 414, *414*
Old Shales (Trotter stallion) 133
Oldenburg 74–5, *74, 75*
oleander 203
Olympic Bonfire (Oldenburg
  dressage champion) 75, *75*
Olympic Games 384
"one-ear" bridles 426, *426*
open-fronted boots 481
opening the hand *272*
Oppenheim LXII (Suffolk
  stallion) 51
Orange I (Brabant stallion) 49
Original Shales (Trotter
  ancestor) 82

Orlov Trotter 116–17, *116, 117*
outside hand and leg 246, *247*
over at the knee 31
overcheck bridoons 435, *435*
overcheck reins 450
overgirths 411
overo horses 177, *177*
overreach 232
overreach boots 482, *483*

P

pacers 133
paces *see* gaits
Packington Blind Horse (Shire
  stallion) 85
paddock sheets 474, *474*
paddocks *196, 197, 197*
  and exercise 224
  feeding horses at grass 219
  fencing 198–9, *198, 199*
  gates 200, *200*
  grass management 205
  poisonous plants 202–3, *203*
  shelters 201, *201*
  water supply 204, *204*
pads *see* bandages and pads
Paint Horse 33, *170*, 176–7, *176,
  177*
Palomino 172–3, *172, 173*
panniers 419, *419*
paper bedding, shredded 212, *213*
parade saddles 404, *405*
parallel grids (oxer grids) 321,
  321, 322, 323
parers, hoof 238
Paso, Peruvian 143, *143*
pasterns *30*, 31
Peacock safety stirrups 416, *416*

peat moss bedding 212
pedal osteitis 241
pelham bits 431, *431*
pelham roundings 431, *431*, 436
Percheron 64–5, *64, 65*
periople (hooves) 236, *236*
perioplic ring 236, *236*
Peruvian Paso 143, *143*
Pessoa training system 451, *451*
petal boots 482, *483*
Philip, Prince 81, *81*
Piaff (Swedish Warmblood
  dressage horse) 123
pigeon toes 31, *240*
pin worms 229
pincers, farrier's 238, *238, 239*
Pinto 33, 177, *177*
Pinzgauer Noriker 79
pirouette 366, *367*
plaiting:
  manes 468, *468*
  tails 468–9, *469*
plants, poisonous 202–3, *203*
Pliohipphus 27
Pluto (Frederiksborg stallion) 50
point of tree *398*
point-to-point 392, *393*
poles:
  canter 311, *311*
  trot *310*, 311
Polkan (stallion) 116
poll *427, 427, 430, 431, 432, 433*
poll guards 488, *489*
polo 183, 370, *370, 371*
  equipment 370
  the game 370–1
  skills required 371
Polo Pony 183, *183*
polo saddles 400, *401*
polo wraps 486, *486, 487*
polocrosse 373, *373*
Poly pads 417, *417*
polymer stirrups 414, *415*
pommels *398*, 402
ponies 145, *188*
Pony Club 346, 351, 352, 372
Pony of the Americas 168, *168*
pony saddles 407, *407*
Pony Type 1 27, *27*
Pony Type 2 *26*, 27
ported mouthpieces 429, 430
Porter boots 486, *486*
Portuguese breeds of horse 108–9
Portuguese breeds of pony 147
position, riding:
  common faults 262

hands *259, 262,* 263, *263*
  ideal 261–2, *261, 262*
  and jumping skills 316, *316*
  legs *261,* 264–5, *264, 265*
post and rail fencing 198–9, *198*
Postier 66
posture (horse's),
    communication 29
posture (rider's) *see* position,
    riding
pouches, saddle 419, *419*
poultices 234, *234*
precision riding stirrups 416, *416*
prices of horses 188
pricker pads *443*
Prince of Wales (Clydesdale
    stallion) 89
Prince of Wales spur, 498
pritchels 238
private vendors 190, *190,* 191
privet 203, *203*
Pro-lite relief pads 418, *418*
proportions (conformation) 30
protective clothing 251, *251,* 495,
    496
Proteq saddle pads 417–18, *418*
proud flesh *232,* 233
Prussian side open bottom
    stirrups 414, *414*
Przewalski Horse 27, 36–7, *36*
public sales 190, *190,* 191
Puckle nosebands 439, *439*
pulse rates 228, *228*
puncture wounds 233

Q

Quarter Horse 128–9, *128, 129,*
    172, 173, 365, *365*
quarter marks *458,* 468, 469
quartering (grooming) 463
quarters-in (haunches-in) 286, *287*
Quito de Baussy (Selle Français
    show jumper) 61

R

race exercise saddles 406, *406*
race riding 392, *393*
  Arab racing 392–3
  equipment needed 392
  point-to-point 392, *393*
  pony and horse 393
  professional flat and jump 393
  skills required *392,* 393
racehorses:
  Quarter Horse 128–9
  Thoroughbred *31,* 44–5, *44, 45,* 46

racing 44–5
racing breastplates 412, *412*
racing girths 410, *411*
racing saddles 406, *406*
racing snaffle bits, loose-ring 434,
    434
racing stirrup leathers 416, *416*
racing surcingles 411, *411*
racing weight saddle cloths 418,
    418
ragwort 202–3, *203*
rain scald 231
rain sheets 476
rasps, farrier's 238, *238, 239*
RDA (Riding for the Disabled
    Association) saddles 407, *407*
red worms 228–9
Regal Realm (Australian Stock
    Horse three-day eventer) 141
rein back 286, *287,* 366–7
rein stops *443,* 448
reins *424,* 440, *440, 445*
  attachments 441, *441*
  and bits 431, 432
  communication with horse 246–7
  endurance bridles 426, *426*
  holding when mounted *258–9*
  lead 455, *455*
  lungeing 452–3, *452, 453, 454*
  neck reining 348
  riding on the right and left
      rein 246, *247*
  training 450–1, *450, 451*
  Western 426, *426*
related distance (jumps) 324
relationship with horses 248
Rembrandt (Westphalian dressage
    champion) 77
removes (horseshoes) 237

respiratory rates 228
rhododendron 203, *203*
rhythm:
  and jumping skills 310–11, *310,*
      311, 316, 318
  maintaining 290, *290–1*
riding boots 250–1, *250,* 494, 495,
    496
Riding for the Disabled
    Association (RDA)
    saddles 407, *407*
riding hats 250, *250,* 495, *495*
Riding Pony 167, *167*
riding schools 190, 249
riding skills and techniques 246–7,
    333
  absorbing the movement 270,
      270
  adjusting tack when
      mounted 258, *258–9*
  bend and flexion 292–5, *292,*
      293, 294, 295
  canter 278, *278, 279,* 280, *280*
  changing direction 272–3, *272,*
      273
  collection and extension of
      gaits 304, *304*
  counter canter 305, *305*
  dismounting 260, *260*
  dressage 307, *307,* 357
  flying change 306, *306*
  gallop 281, *281*
  half-halt 298–9, *298, 299*
  the hands 263, *263,* 288, *288*
  the ideal position 261–2, *261, 262*
  lateral work 286, *286, 287,*
      300–1, *300, 301*
  the legs 264–5, *264, 265,* 289, *289*
  lightening the forehand 285, *285*

lungeing exercises 266, *266, 267*
maintaining a rhythm 290, *290–1*
mounted games 347–50
mounting 256–7, *256, 257*
moving to left and right 284, *284*
right and left rein 246, *247*
tacking up 254, *254–5*
transitions 271, *271*
trot 274–5, *274, 275, 276,*
    277
understanding horses 248
variations within each gait 302,
    302, 303
Western riding 364–5, *364,*
    365–7, *366, 367*
where to learn 249
right:
  moving to the *284*
  turning 272, *273*
right rein, riding on the 246, *247*
ringbone 241
ringworm 231
rising trot 274, *274, 275*
roach back 31
roadwork 225, 226
Roan Barbary (Richard II's
    horse) 40
roaring 28–9
Robie, Wendall T. 363
rollback 366
rolled Arab slips 456, *457*
roller mouthpieces 429, *429*
rollers:
  lunge and breaking 452, *452,*
      453, 454
  rug 479, *479*
Roman (Westphalian show
    jumper) 77
rope cavesson nosebands 437, *437*
rope halters 456, *456*
roughage feeds 216, *216*
"Round the World" exercise *267*
roundings 432, *432,* 436
Roussin 66
rubber matting for
    bedding 212–13, *213*
rubber treads for stirrups 414,
    415
rug bibs 476, *477*
Rugby pelham bits 431, *431*
rugs 254, 463
  coolers 474, *475*
  fitting 478, *478*
  removing *478*
  rug rollers and surcingles 479,
      479

sheets 474, *474*
specialist 476, *476, 477*
stable 473, *473*
turnout 472, *472, 478*
running cheeks 432, *432*
running martingales 448, *448*
running reins 450, *450*
Russian breeds of horse 110–19
Russian Heavy Draught 119
rye grass 205

S

Sable Island Pony 37
saddle bags 419, *419*
saddle cloths *255*, 417–18, *417, 418*
saddle flaps *398*, 400, 402, 406
saddle patches 464, *466*
Saddlebred 130–1, *130, 131*, 136, 173
Saddlebred saddles 402, *403*
saddles 225, *396, 397*
  breastplates and cruppers 412, *412, 413*
  carrying *420*
  ceremonial 408, *408, 409*
  cleaning *420–1*
  girths, cinches and surcingles 410–11, *410, 411*
  learner 407, *407*
  numnahs and saddle cloths *255*, 417–18, *417, 418*
  points of the saddle 398, *398, 399*
  racing 406, *406*
  riding and competing *255*, 400, *400, 401*
  saddle bags 419, *419*
  saddling up *255, 421*
  showing 402, *402, 403*
  and side reins *454*
  stirrups 414, *414, 415*, 416, *416*
  storage *420*
  trail-riding and working 404, *404, 405*
safety gear 250, 495, *495*
safety stirrups 416, *416*
Saint-Lö Stud, Normandy 55
Salerno 102
sales, public 190, *190*, 191
salt licks *219*
sandcracks *240*, 241
sausage boots 232, 482, *482*
Scamperdale pelham bits 431, *431*
Scawbrig bridles 426
Schleswig 51, 78, *78*

schooling 227, *227*
schooling whips *250*
Schoolmasta training aid 451, *451*
Schweiken 68
scissors *460*
Scot Shales (Hackney stallion) 82
scourier bits 434, *434*
screaming 29
Scurry Driving 375
searchers, farrier's 238
seat jockeys *399*
seat (rider's):
  as an aid 299
  belongs in the saddle 270
  communication with horse 246
  cross-country riding 331
  an independent 247, *247*
  when jumping fences 312, *312*
seat (saddle's) 398, *398, 399*
seat savers, sheepskin 411, *411*
seed hay 216, *216*
seedy toe 241
Selim Mare (Thoroughbred mare) 47
Selle Français 60–1, *60, 61*
sesamoid boots *480*, 481
set fast 230
sexual communication between horses 29
Shagya 10, 94–5, *94, 95*
sheaths 463
sheepskin nosebands 439, *439*
sheepskin seat savers 411, *411*
sheepskin sleeves (covers) 412, *413*
sheets 474, *474*, 476, *476*
shelters in paddocks 201, *201*
Sherman Morgan (Morgan stallion) 126
Shetland Pony 29, 158–9, *158, 159*, 169
Shire 84–5, *84, 85*, 89
shock-absorbing pads 418, *418*
shoes and shoeing 237, 238, *238*
shoulder-in 300–1, *300*
shoulders 30, 31
show jumping 343, 384, *384*
  competitions 384–6, *387*
  equipment needed 385
  eventing 388, *388, 389*

opportunities 387
  skills required 385, 386–7, *386, 387*
showing 358, *358, 359*
  breed classes 359–60, *360*
  equipment 358
  equitation classes *361*
  grooming final touches for turnout 469
  in-hand 358, 359, *360*
  ring craft 359
  show-ring driving 374, *374*, 375
  side-saddle classes 361, *361*
  type classes 180, 181, 360, *360*
  Western classes 367
showing bits 435, *435*
showing saddles 402, *403*, 502
shrubs, poisonous 202–3, *203*
sickle hocks 31
side pass 366
side reins 452–3, *453, 454*
sidebones 241
side-saddle show classes 361, *361*
side-saddle stirrup leathers 416, *416*
side-saddle stirrups 414, *415*
side-saddles *399*, 402, *402*, 408, *409*
Simona (Hanoverian show jumper) 71
Simplex stirrups, Australian 416, *416*
single-jointed bits 429
single-link curb chains 436, *436*
Sir George (Hackney stallion) 83
sitting trot 274, *274, 275*
skeleton knee boots 482, *482*
skid boots 481, *481, 484*
skijoring 63
skirts (saddles) *398, 399*
skull caps 250, *250*, 495, *495*
slab-sided 31
sliding halt *366*, 367
Sloothaak, Franke 75
smell (communication between horses) 29
Smetanka (Arab stallion) 116
snaffle bits 428–9, *428, 429*, 433, *433, 434, 434*
snaffle bridles 225, *225*, 424, *424*
snip facial marking *32*

sole (hooves) 236, *236*
Sommier 66
Sorraia Pony 37, 147, *147*
South German 79, *79*
Southern Plantation Riding Horse 136
Soviet Heavy Draught 119
Spahis (cavalrymen) 41
Spanish horse breeds 42–3
Spanish jumping bits 431, *431*
Special Envoy (Irish Draught show jumper) 99
speedicut boots 480, *481*
spin 366, *367*
splay-footed 31
splint boots *see* brushing boots
splints 232–3
"split-ear" bridles 426, *426*
Spotted Pony 179, *179*
spurs 246, *251*, 498, *498, 499*
squealing 28
stable bandages 486, *486*
stable rubbers 460
stable rugs 473, *473*
stable sheets 474, *474*
stable "vices" 193, 224, 490–1
stabling 189, *206, 207*
  bedding 210–13, *210, 211, 212, 213*
  buildings 208–9, *208, 209*
  feeding 218–19, *218, 219*
  feeds 216–17, *216, 217*
  importance of exercise 224
  management of beds 214–15, *214, 215*
  water supply 220–1, *220, 221*
stallions 28, 29, 189
stamps, farrier's 238
Standardbred 132–3, *132, 133*
standing martingales 448, *449*
star facial markings *32*
Stavropol Stud, Russia 115
sticks, riding 250
stirrup leathers *399*, 416, *416*
  adjusting when mounted 258, *259, 264*
  positioning *259*
stirrups *399*, 414, *414, 415*
  checking length 264, *264*
  riding without 266
  safety 416, *416*
Stock Horse, Australian 140, *140, 141*
stone walls 199
stopping *see* halt
straight bar mouthpieces 429

straightness in a horse 292
strangles 231
straw bedding 210–11, *210*
Strelets 115
Strongylus vulgaris (red
    worm) 228–9
stud guard girths 410, *411*
stud guards 410, *411*
stud hooks 441
studs 238–9, *239*
Suffolk 51, 86–7, *86, 87*, 223
Suffolk Punch *see* Suffolk
sugar beet 217, *217*
summer sheets 474, *474*
suppliers 500–1
surcingles *399*, 411, *411*
    rug 479, *479*
sway back 31
sweat flaps *398*, 400
sweat scrapers 461
Swedish breeds of horse 120–3
Swedish Warmblood 122–3, *122,
    123*
sweet itch *230*, 231

T
tack:
    adjusting when mounted 258,
        258–9
    tacking up 254, *254–5*
    Western *364*
    see also bits; bridles; reins; saddles
tail bandages *463*, 486, *486*
tail guards 488, *489*
tails:
    docking 55
    grooming 462–3, *463, 466, 467*
    plaiting or braiding 468–9, *469*
tallest horse 65
tapadero 414
Tarpan 27, 37, *37*
Tartar (Thoroughbred stallion) 45
Tattersall ring bits 435, *435*
teachers, riding 249
team chases 383, *383*
teeth, evolution 26, 27
temperament of a horse 188, 192,
    248
temperature 228, *228*
Tenderfoot sox 485
tendon boots 481, *481*
tendon-hosing boots *235*, 485, *485*
tendons 228, 233
Tennessee Pacer 136
Tennessee Walking Horse 136–7,
    136, 137, 173

Tersk 115, *115*
tetanus 231
thatching 463
Theidemann, Fritz 73
therapy boots 485, *485*
Thoroughbred *31*, 44–5, *44, 45,
    46*, 60, 140, 167, 464, 471
three-day eventing 388–90, *388,
    389, 390*
three-fold leather girths 410, *410*
three-ring gag snaffles 432, *432*
throatlatches *254*, *424, 425, 426,
    444*
thrush 241
tie strap holders *399*
tied in below the knee 31
Tigre (Hanoverian show
    jumper) 71
tobiano horses 177, *177*
todsloan saddle flaps 406
toe covers 414, *415*
toes:
    evolution 26, 27, *27*
    see also feet
tongs, shoe 238, *239*
tongue 427, *427*, 429
tongue bits 434, *434*
tongue guards 443
Top Gun (Hanoverian show
    jumper) 71
touch, horse's sense of 29
toveros horses 177

trace clip 464, *464*
trail pads 419, *419*
trail riding 362, 367
trail-riding saddles 404, *404, 405*
training aids 447
    bits 435, *435*
    corrective equipment 490, *490*
    headcollars and halters 456, *456,
        457*
    lead reins and ropes 455, *455*
    lungeing 452–3, *452, 453, 454*
    martingales 448–9, *448, 449*
    training reins 450–1, *450, 451*
Trait du Nord 59
Trakehner *35*, 68–9, *68, 69*, 107
transitions 271, *271*
transport 342
travelling bandages 486, *486*
travelling equipment 343, 488,
    488, 489
Traventhall Stud, Schleswig-
    Holstein 72
treads for stirrups, rubber 414, *415*
tree (saddle) 398
trees, poisonous 202–3, *203*
trimmers, hoof 238, *238*
trimming *see* clipping and
    trimming
trooper saddles 404, *405*
Trooping of the Colour 408
trot 274
    collected *301*

extended *303*
fitness training 226–7
fox 134–5, *135*
from trot to canter to trot *279*
from walk to trot to walk *277*
half-halt at *298*
medium *301*
rising 274, *274, 275*
sitting 275, *275, 276*
to a fence *317*
working *302*
trot poles 310, 311, *321*
trotters:
    French Trotter 61, 62–3, *62, 63*
    Orlov Trotter 116–17, *116, 117*
    Standardbred 132–3, *132, 133*
trotting races 62, 63
troughs, water 204, *204*
trousers, riding *250*, 251, 496
trust, rider in horse, jumping
    skills 318
"Tschiffely's Ride" 142
tubbing for foot wounds 234–5,
    235
Turkmen 124–5, *124, 125*
turning 272, 349
    left *273*
    right 272, *273*
    Western skills 366, *367*
turnout rugs 472, *472, 478*
Twist la Beige (three-day
    eventer) 47

twisted mouthpieces 429, *429*
Two Step (Westphalian show
    jumper) *77*
tying-up 230
Type 1 Pony 27, *27*
Type 2 Pony *26*, 27
Type 3 Horse *26*, 27
Type 4 Horse 27, *27*
type show classes 180, 181, 360,
    360

U

under rugs 473, *477*
United States of America:
    breeds of horse 126–39
    breeds of pony 168–9
Universal wicking rugs 474,
    475

V

vaulting 368, *368*
    competitions 368–9
    display teams *368*, 369
    on and off skills for Pony Club
        games *347*, 350
    skills required *368*, 369
veterinary surgeons, examination
    of proposed purchases 192–3,
    192, *193*
"vices", stable 193, 224,
    490–1

Victoria, Queen 408
Vladimir Heavy Draught 118–19,
    118
vocabulary, horse 28–9
voice communication between
    rider and horse 246, 248, 289

W

W mouthpieces 429, *429*
waists (saddles) *398*
Wald (Swedish Warmblood
    dressage horse) 123
Waler 140
walk 270
    free *303*
    halt to walk and walk to halt 271,
        271
    medium *302*
    walk to trot to walk *277*
Walkaloosas 175
Walking Horse, Tennessee 136–7,
    136, *137*, 173
wall (hooves) 236, *236*
Walzerkönig (Hanoverian show
    jumper) *71*
Warendorf, Germany 76
warranties 191
water:
    cross-country 332–3, *332*, *333*
    eventing 391, *391*
    show jumping *387*

water brushes 460, *460*, 463
water supply:
    paddocks 204, *204*
    stables 220–1, *220*, *221*
Waterford bits 429, *429*
Wayne, John 408
weight saddle cloths 418, *418*
Weihaiwej (Oldenburg show
    jumper) 75
Welsh Cob 154–5, *154*, *155*, 173
Welsh Mountain Pony 152, *152*
Welsh Pony 152
Welsh Pony of Cob Type 155
Western bits 426, 433, *433*
Western breastplates 412, *412*
Western browbands 426, 442, *442*
Western leather curb straps 436,
    436
Western Pleasure class 367
Western reins 426, 440, *440*, 441,
    441
Western riding 363–4
    cattle-handling classes 367
    equipment 364, *364*, *366*
    horses 129, *129*, 174, 365, *365*
    showing classes 367
    skills required 364–5, *364*,
        365–7, *366*, *367*
Western saddles *399*, 411
    pleasure 404, *405*
    reining 404, *404*

Western show halter 456, *457*
Western stirrups 414, *415*
Westphalian 76–7, *76*, *77*
Weymouth bits 430, *430*
whips 246, *250*, 498, *498*, *499*
    lunge 266, *266*
white line (hooves) 236, *236*
white markings 32, *32*, 33
wicking exercise sheets 474
wild horses 27, 28–9, 36–7
    Asiatic Wild Horse 27, 36–7, *36*
    Brumby 37
    Camargue *29*, 37, 56–7, *56*, *57*
    Mustang *34*, 37, 138–9, *138*, *139*
    Przewalski Horse 27, 36–7, *36*
    Sorraia Pony *37*, 147, *147*
    Tarpan 27, 37, *37*
Wilson, Christopher Wyndham 83
Wilson snaffle bits 434, *434*
wind-sucking bridoons 434, *434*
Wintec girths *410*
wire fencing 199
wisping 461, 463
wither pads 417, *417*
withers *30*, 31
Woermann (Swedish Warmblood
    dressage horse) 123
wood shavings for bedding 211,
    211
Woodbury Morgan (Morgan
    stallion) 126
wooden post and rail
    fencing 198–9, *198*
working hunter saddles 402, *403*
working saddles 404, *404*, *405*
worms 205, 228–9
wounds and their treatment *232*,
    233
Wug turnout rugs 472, *472*

Y

yard system of stabling 209
yew 202, 203, *203*
Yorkshire Coach Horse 51, 72,
    80
Yorkshire Trotter 82
Young Rattler ("the French
    Messenger") 63

Z

zebra 26